Lecture Notes in Computer Science   13751

More information about this series at https://link.springer.com/bookseries/558

Stéphane Devismes · Franck Petit ·
Karine Altisen · Giuseppe Antonio Di Luna ·
Antonio Fernandez Anta (Eds.)

Stabilization, Safety, and Security of Distributed Systems

24th International Symposium, SSS 2022
Clermont-Ferrand, France, November 15–17, 2022
Proceedings

Editors
Stéphane Devismes ⓘ
University of Picardie Jules Verne
Amiens, France

Karine Altisen ⓘ
Grenoble Alpes University
Saint-Martin-d'Hères, France

Antonio Fernandez Anta ⓘ
IMDEA Networks Institute
Madrid, Spain

Franck Petit ⓘ
Sorbonne University
Paris, France

Giuseppe Antonio Di Luna ⓘ
Sapienza University of Rome
Rome, Italy

ISSN 0302-9743 ISSN 1611-3349 (electronic)
Lecture Notes in Computer Science
ISBN 978-3-031-21016-7 ISBN 978-3-031-21017-4 (eBook)
https://doi.org/10.1007/978-3-031-21017-4

This Springer imprint is published by the registered company Springer Nature Switzerland AG
The registered company address is: Gewerbestrasse 11, 6330 Cham, Switzerland

Preface

The papers in this volume were presented at the 24th International Symposium on Stabilization, Safety, and Security of Distributed Systems (SSS), held during November 15–17, 2022 in Clermont-Ferrand, France.

SSS is an international forum for researchers and practitioners in the design and development of distributed systems with a focus on systems that are able to provide guarantees on their structure, performance, and/or security in the face of an adverse operational environment.

SSS started as a workshop dedicated to self-stabilizing systems, the first two editions were held in 1989 and 1995, in Austin (USA) and Las Vegas (USA), respectively. From then, the workshop was held biennially until 2005 when it became an annual event. It broadened its scope and attracted researchers from other communities. In 2006, the name of the conference was changed to the International Symposium on Stabilization, Safety, and Security of Distributed Systems (SSS).

This year the Program Committee was organized into three tracks reflecting major trends related to the conference: *(i)* Self-stabilizing Systems: Theory and Practice, *(ii)* Concurrent and Distributed Computing: Foundations, Fault-tolerance, and Security, and *(iii)* Dynamic, Mobile, and Nature-Inspired Computing.

We received 58 submissions. Each submission was reviewed in a double blind fashion by at least three Program Committee members with the help of external reviewers. Out of the 58 submitted papers, four were (reviewed) invited papers and 17 were selected as regular papers. The proceedings also included seven brief announcements. Selected papers from the symposium will be published in a special issue of Theoretical Computer Science (TCS) journal.

We are grateful to the external reviewers for their valuable and insightful comments. We also thank the members of the Steering Committee for their invaluable advice. We gratefully acknowledge the Local Organization Chairs, Anaïs Durand and Pascal Lafourcade, both from Université Clermont Auvergne (France) for their time and invaluable effort that greatly contributed to the success of this symposium. Last but not least, on behalf of the Program Committee, we thank all the authors who submitted their work to SSS 2022.

Finally, the process of paper submission, selection, and compilation in the proceedings was greatly simplified due to the strong and friendly interface of the EasyChair system (http://www.easychair.org).

November 2022
Karine Altisen
Stéphane Devismes
Giuseppe Antonio Di Luna
Antonio Fernández Anta
Franck Petit

Organization

General Chairs

Stéphane Devismes   MIS, Université de Picardie Jules Verne, France
Franck Petit   LIP6, CNRS and Sorbonne Université, France

Track Chairs

Track A - Self-stabilizing Systems: Theory and Practice

Karine Altisen   Verimag, France

Track B - Concurrent and Distributed Computing: Foundations, Fault-tolerance, and Security

Antonio Fernández Anta   IMDEA Networks Institute, Spain

Track C - Dynamic, Mobile, and Nature-Inspired Computing

Giuseppe Antonio Di Luna   Sapienza University of Rome, Italy

Program Committee

Karine Altisen	VERIMAG, Université de Grenoble Alpes, France
Andrew Berns	University of Northern Iowa, USA
Silvia Bonomi	Sapienza University of Rome, Italy
Janna Burman	Université Paris-Saclay, CNRS, Laboratoire Interdisciplinaire des Sciences du Numérique, France
Stéphane Devismes	MIS, Université de Picardie Jules Verne, France
Giuseppe Antonio Di Luna	Sapienza University of Rome, Italy
Yuval Emek	Technion, Israel
Antonio Fernandez Anta	IMDEA Networks Institute, Spain
Paola Flocchini	University of Ottawa, Canada
Alexey Gotsman	IMDEA Software Institute, Spain
Vincent Gramoli	University of Sydney, Australia
David Ilcinkas	CNRS, LaBRI, Université de Bordeaux, France
Taisuke Izumi	Osaka University, Japan
Tomasz Jurdziński	University of Wroclaw, Poland
Sayaka Kamei	Hiroshima University, Japan

Dariusz Kowalski	Augusta University, USA
Anissa Lamani	Université de Strasbourg, France
Othon Michail	University of Liverpool, UK
Alessia Milani	Aix-Marseille Université, LIS, CNRS, France
Miguel Mosteiro	Pace University, USA
Mikhail Nesterenko	Kent State University, USA
Nicolas Nicolaou	University of Cyprus, Cyprus
Franck Petit	LIP6, CNRS and Sorbonne Université, France
Giuseppe Prencipe	Università di Pisa, Italy
Sergio Rajsbaum	UNAM, Maxico
Ivan Rapaport	Universidad de Chile, Chile
Christopher Thraves	Universidad de Concepción, Chile
Lewis Tseng	Boston College, USA
Sara Tucci-Piergiovanni	Sapienza University of Rome, Italy
Volker Turau	Hamburg University of Technology, Germany
Giovanni Viglietta	JAIST, Japan
Prudence Wong	University of Liverpool, UK
Yukiko Yamauchi	Kyushu University, Japan

Additional Reviewers

Almalki, Nada
Almethen, Abdullah
Beauquier, Joffroy
Blin, Lelia
Bonnet, François
Castañeda, Armando
Connor, Matthew
Dufoulon, Fabien
Godard, Emmanuel
Gonzalez Vasco, Maria Isabel
Guidi, Barbara

Montealegre, Pedro
Naser, Alejandro
Oglio, Joseph
Paz, Ami
Querzoni, Leonardo
Scheideler, Christian
Shibata, Masahiro
Skretas, George
Sudo, Yuichi
Trigeorgi, Andria

Contents

Brief Announcements

Invited Papers

Invited Paper: Simple, Strict, Proper, Happy: A Study of Reachability in Temporal Graphs

Arnaud Casteigts[1(✉)], Timothée Corsini[1], and Writika Sarkar[2]

[1] LaBRI, CNRS, Univ. Bordeaux, Bordeaux INP, Talence, France
{arnaud.casteigts,timothee.corsini}@labri.fr
[2] Chennai Mathematical Institute, Chennai, India
writika@cmi.ac.in

Abstract. Dynamic networks are a complex topic. Not only do they inherit the complexity of static networks (as a particular case) while making obsolete many techniques for these networks; they also happen to be deeply sensitive to specific definitional subtleties, such as *strictness* (can consecutive edges of a same path be used at the same time instant?), *properness* (can adjacent edges be present at the same time?) and *simpleness* (can an edge be present more than once?). These features, it turns out, have a significant impact on the answers to various questions, which is a frequent source of confusion and incomparability among results. In this paper, we explore the impact of these notions, and of their interactions, in a systematic way. Our conclusions show that these aspects really matter. In particular, most of the combinations of the above properties lead to distinct levels of expressivity of a temporal graph in terms of reachability. Then, we advocate the study of an extremely simple model – happy graphs – where these distinctions vanish.

1 Introduction

In the context of this paper, a temporal graph is a labeled graph $\mathcal{G} = (V, E, \lambda)$ where V is a finite set of vertices, $E \subseteq V \times V$ a set of directed or undirected edges (only undirected, in this paper), and $\lambda : E \to 2^{\mathbb{N}}$ a function assigning at least one time label to every edge, interpreted as presence times. These graphs can model various phenomena, ranging from dynamic networks – networks whose structure changes over the time – to dynamic interactions over static (or dynamic) networks. They have found applications in fields as various as biology, transportation, social networks, robotics, scheduling, distributed computing, and self-stabilization. Although more complex formalisms have been defined and extensively studied (see e.g. [13] or [27]), several features of temporal graphs remain not well understood even in very restricted settings.

A fundamental aspect of temporal graphs is reachability. The reachability of a temporal graph $\mathcal{G}$ is commonly characterized in terms of the existence of

---

The full version of this paper is available at https://arxiv.org/abs/2208.01720.

S. Devismes et al. (Eds.): SSS 2022, LNCS 13751, pp. 3–18, 2022.
https://doi.org/10.1007/978-3-031-21017-4_1

temporal paths; i.e., path which traverses edges in chronological order. There has been a large number of studies related to temporal reachability in the past decade, seen from various perspectives, e.g. k-connectivity and separators [18,23,26], components [2,4,6,28], feasibility of distributed tasks [3,8,13,24], schedule design [10], data structures [9,11,28,30], reachability minimization [20], reachability with additional constraints [11,14], temporal spanners [2,4,7,15], path enumeration [21], random graphs [5,16], exploration [19,22,25], and temporal flows [1,29], to name a few (many more exist). Over the course of these studies, it has become clear that temporal connectivity differs significantly from classical reachability in static graphs. To start with, it is non-transitive, which implies that two temporal paths (also called journeys) are not, in general, composable, and consequently, connected components do not form equivalence classes. This explains, in part, why many tractable problems in static graphs become hard when transposed to temporal graphs. Further complications arise, such as the conceptual impact of having an edge appearing multiple times, and that of having adjacent edges appearing at the same time. These aspects, while innocent-looking, have a deep impact on the answers to many structural and algorithmic questions.

In this paper, we take a step back, and examine methodically the impact of such aspects; in particular *strictness* (can consecutive edges of a same path be used at the same time instant?), *properness* (can adjacent edges be present at the same time?) and *simpleness* (can an edge have more than one presence times?) in the case of *undirected* temporal graphs. We look at these aspects from the point of view of temporal reachability. The central tool is the notion of closure of journeys, defined as the static directed graph where an arc exists if and only if a journey exists in the original temporal graph. It turns out that each of these aspects has a strong impact on reachability. Precisely, we prove a number of separations (four) between the sets of closures that such combinations (or *settings*) can produce. We also present three constructions that transform temporal graphs from a certain setting into another, while preserving various aspects of its reachability. By combining the separations and transformations with arguments of containment among temporal graph classes, we obtain an almost complete hierarchy of expressivity of these settings in terms of closures.

All these aspects are a frequent source of confusion and of incomparability of results in the literature. Since many basic questions remain unresolved at this stage, we advocate the study of a particular setting, called happy temporal graphs, where all the above subtleties vanish. To motivate further research in this direction, we show that happy graphs, despite being the least expressive setting, remain general enough to capture several negative results from the literature, in particular, the non-existence of $o(n^2)$-sparse temporal spanners and the computational hardness of finding maximum temporal components. We conclude with a list of open questions related to happy graphs, and to some missing relations in the above hierarchy.

The paper is organized as follows. In Sect. 2, we give some definitions and motivation. In Sect. 3, we present the separations and the transformations,

together with the resulting hierarchy. In Sect. 4, we focus on the particular case
of happy temporal graphs. Finally, we conclude in Sect. 5 with some remarks
and open questions.

2   Temporal Graphs

Given a temporal graph $\mathcal{G}$, the static graph $G = (V, E)$ is called the *footprint*
of $\mathcal{G}$. Similarly, the static graph $G_t = (V, E_t)$ where $E_t = \{e \in E \mid t \in \lambda(e)\}$
is the *snapshot* of $\mathcal{G}$ at time t. A pair (e, t) such that $e \in E$ and $t \in \lambda(e)$ is a
contact (or temporal edge). The range of λ is called the *lifetime* of $\mathcal{G}$, and τ its
length. A *temporal path* (or journey) is a sequence of contacts $\langle(e_i, t_i)\rangle$ such that
$\langle e_i \rangle$ is a path in G and $\langle t_i \rangle$ is non-decreasing.

A central concept in temporal graphs is the one of *temporal reachability*,
which defines reachability in terms of temporal paths. This relation can be captured by the *closure* of journeys [6], i.e. a static directed graph $closure(\mathcal{G}) =
(V, E_c)$, such that $(u, v) \in E_c$ if and only if u can reach v by a journey in $\mathcal{G}$. A
graph $\mathcal{G}$ is *temporally connected* if all the vertices can reach each other at least
once. The class of temporally connected graphs (TC) is arguably one of the most
basic classes of temporal graphs. The distributed community is perhaps more
familiar with TC^R, its infinite lifetime analog where temporal connectivity is
achieved infinitely often (i.e. recurrently).

2.1   Strictness/Properness/Simpleness

The above definitions can be restricted in various ways. In particular, one can
identify three restrictions which are common in the literature, although they are
sometimes considered implicitly and/or under various names:

- *Strictness*: A temporal path $\langle(e_i, t_i)\rangle$ is *strict* if $\langle t_i \rangle$ is increasing.
- *Properness*: A temporal graph is *proper* if $\lambda(e) \cap \lambda(e') = \emptyset$ whenever e and e'
  are incident to a same vertex.
- *Simpleness*: A temporal graph is *simple* if λ is single-valued; i.e., every edge
  has a single presence time.

Strictness is perhaps the easiest way of accounting for non-zero traversal
time for the edges. Without such restriction (i.e., in the *non-strict* setting),
a journey could use an arbitrary number of consecutive edges having the same
time label, whereas this is not allowed for strict journeys (the times must strictly
increase). The notion of *properness* is related to the one of strictness, although
not equivalent. Properness forces all the journeys to be strict, because adjacent
edges always have different time labels. However, if the graph is non-proper, then
considering strict or non-strict journeys does have an impact.

Application-wise, proper temporal graphs arise naturally in some distributed
settings, when the contacts correspond to mutually exclusive pairwise interactions (such as with population protocols). Proper graphs also have the advantage

that λ induces a proper coloring of the contacts (interpreting the labels as colors). Finally, *simpleness* naturally accounts for distributed scenarios where two entities interact only once. It is somewhat unlikely that a real-world system has this property; however, this restriction has been extensively considered in well-known areas (e.g. in gossip theory), and these graphs capture many interesting features of general temporal graphs.

Note that simpleness and properness are properties of the *graphs*, whereas strictness is a property of the *journeys*. Therefore, one may either consider a strict or a non-strict setting for the same temporal graph. The three notions (of strictness, simpleness, and properness) interact in subtle ways, these interactions being a frequent source of confusion and incomparability among results. Before focusing on these interactions, let us make a list of the possible combinations. The naive cartesian product of these restrictions leads to eight combinations. However, not all of them are meaningful, since properness removes the distinction between strict and non-strict journeys. Overall, this results in six meaningful combinations, illustrated in Fig. 1.

- Non-proper, non-simple, strict (1)
- Non-proper, non-simple, non-strict (2)
- Non-proper, simple, strict (4)
- Non-proper, simple, non-strict (5)
- Proper, non-simple (3)
- Proper, simple (= happy) (6)

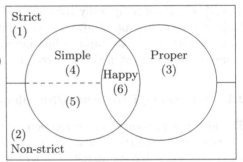

Fig. 1. Settings resulting from combining the three properties

In the name of the settings, "non-proper" refers to the fact that properness is *not required*, not to the fact that it is necessarily not satisfied. In other words, proper graphs are a particular case of non-proper graphs, and similarly for "non-simple", as simple graphs are also a particular case of non-simple graphs. Thus, whenever non-proper or non-simple graphs are considered, we will omit this information from the name. For instance, setting (1) will be referred to as the (general) strict setting. We do not use this terminological simplification for strictness, as it does not correspond to different temporal graph classes and may actually result in two orthogonal settings.

2.2   Does It Really Matter? (Example of Spanners)

While innocent-looking, the choice for a particular setting may have tremendous impacts on the answers to basic questions. For illustration, consider the spanner problem. Given a graph $\mathcal{G} = (V, E, \lambda)$ such that $\mathcal{G} \in TC$, a *temporal spanner* of $\mathcal{G}$ is a graph $\mathcal{G}' = (V, E', \lambda')$ such that $\mathcal{G}' \in TC$, $E' \subseteq E$, and for all e in E', $\lambda'(e) \subset \lambda(e)$. In other words, $\mathcal{G}'$ is a temporally connected spanning subgraph of $\mathcal{G}$. A natural goal is to minimize the size of the spanner, either in terms of number of labels or number of underlying edges. More formally,

---

MIN-LABEL SPANNER

Input: A temporal graph $\mathcal{G}$, an integer k

Output: Does $\mathcal{G}$ admit a temporal spanner with at most k contacts?

MIN-EDGE SPANNER

Input: A temporal graph $\mathcal{G}$, an integer k

Output: Does $\mathcal{G}$ admit a temporal spanner of at most k edges (keeping all their labels)?

The search and optimization versions of these problems can be defined analogously. Observe that, unlike spanners in static graphs, this definition does not consider stretch factors, due to the fact that it is not even guaranteed that small spanners exist without additional constraints. In the following, we illustrate the impact of the notions of strictness, simpleness, and properness (and their interactions) using such problems. The impact of strictness is pretty straightforward. Consider the graph $\mathcal{G}_1$ on Fig. 2. If non-strict journeys are allowed, then this graph admits $\mathcal{G}_2$ as a spanner, this spanner being optimal for both versions of the problem (3 labels, 3 edges). Otherwise, the minimum spanners are bigger (and different) for both versions: $\mathcal{G}_3$ minimizes the number of labels (4 labels, 4 edges), while $\mathcal{G}_4$ minimizes the number of edges (3 edges, 5 labels). If strictness is combined with non-properness, then there exist a pathological scenario (already identified in [26]) where the input is a complete temporal graph (see $\mathcal{G}_5$, for example) no edges of which can be removed without breaking temporal connectivity! Observe that $\mathcal{G}_5$ is also a simple temporal graph. Independently from this particular scenario, simpleness has strong consequences. For example, if the input graph is simple and proper, then it cannot admit a spanning tree (i.e. a spanner of $n-1$ edges) and requires at least $2n-4$ edges (or labels, equivalently, since the graph is simple) [12]. If the input graph is simple and non-proper, then it does not admit a spanning tree if strictness is required, but it does admit one otherwise if and only if at least one of the snapshots is a connected graph. Finally, none of these affirmations hold in general for non-simple graphs.

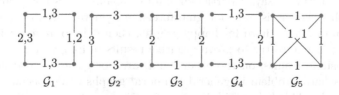

Fig. 2. Some temporal graphs on four vertices

If the above discussion seems confusing to the reader, it is not because we obfuscated it. The situation is intrinsically subtle. In particular, one should bear in mind the above subtleties whenever results from different settings are compared with each other. To illustrate such pitfalls, let us relate a recent mistake (fortunately, without consequences) that involved one of the authors. In [4], Axiotis and Fotakis construct a (non-trivial) infinite family of temporal graphs which do not admit $o(n^2)$-sparse spanners. Their construction is given in the setting of simple temporal graphs, with non-proper labeling and non-strict journeys allowed. The same paper actually uses many constructions formulated in this setting, and a general claim is that these constructions can be adapted to proper graphs (and so strict journeys). Somewhat hastily, the introduction of [16] infers that the counterexample from [4] holds in the same model as in [16], which is that of proper *and* simple temporal graphs. (A similar comment holds for the introduction of [15]). The pitfall is that, for some of the constructions in [4], giving up on non-properness (and non-strictness) is only achievable at the cost of using *multiple* labels per edge – a conclusion that we reached after several failed attempts. To be fair, the authors of [4] never claimed that these adaptations could preserve simpleness, so their claim is actually correct.

Apart from illustrating the inherent subtleties of these notions, the previous observations imply that the question of worst-case instances for temporal spanners in temporal graphs that are both proper and simple was in fact still open. In Sect. 4, we show that the spanner construction from [4] can indeed be adapted to proper *and* simple graphs.

2.3 Happy Temporal Graphs

A temporal graph $\mathcal{G} = (V, E, \lambda)$ is *happy* if λ is both single-valued and locally injective (no two adjacent edges have the same presence time); in other words, if it is both simple and proper. These graphs have sometimes been referred to as *simple temporal graphs* without further mention of their proper nature, which the present paper argues is insufficiently precise. Happy graphs are "happy" for a number of reasons. First, the distinction between strict journeys and non-strict journeys can be safely ignored (due to properness), and the distinction between contacts and edges can also be ignored (due to simpleness). Clearly, these restrictions come with a loss of expressivity, but this does not prevent happy graphs from being relevant more generally in the sense that negative results carry on by containment of happy graphs in more general settings. For instance, if a certain substructure – say, a particular kind of spanner – is not guaranteed in happy graphs, then it is also not guaranteed in general. Similarly, if a problem is computationally hard for happy graphs, then it is so in general. Thus, it seems good practice to try to prove negative results in happy graphs, whenever possible. Positive results, on the other hand, are not generally transferable; in particular, a hard problem in general temporal graphs could become tractable in happy graphs. This being said, if a certain graph contains a happy subgraph, then whatever pattern can be found in the latter also exists in the former, which enables *some form* of transferability for structural results.

In fact, happy graphs coincide with a vast body of literature. Many studies in *gossip theory* consider the same restrictions, and the so-called *edge-ordered graphs* [17] can also be seen as a particular case of happy graphs. In addition, a number of existing results in temporal graphs, independently from these two fields, actually consider the same restrictions. Finally, up to time-distortion that preserve the local ordering of the edges, the number of happy graphs on a certain number of vertices is *finite* – a convenient property for verifying experimentally that certain properties hold for *all* happy graphs of a certain size.

The above arguments, together with the fact that many basic questions remain unsolved even in this restricted model, makes happy graphs a compelling class of temporal graphs to be studied in the current state of knowledge.

3   Expressivity in Terms of Reachability

As already said, a fundamental aspect of temporal graphs is the reachability induced by temporal paths. There are several ways of characterizing the extent to which two temporal graphs G_1 and G_2 have similar reachability. The first three, below, are presented in gradual order of strength. The fourth is weaker.

Definition 1 (Closure equivalence). *Let G_1 and G_2 be two temporal graphs built on the same set of vertices. These graphs are* closure-equivalent *if $closure(G_1) \simeq closure(G_2)$ (i.e. both closures are isomorphic). By abuse of language, we say that G_1 and G_2 have the "same" closure.*

Definition 2 (Support equivalence). *Let G_1 and G_2 be two temporal graphs built on the same set of vertices. These graphs are* support-equivalent *if for every journey in either graph, there exists a journey in the other graph whose underlying path goes through the same sequence of vertices. By abuse of language, we say that both journeys have the "same" underlying path.*

Definition 3 (Bijective equivalence). *Let G_1 and G_2 be two temporal graphs built on a same set of vertices. These graphs are* bijectively equivalent *if there is a bijection σ between the set of journeys of G_1 and that of G_2, and σ is support-preserving (the journeys in bijection have the same underlying path).*

Definition 4 (Induced-closure equivalence). *Let G_1 and G_2 be two temporal graphs built on vertices V_1 and V_2, respectively, with $V_1 \subseteq V_2$. G_2 is* induced-closure equivalent *to G_1 if $closure(G_2)[V_1] \simeq closure(G_1)$. In other words, the restriction of $closure(G_2)$ to the vertices of V_1 is isomorphic to $closure(G_1)$.*

Observe that bijective equivalence implies support-equivalence, which implies closure equivalence, which implies induced-closure equivalence. Furthermore, support-equivalence forces both footprints to be the same (the converse is not true). In this section, we show that some of the settings presented in the previous section differ in terms of reachability, whereas others coincide. We first prove a number of *separations*, by constructing temporal graphs in a setting, whose closure cannot be obtained in another setting. Then, we present three *transformations* that establish various levels of equivalences. Finally, we infer more relations by combining separations and transformations, together with further discussions. A complete diagram illustrating all the relations is given in the end of the section (Fig. 3 on page 12).

3.1   Separations

In view of the above discussion, a separation in terms of closure is pretty general, as it implies a separation for the two stronger forms of equivalences (support-preserving and bijective ones). Before starting, let us state a simple lemma used in several of the subsequent proofs.

Lemma 1. *Unless strict journeys are required, if two vertices are at distance two in the footprint, then at least one of them can reach the other (i.e. the closure must have at least one arc between these vertices).*

3.1.1   "Simple & Strict" *vs.* "Strict"

Lemma 2. *There is a graph in the "non-simple & strict" setting whose closure cannot be obtained from a graph in the "simple & strict" setting.*

Proof. Consider the following non-simple graph $\mathcal{G}$ (left) in a strict setting and the corresponding closure (right). We will prove that a hypothetical simple temporal graph $\mathcal{H}$ with same closure as $\mathcal{G}$ cannot be built in the strict setting. First, observe that the arc (a, c) in $closure(\mathcal{G})$ exists only in one direction. Thus, a and c cannot be neighbors in $\mathcal{H}$. Since $\mathcal{H}$ is simple and the journeys are strict (and a has no other neighbors in $closure(\mathcal{G})$), the arc (a, c) can only result from the label of ab being strictly less than bc. The same argument holds between bc and cd with respect to the arc (b, d) in $closure(\mathcal{G})$. As a result, the labels of ab, bc, and cd must be strictly increasing, which is impossible since (a, d) does not exist in $closure(\mathcal{G})$.

$$\mathcal{G} = \overset{a}{\circ}\!\!\underset{1}{\rule{1.2cm}{0.4pt}}\!\!\overset{b}{\circ}\!\!\underset{1,2}{\rule{1.2cm}{0.4pt}}\!\!\overset{c}{\circ}\!\!\underset{2}{\rule{1.2cm}{0.4pt}}\!\!\overset{d}{\circ} \quad closure(\mathcal{G}) =$$

$\square$

As simple graphs are a particular case of non-simple graphs, the following corollary follows.

Corollary 1. *The "simple & strict" setting is strictly less expressive than the "strict" setting in terms of closure.*

3.1.2 "Non-strict" *vs.* "Simple & Strict"

Lemma 3. *There is a graph in "simple & strict" whose closure cannot be obtained from a graph in "non-strict".*

Proof. Consider the following simple temporal graph $\mathcal{G}$ (left) in a strict setting and the corresponding closure (right). Note that a and c are not neighbors in the closure, due to strictness. For the sake of contradiction, let $\mathcal{H}$ be a temporal graph whose non-strict closure is isomorphic to that of $\mathcal{G}$. First, observe that the footprint of $\mathcal{H}$ must be isomorphic to the footprint of $\mathcal{G}$, as otherwise it is either not connected or complete. Call b the vertex of degree two in $\mathcal{H}$. If $\lambda_{\mathcal{H}}(ab) \neq \lambda_{\mathcal{H}}(bc)$, then either a can reach c or c can reach a, and if $\lambda_{\mathcal{H}}(ab) = \lambda_{\mathcal{H}}(bc)$, then both can reach each other through a non-strict journey. In both cases, $closure(\mathcal{H})$ contains more arcs than $closure(\mathcal{G})$.

$$\mathcal{G} = \overset{a}{\circ} \underset{1}{\rule{1.5em}{0.4pt}} \overset{b}{\circ} \underset{1}{\rule{1.5em}{0.4pt}} \overset{c}{\circ} \qquad closure(\mathcal{G}) = \overset{a}{\circ} \rule{1.5em}{0.4pt} \overset{b}{\circ} \rule{1.5em}{0.4pt} \overset{c}{\circ}$$

$\square$

3.1.3 "Simple & Non-strict" *vs.* "Proper"

Lemma 4. *There is a proper graph whose closure cannot be obtained from a simple graph in the non-strict setting.*

Proof. Consider the following proper temporal graph $\mathcal{G}$ (left). Its closure (right) is a graph on four vertices, with an edge between any pair of vertices except a and d (i.e., a diamond). For the sake of contradiction, let $\mathcal{H}$ be a simple temporal graph in the non-strict setting, whose closure is isomorphic to that of $\mathcal{G}$. First, observe that no arcs exist between a and d in the closure, thus a and d must be at least at distance 3 in the footprint (Lemma 1), which is only possible if the footprint is a graph isomorphic to P_4 (i.e. a path graph on four vertices) with endpoints a and d. Now, since $\{a, b, c\}$ is a clique in the closure (whatever the way identifiers b and c are assigned among the two remaining vertices), they must be temporally connected in $\mathcal{H}$, which forces that $t_1 = t_2$ (otherwise both edges could be travelled in only one direction). Similarly, the fact that $\{b, c, d\}$ is a clique in the closure forces $t_2 = t_3$. As a result, there must be a non-strict journey between a and d, which contradicts the absence of arc between a and d in the closure.

$$\mathcal{G} = \overset{a}{\circ} \underset{2}{\rule{1.5em}{0.4pt}} \overset{b}{\circ} \underset{1,3}{\rule{1.5em}{0.4pt}} \overset{c}{\circ} \underset{2}{\rule{1.5em}{0.4pt}} \overset{d}{\circ} \qquad closure(\mathcal{G}) =$$

$\square$

The next corollary follows by inclusion of proper graphs in the non-strict setting.

Corollary 2. *The "simple & non-strict" setting is strictly less expressive than the "non-strict" setting in terms of closure.*

3.1.4   "Simple & Proper (i.e. Happy)" *vs.* "Simple & Non-strict"

Lemma 5. *There is a graph in the "simple & non-strict" setting whose closure cannot be obtained from a happy graph.*

Proof. Consider the following simple temporal graph $\mathcal{G}$ (left) in a non-strict setting and the corresponding closure (right). For the sake of contradiction, let $\mathcal{H}$ be a happy temporal graph whose closure is isomorphic to that of $\mathcal{G}$.

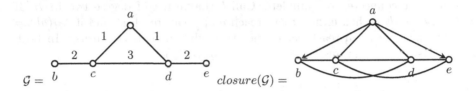

Since a is not isolated in the closure, it has at least one neighbor in $\mathcal{H}$. Vertices b and e cannot be such neighbors, the arc being oneway in the closure, so its neighbors are either c, d, or both c and d. *Wlog*, assume that c is a neighbor (the arguments hold symmetrically for d), we first prove an intermediate statement

Claim. The edge bd does not exists in the footprint of $\mathcal{H}$.

Proof (by contradiction). If $bd \in \mathcal{H}$, then $de \notin \mathcal{H}$, as otherwise d and e would be at distance 2 and share at least one arc in the closure (Lemma 1). However, e must have at least one neighbor, thus $ce \in \mathcal{H}$, and by Lemma 1 again $bc \notin \mathcal{H}$. At this point, the footprint of $\mathcal{H}$ must look like the following graph, in which the status of ad and cd is not settled yet.

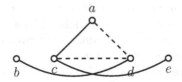

In fact, ad must exist, as otherwise there is no way of connecting d to a and a to d. Also note that the absence of (e, a) in the closure forces $\lambda(ac) < \lambda(ce)$ (remember that $\mathcal{H}$ is both proper and simple), which implies that no journey exists from e to d unless cd is also added to $\mathcal{H}$ with a label $\lambda(cd) > \lambda(ce)$. In the opposite direction, d needs that $\lambda(ad) < \lambda(ac)$ to be able reach e. Now, c needs that $\lambda(cd) < \lambda(bd)$ to reach b. In summary, we must have $\lambda(ad) < \lambda(ac) < \lambda(ce) < \lambda(cd) < \lambda(bd)$, which implies that b cannot reach c.   □

By this claim, $bd \notin \mathcal{H}$, thus $bc \in \mathcal{H}$ and consequently $cd \notin \mathcal{H}$ (by Lemma 1). From the absence of (b, a) in the closure, we infer that $\lambda(bc) > \lambda(ac)$. In order for b to reach d, we need that cd exists with label $\lambda(cd) > \lambda(bc)$. To make d to b mutually reachable, there must be an edge ad with time $\lambda(ad) < \lambda(ac)$. Now, the only way for c to reach e is through the edge de, and since there is no arc (e, a), its label must satisfy $\lambda(de) > \lambda(ad)$. Finally, c can reach e (but not through a), so $\lambda(de) > \lambda(cd)$ and c cannot reach e, a contradiction. $\square$

By inclusion of happy graphs in the "simple & non-strict" setting, we have

Corollary 3. *The "simple & proper (i.e. happy)" setting is strictly less expressive than the "simple & non-strict" setting in terms of closure.*

3.2 Transformations

In this section, we present three transformations. First, we present a transformation from the general non-strict setting to the setting of proper graphs, called the *dilation technique*. Since proper graphs are contained in both the non-strict and strict setting, this transformation implies that the strict setting is at least as expressive as the non-strict setting. This transformation is *support-preserving*, but it suffers from a significant blow-up in the size of the lifetime. Another transformation called the *saturation technique* is presented from the (general) non-strict setting to the (general) strict setting, which is only *closure-preserving* but preserves the size of the lifetime. Finally, we present an induced-closure-preserving transformation, called the *semaphore technique*, from the general strict setting to happy graphs. If the original temporal graph is non-strict, one can compose it with one of the first two transformations, implying that *all* temporal graphs can be turned into a happy graph whose closure contains that of the original temporal graph as an induced subgraph, which makes happy graphs universal in a weak sense. Due to space limitations, the content of the section is available only in the full version of the paper.

3.3 Summary and Discussions

Let S_1 and S_2 be two different settings, we define an order relation $\preceq$ so that $S_1 \preceq S_2$ means that for any graph $\mathcal{G}_1$ in S_1, one can find a graph $\mathcal{G}_2$ in S_2 such that $closure(\mathcal{G}_1) \simeq closure(\mathcal{G}_2)$. We write $S_1 \precnsim S_2$ if the containment is strict (i.e., there is a graph in S_2 whose closure cannot be obtained from a graph in S_1). Finally, we write $S_1 \approx S_2$ if both sets of closures coincide. Several relations follow directly from containment among graph classes, e.g. the fact that simple graphs are a particular case of non-simple graphs. The above separations and transformations also imply a number of relations, and their combination as well. For example, proper graphs are contained both the strict and non-strict settings, and since there is a transformation from non-strict graphs (in general) to proper graphs, we have the following striking relation:

Corollary 4. *"Proper" $\approx$ "non-strict".*

Similarly, combining the fact that "simple & non-strict" is contained in "non-strict", and there exists a closure-preserving (in fact, support-preserving) transformation from "non-strict" to "proper", we also have that

14   A. Casteigts et al.

Corollary 5. *"Simple & non-strict"* $\npreceq$ *"proper"*.

Finally, the fact that there is a closure-preserving transformation from "non-strict" to "strict" (the saturation technique), and some closures from "simple & strict" are unrealizable in "non-strict" (by Lemma 3), we also have

Corollary 6. *"Non-strict"* $\npreceq$ *"strict"*.

A summary of the relations is shown in Fig. 3, where green thick edges represent the transformations that are support-preserving, green thin edges represent transformations that are closure-preserving, red edges with a cross represent separations (i.e. the impossibility of such a transformation), black dashed edges represent the induced-closure-preserving transformation to happy graphs. Finally, inclusions of settings resulting from containment of graph classes are depicted by short blue edges. Some questions remain open. In particular,

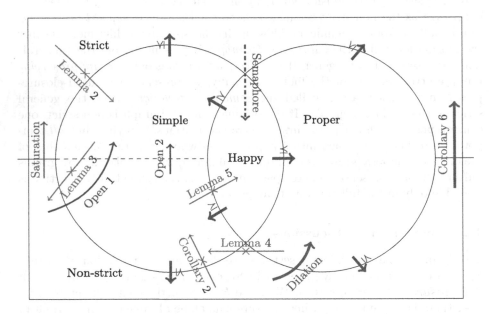

Fig. 3. Separations, transformations, and inclusions among settings. (Color figure online)

Question 1. Does "non-strict" $\preceq$ "simple & strict"? In other words, is there a closure-preserving transformation from the latter to the former?

By Lemma 3, we know that both settings are not equivalent, but are they comparable? If not, a similar question holds for "simple & non-strict":

Question 2. Does "simple & non-strict" $\preceq$ "simple & strict"? In other words, is there a closure-preserving transformation from the latter to the former?

To conclude this section, Fig. 4 depicts a hierarchy of the settings ordered by the above relation $\preceq$; i.e. by the sets of closures they can achieve.

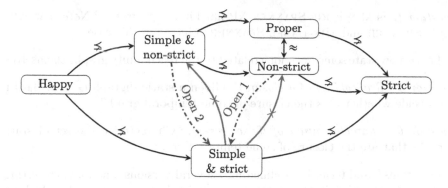

Fig. 4. Ordering of temporal graph settings by sets of realizable closures.

4   More Facts About Happy Temporal Graphs

From the previous section, happy graphs are the least expressive setting. In this section, however, we argue that they remain expressive enough to strengthen existing negative results for well-studied problems. First, we show that the construction from [4] can be made happy, which implies that $o(n^2)$-sparse spanners do not always exist even in happy graphs. We also show that the reduction from clique to maximum components in [6] can be made happy, which implies that finding maximum components is NP-hard problem even in happy graphs. Due to space limitations, the content of the section is available only in the full version of this paper.

5   Concluding Remarks and Open Questions

This paper explored the impact of three particular aspects of temporal graphs: *strictness*, *properness*, and *simpleness*. We showed, through a number of separations, that these aspects have a concrete impact on reachability. On the other hand, our results imply the striking fact that the "proper" setting is as expressive as the "non-strict" setting. Some relations remain unknown, such as the relative status of the "non-strict" setting and the "simple & strict" setting.

Clearly, happy graphs are the most basic setting. Yet, several fundamental questions remain open about them. In particular, our adaptation of Axiotis and Fotakis result implies that spanners of size $o(n^2)$ do not always exist in happy graphs. On the positive side, spanners of size $O(n \log n)$ always exist when the footprint is a clique [15], which raises the following natural question.

Question 3 (also in [15]). Do happy graphs always admit spanners of size $O(n)$ when the footprint is a clique? If so, do they admit spanners of size $2n - 3$?

On the algorithmic side, two independent results [2,4] establish that MIN-LABEL SPANNER is hard in general temporal graphs (indeed, APX-hard). However, the techniques do not seem to carry over to happy graphs (at least, not straightforwardly), which suggests the following important question:

Question 4. Is MIN-EDGE SPANNER NP-hard in happy graphs? Note that MIN-EDGE SPANNER and MIN-LABEL SPANNER coincide in this case.

Let us now state some questions related to the reachability graphs themselves:

Question 5 (Realizability of a closure). Given a static digraph G, how hard is it to decide whether G is the closure of some temporal graph?

Question 6 (Characterization of the closures). Characterize the set of static digraphs that are the closure of some temporal graph.

Questions 5 and 6 can be declined into several versions, one for each setting. To conclude, the work in this paper considered only temporal graphs which are *undirected*. It would be interesting to see if the expressivity of *directed* temporal graphs shows similar separations and transformation.

Question 7 (Directed temporal graphs). Does the expressivity of directed temporal graphs admit similar separations and transformations as in the case of undirected temporal graphs?

References

1. Akrida, E.C., Czyzowicz, J., Gasieniec, L., Kuszner, Ł., Spirakis, P.G.: Temporal flows in temporal networks. J. Comput. Syst. Sci. **103**, 46–60 (2019)
2. Akrida, E.C., Gasieniec, L., Mertzios, G.B., Spirakis, P.G.: The complexity of optimal design of temporally connected graphs. Theory Comput. Syst. **61**(3), 907–944 (2017)
3. Altisen, K., Devismes, S., Durand, A., Johnen, C., Petit, F.: On implementing stabilizing leader election with weak assumptions on network dynamics. In: Proceedings of the 2021 ACM Symposium on Principles of Distributed Computing, pp. 21–31 (2021)
4. Axiotis, K., Fotakis, D.: On the size and the approximability of minimum temporally connected subgraphs. In: 43rd International Colloquium on Automata, Languages, and Programming (ICALP), pp. 149:1–149:14 (2016)
5. Baumann, H., Crescenzi, P., Fraigniaud, P.: Parsimonious flooding in dynamic graphs. Distrib. Comput. **24**(1), 31–44 (2011)
6. Bhadra, S., Ferreira, A.: Complexity of connected components in evolving graphs and the computation of multicast trees in dynamic networks. In: Pierre, S., Barbeau, M., Kranakis, E. (eds.) ADHOC-NOW 2003. LNCS, vol. 2865, pp. 259–270. Springer, Heidelberg (2003). https://doi.org/10.1007/978-3-540-39611-6_23
7. Bilò, D., D'Angelo, G., Gualà, L., Leucci, S., Rossi, M.: Sparse temporal spanners with low stretch. arXiv preprint arXiv:2206.11113 (2022)
8. Bramas, Q., Tixeuil, S.: The complexity of data aggregation in static and dynamic wireless sensor networks. In: Pelc, A., Schwarzmann, A.A. (eds.) SSS 2015. LNCS, vol. 9212, pp. 36–50. Springer, Cham (2015). https://doi.org/10.1007/978-3-319-21741-3_3
9. Brito, L.F.A., Albertini, M.K., Casteigts, A., Travençolo, B.A.N.: A dynamic data structure for temporal reachability with unsorted contact insertions. Soc. Netw. Anal. Min. **12**(1), 1–12 (2022)

10. Brunelli, F., Crescenzi, P., Viennot, L.: On computing pareto optimal paths in weighted time-dependent networks. Inf. Process. Lett. **168**, 106086 (2021)
11. Bui-Xuan, B., Ferreira, A., Jarry, A.: Computing shortest, fastest, and foremost journeys in dynamic networks. Int. J. Found. Comput. Sci. **14**(02), 267–285 (2003)
12. Bumby, R.T.: A problem with telephones. SIAM J. Algebraic Discrete Methods **2**(1), 13–18 (1979)
13. Casteigts, A., Flocchini, P., Quattrociocchi, W., Santoro, N.: Time-varying graphs and dynamic networks. Int. J. Parallel Emergent Distrib. Syst. **27**(5), 387–408 (2012)
14. Casteigts, A., Himmel, A.-S., Molter, H., Zschoche, P.: Finding temporal paths under waiting time constraints. Algorithmica **83**(9), 2754–2802 (2021)
15. Casteigts, A., Peters, J.G., Schoeters, J.: Temporal cliques admit sparse spanners. J. Comput. Syst. Sci. **121**, 1–17 (2021)
16. Casteigts, A., Raskin, M., Renken, M., Zamaraev, V.: Sharp thresholds in random simple temporal graphs. In: 2021 IEEE 62nd Annual Symposium on Foundations of Computer Science (FOCS), pp. 319–326. IEEE (2022)
17. Chvátal, V., Komlós, J.: Some combinatorial theorems on monotonicity. Can. Math. Bull. **14**(2), 151–157 (1971)
18. Conte, A., Crescenzi, P., Marino, A., Punzi, G.: Enumeration of s-d separators in DAGs with application to reliability analysis in temporal graphs. In: 45th International Symposium on Mathematical Foundations of Computer Science (MFCS 2020). Schloss Dagstuhl-Leibniz-Zentrum für Informatik (2020)
19. Di Luna, G., Dobrev, S., Flocchini, P., Santoro, N.: Distributed exploration of dynamic rings. Distrib. Comput. **33**(1), 41–67 (2020)
20. Enright, J., Meeks, K., Mertzios, G.B., Zamaraev, V.: Deleting edges to restrict the size of an epidemic in temporal networks. In: 44th International Symposium on Mathematical Foundations of Computer Science (MFCS 2019). Schloss Dagstuhl-Leibniz-Zentrum fuer Informatik (2019)
21. Enright, J., Meeks, K., Molter, H.: Counting temporal paths. arXiv preprint arXiv:2202.12055 (2022)
22. Erlebach, T., Spooner, J.T.: Parameterized temporal exploration problems. In: 1st Symposium on Algorithmic Foundations of Dynamic Networks (SAND 2022). Schloss Dagstuhl-Leibniz-Zentrum für Informatik (2022)
23. Fluschnik, T., Molter, H., Niedermeier, R., Renken, M., Zschoche, P.: Temporal graph classes: a view through temporal separators. Theoret. Comput. Sci. **806**, 197–218 (2020)
24. Gómez-Calzado, C., Casteigts, A., Lafuente, A., Larrea, M.: A connectivity model for agreement in dynamic systems. In: Träff, J.L., Hunold, S., Versaci, F. (eds.) Euro-Par 2015. LNCS, vol. 9233, pp. 333–345. Springer, Heidelberg (2015). https://doi.org/10.1007/978-3-662-48096-0_26
25. Ilcinkas, D., Klasing, R., Wade, A.M.: Exploration of constantly connected dynamic graphs based on cactuses. In: Halldórsson, M.M. (ed.) SIROCCO 2014. LNCS, vol. 8576, pp. 250–262. Springer, Cham (2014). https://doi.org/10.1007/978-3-319-09620-9_20
26. Kempe, D., Kleinberg, J., Kumar, A.: Connectivity and inference problems for temporal networks. J. Comput. Syst. Sci. **64**(4), 820–842 (2002)
27. Orda, A., Rom, R.: Minimum weight paths in time-dependent networks. Networks **21**(3), 295–319 (1991)
28. Rannou, L., Magnien, C., Latapy, M.: Strongly connected components in stream graphs: computation and experimentations. In: Benito, R.M., Cherifi, C., Cherifi,

H., Moro, E., Rocha, L.M., Sales-Pardo, M. (eds.) COMPLEX NETWORKS 2020. SCI, vol. 943, pp. 568–580. Springer, Cham (2020)

29. Vernet, M., Drozdowski, M., Pigné, Y., Sanlaville, E.: A theoretical and experimental study of a new algorithm for minimum cost flow in dynamic graphs. Discret. Appl. Math. **296**, 203–216 (2021)

30. Whitbeck, J., de Amorim, M.D., Conan, V., Guillaume, J.-L.: Temporal reachability graphs. In: Proceedings of the 18th Annual International Conference on Mobile Computing and Networking, pp. 377–388 (2012)

Invited Paper: One Bit Agent Memory is Enough for Snap-Stabilizing Perpetual Exploration of Cactus Graphs with Distinguishable Cycles

Kohei Shimoyama[1], Yuichi Sudo[2], Hirotsugu Kakugawa[3],
and Toshimitsu Masuzawa[1(✉)]

[1] Osaka University, Osaka, Japan
masuzawa@ist.osaka-u.ac.jp
[2] Hosei University, Tokyo, Japan
sudo@hosei-u.ac.jp
[3] Ryukoku University, Kyoto, Shiga, Japan
kakugawa@rins.ryukoku.ac.jp

Abstract. This paper considers perpetual exploration of anonymous cactus graphs with distinguishable cycles by a single mobile agent under the restriction that nodes have no storage (*e.g.,* whiteboards or token places). A cactus with distinguishable cycles allows the agent to distinguish at each node the two incident edges contained in each cycle from other incident edges. This paper introduces the concept of snap-stabilization into the perpetual exploration and shows that snap-stabilizing perpetual exploration is possible when the agent has one-bit persistent memory. The exploration time of the presented algorithm exactly matches a trivial lower bound. This paper also shows the necessity of one-bit agent memory by showing that any oblivious (or memory-less) agent cannot explore a cactus graph even when it has only a single distinguishable cycle. Finally, this paper shows that snap-stabilizing perpetual exploration by an oblivious agent is possible when a cactus graph with distinguishable cycles has a sense of direction.

Keywords: Mobile agent · Graph exploration · Cactus graph · Snap-stabilization

1 Introduction

Distributed computing by mobile entities called agents or robots has been much investigated in the last two decades [14]. *Graph exploration* by mobile entities, which requires that each node of a graph be visited by at least one entity, is one of the most fundamental problems in this field [7,19]. This paper considers the exploration of *port-numbered anonymous graphs* (where nodes have no identifiers but incident edges at each node are distinguished by port numbers) by a *single mobile agent* under the restriction that nodes have *no storage* (*e.g.,* whiteboards or token places) to store information the agent can read from and write into.

© The Author(s), under exclusive license to Springer Nature Switzerland AG 2022
S. Devismes et al. (Eds.): SSS 2022, LNCS 13751, pp. 19–34, 2022.
https://doi.org/10.1007/978-3-031-21017-4_2

Exploration of anonymous graphs without node storage is practically important since some applications prohibit agents from accessing the node identifiers and storage for security reasons.

The graph exploration is classified into *terminating exploration* (sometimes further classified into exploration with stop and exploration with return) and *perpetual exploration* [9]. The terminating exploration requires agents to terminate after all nodes are visited and the perpetual exploration requires agents to keep visiting all nodes periodically.

This paper considers the perpetual exploration by a single agent since the terminating exploration is impossible regardless of the agent memory size even in anonymous rings when nodes have no storage and the agent has no knowledge of the ring size [7]. A perpetual exploration algorithm for a single agent allows the agent regardless of its starting node to visit all nodes periodically. Its efficiency is mainly measured by the *exploration time*, the *agent (persistent) memory size* and the *node storage size*. The exploration time is the maximum length of the interval between two consecutive visits of the same node.

Self-stabilization is a promising paradigm for designing distributed algorithms with high adaptability to transient faults and dynamical changes of graphs. It is originally introduced by Dijkstra [8] for token circulation in rings and has been extensively investigated for a wide range of problems [1,12]. A self-stabilizing algorithm eventually realizes its intended behavior even when starting from an arbitrary initial configuration (or global state). Thus, it can tolerate any finite number and type of transient faults in the sense that it can recover in a finite time a correct behavior from the corrupted configuration. A self-stabilizing perpetual exploration algorithm for a single agent allows the agent to *eventually* start visiting every node periodically with some exploration time regardless of the initial configuration. But it may require the *stabilization time* longer than the exploration time before starting the periodical exploration. *Snap-stabilization* was first introduced by Bui *et al.* [4] as a desired extreme of self-stabilization, which is self-stabilization with stabilization time of zero. Thus, a snap-stabilizing perpetual exploration algorithm allows the agent to *immediately* (not eventually) start visiting every node periodically with some exploration time.

Our Contribution. This paper focuses on the perpetual exploration by a single agent of *cactus graphs with distinguishable cycles* under the restriction that nodes have no storage. A *cactus graph* can contain cycles but only allows any two distinct cycles to share at most one node, which implies that any edge is never contained in two or more cycles. For each cycle of a cactus graph, each node in the cycle has exactly two incident edges of the cycle. A cactus graph is called the one *with distinguishable cycles* when, at each node, every pair of incident edges contained in the same cycle can be recognized using the port numbers.

This paper introduces for the first time the concept of snap-stabilization into the perpetual graph exploration and shows the following results on the perpetual exploration by a single agent of cactus graphs with distinguishable cycles.

1. Snap-stabilizing perpetual exploration is possible when one-bit agent persistent memory is available. The exploration time of the presented algorithm

is $c + 2t$ where c (resp. t) is the number of edges in cycles (resp. not in any cycle), which exactly matches a trivial lower bound.

2. Exploration is impossible for an *oblivious* (or memory-less) agent even when a cactus graph contains only a single distinguishable cycle.

3. Snap-stabilizing perpetual exploration is possible for an oblivious agent when a cactus graph with distinguishable cycles has a *sense of direction*.

Related Works. Exploration of port-numbered graphs by a single agent has been extensively investigated in much literature [7]. When each node has a *unique identifier*, a depth-first-traversal realizes terminating exploration in time $2m$ (or $2m$ moves) where m is the number of edges in the graph. Panaite *et al.* improved the time for exploration to $m + 3n$ where n is the number of nodes [23].

Terminating exploration of *anonymous* graphs in time $2m$ is possible by the depth-first traversal when $O(\log \Delta)$-bit storage is available at each node or the agent has a single token (or pebble) and $O(D \log \Delta)$-bit memory [16], where Δ is the maximum node degree and D is the diameter of the graph.

For exploration of anonymous graphs with *no node storage*, Reingold [25] proposed a *universal exploration sequence* that allows an agent with $O(\log n)$-bit memory to explore any graph. The matching lower bound of the agent memory was proved by Fraigniaud *et al.* [15]. Disser *et al.* [10] showed that the agent memory size can be reduced to $O(1)$ when the agent can use $O(\log \log n)$ distinguishable tokens and that $\Omega(\log \log n)$ tokens are necessary for the agent with sublogarithmic-bit memory. Exploration of specific graph classes has been investigated, *e.g.*, trees [2,9], grids and tori [3], hypercubes [13] and so on.

Label-guided exploration introduced by Cohen *et al.* [5] and Dobrev *et al.* [11] uses preprocessing for leaving some fixed information at each node to guide the agent to efficient exploration. Cohen *et al.* [5] showed that assigning appropriate 2-bit label (actually taking three different values) to each node enables exploration in $O(m)$ time by an $O(1)$-bit agent and appropriate 1-bit node label enables exploration in $O(\Delta^{O(1)} m)$ time by an $O(\log \Delta)$-bit agent. Most of literature including the above all assumes that the *port number assignment* (also called *local orientation*) at each node is arbitrary and considers the complexities of the worst case of the assignments. Dobrev *et al.* [11] showed that appropriate assignment of port numbers at each node enables an oblivious agent to perpetually explore any graph with exploration time $10n$. Following the works of [17,18], the exploration time using appropriate port numbers was improved to $3.5n - 1$ at the cost of $O(1)$ agent memory by Czyzowicz *et al.* [6]. The exploration time for an oblivious agent was investigated in [6,20] and improved to $4n - 2$ by Kosowski *et al.* [20]. The label-guided approach using the appropriate port numbers is closely related to this paper since cactus graphs with distinguishable cycles allow arbitrary assignment of port numbers under some restriction.

The well-known right-hand-on-the-wall traversal (*e.g.*, [9]) on trees realizes *snap-stabilizing* perpetual exploration by an *oblivious* agent. The rotor-router (originally called the Eulerian walkers model) introduced by Priezzhev *et al.* [24] realizes *self-stabilizing* perpetual exploration of any graph by an oblivious agent.

It uses $O(\log \Delta)$-bit storage and its exploration time is $2m$. Yanovski *et al.* [26] showed its stabilization time is $O(mD)$. Optimality of the storage space and stabilization time was proved by Menc *et al.* [22]. Another self-stabilizing perpetual exploration algorithm is proposed by Masuzawa *et al.* [21] to realize gossiping among multiple agents. The label-guided perpetual exploration proposed by Ilcinkas [18] is also self-stabilizing.

2   Preliminaries

2.1   Cactus Graph

A (simple) graph (or network) $G = (V, E)$ consists of a node set V and an edge set $E$where an edge connects two distinct nodes. An edge connecting $u, v \in V$ is denoted by $\{u, v\}$ and no two edges connect the same pair of nodes. Node u is called a *neighbor* of v (and vice versa) when G has edge $\{u, v\}$. The *degree* of a node v is the number of edges incident to v and is denoted by δ_v. A *walk* is a sequence of nodes $(v_0, v_1, \ldots, v_k)$ satisfying $\{v_i, v_{i+1}\} \in E$ for each i ($0 \leq i \leq k - 1$). This walk is called a *closed* walk if $v_0 = v_k$. A *cycle* is a closed walk $(v_0, v_1, \ldots, v_k(= v_0))$ satisfying $k \geq 3$ and $v_i \neq v_j$ for any $0 \leq i < j \leq k - 1$.

A graph G is a *cactus* graph if any two distinct cycles of G share at most one node in common. Edges of a cactus graph can be partitioned into two sets, *cycle edges* and *tree edges*. An edge is called a cycle edge if it is included in a cycle and is called a tree edge otherwise. The number of the cycle edges (resp. the tree edges) in G is denoted by $c(G)$ (resp. $t(G)$). Figure 1 presents a cactus graph G with three cycles. Edges $\{f, b\}, \{f, g\}, \{f, h\}$ and $\{f, k\}$ are cycle edges and $\{f, a\}$ and $\{f, d\}$ are tree edges incident to node f. Graph G has 10 cycle edges and 11 tree edges (*i.e.*, $c(G) = 10$ and $t(G) = 11$).

A *port-numbered graph* $G = (V, E, PN)$ is a graph $G = (V, E)$ such that a connecting point called a *port* is virtually introduced between a node and each of its incident edges and *port numbering* PN assigns the ports of each node v distinct *port numbers* chosen from $\{0, 1, \ldots, \delta_v - 1\}$. The port set of node v is denoted by P_v. In the following, a port-numbered graph is simply called a graph.

This paper considers only a (port-numbered) cactus graph as a target of perpetual exploration by a single agent. Similarly to edges, a port is called a *cycle port* if it is connecting to a cycle edge and is called a *tree port* otherwise. The number of cycle ports (resp. tree ports) of node v is denoted by $c(v)$ (resp. $t(v)$). Thus $\delta_v = c(v) + t(v)$, $c(G) = \sum_{v \in V} c(v)/2$ and $t(G) = \sum_{v \in V} t(v)/2$ hold. Notice that $c(v)$ is even since node v is incident to exactly two edges included in the same cycle.

We assume that cycle ports of v can be distinguished from tree ports of v. Moreover, for each cycle port $a \in P_v$, the other cycle port $b \in P_v \setminus \{a\}$ connecting to the same cycle as a can be identified. More precisely, function $f_v : P_v \to P_v \cup \{\bot\}$ is available at node v such that $f_v(a) = b$ (also $f_v(b) = a$) holds for distinct cycle ports $a, b \in P_v$ included in the same cycle (if exist), and $f_v(c) = \bot$ holds for tree port $c \in P_v$. A cactus graph is called a cactus graph with *distinguishable cycles* if the function f_v is available at every node v. We consider only cactus

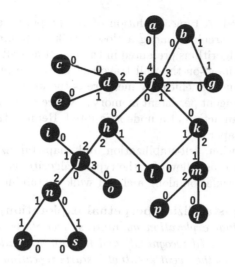

Fig. 1. A cactus graph with distinguishable cycles G

graphs with distinguishable cycles and simply call them cactus graphs. Without loss of generality, we assume that ports $\{0, 1, \ldots, c(v) - 1\} \subseteq P_v$ are cycle ports and satisfy $f_v(2i) = 2i + 1$ for each i $(0 \le i \le c(v)/2 - 1)$. The remaining ports $\{c(v)(= \delta_v - t(v)), c(v) + 1, \ldots, \delta_v - 1\} \subseteq P_v$ are tree ports. Figure 1 presents such a cactus graph.

2.2   Mobile Agent and Graph Exploration

A *mobile agent* operating on a graph $G = (V, E, PN)$ is a mobile state machine that can move from node to node along edges of the graph. Nodes are *anonymous*, that is, nodes have no identifiers that an agent can refer to. Nodes have *no storage* (*e.g.*, whiteboard or token place) to store information that an agent can read from and write into. When an agent reaches a node v, it can recognize the degree δ_v of v and the *incoming port* through which it has entered v. Thus, the agent action at node v depends only on its current state, the incoming port and the degree δ_v, which changes the agent state and chooses the *outgoing port* through which the agent leaves v. The agent action is precisely defined by an *agent algorithm* (shortly an algorithm). An agent has *agent memory* whose contents define the agent state. The agent memory is *persistent*, that is, it can keep the contents when the agent moves from a node to another.

The *graph exploration* problem (shortly exploration problem) requires agents in a graph to visit all nodes. We consider the *perpetual exploration* by a *single agent* that requires the agent to visit every node periodically. One of efficiency measures of perpetual exploration is the *exploration time*, which is the maximum length of the time interval between two consecutive visits of the same node under the assumption that the agent can move from a node to its neighbor in one time unit called a *step* and the time required to execute an action at a node can be ignored. A typical solution of the perpetual exploration is that the agent repeatedly circulates along a closed walk containing all nodes of the graph. Actually the algorithms presented in this paper as well as several previous ones (*e.g.*, the right-hand-on-the-wall traversal and those proposed in [21, 24]) are such solutions. Another efficiency measure is the *agent memory size* (or the number of bits of the agent persistent memory). Notice that the working memory required to execute an action at a node is ignored. Remind that node storage is not allowed in this paper.

For ease of definition, self-stabilization and snap-stabilization in perpetual exploration are defined as follows for the typical algorithms such that the agent eventually repeats circulation along a closed walk containing all nodes.

Definition 1 (Snap-stabilizing perpetual exploration). *A self-stabilizing algorithm for perpetual exploration guarantees, regardless of the initial state, the initial incoming port (if recognized) and the initial location (or the starting node) of the agent, that the agent eventually starts repeating circulation along a closed walk containing all nodes. The time required before starting the repeated circulation along the closed walk is called the* stabilization time.

A snap-stabilizing algorithm for perpetual exploration is a self-stabilizing one with stabilization time of zero.   □

Let $\mathcal{G}$ be a class of port-numbered graphs. We say that an algorithm solves the perpetual exploration problem in $\mathcal{G}$ when it can solve the problem in any graph $G \in \mathcal{G}$. Self- or snap-stabilizing algorithms for $\mathcal{G}$ are similarly defined.

3   Snap-Stabilizing Perpetual Exploration

This section presents a snap-stabilizing perpetual exploration algorithm for a single agent with one-bit agent memory in a cactus graph G. Its exploration time is $c(G) + 2t(G)$, which exactly matches an obvious lower bound.

3.1   Port Traversal Graph

The strategy of the proposed algorithm is to traverse a cactus graph G by circulating a ring graph called a *port traversal graph* that is virtually constructed from G. Before presenting the algorithm, we introduce the port traversal graph.

Definition 2 (Port traversal graph). *For a given cactus graph $G = (V, E, PN)$, the* port traversal graph *$P(G) = (P(V), P(E))$ is defined as follows.*

- *$P(V) = \{p \mid p$ is a cycle port$\} \cup \{p^\ominus \mid p$ is a tree port$\} \cup \{p^\oplus \mid p$ is a tree port$\}$. That is, $P(V)$ contains all cycle ports of G, and $p^\ominus$ and $p^\oplus$ for each tree port p. Nodes of $P(G)$ are called* p-nodes *to distinguish them from nodes and ports in G, and are also called* cycle p-nodes *or* tree p-nodes *depending on the corresponding ports in G.*

For each node $v \in V$, its port with port number i $(0 \le i \le \delta_v - 1)$ is denoted by v^i. The cycle p-node corresponding to v^i $(0 \le i \le c(v) - 1)$ is also denoted by v^i. The tree p-nodes corresponding to $v^j (c(v) \le j \le \delta_v - 1)$ are denoted by $v^{j\ominus}$ and $v^{j\oplus}$.

– $P(E)$ is the set constituted by the following edges. Edges in $P(G)$ are called p-edges to distinguish them from edges in G.

1. For every cycle edge $\{u, v\} \in E$ connecting ports $u^i \in P_u$ and $v^j \in P_v$, p-edge $\{u^i, v^j\}$ is in $P(E)$. This p-edge is called a cycle p-edge.

2. For every tree edge $\{u, v\} \in E$ connecting ports $u^i \in P_u$ and $v^j \in P_v$, two p-edges $\{u^{i\ominus}, v^{j\oplus}\}$ and $\{u^{i\oplus}, v^{j\ominus}\}$ are in $P(E)$. These p-edges are called tree p-edges.

3. For every node v and every cycle port v^i with an odd port number i $(\in \{1, 3, \ldots, c(v) - 1\}$, a single p-edge $\{v^i, v^{i+1 \bmod \delta_v}\}$ (when $v^{i+1 \bmod \delta_v}$ is a cycle port) or $\{v^i, v^{(i+1 \bmod \delta_v)\ominus}\}$ (when $v^{i+1 \bmod \delta_v}$ is a tree port) is in $P(E)$. This p-edge is called an intra-node edge.

4. For every node v and every tree port v^j $(c(v) \le j \le \delta_v - 1)$, a single p-edge $\{v^{j\ominus}, v^{(j+1 \bmod \delta_v)\oplus}\}$ (when $v^{j+1 \bmod \delta_v}$ is tree port) or $\{v^{j\ominus}, v^0\}$ (when $j = \delta_v - 1$ and v^0 is a cycle port) is in $P(E)$. This edge is also called an intra-node edge.   □

Figure 2 shows (a) node v in a cactus graph and (b) the part of the port traversal graph corresponding to node v. Node v has four cycle ports v^0, v^1, v^2, v^3 and four tree ports v^4, v^5, v^6, v^7. To construct the port traversal graph, cycle ports v^0, v^1, v^2, v^3 become members of $P(V)$ as well as $v^{4\ominus}, v^{5\ominus}, v^{6\ominus}, v^{7\ominus}, v^{4\oplus}, v^{5\oplus}, v^{6\oplus}, v^{7\oplus}$ that are obtained from the tree ports. Each of the cycle p-nodes is connected by a cycle p-edge to a cycle p-node of a neighbor in G. Similarly, each of the tree p-nodes is connected by a tree p-edge to a tree p-node of a neighbor in G. Notice that two tree p-nodes $v^{i\ominus}, v^{i\oplus}$ are introduced in $P(G)$ for tree port v^i of G and $v^{i\ominus}$ (resp. $v^{i\oplus}$) is connected to a tree p-node $u^{j\oplus}$ (resp. $u^{j\ominus}$) of the neighbor, say u. The meaning of the two tree p-nodes, one with $\ominus$ and the other with $\oplus$, and their connection pattern by tree p-edges (i.e., a tree p-node with $\ominus$ is connected to the one with $\oplus$) is explained in the next subsection.

Figure 3 shows the port traversal graph of the cactus graph of Fig. 1. In the following, we omit "mod δ_v" in the port number at node v. The following Proposition summarizes some properties of the port traversal graph.

Proposition 1. *The port traversal graph $P(G) = (P(V), P(E))$ of any cactus graph $G = (V, E, PN)$ has the following properties.*

(1) Each cycle p-node v^i is incident to one cycle p-edge and one intra-node edge connecting to v^{i-1} or $v^{(i-1)\ominus}$ (if i is even), or v^{i+1} or $v^{(i+1)\oplus}$ (if i is odd).

(2) Each tree p-node $v^{i\ominus}$ (resp. $v^{i\oplus}$) is incident to one tree p-edge and one intra-node edge connecting to v^{i+1} or $v^{(i+1)\oplus}$ (resp. v^{i-1} or $v^{(i-1)\ominus}$).

The following lemma shows that the port traversal graph is a ring graph.

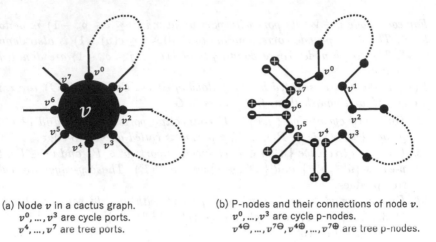

(a) Node v in a cactus graph.
$v^0, ..., v^3$ are cycle ports.
$v^4, ..., v^7$ are tree ports.

(b) P-nodes and their connections of node v.
$v^0, ..., v^3$ are cycle p-nodes.
$v^{4\ominus}, ..., v^{7\ominus}, v^{4\oplus}, ..., v^{7\oplus}$ are tree p-nodes.

Fig. 2. The part of the traversal graph corresponding to node v

Lemma 1. *The port traversal graph $P(G) = (P(V), P(E))$ of any cactus graph $G = (V, E, PN)$ is a ring graph.*

Proof. From Proposition 1, the degree of every p-node is two. It remains to show that the port traversal graph $P(G)$ is a connected graph.

We first show that all the p-nodes of each node $v \in V$ are connected. Consider two cycle p-nodes (if exist) v^{2a} and v^{2a+1} for each a ($0 \le a \le c(v)/2 - 1$). These two p-nodes are not neighbors in $P(G)$ if v has a port other than these ports, but they are incident to cycle p-edges constituting the same cycle C_G of G. Consider the cycle C_P of $P(G)$ that contains v^{2a} and traverse C_P from p-node v^{2a} and its incident cycle p-edge. The traversal of C_P returns to a p-node of v and the structure of the cactus graph implies that the first return to v should come through the cycle p-edge that is contained in C_G, which is incident to v^{2a+1} in $P(G)$. Thus, p-nodes v^{2a} and v^{2a+1} are connected (or reachable each other) in $P(G)$. Since cycle p-node v^{2a} is connected to cycle p-node v^{2a-1} (if exists) by an intra-node edge, all the cycle p-nodes of v are connected. Similarly, we can show that two tree p-nodes (if exist) $v^{b\ominus}$ and $v^{b\oplus}$ for each b ($c(v) \le b \le \delta_v - 1$) are connected, and thus, all the tree p-nodes of v are connected. If v has both a cycle p-node and a tree p-node, cycle p-node v^0 is connected to tree p-node $v^{(\delta_v - 1)\ominus}$ by an intra-node edge, which implies that all the p-nodes in $P(G)$ of each node $v \in V$ are connected.

For any neighbors $u, v \in V$ of G, there exist p-nodes neighboring in $P(G)$, one from u and the other from v, since all edges of G are also p-edges of $P(V)$ (although each tree edge, say $\{w^a, x^b\}$, are replaced with two tree p-edges $\{w^{a\ominus}, x^{b\oplus}\}$ and $\{w^{a\oplus}, x^{b\ominus}\}$). This implies that any two p-nodes of neighbors u and v of G are connected since all the p-nodes of a node are connected as proved above. It follows that all p-nodes of $P(G)$ are connected since G is a connected graph. Consequently, $P(G)$ is a connected graph. $\square$

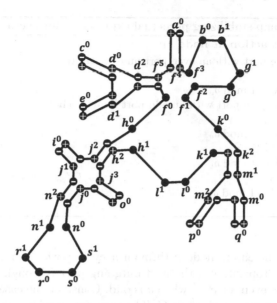

Fig. 3. The port traversal graph of the cactus in Fig. 1

From Proposition 1 and Lemma 1, the following proposition clearly holds.

Proposition 2. *The port traversal graph (or a ring) $P(G) = (P(V), P(E))$ of any cactus graph $G = (V, E, PN)$ is a ring formed by an alternating sequence of cycle/tree p-edges and intra-node edges.* □

Proposition 3. *In the port traversal graph (or a ring) $P(G) = (P(V), P(E))$ of any cactus graph $G = (V, E, PN)$, p-nodes of node v appear in a cyclic shift order of*

$$v^0, v^1, \ldots, v^{c(v)-1}, v^{c(v)\oplus}, v^{c(v)\ominus}, v^{(c(v)+1)\oplus}, v^{(c(v)+1)\ominus}, \ldots, v^{(\delta_v-1)\oplus}, v^{(\delta_v-1)\ominus}$$

or its reverse. □

In the port traversal graph of Fig. 3, when the ring starts with a p-node of node a and goes in the counter-clockwise direction, p-nodes of node f appear in the order of $f^{4\ominus}, f^{5\oplus}, f^{5\ominus}, f^0, f^1, f^2, f^3, f^{4\oplus}$ (or in ascending order of port numbers) and p-nodes of node h appear in the order of $h^0, h^{2\ominus}, h^{2\oplus}, h^1$ (or in descending order of port numbers).

3.2 Algorithm for a Single Agent with One-Bit Agent Memory

The fundamental strategy of the snap-stabilizing perpetual exploration algorithm for a cactus graph G is to traverse the edges of G in the order that they appear in the port traversal graph $P(G)$. In other words, the agent traverses $P(G)$ with skipping the intra-node edges.

Algorithm 1. Snap-stabilizing perpetual exploration for cactus graphs

---

algorithm (agent action at node v):

1: **if** IN is a cycle port with an even port number **then**
2:      $dir \leftarrow' \ominus'$
3:      $OUT \leftarrow IN - 1 \bmod \delta_v$
4: **else if** IN is a cycle port with an odd port number **then**
5:      $dir \leftarrow' \oplus'$
6:      $OUT \leftarrow IN + 1 \bmod \delta_v$
7: **else if** $dir =' \ominus'$ **then**   ▷ IN is a tree port
8:      $OUT \leftarrow IN - 1 \bmod \delta_v$
9: **else**   ▷ IN is a tree port and $dir =' \oplus'$
10:      $OUT \leftarrow IN + 1 \bmod \delta_v$
11: **end if**

When the agent enters node v through a cycle port v^a of G, it can easily determine, from Proposition 1, the next outgoing port (through which it leaves v): v^{a-1} when a is even, or v^{a+1} when a is odd. Consider the case that the agent enters v through a tree port v^b of G. The port traversal graph $P(G)$ has two tree p-nodes $v^{b\ominus}$ and $v^{b\oplus}$ corresponding to port v^b of G. From Proposition 1, the agent should leave v through port v^{b+1} of G when the arrival p-node is $v^{b\ominus}$, or through port v^{b-1} when the arrival p-node is $v^{b\oplus}$. However, G has only port v^b corresponding to $v^{b\ominus}$ and $v^{b\oplus}$. Thus we use a binary agent state to distinguish $v^{b\ominus}$ and $v^{b\oplus}$. More precisely in G, when the agent enters v through a tree port v^b, the next outgoing port depends on the incoming port of v previous to v^b: from Proposition 3 the agent should leave through v^{b-1} if the previous incoming port was v^{b+1} (*i.e.*, the ports of v are used in *descending* order), or through v^{b+1} otherwise (*i.e.*, the ports of v are used in *ascending* order). In the proposed algorithm, the agent has only a single binary variable dir to store the order. The variable dir is overwritten every time the agent enters a node through a cycle port. But when the agent comes back to node v through a tree port, variable dir stores the correct direction for v as we prove later.

Algorithm 1 presents a snap-stabilizing perpetual exploration algorithm for a cactus graph G, which describes the action of the agent when it enters node v. We regard the agent action at a node as an atomic action. This implies that Algorithm 1, though it is snap-stabilizing, is executed from line 1 (not from the middle) every time the agent enters a node. The agent determines by the algorithm the outgoing port based on the agent state, the incoming port and the degree δ_v of v. Locally-working (not persistent) variables IN and OUT in Algorithm 1 denote the incoming and the outgoing ports respectively. The agent has only one binary variable $dir \in \{\ominus, \oplus\}$ as its persistent variable, that is, the agent has only two states. When the agent enters v through a tree port, value $\ominus$ (resp. $\oplus$) in variable dir implies that the ports of v are used in descending (resp. ascending) order of the port numbers.

Let G be any cactus graph, $P(G)$ be the port traversal graph of G, and C_P be the alternating sequence of cycle/tree p-edges and intra-node edges forming the ring of $P(G)$. A *traversal walk* of G is defined as the edge sequence obtained from C_P by removing the intra-node edges.

Theorem 1. *Algorithm 1 presents a snap-stabilizing perpetual exploration algorithm for a single agent in any cactus graph G. The agent uses one-bit agent memory and the exploration time is $c(G) + 2t(G)$, which exactly matches a lower bound.*

Proof. We transform the traversal route of the agent in G into a sequence W of edges in its port traversal graph $P(G)$ and shows that W is a walk in $P(G)$ repeatedly circulating the ring of $P(G)$. The transformation is done as follows.

Initially, W is an empty sequence. We trace the traversal route of the agent in G from the beginning. When the agent executes Algorithm 1 at node v and moves to a neighbor u, a pair of an intra-edge and a cycle/tree p-edge of $P(G)$ is appended to W as follows. In the following, let $IN = v^a$ hold when Algorithm 1 is executed at v and u^b be the port of u that connects to edge $\{u, v\}$.

(a) Case that the agent executes lines 2–3 (and leaves through v^{a-1}):
When v^{a-1} is a cycle port, $\{v^a, v^{a-1}\}, \{v^{a-1}, u^b\}$ are appended to W.
When v^{a-1} is a tree port, $\{v^a, v^{(a-1)\ominus}\}, \{v^{(a-1)\ominus}, u^{b\oplus}\}$ are appended to W.
(b) Case that the agent executes lines 5–6 (and leaves through v^{a+1}):
When v^{a+1} is a cycle port, $\{v^a, v^{a+1}\}, \{v^{a+1}, u^b\}$ are appended to W.
When v^{a+1} is a tree port, $\{v^a, v^{(a+1)\oplus}\}, \{v^{(a+1)\oplus}, u^{b\ominus}\}$ are appended to W.
(c) Case that the agent executes line 8 (and leaves through v^{a-1}):
When v^{a-1} is a cycle port, $\{v^{a\oplus}, v^{a-1}\}, \{v^{a-1}, u^b\}$ are appended to W.
When v^{a-1} is a tree port, $\{v^{a\oplus}, v^{(a-1)\ominus}\}, \{v^{(a-1)\ominus}, u^{b\oplus}\}$ are appended to W.
(d) Case that the agent executes line 10 (and leaves through v^{a+1}):
When v^{a+1} is a cycle port, $\{v^{a\ominus}, v^{a+1}\}, \{v^{a+1}, u^b\}$ are appended to W.
When v^{a+1} is a tree port, $\{v^{a\ominus}, v^{(a+1)\oplus}\}, \{v^{(a+1)\oplus}, u^{b\ominus}\}$ are appended to W.

First, we show the following claim by induction on the number k of agent moves (*i.e.*, the number of the pair appendices described above).

Claim. The p-edge sequence W_k (of length $2k$) obtained by applying the above appendices k times is a walk in $P(G)$ and ends with an p-edge connecting to the node the agent currently stays at. Moreover, when the last p-edge of W_k is a tree p-edge, the last p-node is $u^{b\oplus}$ (resp. $u^{b\ominus}$) for some b if $dir =' \ominus'$ (resp. $dir = ''\oplus'$) holds immediately after the k-th move of the agent.

When $k = 1$, we consider the four cases of the first appendix. In case (a), v^a ($= IN$) is a cycle port with an even port number. From Proposition 1 (1), the first p-edge $\{v^a, v^{a-1}\}$ or $\{v^a, v^{(a-1)\ominus}\}$ of W_1 is an intra-edge of $P(G)$. The second p-edge $\{v^{a-1}, u^b\}$ (resp. $\{v^{(a-1)\ominus}, u^{b\oplus}\}$) of W_1 is a cycle p-edge (resp. a tree p-edge) of $P(G)$ from the definition of $P(G)$. Moreover, when tree p-edge $\{v^{(a-1)\ominus}, u^{b\oplus}\}$ is appended, $dir =' \ominus'$ holds after the first move, which verifies the claim for case (a). The claim holds similarly for case (b). In case (c), v^a ($= IN$) is a tree port and $dir =' \ominus'$ initially holds (and remains unchanged in the first action of the agent). We can see that W_1 is a walk of $P(G)$ and the last p-node is $u^{b\oplus}$ when the last p-edge is a tree p-edge, which verifies the claim for case (c). The claim holds similarly for case (d).

Assume that the claim holds for W_k, we prove that the claim holds for W_{k+1}. In case (a), the inductive assumption implies that W_k is a walk of $P(G)$ ending with a cycle port v^a such that $IN = v^a$ holds at the beginning of the $(k+1)$-st agent action. Thus, W_{k+1} obtained by appending $\{v^a, v^{a-1}\}, \{v^{a-1}, u^b\}$ or $\{v^a, v^{(a-1)\ominus}\}, \{v^{(a-1)\ominus}, u^{b\oplus}\}$ to W_k is a walk in $P(G)$. Moreover, when tree p-edge $\{v^{(a-1)\ominus}, u^{b\oplus}\}$ is appended, $dir =' \ominus'$ holds after the $(k+1)$-st move, which verifies the claim for case (a). The claim holds similarly for the other cases.

The claim we've just proved implies that the traversal of G by the agent can be considered as a walk W in $P(G)$. Notice that W is a walk in a ring since $P(G)$ is a ring. Proving that the agent never changes the direction in W suffices for showing that Algorithm 1 is a snap-stabilizing perpetual exploration algorithm with exploration time $c(G) + 2t(G)$. To change the direction in ring traversal, the same edge has to be used consecutively. However, the construction of W guarantees that W is an alternating sequence of intra-node edges and cycle/tree p-edges, which implies that W is a walk repeatedly traversing $P(G)$ in a fixed direction.

We can show by considering a cactus graph consisting of a ring and a line that the exploration time $c(G) + 2t(G)$ exactly matches a lower bound.   □

4   Exploration by an Oblivious Agent

This section considers exploration of cactus graphs by an *oblivious* (or memoryless) agent. We first show impossibility of exploration even for a cactus graph containing only a single cycle where the cycle ports are distinguishable. This impossibility result shows the one-bit agent memory used in Algorithm 1 is necessary for exploration of cactus graphs.

Theorem 2. *No exploration algorithm exists for an oblivious agent in a graph containing only a single cycle.*

Proof. Since the agent is oblivious, the outgoing port OUT from node v is determined from the incoming port IN and the numbers of cycle ports $c(v)$ and tree ports $t(v)$. Consider the graphs G_1 and G_2 in Fig. 4 and the case that the initial node of the agent is x. The agent executes the same action at node u, v and w since each of them has two cycle ports and one tree port. We define function $OUT : \{0, 1, 2\} \to \{0, 1, 2\}$ that determines at these nodes the outgoing port from the incoming port.

When agent reaches u from x in G_1, it has to move v or w, otherwise it repeatedly moves only between u and x. We assume that the agent moves to v, that is, $OUT(2) = 0$ holds. When the agent moves to w, we exchange the port numbers 0 and 1 in the following proof. Thus this assumption does not lose

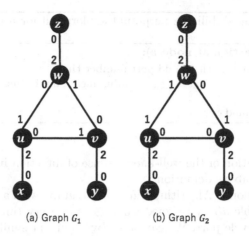

(a) Graph G_1 (b) Graph G_2

Fig. 4. The graphs for proving the impossibility of exploration by an oblivious agent

generality. Now consider the agent action when it reaches v in G_1. It can move to u, w or y next (or $OUT(1) = 1, 0$ or 2 respectively).

(a) Case of $OUT(1) = 0$: The agent repeatedly circulates w, u and v in this order. It cannot visit y or z.
(b) Case of $OUT(1) = 1$: The agent moves back to u and then has to move to w (or $OUT(0) = 1$), otherwise it repeatedly moves between u and v or among x, u and v. Setting $OUT(0) = 1$ makes the agent repeatedly circulates u, w and v in this order, and the agent cannot visit y or z.
(c) Case of $OUT(1) = 2$: The agent succeeds to make perpetual exploration in G_1. But in G_2, it will never visit z irrespective of setting $OUT(0)$, thus it fails to explore G_2. This is because, if we set $OUT(0) = 0$ (resp. $OUT(0) = 1$, and $OUT(0) = 2$), the agent repeatedly moves between u and v (resp., among x, u, v and w, and among x, u, v and y).

Thus, we have no function OUT for u, v and w that allows exploration in both G_1 and G_2. □

The above impossibility is proved for exploration that requires that each node be visited *at least once*, and thus holds for (snap-stabilizing) perpetual exploration.

In the remaining part of this section, we introduce the restriction on the port numbering, a *sense of direction*, into a cactus graph G so that an oblivious agent can perpetually explore G in a snap-stabilizing fashion.

As in the previous section, we assume for a cactus graph G that cycle ports at each node v are assigned port numbers from $0, 1, \ldots, c(v) - 1$ so that the ports numbered with $2a$ and $2a + 1$ are connecting to edges in the same cycle of G for each a ($0 \leq a \leq c(v)/2 - 1$). We say G has a sense of direction if, for each cycle edge $\{u, v\}$, the port of u connecting to $\{u, v\}$ is assigned an even port number if and only if the port of v connecting to $\{u, v\}$ is assigned an odd port number.

Algorithm 2. Snap-stabilizing perpetual exploration for a cactus graph with sense of direction

algorithm (agent action at node v):
1: **if** IN is a cycle port with an odd port number **then**
2:     $IN \leftarrow IN - 1$ ▷ Adjustment only in the initial configuration
3: **end if**
4: $OUT \leftarrow IN - 1 \bmod \delta_v$

This is a generalization of the well-known sense of direction in a ring as that in a ring satisfies the above definition.

Consider execution of Algorithm 1 in a cactus graph with a sense of direction. Remind that variable dir is assigned value $\ominus$ or $\oplus$ every time the agent enters a node through a cycle port. We can show by argument similar to the proof of Theorem 1 that the agent leaves a node through an odd-numbered cycle port if and only if $dir = \ominus$ holds. The sense of direction guarantees that the agent leaving through an odd-numbered (resp. even-numbered) cycle port enters the next node through an even-numbered (or odd-numbered) cycle port. Proposition 3 guarantees that the next cycle port through which the agent leaves after entering through an even-numbered (or odd-numbered) cycle port has an odd (resp. even) port number. The above implies that variable dir remains unchanged during the perpetual exploration, and thus variable dir is unnecessary.

Algorithm 2 presents a snap-stabilizing perpetual exploration for cactus graphs assuming a sense of direction. The traversal route of the agent is exactly same as that in Algorithm 1 with keeping $dir = \ominus$. When the initial value of IN (the incoming port) designates an odd-numbered cycle port, the algorithm adjusts the initial value of IN so that the traversal direction coincides with that in Algorithm 1 with $dir = \ominus$. This determines the next outgoing port as $IN - 1$ when the agent enters a node through a tree port.

Theorem 3. *Algorithm 2 presents a snap-stabilizing perpetual exploration algorithm for a single oblivious agent in any cactus graph G with a sense of direction. Its exploration time is $c(G) + 2t(G)$, which exactly matches a lower bound.*

Acknowledgements. This work was partially supported by JSPS KAKENHI Grant Numbers 19H04085, 19K11826, 20H04140, and 20KK0232.

References

1. Altisen, K., Devismes, S., Dubois, S., Petit, F.: Introduction to Distributed Self-Stabilizing Algorithms. Synthesis Lectures on Distributed Computing Theory. Morgan & Claypool Publishers, San Rafael (2019)
2. Ambühl, C., Gasieniec, L., Pelc, A., Radzik, T., Zhang, X.: Tree exploration with logarithmic memory. ACM Trans. Algorithms **7**(2), 17:1–17:21 (2011)
3. Becha, H., Flocchini, P.: Optimal construction of sense of direction in a torus by a mobile agent. Int. J. Found. Comput. Sci. **18**(3), 529–546 (2007)

4. Bui, A., Datta, A.K., Petit, F., Villain, V.: State-optimal snap-stabilizing PIF in tree networks. In: Proceedings of ICDCS Workshop on Self-stabilizing Systems, pp. 78–85 (1999)
5. Cohen, R., Fraigniaud, P., Ilcinkas, D., Korman, A., Peleg, D.: Label-guided graph exploration by a finite automaton. ACM Trans. Algorithms 4(4), 42:1–42:18 (2008)
6. Czyzowicz, J., et al.: More efficient periodic traversal in anonymous undirected graphs. Theor. Comput. Sci. **444**, 60–76 (2012)
7. Das, S.: Graph explorations with mobile agents. In: Flocchini, P., Prencipe, G., Santoro, N. (eds.) Distributed Computing by Mobile Entities, Current Research in Moving and Computing. LNCS, vol. 11340, pp. 403–422. Springer, Cham (2019). https://doi.org/10.1007/978-3-030-11072-7_16
8. Dijkstra, E.W.: Self-stabilizing systems in spite of distributed control. Commun. ACM **17**(11), 643–644 (1974)
9. Diks, K., Fraigniaud, P., Kranakis, E., Pelc, A.: Tree exploration with little memory. J. Algorithms **51**(1), 38–63 (2004)
10. Disser, Y., Hackfeld, J., Klimm, M.: Tight bounds for undirected graph exploration with pebbles and multiple agents. J. ACM **66**(6), 40:1–40:41 (2019)
11. Dobrev, S., Jansson, J., Sadakane, K., Sung, W.-K.: Finding short right-hand-on-the-wall walks in graphs. In: Pelc, A., Raynal, M. (eds.) SIROCCO 2005. LNCS, vol. 3499, pp. 127–139. Springer, Heidelberg (2005). https://doi.org/10.1007/11429647_12
12. Dolev, S.: Self-Stabilization. MIT Press, Cambridge (2000)
13. Flocchini, P., Huang, M.J., Luccio, F.L.: Decontamination of hypercubes by mobile agents. Networks **52**(3), 167–178 (2008)
14. Flocchini, P., Prencipe, G., Santoro, N. (eds.): Distributed Computing by Mobile Entities, Current Research in Moving and Computing. LNCS, vol. 11340. Springer, Cham (2019). https://doi.org/10.1007/978-3-030-11072-7
15. Fraigniaud, P., Ilcinkas, D., Peer, G., Pelc, A., Peleg, D.: Graph exploration by a finite automaton. Theor. Comput. Sci. **345**(2–3), 331–344 (2005)
16. Fraigniaud, P., Ilcinkas, D., Rajsbaum, S., Tixeuil, S.: Space lower bounds for graph exploration via reduced automata. In: Pelc, A., Raynal, M. (eds.) SIROCCO 2005. LNCS, vol. 3499, pp. 140–154. Springer, Heidelberg (2005). https://doi.org/10.1007/11429647_13
17. Gasieniec, L., Klasing, R., Martin, R.A., Navarra, A., Zhang, X.: Fast periodic graph exploration with constant memory. J. Comput. Syst. Sci. **74**(5), 808–822 (2008)
18. Ilcinkas, D.: Setting port numbers for fast graph exploration. Theor. Comput. Sci. **401**(1–3), 236–242 (2008)
19. Ilcinkas, D.: Oblivious robots on graphs: exploration. In: Flocchini, P., Prencipe, G., Santoro, N. (eds.) Distributed Computing by Mobile Entities, Current Research in Moving and Computing. LNCS, vol. 11340, pp. 218–233. Springer, Cham (2019). https://doi.org/10.1007/978-3-030-11072-7_9
20. Kosowski, A., Navarra, A.: Graph decomposition for memoryless periodic exploration. Algorithmica **63**(1–2), 26–38 (2012)
21. Masuzawa, T., Tixeuil, S.: Quiescence of self-stabilizing gossiping among mobile agents in graphs. Theor. Comput. Sci. **411**(14–15), 1567–1582 (2010)
22. Menc, A., Pajak, D., Uznanski, P.: Time and space optimality of rotor-router graph exploration. Inf. Process. Lett. **127**, 17–20 (2017)
23. Panaite, P., Pelc, A.: Exploring unknown undirected graphs. J. Algorithms **33**(2), 281–295 (1999)

24. Priezzhev, V.B., Dhar, D., Dhar, A., Krishnamurthy, S.: Eulerian walkers as a model of self-organized criticality. Phys. Rev. Lett. **77**, 5079–5082 (1996)
25. Reingold, O.: Undirected connectivity in log-space. J. ACM **55**(4), 17:1–17:24 (2008)
26. Yanovski, V., Wagner, I.A., Bruckstein, A.M.: A distributed ant algorithm for efficiently patrolling a network. Algorithmica **37**(3), 165–186 (2003)

Invited Paper: Towards Practical Atomic Distributed Shared Memory: An Experimental Evaluation

Andria Trigeorgi[1,2]($\boxtimes$), Nicolas Nicolaou[1], Chryssis Georgiou[2],
Theophanis Hadjistasi[1], Efstathios Stavrakis[1], Viveck Cadambe[3],
and Bhuvan Urgaonkar[3]

[1] Algolysis Ltd., Limassol, Cyprus
[2] Department of Computer Science, University of Cyprus, Nicosia, Cyprus
trigeorgi.andria@ucy.ac.cy
[3] Pennsylvania State University, State College, PA, USA

Abstract. Distributed Shared Storage Services may serve as building blocks to yield complex, decentralized, cloud applications in emerging technologies (e.g., IoT, VR/AR), as they offer a transparent cloud storage space where distributed applications can store, retrieve, and coordinate over shared data. Ideally, distributed applications would like to communicate through a "cloud" memory layer that may provide similar guarantees as a centralized sequential memory. Atomic Distributed Shared Memory (ADSM) provides the illusion of a sequential memory space despite asynchrony, network perturbations, and device failures. A plethora of algorithmic solutions along with proven correctness guarantees have been proposed to provide ADSM in a message passing system. None of them, however, has been adopted in a real working solution: commercial solutions avoid the use of ADSM algorithms, mainly due to their communication overhead. *But what is exactly the performance overhead of an ADSM algorithm over existing commercial solutions?* In this work we want to provide a first answer to this question by performing an in-depth experimental comparison of the state-of-the-art dynamic ADSM algorithm ARES, with two well-established open-source distributed storage solutions, CASSANDRA and REDIS. The results show that ARES's performance is comparable with the commercial systems, with respect to scalability, object size and throughput.

Keywords: Distributed storage · Strong consistency · Erasure code · Reconfiguration · Fault-tolerance

1 Introduction

Motivation and Prior Work. Emulating a shared memory over a set of distinct, often geographically dispersed devices, is a fundamental problem in

Supported by the EU's NGIAtlantic.eu cascading grant agreement no. OC4-347; https://projects.algolysis.com/ares-ngi/.

distributed computing, and an important tool for the development of dependable and robust distributed applications [6,14]. A Distributed Shared Memory (DSM) service promises to provide an available, accessible, and survivable shared memory space over an asynchronous, fail prone, message passing environment. To preserve these properties, data are replicated in multiple devices, referred to as servers or replica hosts, raising the challenge on how to preserve *consistency* between the replica copies. Different consistency guarantees were rigorously defined over the years [16]. *Atomicity* is a venerable notion of consistency, introduced by Lamport [19]. To this day it remains the most natural type of consistency because it provides an illusion of equivalence with the serial object type that software designers expect. For more than two decades, a series of works, e.g., [4,7,9–11,13,20,21], suggested solutions for building Atomic DSM (ADSM) emulations, for both static, i.c., where replica participation does not change over time, and dynamic (reconfigurable) environments, i.e., where failed replicas may retire and new replicas may join the service in a non-blocking manner.

It is apparent that those solutions cannot be found readily and were not adopted by commercial distributed storage applications. Commercial Distributed Storage Systems (DSS), such as Dropbox, HDFS, CASSANDRA and REDIS, avoid providing strong consistency guarantees (such as atomicity) as they are considered costly and difficult to implement in an asynchronous, fail prone, message passing environment. Hence, such solutions either choose to offer weaker or tunable guarantees to achieve better performance when atomicity is not preserved.

Indeed, initial implementations of ADSM had high demands in communication, storage, and sometimes computation. Recent works, however, e.g., [12,21], invest in algorithms that may reduce the overheads on the aforementioned parameters. ARES [21] is a recent ADSM algorithm, which proposes a modular approach for providing a *dynamic* shared memory space. ARES may use any ADSM algorithm at its core, providing the flexibility to adjust its performance based on the application demands. Fragmented ARES [12] is an extension of ARES that supports versioning and fragmentation for efficiently handling large objects, such as files.

Experimental results presented in [12,21], demonstrated a promising performance of the algorithm under various environmental conditions and data loads. *But how such an algorithm may compare to commercially used solutions?* That is, no evidence exists to date to examine what are the gains from commercial solutions to adopt less than intuitive guarantees. In this work we set to put ADSM and chosen open-source, commercial solutions in a head-to-head comparison in order to answer the question: *Is it worth to trade consistency for performance?*

Contributions. In this work we perform an in-depth experimentation on ARES [21] and we present extensive comparison with two open-source widely used distributed storage solutions: (*i*) CASSANDRA [1], and (*ii*) REDIS [2]. To this respect, we have developed our own implementation of ARES, and we have utilized the open source code of CASSANDRA and REDIS.

Our experimental study focuses on measuring the average operation latency (communication and computation), in the following three test categories:

- **Scalability Tests:** Aim to test the ability of the service while the set of service participants grows.
- **Stress Tests:** Aim to test the performance of the service under various loads, concurrency patterns, and topology deployments.
- **Fault-Tolerance Tests:** Aim to test the tolerance of the service to node failures and its performance in necessary reconfigurations.

We deployed our experiments in real testbeds, distributed in the European Union (EU) and the USA. Such deployment helped us obtain real-condition results and evaluate the algorithms over cross-Atlantic setups. To the best of our knowledge, this is the first work to conduct such comparison. Our experimentation results suggest, perhaps surprisingly, that ARES has a similar or sometimes better performance than the competition, even without any optimization.

2   Algorithms Overview

In this section we provide a high-level description of the algorithms we examine in this work, highlighting their main differences.

2.1   ARES

ARES [21] is a modular framework, designed to implement dynamic, reconfigurable, fault-tolerant, read/write distributed atomic shared memory objects. Similar to traditional implementations, ARES uses $\langle tag, value \rangle$ pairs to order the operations on a shared object. In contrast to existing solutions, ARES does not define the exact methodology to access the object replicas. Rather, it relies on three, so called, *data access primitives* (DAPs): (i) the get-tag, which returns the tag of an object, (ii) the get-data, which returns a $\langle tag, value \rangle$ pair, and (iii) the put-data($\langle tag, v \rangle$), which accepts a $\langle tag, value \rangle$ as an argument.

DAPs. As detailed in [21], these DAPs may be used to express the data access strategy, i.e., how they retrieve and update the object data, of different shared memory algorithms (e.g., [6]). Using the DAPs, ARES achieves a modular design, agnostic of the data access strategies, and enables the use of different DAP implementation per configuration (something impossible for other solutions). For the DAPs to be useful, they need to satisfy *Property 1* [21], which informally states that a get-data (or get-tag) DAP returns a value (or tag) at least as recent as the one written by a put-data.

To demonstrate the flexibility that DAPs provide, the authors in [21] expressed two different atomic shared R/W algorithms in terms of DAPs. These are the DAPs for the well celebrated ABD [7] algorithm, and the DAPs for an erasure coded based approach presented for the first time in [21]. In the rest of the manuscript we refer to the two DAP implementations as ABD-DAP and EC-DAP. In EC-DAP, an $[n, k]$-MDS erasure coding algorithm (e.g., Reed-Solomon [25]) encodes k object fragments into n coded elements, which consist of the k encoded data fragments and m encoded parity fragments. The n coded fragments are distributed among a set of n different servers. Any k of the n coded fragments can then be used to reconstruct the initial object value. As servers maintain a fragment instead of the whole object value, EC-based approaches claim significant storage benefits. To reduce the communication overhead and yet preserve atomicity, servers maintain the last δ values they have seen, such that $\delta = |W|$ the set of writers, and thus the number of concurrent write operations. By utilizing the EC-DAP, ARES became *the first* erasure coded dynamic algorithm to implement an atomic R/W object. We refer as ARES-ABD and ARES-EC the versions of ARES using ABD-DAP and EC-DAP, respectively.

We now provide a high-level description of the two main functionalities supported by ARES: (i) the reconfiguration of the servers, and (ii) the read/write operations on the shared object.

Reconfiguration. Reconfiguration is the process of changing the set of servers. In high-level, ARES maintains a sequence of configuration ids. Whenever a server wants to introduce a new configuration, it performs the following steps: (1) it parses the configuration sequence to find the last configuration id proposed, (2) it proposes a new configuration to extend the sequence via an external *consensus* service, and (3) if its proposal is accepted, it moves the value of the object from the old configurations to the new, and then appends the id of the new configuration to the end of the sequence. The reconfiguration protocol ensures that the sequence remains connected, does not have any gaps, and it is the same for any participant in the system. The whole process is *non-blocking*, that it, the reconfiguration does not block the read/write operations on the object.

Reads/Writes. Read and write operations act as follows: (1) parse the sequence to find the latest configuration (read-config), (2) read the "latest" (based on the *tag*) value (if it is a read) or only the tag (if it is a write) of the object from that configuration (using DAPs), (3) get in a loop to propagate the latest (if its a read) or the new (if its a write) value to the latest configuration in the sequence (using DAPs and read-config), (4) terminate if no new configuration is discovered. The last two steps serve to propagate the value to new configurations as they become available. Essentially read and writes catch up with the latest configuration. Detailed analysis appears in [21].

Implementation. As we already mentioned, for the purposes of this study we have developed our own implementation of ARES. Our implementation is based on the architecture depicted in Fig. 1. This includes the modules composing the infrastructure as well as the communication layer between these modules. The system is composed of two main modules: (i) a Manager, and (ii) a Distributed Shared Memory Module (DSMM). The manager provides an interface to each client for accessing the DSM (in our case a command line interface - CLI). Following this architecture, clients may access the file system through the Manager, while the shared objects are maintained by the servers through the DSMM. Notice that the Manager uses the DSMM as an external service to write and read objects to the shared memory. To this respect, our architecture is flexible enough to utilize any underlying DSM algorithm to implement the DSMM. In our case

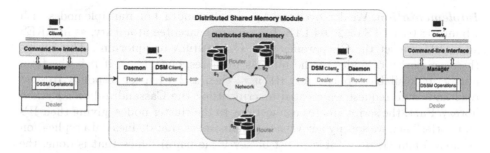

Fig. 1. The architecture of our ARES implementation.

we implemented two algorithms. At first, we integrated algorithm ABD to our DSM Module. Next, we implemented algorithm ARES with two different DAPs (ABD and EC) and then we integrated that implementation to the DSM Module. Python was chosen as the programming language and ZeroMQ [27] messaging library written in Python (the Dealer-Router paradigm) for the underlying communication. For the EC algorithm, we use the standard Reed-Solomon implementation provided by liberasurecode from the PyEClib Python library [23]. Notice that the implementation of ARES requires a consensus algorithm to be implemented as well. So, we implemented the RAFT [22] consensus algorithm, utilizing an open-source implementation of RAFT, also written in Python [24].

2.2 CASSANDRA

CASSANDRA [1] is a NoSQL distributed database offering continuous availability, high performance, horizontal scalability, and a flexible approach with tunable parameters. It was initially developed by Facebook for their inbox search feature. Today, it is an open-source application of Apache Hadoop. CASSANDRA uses peer-to-peer communication where each node is connected to all other nodes. The protocol used to achieve this communication is gossip, in which nodes periodically exchange state information about themselves. All the nodes in a cluster can serve read and write requests. Thus, when a request is sent to any node, this node acts as the coordinator. The coordinator distributes execution around the cluster, gathers the responses from the replicas, and responds back to the client. By default, CASSANDRA guarantees *eventual consistency*, which implies that all updates reach all replicas eventually. However, CASSANDRA offers tunable consistency for read and write operations, so that the system can guarantee weaker or stronger consistency, as required by the client application. The required consistency can be achieved by tuning the consistency level (CL) and the replication factor (RF) parameters. RF specifies how many copies of a store object (i.e., a row in CASSANDRA's Database) is kept among the participants. Given the value of the RF, the CL controls how many responses the coordinator waits for before the operation is considered complete. Finally, CASSANDRA allows the removal and addition of a single node at a time, in contrast to ARES that allows a complete modification of the configuration (reconfiguration) in a single operation.

Implementation. We deployed the Apache Cassandra 4 on multiple nodes with Ubuntu 18.04.1 LTS or 20.04 LTS. In order to guarantee atomicity, as in ARES and ABD, we set the CL parameter of CASSANDRA to "quorum". This means that a majority of nodes of the replicas must respond. Thus, if n is the total number of available replicas, and RF is n, then $n/2 + 1$ must respond. To send read and write request we created a script using the Cassandra-driver Python library. First, the script creates connections to the cluster nodes, giving their IPs and ports. Then we specify a keyspace (a namespace that defines data replication on nodes) and create a table (a list of key-value pairs). Once that is done, the client can send write and read requests, using the *insert* and *select* statements, respectively. A writer inserts a tuple ($fileid, value$), where the value is a byte string of type blobs (binary large objects) in CASSANDRA. A reader selects the value providing the file's id.

2.3 REDIS

REDIS [2] is an open source, in-memory key-value store. The read/write response time for REDIS is extremely fast since all the data is in memory. REDIS is based on a Master-Slave architecture, i.e., it enables replication of master REDIS instances in replica REDIS instances. The use of REDIS is rather easy; REDIS will internally store the key and value when users execute commands like set key value. REDIS returns the value with a simple get key command from the user. The data size cannot exceed the main memory limit because all the data are in main memory. REDIS has two persistence mechanisms: RDB (Redis Database Backup) and AOF (Append Only File). RDB persistence provides point-in-time snapshots of the database at specified intervals. AOF persistence logs every write operation. When the database server starts, REDIS reads the AOF log to reconstruct the database. RDB is perfect for backup, but if RDB stops working all data changes since the last snapshot are lost. In comparison, AOF has better durability, although adopting AOF persistence may result in performance loss. REDIS has a command called "WAIT" in order to implement synchronous replication. This command blocks the current client until all the previous write commands are successfully transferred and acknowledged by at least the specified number of replicas. REDIS provides eventual consistency. Even though a write may wait until all replicas reply, reads do not wait and always terminate as soon as they receive messages from the master. So, we consider REDIS as a benchmark providing eventual consistency, however, due to the use of the "WAIT" function, in most scenarios (as claimed in [2]), it may provide atomic consistency.

Implementation. We deployed REDIS 5 on multiple nodes with Ubuntu 18.04.1 LTS or 20.04 LTS. We implement two variants of REDIS, with and without the WAIT command during a write operation, i.e., REDIS_W and REDIS, respectively. For the REDIS_W, we specified the number of waiting write acknowledgments with a majority, i.e., $n/2 + 1$, to match the ABD algorithm. To send read and write requests we created a script using the Redis-driver Python library. First, the script creates a connection to REDIS, giving the IP and port of the master node. Once connected to REDIS, the client can write and read with REDIS command functions, *set* and *get* respectively. A writer assigns a file's byte string value to the REDIS key; it uses the file's id as the key, while a reader gets the value giving the file's id. We note that the number of reader clients can dynamically increase or decrease. However, if the Master crashes, the writes will be blocked, as the replica nodes are read only, until a new replica becomes the new master; with this respect, reconfiguration in REDIS is blocking.

3   Experimental Evaluation

In this section we provide a description of our experiments and the results we have obtained in this study. Section 3.1 presents the setup of the distributed system we considered and the tools we used for the experiment deployment. Section 3.2 presents the different scenarios we examined and the purpose of each scenario. We conclude with our results and their analysis in Sect. 3.3. The collected data are available in [3], in case one would like to validate our analysis.

3.1   Experimentation Setup

Our main goal was to conduct real-life experiments, exposed to the perturbations, delays, and uncertainty of network communication. We picked devices both in the EU and the USA, thus, examining the impact of long (cross-Atlantic) communication on the performance of each algorithm. We used two main tools to deploy and execute our experiments: (*i*) jFed [18], and (*ii*) Ansible [5].

Experiment Deployment. jFed is a GUI tool that was developed within the Fed4FIRE+ project and was used to get access and reserve virtual and physical machines in various experimental testbeds. Through the tool we were able to define our node deployment strategy, and specify the connectivity between the reserved nodes, their external interfaces, the resources and the OS image to use, and launch those machines in their respective testbeds, *for all algorithms*.

We used machines from four different testbeds (in the EU and the USA), that are supported by JFed: (*i*) imec Virtual Wall 1/2 [26] (Belgium – EU), (*ii*) Cloudlab [8] (Utah – USA), (*iii*) InstaGENI [17] (NYU, UCLA, and Utdallas – USA) and (*iv*) Grid5000 [15] (France – EU). In total, we used 39 nodes, where the InstaGENI ones are XEN VMs with Ubuntu 18.04.1 LTS and routable IPs, and the rest are physical machines with Ubuntu 20.04 LTS. Due to the similarity on machine specifications and the high demands in those testbeds we did not use a specific set of spec configuration but rather we were reserving random available nodes for each experiment. A reserved machine can either act as a client or a server in any given experimental run. We avoided having a machine with both roles, preventing giving a communication advantage to clients residing in the same machine with a server. Each server is deployed on a different machine, and clients are all deployed in the remaining machines in a round robin fashion (i.e., a machine may execute multiple client instances). For example, with 10 machines,

4 servers, 6 writers and 6 readers, servers would have been deployed on the first 4 machines and each other machine would contain one writer and one reader.

Experiment Execution. Ansible was mainly used for the execution of the experiments as it is a tool to automate different IT tasks, such as cloud provisioning, configuration management, application deployment, and intra-service orchestration. There are two main steps to run an experiment: (*i*) booting up the client (either writer or reader) and the server nodes, and (*ii*) executing each scenario using Ansible Playbooks, scripts written in the YAML language. The scripts get pushed to target machines, they are executed, and then get removed. In our experiments, one instance node was dedicated as a controller to orchestrate the experiments. For the execution of the experiment, Ansible automated the provision of the executables in each machine, the execution of the operations in the experiment, and the collection of the logs for our analysis.

Operations. In throughput experiments, operations are invoked without any delay (i.e., an operation is invoked once the previous operation by the same client is completed), and the clients perform 1000 operations each. For all other experiments we use a stochastic invocation scheme: each client waits a **random interval** each time it terminates an operation and before invoking the next one. Reads and writes are scheduled at a random interval between $[1 \ldots 3]$ s. In total, each writer performs 50 writes and each reader 50 reads. Each reconfigurer invokes one operation every 15 s and performs a total of 15 reconfigurations.

Performance Metric. The performance of the algorithms is measured in terms of the time it takes for their operations to terminate. Thus, for each algorithm, we measure the *average operation latency*, starting at the invocation to the response, and taking into account both the communication as well as the computation overhead. Notice that the operation latency is computed as the average of all clients' average operation latencies. Note that in the case of CASSANDRA, we omitted to account some "unsuccessful operations", i.e., operations where the client invoking them did not receive replies from a majority of servers.

3.2 Scenarios

Scenarios aim to capture the performance of the algorithms in the three performance parameters (tests) we mentioned in Sect. 1. Our scenarios are:

Scalability Test – Participation (All Algorithms). This scenario is constructed to compare the read and write latencies of the algorithms, as the number of the service participants increases. We varied the number of readers $|R|$ from 5 to 250 and the number of writers $|W|$ from 5 to 20. The number of servers $|S|$ is set to two different values, 3 and 11. To reduce the amount of combinations, we fixed the number of writers to 5 when testing all possible values of readers, and the readers to 5 when testing all possible combinations of writers. The size of the object is 1 MB. We used a different parity for ARES-EC, m, based on the number of servers used: m is set to $m = 1$ for $|S| = 3$ and $m = 5$ for $|S| = 11$.

Stress Test – Topology (All Algorithms). This scenario aims to measure how the performance of the algorithms is affected under different topologies and server participation. In this case we measure the throughput (average number of operations per second) of each algorithm. To avoid any delays due to operation contention, we chose to use 2 clients (1 reader and 1 writer), the minimum number of servers to form a majority, i.e. 3, and a simple object of 32 B. As we deployed machines on both EU and USA, our servers are split in such a way to either force all of them or their majority to be in a single continent. In particular, the 3 servers selected based the following topologies: $0E+3U$, $1E+2U$, $2E+1U$, $3E+0U$, where xY means that x servers are deployed in Y continent for $E = EU$ and $U = USA$. Similarly we deployed the clients either close (i.e., to the same continent) or away from the server majority. Last, we tested the throughput of the algorithms when the number of servers is growing from 3 to 15. In this case, for every server deployed in EU, we deployed 2 servers in the USA.

Stress Test – Object Size (All Algorithms). This scenario is made to evaluate how the read and write latencies are affected by the size of the shared object. The file size doubled from 64 kB to 8 MB. The number of servers is fixed to 11. The number of writers and the number of readers is fixed to 5. For ARES, there are two separated runs, one for ARES-ABD and one for ARES-EC. The parity value of ARES-EC is set to $m = 5$, and thus the fragmentation parameter is $k = 6$. The quorum size of the ARES-EC is $\left\lceil \frac{|S|+k}{2} \right\rceil = \left\lceil \frac{11+6}{2} \right\rceil = 9$, while the quorum size of ARES-ABD is $\left\lfloor \frac{|S|}{2} \right\rfloor + 1 = \left\lfloor \frac{11}{2} \right\rfloor + 1 = 6$. For CASSANDRA, we set the consistency level (CL) to the majority, i.e., 6. The writers of REDIS_W also wait for a majority (6) servers to reply.

Stress Test – Fragmentation Parameter k (Only ARES-EC). This scenario applies only to ARES-EC since we examine how the read and write latencies are affected as we modify the erasure-code fragmentation parameter k (a parameter of Reed-Solomon). We assume 11 servers and we increase k from 2 to 10. The number of writers (and hence the value of δ) are set to 5. The number of readers is fixed to 15. The size of the object used is 4 MB.

Fault-Tolerance Test – Node Crashes (Only ARES). In this scenario, we introduced server fail-crashes in the ARES algorithm to verify the fault-tolerance guarantees and the responsiveness of the system, *especially with respect to reconfigurations*. The number of servers $|S|$ is set to 11 with $m = 5$. The number of writers and readers are fixed to 5 and 15, respectively. The size of the file used is 1 MB. We execute 2 crashes during each experimental run, server $s0$ crashes 100 s within the experiment and $s3$ crashes 200 s after. Both failed servers are from the imec Virtual Wall 2 testbed (EU), since we observed that they are included in the most quorum replies. We assign a unique id to each quorum. However, the quorum of each DAP differs in size. The size of each quorum (majority) in ARES-ABD is 6, while the quorum size of ARES-EC is 9. In total, ARES-ABD has 462 quorums and ARES-EC has 55. For ease of visualization, we categorize the quorums of the two DAPs into three groups: (i) one which includes all quorums, (ii) one which excludes quorums involving $s0$; and (iii) one which excludes quorums involving either $s0$ or $s3$. During the same scenario we tested the reconfiguration ability of the algorithm. In particular, we varied the number of reconfigurers with values in $\{1, 3, 5\}$ and each reconfiguration was switching between the two DAPs.

3.3   Experimental Results

Our analytical results aim to expose how a strongly consistent, reconfigurable service like ARES, compares in performance with the two commercial storages of our choice, namely CASSANDRA and REDIS. Moreover, it helps us identify bottlenecks and shortcomings of ARES for future optimizations, and, in some scenarios, we demonstrate the ability of ARES to utilize erasure-coding and to cope with failures and dynamic reconfiguration.

Table 1 provides a comprehensive list of the variables we used in our scenarios. Experiments were conducted for a selection of those parameters. In this section we highlight some representative outcomes in each scenario. *More results may be found in the website of the project*[1] *presented in interactive plots where the user may choose the parameters to apply.* The results shown are compiled as averages over 3 samples per each scenario and 5 samples for the topology scenario.

Table 1. Experimental variables

Variable	Possible values	Description
Topology	{ *0E+3U, 1E+2U, 2E+1U, 3E+0U* }	Distribution of servers in EU and US. For the scenarios with more than 3 servers we use two servers in US for every server in EU
ClientContinent	{ *EU, US* }	Location of the clients (for throughput scenario)
$\mathcal{S}$	{ 3, 5, 7, 9, 11 }	The number of servers
$\mathcal{W}$	{ 0, 1, 5, 10, 15, 20 }	The number of writers
$\mathcal{R}$	{ 0, 1, 5, 15, 50, 100, 150, 250 }	The number of readers
$\mathcal{G}$	{ 0, 1, 3, 5 }	The number of reconfigurers
k	{ 1, 2, 3, 4, 5, 6, 7, 8, 9 }	Erasure-coding data fragments
fsize	{ 64 kB, 128 kB, 256 kB, 512 kB, 1 MB, 2 MB, 4 MB, 8 MB }	The size of the file (object)
Recontype	{ *sameDAP, switchingDAP, switchingDAP & andomServers* }	The way the reconfigurers work: (i) reconfiguring to the same DAP, (ii) reconfiguring the DAP alternately, (iii) reconfiguring the DAP alternatively and servers randomly

---

[1] https://projects.algolysis.com/ares-ngi/results/.

Scalability Tests. Some of the results obtained while increasing the number of participants in the system appear in Figs. 2, 3 and 4. At a first glance, CASSANDRA seems to struggle to keep up as the readers grow in all cases, while REDIS_W does not seem to be affected. Similar observation can be made for the two ABD based algorithms (ABD and ARES-ABD) as they remain at low levels as $|\mathcal{R}|$ increases. ARES-EC exposes an interesting behavior as it is the worst performing algorithm when few servers are used, and becomes faster when more servers are deployed. This can be seen in Figs. 3 and 4. The more the servers the more the encoded elements to be distributed and the bigger can be the fragmentation parameter k. Thus, each object fragment becomes smaller, resulting in tremendous benefits on the communication delays. Worth observing is that the latency of the write operation of ARES-EC matches the one of REDIS_W when $|\mathcal{S}| = 11$.

Similar findings can be seen as the number of writers $|\mathcal{W}|$ grows. CASSANDRA has the larger write latency despite the fact that it shows a more stable behavior, and the read latency of ARES-EC is the worst when $|\mathcal{S}| = 3$.

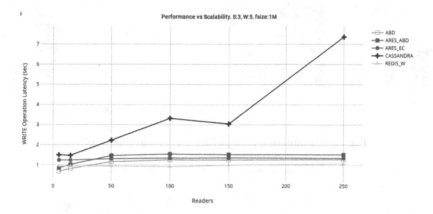

Fig. 2. Readers scalability vs write latency, $|\mathcal{S}| = 3$.

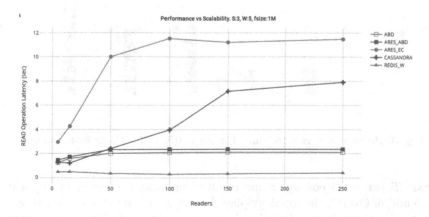

Fig. 3. Readers scalability vs read latency, $|\mathcal{S}| = 3$.

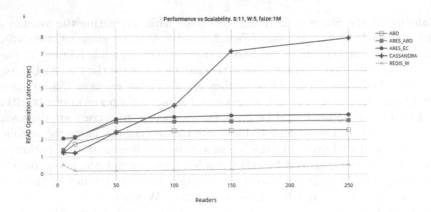

Fig. 4. Readers scalability vs read latency, $|\mathcal{S}| = 11$.

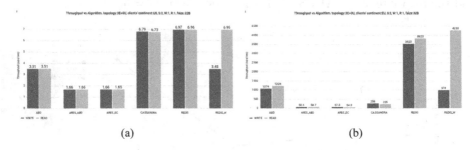

(a)   (b)

Fig. 5. Throughput vs algorithm. Topology: $3E + 0U$

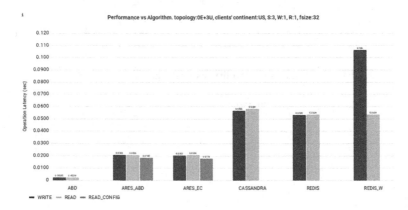

Fig. 6. Performance vs algorithm. Topology: $0E + 3U$ (Color figure online)

Stress Tests – Topology. Some results from these experiments appear in Figs. 5 and 6. Overall the topology played a major role on the performance, and in particular throughput, of all the algorithms we studied. All of the algorithms (including the ADSM algorithms we implemented, i.e., ABD, ARES-ABD, and

ARES-EC), achieve their maximum read and write throughput when the servers and the clients are deployed in the same continent.

For the ADSM algorithms, there appears to be no difference when the experiment contains non-concurrent or concurrent operations. The small $fsize$ (32 B), amplified the impact of the stable overhead of read-config operations, and they constitute a significant percentage of the total operation latency (see blue bar in Fig. 6). From the same figure we interestingly observe that the setup where all servers and clients are deployed in the USA, favored the ADSM algorithms over both CASSANDRA and REDIS.

On the other hand, CASSANDRA shows different behavior. It achieves the maximum read throughput when both servers and clients are deployed in the EU. It demonstrates a small lead over the ADSM algorithms in most cases on both operations. However, it shows some performance degradation when write and read operations are invoked concurrently.

Finally, REDIS and REDIS_W outperform the rest of the algorithms in most scenarios. REDIS shows consistent performance for both reads and writes due to the weaker consistency requirements and thus smaller communication footprint. The impact of the communication overhead is obvious in REDIS_W, where the writer waits before completing.

Stress Tests – Object Size. The results for the write performance in these experiments are captured in Fig. 7. We observe that the write latencies of all operations, except ARES-EC and REDIS_W, grow significantly, as the $fsize$ increases. The fragmentation applied by the ARES-EC benefits its write operations, which follow a slower increasing curve like the REDIS_W. The write latencies of all other algorithms are close to each other. Results show that the read operations of ARES-EC suffer the most delays until 4 MB. The first phase of the read operation does decoding, which is slower than the first phase of the write, which simply finds the maximum tag, contributed to this overhead. However, at larger file sizes (8 MB) CASSANDRA has the slowest read operations. As

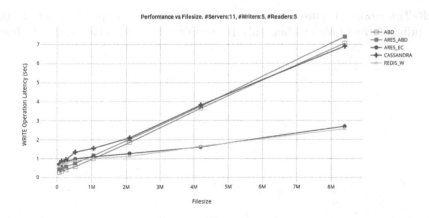

Fig. 7. Filesize results.

expected, the REDIS_W read operations provide the best results, and its write operations with the WAIT command have higher latency compared to the read operations. However, both of them remain at low levels as the $fsize$ increases.

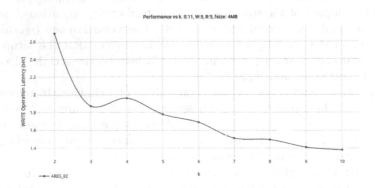

Fig. 8. k scalability results.

Stress Tests – Fragmentation Parameter k. From Fig. 8 we can infer that when smaller k are used, the write and read latencies reach their highest values. In both cases, small k results in the generation of a smaller number of data fragments and thus bigger sizes of the fragments and higher redundancy. For example, we can see that for $RS(11, 7)$ and $RS(11, 6)$ we have the same size of quorum, equal to 9, whereas the latter has more redundant information. As a result, with a higher number of m (i.e., smaller k) we achieve higher levels of fault-tolerance. The write latency seems to be less affected by the value of k since the write operation does only encoding, and not decoding, while the read operation does both. In conclusion, there appears to be a trade-off between operation latency and fault-tolerance in the system: the further increase of k (and thus lower fault-tolerance), the smaller the latency of read/write operations.

Fault-Tolerance. Figure 9 shows to which quorum group (0, 1, or 2) the responding servers belong when only 1 reconfigurer exists. That is, Fig. 9 shows

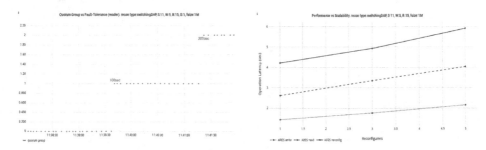

Fig. 9. Quorum replies to reader6.

Fig. 10. Reconfiguring DAP alternately and 2 server fails.

the quorum group that sends to reader6 every 1 s interval. Until the first 100 s of each operation, quorum group is 0, e.g., all quorums were active. From that moment on, the clients receive responses only from group 1, e.g., quorums excluded server0. With the second kill, after 200 s, only the quorums included in group 2 remain active. Figure 10 shows the read, write, and reconfig operation latency as the number of reconfigurers increases. During each experiment, the two server failures took place, but our system kept running without interruptions.

4 Conclusions

As a general finding, achieving strong consistency is more costly than providing weaker semantics as we experienced with REDIS and REDIS_W. However, the performance gap is not prohibitively large and future optimizations of ARES may close it enough so as to substantiate trading performance for consistency. Compared to the atomic version of CASSANDRA, ADSM algorithms seem to scale better, but lack behind in the throughput when dealing with small objects. Both approaches seem to be affected by the object size, but ARES-EC suggests that fragmentation may be the solution to this problem. Finally, we demonstrated that ARES may handle efficiently failures in the system, and reconfiguring from one DAP to another without service interruptions. Also, by examining the fragmentation parameter, we exposed trade-offs between operation latency and fault-tolerance in the system: the further increase of the parity (and thus higher fault-tolerance), the larger the latency.

ARES, an algorithm that always offers provable guarantees, competes closely and in many cases outperforms existing DSS solutions (even when offering weaker consistency guarantees). It would be interesting to study how optimizations may improve the performance of ARES. For example, fragmentation techniques as presented in [12] may have a positive impact on the performance of the algorithm.

References

1. Cassandra. https://cassandra.apache.org/_/index.html
2. Redis. https://redis.io
3. Data repository. https://github.com/nicolaoun/ngiatlantic-public-data
4. Aguilera, M.K., Keidar, I., Malkhi, D., Shraer, A.: Dynamic atomic storage without consensus. J. ACM **58**(2), 7:1–7:32 (2011)
5. Ansible. https://www.ansible.com/overview/how-ansible-works
6. Attiya, H.: Robust simulation of shared memory: 20 years after. Bull. EATCS **100**, 99–114 (2010)
7. Attiya, H., Bar-Noy, A., Dolev, D.: Sharing memory robustly in message-passing systems. J. ACM **42**(1), 124–142 (1995)
8. CloudlabUtah. Cloudlab Utah. https://www.cloudlab.us
9. Dutta, P., Guerraoui, R., Levy, R., Chakraborty, A.: How fast can a distributed atomic read be? In: Proceedings of PODC, pp. 236–245 (2004)

10. Georgiou, C., Nicolaou, N., Shvartsman, A.: Fault-tolerant semifast implementations of atomic read/write registers. JPDC **69**(1), 62–79 (2009)
11. Georgiou, C., Hadjistasi, T., Nicolaou, N., Schwarzmann, A.A.: Implementing three exchange read operations for distributed atomic storage. JPDC **163**, 97–113 (2022)
12. Georgiou, C., Nicolaou, N., Trigeorgi, A.: Fragmented ARES: dynamic storage for large objects. In: Proceedings of DISC (2022, To appear). arXiv:2201.13292
13. Gilbert, S., Lynch, N.A., Shvartsman, A.A.: RAMBO: a robust, reconfigurable atomic memory service for dynamic networks. Dist. Comp. **23**(4), 225–272 (2010)
14. Gramoli, V., Nicolaou, N., Schwarzmann, A.A.: Consistent Distributed Storage. Synthesis Lectures on DC Theory. Morgan & Claypool Publishers, San Rafael (2021)
15. GRID5000. https://www.grid5000.fr/w/Grid5000:Home
16. Herlihy, M., Wing, J.: Linearizability: a correctness condition for concurrent objects. ACM TOPLAS **12**(3), 463–492 (1990)
17. InstaGENI. https://groups.geni.net/geni/wiki/GeniAggregate
18. jFed. https://jfed.ilabt.imec.be
19. Lamport, L.: On interprocess communication, parts I and II. Distrib. Comput. **1**(2), 77–101 (1986)
20. Lynch, N., Shvartsman, A.: Robust emulation of shared memory using dynamic quorum-acknowledged broadcasts. In: Proceedings of FTCS, pp. 272–281 (1997)
21. Nicolaou, N., et al.: ARES: adaptive, reconfigurable, erasure coded, atomic storage. ACM Trans. Storage (TOS) (2022, To appear). arXiv:1805.03727
22. Ongaro, D., Ousterhout, J.: In search of an understandable consensus algorithm. In: Proceedings of USENIX ATC, pp. 305–320 (2014)
23. PyEClib. https://github.com/openstack/pyeclib
24. PySyncObj. https://github.com/bakwc/PySyncObj
25. Reed, I.S., Solomon, G.: Polynomial codes over certain finite fields. J. Soc. Ind. Appl. Math. **8**, 300–304 (1960)
26. VirtualWall. https://doc.ilabt.imec.be/ilabt/virtualwall/
27. ZeroMQ. https://zeromq.org

Invited Paper: Cross-Chain State Machine Replication

Yingjie Xue[ID] and Maurice Herlihy[✉][ID]

Department of Computer Science, Brown University, Providence, RI 02912, USA
maurice.herlihy@gmail.com

Abstract. This paper considers the classical state machine replication (SMR) problem in a distributed system model inspired by cross-chain exchanges. We propose a novel SMR protocol adapted for this model. Each state machine transition takes $O(n)$ message delays, where n is the number of active participants, of which *any number* may be Byzantine. This protocol makes novel use of path signatures [8] to keep replicas consistent. This protocol design cleanly separates application logic from fault-tolerance, providing a systematic way to replace complex *ad-hoc* cross-chain protocols with a more principled approach.

1 Introduction

In the *state machine replication* (SMR) problem, a service, modeled as a state machine, is replicated across multiple servers to provide fault tolerance. SMR has been studied in models of computation subject to crash failures [10] and Byzantine failures [2].

This paper proposes an SMR protocol for a model of computation inspired by, but not limited to, transactions that span multiple blockchains. The service's state is replicated across multiple automata. These replicas model smart contracts on blockchains: they are *trustworthy*, responding correctly to requests, but *passive*, meaning they undergo state changes only in response to outside requests. Like smart contracts, replicas cannot communicate directly with other replicas or observe their states. Active *agents* initiate replica state changes by communicating with the replicas over authenticated channels. Agents model blockchain users: any number of them may be *Byzantine*, eager to cheat other agents in arbitrary (but computationally-bounded) ways.

This SMR protocol guarantees *safety*, meaning that Byzantine agents cannot victimize honest agents, and *liveness*, meaning that if all agents are honest, then all replicas change state correctly.

Although cross-chain SMR and conventional SMR have (essentially) the same formal structure, their motivations differ in important ways. Conventional SMR embraces distribution to make services fault-tolerant. By contrast, individual blockchains are already fault-tolerant. Instead, cross-chain SMR is motivated by the need for *interoperability* across multiple independent chains. For example, suppose Alice and Bob have euro accounts on a chain run by the European

S. Devismes et al. (Eds.): SSS 2022, LNCS 13751, pp. 51–65, 2022.
https://doi.org/10.1007/978-3-031-21017-4_4

Central Bank, and dollar accounts on a chain run by the Federal Reserve. They agree to a trade: Alice will transfer some euros to Bob if Bob transfers some dollars to Alice. Realistically, however, Alice and Bob will never be able to execute their trade on a single chain because for political reasons the dollar chain and the euro chain will always be distinct. They could use an *ad hoc* cross-chain swap protocol [8,15], but an SMR protocol has a cleaner structure, and generalizes more readily to more complex exchanges. So Alice and Bob codify their trade as a simple, centralized state machine that credits and debits their accounts. They place a state machine replica on each chain, and execute the trade through an SMR protocol that keeps those replicas consistent. While both replicas formally execute the same steps, the euro chain replica actually transfers the euros, the dollar chain replica actually transfers the dollars, and the SMR protocol ensures these transfers happen atomically.

A conceptual benefit of SMR over *ad-hoc* protocols is separation of concerns. Expressing a complex financial exchange as a (non-distributed) state machine frees the protocol designer to focus on the exchange's incentives, payoffs, and equilibria, without simultaneously having to reason about distributed issues such as timeout durations or faulty communication.

Prior SMR protocols assume some fraction of the participants (usually more than one-half or two-thirds) to be non-faulty. By contrast, for cross-chain applications it does not make sense to assume a limit on the number of Byzantine agents. Instead, this model's SMR protocol protects agents who honestly follow the protocol from those who don't, all while ensuring progress when enough agents are honest.

This paper makes the following contributions. We are the first to consider the classical SMR coordination problem in a distributed system model inspired by cross-chain exchanges. The model itself is a formalization of models implicit in earlier, more applied works [8,9]. Fundamental coordination problems in this model have received little formal analysis. We propose a novel SMR protocol adapted for this model. Each state machine transition takes $O(n)$ message delays, where n is the number of agents, of which *any number* may be Byzantine. This protocol makes novel use of path signatures [8] to keep replicas consistent. This SMR structure cleanly separates application logic from fault-tolerance, providing a systematic way to replace complex *ad-hoc* cross-chain protocols with a more principled approach.

This paper is organized as follows. Section 2 describes the cross-chain model of computation, Sect. 3 gives examples of automata representing various kinds of cross-chain exchanges, Sect. 4 describes our cross-chain SMR protocol, Sect. 5 discusses optimizations and extensions, and Sect. 6 surveys related work.

2   Model of Computation

Our model is motivated by today's blockchains and smart contracts, but it does not assume any specific blockchain technology, or even blockchains as such. Instead, we focus on computational abstractions central to any systematic approach to exchanges of value among untrusting agents, whatever technology underlies the shared ledger.

The system consists of a set of communicating automata. An automaton is either an active, untrusted *agent*, or a passive, trusted *replica*. An agent automaton models a blockchain client such as a person or an organization, and is untrusted. A replica automaton models a *smart contract* (or *contract*), a chain-resident program that manipulates ledger state. Contract code and state are public, and that code is reliably executed by validators who reach consensus on each call. Replicas are trusted because they model trusted contracts.

Reflecting the limitations of today's blockchains, agents communicate only with replicas (clients can only call contract functions), and replicas do not communicate with other replicas (contracts on distinct chains cannot communicate). Replica A can learn of a state change at replica B only if some agent explicitly informs A of B's new state. Of course, A must decide whether that agent is telling the truth.

Like prior work [8,9,15], we assume a *synchronous* network model where communication time is known and bounded. There is a time bound $\Delta > 0$, such that when an agent initiates a state change at a replica, that change will observed by all agents within time Δ. We do not assume clocks are perfectly synchronized, only that clock drifts are kept small in comparison to Δ.

We make standard cryptographic assumptions. Each agent has a public and a private key, with public keys known to all. Messages are signed so they cannot be forged, and they include single-use labels ("nonces") so they cannot be replayed.

The agents participating in an exchange agree on a common *protocol*: rules that dictate when to request replica state changes. Instead of distinguishing between faulty and non-faulty agents, as in classical SMR models, we distinguish only between *compliant* (i.e. *honest*) agents who honestly follow the common protocol, and *deviating* (i.e. *Byzantine*) agents who do not. Unlike prior SMR models, which require some fraction of the agents to be compliant, we tolerate any number of Byzantine agents[1].

3   State Machines

Because applications such as cross-chain auctions or swaps are typically structured as multi-step protocols where agents take turns transferring assets in and out of escrow accounts [9,15], the state machine is structured as a multi-agent game. For simplicity, agents make moves in round-robin order. (In practice, agents can sometimes skip moves or move concurrently, discussed in Remarks in full version paper [19].)

Formally, a *game* is defined by a decision tree $G = (\mathcal{A}, \mathcal{M}, \mathcal{S}, \mathcal{F}, moves, enabled, succ, util)$, where $\mathcal{A}$ is a set of $n > 1$ *agents*, $\mathcal{M}$ is a set of *moves*, $\mathcal{S}$ is a set of *non-final states*, and $\mathcal{F}$ is a set of *final states* disjoint from $\mathcal{S}$. $\mathcal{S}$ includes a distinguished *initial state* s_0. The function

---

[1]   If all agents are Byzantine, then correctness becomes vacuous.

moves : $\mathcal{S} \rightarrow 2^{\mathcal{M}}$ defines which moves are enabled at each non-final state, *enabled* : $\mathcal{S} \rightarrow \mathcal{A}$ defines which agent chooses the next move at each non-final state, *succ* : $\mathcal{S} \times \mathcal{M} \rightarrow \mathcal{S} \cup \mathcal{F}$, defines which state is reached following a move in a non-final state. This successor function induces a tree structure on states: for $s_1, s_2 \in \mathcal{S}$ and $m_1, m_2 \in \mathcal{M}$, if $succ(s_1, m_1) = succ(s_2, m_2)$ then $s_1 = s_2$ and $m_1 = m_2$. Finally, the utility function $util : \mathcal{A} \times \mathcal{F} \rightarrow \mathbb{R}^n$ is given by a vector of real-valued functions on final states, indexed by agent: $(util_P : \mathcal{F} \rightarrow \mathbb{R} \mid P \in \mathcal{A})$. For each agent $P \in \mathcal{A}$ and state $z \in \mathcal{F}$, $util_P(z)$ measures P's preference for z compared to its preference for the initial state. Informally, $util_P(z)$ is negative for states where P ends up "worse off" than it started, positive for states where P ends up "better off", and zero for states where P is indifferent. An *execution* from state s_0 is a sequence $(s_0, P_1, \mu_1, \ldots, s_{i-1}, P_i, \mu_i, \ldots, s_k)$ where each $P_i = enabled(s_{i-1})$, $\mu_i \in moves(s_{i-1})$, $s_i = succ(s_{i-1}, \mu_i)$, and $s_k \in \mathcal{F}$. We divide executions into *rounds*: move μ_i takes place at round i. Game trees are finite and deterministic, hence so are executions.

Not all game trees make sense as abstract state machines. We are not interested in games like chess or poker where one agent's gain is another agent's loss. Instead, we are interested in games where all agents stand to gain. A *protocol* $\Pi : \mathcal{S} \rightarrow 2^{\mathcal{M}}$ is a rule for choosing among enabled moves. As mentioned, agents that follow the protocol are *compliant*, while those who do not are *deviating*. More precisely, P is compliant in an execution $(s_0, P_1, \mu_1, \ldots, s_{i-1}, P_i, \mu_i, \ldots, s_k)$ if it follows the protocol: if $P = enabled(s_{i-1})$, then $\mu_i \in \Pi(s_{i-1})$. An execution is compliant if every agent follows the protocol: for $i \in 1 \ldots k$, $\mu_i \in \Pi(s_{i-1})$.

A *mutually-beneficial protocol* guarantees:

- *Liveness*: Every compliant execution leads to a final state z where $util_P(z) > 0$ for all $P \in \mathcal{A}$.
- *Safety*: Every execution in which agent P is compliant leads to a final state z where $util_P(z) \geq 0$.

The first condition says that if all agents are compliant, they all end up strictly better off. The second says that a compliant agent will never end up worse off, even if others deviate. Establishing these properties is the responsibility of the game designer, and preserving them is the responsibility of the SMR protocol.

Both agents and the state machine itself can own and exchange *assets*. We keep track of ownership using *addresses*: each agent P has an *address*, $addr(P)$, and the state machine has an address *Self*. Let $\mathcal{ADDR}$ be the domain of addresses, and $\mathcal{ASSET}$ the domain of assets.

We represent state machines in procedural pseudocode. The block marked **State** defines the machine's state components. The state includes an *account* map, *account* : $\mathcal{ADDR} \times \mathcal{ASSET} \rightarrow \mathbb{Z}$, mapping addresses and assets to account balances. We will often abuse notation by writing $account(P, A)$ in place of $account(addr(P), A)$ when there is no danger of confusion. Other state components may include counters, flags, or other bookkeeping structures.

At the start of the state machine execution, the agents (optionally) *initialize* the state by executing the block marked **Initialize**($\ldots$). An agent triggers a state transition by issuing a *move*, which may take arguments. Each move has an implicit *Sender* argument that keeps track of which agent originated that move. In examples, a move is defined by a **Move** block, which checks preconditions and enforces postconditions. To capture the Byzantine nature of agents, every non-final state has an implicit enabled *Skip* move, which leaves the state unchanged, except for moving on to the next turn. (Usually, *Skip* deviates from the protocol.) The keyword **halt** ends the execution for the sender.

The example state machines illustrated in this section favor readability over precision when meanings are clear. For clarity and brevity, we omit some routine sanity checks and error cases. Our examples are all applications that exchange assets because these are the applications that make the most sense for the cross-chain model.

3.1 Example: Simple Swap

State Machine 1 Simple Swap

State:
1: *account* : $\mathcal{ADDR} \times \mathcal{ASSET} \to \mathbb{Z}$
2: *Alice Yes, Bob Yes, AllDone*: bool := *false, false, false*
Move: Agree()   ▷ Each agent agrees to swap
3: **if** *Sender* = Alice $\land$ *account*(Alice, florin) ≥ 1 **then**
4:     *Alice Yes* := *true*
5: **else if** *Sender* = Bob $\land$ *account*(Bob, ducat) ≥ 1 **then**
6:     *Bob Yes* := *true*
Move: Complete()   ▷ Any agent can complete the swap
7: **if** ¬*AllDone* **then**   ▷ Not yet completed?
8:     **if** *Alice Yes* $\land$ *Bob Yes* **then**   ▷ Both agents agreed?
9:         *account*(Alice, florin) := *account*(Alice, florin) − 1
10:        *account*(Bob, florin) := *account*(Bob, florin) + 1
11:        *account*(Bob, ducat) := *account*(Bob, ducat) − 1
12:        *account*(Alice, ducat) := *account*(Alice, ducat) + 1
13:    *AllDone* = *true*
14: **halt**

Algorithm 1 shows pseudocode for a *simple swap* state machine, where Alice and Bob swap one of her florins for one of his ducats. The block marked **State** defines the state components: the accounts map, and various control flags. Each agent agrees to the swap (Line 3, Line 5), checking that the caller has sufficient funds. After both have agreed, either agent can complete the transfers (Line 8). If either agent tries to complete the transfer before both have agreed, the transfer fails, and no assets are exchanged.

State Machine 2 DAO State Machine

State:
1: $account : \mathcal{ADDR} \times \mathcal{ASSET} \to \mathbb{Z}$ ▷ Initially 0
2: $yesVotes : \mathcal{A} \to \mathbb{Z}, noVotes : \mathcal{A} \to \mathbb{Z}$ ▷ Initially 0
3: $voted : \mathcal{A} \to \{true, false\}$ ▷ Initially *false*
Initialize():
4: **if** $account(Self, \text{florin}) < 100$ **then**   ▷ Make sure DAO has funds
5:      **halt**
Move: VoteYes$(k : \mathbb{Z})$ ▷ LP casts k votes
6: **if** *Sender* is enabled **then**
7:      **if** $account(Sender, \text{token}) \geq k$ **then**   ▷ Sender has enough tokens
8:          $yesVotes(Sender) := k$
9:          $voted(Sender) := true$
Move: VoteNo$(k : \mathbb{Z})$ ...   ▷ Symmetric with *VoteYes*
Move: *Skip()*
10: do nothing
Move: Resolve()
11: **if** *Sender* is enabled and threshold voted YES **then**   ▷ Fund 100 to Alice
12:     $account(Self, \text{florin}) := account(Self, \text{florin}) - 100$
13:     $account(\text{Alice}, \text{florin}) := account(\text{Alice}, \text{florin}) + 100$
14:     **halt**

3.2   Example: Decentralized Autonomous Organization (DAO)

Consider a venture fund organized as a *decentralized autonomous organization* (DAO), where liquidity providers (LPs) vote on how to invest their funds. Algorithm 2 shows a state machine where the DAO's LPs vote on whether to fund Alice's request for 100 florins. Each LP holds some number of *governance tokens*, each of which can be converted to a vote. After the LPs vote, a *director* tallies their votes, and if there are enough YES votes, transfers the funds. The state consists of accounts, $account : \mathcal{ADDR} \times \mathcal{ASSET} \to \mathbb{Z}$, and maps $yesVotes : \mathcal{A} \to \mathbb{Z}$ and $noVotes : \mathcal{A} \to \mathbb{Z}$ counting YES and NO votes.

Initialization (Line 4) ensures that the DAO's own account is funded. Each LP votes in turn whether to approve Alice's request (Lines 6 to 9). (As discussed in full version paper [19], these votes could be concurrent.) If an LP skips its turn, the tallies are unchanged (Line 10). After every LP has had a chance to vote, the director can ask for a resolution (Lines 11 to 14). If the caller is authorized and if a threshold number of votes were YES (Line 11), the funds are transferred to Alice from the DAO's account. In either case, the execution ends.

An example for sealed-bid auction can be found in our full version paper [19].

4   State Machine Replication Protocol

In this section, we define an SMR protocol by which multiple *replica* automata emulate a (centralized) state machine as defined in the previous section.

There are n agents and m assets, where each asset is managed by its own replica. Each replica maintains its own copy of the shared state. The SMR protocol's job is to keep those copies consistent. We assume that agents have some way to find one another, to agree on the state machine defining their exchange, and to initialize replicas that begin execution with synchronized clocks.

The core of the SMR protocol is a reliable delivery service that ensures that the moves issued by the agents are delivered to the replicas reliably, in order. Reliable ordered delivery in the presence of Byzantine failures is well-studied [7, 12], but the cross-chain model requires new protocols because the rules are different. The principal difference is the asymmetry between *agents*, active automata who cannot be trusted, and *replicas*, purely reactive automata who can observe only their own local states, but who can be trusted to execute their own transitions correctly.

For example, suppose the protocol calls for Alice to send a move to replicas A and B, instructing them to transition to state s. Each replica that receives the move validates Alice's signature, checks that it is Alice's turn, and that the move is enabled in the current state.

There are several ways Alice might deviate. First, she might send her move to replica A but not B. In the SMR protocol, however, agents monitor one another. Another compliant agent, Bob, will notice that B has not received Alice's move. Bob will sign and relay that move from A to B, causing B to receive that move at most Δ later than A. As long as there is at least one compliant agent, each move will be delivered to each replica within a known duration.

Second, Alice might deviate by sending conflicting moves, such as "transition to s" to A, but "transition to s'" to B. Here, too, Bob will notice the discrepancy and relay both moves to A and B, presenting each replica with proof that Alice deviated. Each replica will discard the conflicting moves, acting as if Alice had skipped her turn.

Third, Alice might send a move to A that is not enabled in the current state. Replica A simply ignores that move, acting as if Alice had skipped her turn.

Finally, Alice might not send her move to either replica. Each replica that goes long enough without receiving a move will act as if Alice had skipped her turn. In short, reliable delivery has only two outcomes: a valid move from Alice delivered to every replica, or no valid move delivered, interpreted as a *Skip*, all within a known duration.

To summarize, the SMR protocol consists of three modules.

- The *front-end* automata (Algorithm 5), one for each agent, provide functions called by agents, including initial asset transfers into the state machine, the moves, and final asset transfers out of the state machine. (Every compliant agent is in charge of ensuring that final asset transfers take place.)
- The *relay* service (Algorithm 3) guarantees that moves issued by front-ends are reliably delivered to the replicas as long as at least one agent is compliant.
- The *replicas* (Algorithm 4), one for each asset, process function calls sent by agents from front-end, maintain copies of the state, and manage individual assets.

4.1   Path Signatures

A *request* req is a triple (P, μ, r), used to indicate that agent P requests move μ at the start of round r. Let $sig_P(P, m)$ denote the result of signing a message m with P's secret key. A *path* p of length k is a sequence $[P_1, \ldots, P_k]$ of distinct agents. We use $[]$ for the empty sequence, and $[p, Q]$ to append Q to the sequence p: $[[P_1, \ldots, P_k], Q] = [P_1, \ldots, P_k, Q]$. A *path signature* [8,9] for p is defined inductively:

$$p(P, \mu, r) := \begin{cases} (P, \mu, r) & \text{If } p = [], \\ sig_Q(Q, q(P, \mu, r)) & \text{if } p = [q, Q] \end{cases}$$

Informally, path signatures work as follows. The rth round starts at time $t - (r - 1)n\Delta$ after initialization. Within time $t + \Delta$ after the start of round r, a receiver accepts the path signature $[\text{Alice}](\text{Alice}, \mu, r)$ directly from Alice. Within time $t + 2\Delta$, a receiver accepts $[\text{Alice}, \text{Bob}](\text{Alice}, \mu, r)$ originating from Alice and relayed through Bob, and within time $t + k\Delta$, a receiver accepts a message originating from Alice and relayed through $k - 1$ distinct agents. A path signature of length k is *live* for a duration of $k\Delta$ after t. If no message is received for a duration of $n\Delta$ after t, then no message was sent.

Function $now()$ returns the current time. Define the following functions and predicates on path signatures of length k:

$$age(p(P, \mu, r)) := now() - (r - 1)n\Delta$$
$$live(p(P, \mu, r)) := age(p(P, \mu, r)) \le k\Delta$$
$$ready(p(P, \mu, r)) := age(p(P, \mu, r)) > n\Delta$$

The $age()$ function is the time elapsed since the start of the current round. The SMR protocol uses $live()$ to determine whether a message should be accepted by replicas, and $ready()$ to determine whether the accepted message's move can be applied. A path signature is *well-formed* if the signatures are valid and the signers are distinct. For brevity, replica pseudocode omits well-formedness checks. We use $\mathcal{REQ} = \mathcal{A} \times \mathcal{M} \times \mathbb{Z}$ for the domain of requests, and $\mathcal{PS}$ for the domain of path signatures.

4.2   Reliable Delivery

The n agents act as *senders* (indexed by $\mathcal{A}$) and the m replicas act as *receivers* (indexed by $\mathcal{ASSET}$).

Each receiver A has a component: $buffer_A : \mathcal{A} \to 2^{\mathcal{PS}}$, where $buffer_A(P)$ holds path signatures for moves originally issued by agent P and received at chain A.

Property 1. Here is the specification for the reliable delivery protocol.

- *Authenticity*: Every move contained in a path signature in $buffer_A(P)$ was signed by P.
- *Consistency*: If any receiver receives a path signature indicating P's move, then, within Δ, so does every other receiver.
- *Fairness*: If a compliant P issues a move, then every receiver receives a path signature containing that move within Δ.

Note that a deviating sender may deliver multiple moves to the same receiver.

Before issuing a move, a compliant agent P waits until that move is enabled at some replica's state (not shown in pseudocode). To issue the move, P sends the path signature $[P](P, \mu, t)$ to every replica (Algorithm 5 Line 10). When replica A receives a live path signature with a move originally issued by P, A places that message in $buffer_A(P)$ (Algorithm 4 Line 12). From that point, the relay service is in charge of delivery.

A natural way to structure the relay service is to have each (compliant) sender run a dedicated thread that repeatedly reads replica buffers and selectively relays messages from one replica to the others (Algorithm 3). Lines 3 to 8 shows the pseudocode for relaying moves. Each relaying agent Q reads each receiver's buffer (Line 4), and selects messages (more specifically, requests of moves) (P, μ, r) which are not already relayed by Q (Line 5). Each such message is sent to the other receivers (Line 6) by adding Q to the path p and produces $[p, Q](P, \mu, r)$, and the message is recorded to avoid later duplication (Line 7). After reading the buffers, Q calls each replica's *deliver()* function (Line 8) which causes the replica to check whether it can execute a move (see below).

State Machine 3 Relay Protocol for $Q \in \mathcal{A}$

1: $seen : 2^{\mathcal{REQ}}$ ▷ Initially empty
2: **while** Exchange is in progress **do**
3:     **for all** $A \in \mathcal{ASSET}, P \in \mathcal{A}$ **do**
4:         **for all** $p(P, \mu, r) \in buffer_A(P)$ **do**   ▷ Inspect every path signature
5:             **if** $(P, \mu, r) \notin seen$ **then**   ▷ Does it need to be relayed?
6:                 **for all** $B \in \mathcal{ASSET}$ **do** $B.send([p, Q](P, \mu, r))$ ▷ Append signature and relay
7:                 $seen := seen \cup \{(P, \mu, r)\}$ ▷ Don't relay again
8:         **for all** $A \in \mathcal{ASSET}$ **do** $A.deliver()$ ▷ Wake up replicas

---

Properties of our relay protocol and proof can be found in our full version paper [19].

4.3 Initialization, Moves, and Settlement

Each replica manages a unique asset. On the replica that manages asset A, each agent P has a *long-lived account*, denoted $LongAccount_A(P)$, that records how many units of A are owned by P. While an execution is in progress, each agent

P has a *short-lived account* at A, denoted $ShortAccount_A(P, B)$, tracking how many units of asset B have been tentatively assigned to P at replica A. Each replica A has address $Self_A$. Long-lived and short-lived accounts are related by the following invariant:

$$LongAccount_A(Self_A) = \sum_{P \in \mathcal{A}} ShortAccount_A(P, A).$$

We assume replica A is authorized to transfer A assets, in either direction, between the calling agent's long-lived account: $LongAccount_A(Sender)$, and the replica's own long-lived account: $LongAccount_A(Self)$.

At the start of the execution, each agent P escrows funds by transferring some quantity of each asset A from $LongAccount_A(P)$ to $LongAccount_A(Self)$ (Algorithm 4, Line 6). If that transfer is successful, the replica credits P's short-lived accounts: for all $B \in \mathcal{ASSET}$, P sets $ShortAccount_B(P, A)$ equal to the amount funded (Line 8). Agent P is then marked as funded (Line 9). Only properly funded agents can execute moves (Line 11).

What could go wrong? The transfer from $LongAccount_A(P)$ to $LongAccount_A(Self)$ might fail because $LongAccount_A(P)$ has insufficient funds. The replica at A can detect and react to such a failure, but the other replicas cannot. To protect against such failures, each agent calls the function *verifyAccounts()* (Algorithm 5, Lines 6 to 8), which checks that all replicas' account balances are consistent. Finally, each agent checks that every other agent has transferred the agreed-upon amounts (Line 3). This last test is application-specific: for the swap example, agents would check that the others transferred a specified amount of coins, while in the DAO example, LPs can transfer as many governance tokens as they like. If either test fails, the front-end refunds that agent's assets (by invoking *redeem()* in Algorithm 5). In this way, if some agents drop out before initialization, they are marked as unfunded, and the remaining funded agents may or may not choose to continue. In the meantime, *safety* is preserved since each compliant agent who continues sees a consistent state across all replicas. Each compliant agent who leaves the execution gets their funds back, ensuring they end up no worse off.

This funding step takes time at most Δ. Each agent then verifies that replicas are funded consistently. If not, the agent calls *redeem()* to reclaim its funding, and drops out. This verification takes time $n\Delta$, like any other move. For an execution starting at time t, initialization completes before $t + (n + 1)\Delta$.

While the execution is in progress, transfers of asset A between P and Q are expressed as transfers between $ShortAccount_A(P, A)$ and $ShortAccount_A(Q, A)$, leaving the balance of $LongAccount_A(Self)$ unchanged. Replica A also tracks P's balances for other assets: $ShortAccount_A(P, B)$ is A's view of P's current short-lived balance for each asset $B \neq A$.

When the execution ends, each P calls each replica's *redeem()* function (Algorithm 5, Line 20), to get its assets back. This function transfers $ShortAccount_A(P, A)$ units of asset A from $LongAccount_A(Self)$ to $LongAccount_A(P)$ (Algorithm 4, Line 31). Once an agent's funds are redeemed, that agent is marked as not funded (Line 32). The *redeem*() function serves two roles: it can *refund* an agent's original assets if the exchange fails, or it can *claim* an agent's new assets if the exchange succeeds. If all agents are conforming and no one drops out, the execution proceeds and every agent ends up with a better payoff, ensuring liveness. Any compliant agent can drop out, either early with a refund (say, if it observes inconsistent funding), or at the execution's end. Both choices ensure that all assets in short-lived accounts are moved to long-lived accounts.

Each replica (Algorithm 4) has its own copy of the state machine (Line 3). The replica can apply moves to the copy (Line 15), and the replica can determine whether a proposed move by a particular agent is currently enabled (Line 13).

Replica A's *deliver*() function determines whether there is a unique move in $buffer_A(P)$ to execute. Each time replica A starts a round, it records the time (Line 16). If $n\Delta$ time then elapses without delivering the next move (Line 17), the missing move is deemed to be a *Skip* (Line 18).

4.4 Dynamic Funding

The protocol provided above assumes no additional funding after initialization. However, sometimes, it is good to allow parties to add more funding during the execution of the game, for example, in auctions. We provide protocols for dynamic funding. Our full version paper [19] provides more details.

5 Remarks

In this paper, we present a cross-chain state machine replication protocol for cross-chain transactions. Cross-chain transactions are formalized as state machines and each blockchain's smart contract represents a replica. Although it is mostly straightforward to implement replica automata as smart contracts, there are practical, blockchain-specific details (such as analyzing gas prices) that are beyond the scope of this paper. See more discussions on optimization in our full version paper [19].

6 Related Work

State machine replication is a classic problem in distributed computing. Protocols such as Paxos [10], Raft [4], and their immediate descendants were designed to tolerate crash failures. Later protocols (see Distler's survey [5]) tolerate Byzantine failures. These protocols are not applicable to cross-chain exchanges because of differences in the underlying trust and communication models.

Prior Byzantine fault-tolerant (BFT) SMR protocols [5] assume replicas may be Byzantine but clients are honest. By contrast, in our cross-chain model, replicas are correct (because they represent blockchains), but clients can be Byzantine (because they may try to steal one another's assets). Most prior BFT-SMR protocols assign one replica to be the *leader*, and the rest to be *followers* (sometimes

---

State Machine 4 Replica for asset A

State:
1: $buffer_A : \mathcal{A} \rightarrow 2^{\mathcal{PS}}$ ▷ initially all $\emptyset$
2: $funded_A : \mathcal{A} \rightarrow \{true, false\}$ ▷ initially all $false$
3: $machine$ ▷ Replica of state machine
4: $delivered_A : 2^{\mathcal{REQ}}$ ▷ Next move to execute
5: $startTime : \mathbb{Z} \rightarrow \mathbb{Z}$ ▷ Each round's start time
Initialize($fund : \mathcal{ASSET} \rightarrow \mathbb{Z}$):   ▷ Initial funding
6: transfer $fund(A)$ units of A from $LongAccount_A(Sender)$ to $LongAccount_A(Self)$
7: **if** transfer was successful **then**
8:      **for all** $B \in \mathcal{ASSET}$ **do** $ShortAccount_B(Sender, A) := fund(A)$
9:      $funded_A(Sender) := true$
10: $startTime(1) := (n+1)\Delta$ ▷ Set start time for round 1
Move: send $p(P, \mu, t)$ ▷ Forward move to relay protocol
11: **if** $live(p(P, \mu, t)$ and $funded_A(P)$ **then**   ▷ Relay only live moves by funded agents
12:      $buffer_A(P) := buffer_A(P) \cup \{p(P, \mu, r)\}$
Move: $deliver()$ ▷ Relayer: check for executable move
13: $delivered := \{(P, \mu, r) \mid p(P, \mu, r) \in buffer_A(P) \wedge ready(p(P, \mu, r)) \wedge P \in enabled(machine) \wedge \mu \in moves(machine)\}$ ▷ Execute if enough time has elapsed
14: **if** $delivered = \{(P, \mu, t)\}$ **then**   ▷ Unique executable move?
15:      $machine.\mu()$ ▷ Execute it
16:      $startTime(r+1) := startTime(r) + n\Delta$ ▷ Set the start time of next round
17: **else if** $now() - startTime(r) > n\Delta$ **then**   ▷ Did we time out?
18:      $machine.Skip()$ ▷ Agent chose not to move
19:      $startTime(r+1) := startTime(r) + n\Delta$ ▷ Set the start time of next round
Move: $topUp(fund : \mathcal{ASSET} \rightarrow \mathbb{Z})$ ▷ Dynamically add funding
20: **if** $funded_A(Sender)$ **then**
21:      transfer $fund(A)$ units of A from $LongAccount_A(Sender)$ to $LongAccount_A(Self)$
22:      **if** transfer was successful **then**
23:          $(\forall B \in \mathcal{ASSET}) ShortAccount_B(Sender, A) := ShortAccount_B(Sender, A) + fund(A)$ ▷ Credit accounts
24:      **else**
25:          $funded_A(Sender) := false$ ▷ Freeze accounts
Move: $defund(defundVote : \mathcal{A} \rightarrow \{true, false\})$
26: **if** $Sender = leader$ **then**   ▷ check authorization
27:      **for all** $P \in \mathcal{A}$ **do**
28:          **if** $defundVote(P)$ **then**
29:              $funded_A(P) := false$
Move: $redeem()$ ▷ Settle accounts at end
30: **if** $funded_A(Sender)$ **then**
31:      transfer $ShortAccount_A(A, Sender)$ units of A from $LongAccount_A(Self)$ to $LongAccount_A(Sender)$
32:      $funded_A(Sender) := false$ ▷ No moves allowed after cashing out

---

State Machine 5 Front-end for agent P

Initialize($fund_P : \mathcal{ASSET} \to \mathbb{Z}$):
1: **for all** $A \in \mathcal{ASSET}$ **do** A.**Initialize**($fund_P$)
2: $verifyAccounts()$
3: **if** $(\exists A \in \mathcal{ASSET}, P \in A)ShortAccount_A(P, A)$ is not the agreed-upon amount **then**
4:     $redeem()$ ▷ Get assets refunded
5:     **halt**
Move: $verifyAccounts()$ ▷ Check for malformed funding data
6: **if** $(\exists A, B \in \mathcal{ASSET}, Q \in A)$ $funded_A(Q) \wedge (ShortAccount_A(Q, A) \neq ShortAccount_B(Q, A))$ **then**
7:     $redeem()$ ▷ Ask for asset refund
8:     **halt**
Move: $send(\mu)$
9: **for all** $A \in \mathcal{ASSET}$ **do**
10:     $A.send([P](P, \mu, t))$ ▷ Add path sig and broadcast
Move: $topUp(fund_P : \mathcal{ASSET} \to \mathbb{Z})$
11: **for all** $A \in \mathcal{ASSET}$ **do** $A.topUp(fund_P)$ ▷ Send path sig
12: $verifyAccounts()$
Move: $topUpVerified(fund : \mathcal{ASSET} \to \mathbb{Z})$
13: $topUp(fund_p)$ ▷ Call regular top-up
14: **if** $Self = leader$ **then**   ▷ Authorized to accept or reject top-up
15:     **for all** $P \in \mathcal{A}$ **do**
16:         $defundVote(P) := (\exists A, B \in \mathcal{ASSET})ShortAccount_A(P, A) \neq ShortAccount_B(P, A)$
17:     **for all** $A \in \mathcal{ASSET}$ **do** $A.defund(defundVote)$
18: **else**
19:     wait for leader to deliver defund votes
20: $verifyAccounts()$
Move: $redeem()$ ▷ Reclaim assets
21: **for all** $A \in \mathcal{ASSET}$ **do** $A.redeem()$ ▷ Redeem assets from each replica

---

"validators"). These protocols tolerate only a certain fraction of faulty replicas. Our cross-chain SMR protocol, by contrast, does not distinguish between leaders and followers, and tolerates any number of faulty agents.

An individual blockchain's consensus protocol can be viewed as an SMR protocol, where the ledger state is replicated among the validators (miners). Validators are typically rewarded for participating [18]. Validators might deviate in various ways, including *selfish mining* [6], front-running [3], or exploiting the structure of consensus rewards [1]. Individual blockchain SMR protocols are not applicable for cross-chain SMR because of fundamental differences in models and participants' incentives.

An alternative approach to cross-chain interoperability is allowing blockchains to communicate states to one another. As shown in a recent survey [17], these protocols usually adopt external relayers/validators to relay/validate messages across chains. Any failure of those external players can harm the safety of the cross-chain system.

In failure models of some prior work, parties are classified as either rational, seeking to maximize payoffs, or Byzantine, capable of any behavior. First proposed for distributed systems [14], this classification has been used for chain consensus protocols [11]. The rational vs Byzantine classification is equivalent to our compliant vs deviating classification for cross-chain exchanges where compliance is rational, a property one would expect in practice.

The notion of replacing an *ad-hoc* protocol with a generic, replicated state machine was anticipated by Miller *et al.* [13], who propose generic *state channels* as a cleaner, systematic replacement for prior payment channels of the kind used in the Lightning network [16].

Acknowledgement. This research is supported by NSF grant 5260383.

References

1. Buterin, V., Reijsbergen, D., Leonardos, S., Piliouras, G.: Incentives in Ethereum's hybrid Casper protocol. Int. J. Netw. Manag. **30**(5) (2020). https://doi.org/10.1002/nem.2098. https://onlinelibrary.wiley.com/doi/10.1002/nem.2098
2. Castro, M., Liskov, B.: Practical Byzantine fault tolerance. In: Proceedings of the Third Symposium on Operating Systems Design and Implementation, OSDI 1999, New Orleans, Louisiana, USA, pp. 173–186. USENIX Association, Berkeley (1999). https://dl.acm.org/citation.cfm?id=296806.296824. tex.acmid: 296824
3. Daian, P., et al.: Flash boys 2.0: frontrunning, transaction reordering, and consensus instability in decentralized exchanges. arXiv:1904.05234 [cs] (2019)
4. Ongaro, D., Ousterhout, J.: In search of an understandable consensus algorithm. In: 2014 USENIX Annual Technical Conference, pp. 305–319. USENIX Association, Philadelphia (2014). https://www.usenix.org/conference/atc14/technical-sessions/presentation/ongaro
5. Distler, T.: Byzantine fault-tolerant state-machine replication from a systems perspective. ACM Comput. Surv. **54**(1), 1–38 (2021). https://doi.org/10.1145/3436728
6. Eyal, I., Sirer, E.G.: Majority is not enough: bitcoin mining is vulnerable. In: Christin, N., Safavi-Naini, R. (eds.) FC 2014. LNCS, vol. 8437, pp. 436–454. Springer, Heidelberg (2014). https://doi.org/10.1007/978-3-662-45472-5_28
7. Guerraoui, R., Kuznetsov, P., Monti, M., Pavlovic, M., Seredinschi, D.A., Vonlanthen, Y.: Scalable Byzantine reliable broadcast (extended version). arXiv:1908.01738 [cs] (2020). https://doi.org/10.4230/LIPIcs.DISC.2019.22
8. Herlihy, M.: Atomic cross-chain swaps. In: Proceedings of the 2018 ACM Symposium on Principles of Distributed Computing, PODC 2018, Egham, UK, pp. 245–254. ACM, New York (2018). https://doi.org/10.1145/3212734.3212736. tex.acmid: 3212736
9. Herlihy, M., Liskov, B., Shrira, L.: Cross-chain deals and adversarial commerce. Proc. VLDB Endow. **13**(2), 100–113 (2019). https://doi.org/10.14778/3364324.3364326. https://arxiv.org/abs/1905.09743
10. Lamport, L.: The part-time parliament. ACM Trans. Comput. Syst. **16**(2), 133–169 (1998)

11. McMenamin, C., Daza, V., Pontecorvi, M.: Achieving state machine replication without honest players. arXiv:2012.10146 [cs] (2021)
12. Mendes, H., Tasson, C., Herlihy, M.: Distributed computability in Byzantine asynchronous systems. arXiv:1302.6224 [cs] (2014)
13. Miller, A., Bentov, I., Kumaresan, R., McCorry, P.: Sprites: payment channels that go faster than lightning. CoRR abs/1702.05812 (2017). http://arxiv.org/abs/1702.05812 tex.bibsource: dblp computer science bibliography. http://dblp.org/rec/bib/journals/corr/MillerBKM17
14. Moscibroda, T., Schmid, S., Wattenhofer, R.: When selfish meets evil: Byzantine players in a virus inoculation game. In: Proceedings of the Twenty-Fifth Annual ACM Symposium on Principles of Distributed Computing, PODC 2006, Denver, Colorado, USA, p. 35. ACM Press (2006). https://doi.org/10.1145/1146381.1146391
15. Nolan, T.: Atomic swaps using cut and choose (2016). https://bitcointalk.org/index.php?topic=1364951
16. Poon, J., Dryja, T.: The bitcoin lightning network: scalable off-chain instant payments (2016). https://lightning.network/lightning-network-paper.pdf
17. Robinson, P.: Survey of crosschain communications protocols. Computer Networks (2021). https://arxiv.org/pdf/2004.09494.pdf
18. Roughgarden, T.: Transaction fee mechanism design for the ethereum blockchain: an economic analysis of EIP-1559. arXiv:2012.00854 [cs, econ] (2020)
19. Xue, Y., Herlihy, M.: Cross-chain state machine replication (2022). https://doi.org/10.48550/ARXIV.2206.07042

Regular Papers

Plateau: A Secure and Scalable Overlay Network for Large Distributed Trust Applications

John Augustine[1]($\boxtimes$) (iD), Wahid Gulzar Bhat[1] (iD), and Sandip Nair[2] (iD)

[1] Indian Institute of Technology Madras, Chennai, India
augustine@iitm.ac.in
[2] Columbia University, New York, USA
sdn2124@columbia.edu

Abstract. We propose a novel two-tiered overlay network design called *plateau*. It has two levels: a small upper-level that regulates entry of new nodes into the network, and a lower-level comprising all nodes. The lower level is a well-connected expander that is ideal for building peer-to-peer distributed trust applications. It is designed to be secure despite the presence of adversarial Byzantine nodes and resilient to large amounts of churn. The good nodes only need to communicate with their neighbors in the network, thus making plateau fully distributed. Membership in the network must be earned through proof-of-work that is verified by the upper-level nodes. Plateau is robust despite heavy churn controlled by an adversary, i.e., up to $C = \text{poly}(n)$ number of nodes can join and leave the network per round without disrupting the network structure; n is the total number of good nodes in the network. As long as the compute power controlled by the Byzantine adversary is bounded, the number of Byzantine nodes in the network is kept in check and, more importantly, they will not be able to disrupt the structure or functioning of the overlay network. Additionally, we show that all resources needed to operate this network is bounded polylogarithmically with respect to n.

1 Introduction

Since the invention of Bitcoin by Satoshi Nakamoto [29], we have seen a significant increase in peer-to-peer distributed trust systems. A large number of cryptocurrencies have sprouted over the years and a tremendous amount of research has been invested in this technology in the last decade. The key innovation in Nakamoto's work that is driving this surge is blockchains, a technology by which a peer-to-peer network can maintain a trustworthy record of transactions. Thus, blockchains appeal to a much wider class of applications that require trust between parties. An important aspect of all of these applications is the large volume at which they are intended to operate essentially catering to large populations at national, continental and global scale.

Current blockchain implementations are unfortunately not built for scale [10]. There are many factors that limit them. While some issues like the energy cost of

© The Author(s), under exclusive license to Springer Nature Switzerland AG 2022
S. Devismes et al. (Eds.): SSS 2022, LNCS 13751, pp. 69–83, 2022.
https://doi.org/10.1007/978-3-031-21017-4_5

consensus have drawn significant attention, others have been largely ignored. The actual peer-to-peer network on which the blockchains operate are surprisingly small when compared to the scope and scale of their applications. For example, despite significant use of bitcoin, the actual number of peers that operate is quite small. As of 2018, measurements show that the number of peers is about 14000 [30]. We posit that this small scale of the peer-to-peer network will be a limiting factor as large countries and economic blocs like USA, EU, China, and India seek to employ public blockchain based distributed trust applications for their citizens. If we contrast this with the penetration of the Internet into households across the globe, we realize that distributed trust applications built on current peer-to-peer networks are a far cry from the scale we need for the applications we wish to build on them.

Much of the research in consensus mechanisms abstract away the network issues by assuming that flooded messages reach most nodes within some time period. Such convenience assumptions are acceptable for small networks that are currently deployed. The widely used approach is to maintain the peer-to-peer network as an unstructured random graph. New nodes that wish to join the network connect to random peers obtained from established seeders who crawl through the network and maintain current a list of peers [8]. Such seeders have two drawbacks. Firstly, while they operate well in small networks, their performance in large systems is more challenging. It will be very hard for seeders to publish a list of current nodes at billion nodes scale. Secondly, there is very little mathematical basis for their guarantees. With large amounts of churn, the data they hold can quickly become stale. This, in turn, can lead to poorly connected or even disconnected networks.

Thus, we need to design peer-to-peer networks that can scale well in practice to reach close to Internet scale. At the same time, given the high stakes, we also require strong guarantees backed by rigorous mathematical proofs. A peer-to-peer network capable of hosting large scale distributed trust applications must reliably and efficiently provide some basic functions and properties. Perhaps, the most important function is efficient information spreading, which requires the network to be well connected with good network expansion [25] and of low diameter. The (vertex) expansion of a network graph $G = (V, E)$ is defined as $\min_{S \subset V, |S| \leq |V|/2} |N(S)|/|S|$, where $N(S)$ is the open neighborhood of S (i.e., excluding S). G is said to be an expander if its expansion is bounded from below by a constant. Creating such expander networks with efficient information spreading properties require fast and reliable sampling of random peer nodes [27]. Sampling is straightforward in small networks because the full list of nodes can be effectively maintained by seeders (as it is currently done). However, when the network becomes large, we will need a more distributed mechanism typically employing random walks [14].

To make matters worse, there are several security challenges. Peer-to-peer networks are permissionless allowing any node to participate – including those that are potentially malicious (also called Byzantine nodes). Such Byzantine nodes can affect the network in many ways. They can create cuts in the network and hinder the flow of information across the cut, thereby causing eclipse attacks [18]. It can also be hard to pin down the true identity of participants because of Sybil attacks whereby multiple IP addresses can be created [16, 17]. Furthermore, a large number of malicious nodes can engage in a denial-of-service attack wherein they target some nodes and send repeated messages that overwhelm those nodes and render them unresponsive.

Finally, any peer-to-peer network must be able to tolerate large amounts of churn and other forms of network dynamics. Studies have shown that up to 97% of the nodes exhibit intermittent network connectivity [19]. Moreover, nodes will only participate as long as there is an immediate benefit to them and will leave when there is none. In fact, it has long been established that up to 50% of the nodes can be renewed within an hour, but the number of active peers does not change dramatically because the number of joins and leaves are about the same within small time frames [37]. It is therefore in the interest of peer-to-peer network designers to allow peers to efficiently join and leave without disrupting the network. Sybil attacks and churn coupled together can be quite damaging because the mechanisms in place to let new nodes join the network must be smart enough to ensure that sybils do not abuse the churn facility.

The key mechanism that researchers have used in order to tackle this combination of malicious behavior and churn is to make the participants pay a price in the form of resource burning [17]. This is a mechanism by which the participants are able to prove that they spent some effort or resource to earn their place in the peer-to-peer network. In fact, Gupta *et al.* [16, 17] argue game theoretically that resource burning is a crucial requirement that cannot be avoided when dealing with malice and churn, a position that we share as well. The most common form of resource burning is a mechanism called proof-of-work where a computational puzzle is solved – typically, one that is hard to solve but easy to verify. It is of course a widely used technique for consensus in bitcoin and other cryptocurrencies. Of course, while we may not be able to avoid resource burning, from a sustainability point of view, it is imperative that we minimize its use. In the rest of the paper, we use the term proof-of-work out of deference to its familiarity, but our ideas will go through under any other reasonable form of resource burning as well. Finally, we note that – as in every other proof-of-work based system – we must limit the computation power of the Byzantine adversary to within a fraction of the computational power vested with good participants.

1.1   Our Contribution

In this work, we have made first steps towards designing a secure peer-to-peer overlay network called *Plateau* that can arguably scale well, handle large amounts of churn, and resilient to Byzantine nodes. Our emphasis is on ensuring that the desired properties can be formally proved. Towards this goal, we empower a single adversary to orchestrate the behavior of Byzantine nodes *and* the nature of churn. We assume that the adversary is vested with 1/4 fraction of the compute power that good nodes possess. Section 2 provides a detailed description of our model. The only cryptographic tools assumed are private channels between nodes and a proof-of-work mechanism. We do not assume public key infrastructure. The non-triviality of this work comes from carefully designing network and the maintenance protocols so that the properties described below (and formally stated in Theorem 2) hold with high probability (whp)[1].

Plateau is fully distributed. Nodes need to only be aware of their neighbors' IDs and interact with them. Nevertheless, membership is globally secure in the sense that nodes cannot arbitrarily enter the network. Membership in the network must be earned through proof-of-work that is verified by the nodes in the upper level.

The overlay has low diameter and is sparse with both diameter and degree at most logarithmic in the size of the network. The network graph induced by the good nodes is well-connected in the form of an expander, specifically in the sense that its vertex expansion is lower bounded by a constant. Thus, our network is resistant to eclipse attacks. We exploit this expansion to provide a sampling mechanism based on random walks that is resilient to Byzantine behavior. Furthermore, Plateau is designed with judicious use of proof-of-work that makes it resilient to Sybil and DoS attacks. Plateau is robust despite heavy churn controlled by the adversary. Up to $C \in O(n/\text{polylog}(n))$ nodes can join and leave the network per round without disrupting the network.

Its scalability is highlighted by the fact that all resources used are small compared to the overall size of the network and more importantly competitive with the amount of churn. Communication between nodes is via small messages of $\text{polylog}(n)$ bits. Each node has at most $\text{polylog}(n)$ neighbors at any point in time and only needs to communicate with its neighbors. The total number of messages sent/received by all nodes during any round is at most $\tilde{O}(C)$.

Prior works typically assume that the new nodes are automatically connected to appropriate nodes within the network. This is in stark contrast to reality where new nodes must depend on information provided by seeders [8]. Our work formally includes this aspect in that our protocol requires a dynamic whiteboard[2] with $\tilde{O}(C)$ bits that is visible to any new node that seeks to join the network. Each new node samples (from the whiteboard) a random $\text{polylog}(n)$ sized chunk of information that includes a suitable proof-of-work puzzle that the new node must solve. It also includes IDs of the appropriate nodes within the network that it must connect to and submit the solution to the puzzle in order to gain entry into the network. Our protocol updates the whiteboard at the rate of $\tilde{O}(C^2/n)$

---

[1] We say that an event E holds with high probability (whp) if $\text{Prob}[E] \geq 1 - 1/n^\eta$ for any fixed parameter η that is independent of n, but may depend on constants used in the algorithm.

[2] We use the term whiteboard to abstract out the ability to expose information about the network to the world. This is a crucial requirement for any network to handle churn. Otherwise, new nodes will not know where to connect. In current cryptocurrency systems like Bitcoin, we have specialized servers called *seeders* that provide this service [8]. Other alternatives include using the blockchain itself to expose this information [1]. The main design issue is to ensure that the whiteboard only needs to store a bounded amount of information and that updates to the whiteboard are not too fast.

bits per round in order to keep up with the dynamic updates within the network. Thus, as long as the churn rate is $\tilde{O}(\sqrt{n})$, the update rate is at most polylog(n). When C is larger, the whiteboard must be updated at a commensurately larger rate. This is essentially the best we can do because we prove a matching lower bound (within polylog(n) factor) for the update rate.

Importantly, our work assumes that an adversary controls the behavior of all Byzantine nodes including when to seek membership, when to exit, whether to send messages, and what messages to send. The adversary controls churn amongst good nodes in the following oblivious manner that models the worst case (but not malicious) behavior. At the time when a new good node enters the network, the adversary decides how long it will stay in the network. This choice must not violate the churn rate C. Specifically, the adversary is not allowed to churn out more than C nodes per round. Thus, the adversary can impose worst case patterns by which good nodes can churn in and out, but it cannot maliciously and/or adaptively decide when to churn out good nodes.

The main novelty in plateau's design is its two levels. The upper-level is smaller and commensurate in size with the rate at which new nodes join. It consists nodes that act as juries and regulate entry into the network. The lower-level is the essential peer-to-peer (P2P) network that is scalable to large sizes. It is well-connected with good expansion (thereby allowing us to spread information fast and also sample random nodes via random walks) making it ideal for building peer-to-peer distributed trust applications. We show that Plateau can be maintained despite the Byzantine adversary possessing up to a fixed $\beta < 1/4$ of the computational power possessed by good nodes.

1.2 Related Works

In the early years of P2P networks, several prominent overlay network designs like Chord [36], CAN [34], Pastry [35], Tapestry [39] were proposed. Following those early proposals, there has been extensive research on designing robust overlay networks with a variety of useful and rigorously proved characteristics like well-connectedness, low diameter, expansion, low degree, and robustness to network churn and malicious behaviour [3–5,9,11,20,21,24–26,31–33]. For our purpose, we will highlight a few works that are relevant to our goals and design principles of maintaining large scale well connected overlay networks that are robust against Byzantine behavior and adversarial churn.

One of the earliest works in this regard was by Fiat and Saia [13] where items can be stored in a network and most items can be retrieved efficiently despite an adversarial removal of a large fraction of the nodes. In fact, their solution can be adapted to situations where the adversary takes control of a fraction of the nodes (not just remove them). Unfortunately, it is unclear how their overlay can be maintained in the presence of heavy churn. More recently, Guerroui et al. [15] presented a Byzantine resilient overlay maintenance protocol called Neighbors on Watch (NOW) that bears significant resemblance to our protocol. They also maintain a expander graph on supernodes (containing $\Theta(\log n)$ peer nodes) and ensure random distribution of peers within the supernodes. They show how a new node can join or an old node can leave. To the best of our understanding, their design and analysis is limited to just a few nodes (up to $O(\log n)$ nodes) joining or leaving at a time. To their credit, they employ a much strong form of adversary that can churn out any choice of nodes at any time.

Several gossip based sampling protocols have been studied in the past [9, 22,23]. The work by Bortnikov et al. [9] is quite relevant to ours. It has two components: the sampling component and the gossiping component. The sampling component maintains a list of uniform samples from the set of IDs that passed through the node. The gossiping component spreads IDs across the network and maintains the dynamic view of the system. There are, however, two significant drawbacks. Firstly, the protocol requires each node to store $\Theta(n^{1/3})$ IDs locally. Secondly, the analysis of convergence to uniform random samples holds only when the churn ceases, which is unfortunately not the case in the real world. Jesi et al. [22] provide a Byzantine resilient peer sampling mechanism that employs identifying and blacklisting nodes that behave maliciously. Johansen et al. [23] provide a robust pseudorandom structure that is useful for good nodes to maintain correct membership views. Their work maintains a complete membership view, which is unfortunately unscalable for very large networks.

Peer-to-peer networks, as we have mentioned before, experience heavy network churn [19,37]. Quite a bit of research has gone into designing overlays that are resilient to heavy churn [3,4,6,11]. Awerbuch and Scheideler [6] employed the cuckoo rule by which new nodes can join with minimum displacement of existing nodes. An interesting deterministic P2P overlay network was proposed by Kuhn et al. [24], but the price of determinism is that their approach only works with a very small rate of joins and leaves. Augustine et al. [3] show how to maintain an overlay network with good expansion despite heavy churn. They employ random walks to sample random nodes and place new nodes in random locations in order to maintain good expansion. Drees et al. [11] design an overlay network that can handle heavy adversarial churn, but their model requires nodes to join and leave gracefully with a forewarning of at least $\Omega(\log\log n)$ rounds. Augustine and Sivasubramanian [4] provide an overlay design called Spartan that has many similarities to our approach. Both [24] and [4] employ supernodes (or committees) of size $\Theta(\log n)$ nodes. The major drawback of all these works is that they are not shown to be resilient to Byzantine failures.

In a recent work [1], Aradhya et al. show how to maintain a Byzantine resilient blockchain overlay network using the blockchain itself as a means to share information among the peers. This work bears many common features with ours. They also show how the network can tolerate churn. While our work uses arbitrary expander graph structure, they use a hypercubic network structure for the overlay. Their work is specific to blockchain systems, but our work is more general and applicable to any secure peer-to-peer network.

Organization. We begin with a formal description of the model in Sect. 2 and also describe a few important tools that we use in our design. We then present a detailed description of Plateau's design in Sect. 3. Proofs and pseudocode have not been included due to insufficient space.

2   Model and Preliminaries

We begin with a formal description of our network model. Our goal is to design a sustainable peer-to-peer overlay network that can serve as a platform for building large scale distributed trust applications. See Fig. 1 for a schematic. We use the term *node* to refer to the peers that participate in the system. Some of these nodes will be Byzantine (i.e., malicious) while others are good. Moreover, network must also tolerate churn whereby nodes can join and leave. The *System* comprises both the network and all the nodes (both Byzantine and good) that are actively seeking membership within the network. For simplicity, we assume that the number of good nodes n in the system at any point in time is stable.

For simplicity, we assume that the system operates synchronously with rounds being the basic unit of time. Due to churn, up to C good nodes, for some $C \in [0, n/\operatorname{polylog}(n)]$, can leave the system per round and an equal number[3] must enter the system per round in order to maintain a stable number of good nodes in the system. When a node enters the system, it must be integrated into the network by a protocol that maintains the network (and this may take some time). The nodes in the system, but not yet integrated into the network are called *seekers* because they are nodes seeking membership within the network.

We assume that each good node has a unique ID – typically its IP address – that can be used both to uniquely identify it as well as to form network connections. Moreover, each good node is capable of a bounded amount of computational work (or just work). The Byzantine nodes are controlled by a single Byzantine adversary that can create as many Byzantine nodes as it needs, but the overall computational power of the Byzantine adversary is limited to a positive fraction $\beta < 1/4$ (known as the *Byzantine power parameter*) of the total compute power of good nodes.

The goal is to design a network that is robust despite churn and Byzantine nodes. In particular, the good nodes must maintain a degree of at most $O(\log n)$ and must induce an expander graph with vertex expansion bounded from below by a constant. The specific network we present is called the *Plateau network* (or just network) and for this reason, we refer to the system as the *Plateau system*. Plateau must ensure that, at any point in time, all

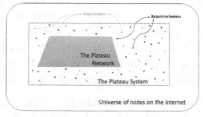

Fig. 1. The Plateau System and the Plateau network.

but $O(C)$ good seekers are integrated into the network. It is inevitable that the network may have integrated some Byzantine nodes as well but we wish to ensure that they are at most $\beta^* n$ at any point in time for some fixed fraction $\beta^* < 1/2$. Moreover, those Byzantine nodes must be incapable of compromising the guar-

---

[3] Our design is sufficiently robust to admit variation between the number of nodes joining and leaving as long as the total number of good nodes stays bounded within some reasonable $\Theta(n)$.

antees offered by the network. The term *Plateau system* (or just *system*) denotes the network and the seekers; see Fig. 1 for a schematic of the system and the network.

Churn Model. We now describe the churn process in bit more detail. A node that is neither a member nor a seeker is called an *external node* and such an external node can become a seeker at any time; we call this *churning in*. Likewise, a node in the system (regardless of whether it is a member or a seeker) can leave the system and become an external node; we call this *churning out*. The Byzantine adversary controls nodes churning in and out subject to the following constraints.

At most C good nodes can be *churned in* per round and an equal number churned out. Any number of Byzantine nodes can be churned in and churned out. An *epoch* is defined to be n/C rounds and corresponds to the time required by an adversary to completely replace the current set of nodes with a new set of nodes. The network must ensure that good seekers gain entry into the network in a timely fashion through a process called *integration*. Specifically, we wish to ensure that the number of good seekers is no more than $O(C)$ at any time (whp). Moreover, every good seeker node should be integrated into the network within $O(\log n)$ rounds (whp).

Nodes can be *churned out* either by the protocol or by the adversary. When all good nodes drop their connections with a node u, then it is considered churned out by the protocol (as long as it is clear that good nodes cannot be tricked into forming connections with u later on). Such churn outs are expected to happen when a node is unable to provide proof of work that the protocol may require of it from time to time. The protocol must be designed to ensure that good nodes are not churned out in this manner because they are expected to be willing to spend one unit of computational power per epoch. The time when a good node v is churned out by the adversary must be specified when the node is churned in. (A good node will not be aware of its churn out time.) There is no incentive for the adversary to actively churn out Byzantine nodes. However, since the computational power of the adversary is bounded, Byzantine nodes that are unable to provide proof-of-work must be churned out by the protocol.

Communication Model. Nodes can communicate with each other in one of two modes: either through established overlay links (e.g., TCP sessions) or through ports that are open. Formation of an overlay link between two nodes u and v must be initiated by one node and consented by the other; such a link can be formed in one round. We assume that each node can maintain $O(\log n)$ overlay links. Alternatively, each node has $O(\log n)$ ports numbered $\{1, 2, \ldots, O(\log n)\}$ through which it can listen for new messages or new connections. Thus, if a node u knows the ID of node v, then u can send v a message through some port x. The message will be delivered to v if no other node is also attempting to send a message to v through x at the same time. Messages will be dropped when such conflicts occur. We assume that u will be aware of whether the message reached v or not. We require each message (sent through either mode) to be small in size, i.e., at most $O(\text{polylog}\, n)$ bits. Furthermore, We wish to ensure that the total number of messages sent by good nodes are at most $M \in O(C \log n)$ per round. We similarly limit the number of messages sent by Byzantine nodes to also be within the same limit M.

Public Whiteboard. To facilitate integration, the network is allowed to publish information on a *whiteboard* that is available for public viewing. For the purpose of this paper, we abstract away the details of how such a whiteboard may be implemented. The whiteboard, however, must be limited to displaying $\tilde{O}(C)$ bits of information that is updated at the rate of $o(C)$ bits per round, i.e., at most $o(C)$ bits can be erased and at most $o(C)$ bits can be written per round.

Proof-of-Work. We assume that proof-of-work puzzles can be solved by expending one unit of compute power[4]. To solve such a puzzle, a node u requires an input bit string r and its own ID and computes a nonce bit string q such that $h(r|ID(u)|q)$ has sufficiently many leading zeros, where h is a random oracle hash function. Each good node must be willing to spend 1 unit of computational power for integration and subsequently spend one unit of computational power per epoch. The number of rounds required to solve one proof of work puzzle is assumed to be within $O(\log n)$ rounds. The total computational power of the Byzantine adversary is assumed to be βn per epoch, where $\beta > 0$ known as the *Byzantine power parameter* is a fixed constant bounded strictly below $1/4$. I.e., the Byzantine nodes, in total, can solve $n/4$ proof-of-work puzzles per epoch. Additionally, whenever a good node is churned in, the Byzantine adversary is credited with β units of computational power that must be spent within $O(\log n)$ rounds. This is to ensure that the Byzantine adversary is empowered to churn in Byzantine nodes into the network.

Useful Tools and Techniques. We use several standard tools and techniques that we explain in greater detail in the full version. We rely on expander graphs [38] for fast mixing time, low diameter (i.e., both logarithmig in the size of the network) and established tools for creating and maintaining them in dynamic environments [3,32]. Furthermore, we assume that Byzantine agreement [12] and collective coin tossing [28] can be executed $O(\log n)$ rounds whp.

3 The Plateau Network Design and Statement of Results

We now describe our proposed network design. It relies crucially on sets of $\Theta(\log n)$ nodes called *supernodes* that are interconnected to form the Plateau network. The supernodes partition the set of nodes, thus there are $n/c \log n$ supernodes for some sufficiently large constant c. We say that a supernode is b-Byzantine-Bounded for some $b \in [0, 1]$ if *fewer than* b fraction of the nodes in it are Byzantine. The network is said to be b-Byzantine-Bounded if all supernodes in it are b-Byzantine-Bounded. Our goal is to guarantee that the Plateau network is $(1/3)$-Byzantine-Bounded (i.e., every supernode is $(1/3)$-Byzantine-Bounded).

---

[4] This is a simplifying assumption. We can also model the compute power required to solve a puzzle as an exponential random variable.

Thanks to this limited influence by the Byzantine adversary, supernodes can serve as committees that decisively act by invoking Byzantine Agreement [12].

The list of nodes in a supernode s is maintained as common knowledge among all nodes in s. Thus, whenever all good nodes in s unanimously propose a value, they can initiate Byzantine Agreement and ensure that s (as a single entity) will be able to decide on one of those values. Moreover, each supernode can execute Micali and Rabin's unbiased coin tossing protocol and generate unbiased random bits that all good nodes within s agree upon.

Two supernodes s_1 and s_2 are said to be connected by a *logical link* if every good node in s_1 (resp., s_2) is aware of all members in s_2 (resp., s_1) and has successfully established an overlay link with every good node in s_2 (resp., s_1).

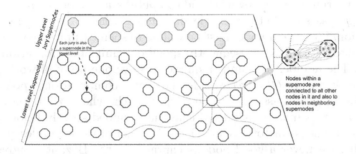

Fig. 2. The Plateau network architecture comprising (1/3)-Byzantine-Bounded supernodes in two levels. Each jury supernode is also a supernode in the lower level. The supernodes in the lower level (resp., juries in the upper level) are connected via logical links (not shown) to form an expander graph G (resp., H).

The Two-Tier Plateau Structure. As mentioned before, Plateau comprises two levels: the lower level comprising the set of all supernodes S and the upper level comprising a (dynamic) set of $\Theta(M)$ supernodes J called juries. Note that juries will have to continue their role in the lower level even while serving as juries. See Fig. 2 for a schematic of the Plateau architecture.

The supernodes at both levels are connected via logical links in the form of (constant degree) expander graphs: $G = (S, E)$ for the lower level and $H = (J, E')$ for the upper level. Our design therefore ensures that each supernode has established logical links to at most $O(1)$ other supernodes. Thus, the number of overlay links at each individual node is at most $O(\log n)$.

Secure Messages. Two supernodes s_1 and s_2 that are connected by a logical link can communicate with each other at will via *secure messages* (explained shortly) with the twin security guarantees of authentication and integrity. When the (good) nodes in (say) s_1 wish to send a secure message to the nodes in s_2, they individually send the same message to every node in s_2. At the receiving end, i.e., at s_2, the good nodes accept all messages sent by at least a 2/3 fraction of the nodes in s_1. Any message sent by fewer than a 2/3 fraction is discarded. Such a message sent by all good nodes in s_1 to all good nodes in s_2 in this coordinated manner is deemed a secure message. Notice that s_2 receives a secure message from s_1 iff s_1 sends a secure message to s_2. Thus, as long as all the good nodes in s_1 are agreed on what message to send, the recipient s_2 knows that the message indeed originated at s_1 (i.e., the sender's authenticity is guaranteed) and that the message has not been tampered with (i.e., its integrity is guaranteed). Notice however that these secure messages are not guaranteed to be private. If either s_1 or s_2 has even one Byzantine node, the Byzantine adversary will be able to learn the contents of the secure message.

A node u cannot become a member of a supernode without proper credentials. If u is a seeker and has performed the requisite proof-of-work, a jury supernode will admit it into the network and move u to a random supernode s via a secure random walk (described shortly). Importantly, u cannot influence the choice of s. Subsequently u may be moved around via secure random walks roughly once every epoch. Thus, there is no provision for a node u to join an arbitrary supernode. Node u can only join a supernode s as a consequence of secure random walks that explicitly introduce u to s.

Plateau Maintenance. To maintain Plateau, we operate in *maintenance cycles* of $m \in \Theta(\log n)$ rounds. In each cycle, $\tilde{\Theta}(1 + \frac{C^2 \log^3 n}{n})$ juries are replaced by randomly chosen supernodes from the lower level and an expected C nodes are moved to random locations. Simultaneously, new nodes that wish to join are integrated into Plateau after proper vetting of their proof of work.

Replacement of Juries. The juries $J \subset S$ (chosen uniformly at random) regulate the entry of new nodes into the network. We rotate in new jury supernodes during each maintenance cycle and simultaneously evict an equal number from the upper level. All the IDs of nodes in the newly inducted juries are added to the whiteboard and the IDs of nodes in the evicted juries are deleted from the whiteboard. The rotation of juries ensures that the list of nodes in juries written to the whiteboard are sufficiently current.

Let $\mathbf{r} = \tilde{\Theta}(1 + \frac{C^2 \log^3 n}{n})$ denote the *refresh rate*, i.e., the rate at which juries are rotated in and out of the upper level per round. At the start of every maintenance cycle, the protocol picks $\mathbf{r}m \in O(\mathbf{r}\log n)$ random juries j and marks them for replacement. Simultaneously, an equal number of random lower level supernodes s are called for jury duty and are installed in H, with each s in the same neighborhood of a corresponding j in H; juries marked for deletion can now be deleted from H. Thus, the topology of H remains stable, but its vertices are rotated in and out regularly. Note that the random choices of j and s can be made via secure random walks of length $\Theta(\log n)$ performed on H and G, respectively. The full version contains formal pseudocode.

Information Published on the Whiteboard. The whiteboard maintains a current list of juries and the constituent nodes within those juries (including Byzantine nodes). It also includes a random bit string r that is updated every cycle. The whiteboard will only accept updates given by secure messages from current juries. Whenever a jury j leaves the upper level, it informs the whiteboard and is erased from the whiteboard. When a new jury j enters the upper level, a pre-existing jury j' (typically a neighbor of j in H) must inform the whiteboard so that j and its constituent members can be included in the whiteboard. We also maintain a designated lead jury j^* that generates a random bit string r in each cycle and updates the whiteboard with r (while the earlier string is erased).

Reassignment of Nodes. Byzantine nodes can selectively sever ties with nodes both within its own supernode as well as neighboring supernodes. Moreover, we must ensure that Byzantine nodes don't freeload or selectively stagnate and pile up in some supernode. To avoid these issues, each node u in each supernode s is reassigned once every (expected) n/mC cycles to a new supernode s' chosen randomly through a secure random walk. The choice of u is via collective coin tossing by nodes within s such that the time between two consecutive reassignments for u is geometrically distributed with $p = mC/n$. When chosen for reassignment, u must first show proof of work requiring a one unit of computation. Then the nodes in s vote on whether (i) u has shown the correct proof of work *and* (ii) has correctly executed all protocols during the last epoch and perform a Byzantine agreement to decide whether to retain u or churn it out. If the agreement is not in favor of u, all good nodes in s will sever their links with u and also inform all neighboring supernodes through secure messages, thereby effectively churning out u. If u survives, it is forced to make a secure random walk for $\ell_G \in \Theta(\log n)$ steps where u will be chaperoned to a new random supernode s'.

Integrating Seekers into the Network. Each seeker x reads the current random string r from the whiteboard and solves the puzzle pertaining to $(r|ID(x))$. The solution is a nonce bit string t such that $h(r|ID(x)|t)$ has at least ℓ leading zeros for some predefined ℓ and a commonly agreed random oracle hash function h. This requires a 1 unit of compute power and time that is at most $O(\log n)$ rounds. The seeker x then picks a random jury j and sends its proof of work to every node in j (listed in the whiteboard) through randomly chosen ports. If more than half of the members of j receive the proof and acknowledge it, then x sends an accept message to nodes in j and waits for j to integrate x into the network. Otherwise, x sends a reject message to nodes in j and repeats the process with a new random jury. The juries wait for seekers to send proof and acknowledge them. When a seeker x sends an accept, the jury begins Byzantine agreement to either approve or reject the request. If approved, a secure random walk is initiated and x is chaperoned to a random supernode in G.

Our results are formalized by the following two theorems.

Theorem 1. *Any whiteboard based P2P network (with whiteboard size $O(C)$) that experiences churn at the rate of C nodes per round must update the whiteboard at the rate of $\tilde{\Omega}(C^2/n)$ bits per round.*

Theorem 2. *The Plateau system is designed with the following guarantees that hold with high probability as long as the Byzantine power parameter β is a fixed constant that is bounded strictly below $1/4$ and the churn rate $C \in [0, n/\operatorname{polylog}(n)]$.*

Byzantine Boundedness. *The Plateau network will be (1/3)-Byzantine-Bounded for at least $T \in \Omega(n^k)$ rounds for fixed k.*

Network Properties. *The network induced by the good nodes within the Plateau network forms an expander with vertex expansion bounded from below by a constant. Thus, its diameter is $O(\log n)$. Moreover, the number of overlay edges incident to any good node is at most $O(\log n)$.*

Quick Integration. *Seekers will integrate within $O(1)$ rounds on expectation and the expected number of seekers waiting to be integrated will be at most $O(C)$ at any time.*

Efficient Whiteboard. *The whiteboard employed by Plateau is of size at most $\tilde{O}(C)$ and is updated at the rate of $\tilde{O}(C^2/n) \in o(C)$ bits per round when C is at most $n/\text{polylog}(n)$. In fact, the update rate is at most $\tilde{O}(1)$ if $C \in \tilde{O}(\sqrt{n})$ and this is optimal to within a $\text{polylog}(n)$ factor.*

4 Concluding Remarks and Future Work

We have presented a P2P network architecture called Plateau that is able to regulate the entry and exit of nodes even at high churn rates. Our design is quite generic and can be easily adapted in a variety of ways. Our choice of expander graph structure is in keeping with the long line of works on P2P networks that rely on expansion [15,25,31]. Moreover, it closely resembles the P2P networks we see in practice and they are known to be robust even under adversarial deletions [7]. However, expander graphs can be replaced by other structures that have good sampling properties (e.g., hypercubes [2] and butterflies) with potential benefits. For example, the Spartan structure [4] that is based on the butterfly network facilitates addressable supernodes and efficient routing between them. This can be used to build distributed hash tables.

Furthermore, for simplicity, we assumed that the number of good nodes is stable at n. However, we can easily adapt Plateau's design to varying values of n. This can be done very robustly when the rate of change of n is $\text{polylog}(n)$ per round by adapting G using [32]. For more dramatic changes, we can use a more structured approach wherein G is a hypercube or a butterfly. When n increases or decreases dramatically, such structures can be expanded or contracted by incrementing or decrementing their dimension using ideas from [2].

We believe that a thorough simulation of Plateau will greatly help in understanding its viability in practice. Moreover, the current paper is limited to synchronous systems. Extending these ideas to asynchronous systems is an important next step. Finally, the current work abstracts away the details pertaining to implementing a whiteboard, but these details need to be worked out for Plateau to work in practice.

Acknowledgements. We thank Seth Gilbert and Aquinas Hobor for preliminary discussions in which they suggested the idea of using a whiteboard to facilitate new nodes joining the network. The first author was supported in part by Extra-Mural Research Grant (file number EMR/2016/003016) and MATRICS grant (file number MTR/2018/001198). He is currently supported by the potential Centre of Excellence in Cryptography Cybersecurity and Distributed Trust (CCD) under the IIT Madras Institute of Eminence scheme. The third author worked on this project as an intern at IIT Madras supported by an Information Security Education and Awareness (https://isea.gov.in/) Phase II project (CCECEP22VK&CPCSE1415).

References

1. Aradhya, V., Gilbert, S., Hobor, A.: OverChain: building a robust overlay with a blockchain (2022). https://arxiv.org/abs/2201.12809
2. Augustine, J., Chatterjee, S., Pandurangan, G.: A fully-distributed scalable peer-to-peer protocol for Byzantine-resilient distributed hash tables. In: SPAA, pp. 87–98 (2022)
3. Augustine, J., Pandurangan, G., Robinson, P., Roche, S.T., Upfal, E.: Enabling robust and efficient distributed computation in dynamic peer-to-peer networks. In: FOCS (2015)
4. Augustine, J., Sivasubramaniam, S.: Spartan: a framework for sparse robust addressable networks. In: 2018 International Parallel and Distributed Processing Symposium (IPDPS), pp. 1060–1069 (2018)
5. Awerbuch, B., Scheideler, C.: The hyperring: a low-congestion deterministic data structure for distributed environments. In: SODA (2004)
6. Awerbuch, B., Scheideler, C.: Towards a scalable and robust DHT. Theory Comput. Syst. **45**(2), 234–260 (2009)
7. Bagchi, A., Bhargava, A., Chaudhary, A., Eppstein, D., Scheideler, C.: The effect of faults on network expansion. Theory Comput. Syst. **39**(6), 903–928 (2006)
8. Bitcoin P2P network official documentation. https://developer.bitcoin.org/devguide/p2p_network.html. Accessed 25 Apr 2022
9. Bortnikov, E., Gurevich, M., Keidar, I., Kliot, G., Shraer, A.: Brahms: Byzantine resilient random membership sampling. Comput. Netw. **53**(13), 2340–2359 (2009)
10. Croman, K., et al.: On scaling decentralized blockchains. In: Clark, J., Meiklejohn, S., Ryan, P.Y.A., Wallach, D., Brenner, M., Rohloff, K. (eds.) FC 2016. LNCS, vol. 9604, pp. 106–125. Springer, Heidelberg (2016). https://doi.org/10.1007/978-3-662-53357-4_8
11. Drees, M., Gmyr, R., Scheideler, C.: Churn-and DoS-resistant overlay networks based on network reconfiguration. In: SPAA 2016, pp. 417–427. ACM (2016)
12. Feldman, P., Micali, S.: An optimal probabilistic protocol for synchronous Byzantine agreement. SIAM J. Comput. **26**(4), 873–933 (1997)
13. Fiat, A., Saia, J.: Censorship resistant peer-to-peer networks. Theory Comput. **3**(1), 1–23 (2007). https://doi.org/10.4086/toc.2007.v003a001. https://www.theoryofcomputing.org/articles/v003a001
14. Gkantsidis, C., Mihail, M., Saberi, A.: Random walks in peer-to-peer networks: algorithms and evaluation. Perform. Eval. **63**(3), 241–263 (2006). P2P Computing Systems
15. Guerraoui, R., Huc, F., Kermarrec, A.M.: Highly dynamic distributed computing with Byzantine failures. In: PODC 2013 (2013)
16. Gupta, D., Saia, J., Young, M.: Resource burning for permissionless systems (invited paper). In: Richa, A.W., Scheideler, C. (eds.) SIROCCO 2020. LNCS, vol. 12156, pp. 19–44. Springer, Cham (2020). https://doi.org/10.1007/978-3-030-54921-3_2
17. Gupta, D., Saia, J., Young, M.: Bankrupting sybil despite churn. In: ICDCS, pp. 425–437 (2021)

18. Heilman, E., Kendler, A., Zohar, A., Goldberg, S.: Eclipse attacks on bitcoin's peer-to-peer network. In: 24th USENIX Security Symposium (USENIX Security 2015) (2015)
19. Imtiaz, M.A., Starobinski, D., Trachtenberg, A., Younis, N.: Churn in the bitcoin network: characterization and impact. In: 2019 IEEE International Conference on Blockchain and Cryptocurrency (ICBC), pp. 431–439 (2019)
20. Jacob, R., Richa, A., Scheideler, C., Schmid, S., Täubig, H.: SKIP+: a self-stabilizing skip graph. J. ACM **61**(6), 36:1–36:26 (2014)
21. Jacobs, T., Pandurangan, G.: Stochastic analysis of a churn-tolerant structured peer-to-peer scheme. Peer-to-Peer Netw. Appl. **6**(1) (2013)
22. Jesi, G.P., Montresor, A., van Steen, M.: Secure peer sampling. Comput. Netw. **54**(12), 2086–2098 (2010)
23. Johansen, H.D., Renesse, R.V., Vigfusson, Y., Johansen, D.: Fireflies: a secure and scalable membership and gossip service. ACM Trans. Comput. Syst. **33**(2) (2015)
24. Kuhn, F., Schmid, S., Wattenhofer, R.: Towards worst-case churn resistant peer-to-peer systems. Distrib. Comput. **22**(4), 249–267 (2010)
25. Law, C., Siu, K.Y.: Distributed construction of random expander networks. In: IEEE INFOCOM 2003, vol. 3, pp. 2133–2143 (2003)
26. Mahlmann, P., Schindelhauer, C.: Peer-to-peer networks based on random transformations of connected regular undirected graphs. In: SPAA, pp. 155–164 (2005)
27. Mao, Y., Deb, S., Venkatakrishnan, S.B., Kannan, S., Srinivasan, K.: Perigee: efficient peer-to-peer network design for blockchains. In: PODC 2020, pp. 428–437 (2020)
28. Micali, S., Rabin, T.: Collective coin tossing without assumptions nor broadcasting. In: Menezes, A.J., Vanstone, S.A. (eds.) CRYPTO 1990. LNCS, vol. 537, pp. 253–266. Springer, Heidelberg (1991). https://doi.org/10.1007/3-540-38424-3_18
29. Nakamoto, S.: Bitcoin: a peer-to-peer electronic cash system (2009)
30. Neudecker, T.: Characterization of the bitcoin peer-to-peer network (2015–2018). Technical report. 1, Karlsruher Institut für Technologie (KIT) (2019)
31. Pandurangan, G., Raghavan, P., Upfal, E.: Building low-diameter peer-to-peer networks. IEEE J. Sel. Areas Commun. **21**(6), 995–1002 (2003)
32. Pandurangan, G., Robinson, P., Trehan, A.: DEX: self-healing expanders. Distrib. Comput. **29**(3), 163–185 (2016)
33. Pandurangan, G., Trehan, A.: Xheal: a localized self-healing algorithm using expanders. Distrib. Comput. **27**(1), 39–54 (2014)
34. Ratnasamy, S., Francis, P., Handley, M., Karp, R., Shenker, S.: A scalable content-addressable network. Comput. Commun. Rev. **31**(4), 161–172 (2001)
35. Rowstron, A., Druschel, P.: Pastry: scalable, decentralized object location, and routing for large-scale peer-to-peer systems. In: Guerraoui, R. (ed.) Middleware 2001. LNCS, vol. 2218, pp. 329–350. Springer, Heidelberg (2001). https://doi.org/10.1007/3-540-45518-3_18
36. Stoica, I., Morris, R., Karger, D., Kaashoek, M.F., Balakrishnan, H.: Chord: a scalable peer-to-peer lookup service for internet applications. Comput. Commun. Rev. **31**(4), 149–160 (2001)
37. Stutzbach, D., Rejaie, R.: Understanding churn in peer-to-peer networks. In: SIGCOMM, New York, NY, USA (2006)
38. Vadhan, S.P.: Pseudorandomness. Found. Trends® Theor. Comput. Sci. **7**(1–3), 1–336 (2012)
39. Zhao, B.Y., Kubiatowicz, J., Joseph, A.D.: Tapestry: a fault-tolerant wide-area application infrastructure. Comput. Commun. Rev. **32**(1), 81 (2002)

The Limits of Helping in Non-volatile Memory Data Structures

Ohad Ben-Baruch[1]([⊠]) and Srivatsan Ravi[2]

[1] Ben-Gurion University of the Negev, Be'er Sheva, Israel
ohadben@post.bgu.ac.il
[2] University of Southern California, Los Angeles, USA
srivatsr@usc.edu

Abstract. Linearizability, the traditional correctness condition for concurrent data structures is considered insufficient for the non-volatile shared memory model where processes recover following a crash. For this crash-recovery shared memory model, strict-linearizability is considered appropriate since, unlike linearizability, it ensures operations that crash take effect prior to the crash or not at all. This work formalizes and answers the question of whether an implementation of a data type derived for the crash-stop shared memory model is also strict-linearizable in the crash-recovery model.

This work presents a rigorous study to prove how helping mechanisms, typically employed by non-blocking implementations, is the algorithmic abstraction that delineates linearizability from strict-linearizability. We first formalize the crash-recovery model and how explicit process crashes and recovery introduces further dimensionalities over the standard crash-stop shared memory model. We make the following technical contributions that answer the question of whether a help-free linearizable implementation is strict-linearizable in the crash-recovery model: (i) we prove surprisingly that there exist linearizable implementations of object types that are help-free, yet not strict-linearizable; (ii) we then present a natural definition of help-freedom to prove that any obstruction-free, linearizable and help-free implementation of a total object type is also strict-linearizable. The next technical contribution addresses the question of whether a strict-linearizable implementation in the crash-recovery model is also help-free linearizable in the crash-stop model. To that end, we prove that for a large class of object types, a non-blocking strict-linearizable implementation cannot have helping. Viewed holistically, this work provides the first precise characterization of the intricacies in applying a concurrent implementation designed for the crash-stop model to the crash-recovery model, and vice-versa.

1 Introduction

Concurrent data structures for the standard volatile shared memory model typically adopt linearizability as the traditional safety property [11]. The emergence of systems equipped with non-volatile shared memory draws attention to the

S. Devismes et al. (Eds.): SSS 2022, LNCS 13751, pp. 84–98, 2022.
https://doi.org/10.1007/978-3-031-21017-4_6

crash-recovery model [5] where processes *recover* following a crash. In such systems linearizability is considered insufficient since it allows object operations that crash to take effect anytime in the future. Aguilera and Frølund proposed to strengthened linearizability to force crashed operations to take effect before the crash or not take effect at all, so-called *strict-linearizability* [1]. While there exists a well-studied body of linearizable data structure implementations in the crash-stop model [3], concurrent implementations in the crash-recovery model are comparatively nascent. Consequently, it is natural to ask: under what conditions is a linearizable implementation in the crash-stop also strict-linearizable in the crash-recovery model?

Non-blocking implementations in the crash-stop model employ *helping*: i.e., apart from completing their own operation, processes perform additional work to help *linearize* concurrent operations and make progress. It has been shown that for many objects, any linearizable implementation using a set of well-known atomic operations must introduce helping [6]. This helping mechanism enables an operation invoked by a process p_i to be linearized by an event performed by another process p_j, but possibly after the crash of p_i. However, strict-linearizability stipulates that the operation invoked by p_i be linearized before the crash event. Intuitively, this suggests that a linearizable implementation with helping mechanism is not strict-linearizable (also conjectured in [5]: section 2), while one that is *help-free* must be strict-linearizable. This work formalizes and answers this precise question: whether a help-free implementation of a data type derived for the crash-stop model can be used *as it is* in the crash-recovery model. Answering this question could be very important from a practical standpoint as we transition towards byte-addressable non-volatile memory: if the answer is in the affirmative, then we could take a linearizable concurrent data structure that is provably help-free and it would be correct (i.e. strict-linearizable) when deployed for non-volatile shared memory.

Precisely answering this question necessitates the formalization of the crash-recovery shared memory model. Explicit process crashes introduce further dimensionalities to the set of executions admissible in the crash-recovery model over the well formalized crash-stop shared memory [3]. Processes may crash on an individual basis, i.e., an event in the execution corresponds to the crash of a single process (we refer to this as the *individual crash-recovery model*). An event may also correspond to m $(1 < m \le n)$, process crashes where n is total number of processes participating in the concurrent implementation (when $m = n$ it is the *full-system crash-recovery model*). Following a crash event in this model, the local state of the process is reset to its initial state when it recovers and restarts an operation assuming the *old identifiers crash-recovery model* (and resp. *new identifiers crash-recovery model*) with the original process identifier (and resp. new process identifier). Our contributions establish equivalence and separation results for crash-stop and the identified crash-recovery models, thus providing a precise characterization of the intricacies in applying a concurrent implementation designed for the crash-stop model to the crash-recovery model, and vice-versa.

1.1   Contributions

First, we define the crash-recovery model and its characteristics. We show that there exist sequential implementations of object types in the crash-stop model that have inconsistent sequential specifications in the old identifiers crash-recovery model (Lemma 1). The result is intuitive, since stopping and restarting an operation execution may cause inconsistency.

We then consider how data structures use helping in the crash-stop model by adopting the definitions of *linearization-helping* [6] and *universal-helping* [2]. When considering an execution with two concurrent operations, the linearization of these operations dictates which operation takes effect first. The definition of linearization-helping considers a specific event e, in which it is *decided* which operation is linearized first. In an implementation that does not have linearization-helping, e is an event by the process whose operation is decided to be the one that comes first. Universal-helping requires that the progress of some processes eventually ensures that all pending invocations are linearized, thus forcing a process to ensure concurrent operations of other processes are eventually linearized.

The first technical contribution of this paper is proving that some pairs of conditions are incomparable. That is, satisfying one of the conditions does not imply the other condition holds as well. For that, we present an implementation such that one condition holds while the other does not hold. Moreover, we also present implementations such that both conditions hold, and such that none holds. As a result, arguing about one of the conditions does not imply any result regarding the other condition.

- There exists an implementation that satisfies universal-helping (and resp. linearization-helping) but does not satisfy linearization-helping (and resp. universal-helping) (Lemma 2).
- A strict-linearizable implementation in the crash-recovery model can either have or not have linearization-helping in the crash-stop model (Lemma 4).
- A strict-linearizable implementation in the crash-recovery model can either have or not have universal-helping in the crash-stop model (Lemma 6).

We find this set of results to be somewhat counter intuitive. It is known that linearization-helping does not imply universal-helping. However, the other direction may be misleading, since in most cases universal-helping implies linearization-helping. As we prove, this is not always the case, and one can use different linearization orders for the same set of executions in order to prove universal-helping does hold, while linearization-order does not hold. In addition, it was speculated that strict-linearizability precludes any kind of helping [5]. Surprisingly, there is an implementation that is strict-linearizable in the crash-recovery model while also having linearization-helping or universal-helping in the crash-stop model.

The key implications of these results is that, in general, it is not the case that a help-free implementation of a data type derived for the crash-stop model can be used *as it is* in the crash-recovery model and still be strict-linearizable. However, our second technical contribution is to show that under certain restrictions there is a correlation between some of the above conditions for an important class of concurrent data structures.

- Note that as part of Lemma 4, we present a linearizable implementation of a *sticky-bit* object that does not satisfy linearization-helping (Claim 4.1), yet is not strict-linearizable. This result is surprising and made possible because linearization-helping permits some unintuitive linearizations: it may linearize operations of some history H in different order for different extensions of H. Restricting the definition of linearization-helping to be *prefix-respecting*, we prove that linearization-help free implies strict-linearizability. More specifically, any *obstruction-free* implementation of a *total* object type that is linearizable and has no linearization-helping in the crash-stop model is also strict-linearizable in the new identifiers individual crash-recovery model (Corollary 1). Thus, from a practical standpoint, this result establishes an important equivalence between linearizability and strict-linearizability for a large class of concurrent implementations.
- We prove that any non-blocking implementation of an *order-dependent* type that is strict-linearizable in the crash-recovery model has no universal-helping in the crash-stop model (Lemma 7). Order-dependent types are closely related to *exact-order* types [6] and include popular objects like queues and stacks (Sect. 3). From a practical standpoint, our result implies that if an order-dependent object has universal-helping in the crash-stop model, then it is *not* going to be strict-linearizable in the crash-recovery model.

Roadmap. The contributions in this paper are structured as follows: Sect. 2 presents our characterization of the dimensionalities of the crash-recovery shared memory model (for the standard crash-stop shared memory model please see [4]) Sect. 3 recalls universal-helping, linearization-helping, valency-helping and presents new results on implementations satisfying these definitions. Section 4 discusses the correlation between strict-linearizable implementations and linearization-helping, and proves that help-freedom does not imply strict-linearizability in general, but under a natural definition of help-freedom it does follow. Section 5 proves that strict-linearizability and universal-helping are incomparable . However, for a large class of objects, strict-linearizability implies universal-help freedom.

The full paper [4] contains full proofs and detailed results that are omitted from the main paper due to space constraints. It also expends the results as follows. We consider the implications of our results for weaker (than strict-linearizability) conditions [5,12] which, unlike strict-linearizability, do not preclude helping. For the sake of completion, we also study the relationship between strict-linearizability and *valency-helping* [2] which unlike linearization-helping and universal-helping is defined on operation responses.

1.2 Related Work

Strict-linearizability was proposed by Aguilera et al. [1] which proved that it precludes wait-free implementations of multi-reader single-writer registers from single-reader single-writer registers. [5] showed that this is in fact possible with linearizability thus yielding a separation between the crash-stop and crash-recovery models. That helping mechanisms, typically employed by non-blocking implementations, is the algorithmic abstraction that may delineate linearizability from strict-linearizability was also conjectured in [5]. This is the first work to conclusively answer this question by providing the first precise characterization of the intricacies in applying a shared memory concurrent implementation designed for the crash-stop model to the crash-recovery model, and vice-versa. We prove that although in general helping does not contradict strict-linearizability, under very natural definitions and in many cases helping does not go hand in hand with strict-linearizability.

Censor-Hillel et al. [6] formalized linearization-helping and showed that without it, certain objects called *exact-order* types lack wait-free linearizable implementations (assuming only read, write, compare-and-swap, fetch-and-add primitives) in the standard crash-stop shared memory model. Universal-helping and valency-helping were defined by Attiya et al. [2]. Informally, it was shown in [2] that a non-blocking n-process linearizable implementation of a queue or a stack with universal-helping can be used to solve n-process consensus. This result was also extended to *strong-linearizability* [8] which requires that once an operation is linearized, its linearization order cannot be changed in the future. The definition of strong-linearizability does bear resemblance with the proposed helping definitions in [2,6]; however, it is defined as restriction of linearizability and is incomparable to helping. Indeed, [6] makes the observation that strong-linearizability is incomparable with linearization-helping. The results in this paper study the implications of the universal, linearization and valency helping definitions for strict-linearizability in the crash-recovery, which has not been studied carefully thus far.

2   Characterization of the Crash-Recovery Model

Processes and Non-volatile Shared Memory. We extend the standard crash-stop model (for formal definitions please see [4]) by allowing any process p_i to *fail by crashing*; following a crash, process p_i does not take any steps until the invocation of a new operation. Following a crash, the state of the shared objects remains the same as before the crash; however, the local state of crashed process is set to its initial state.

Executions and Configurations. An *event* of a process p_i in the crash-recovery model is any step admissible in the crash-stop model as well as a special $\perp_{\mathbb{P}}$ crash step; $\mathbb{P}$ is a set of process identifiers. The $\perp_{\mathbb{P}}$ step performs the following actions: (i) for each $i \in \mathbb{P}$, the local state of p_i set to its initial state, (ii) the execution $E_1 \cdot \perp_{\mathbb{P}} \cdot E_2$ where E_2 is $\mathbb{P}$-free, is indistinguishable to every process $j \notin \mathbb{P}$ from the execution $E_1 \cdot E_2$. In other words, processes are not aware of crash events.

Process Crash Model. We say that an execution E is admissible in the *individual crash-recovery model* if for any event $\perp_{\mathbb{P}}$ in E, $|\mathbb{P}| = 1$. If $|\mathbb{P}| = \mathbb{N}$ for any event $\perp_\mathbb{P}$ in E, we refer to it as the *system-wide crash-recovery model*. We say that an implementation I is admissible in the *system-wide crash-recovery model* (resp. *system-wide crash-recovery model*) if every execution of I is admissible in the *individual crash-recovery model* (resp. *system-wide crash-recovery model*).

We note that the system-wide crash-recovery model is closer in nature to real-world systems, where in case of a crash such as power loss all processes crash together. However, in this paper we use the individual crash-recovery model in order to derive stronger results which hold for both models.

Safety Property: Strict-Linearizability. A history H is *strict-linearizable* with respect to an object type τ if there exists a sequential history S equivalent to H^c, a *strict completion of H*, such that (1) $\to_{H^c}\subseteq\to_S$ and (2) S is consistent with the sequential specification of τ.

A strict completion of H is obtained from H by inserting matching responses for a subset of pending operations after the operation's invocation and before the next crash step (if any), and finally removing any remaining pending operations and crash steps.

Liveness. An object implementation is *obstruction-free* if for any execution E and any pending operation π_i by process p_i, π returns a matching response in $E \cdot E'$ or crashes where E' is the complete *solo-run* (E' only contains steps of p_i executing π) execution fragment of π by p_i. An object implementation is *non-blocking* if in every execution, at least one of the *correct* processes completes its operation in a finite number of steps or it crashes. An object implementation is *wait-free* if in every execution, every *correct* process completes its operation within a finite number of its own steps or crashes. Obviously, liveness in the crash-stop model is identical to the above without the option of process crashing.

Old Identifiers Crash-Recovery Model. Consider an execution E and a process p_i that crashes in E. We say that an execution E is admissible in the *old identifiers crash-recovery model* if for any process p_i and any event $\perp_\mathbb{P}$ in E such that $i \in \mathbb{P}$, p_i takes its first step in E after the crash by invoking a new operation.

New Identifiers Crash-Recovery Model. We say that an execution E is admissible in the *new identifiers crash-recovery model* if for any process p_i and any event $\perp_\mathbb{P}$ in E such that $i \in \mathbb{P}$, process p_i no longer takes steps following $\perp_\mathbb{P}$ in E. Note that even in this model, there are at most $\mathbb{N}$ *active* processes in an execution, i.e., processes that have not crashed.

Aguilera and Frølund [1] showed that there exist object types for which there exists a wait-free linearizable implementation in the crash-stop model, while there exists no wait-free strict-linearizable implementation in the crash-recovery model. Lemma 1 further strengthen this result by proving that given an implementation in the crash-stop model, using it as is in the old identifiers crash-recovery model may result a sequential execution (i.e., an execution with no concurrency) in which a process returns an invalid response. For lack of space, a proof can be found in [4]. These results suggest that it is not trivial to transform an implementation from the crash-stop model to the old identifiers crash-recovery model.

Izraelevitz et al. defined the new-identifiers crash-recovery model as it is closer to real-world systems [12]. Under the new identifier crash-recovery model any execution with crash events is indistinguishable to all non-crashed processes from an execution in the crash-stop model in which every crashed process simply halts, and vice-versa. Thus, and by abuse of notation, we can consider the same execution in both models in the context of deriving proofs for a given implementation. Notice however that although we can consider the same executions in both models, the correctness conditions are different.

For this reason, all results in this work concern the new identifiers crash-recovery model, thus we do not state the model explicitly. We note that all impossibility results in this paper hold also for the old identifiers crash-recovery model. This stems from the fact that given an execution in the new identifiers crash-recovery model, it can be seen as an execution in the old identifiers crash-recovery model when $\mathbb{N}$, the total number of processes in the system, is larger than the number of processes taking steps in the execution.

Lemma 1. *There exists a sequential implementation A of a type τ in the crash-stop model providing sequential liveness, such that A is not consistent with τ's sequential specification in the old identifiers system-wide crash-recovery model.*

3   Process Helping

In this section we present the various variants of helping based on previous works [2,6]. We then show that linearization-helping and universal-helping are not comparable, i.e., one does not imply the other.

Linearization-Helping ([6], Rephrased). We say that f is a *linearization function* over a set of histories $\mathcal{H}$, if for every $H \in \mathcal{H}$, $f(H)$ is a linearization of H. We say that operation π_1 is decided before π_2 in H with respect to f and a set of histories $\mathcal{H}$, if there exists no $S \in \mathcal{H}$ such that H is a prefix of S and $\pi_2 <_{f(S)} \pi_1$. Throughout the paper, the binary relation $<$ is used to denote that the linearization of one operation precedes another.

A set of executions $\mathcal{E}$ is *linearization-help free* if there exists a linearization function f over $\mathcal{E}$, such that for any execution $E \in \mathcal{E}$, and for any two operations $\pi_1, \pi_2 \in E$ and a single step γ such that $E \cdot \gamma \in \mathcal{E}$, it holds that if π_1 is decided before π_2 in $E \cdot \gamma$ and π_1 is not decided before π_2 in E, then γ is a step of π_1 by the process that invoked π_1. We say that an implementation is *linearization-help free* if the set of admissible histories is linearization-help free.

Universal-Helping ([2], Rephrased). For simplicity and without loss of generality, for the purposes of defining universal-helping, we assume that the first step of every operation is to publish its signature (i.e., the operation type and its operands). Consider an n-process linearizable implementation A of an object type τ and a function $t : \mathbb{N} \mapsto \mathbb{N}$. Then, A has *t-universal-helping* (when t is clear from the context, we leave it out) if for every finite execution $E \cdot E'$ such that some process completes $t(n)$ or more operations in E' whose invocations are contained in E', there is a linearization of $E \cdot E'$ satisfying the following conditions:

- the linearization of $E \cdot E'$ contains every operation that is incomplete in E
- for every extension E'', the execution $E \cdot E' \cdot E''$ has a linearization such that the linearization of $E \cdot E'$ is the same

Otherwise, we say that A is *universal-help free*.

[2] proved that universal-helping implies linearization-helping. However, a careful inspection of the proof reveals an implicit assumption on the object type was made. Roughly speaking, [2] conclude that if a pending operation needs to be linearized by steps of another process due to universal helping then this implies linearization-helping. Although it is the case for many objects, the key point to consider is that universal-helping and linearization-help free definitions requires the existence of a linearization function satisfying specific conditions. Exploiting this flexibility we prove an implementation has universal-helping using some linearization function, while proving it is also linearization-help free using a different linearization function.

Claim. There exists a wait-free strict-linearizable implementation A of an object type τ in the individual crash-recovery model, such that A has universal-helping and it is linearization-help free in the crash-stop model.

Proof. A k-bounded Counter τ is an object type supporting a single operation FETCH&INCREMENT (F&I). The initial value of τ is 0. A F&I operation π applied to τ with value l changes the value of the object to $l + 1$ and returns l if $l < k$, otherwise $l = k$ and π returns k without changing τ's value. Algorithm 1 is a wait-free implementation of a k-bounded Counter using CAS (compare-and-swap) primitive.

Linearization-Help Free. To prove Algorithm 1 is linearization-help free, it is enough to present a linearization function such that each operation π is linearized at a step by the process performing it. Consider the following linearization function: for any execution E and an operation $\pi \in ops(E)$, π is linearized at its successful CAS event, if such exists. Otherwise, if π reads the value k in Line 2, this is the linearization point of π.

Universal-Helping. We present a linearization function satisfying the conditions of the definition for universal-helping. An operation π performing a successful CAS operation is linearized at the point of the CAS. In addition, once some operation π changes the value of count to k, any other pending operation that is yet to be linearized, is linearized (in an arbitrary order) immediately after π. From that point on, any new invoked operation is linearized on its first step. Let π be a pending F&I operation in an execution E. The following holds – either π already have a linearization point in E; or if any other process completes k operations starting from E then π have a linearization point. Moreover, the assignment of linearization points is the same for any extending execution.

Strict-Linearizability. The linearization function presented above to prove Algorithm 1 is linearization-help free, can also be used to prove it is strict-linearizable, that is, the same linearization points can be used even if the execution contains crash events. Any operation π is linearized on a step by its owner. Hence, if process p_i crashes while executing an operation π, either the operation was linearized before the crash of p_i, or π has no linearization point in any extending execution.

Algorithm 1: k-bounded `Counter`. Code for process p_i

Shared variables: count $:= 0$

Procedure *Fetch&Increment*()

```
1  while true do
2      val := count
3      if val = k then  return k  if CAS(count, val, val + 1) then
4          return val
5
```

Lemma 2. *There exists an implementation of a data type that satisfies universal-helping (resp. linearization-helping), but does not satisfy linearization-helping (resp. universal-helping).*

Proof Sketch. The bounded counter implementation from Claim 3 gives the proof for one direction of Lemma 2. To prove the other direction, we observe that any implementation in which only a subset of the operations are getting help has linearization-helping but no universal-helping. For example, in the Binary Search Tree implementation of Ellen et al. [7] update operations help each other to complete, while find operations do not complete any incomplete update operation. Therefore, intuitively two update operations can prove linearization-helping. However, an infinite sequence of find operations does not complete any pending update operation; thus denying universal-helping since every pending operation must be eventually linearized. [2] also describes an implementation satisfying linearization-helping, but not universal-helping.   □

The main results in this work focus on universal and linearization-helping. However, [2] also introduced the definition of *valency-helping* which unlike linearization-helping and universal-helping is defined on operation responses. Since correctness conditions like strict-linearizability only care about linearization order, it is more relevant to discuss help definitions that are defined using the linearization order of operations, and not using the response values. Nonetheless, the full paper discusses also the relation between strict-linearizability and valency-helping [4].

4   Strict-Linearizability vs. Linearization-Helping

We first prove that strict-linearizability and linearization-helping are incomparable. That is, a strict-linearizable implementation in the crash-recovery model can either have or not have linearization-helping in the crash-stop model.

Claim 3 proves that an implementation can be strict-linearizable in the crash-recovery model while being linearization-help free in the crash-stop model. Claim 4 below proves that there in fact exist linearizable object type implementations that are wait-free with both linearization-helping and universal-helping, but are also strict-linearizable. We find this result to be somewhat surprising, since intuitively helping seems to contradict strict-linearizability – an operation can be linearized by steps of other processes, thus if the owner of the operation crash the linearization point of the crashed operation may be after the crash. As we show, one can consider different linearization functions to prove the different properties of the implementation. For lack of space a detailed proof can be found in [4].

Claim. There exists an implementation A of an object type τ such that A is linearizable, wait-free and has both linearization-helping and universal-helping in the crash-stop model. Moreover, A is strict-linearizable in the individual crash-recovery model.

Lemma 3. *An implementation being strict-linearizable in the crash-recovery model is independent of it satisfying linearization-helping in the crash-stop model.*

The proof follows directly from Claims 3 and 4.

Next we prove an implementation can have no helping (both linearization and universal helping) while still being not strict-linearizable. The result is counter intuitive, since no linearization-helping seems to imply only the owner of an operation p can cause it to be linearized by its own step. Hence, in case of a crash, either the pending operation was already linearized by a step of p, or that it is yet to be linearized and p takes no more steps after the crash, thus the operation will have no linearization point. As we prove, forcing a linearization function to have no decided-before relation between two operations, even after the operations are linearized and completed, allows us to derive such a counter-example.

We then preclude such behaviours by posing a condition on the linearization function. In a nutshell, we consider only functions such that after two operations are linearized, in any extending execution the linearization function must linearized both in the same order. We note that to the best of our knowledge, any known linearizable implementation has such a linearization function. Under this restriction, linearization-help free indeed implies strict-linearizability.

4.1   Sticky-Bit Object

A `Sticky-Bit` object type τ is the most simple form of multi-reader multi-writer register. Its value is initially 0, and it supports SET and READ operations. A

SET operations returns ack, while a READ operation returns 0 if there is no SET preceding it in the history, and 1 otherwise. We present a Sticky-Bit implementation I using single bit registers, such that I is linearizable, wait-free, linearization-help free, and universal-help free in the crash-stop model. However, as we prove, I is not strict-linearizable in the system-wide crash-recovery model.

SET operation simply writes 1 to val. However, p_0 and p_1 executes SET in a different manner, by first announcing their operation by setting a bit in an ann array, and only then writing 1 to val. Two different READ implementations are provided. For clarity, we refer to them as READ1 and READ2. READ1 simply returns the value stored in val while READ2 first sets val to 1 if both bits in the ann array set, and then returns the value stored in val. We assume some processes use only READ1, and all others use only READ2. As we prove, the claim holds as long as there is at least one process different than p_0, p_1 using READ1, and at least one such process using READ2. As such, we assume it holds, and do not specify the exact set of processes using each of the different READ implementations. The code together with detailed proofs can be found in [4]. Wait-freedom follows directly from the code.

Linearizability holds since once val is set it remains so for the rest of the execution and all READ returns 1. The implementation does not satisfy strict-linearizability since a READ2 operation helps the SET operations of p_0 and p_1 to set val. Thus, if both p_0 and p_1 write to ann followed by a system-wide crash, after the crash a READ1 still returns 0, while a later READ2 operation will complete the SET and return 1. This implies the linearization point of at least one of the SET operations is after the crash. Universal-help free follows from the following scenario - process p_0 invokes a SET operation, write to ann and halts. Then, a process $p \neq p_0$ performs an infinite sequence of READ1 operations, all returns 0, implying the SET is pending and have no linearization point.

To prove the implementation is linearization-help free we note that even in the case where READ2 helps to set val due to SET operations Set_0, Set_1 by p_0, p_1 respectively, we can linearize the operations in any order that we want. Thus, we can choose a linearization function f such that in different extensions it sometimes linearizes Set_0 before Set_1 and vice versa (for example, based on the number of operations in the execution – odd or even). Hence, by definition Set_0 is not decided before Set_1 at any point, and vice versa. In other words, function f proves the implementation is linearization-help free.

Claim. There exists a wait-free linearizable implementation I of an object type τ such that I is linearization-help free and universal-help free in the crash-stop model, while I is not strict-linearizable in the system-wide crash-recovery model.

Remark 1. Implementation I being not strict-linearizable in the system-wide new identifiers crash-recovery model imply I is also not strict-linearizable in all other crash-recovery models - individual (system-wide) new (old) identifiers crash-recovery model. Therefore, Claim 4.1 holds for all crash-recovery models.

Lemma 4. *Strict-linearizability and linearization-helping are incomparable*

Proof Sketch. Lemma 3 proves an implementation can be strict-linearizable in the crash-recovery model while having or not linearization-helping in the crash-stop model. For the not strict-linearizable case, Claim 4.1 proves an implementation can be not strict-linearizable in the crash-recovery model, while being linearization-help free in the crash-stop model. The last case to consider is an implementation being not strict-linearizable in the crash-recovery model, while satisfying linearization-helping in the crash-stop model. This case is almost trivial, and can be proven using many known implementations with linearization-helping. For example, in the Binary Search Tree implementation of Ellen et al. [7], an update operation may mark a node, and later in the execution the operation can be completed by a different process. To prove the implementation is not strict-linearizable, consider the scenario where a process crash after the marking. The operation will be completed and linearized after the crash by a different process.   □

4.2   An Equivalence Between Linearizability and Strict-Linearizability

The formalization of linearization-helping specifies a linearization function f such that for any history H it produce its linearization order $f(H)$. As the sticky-bit implementation demonstrates, the formalization of linearization-helping leads to executions where the decided-before order is not well-defined, and this may break the concept of helping leading to non-intuitive results. Specifically, f can linearize operations of some history H in different order for different extensions of H. For example, consider a stack implementation, and a history H where two *pop* operations π_1, π_2 are executed concurrently to completion starting from the initial configuration. Both operations returns empty and can be linearized in any order. Therefore, f may linearize π_1 before π_2 or vice versa for different extensions of H. Thus, although both operations completed, there is no decided-before order between the two.

In this section we restrict the discussion to a more natural *prefix-respecting* linearization function precluding such a behaviour. To the best of our knowledge, any known implementation has such a linearization function.

Definition 1. *We say that a linearization function f is* prefix-respecting *if for any execution E and an execution F extending it, $<_{f(E)} \subseteq <_{f(F)}$. In other words, for any two operations $\pi_1, \pi_2 \in E$, if $\pi_1 <_{f(E)} \pi_2$ then $\pi_1 <_{f(F)} \pi_2$.*

Strong-linearizability [8] requires the linearization order of an execution E to be a prefix of the linearization order of any extension of E. Although this seems to bear similarity to prefix-respecting, strong-linearizability is a more restrictive requirement. Given an execution E, strong-linearizability requires that if an operation π is linearized in $f(E)$, then in any extending execution no operation σ that is pending in E can be linearized before π, even if σ was invoked before π and it is not linearized in $f(E)$. On the other hand, prefix-respecting allows such a scenario, as long as one does not change the linearization order of operations that are already linearized in $f(E)$.

A key feature of prefix-respecting linearization function is that given an execution E, if some operation π_1 is linearized before π_2 in $f(E)$, then it holds that π_1 is decided before π_2 in E (with respect to f). Hence, and by abuse of notation, we may say π_1 is linearized before π_2 while referring to the decided before order. Restricting our discussion to linearization-helping based on prefix-respecting linearization functions only, we prove that a linearization-help free implementation A of an object type τ in the crash-stop model is also strict-linearizable in the crash-recovery model. Roughly speaking, under this restriction, if A is linearization-help free and some operation π crashes, then either it has a linearization point before the crash, or that it has no linearization point in any extending execution, as steps by other processes can not cause it to be linearized. For a full proof we refer the reader to [4].

Lemma 5. *Let A be an obstruction-free implementation of a total object type τ such that A is not strict-linearizable in the individual crash-recovery model. Then, any prefix-respecting linearization function f of A imply linearization-helping in the crash-stop model.*

Corollary 1. *Let A be an obstruction-free implementation of a total object type τ such that A is linearizable and linearization-help free in the crash-stop model. Then A is strict-linearizable in the individual crash-recovery model.*

5   Strict-Linearizability vs. Universal-Helping

In this section we prove that strict-linearizability and universal-helping are incomparable. We then prove that for a large class of object types, any strict-linearizable implementation in the crash-recovery model is universal-help free in the crash-stop model.

Lemma 6. *Strict-linearizability and universal-helping are incomparable*

Proof Sketch. We prove the existence of each of the four combinations separately.

Strict-Linearizability + Universal-Helping. Follows from Claim 3 and 4.

Strict-Linearizability + Universal-Help Free. This direction is intuitive, since naturally strict-linearizability seems to contradict universal-helping. Indeed, any strict-linearizable implementation we are familiar with is universal-help free in the crash-stop model. For example, consider the well-known Harris linked-list [9]. It is strict-linearizable in the crash-recovery model since any operation is linearized on a step by its owner process. However, it is universal-help free in the crash-stop model since processes do not help each other (except for physical removal of nodes), thus an insert operation will never be completed if its owner halts before adding the key to the list.

not Strict-Linearizable + Universal-Helping. This direction is intuitive as well, since in most cases universal-helping contradicts strict-linearizability. Consider Herlihy universal-construction [10] applied to a stack object type. It has universal-helping in the crash-stop model. However, it is not strict-linearizable in the crash-recovery model, since a process may crash after announcing a pop operation, and later that operation can be completed by a different process. This may affect a return value of a push operation which was invoked after the crash. This implies the linearization point of the pop operation must be after the crash.

not Strict-Linearizable + Universal-Help Free. Follows from Claim 4.1 $\square$

5.1 Equivalence Between Strict-Linearizability and Universal-Help Freedom

Notation. Given a sequential history H and an operation π, we denote by $H + \pi$ the set of all sequential histories obtained by including π (i.e., its invocation and response) in H. The same is defined for more than one operation. Two sequential histories H_1, H_2 are *distinct* if there exists an operation π in both such that its response is different. If π is in some (common) sub-history H, we say that H_1, H_2 are *distinct for an operation in H*.

Definition 2 (Order-dependent type). *An object type τ is* order-dependent *if there exists an infinite sequential history H and two operations π_1, π_2 such that the following holds:*

OD1: *For any histories $H_1 \in (H + \pi_1) \cup (H + \pi_2)$, $H_2 \in H + \pi_1 + \pi_2$, any two histories in $\{H, H_1, H_2\}$ are distinct for some operation in H.*
OD2: *$\pi_1 \cdot \pi_2 \cdot H$ and $\pi_2 \cdot \pi_1 \cdot H$ are distinct for some operation in H.*

Order-dependant types include many known objects, such as queue and stack. In a nutshell, an order-dependent type has two operations such that adding exactly one of them or both changes the response of some other operation. Moreover, the order in which both operations are performed (starting from the initial configuration) effects the response of some other operation.

Order-dependant are closely related to *exact-order* types [6]. Roughly speaking, exact-order types are types in which operations are non-commutative, that is, switching the order of two operations changes the response of future operations. [6] proved that an exact-order type precludes a linearizable wait-free and linearization-help free implementation using read, write, compare-and-swap and fetch-and-add primitives. Order-dependant type and exact-order type are incomparable [4].

Lemma 7 below proves that for an order-dependent object type, strict-linearizability implies universal-help free. The full proof can be found in [4].

Lemma 7. *Let A be a non-blocking implementation of an order-dependent total type τ, such that A is strict-linearizable in the system-wide crash-recovery model. Then A is linearizable and universal-help free in the crash-stop model.*

Corollary 2. *Let A be a non-blocking implementation of an order-dependent total object τ such that A has universal-helping in the crash-stop model. Then A is not strict-linearizable in the system-wide crash-recovery model.*

Remark 2. An implementation I that is not strict-linearizable in the system-wide new identifiers crash-recovery model imply I is also not strict-linearizable in all other crash-recovery models - individual (system-wide) new (old) identifiers crash-recovery model. Therefore, Lemma 7 and Corollary 2 holds for all crash-recovery models.

References

1. Aguilera, M.K., Frolund, S.: Strict linearizability and the power of aborting. Technical report, HP Laboratories Palo Alto (2003)
2. Attiya, H., Castañeda, A., Hendler, D.: Nontrivial and universal helping for wait-free queues and stacks. J. Parallel Distrib. Comput. **121**, 1–14 (2018)
3. Attiya, H., Welch, J.: Distributed Computing. Fundamentals, Simulations, and Advanced Topics. McGraw-Hill (1998)
4. Ben-Baruch, O., Ravi, S.: Separation and equivalence results for the crash-stop and crash-recovery shared memory models. CoRR abs/2012.03692 (2020). https://arxiv.org/abs/2012.03692
5. Berryhill, R., Golab, W.M., Tripunitara, M.: Robust shared objects for non-volatile main memory. In: 19th International Conference on Principles of Distributed Systems, OPODIS 2015, Rennes, France, 14–17 December 2015, pp. 20:1–20:17 (2015)
6. Censor-Hillel, K., Petrank, E., Timnat, S.: Help! In: Proceedings of the 2015 ACM Symposium on Principles of Distributed Computing, PODC 2015, Donostia-San Sebastián, Spain, 21–23 July 2015, pp. 241–250 (2015)
7. Ellen, F., Fatourou, P., Ruppert, E., van Breugel, F.: Non-blocking binary search trees. In: Proceedings of the 29th Annual ACM Symposium on Principles of Distributed Computing, PODC 2010, Zurich, Switzerland, 25–28 July 2010, pp. 131–140 (2010)
8. Golab, W.M., Higham, L., Woelfel, P.: Linearizable implementations do not suffice for randomized distributed computation. In: Proceedings of the 43rd ACM Symposium on Theory of Computing, STOC 2011, San Jose, CA, USA, 6–8 June 2011, pp. 373–382 (2011)
9. Harris, T.L.: A pragmatic implementation of non-blocking linked-lists. In: Welch, J. (ed.) DISC 2001. LNCS, vol. 2180, pp. 300–314. Springer, Heidelberg (2001). https://doi.org/10.1007/3-540-45414-4_21
10. Herlihy, M.: Wait-free synchronization. ACM Trans. Progr. Lang. Syst. **13**(1), 123–149 (1991)
11. Herlihy, M., Wing, J.M.: Linearizability: a correctness condition for concurrent objects. ACM Trans. Program. Lang. Syst. **12**(3), 463–492 (1990)
12. Izraelevitz, J., Mendes, H., Scott, M.L.: Linearizability of persistent memory objects under a full-system-crash failure model. In: Gavoille, C., Ilcinkas, D. (eds.) DISC 2016. LNCS, vol. 9888, pp. 313–327. Springer, Heidelberg (2016). https://doi.org/10.1007/978-3-662-53426-7_23

Treasure Hunt in Graph Using Pebbles

Adri Bhattacharya[1], Barun Gorain[2], and Partha Sarathi Mandal[1(✉)] ⓘ

[1] Indian Institute of Technology Guwahati, Guwahati 781039, India
{a.bhattacharya,psm}@iitg.ac.in
[2] Indian Institute of Technology Bhilai, Bhilai, India
barun@iitbhilai.ac.in

Abstract. In this paper, we study the treasure hunt problem in a graph by a mobile agent. The nodes in the graph $G = (V, E)$ are anonymous and the edges incident to a vertex $v \in V$ whose degree is $deg(v)$ and they are labeled arbitrarily as $0, 1, \ldots, deg(v) - 1$. At a node t in G a stationary object, called *treasure* is located. The mobile agent that is initially located at a node s in G, the starting point of the agent, must find the treasure by reaching the node t. The distance from s to t is D. The *time* required to find the treasure is the total number of edges the agent visits before it finds the treasure. The agent neither have any prior knowledge about the graph nor the position of the treasure. An oracle that knows the graph, the agent's initial position, and the position of the treasure, places some pebbles on the nodes, at most one per node, of the graph to guide the agent towards the treasure.

This paper aims to study the trade-off between the number of pebbles provided and the time required to find the treasure. To be specific, we aim to answer the following question:
  - "What is the minimum time for treasure hunt in a graph with maximum degree Δ and diameter D if k pebbles are placed?"
We answer the above question when $k < D$ and $k = cD$ for some positive integer c. We design efficient algorithms for the agent for different values of k. We also propose an almost matching lower bound result for $k < D$.

Keywords: Treasure hunt · Mobile agent · Anonymous graph · Pebbles · Deterministic algorithms

1 Introduction

1.1 Background and Motivation

Treasure hunt problem is well studied in varying underlying topologies such as graphs and planes [2,3,6–9]. In this paper, we have delved into the treasure hunt

A. Bhattacharya—Supported by CSIR, Govt. of India, Grant Number: 09/731(0178)/2020-EMR-I

B. Gorain—Partially supported by SERB, Govt. of India (Grant Number: CRG/2020/005964 and Grant Number: MTR/2021/000118) and Research Initiation Grant supported by the IIT Bhilai, India.

P. S. Mandal—Partially supported by SERB, Govt. of India, Grant Number: MTR/2019/001528.

S. Devismes et al. (Eds.): SSS 2022, LNCS 13751, pp. 99–113, 2022.
https://doi.org/10.1007/978-3-031-21017-4_7

problem using mobile agents on graphs. The main idea of this problem is that the mobile agent starting from a position, has to find a stationary object, called treasure, placed at some unknown location in the underlying topology. There are many real-life applications to this problem. Consider a scenario where a miner is stuck inside a cave and needs immediate assistance. In network applications, consider a network containing a virus, the agent being a software agent has the task assigned to find the virus in an unknown location inside the network. For any graph with maximum degree Δ, the agent can find the treasure located at a distance D, by performing a breadth-first search (BFS) technique in $\mathcal{O}(\Delta^D)$ time. But this naive strategy is expensive as many real-life problems require a much more efficient solution. Suppose a person is stuck inside a building that has caught fire. He needs to find the fire exit and then evacuate within a short period time. These kind of emergencies require a faster solution. The person needs external help guiding him toward the fire exit. Similar to that finding the treasure, the agent needs some external help to guide the agent toward the treasure. This external help is provided to the mobile agent by the oracle. The external information provided by the oracle is in the form of pebbles placed at the graph's vertices (nodes) [6], also termed as *advice*. This advice guides the agent towards the treasure. The pebbles are placed at the nodes, so the agent visiting those nodes gains some knowledge and finds the treasure using that information. The oracle places pebbles, at most one at a node, by knowing the underlying graph topology, initial position of the agent, and treasure's location. Gorain et al. [6] recently studied the treasure hunt problem in an anonymous graph. They studied the question, what is the fastest treasure hunt algorithm regardless of any number of pebbles placed? In that paper, they obtained an efficient algorithm that finds the treasure, irrespective of the number of pebbles placed. So, now a natural question arises that they did not address. Given k many pebbles, what is the fastest possible treasure hunt algorithm. In this paper, we find the solution to the question: *Given k pebbles, what is the fastest algorithm which solves the treasure hunt problem in an anonymous graph?*

1.2   Model and Problem Definition

The search domain by the agent for finding the treasure is considered as a simple undirected connected graph $G = (V, E)$ having $n = |V|$ vertices that are anonymous, i.e., unlabeled. The vertices are also termed as nodes in this paper. An edge $e = (u, v)$ must have two port numbers one adjacent to u, which is termed as *outgoing* port from u and the other adjacent to v, termed as *incoming* port of v (refer the edge (v_i, v_{i+1}) in Fig. 3, where ρ_4 is the outgoing port from v_i and ρ_0 is the incoming port of v_{i+1}). Δ is denoted as the maximum degree of the graph. A node $u \in V$ with $deg(u)$ is connected with its neighbors $u_0, u_1, \cdots, u_{deg(u)-1}$ via outgoing port numbers which have arbitrary but fixed labeling $\rho_0, \rho_1, \cdots, \rho_{deg(u)-1}$, respectively. Initially, the agent only knows the degree of the initial node. Further, while the agent visits a node it can read the port numbers when entering and leaving a node, as stated in the paper [4]. Moreover, when the agent reaches a node v from a node u, it learns the outgoing port from u and the incoming port at v, through which it reaches v. The first half of u's neighbors are the nodes corresponding to the outgoing port numbers $\rho_0, \rho_1, \cdots, \rho_{\frac{deg(u)}{2} - 1}$, whereas the second half of u's neighbors are the nodes corresponding to the outgoing port numbers $\rho_{\frac{deg(u)}{2}}, \cdots, \rho_{deg(u)-1}$. The agent is initially placed at a node s and the treasure t is located on a node of G at a distance D from s, which is unknown to the agent. The oracle places the pebbles at the nodes of the graph G, in order to guide the agent towards the treasure. Moreover, at most one pebble is placed at a node. The agent has no prior knowledge about the underlying topology, nor any knowledge about the position of treasure, pebble positions, and the number of pebbles deployed by the oracle. Further, it has no knowledge about the value of D as well. The agent has unbounded memory and it can only find the treasure or a pebble whenever it reaches the node containing the treasure or a pebble. Distance is considered as the number of edge traversal. We denote the shortest distance between any two nodes $u, v \in G$ by $dist(u,v)$, hence $dist(s,t) = D$. The *time* of the treasure hunt is defined as the number of edges traversed by the agent from its initial position until it finds the treasure.

1.3 Contribution

We study the trade-off between the number of pebbles (k) provided by the oracle and the associated time required to find the treasure. The contributions in this paper are mentioned below.

- For $k < \frac{D}{2}$ pebbles, we propose an algorithm that finds the treasure in a graph at time $\mathcal{O}(D\Delta^{\frac{D}{(2\eta+1)}})$, where $\eta = \frac{k}{3}$.
- For $\frac{D}{2} \leq k < D$, we propose a treasure hunt algorithm with time complexity $O(k\Delta^{\frac{D}{k+1}})$.
- In case of bipartite graphs, the proposed algorithm for treasure hunt has time complexity $\mathcal{O}(k\Delta^{\frac{D}{k}})$ for $0 < k < D$.
  For $k = cD$ where c is any positive integer, we give an algorithm that finds the treasure in time $\mathcal{O}\left[cD(\frac{\Delta}{2^{c/2}})^2 + cD\right]$
- We propose a lower bound result $\Omega((\frac{k}{e})^{\frac{k}{k+1}}(\Delta - 1)^{\frac{D}{k+1}})$ on time of treasure hunt for $0 < k < D$.

1.4 Related Work

Several works have been done on searching for a target by one or many mobile agents under varied underlying environments. The underlying environment can be a graph or a plane. Also the search algorithm can be deterministic or randomized. The paradigm of *algorithm with advice* was mainly studied for networks, where this advice (or information) enhances the efficiency of the solutions in [5]. In the past few decades, the problem of treasure hunt has been explored in many papers, some of them are [3,9]. The treasure hunt problem is mainly studied in a

continuous and discrete model. Bouchard et al. [3] studied the problem of treasure hunt in the Euclidean plane, where they showed an optimal bound of $\mathcal{O}(D)$
with angular hints at most π. Pelc et al. [8] provided a trade-off between time
and information of solving the treasure hunt problem in the plane. Pelc et al.
[9] gave an insight into the amount of information required to solve the treasure
hunt in geometric terrain at $\mathcal{O}(L)$ time, where L is the shortest path of the
treasure from the initial point. Further, Pelc [7] investigated the treasure hunt
problem in a plane with no advice for static and dynamic cases. Gorain et al.
[6] studied the treasure hunt problem in the graphs with pebbles and provided
a lower bound of the run time complexity using any number of pebbles. Our
problem is a more generalized version of the paper by Gorain et al. [6], where
they have used an infinite number of pebbles to give a $\theta(D \log \Delta)$ time algorithm.
This paper tries to find an efficient algorithm for a given number of pebbles.

The rest of the paper is organized as follows. In Sect. 2, given $k < D$ pebbles,
we provide a treasure hunt algorithm for a general graph. Further, in Sect. 3,
given $k \geq D$, we propose the treasure hunt algorithm for a general graph. In
Sect. 4, we propose a lower bound for the case $k < D$. Finally, concluded in
Sect. 5. All proofs are available in the full version of the paper [1]. In the following
sections, we propose different algorithms for different graph topology and their
analysis.

2 Treasure Hunt Algorithm When $k < D$

In this section, we provide algorithms and their analysis for the case when the
number of pebble k is less than D. We introduce our idea for the general graph,
with the help of a new paradigm termed as *markers*.

As the nodes in the graph are anonymous, i.e., there is no id for the nodes.
The agent can't distinguish between a node that is visited or not, this creates
an issue. Suppose the agent is currently searching from some node containing a
pebble at level L_i (where L_i is the i-th level in the BFS tree corresponding to the
graph G), then how to determine the fact that the pebble found is at level L_j,
where $i < j$ but not $j < i$ or $j = i$. Hence if these two issues are not resolved, the
agent may move inside a cycle for infinite time in the worst case. So, in the next
two sections, we deal with the issues related to the general graph. We provide
algorithms and their analysis for the agent to find treasure when $\frac{D}{2} \leq k < D$
and $k < \frac{D}{2}$.

2.1 $\frac{D}{2} \leq k < D$

In this case, the oracle places a pebble along the path P at alternative levels,
i.e., at the nodes v_j, where $1 \leq j \leq D$ and j is even. The agent searches every
possible path of length $\frac{D}{k+1}$ $(=l)$ until a pebble or the treasure is encountered
from *SearchNode*. The path length between two pebbles, in this case is at most 2,
i.e., $l \leq 2$ as $k \geq \frac{D}{2}$. So, by searching a path of length at most 2 from *SearchNode*,
the agent cannot return to itself, i.e., the current *SearchNode*. The reason is that

G has no multiple edges and self-loops. Further, the agent cannot go to the previous *SearchNode* as well. The reason is, suppose the *SearchNode* is at level L_i, then all the incoming ports from the level L_{i-1} to the *SearchNode* is already saved. Further, the agent cannot use these saved ports while searching a BFS of length l from *SearchNode*. Hence the length of the path from L_i to any node in L_k (where $k < i$) containing pebble is at least $l+1$. So, the issue of circling it's way back to itself (i.e. *SearchNode*) and going back to the previous level is restricted. Hence, the agent can only move forward along P and ultimately finds the treasure. The time taken to search all possible paths of length $\frac{D}{k+1}$ is $\mathcal{O}(\Delta^{\frac{D}{k+1}})$ and it is done from each k pebbles. Hence the total time to find the treasure is at most $\mathcal{O}(k\Delta^{\frac{D}{k+1}})$.

Now in the case of a general graph with $\frac{D}{2} \leq k < D$ pebbles, the placement of pebbles at alternate levels ensures that there is no returning back to previous level and also to the *SearchNode*. But this fact is not valid for general graphs with $k < \frac{D}{2}$ pebbles. This is explained with the help of the following example.

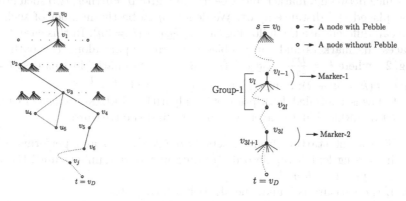

Fig. 1. Impossibility case in General Graph

Fig. 2. Pebble Placement in General Graph with Multiple Markers

Example: Consider the example in Fig. 1, where the *SearchNode* is v_3 and $l = 3$. The correct path from v_3 to the treasure is along $v_3 \longrightarrow v_4 \longrightarrow v_5 \cdots v_j \cdots \longrightarrow t$. But when it performs a BFS of length l from *SearchNode*, it is not possible for the agent to distinguish between the paths $v_3 \longrightarrow v_4 \longrightarrow v_5 \longrightarrow v_6$ and $v_3 \longrightarrow u_4 \longrightarrow u_5 \longrightarrow v_3$. In both the cases after traversing a *dist* of l from v_3, the agent encounters a pebble. In the worst case, the agent may traverse this wrong path each time and never reach the treasure. Moreover, the number of pebbles must be at least 2, as with a single pebble, the agent can't find the treasure. Consider the Fig. 1, where a pebble is placed at v_3 only. In this case, the agent may never find the treasure. It is because, for every search from v_3, the agent may circle its way back to v_3 again and again (as the nodes and pebbles are anonymous) rather than encountering the treasure. Now this can be resolved with the help of *Markers*, which is defined as follows.

Marker: To deal with this scenario, we create a notion of markers. The idea of *markers* came from the concept of colors. Colors are always helpful in distinguishing certain characteristics. In our case, it helps to identify whether a node is already visited or not, but no concept of colors is used in our model. We replicate the idea of colors by using a certain combination of pebbles, and this combination is termed as *Marker*. To denote a marker, the oracle places two pebbles adjacent to each other along the path P. When the agent finds a pebble in one of the adjacent nodes of the current pebble, it understands that it has found a marker. We generalize our idea in general graphs with markers.

2.2 $k < \frac{D}{2}$

In this section, we discuss how multiple marker helps the agent, find the treasure in a general graph. The pebble placement strategy is discussed as follows.

We define a group as a marker together with the immediate next pebble. Markers and pebbles are placed alternatively, as shown in Fig. 2. Let l be the distance between a marker and a pebble in a group. Further, two such groups are also placed at l distance apart. We denote η to be the number of such groups. We can differentiate the following cases. *Case-1* ($k = 3\eta$): In this case, the oracle places the markers and the pebbles l distance apart along the path P (refer Fig. 2), where $l = \frac{D-\eta}{2\eta+1}$. *Case-2* ($k = 3\eta + 1$): Similarly, in this case $l = \frac{D-\eta}{2\eta+2}$. *Case-3* ($k = 3\eta + 2$): Similarly, in this case as well, $l = \frac{D-\eta-1}{2\eta+2}$.

Below is a detailed description of the algorithm TREASUREHUNTFORGRAPH-WITHMARKER that the agent executes to find the treasure.

1. The agent starting from s, sets *SearchNode* $= s$ and performs a BFS in increasing lexicographic order of outgoing port numbers until the treasure or a pebble is found.
2. If the treasure is found, the algorithm terminates.
3. If the treasure is not found and a pebble is found. Then the agent sets the *dist* between s and this node containing the pebble as $l - 1$. Also consider that the node containing the pebble is v_{l-1} at L_{l-1}-th level.
4. Further from v_{l-1}, the agent performs two tasks. Firstly it searches the neighbors of v_{l-1}, and finds another pebble at the node v_l in level L_l. Further, it stores the path length l from *SearchNode* to v_l and identifies that a marker is found. Secondly it stores the incoming port number ρ_{l-1} of the edge (v_{l-1}, v_l).
5. Reset *SearchNode* $= v_l$.
6. The agent performs a BFS of length l from *SearchNode* until the treasure or a pebble is found.
7. If the treasure is found, then the algorithm terminates.
8. If the treasure is not found and whenever a pebble is found, there are two possibilities: *P1* and *P2*. *P1:* The agent has returned to *SearchNode* as the underlying graph topology is a general graph. *P2:* The agent has encountered a new pebble along path P. Now to understand which of these possibilities the agent has encountered. The agent travels the stored sequence of port

numbers, in this case ρ_l of length 1. If in this traversal, a marker is found, then the agent has encountered *P1* and searches a different path. Otherwise, if the marker is not found then it is possibility *P2*.

9. If the agent encounters *P2*, i.e., it has found a pebble for the first time at the node v_{2l} in L_{2l}-th level. The agent performs the following tasks. Firstly, it stores the sequence of incoming port numbers of the shortest path from $v_{l-1} \longrightarrow SearchNode \longrightarrow v_{2l}$ of length $l + 1$. Secondly, it completes the BFS search at the L_{2l-1} level. Whenever another pebble is encountered, the agent stores the incoming port number of the incoming edge of that node containing a pebble, i.e., the edge from the node with pebble in level L_{2l-1} and v_{2l}. Sets $SearchNode = v_{2l}$.

10. From $SearchNode$, it performs a BFS of length l using the ports except for the stored incoming ports until the treasure or a pebble is encountered. If the treasure is encountered, go to step 7. If a pebble is encountered, then perform only step 8. Further if *P2* arises then search the neighbor of $SearchNode$ (i.e., v_{3l}).

11. If a pebble is found at one of its neighbor node v_{3l+1}, then identify a new marker is found and store the incoming port ρ_{3l} of the incoming edge (v_{3l}, v_{3l+1}). Then go to step 5. If no pebble is found, go to step 9.

Lemma 1. *Given* $k < \frac{D}{2}$ *pebbles, the agent following* TREASUREHUNTFOR-GRAPHWITHMARKER *algorithm successfully finds the treasure in a general graph with the help of multiple markers.*

Theorem 1. *The agent finds the treasure in* $\mathcal{O}(D\Delta^{\frac{D}{(2\eta+1)}})$ *time, where* $\eta = \frac{k}{3}$.

Lemma 2. *Given* $k < \frac{D}{2}$ *pebbles, the agent following* TREASUREHUNTFOR-BIPARTITEGRAPH *algorithm successfully finds the treasure in a bipartite graph.*

Theorem 2. *Given* $k < \frac{D}{2}$, *the agent finds the treasure in* $\mathcal{O}(k\Delta^{\frac{D}{k}})$ *time in a bipartite graph.*

3   Treasure Hunt Algorithm When $k \geq D$

In this section, we explore the case when $k = cD$ pebbles are provided by the oracle, where c is any positive integer. We propose an algorithm that finds the treasure in $\mathcal{O}\left[cD(\frac{\Delta}{2^{c/2}})^2 + cD\right]$ time.

Let G be a graph with maximum degree $\Delta \geq 10(c+1)+6$ [1]. Let us consider $\beta = 10(c+1)+6$. The case where $\Delta < \beta$ is dealt with a different strategy, which is explained ahead. The path P from s to t may have two scenarios. *Scenario-1:* The path P may not contain any node of degree β which is similar to solving the case in which G has maximum degree $\Delta < \beta$. *Scenario-2:* The path P contains at least one node of degree β.

All these cases are dealt separately and are discussed ahead. So, before proceeding to general graphs, we first describe our algorithm and pebble placement strategy in trees and then further extend our idea for general graphs keeping in mind the additional difficulties.

3.1   Idea of Treasure Hunt in Tree for $k = cD$ Pebbles

Let G be a rooted tree, where initial node s is the root of the tree. The nodes at the level L_i are located at a distance i from s. The treasure t is located at a distance D from s at the level L_D. Let $P = v_0, v_1, \cdots, v_D$ (where $v_0 = s$ and $v_D = t$) be the shortest path from s to t.

If $k = D$ pebbles are given, then the oracle places a pebble on each D many nodes along P, i.e., one pebble is placed on each v_i, where $0 \leq i \leq D - 1$ and $v_i \in P$. Now if more than D pebbles are provided, i.e., $k > D$, then along with placing D pebbles on each node v_i, the oracle further places the remaining pebbles along the neighbors of v_i's. These remaining pebbles help the agent to reduce its search domain to find the next node v_{i+1} along P. The agent from v_i, obtains a binary string by visiting the neighbors of v_i along which some of the remaining $k - D$ pebbles are placed. This binary string gives the knowledge to the agent, about the collection of outgoing ports along which the agent must search in order to encounter the pebble placed at the node v_{i+1}. Next, we discuss how a string is represented with respect to the pebbles placed.

String Representation with Pebbles: Among the neighbors of v_i which are used for encoding a string: if the node contains a pebble, it is termed as '1' in the j-th bit of the binary string, whereas no pebble represents '0'. Now suppose all the neighbors are not used for encoding. So, to learn where the encoding has ended, the following strategy is used [6]. Instead of a simple binary representation, we provide a *transformed* binary representation in which we replace '1' by '11' and '0' by '10'. This transformation ensures no '00' substring exists in the transformed binary string. As an example $\gamma = 0010$ will be transformed to $\gamma^t = 10101110$. So, when the agent finds two consecutive '0's, it learns that the encoding has ended. The process is explained with the following example.

Example: Given $k = 2D$ pebbles, the example shown in Fig. 3 explains the algorithm's execution when the agent reaches the node $v_i \in P$ along the incoming port ρ_0. Let $deg(v_i) = 12$ and the node v_{i+1} is connected to v_i with the edge having outgoing port number ρ_i, where $\rho_i \in \{\rho_1, \cdots, \rho_{\frac{deg(v_i)}{2}-1}\}$ (i.e., ρ_4 to be exact). Further, the pebbles for encoding are placed along the nodes corresponding to the outgoing ports $\{\rho_{\frac{deg(v_i)}{2}}, \cdots, \rho_{deg(v_i)-1}\}$. The j-th bit of the binary string is '1' if the node corresponding to the outgoing port number $\rho_{(\frac{deg(v_i)}{2}+(j-1))}$ contains a pebble otherwise, if no pebble is found then the j-th bit is '0'. So, the agent currently at v_i obtains the transformed binary string $\gamma^t = 11$ (as the '00' obtained stops the agent from further search) by searching the nodes corresponding to the outgoing ports $\{\rho_{\frac{deg(v_i)}{2}}, \cdots, \rho_{deg(v_i)-1}\}$. Hence the binary string is $\gamma = 1$. Now as the length of γ obtained is 1, it divides the first $\frac{deg(v_i)}{2}$ neighbor nodes of v_i into $2^{|\gamma|}$ (where $|\gamma| = 1$) partitions each of size at most $\lceil \frac{deg(v_i)}{2^{1+1}} \rceil = \lceil \frac{12}{4} \rceil = 3$. Further, it searches the outgoing ports corresponding to the 2nd partition (as the value 0 represents the 1st partition, whereas the value 1 represents the second partition of $\frac{deg(v_i)}{2}$ neighbors of v_i) out of 2^1 partitions each consisting of exactly 3 ports. This means the agent searches only the nodes corresponding to the outgoing ports ρ_4, ρ_5 and ρ_6 and finds the desired node v_{i+1} containing a pebble via the outgoing port ρ_4.

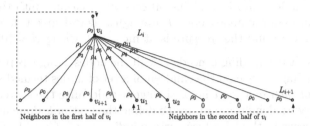

Fig. 3. Represents the encoding to reach v_{i+1} from v_i. Pebbles are placed at the nodes u_1 and u_2, to represent the *transformed* binary string 11, which the agent obtains. This string localizes the search of only the outgoing ports ρ_3, ρ_4 and ρ_5. The node v_{i+1} corresponds to the port ρ_4.

This idea is simple for trees, but it will not work for any arbitrary graph. So, we make necessary modifications and explain them in the next section.

3.2 Extending the Idea for General Graphs

The above idea for trees cannot be directly extended to general graphs. The reason being any tree can be transformed into a rooted tree with root s, in which the edges go from level L_i to L_{i+1} (where $i \geq 0$), creating an acyclic structure. It is because there is a unique path between two nodes in a tree, i.e., no two nodes have common children. Similarly, we can create a BFS tree of any arbitrary graph rooted at s. But any arbitrary graph may contain cycles. So, there may also be edges in between levels in the BFS tree. Now recalling the pebble placement idea for trees, the encoding in the neighbors of a node v does not affect the encoding in the neighbors of node u as there are no common children. But this is not true for general graphs. The encoding done for the node u can hamper the encoding for the node v. To resolve this issue, we place the pebbles for encoding on high degree nodes that are not 'close'. We call these high degree nodes *fat* nodes, which are defined below. A node is fat if its degree is at least β, where $\beta = 10(c+1) + 6$. Otherwise, it is *light*.

Now we have the following cases, and we deal with them separately. <u>*Case-1:*</u> Every node $v_i \in P$, $0 \leq i \leq D-1$, is light. <u>*Case-2:*</u> There exists at least one node in P, which is fat.

<u>*Case-1:*</u> In this case no encoding is needed. The oracle places a single pebble at each level of the BFS tree along the path P. So, the agent starting from s, sets $SearchNode = s$. If a pebble is found at s then it searches the neighbors having a pebble along the outgoing port $\{\rho_0, \ldots, \rho_{(\frac{deg(s)}{2}-1)}\}$. Otherwise if no pebble is found at s then it searches the neighbors having a pebble along the outgoing ports $\{\rho_{(\frac{deg(s)}{2})}, \ldots, \rho_{deg(s)-1}\}$. Whenever the next pebble is found at a node

v_1, it sets the $SearchNode = v_1$. At each subsequent steps the agent visits all the neighbors of the $SearchNode$ for a pebble, except the incoming port which connects the current $SearchNode$ to the previous $SearchNode$ (i.e., except the port ρ_0 for the node v_i in Fig. 3). This process will continue until the treasure is found. Now, since all the nodes along P are light, their degree is less than β. So, the time required to find the treasure is at most βD, where $\beta = 10(c+1) + 6$.

Case-2: In this case, encoding is needed as all the nodes along the path P are not light. The encoding is done on the children of a set of nodes termed as *milestone*. The presence of each *milestone* helps the agent to localize the search domain for the next few nodes along the path P. To define the first *milestone* node, we have the following cases in the BFS tree corresponding to G. *Case-A:* The node s is fat. This implies the first *milestone* is s. *Case-B:* The node s is light but the node $v_1 \in P$ at level L_1 is fat. This implies the first *milestone* is v_1. *Case-C:* The nodes $s, \cdots, v_j \in P$ (where $j \geq 2$) are light whereas the node v_{j+1} at level L_{j+1} is fat. This implies the first *milestone* is v_{j+1} along P.

The subsequent milestones are defined recursively. For $i \geq 1$, let the i-th milestone is at the level L_j (where $j \geq 0$). Then the $(i+1)$-th milestone node should be at level L_k, where $k - j \geq 5$, i.e., the distance between any two milestones is at least 5. This distance is maintained to avoid having a common neighbor between any two pair of milestones. Since the agent does not know the underlying topology, hence it cannot distinguish between light or milestone nodes. The placement of pebbles for encoding not only gives the binary representation but also determines whether a node is a milestone node or a light node (refer CHECKERFORMILESTONE algorithm). The pebble placement strategy is discussed below.

Pebble Placement: There are two reasons for pebble placement. One is for giving the direction to the treasure along P. The other is for encoding, that reduces the search domain for the next node along P. Pebbles are placed at every node along the path P, except at a node which is 2 *dist* apart from a milestone node. More precisely, if v_i is a milestone node at level L_i along P, then no pebble is placed at the node v_{i+2} at level L_{i+2} along P (refer the node v_2 in Fig. 4, where s is the first milestone). The agent's goal is to locate the next pebble along P. In the worst case, the agent may have to search all the neighbors. To reduce this search domain, encoding is incorporated. So, encoding will be done only at the neighbors of the milestone. Now the question is, which neighbors of the milestone are used for encoding. As the oracle knows which neighbor of the milestone a pebble is placed for the desired path. It accordingly, uses the other half of the neighbors to place the pebbles for encoding. As shown in the Fig. 4, where s is a milestone and v_1 is the next node along P, the pebbles for encoding are placed along the other half of neighbors of s.

Strategy for Encoding: The number of available neighbors for encoding is $\frac{deg(v)}{2}$, where v is a milestone. Out of cD pebbles, D many pebbles are placed along P. The remaining $(c-1)D$ pebbles are used for encoding. The length of each encoding should be at most $c - 1$. The oracle leaves two consecutive neighbors

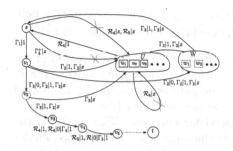

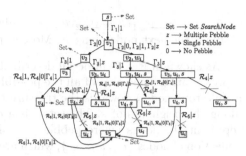

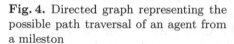

Fig. 4. Directed graph representing the possible path traversal of an agent from a mileston

Fig. 5. Flow Chart representing possible traversals from a milestone s

without pebbles to distinguish between two separate encoding. To understand the termination of the encoding, another three consecutive neighbors are kept empty. To encode α many binary strings, we need at least $\alpha((c-1)+2)+3$ neighbors. So, the relation between $deg(v)$ and α is $\frac{deg(v)}{2} \geq \alpha(c+1)+3$. Further, we define the set $\mathcal{R}$, as the set of two outgoing port numbers and all the incoming port numbers of the neighbors of the milestone node along which pebbles are placed. The cardinality of $\mathcal{R}$ is at most $\alpha(c-1)+2$. The reason is, from a milestone α binary strings are encoded, each having a length at most $(c-1)$, and a single pebble is placed at the desired node along the desired path. As shown in Fig. 3 the set $\mathcal{R} = \{\rho_4, \rho_6, \rho_0, \rho_0, \rho_0\}$, corresponding to the nodes v_{i+1}, u_1 and u_2, respectively.

Below is a detailed description of the CHECKERFORMILESTONE algorithm, for the agent to determine whether a node is a milestone or light.

1. The agent is at a node v. It checks the node along the outgoing port ρ_1.
2. If a pebble is found, then it searches the next four consecutive neighbors, i.e., the nodes with outgoing ports ρ_2, ρ_3, ρ_4 and ρ_5, respectively. If more than one pebble is found, then the agent concludes v is a milestone, and the encoding is done along the first half of its neighbors, except the parent. It further concludes that the next node along P is present in the other half of its neighbors. Otherwise, if a single pebble is found, corresponding to the nodes with outgoing ports $\rho_1, \rho_2, \rho_3, \rho_4$ and ρ_5, then the node having a pebble is the next node along P. It further checks the node with outgoing port $\rho_{\frac{deg(v)}{2}+1}$, if a pebble is found, then v is a milestone, otherwise v is light.
3. Moreover if no pebble is found at the node with outgoing port ρ_1, then the agent checks the nodes with outgoing port $\rho_{\frac{deg(v)}{2}}, \rho_{\frac{deg(v)}{2}+1}, \rho_{\frac{deg(v)}{2}+2}$, $\rho_{\frac{deg(v)}{2}+3}$ and $\rho_{\frac{deg(v)}{2}+4}$, respectively. If more than one pebble is found, then the agent concludes v is a milestone and the encoding is done along the second half of its neighbors, except the parent. It further concludes that the next node along P is present in the other half of its neighbors. Otherwise, if a single pebble is found, corresponding to the nodes with outgoing ports

$\rho_{\frac{deg(v)}{2}}, \rho_{\frac{deg(v)}{2}+1}, \rho_{\frac{deg(v)}{2}+2}, \rho_{\frac{deg(v)}{2}+3}$ and $\rho_{\frac{deg(v)}{2}+4}$, then the node having pebble is the next node along P. Moreover, conclude that the node v is light.

As shown in Fig. 4 (in detail described in Fig. 5), we create a directed graph representation consisting of all the possible paths that the agent can travel from a milestone node s towards the treasure t. The pebbles for encoding are placed along the neighbors of s. The set U is a collection of nodes $\{u_1, u_2 \cdots\}$, which represent the nodes where pebbles are placed for encoding. The set W is the collection of nodes $\{w_1, w_2, \cdots\}$, which are at the same level as v_1 and no pebbles are placed on them. The nodes along the desired path from s to t are depicted by circles, in which pebbles are placed at every node, except at v_2 (marked by a red circle) and t. Let Γ_i be the integer value of the binary string γ_i (where $1 \leq i \leq \alpha$) encoded along the neighbors of s. The edge (u, v) denoted by $\Gamma|n$ implies that the agent after searching some Γ partition of u's neighbor, encountered n many pebbles. The edge (u, v) denoted by $\mathcal{R}|n$ implies that the agent after searches the nodes corresponding to the set $\mathcal{R}$ of u's neighbor, encountered n many pebbles. The notation $\mathcal{R}|0|\Gamma|n$ along an edge (u, v), represents the fact that the agent after searching the nodes corresponding to the set $\mathcal{R}$ of u's neighbor and encounters no pebble, further it searches its Γ partition of neighbors and encounters n many pebbles. The red cross on edge denotes a path in which the agent detects inconsistency and stops further exploration along this path. As shown in Fig. 4, z is an integer greater than 1.

Below is a detailed description of the TREASUREHUNTFORGRAPH algorithm for the agent to find the treasure.

1. The agent starting from s, sets $SearchNode = s$, checks for a pebble at s. If no pebble is found at s, then it searches the first half of its neighbors for a node with a pebble. If a pebble is found at s, then it performs the CHECKERFORMILESTONE algorithm to check whether the node is light or a milestone.

2. If s is light, then it searches the second half of its neighbors until a treasure or a pebble is encountered. If the treasure is found, then the algorithm terminates. Otherwise if a pebble is found at a node v_1, then set $SearchNode = v_1$.

3. If s is a milestone, then it decodes the α many binary strings by visiting the second half of its neighbors (node u_i's in Fig. 3) and accordingly updates the set $\mathcal{R}$ and performs the following task.

    (a) The agent first obtains the binary strings $\gamma_1, \cdots, \gamma_\alpha$ (of size at most $\frac{c-1}{2}$) from the *transformed* binary strings (of size at most $c - 1$), as explained in pebble placement strategy of Sect. 3.2.

    (b) The agent divides the first half of neighbors of $SearchNode$ into $2^{|\gamma_1|}$ partitions. Each partition consisting of $\frac{deg(SearchNode)}{2^{|\gamma_1|}}$ neighbors. Then it searches Γ_1-th partition, where Γ_1 is the integer value of γ_1. If the treasure is found, then the algorithm terminates. Otherwise a pebble is found at a node v_1 (say), set $SearchNode = v_1$ (as shown by the edge (s, v_1) in Fig. 5).

(c) The agent searches Γ_2 partition of *SearchNode* neighbors. The agent finds either no pebble or at least one pebble (refer the edges (v_1, v_2), (v_1, u_i) and (v_1, w_i) in Fig. 4).

Irrespective of the number of nodes encountered without pebbles, after searching Γ_2 partition of its neighbors. The agent visits each such node without a pebble one at a time, by maintaining a stack. Then it searches its Γ_3 partition of its neighbors. If no pebble is encountered, then the agent returns to its parent. Otherwise, there can be a single or multiple pebbles encountered (refer to the edges with notation $\Gamma_3|1$ and $\Gamma_3|z$, respectively in Fig. 4).

If a single pebble is found, then there are multiple possibilities, as shown by the edges denoted by $\Gamma_3|1$ in the Fig. 5.

> *P1:* The agent is currently at some node $w_i \in W$, encounters a pebble at a node in the previous level (refer the edge (w_i, s) with notation $\Gamma_3|1$ in Fig. 4).

> *P2:* The agent is currently at some node $w_i \in W$, encounters a pebble at a node in the same level (refer the edge (w_i, u_i) with notation $\Gamma_3|1$ in Fig. 4).

> *P3:* The agent is currently at the node v_2, encounters a pebble at a node in the next level of v_2, i.e., at v_3 (refer the edge (v_2, v_3) denoted by $\Gamma^3|1$ as shown in Fig. 4) which is indeed the desired path towards the treasure.

Otherwise, *if multiple pebbles are found*, then we have further possibilities, as shown by the edges denoted by $\Gamma_3|z$ in Fig. 5.

> *P1:* The agent is currently at some node $w_i \in W$, encounters a pebble at a node in the previous level, i.e., at s (refer the edge (w_i, s) with notation $\Gamma_3|z$ in Fig. 4) and all the remaining pebbles along the nodes in the same level, i.e., along u_i (refer the edge (w_i, u_i) with notation $\Gamma_3|z$ in Fig. 4).

> *P2:* The agent is currently at some node $w_i \in W$, encounters all the pebbles at a node in the same level, i.e., along u_i (refer the edge (w_i, u_i) with notation $\Gamma_3|z$ in Fig. 4).

> *P3:* The agent is currently at v_2, encounters a pebble at a node in the next level, i.e., at v_3 (refer the edge (v_2, v_3) with notation $\Gamma_3|z$ as shown in Fig. 4) which is indeed the desired path towards the treasure. The remaining pebbles are found along the nodes in the previous level, as shown by the edge (v_2, u_i) with notation $\Gamma_3|z$ in Fig. 4.

So, irrespective of the number of pebbles encountered, the agent visits each one of them and searches the nodes corresponding to the ports in the set $\mathcal{R}$. *If no pebble is encountered*, then the agent is at v_3 and it searches the Γ_4 partition of its neighbors and encounters v_4 (refer the edge (v_3, v_4) with notation $\mathcal{R}_4|0|\Gamma_4|1$ in Fig. 4). From v_4, it further searches Γ_5 partition of its neighbors and finds v_5. It sets *SearchNode* $= v_5$.

If a single pebble is found then we have the following possibilities.

> *P1:* If the agent is currently at some node $u_i \in U$, then the pebble encountered is at the node s (refer the edge (u_i, s) in Fig. 4).

> *P2:* If the agent is at a node v_3, then the pebble encountered is at the node v_4 (refer the edge (v_3, v_4) with notation $\mathcal{R}_4|1$ in Fig. 4) which is the desired path.

In this case, the agent searches the nodes corresponding to the ports in the set $\mathcal{R}$, from the node where a single pebble is encountered. Then we have further possibilities:

> *P1:* If no pebble is encountered, then the agent is at v_4. In this case, the agent further searches the Γ_5 partition of its neighbors and encounters v_5 (refer the edge (v_4, v_5) with notation $\mathcal{R}_5|0|\Gamma_5|1$ in Fig. 4). It sets *SearchNode* $= v_5$.

> *P2:* If a single pebble is encountered (refer the edge (v_4, v_5) with notation $\mathcal{R}_5|1$ in Fig. 4), then this is the correct path, and the agent will reach to the node v_5, and set *SearchNode* $= v_5$.

> *P3:* If multiple pebbles are encountered, then return to its parent (refer to all the crossed edges denoted by $\mathcal{R}_5|z$ in Fig. 4 and in Fig. 5).

If *multiple pebbles are found* along this search, then the agent returns to its parent, as referred by the crossed red edges denoted by $\mathcal{R}_4|z$ in Fig. 4 and Fig. 5.

In each case, by rejecting every wrong path (referred as crossed red edges in Fig. 5), the agent will ultimately return to the node v_5 (refer all the edges denoted as $\mathcal{R}_5|1$ and $\mathcal{R}_5|0|\Gamma_5|1$ in Fig. 5) and set *SearchNode* $= v_5$.

(d) Further from v_5, i.e., *SearchNode*. The agent searches the Γ_6 partition of v_5 and encounters a pebble at the node v_6. Then it sets *SearchNode* $= v_6$. This process continues until *SearchNode* $= v_\alpha$.

4. If *SearchNode* is light, search all its neighbor until a pebble or the treasure is encountered. If the treasure is found, then the algorithm terminates. If a pebble is found at a node v_j, set *SearchNode* $= v_j$, where $(j \geq 2)$.

5. If *SearchNode* is a milestone, then it searches its corresponding half of neighbors determined by the algorithm CHECKERFORMILESTONE, and then go to step 3.

Lemma 3. *Given $k = cD$ pebbles, the agent following the* TREASUREHUNTFORGRAPH *algorithm successfully finds the treasure.*

Lemma 4. *The agent following* TREASUREHUNTFORGRAPH *algorithm takes* $\mathcal{O}\left(c(\frac{\Delta}{2^{c/2}})^2 + c\right)$ *time to reach from a milestone to another milestone.*

Theorem 3. *Given $k = cD$ pebbles, the agent following the* TREASUREHUNTFORGRAPH *algorithm finds the treasure in* $\mathcal{O}\left[cD(\frac{\Delta}{2^{c/2}})^2 + cD\right]$ *time.*

4   Lower Bound

In this section, we provide a lower bound result on time of treasure hunt for the case when the number of pebbles k is at most $D - 1$.

Let T be a complete tree with n nodes and of height D where the degree of the root r and each internal node is Δ. There are $\Delta \cdot (\Delta - 1)^{D-1}$ leaves in T.

Let $p = \Delta \cdot (\Delta - 1)^{D-1}$ and $u_1, \ldots, u_p$ be the leaves of T in the lexicographical ordering of the shortest path from the root r to the leaves. For $1 \leq i \leq p$, we construct an input B_i as follows. The tree T is taken as the input graph, r as the starting point of the agent, and u_i as the position of the treasure. Let $\mathcal{B}$ be the set of all inputs B_i, $1 \leq i \leq p$. Let $\mathcal{A}$ be any deterministic treasure hunt algorithm executed by the mobile agent and, let $\mathcal{L}$ be any pebble placement algorithm for the set of instances $\mathcal{B}$. We prove the following theorem.

Theorem 4. *There exists a tree with maximum degree Δ and diameter D such that any deterministic algorithm must require $\Omega((\frac{k}{e})^{\frac{k}{k+1}}(\Delta - 1)^{\frac{D}{k+1}})$-time for the treasure hunt using at most k pebbles placed on the nodes of T.*

5   Conclusion

In this paper, we study the trade-off between the number of pebbles k and the time for a treasure hunt for $k = cD$, where $c \geq 1$. For $k < D$, our proposed upper bound and lower bound on time of treasure hunt are close. For $k = cD$, we propose an algorithm for the treasure hunt. Therefore, proving a tight lower bound result for both of the above cases is a natural problem to solve in the future. On the other hand, as the previous result [6] proves that the fastest possible treasure hunt algorithm can be achieved with $O(D \log \Delta)$ pebbles, it will be interesting to investigate the case when $k \in w(D)$ and $k \in o(D \log \Delta)$. We propose algorithms which have close upper and lower bounds when $k < D$. In the future, we will like to provide a more tighter lower bound. Further, when $k \geq D$, we have given only the upper bound. A possible future work will be to propose a lower bound for this proof.

References

1. Bhattacharya, A., Gorain, B., Mandal, P.S.: Treasure hunt in graph using pebbles. arXiv preprint arXiv:2209.00857 (2022)
2. Bouchard, S., Dieudonné, Y., Labourel, A., Pelc, A.: Almost-optimal deterministic treasure hunt in arbitrary graphs. In: ICALP 2021, Glasgow, Scotland, 12–16 July 2021. LIPIcs, vol. 198, pp. 36:1–36:20 (2021)
3. Bouchard, S., Dieudonné, Y., Pelc, A., Petit, F.: Deterministic treasure hunt in the plane with angular hints. Algorithmica **82**, 3250–3281 (2020)
4. Dereniowski, D., Pelc, A.: Drawing maps with advice. J. Parallel Distrib. Comput. **72**(2), 132–143 (2012)
5. Fraigniaud, P., Ilcinkas, D., Pelc, A.: Communication algorithms with advice. J. Comput. Syst. Sci. **76**(3–4), 222–232 (2010)
6. Gorain, B., Mondal, K., Nayak, H., Pandit, S.: Pebble guided optimal treasure hunt in anonymous graphs. Theor. Comput. Sci. (2022)
7. Pelc, A.: Reaching a target in the plane with no information. Inf. Process. Lett. **140**, 13–17 (2018)
8. Pelc, A., Yadav, R.N.: Cost vs. information tradeoffs for treasure hunt in the plane. arXiv preprint arXiv:1902.06090 (2019)
9. Pelc, A., Yadav, R.N.: Advice complexity of treasure hunt in geometric terrains. Inf. Comput. **281**, 104705 (2021)

Blockchain in Dynamic Networks

Rachel Bricker, Mikhail Nesterenko[✉], and Gokarna Sharma

Kent State University, Kent, OH 44242, USA
{rbricke2,gsharma2}@kent.edu, mikhail@cs.kent.edu

Abstract. We consider blockchain in dynamic networks. We define the Blockchain Decision Problem. It requires miners that maintain the blockchain to confirm whether a particular block is accepted. We establish the necessary conditions for the existence of a solution. We, however, prove that the solution, even under these necessary conditions is, in general, impossible. We then present two algorithms that solve the Blockchain Decision Problem under either the knowledge of the maximum source pool propagation time or the knowledge of the source pool membership. We evaluate the performance of the two algorithms.

Keywords: Dynamic networks · Blockchain · Consensus

1 Introduction

Blockchain is a means of organizing a decentralized public ledger. The lack of centralized controller potentially makes the blockchain more resilient to network failures and attacks. Blockchain is a popular architecture for a number of applications such as cryptocurrency [17,22], massive Internet-of-Things storage [2] and electronic voting [9].

The major problem of maintaining this ledger is for the participants to achieve consensus on its records despite faults or hostile environment. Classic robust consensus algorithms [5,15] use cooperative message exchanges between peer processes to arrive at a joint decision. However, such algorithms require that each process is aware of all the other processes in the network. In a system with unstable membership, such requirement may be excessive. An alternative is competitive consensus [17] where processes race to have records that they generated added to the blockchain. This competition does not require fixed membership or explicit fault handling. Instead, it organically provides defense against attacks and faults so long as the computing power of correct nodes exceeds those of faulty nodes or adversaries.

Ordinarily, the network underlying the blockchain is considered to be always connected. However, as blockchain finds greater acceptance and new applications, this assumption may no longer be considered as a given. Instead, the blockchain operation under less reliable communication conditions needs to be examined. This requires the study of relation between block generation and its propagation throughout the network.

© The Author(s), under exclusive license to Springer Nature Switzerland AG 2022
S. Devismes et al. (Eds.): SSS 2022, LNCS 13751, pp. 114–129, 2022.
https://doi.org/10.1007/978-3-031-21017-4_8

We use dynamic network to study it. Such network assumes that a connection between any two processes may appear and disappear at any moment. We thus explore how blockchain behaves at the boundaries of connectivity: where message delay and miner participation is tenuous while connection and communication speeds vary greatly.

Related Work. An area related to dynamic networks is population protocols, where passive agents do not control their movement but may exchange information as they encounter each other. See Michail et al. [16] for an introduction to the topic. A system with arbitrary link failures was considered by Santoro and Widmayer [20]. There are several papers that explore the model of link failures in greater detail [1,6,8].

The network that dynamically changes in an arbitrary manner, possibly to the detriment of the problem to be solved, was first formally studied by O'Dell and Wattenhofer [18]. This topic is explored in Kuhn et al. [13]. Several studies [4,10] investigate reliable broadcast in dynamic networks with Byzantine faults. There is a large body of literature on cooperative consensus in dynamic networks [3,14,21]. In particular, Winkler et al. [21] explored the concept of an eventually stably communicating root component necessary for consensus. This is similar to the concept of source communication pool that we introduce in this paper.

Let us discuss the related blockchain research. There are some applied studies [7,12] that consider the operation of blockchain that tolerates extensive delays or temporary disconnections. Hood et al. [11] explores in detail the blockchain operation under network partitioning. However, to the best of our knowledge, this paper is the first to study blockchain in dynamic networks.

Paper Organization and Contribution. In Sect. 2, we introduce the notation and state the Blockchain Decision Problem for dynamic networks: every network miner needs to confirm the acceptance of each block.

In Sect. 3, we establish the conditions for blockchain and the dynamic network so that the problem is at all solvable: there needs to be a single source pool of continuously interacting miners that propagate the blocks they generate to the rest of the network and none of the other miners may generate infinitely many blocks and propagate them back to the source pool. In Sect. 4, we prove that, in general, even if these conditions are met, the problem is impossible to solve. Intuitively, miners may not determine when these outside blocks stop coming.

On the constructive side, in Sect. 5, we present two algorithms that solve the problem with restrictions: *KPT*—if maximum message propagation time is known to all miners, *KSM*—if source pool membership is known to all miners. We evaluate the performance of the two algorithms in Sect. 7. We conclude the paper by Sect. 8.

2   Notation, Definitions and Problem Statement

Network. A network N consists of a fixed number of processes or *miners*. Each miner has a unique identifier which may or may not be known to the other miners in the beginning. The alternative interpretation is that the network membership is either fixed or dynamic.

The network computation proceeds in synchronous rounds. Miners communicate via message passing over uni-directional links connecting the sender miner m_s and receiver miner m_r. This is denoted as $m_s \rightarrow m_r$. The network is dynamic as links may appear or disappear. Existing link is reliable. If there is no link, no messages may be sent.

More specifically, at the beginning of each round i, the receiver miner receives all messages sent to it during the previous round, then carries out calculations and submits messages over the links that exist in round i to be received in the next round. A *computation* is a, possibly infinite, sequence of such rounds.

To simplify the presentation, we first assume that the communication is instantaneous. That is, all the information sent over the link is received in the same round. We also assume that arbitrary amount of information may be communicated in one message. We relax these assumptions later in the paper.

A *journey* in a computation is a sequence of miners and communication links $m_1 \rightarrow \cdots \rightarrow m_i \rightarrow m_{i+1} \rightarrow m_{i+2} \rightarrow \cdots \rightarrow m_x$ such that each round i of the computation, where link $m_i \rightarrow m_{i+1}$ exists, precedes the round with link $m_{i+1} \rightarrow m_{i+2}$. *Journey time* is the number of computation rounds between the first and last link in the journey. Note that journey time may be greater than the total number of links in the journey since it may take more than one round for each subsequent link in the journey to appear.

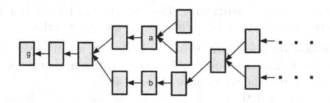

Fig. 1. Blockchain notation illustration. Block g is genesis. It is the ancestor of all blocks. It is accepted if the blockchain is infinite. Block a is rejected because it is an ancestor to only finitely many blocks. Alternatively, a belongs to finite branches only. Block b is accepted since it is an ancestor to infinitely many blocks. That is, b belongs to infinite branches. Block a is a cousin of block of b. In an infinite blockchain, b is accepted if all its cousin branches are finite.

Blockchain. The introduced terms are illustrated in Fig. 1. *Blockchain* is a tree of linked *blocks*. Each mined block is unique and can be distinguished from the others. Further block contents is immaterial. A block may be linked to a single *parent block*. A *child* is a block linked to a parent. *Genesis* is the root of the tree and the only block without a parent. A *leaf* is the block with no children. An *ancestor* of a block b is either a parent of b or, recursively, an ancestor of b. A *descendant* of a block b is any block whose ancestor is b. The *depth* of a block is the number of its ancestors.

A *branch* is the maximal sequence of blocks $b_1, \cdots, b_i, b_{i+1}, \cdots$ such that b_1 is the genesis and for each i, b_i is the parent of b_{i+1}. By this definition, either a branch is infinite or it ends with a leaf. Given a block b that belongs to a branch, all blocks preceding b in this branch are its ancestors and all blocks following b are its descendants. The *length* of a finite branch is the depth of its leaf. The length of an infinite branch is infinite.

A *trunk* of two branches is their longest shared prefix. Thus, the trunk of any two branches is at least the genesis. A branch is a trunk of itself. The blocks of the trunk belong to the branches that share this trunk. Consider a block b that does not belong to the shared trunk of the two branches. *Cousins* of b are the blocks that belong to these branches but neither descendants nor ancestors of b. These blocks belong to a *cousin branch*.

The blockchain of a computation is the collection of all blocks mined during this computation. In the beginning of each computation, each miner stores the same genesis. Each miner in the network stores all the blockchain blocks known to it. That is, miners maintain local copies of the blockchain. However, due to the haphazard link appearance in a dynamic network, local copies of the blockchain may be out of sync.

In an arbitrary round, a miner m may generate or *mine* a new block b linked to the longest branch of the local copy of the blockchain. If m has several branches of the same length, the new block may be mined on any one of them. Multiple processes may mine blocks in the same round. Once linked, the sender sends its entire copy of the blockchain to the receiver. We discuss how to limit the amount of transmitted information later in the paper. By this operation, the number of children for any block, i.e. the arity of the blockchain, is at most $|N|$.

We place few assumptions on the relationship between the relative speed of communication and block mining. However, we assume the following fairness: throughout the computation, a miner either receives infinitely many new blocks or mines infinite many blocks itself.

The Blockchain Decision Problem. A block is *accepted* if it is the ancestor of all but finitely many blocks. A block is *rejected* if it is the ancestor of finitely many blocks.

In the attempt to agree on the common state of the blockchain, each miner decides whether the block is accepted by outputting a *confirm* decision. The decision about block rejection is implied and is not required. To arrive at this decision, the miners may store and exchange arbitrary information. We use the term computation for block mining and blockchain maintenance as well as for the operation of the algorithm that allows the miners to output decision about the blocks of this blockchain. We formulate the decision problem as follows.

Definition 1 (The Blockchain Decision Problem *BDP*). *A solution to the Blockchain Decision Problem satisfies the following properties:*

Decision: *each miner eventually confirms every accepted block;*
Confirmation Validity: *each miner confirms only accepted blocks.*

We explore the solvability of this problem under various connectivity conditions in dynamic networks.

3 Decisive Computations

Globally Decisive Computations. A computation is *globally decisive* if every block of its blockchain is uniquely categorized: either accepted or rejected but not both at once.

Lemma 1. *The blockchain of a globally decisive computation has exactly one infinite branch.*

To put the lemma another way: in a decisive computation, all branches except for one are finite.

Proof. The blockchains that do not conform to the conditions of the lemma either have no infinite branches or have more than one. If a blockchain does not have infinite branches at all, then it has a finite number of blocks. In this case, every block b is the ancestor of finitely many blocks. That is, b is rejected. However, b is also an ancestor of all but finitely many blocks. That is, b is also simultaneously accepted. In a globally decisive computation, a block may be either accepted or rejected but not both.

Let us consider the second case of a blockchain not conforming to the conditions of the lemma: it has multiple infinite branches. Let block b belong to one such branch but not to the shared trunk of all the branches. Since b belongs to an infinite branch, it is an ancestor to an infinite number of blocks. Therefore, b is not rejected. However, there are infinite number of blocks in the infinite cousin branches, i.e. the branches to which b does not belong. That is, b is not an ancestor to an infinite number of blocks. Hence, b is not accepted either.

That is, a blockchain with unique categorization of acceptance and rejection has exactly one infinite branch. A computation must have such a blockchain to be decisive. The lemma follows.   □

Mining Pools. In a certain computation, a *mining pool M* is a maximal set of miners such that each miner $m \in M$ has an infinite number of journeys to every other miner in M. That is, each miner in a pool is reachable from every other miner in this pool infinitely often. If, for some miner m, there are no other miners that are mutually reachable infinitely often, then m forms a pool by itself.

A pool graph $\mathcal{PG}$ for a computation C is a static directed graph formed as follows. Each node in $\mathcal{PG}$ corresponds to a mining pool in C. An edge from node $P_1 \in \mathcal{PG}$ to node $P_2 \in \mathcal{PG}$ exists if there is an infinite number of journeys from miners of pool P_1 to the miners of the pool P_2.

Let us observe that any pool graph $\mathcal{PG}$ is a DAG. Indeed, if there is cycle in $\mathcal{PG}$, then any miner m_1 has an infinite number of journeys to any other miner m_2 in this cycle. Since mining pools are maximal, these miners belong to the same pool. If $\mathcal{PG}$ has a path from pool P_1 to pool P_2, then any miner $m_1 \in P_1$

has an infinite number of journeys to any miner $m_2 \in P_2$. If it does not, then the number of journeys between P_1 and P_2 is finite.

A node in a static graph is a source if it has no incoming edges. Since a DAG has no cycles, it has at least one source. A *source pool* is a pool that corresponds to a source in $\mathcal{PG}$. An infinite branch *belongs* to a pool if it contains a suffix of blocks where every block is mined by a member of this pool.

Lemma 2. *If the blockchain of a computation contains an infinite branch, this branch belongs to a single pool.*

Proof. Assume that there is a computation C whose blockchain has an infinite branch BR that does not belong to a single pool. That is, branch BR contains infinitely many blocks mined by miners in at least two separate pools P_1 and P_2. The pool graph $\mathcal{PG}$ of C contains no cycles. That means that if there is a path from one pool to the other, there is no path in the other direction. Suppose, without loss of generality, that there is no path from P_1 to P_2. This means that there is a finite number of journeys from miners of P_1 to P_2 in C. Let round r be a round of C after the last journey from P_1 to P_2 ends. However, there are infinitely many blocks in BR that are mined by miners in P_1 and in P_2. Consider two blocks b_1 and b_2 of BR mined after round r such that b_1 is mined by miner $m_1 \in P_1$ and b_2 by miner $m_2 \in P_2$. Moreover, b_1 is the ancestor of b_2. If this is the case, there is a journey from m_1 to m_2 in C. However, we assumed that there are no such journeys after round r in C. That is, our assumption is incorrect and C does not exist. This proves the lemma.   □

Locally Decisive Computations. A computation is *locally decisive* if it is globally decisive and each miner receives every accepted block.

Lemma 3. *In a locally decisive computation, infinite branches belong to a source pool.*

Proof. Assume that there is a locally decisive computation C whose blockchain contains an infinite branch BR that does not belong to the source pools of C. According to Lemma 2, BR belongs to some pool P. Since the pool graph of C is a DAG, it must have a source pool SP. A source pool has a finite number of journeys from the miners outside itself.

Computation C is locally decisive. This means that all miners, including the miners in SP, receive all blocks in BR. Yet, BR is infinite. This means that there are infinitely many journeys from miners in P to the miners in SP. This means, contrary to our initial assumption, that SP is not a source pool.   □

Lemma 4. *In a locally decisive computation, there is a single source pool.*

Proof. Assume the opposite: there is a locally decisive computation C with at least two source pools: SP_1 and SP_2. Since a locally decisive computation is also a globally decisive computation, according to Lemma 1, C contains a single infinite branch. According to Lemma 2, this branch belongs to a single pool and, according to Lemma 3, this pool is a source. That is, the infinite branch belongs to either SP_1 or SP_2. Let it be SP_1. This means that miners of SP_1 mine infinitely many blocks that belong to the infinite branch. Since C is globally decisive, these blocks are accepted.

However, SP_2 is also a source, this means that it has a finite number of journeys from miners outside itself. Yet, since C is locally decisive, the miners in SP_2 need to receive the infinite number of blocks mined in SP_1. That is, there are infinite number of journeys from the miners of SP_1 to the miners of SP_2. That is, SP_2 is not a source.   □

The following theorem summarizes the results proven in Lemmas 1, 2, 3 and 4.

Theorem 1. *If a computation is globally and locally decisive, then it has exactly one infinite branch and one source pool. Moreover, this infinite branch belongs to this source pool.*

4 Impossibility

In a solution to the Blockchain Decision Problem, every miner is required to confirm each accepted block. Theorem 1 states necessary conditions for the possibility of the solution. Yet, even if these conditions are satisfied, a miner may make a mistake. Indeed, assume a miner m determines that a certain block b belongs to the longest branches of all processes in the source pool. Miner m confirms it. Yet, a non-source pool miner may later mine a longer cousin branch to b, communicate it to the source pool forcing rejection of b. This makes m's confirmation incorrect. Even though, by definition of the source pool, such links from the outside happen only finitely many times, the time they stop is not predictable. This makes the solution, in the general case, impossible. The below theorem formalizes this intuition.

Theorem 2. *There does not exist a solution to the Blockchain Decision Problem even for globally and locally decisive computations.*

Proof. Assume there is an algorithm A that solves *BDP* for globally and locally decisive computations. Consider a globally and locally decisive computation C_x which contains mining pools P_1 and P_2 such that P_1 is the source pool.

Since C_x is globally and locally decisive, according to Theorem 1, it has a single source pool and a single infinite branch that belongs to this source pool. This means that there are infinite number of blocks in the infinite branch. All these blocks are accepted. After some round r_1 they must be mined in P_1. Let block b be one such block. Since the computation is locally decisive, b has to reach miners in P_2. The Decision Property of *BDP* requires that all miners eventually confirm accepted blocks. This means that miners of P_2 have to eventually confirm b. Let r_2 be the round where some miner $m_2 \in P_2$ confirms b in C_x.

Consider a computation C_y that has an extra pool P_3. Communication in C_y is as follows. Miners of pool P_3 have no links to the outside miners until round

---

Algorithm 1: Known Source Pool Propagation Time Algorithm *KPT*.

---

1 **Constants:**
2 p // miner identifier
3 PT // source pool propagation time, integer

4 **Variables:**
5 T // blockchain tree, initially genesis
6 L // set of tuples $\langle b, l \rangle$, where $b \in T$ and l is either accept or reject initially $\varnothing$, if
   $b \in T$ and $b \notin L$, then b is unlabeled

7 **Actions:**
8 **if** *mined block b* **then**
9 $\lfloor$ add b to T

10 **if** *available link to miner q* **then**
11 $\lfloor$ send T to q

12 **if** *receive T_q from miner q* **then**
13 $\lfloor$ merge T and T_q

14 **if** *exists unlabeled b_1 such that for every $BR(b_1)$, there is a cousin block b_2 such that*
   $depth(b_2) > length(BR(b_1))$ for at least $2 \cdot PT$ rounds **then**
15 $\lfloor$ add $\langle b_1, \text{reject} \rangle$ to L

16 **if** *exists unlabeled b such that for its every cousin c: $\langle c, \text{reject} \rangle \in L$* **then**
17 $\lfloor$ add $\langle b, \text{accept} \rangle$ to L
18 $\lfloor$ confirm b

---

r_2. Since the miners of P_3 do not influence other miners, we construct C_y such that up to the round r_2, the actions of miners of P_1 and of P_2 are the same as in C_x. This includes m_2 confirming block b. We construct the remainder of C_y as follows. Miners of P_3 have only outgoing links to miners of P_1 and P_2 for the remainder of C_y. That is, P_3 is a source. We construct C_y to be locally and globally decisive. That is, we make P_3 its own single infinite branch.

By construction, miners of P_1 never send messages to miners of P_3. This means that block b mined in P_2 does not reach P_3. Hence, b does not belong to the infinite branch. Therefore, b is rejected. However, miner m_2 confirms it in C_x and, therefore, in C_y. This is contrary to the Confirmation Validity property of *BDP*, which stipulates that miners may confirm only accepted blocks. Thus, despite our initial assumption, algorithm A does not solve the Blockchain Decision Problem. Hence, the theorem.   □

5 Solutions

Previously, we considered completely formed infinite blockchain trees. However, to solve the Blockchain Decision Problem, individual miners have to make decisions whether a particular block is accepted or rejected on the basis of a tree that is not yet complete. Moreover, a miner may not be aware of some already mined blocks due to propagation delays. To describe this uncertainty, we introduce additional notation.

A branch BR is *dead* if all miners are mining on cousin branches longer than BR. A branch is *live* otherwise. Notice that once a branch is dead, it may not become live. Thus, if a block belongs to dead branches only, it is rejected. In an infinite computation, a block is accepted if it belongs to all infinite branches. To put another way, a block is accepted if all its cousin branches are dead. The algorithms in this section exploit the miners' ability to detect dead branches for accepted block confirmation.

Per Theorem 2, the solution to the Blockchain Decision Problem is impossible if non-source-pool miners are able to send their mined blocks to the source pool. Alternatively, the miners are not aware whether they are in the source pool or not. We, therefore, consider the following restriction. A mining pool is *initially closed* if its members do not have incoming edges from non-pool members. If source pool is initially closed, to evaluate whether the branch is dead, it is sufficient to consider blocks generated by source pool miners only.

Known Propagation Time. Let m be an arbitrary miner in the source pool. *Source pool propagation time PT* is the time of the longest journey from m to any other miner in the network. If PT is fixed, it takes at most PT rounds for a message sent by m to reach all miners. If PT is known, the solution to BDP seems straightforward as dead branches eventually become shorter than live ones so a miner may just have to wait for one of the branches to outgrow the others. However, this solution is not immediate since, even with fixed PT, the length difference between live branches may be arbitrarily large. Indeed, a miner may mine a number of blocks extending its branch length significantly. However, other miners may subsequently mine on their branches catching up and keeping their branches live. Thus, the solution needs to determine how long a miner waits before it determines whether the particular branch is dead.

Instead, to detect a dead branch, the algorithm that solves BDP, relies on the branch length difference over a certain period of time. We call this algorithm *KPT*. Its code is shown in Algorithm 1. The algorithm operates as follows. Each miner p maintains the local copy of the blockchain tree T and a set of per-block labels L where it stores decisions whether the block is accepted or rejected. If the decision is not reached, the block is unlabeled. Once block b is mined, it is added to the tree T. If a link to some miner q appears, miner p sends its entire blockchain to q.

The decisions are reached as follows. An unlabeled block b_1 is labeled rejected if for its every branch $BR(b_1)$ the following happens. There is a cousin block b_2 such that the depth of b_2 is greater than the length of this branch $BR(b_1)$ for at least $2 \cdot PT$ rounds. An unlabeled block b is accepted if all its cousins are rejected. In the latter case, b is confirmed.

Lemma 5. *Let, at some round r, some miner m observe that there is a block b whose depth is greater than the length of its cousin branch BR. If b's depth is still greater than the length of BR at round $r + 2 \cdot PT$, then BR is dead.*

Proof. Assume some block b is mined by miner m_b of the source pool in round r_b. Let us consider an arbitrary miner in the source pool m_c mining on BR. If, at the time of receipt of r_b, the length of BR is less than the depth of r_b, then m_c switches to the branch with r_b. That is, if miners do not mine enough blocks on BR to extend it past r_b before it arrives, the branch is dead. The latest round

m_c may receive b is $r_b + PT$. This is how long the miners may potentially mine blocks on short branch BR before it dies.

Let us now consider another miner m_d that observes block arrival. The earliest round when m_d may receive b is also r_b. The miners may mine blocks on BR for PT more rounds. These blocks reach m_d in another PT rounds. Hence, if m_d observes the depth of b is greater than the length of BR for $2 \cdot PT$ rounds, then BR is dead. □

Algorithm 2: Known Source Pool Membership Algorithm *KSM*.

1 **Constants:**
2 p // miner identifier
3 SM // set of ids of source pool miners

4 **Variables:**
5 T // blockchain tree, initially genesis
6 P // set of tuples $\langle b, m \rangle$, where $b \in T$ and $m \in SM$, initially $\varnothing$, positions of source pool miners
7 L // set of tuples $\langle b, l \rangle$, where $b \in T$ and l is either accept or reject initially $\varnothing$, if $b \in T$ and $b \notin L$, then b is unlabeled, block labels

8 **Actions:**
9 **if** *mined block b* **then**
10 | add b to T
11 | **if** $p \in SM$ **then**
12 | | update p's entry in P to $\langle b, p \rangle$

13 **if** *available link to miner q* **then**
14 | send T, P to q

15 **if** *receive T_q, P_q from miner q* **then**
16 | merge T and T_q, merge P and P_q
17 | **if** $p \in SM$ **then**
18 | | let b be the deepest block in T
19 | | update p's entry in P to $\langle b, p \rangle$

20 **if** *exists unlabeled b_1 such that for every $BR(b_1)$, for all $m \in SM$ there exists $\langle b_2, m \rangle \in P$ such that $depth(b_2) > length(BR(b_1))$* **then**
21 | add $\langle b_1, \text{reject} \rangle$ to L

22 **if** *exists unlabeled b such that all cousins of b are* reject **then**
23 | add $\langle b, \text{accept} \rangle$ to L
24 | confirm b

Theorem 3. *Known Source Pool Propagation Time Algorithm* KPT *solves the Blockchain Decision Problem with initially closed source pool.*

Proof. Let us consider the Confirmation Validity Property of *BDP*. According to Lemma 5, If PT is known and if miner p observes that some block is deeper than the height of a branch for longer than $2 \cdot PT$ rounds, then this branch is dead. If some block belongs to dead branches only, it is rejected. This is the exact condition under which blocks are labeled rejected in *KPT* (see Line 14). If all cousins are rejected, the block is accepted. This is how the is block is labeled accepted and confirmed in *KPT* (see Line 16). To put another way, *KPT* confirms only accepted blocks which satisfies the Confirmation Validity Property of *BDP*.

Let us now discuss the Decision Property and show that every accepted block is eventually confirmed. Indeed, according to Lemma 5, a miner determines that a branch is dead in at most $2 \cdot PT$ rounds. A block is rejected once all branches that it belongs to are dead. That is, a block rejection is determined in this many rounds after the last branch of the block is dead.

A block is labeled accepted and then confirmed after all its cousins are rejected. To put another way, a block is accepted after at most $2 \cdot PT$ rounds of the rejection of the last cousin block. This proves that all accepted blocks are eventually confirmed and KPT satisfies the Decision Property of BDP. □

Let us describe a couple of simple enhancements of KPT. Since miners never make mistakes in their classification of reject and accept, a miner may send its label set L to help its neighbors make their decisions faster. Also, a miner may determine dead branches quicker if each block is labeled with the round of its mining. In this case, to ascertain that a certain branch BR is dead, it is sufficient to check if there is a cousin block b_2 such that BR does not outgrow b_2 for PT rounds.

Known Source Pool Membership. Miner *position* in a blockchain tree is the block on which it is currently mining. Note that the depth of a miner's position throughout the computation may only increase. Once it is observed that all source pool miners moved to positions longer than a particular branch, the source pool miners may not mine on this branch. That is, the branch is dead. We state this formally in the following lemma.

Lemma 6. *If some miner m observes that there is a branch BR such that the depth of the position of every source pool miner is greater than the length of BR, then BR is dead.*

Determining source pool miner positions directly from mined blocks in the blockchain is not always possible: some source pool miner, even if it is fair, may never mine a block if it keeps receiving longer branches. Instead, the below algorithm relies on miners directly reporting their positions. We call this algorithm KSM. Its code is shown in Algorithm 2. Similar to KPT, it maintains the blockchain tree T and a set of accept/reject labels per each block L. Besides those, KSM also maintains set P where it records the positions of all miners in the source pool. Each miner sends its collected positions together with the blockchain along all outgoing links. A block is rejected if all its branches are shorter than the known positions of the source pool miners. Note that non-source pool miners may still mine on the dead branches and extend them. However, since the source pool is closed and the source pool miners never see these non-source pool generated blocks, they are never added to the live branches. The block labeling is similar to KPT. Once the dead branches are determined and the rejected blocks are labeled, the blocks whose cousins are dead are accepted and confirmed. The correctness argument is similar to that of KPT. It is stated in Theorem 4.

Theorem 4. *Known Source Pool Membership Algorithm* KSM *solves the Blockchain Decision Problem with initially closed source pool.*

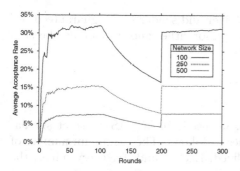
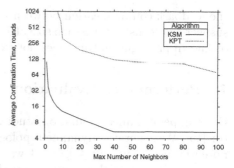

Fig. 2. Acceptance rate change as source pool membership is modified: complete network from rounds 0 to 99, 25% from 100 to 199, and complete network thereafter.

Fig. 3. Confirmation time vs. maximum neighborhood size.

Observe that in *KSM*, all miners know the source pool membership. Thus, a miner that is not in the source pool knows that all the blocks that it mines are rejected. So this miner may either not mine its own blocks at all or discard them as soon as they are mined.

6 Extensions and Optimizations

The algorithm presentation and discussion in the previous sections focused on simplicity. However, there are optimizations that can be implemented to make the algorithms more applicable and more generic. We are going to list them here.

In the previous section, we assumed that the pool is initially closed. However, both algorithms could be modified to operate correctly if there is a known upper bound when the source pool is closed. That is, all miners are aware of the round number after which there are no incoming links for source pool miners from non-source pool miners.

Also, we assumed that each miner is sending the entire copy of its blockchain. This is unnecessary. First, with no modifications, both algorithms operate correctly even if each miner sends only its longest branch. That is, the branch that it is currently mining on. However, further sending optimization is possible. Observe that the operation of the algorithms hinges on the miners communicating infinitely often. Thus, if a miner keeps track of the blocks it already sent, it is sufficient to send only the oldest, i.e. the deepest unsent block over each link. With this modification, the two algorithms, *KPT* and *KSM*, transmit only $\log N$ bytes in every message. That is, the two algorithms use constant size messages.

We assumed that link communication is instantaneous. However, the algorithms remain correct even if a message in each link is delayed arbitrarily long.

It is interesting to consider message loss. If there is fair message loss that allows ultimate progress, the two algorithms operate correctly if each miner sends the entire blockchain or the longest branch in every message. However, since the feedback communication between receiver and sender is not guaranteed, we suspect that constant message size algorithm for either known pool membership or known propagation time does not exist.

7   Performance Evaluation

For our performance evaluation studies, we used QUANTAS abstract simulator [19]. We generated dynamic topologies as follows. The maximum number of potential neighbors $mx \leq |N| - 1$ was fixed. Each round, for every miner, the number of actual neighbors was selected uniformly at random from 0 to mx; the neighbor identifiers were also selected randomly. Miners generated blocks at the rate of 2.5%.

In the first experiment, we studied the dynamics of block acceptance as the source pool membership changed. The results are shown in Fig. 2. We ran the computations for 300 rounds. In the first 100 rounds, the neighbors were selected from the whole network. That is, the complete network was the source pool. In the second 100 rounds, $\lfloor 25 \rfloor\%$ of miners were selected to be the source pool. Specifically, the source pool miners may connect to arbitrary neighbors, i.e. they have no connection restrictions. The remaining miners may connect only to non-source pool miners. In the remaining 100, the restrictions were lifted and all miners formed the single source pool again.

In a particular state of the computation, some block is accepted if it is in the longest branch of every miner. That is, every miner is mining on top of this block. The *acceptance rate* is the ratio of accepted vs. generated blocks. We ran experiments for the network size of 100, 250 and 500 miners. We did 10 experiments per network size and averaged our results.

The results indicate that, as the source pool size is restricted, the block acceptance rate declines. This is due to the source pool neighbors not receiving the blocks from non-source pool neighbors. The acceptance rate sharply rises as the source pool is enlarged to incorporate all miners and long chains of blocks mined outside the source pool are propagated throughout the network. The acceptance rate is lower in the networks of larger size. Indeed, as more concurrent blocks are generated, fewer of them are accepted.

In the next experiment, we observed how the neighborhood size affects the time it takes our algorithms to confirm the blocks. We implemented *KSM* and *KPT* and measured their confirmation time. The *confirmation time* for a particular block is the number of rounds from the round when the block was generated till the round when the last miner outputs the confirmation decision. We counted confirmation time for accepted blocks only. We varied the maximum number of neighbors mx and observed average confirmation time for *KSM* and *KPT*. The network size was 100, the source pool was fixed at 75 miners.

Algorithm *KPT*, needs maximum propagation time PT to be known in advance. To determine PT we ran preliminary computations. For a fixed mx, we computed PT by running 100 computations with this mx and computing the longest recorded propagation time. These preliminary computation lengths were set between 10, 000 and 15, 000 rounds. Then, for measurement computations, to collect sufficiently many confirmed blocks, we set computation lengths to $12 \cdot PT$ rounds. We ran 10 experiments per data point.

The results are shown in Fig. 3. They indicate that, as the maximum possible number of neighbors increases, the blocks are propagating faster and the confirmation time drops. Perhaps surprisingly, *KSM* performed better because each miner can confirm a block as soon as it receives the data from all the known source pool miners, while, in *KPT*, a miner has to wait for twice the maximum propagation time *PT*. This holds even though we ran preliminary computations to select the shortest possible maximum propagation time *PT*.

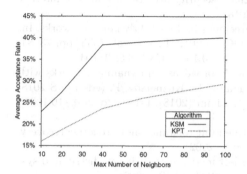
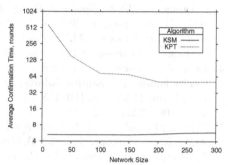

Fig. 4. Acceptance Rate vs. maximum neighborhood size.

Fig. 5. Confirmation time vs. network size.

For the same experiment, we computed average acceptance rate. We show the results in Fig. 4. Algorithm *KSM* has lower confirmation time and, therefore, higher acceptance rate. In the final experiment, we observed the performance of the two algorithms as the network scale changes. The number of source pool members is fixed at $\lfloor 75 \rfloor \%$ of the network size. The computation lengths were set to $12 \cdot PT$ rounds. We ran 10 computations per data point. The results are shown in Fig. 5. As the network scale increases, mx increases also. This increases the number of potential journeys and decreases *PT*, which, in turn, decreases the confirmation time of *KPT* that depends on *PT*. *KSM* exhibits the opposite dynamics. With larger scale, the number of source pool miners increases also. This makes *KSM* run slightly slower as every miner has to wait to hear from a greater number of source pool miners.

Our performance evaluation shows that *KSM* outperforms *KPT* under all conditions. Therefore, *KPT* should be considered only when the source pool membership is not available and *KSM* is not implementable.

8 Conclusion

In this paper we determine that Blockchain Decision Problem is, in general, not solvable in the dynamic network. To overcome this, the two algorithms that we present place rather strict assumptions on either membership or communication delay. This makes them similar to cooperative consensus. Weakening these assumptions and closing the gap between the impossible and the achievable that we establish in this paper is left to future studies.

References

1. Afek, Y., Gafni, E.: Asynchrony from synchrony. In: Frey, D., Raynal, M., Sarkar, S., Shyamasundar, R.K., Sinha, P. (eds.) ICDCN 2013. LNCS, vol. 7730, pp. 225–239. Springer, Heidelberg (2013). https://doi.org/10.1007/978-3-642-35668-1_16
2. Alphand, O., et al.: IoTChain: a blockchain security architecture for the internet of things. In: WCNC, pp. 1–6. IEEE (2018)
3. Biely, M., Robinson, P., Schmid, U.: Agreement in directed dynamic networks. In: Even, G., Halldórsson, M.M. (eds.) SIROCCO 2012. LNCS, vol. 7355, pp. 73–84. Springer, Heidelberg (2012). https://doi.org/10.1007/978-3-642-31104-8_7
4. Bonomi, S., Farina, G., Tixeuil, S.: Reliable broadcast in dynamic networks with locally bounded Byzantine failures. In: Izumi, T., Kuznetsov, P. (eds.) SSS 2018. LNCS, vol. 11201, pp. 170–185. Springer, Cham (2018). https://doi.org/10.1007/978-3-030-03232-6_12
5. Castro, M., Liskov, B.: Practical Byzantine fault tolerance and proactive recovery. ACM Trans. Comput. Syst. **20**(4), 398–461 (2002)
6. Charron-Bost, B., Schiper, A.: The heard-of model: computing in distributed systems with benign faults. Distrib. Comput. **22**(1), 49–71 (2009)
7. Cong, X., Zi, L., Du, D.-Z.: DTNB: a blockchain transaction framework with discrete token negotiation for the delay tolerant network. IEEE Trans. Netw. Sci. Eng. **8**(2), 1584–1599 (2021)
8. Coulouma, E., Godard, E., Peters, J.: A characterization of oblivious message adversaries for which consensus is solvable. TCS **584**, 80–90 (2015)
9. Grontas, P., Pagourtzis, A.: Blockchain, consensus, and cryptography in electronic voting. Homo Virtualis **2**(1), 79–100 (2019)
10. Guerraoui, R., Komatovic, J., Kuznetsov, P., Pignolet, Y.-A., Seredinschi, D.-A., Tonkikh, A.: Dynamic Byzantine reliable broadcast. In: 24th International Conference on Principles of Distributed Systems (2021)
11. Hood, K., Oglio, J., Nesterenko, M., Sharma, G.: Partitionable asynchronous cryptocurrency blockchain. In: 2021 IEEE International Conference on Blockchain and Cryptocurrency (ICBC), pp. 1–9. IEEE (2021)
12. Hu, Y., et al.: A delay-tolerant payment scheme based on the Ethereum blockchain. IEEE Access **7**, 33159–33172 (2019)
13. Kuhn, F., Lynch, N., Oshman, R.: Distributed computation in dynamic networks. In: Proceedings of the Forty-Second ACM Symposium on Theory of Computing, pp. 513–522 (2010)
14. Kuhn, F., Moses, Y., Oshman, R.: Coordinated consensus in dynamic networks. In: Proceedings of the 30th Annual ACM SIGACT-SIGOPS Symposium on Principles of Distributed Computing, pp. 1–10 (2011)
15. Lamport, L., Shostak, R., Pease, M.: The Byzantine generals problem. ACM Trans. Program. Lang. Syst. **4**(3), 382–401 (1982)
16. Michail, O., Chatzigiannakis, I., Spirakis, P.: New models for population protocols. Synth. Lect. Distrib. Comput. Theory **2**(1), 1–156 (2011)
17. Nakamoto, S.: Bitcoin: a peer-to-peer electronic cash system (2008)

18. O'Dell, R., Wattenhofer, R.: Information dissemination in highly dynamic graphs. In: Proceedings of the 2005 Joint Workshop on Foundations of Mobile Computing, pp. 104–110 (2005)
19. Oglio, J., Hood, K., Nesterenko, M., Tixeuil, S.: QUANTAS: quantitative user-friendly adaptable networked things abstract simulator. arXiv preprint arXiv:2205.04930 (2022)
20. Santoro, N., Widmayer, P.: Time is not a healer. In: Monien, B., Cori, R. (eds.) STACS 1989. LNCS, vol. 349, pp. 304–313. Springer, Heidelberg (1989). https://doi.org/10.1007/BFb0028994
21. Winkler, K., Schwarz, M., Schmid, U.: Consensus in rooted dynamic networks with short-lived stability. Distrib. Comput. **32**(5), 443–458 (2019). https://doi.org/10.1007/s00446-019-00348-0
22. Wood, G.: Ethereum: a secure decentralized generalized transaction ledger. Ethereum Project Yellow Paper **151**, 1–32 (2014)

Improving the Efficiency of Report and Trace Ring Signatures

Xavier Bultel[1]([✉]), Ashley Fraser[2], and Elizabeth A. Quaglia[3]

[1] INSA Centre Val de Loire, LIFO, Bourges, France
xavier.bultel@insa-cvl.fr
[2] Department of Computer Science, University of Surrey, Guildford, UK
[3] Information Security Group, Royal Holloway, University of London, London, UK

Abstract. Ring signatures allow signers to produce verifiable signatures and remain anonymous within a set of signers (i.e., the ring) while doing so. They are well-suited to protocols that target anonymity as a primary goal, for example, anonymous cryptocurrencies. However, standard ring signatures do not ensure that signers are held accountable if they act maliciously. Fraser and Quaglia (CANS'21) introduced a ring signature variant that they called report and trace ring signatures which balances the anonymity guarantee of standard ring signatures with the need to hold signers accountable. In particular, report and trace ring signatures introduce a reporting system whereby ring members can report malicious message/signature pairs. A designated tracer can then revoke the signer's anonymity if, and only if, a ring member submits a report to the tracer. Fraser and Quaglia present a generic construction of a report and trace ring signature scheme and outline an instantiation for which it is claimed that the complexity of signing is linear in the size of the ring $|R|$.

In this paper, we introduce a new instantiation of Fraser and Quaglia's generic report and trace ring signature construction. Our instantiation uses a pairing-based variant of ElGamal that we define. We demonstrate that our instantiation is more efficient. In fact, we highlight that the efficiency of Fraser and Quaglia's instantiation omits a scaling factor of λ where λ is a security parameter. As such, the complexity of signing for their instantiation grows linearly in $\lambda \cdot |R|$. Our instantiation, on the other hand, achieves signing complexity linear in $|R|$.

We also introduce a new pairing-free report and trace ring signature construction reaching a similar signing complexity. Whilst this construction requires some additional group exponentiations, it can be instantiated over any prime order group for which the Decisional Diffie-Hellman assumption holds.

1 Introduction

In the context of distributed systems, it is often necessary to balance the competing goals of anonymity and accountability. On the one hand, there is an

A. Fraser—Funded by EPSRC under the DECaDE project P/T022485/1.

S. Devismes et al. (Eds.): SSS 2022, LNCS 13751, pp. 130–145, 2022.
https://doi.org/10.1007/978-3-031-21017-4_9

expectation of privacy by the system's users; on the other, the system must be able to hold misuse accountable. The need to balance these goals is particularly true for cryptocurrencies, which are typically deployed atop a distributed ledger. Indeed, several cryptocurrencies target user anonymity as a primary security goal [3,12,23,24,28], ensuring that users can transact without revealing their identity. In particular, Monero [24] uses a ring signature [26], a cryptographic tool that allows users to sign transactions within a group of users known as the ring, thus ensuring that the signer is anonymous within the ring. However, using a standard ring signature means that tracing a fraudulent transactor is difficult. As such, Monero cannot provide a guarantee of accountability.

The notion of a standard ring signature has been extended to incorporate accountability. Specifically, Xu and Yung introduced accountable ring signatures [32], which introduce a designated tracer that can revoke the anonymity of signers. More recently, Fraser and Quaglia presented report and trace ring (RTR) signatures [14]. This new ring signature variant builds upon the functionality of accountable ring signatures, requiring that the designated tracer can revoke anonymity only if a ring member first sends a report of malicious behaviour to the designated tracer[1].

Report and Trace Ring Signatures. Similar to standard ring signatures, RTR signatures allow signers to generate signatures with respect to a group (i.e., ring) of users, and the signer is anonymous within the ring. Additionally, RTR signatures provide a mechanism whereby ring members can produce a report for a signed message. Upon receiving a report, a designated tracer can trace the signer's identity. Fraser and Quaglia defined report and trace ring signatures in [14], and provided a complete security model for the primitive. Accompanying this formalisation, the authors present a provably secure generic construction and concrete instantiation of an RTR signature.

With respect to the instantiation, we note two drawbacks that we aim to address. Firstly, the instantiation is not as efficient as claimed. In fact, during signing, the instantiation uses Stadler's zero-knowledge proof [30] to prove correct encryption of a reporter token. Stadler's proof must be repeated λ times to be secure, where λ is the security parameter. As such, the complexity of the proof is linear in the security parameter. The efficiency analysis of the instantiation presented in [14] omits the security parameter. That is, signing is claimed to be linear in the size of the ring $|R|$ but is, in fact, linear in $\lambda \cdot |R|$. Secondly, the instantiation relies on a number theoretical group. As a consequence, the instantiation does not reap the efficiency benefits of the most efficient groups such as those based on elliptical curves.

Our Contributions. This work addresses the limitations of the existing RTR signature instantiation. Namely, we introduce a new instantiation of the generic

---

[1] For simplicity, we also consider a single designated tracer in this work. We note, however, that this role can be distributed using standard secret sharing techniques, making it more suitable for decentralised applications.

construction in [14] (Sect. 4) that is more efficient than the instantiation in [14] with respect to signing. Then, we introduce a new RTR signature scheme construction (Sect. 5) that can be instantiated with any group for which the Decisional Diffie-Hellman assumption holds. Here, we provide a brief overview of our results.

In the generic construction of [14], during signing, the signer generates a reporter token that is encrypted to each ring member. The signer also generates a proof of correct encryption of the reporter token. In the instantiation of [14], this functionality is realised with standard ElGamal encryption and Stadler's zero-knowledge proof [30]. In this paper, we introduce a new instantiation which relies on a bespoke pairing-based variant of the ElGamal public-key encryption scheme. Furthermore, we demonstrate that the zero-knowledge proof of correct encryption, which requires proof of equality of pairings for our new variant, can be instantiated using the Fiat-Shamir transformation [13] on the variant of the Schnorr protocol from [10]. Accordingly, the complexity of signing for our instantiation grows linearly only in the size of the ring, improving upon the efficiency of the instantiation from [14]. In Sect. 3, we introduce our new pairing-based public-key encryption scheme and demonstrate how to prove correctness of encryption for our new scheme. We also discuss the security and efficiency of our instantiation.

We then propose a new RTR signature scheme construction in Sect. 5. This new scheme follows the syntax of an RTR signature, as outlined in Sect. 2, but differs from existing constructions, namely, the construction of [14]. Our new construction is pairing-free and can be instantiated with any group in which the Decisional Diffie Hellman assumption holds. Thus, our new construction allows for the use of more efficient and standard prime order groups (e.g., elliptic curves) than our instantiation (Sect. 4) and Fraser and Quaglia's instantiation [14]. We demonstrate that our new construction is secure and can be instantiated using standard cryptographic protocols from the literature. We conclude with a brief discussion of its efficiency, showing that although it requires more group exponentiations for signing and produces signatures that contain more group elements than our instantiation in Sect. 3, it achieves signing complexity that is linear in the size of the ring.

Other Related Work. Several ring signatures [26] variants aim to balance anonymity with accountability. As mentioned in introduction, accountable ring signatures [4,32] allow signers to generate ring signatures and remain anonymous within the ring, unless a designated tracer reveals the signer's identity. Moreover, linkable [22] and traceable [15] ring signatures allow tracers to determine whether two signatures are generated by the same, or different, users. Addressing the balance of anonymity and accountability has frequently arisen with respect to other cryptographic protocols. Notably, many group signature [9] variants introduce measures whereby signer anonymity can be revoked [19,20,27]. Additionally, anonymity and accountability has been discussed in relation to end-to-end encryption [31] and systems that permit the reporting of malicious, and perhaps criminal, behaviour [1,18,21,25].

2 Preliminaries

In this section, we define the notations and the tools that we use in this paper. More detailed and formal definitions are given in the full version of this paper [5]. We also recall the ElGamal encryption scheme and the IND-CPA security definition in the full version.

The Decisional Diffie-Hellman (DDH) assumption. Let $\mathbb{G} = \langle g \rangle$ be a group of prime order p. Picking $b \xleftarrow{\$} \{0,1\}$ and $(x, y, z_1) \xleftarrow{\$} (\mathbb{Z}_p^*)^3$, and setting $z_0 = a \cdot b$ and $(X, Y, Z) = (g^x, g^y, g^{z_b})$, the DDH assumption in $\mathbb{G}$ states that no Probabilistic Polynomial Time (PPT) algorithm is able to return b on input (X, Y, Z) with non-negligible advantage.

Non-interactive Zero-Knowledge Proof of Knowledge (NIZKP). Let $\mathcal{R}$ be a binary relation and let $\mathcal{L}$ be a language such that $s \in \mathcal{L} \Leftrightarrow (\exists w, (s, w) \in \mathcal{R})$. According to the Camenisch-Stadler notation [6], $\mathsf{NIZK}\{w : (s, w) \in \mathcal{R}\}$ denotes a NIZKP of w for the langage $\mathcal{L}$. A NIZKP is said to be extractable when there exists a PPT knowledge extractor that efficiently extracts a witness w from any PPT algorithm that forges valid proofs of knowledge for a given statement s such that $(s, w) \in \mathcal{R}$. Moreover, a NIZKP is said to be zero-knowledge when there exists a PPT simulator that takes a statement s as input and that produces proofs that are indistinguishable from those outputted by the real NIZKP protocol on s.

Signature of Knowledge (SoK). A SoK [7] on a message m, denoted by $\mathsf{SoK}_m\{w : (s, w) \in \mathcal{R}\}$, is similar to a NIZKP except that the message m is embedded in the proof. w is seen as a secret key and s as the corresponding public key. Since the knowledge of w is required to generate a valid SoK on a message m, a SoK is unforgeable, which is the standard security requirement the digital signatures.

3 Syntax and Security Model

We recall the syntax and security model of a report and trace ring (RTR) signature scheme as presented in [14]. In an RTR signature, users sign messages with respect to a ring. The signer cannot be identified (i.e., is anonymous within the ring) unless a ring member generates an anonymous report and transmits the report to the designated tracer, who can then reveal the signer's identity. We adopt the notation conventions of [14], writing T to denote the tracer and U to denote a user from a set of users $\mathcal{U}$.

Definition 1 (RTR signature). *An* RTR *signature scheme is a tuple of algorithms (*Setup, T.KGen, U.KGen, Sign, Verify, Report, Trace, VerTrace*) defined as follows:*

$\mathsf{Setup}(1^\lambda) \to pp$: On input security parameter 1^λ, outputs public parameters pp.

T.KGen(pp) → ($\mathsf{pk_T}, \mathsf{sk_T}$): On input pp, outputs a tracer public key $\mathsf{pk_T}$ and secret key $\mathsf{sk_T}$.

U.KGen(pp) → ($\mathsf{pk_U}, sk_U$): On input pp, outputs a user public key $\mathsf{pk_U}$ and secret key sk_U.

Sign($pp, sk_U, \mathsf{pk_T}, m, R$) → σ: On input pp, sk_U, $\mathsf{pk_T}$, message m and ring R, outputs a signature σ.

Verify($pp, \mathsf{pk_T}, m, R, \sigma$) → $\{0, 1\}$: On input pp, $\mathsf{pk_T}$, m, R and σ, outputs 1 if σ is a valid signature on m with respect to R, and 0 otherwise.

Report($pp, \mathsf{pk_T}, sk_U, m, R, \sigma$) → Rep: On input pp, $\mathsf{pk_T}$, sk_U, m, R and σ, outputs a reporter token Rep.

Trace($pp, sk_T, m, R, \sigma, \mathtt{Rep}$) → ($\mathsf{pk_U}, \mathtt{Tr}, \rho_t$): On input pp, sk_T, m, R, σ and Rep, outputs the signer's identity $\mathsf{pk_U}$, auxiliary information Tr consisting of the reporter token, and a proof of correct trace ρ_t.

VerTrace($pp, \mathsf{pk_T}, m, R, \sigma, \mathsf{pk_U}, \mathtt{Tr}, \rho_t$) → $\{0, 1\}$: On input pp, $\mathsf{pk_T}$, m, R, σ, $\mathsf{pk_U}$, Tr and ρ_t, outputs 1 if the trace is valid, and 0 otherwise.

An RTR signature must satisfy correctness and trace correctness. Informally, correctness requires that algorithm Verify outputs 1 if the signature is the output of algorithm Sign (and setup/key generation is honestly executed) with overwhelming probability. Trace correctness necessitates that algorithm VerTrace outputs the correct signer's identity for a signature output by algorithm Sign with overwhelming probability. Correctness and trace correctness for RTR signatures are introduced and formally defined in [14].

3.1 Security Model

RTR signatures must satisfy anonymity, unforgeability, non-frameability, trace soundness and reporter anonymity. These properties are defined in [14]. Here, we provide an overview of these properties, and present the detailed formal security model in the full version of this paper [5] for reference. The security experiments model an attacker that can register and corrupt/control users (i.e., obtain their honestly-generated secret keys/generate keys on their behalf), and generate signatures, reports and traces through access to several oracles. We present these oracles in detail in the full version [5]. alongside the formal definition of the security model.

Anonymity. Anonymity requires that, on the condition that a signature is not reported and the signer traced, a signature does not reveal the signer's identity. Anonymity for RTR signatures, as defined in [14], adjusts the definition of anonymity against adversarially generated keys in [2]. In doing so, it is assumed that the attacker can control users and reporters. However, the tracer is assumed to be honest. In the anonymity experiment, the adversary outputs a message, ring and two potential signers (who are assumed to be honest). The adversary obtains a signature and outputs a bit to indicate which signer produced the signature. An RTR signature is anonymous if the adversary cannot determine which of the two potential signers generated the signature.

Unforgeability. Unforgeability for RTR signatures is adapted from the standard definition of unforgeability for ring signatures presented in [2]. It requires that an attacker cannot produce a valid ring signature on behalf of a member of an honest ring. An attacker is assumed to control the tracer, and can corrupt and control users. In the security experiment, the adversary outputs a message, ring and signature (which is not obtained via a signing oracle). If the signature is valid, we say that the adversary has produced a valid forgery. An RTR signature scheme satisfies unforgeability if the adversary cannot construct a valid forgery.

Non-frameability. Intuitively, non-frameability captures the property that a non-signer cannot be identified as the signer by the designated tracer. The formal non-frameability experiment models an attacker that can control the tracer, and can corrupt and control signers. The adversary outputs a message, ring, signature and trace, where the traced signer is assumed to be honest. An RTR signature scheme satisfies non-frameability if algorithm VerTrace returns 0.

Trace Soundness. In [4], trace soundness was introduced as a new security property for accountable ring signatures. Trace soundness states that the signer identified by the tracer must be unique. In other words, two users can be verifiably identified as signers. In [14], the trace soundness property is adapted to the syntax of an RTR signature, and, like the original definition in [4], models an attacker that controls the tracer and can corrupt and control all signers. In the formal security experiment, the adversary outputs two traces (where each trace identifies a different ring member as the signer) alongside a message, ring and signature. The trace soundness property is satisfied if algorithm VerTrace does not output 1 for both traces.

Reporter Anonymity. Reporter anonymity requires that a report does not reveal the ring member that produced it, if it is assumed that the reporter is honest. The attacker can control the tracer and corrupt/control a subset of users. In the reporter anonymity experiment, the adversary outputs a message, ring, signature and the two ring members (i.e., two potential reporters). The adversary obtains a report and outputs a bit to indicate which reporter generated the report. An RTR signature satisfies reporter anonymity if the adversary cannot determine which reporter produced the report.

4 An Efficient Instantiation of Fraser and Quaglia's Protocol

Fraser and Quaglia present a generic construction for an RTR signature in [14]. We provide a brief intuition into their construction here and refer the reader to [14] for full details. During key generation, users (i.e., ring members) and the tracer generate a keypair for a public-key encryption (PKE) scheme. To sign a message, signers generate a fresh key pair for a PKE scheme. The fresh secret key is known as the reporter token. The reporter token is encrypted under the public key of each ring member. Then, the signer encrypts their identity under the public key of the tracer and then again under the fresh public key. The signer also constructs a zero-knowledge proof (NIZK) that the reporter token is encrypted to all ring members, and a signature of knowledge (SoK) that the signer's identity is encrypted to the tracer. Ring members can report signatures by decrypting the reporter token using their decryption key for the PKE scheme. A tracer can decrypt the signer's identity using their decryption key and the reporter token.

Fraser and Quaglia also present a concrete instantiation of their construction. A central requirement of their construction is that the signer must prove that a ciphertext encrypts a secret key (i.e., the reporter token) that corresponds to a given public key. Fraser and Quaglia propose to instantiate their construction with the original ElGamal cryptosystem and Stadler's zero-knowledge proof [30], which ensures that an ElGamal ciphertext encrypts a discrete logarithm in a zero-knowledge way. However, this approach has two drawbacks. Firstly, Stadler's proof has complexity linear in the security parameter as the proof must be repeated λ times. Secondly, the proof only works for number-theoretic groups of prime order, and cannot be extended to groups based on elliptic curves.

In what follows, we propose an instantiation of Fraser and Quaglia's construction using a variant of ElGamal based on bilinear maps, overcoming the first drawback (we address the second drawback in Sect. 5). Our new instantiation differs from Fraser and Quaglia's instantiation in the following respect. We use our ElGamal variant to generate the reporter token and encrypt the signer's identity under the reporter token. Then, we modify the zero-knowledge proof for our ElGamal variant. In all other respects, our instantiation is identical. In particular, we use a one-way function to generate the signer's public identity, the SoK of [4], and we use standard ElGamal encryption to encrypt the reporter token to the ring members and the signer's identity to the tracer. Now, we introduce our new ElGamal variant, and then discuss the security and efficiency of our new instantiation.

4.1 A Pairing-Based ElGamal Variant

Let $\mathbb{G}_1$, $\mathbb{G}_2$ and $\mathbb{G}_t$ be groups of prime order p, $g_1 \in \mathbb{G}_1$ and $g_2 \in \mathbb{G}_2$ be generators, and $e : \mathbb{G}_1 \times \mathbb{G}_2 \to \mathbb{G}_t$ be a type-3 bilinear pairing. We first recall the standard ElGamal cryptosystem in $\mathbb{G}_1$, which is used by each ring member to generate their key pair and is specified as follows.

- Choose secret key $\mathsf{sk_{PKE}} \in \mathbb{Z}_p^*$ and let public key $\mathsf{pk_{PKE}} = g_1^{\mathsf{sk_{PKE}}}$.
- To encrypt a message m with randomness r, run $\mathsf{PKE.Enc}(\mathsf{pk_{PKE}}, m; r)$, which retruns $(c_1, c_2) = (g_1^r, \mathsf{pk_{PKE}}^r \cdot m)$.
- To decrypt, run $\mathsf{PKE.Dec}(\mathsf{sk_{PKE}}, (c_1, c_2))$, which returns $m = \frac{c_2}{c_1^{\mathsf{sk_{PKE}}}}$.

Our new ElGamal variant, used by the signer during the signature algorithm to generate a fresh PKE key pair, is defined as follows.

- Generate fresh secret key $\mathsf{sk_{Sign}} \in \mathbb{G}_1$ and define the fresh public key as $\mathsf{pk_{Sign}} = e(\mathsf{sk_{Sign}}, g_2)$.
- $\mathsf{PKE.Enc}(\mathsf{pk_{Sign}}, m; r)$ returns $(c_1, c_2) = (g_2^r, \mathsf{pk_{Sign}^r} \cdot m)$.
- $\mathsf{PKE.Dec}(\mathsf{sk_{Sign}}, c)$ returns $m = \frac{c_2}{e(\mathsf{sk_{Sign}}, c_1)}$.

Note that anyone can transform a ciphertext $(c_1, c_2) = (g_2^r, \mathsf{pk_{Sign}^r} \cdot m)$ of this ElGamal variant into a standard ElGamal ciphertext in $\mathbb{G}_t$ by computing $(e(g_1, c_1), c_2)$.

We show the following result.

Theorem 1. *The proposed variant of ElGamal satisfies* $\mathsf{IND\text{-}CPA}$ *security under the Decisional Diffie-Hellman (DDH) assumption in* $\mathbb{G}_2$.

Proof. Assume that there exists a Probabilistic Polynomial Time (PPT) adversary $\mathcal{A}$ that breaks the $\mathsf{IND\text{-}CPA}$ security of our ElGamal variant with a non-negligible advantage $\epsilon_{\mathcal{A}}(\lambda)$. We show how to build a PPT adversary $\mathcal{B}$ that breaks the DDH assumption in $\mathbb{G}_2$ with a non-negligible advantage $\epsilon_{\mathcal{B}}(\lambda)$ (where λ is the security parameter used to generate $\mathbb{G}_2$).

$\mathcal{B}$ receives the DDH challenge $(X, Y, Z) = (g_2^x, g_2^y, g_2^{z_b})$ and picks $b' \xleftarrow{\$} \{0, 1\}$. It sets $\mathsf{pk_{Sign}} \leftarrow e(g_1, X)$ and sends it to $\mathcal{A}$, which returns a pair of chosen plaintexts (m_0, m_1). $\mathcal{B}$ computes $c_1 \leftarrow Y$ and $c_2 = e(g_1, Z) \cdot m_{b'}$. It sends (c_1, c_2) to $\mathcal{A}$, which returns b''. If $b' = b''$, then $\mathcal{B}$ returns 0, else it returns 1.

We remark that $c_1 = Y = g_2^y$, and $c_2 = e(g_1, Z) \cdot m_{b'} = e(g_1, g_2)^{z_b} \cdot m_{b'}$. If $b = 0$, then $c_2 = e(g_1, g_2)^{x \cdot y} \cdot m_{b'} = e(g_1, g_2^x)^y \cdot m_{b'} = e(g_1, X)^y \cdot m_{b'} = \mathsf{pk_{Sign}^y} \cdot m_{b'}$. In this case, the $\mathsf{IND\text{-}CPA}$ experiment is perfectly simulated for $\mathcal{A}$, so $\mathcal{A}$ returns $b'' = b'$ with the non-negligible advantage $\epsilon_{\mathcal{A}}(\lambda)$. If $b = 1$, then $c_2 = e(g_1, g_2)^{z_1} \cdot m_{b'}$ seems to be random from the point of view of $\mathcal{A}$. In this case, $\mathcal{A}$ has no information about b', so it returns $b'' = b'$ with probability $1/2$ (its advantage is null). Finally, $\epsilon_{\mathcal{B}}(\lambda) = \epsilon_{\mathcal{A}}(\lambda)/2$, so $\epsilon_{\mathcal{B}}(\lambda)$ is non-negligible, which concludes the proof. $\qquad\square$

We will now show how to prove that an ElGamal ciphertext in $\mathbb{G}_1$ encrypts a secret key of our ElGamal variant in a zero-knowledge way. We consider the key pair of our ElGamal variant $\mathsf{sk_{Sign}} \in \mathbb{G}_1$ and $\mathsf{pk_{Sign}} = e(\mathsf{sk_{Sign}}, g_2)$, and the ciphertext $(c_1, c_2) = (g_1^r, \mathsf{pk_{PKE}^r} \cdot \mathsf{sk_{Sign}}) \in \mathbb{G}_1^2$ which encrypts $\mathsf{sk_{Sign}}$ with the public key $\mathsf{pk_{PKE}}$.

We have to prove that $\mathsf{pk_{Sign}} = e\left(\mathsf{PKE.Dec}(pp_{\mathsf{PKE}}, \mathsf{sk_{PKE}}, (c_1, c_2)), g_2\right)$. We have the following equivalences:

$$\mathsf{pk_{Sign}} = e\left(\mathsf{PKE.Dec}(pp_{\mathsf{PKE}}, \mathsf{sk_{PKE}}, (c_1, c_2)), g_2\right)$$

$$\Leftrightarrow \mathsf{pk_{Sign}} = e\left(\frac{c_2}{c_1^{\mathsf{sk_{PKE}}}}, g_2\right) = \frac{e(c_2, g_2)}{e\left(c_1^{\mathsf{sk_{PKE}}}, g_2\right)} = \frac{e(c_2, g_2)}{e\left(g_1^{r \cdot \mathsf{sk_{PKE}}}, g_2\right)} = \frac{e(c_2, g_2)}{e(\mathsf{pk_{PKE}}, g_2)^r}$$

$$\Leftrightarrow e(\mathsf{pk_{PKE}}, g_2)^r = \left(\frac{e(c_2, g_2)}{\mathsf{pk_{Sign}}}\right)$$

On the other hand, we have $e(c_1, g_2) = e(g_1^r, g_2) = e(g_1, g_2)^r$. Finally, in order to prove that the ElGamal ciphertext in $\mathbb{G}_1$ encrypts the secret key of our ElGamal variant in zero-knowledge, we have to prove the following relation, knowing r:

$$\mathsf{NIZK}\left\{ r : e(c_1, g_2) = e(g_1, g_2)^r \wedge e\left(\mathsf{pk}_{\mathsf{PKE}}, g_2\right)^r = \left(\frac{e\left(c_2, g_2\right)}{\mathsf{pk}_{\mathsf{Sign}}}\right) \right\} \qquad (1)$$

This is a proof of discrete logarithm equality in $\mathbb{G}_t$. This zero-knowledge proof can be instantiated with the Fiat-Shamir transform [13] on the variant of the Schnorr protocol given in [10].

4.2 Discussion

We propose to use the above encryptions and NIZK proof to build an *efficient* RTR signature scheme following the generic construction in [14]. We recall that in a type 3 pairing, the DDH assumption holds in $\mathbb{G}_1$, $\mathbb{G}_2$, and $\mathbb{G}_t$, which implies that any construction based on the discrete logarithm assumption, the computational Diffie-Hellman assumption, or the decisional Diffie-Hellman assumption remains secure in each of these groups. The construction of Fraser and Quaglia uses only discrete logarithm-based building blocks, so it remains secure in our new pairing setup. Moreover, in order to prove relations among different elements of the signature, this construction uses Schnorr-based proofs of discrete logarithm relation and discrete logarithm knowledge, which work in any group of prime order, even when the relation is proved over different groups of the same order. Since our new encryption instantiation keep the structure of ElGamal, the other zero-knowledge proofs can be instantiated as in [14].

The NIZK proof outlined above is more efficient than the NIZK used in the instantiation in [14]. More specifically, the above NIZK proof requires a constant number of group exponentiations and pairings[2] (2 and 3, respectively) to prove. Similarly, verification of the NIZK proof requires 4 group exponentiations and 3 pairings. The size of the proof is also constant in size: it consists of 2 group elements and 1 field element. Comparatively, the size of the NIZK proof used in Fraser and Quaglia's instantiation, and the computational costs associated with proving and verification, are linear in $|R| \cdot \lambda$ (where λ is the security parameter). With respect to other costs associated with signing and verification, the two instantiations are identical, as shown above. As such, with respect to signature generation and verification, our instantiation has linear space and time complexity in the size of the ring. Therefore, our approach implies that the generic construction can be instantiated more efficiently than originally proposed, *i.e.*, avoiding the linear increase in the security parameter.

To conclude, as a consequence of the security proofs for the generic construction in [14], our pairing instantiation is secure if our new ElGamal variant satisfies

---

[2] According to [8], type 3 pairings are more efficient than type 1 and 2 pairings, and the computation time of a type 3 pairing is equivalent to 4 exponentiations for the best implementation.

IND-CPA security [16] and our NIZK proof of correct encryption (Eq. 1) satisfies completeness, knowledge soundness and zero-knowledge, as defined in [17]. As such, our instantiation satisfies the RTR signature security model.

5   A New **RTR** Signature Construction

In this section, we present a new RTR signature construction. We describe our protocol and present an instantiation. We conclude this section with a security analysis of our protocol and a brief discussion of its efficiency.

5.1   Description of Our Protocol

We outline our protocol following the syntax of an RTR scheme introduced in Definition 1.

Setup and Key Generation. Our construction uses ElGamal-based keys. Each ElGamal encryption key ek is provided together with a proof of knowledge π of the corresponding secret key sk. We will see why these proofs of knowledge are required later in this section. The public key is the pair $\mathsf{pk} = (\mathsf{ek}, \pi)$ and the secret key is sk. We use the part ek of the user public key as their identity.

$\mathsf{Setup}(1^\lambda)$: Generates a prime order group setup $pp = (\mathbb{G}, p, g)$ such that the Decisional Diffie-Hellman assumption holds in $\mathbb{G}$.

$\mathsf{T.KGen}(pp)$: Picks $\mathsf{sk_T} \xleftarrow{\$} \mathbb{Z}_p^*$, sets $\mathsf{ek_T} \leftarrow g^{\mathsf{sk_T}}$, sets $\pi_\mathsf{T} \leftarrow \mathsf{NIZK}\left\{\mathsf{sk_T} : \mathsf{ek_T} = g^{\mathsf{sk_T}}\right\}$ and outputs $\mathsf{pk_T} \leftarrow (\mathsf{ek_T}, \pi_\mathsf{T})$.

$\mathsf{U.KGen}(pp)$: Picks $\mathsf{sk_U} \xleftarrow{\$} \mathbb{Z}_p^*$, sets $\mathsf{ek_U} \leftarrow g^{\mathsf{sk_U}}$, sets $\pi_\mathsf{U} \leftarrow \mathsf{NIZK}\left\{\mathsf{sk_U} : \mathsf{ek_U} = g^{\mathsf{sk_U}}\right\}$ and outputs $\mathsf{pk_U} \leftarrow (\mathsf{ek_U}, \pi_\mathsf{U})$.

Signature Generation and Verification. The idea of the signature is to separate the public key ek of the signer into two shares S_1 and S_2 such that $S_1 \cdot S_2 = \mathsf{ek}$. The signer picks a coin α at random and uses it to encrypt (using ElGamal) S_2 for each public encryption key ek_i in the ring, outputting $|R|$ ciphertexts denoted c_i. The signer then encrypts S_1 for the tracer encryption key $\mathsf{ek_T}$, outputting ciphertext c. The signer then proves that the ring members' ciphertexts encrypt the same message in zero-knowledge. Note that due to the homomorphic properties of ElGamal, each $c_i \cdot c$ encrypts $S_1 \cdot S_2 = \mathsf{ek}$. Finally, the signer signs the message using a signature of knowledge that proves in zero-knowledge that it knows the secret key sk_i for a secret index i (which is its own secret key $\mathsf{sk}_i = \mathsf{sk_U}$) that decrypts $c_i \cdot c$ on the message $\mathsf{ek}_i = \mathsf{ek_U}$.

$\mathsf{Sign}(pp, \mathsf{sk_U}, \mathsf{pk_T}, m, R)$: Parses $\mathsf{pk_T}$ as $(\mathsf{ek_T}, \pi_\mathsf{T})$. Sets $n \leftarrow |R|$, parses R as $\{\mathsf{pk}_i\}_{i=1}^n$ and each pk_i as (ek_i, π_i). Verifies each π_i (this step preempts a subtle attack on anonymity that we will detail later). If there are two indices i and j such that $\mathsf{pk}_i \neq \mathsf{pk}_j$ and $\mathsf{ek}_i = \mathsf{ek}_j$, or if there is no index i such that $\mathsf{pk_U} = \mathsf{pk}_i$, then it aborts and returns the failure symbol $\perp$. Picks

$\alpha \xleftarrow{\$} \mathbb{Z}_p^*$ and sets $h \leftarrow g^\alpha$. Picks $S_1 \xleftarrow{\$} \mathbb{G}$ and sets $S_2 \leftarrow \mathsf{ek_U}/S_1$. Note that S_1 and S_2 are two shares of the secret identity $\mathsf{ek_U} = S_1 \cdot S_2$. Sets $c \leftarrow \mathsf{ek_T}^\alpha \cdot S_1$. For each $i \in [\![n]\!]$, sets $c_i \leftarrow \mathsf{ek}_i^\alpha \cdot S_2$, if $i > 1$, then sets $\pi_i' \leftarrow \mathsf{NIZK}\left\{\alpha : \left(h = g^\alpha \wedge \left(\frac{c_i}{c_{i-1}}\right) = \left(\frac{\mathsf{ek}_i}{\mathsf{ek}_{i-1}}\right)^\alpha\right)\right\}$, else $\pi_i' \leftarrow \perp$.
The proofs π_i' ensure that each ElGamal ciphertext (h, c_i) encrypts the same message. Note that $(h, c \cdot c_i)$ is the ElGamal encryption of $S_1 \cdot S_2 = \mathsf{ek_U}$ for the public key $(\mathsf{ek_T} \cdot \mathsf{ek}_i)$. Sets $M \leftarrow (pp, \mathsf{pk_T}, m, R, h, c, (c_i, \pi_i')_{i=1}^n)$, and sets $\sigma_M \leftarrow \mathsf{SoK}_M\left\{(\alpha, \mathsf{sk_U}) : \bigvee_{i=1}^n \left(h = g^\alpha \wedge \frac{c \cdot c_i}{\mathsf{ek}_i} = (\mathsf{ek_T} \cdot \mathsf{ek}_i)^\alpha \wedge \mathsf{ek}_i = g^{\mathsf{sk_U}}\right)\right\}$.
The signature of knowledge σ_M ensures that $(h, c \cdot c_i)$ is an ElGamal encryption of one ek_i, and that the signer knows the secret key corresponding to ek_i, which means that ek_i is the identity of the signer. Finally, the algorithm returns $\sigma = (h, c, (c_i, \pi_i')_{i=1}^n, \sigma_M)$.
$\mathsf{Verify}(pp, \mathsf{pk_T}, m, R, \sigma)$: Verify each π_i and σ_M.

Note that, if the keys are honestly generated, the probability that the signature aborts because two encryption keys ek_i and ek_j are equal is negligible.

Report and Trace. To report a signature, a user decrypts the ciphertext c_i that corresponds to their public key in order to learn S_2, and proves the correctness of the decryption using a zero-knowledge proof. To trace the signature, the tracer decrypts c in order to learn S_1, proves the correctness of the decryption using a zero-knowledge proof, and returns the identity that corresponds to the encryption key $\mathsf{ek} = S_1 \cdot S_2$.

$\mathsf{Report}(pp, \mathsf{pk_T}, \mathsf{sk_U}, m, R, \sigma)$: Verifies the signature σ. Sets $n \leftarrow |R|$, parses R as $\{\mathsf{pk}_i\}_{i=1}^n$ and each pk_i as (ek_i, π_i). Let j be the index that verifies $\mathsf{pk}_j = (\mathsf{ek_U}, \pi_j)$. Parses σ as $(h, c, (c_i, \pi_i')_{i=1}^n, \sigma_M)$. Sets $S_2 \leftarrow c_j/h^{\mathsf{sk_U}}$ and $\pi_{\mathsf{Rep}} \leftarrow \mathsf{NIZK}\left\{\mathsf{sk_U} : \bigvee_{i=1}^n \left(\left(\frac{c_i}{S_2}\right) = h^{\mathsf{sk_U}} \wedge \mathsf{ek}_i = g^{\mathsf{sk_U}}\right)\right\}$. The proofs π_{Rep} ensures that one (h, c_i) encrypts S_2. This algorithm returns $\mathsf{Rep} \leftarrow (S_2, \pi_{\mathsf{Rep}})$

$\mathsf{Trace}(pp, \mathsf{sk_T}, m, R, \sigma, \mathsf{Rep})$: Verifies the signature σ. Parses Rep as $(S_2, \pi_{\mathsf{Rep}})$ and σ as $(h, c, (c_i, \pi_i')_{i=1}^n, \sigma_M)$. Verifies the proof π_{Rep}. Sets $S_1 \leftarrow c/h^{\mathsf{sk_T}}$, and $\pi_{\rho_t} \leftarrow \mathsf{NIZK}\left\{\mathsf{sk_T} : \left(\frac{c}{S_1}\right) = h^{\mathsf{sk_T}} \wedge \mathsf{ek_T} = g^{\mathsf{sk_T}}\right\}$.
The proof π_{ρ_t} ensures that one (h, c) encrypts S_1. This algorithm returns $\rho_t \leftarrow (S_1, \pi_{\rho_t})$

$\mathsf{VerTrace}(pp, \mathsf{pk_T}, m, R, \sigma, \mathsf{pk_U}, \mathsf{Tr}, \rho_t):]$ Sets $n \leftarrow |R|$, parses R as $\{\mathsf{pk}_i\}_{i=1}^n$ and each pk_i as (ek_i, π_i). Verifies π_{Rep} and π_{ρ_t}. If one of these proofs is not valid, then it returns the failure symbol $\perp$, else it returns the key pk_i that verifies $\mathsf{ek}_i = S_1 \cdot S_2$.

Instantiation. In the following, we propose an instantiation for each of the proofs and signatures of knowledge used in our protocol. The proof $\mathsf{NIZK}\{x : h = g^x\}$ used in π_U and π_T can be instantiated with the Fiat-Shamir transform on the Schnorr protocol [29]. The proof

NIZK $\{x : h_1 = g_1^x \wedge h_2 = g_2^x\}$ used in π_{ρ_t} and each π_i' can be instantiated with the Fiat-Shamir transform on the variant of the Schnorr protocol given in [10]. The proof NIZK $\{x : \bigvee_{i=1}^n (h_{i,1} = g_{i,1}^x \wedge h_{i,2} = g_{i,2}^x)\}$ used in π_{Rep} can be instantiated with the Cramer-Damgård-Schoenmakers transform [11] (which transforms a zero-knowledge proof of a statement into a zero-knowledge proof of 1-out-of-n statements) and the Fiat-Shamir transform applied on the variant of the Schnorr protocol given in [10]. Finally, the proof NIZK $\{(x,y) : \bigvee_{i=1}^n (h_{i,1} = g_{i,1}^x \wedge h_{i,2} = g_{i,2}^x \wedge h_{i,3} = g_{i,3}^y)\}$ used in σ_M can be instantiated with the Fiat-Shamir transform and the Cramer-Damgård-Schoenmakers transform [11] applied on the successive executions of the Schnorr protocol [29] and the variant of the Schnorr protocol given in [10]. To transform this proof into a signature of knowledge, it suffices to add the message to the hashed elements during the creation of the challenge (this method works with any protocol resulting from the Fiat-Shamir transform [7]).

All these proofs of knowledge use only group operations and do not require any specific tool to be instantiated. The non-interactive version of the proofs and the signature of knowledge require a hash function modeled by a random oracle.

5.2   Security Analysis

Our new construction satisfies the security properties for an RTR signature scheme and, as such, we obtain Theorem 2. The formal proof of this theorem is given in the full version of this paper [5] and we informally explain why these properties hold here.

Theorem 2. *Our protocol instantiated with extractable and zero-knowledge proofs and signatures of knowledge is unforgeable, anonymous, non-frameable, trace sound, and reporter anonymous under the Decisional Diffie-Hellman assumption in the standard model.*

Unforgeability: To forge a signature, an adversary must forge a signature of knowledge σ_M, which requires the knowledge of one of the secret keys of the ring, which is the discrete logarithm of one of the public encryption keys. If an adversary produces such a signature, then the extractor of the signature of knowledge can be used to break the discrete logarithm assumption (which is hard under the Decisional Diffie-Hellman assumption).

Anonymity: To deduce the identity of the signer, the share S_1 of the signer identity is required by the adversary. This share is encrypted using the ElGamal encryption on the honest tracer public key. Thus, breaking the anonymity is at least as difficult as breaking the IND-CPA security of ElGamal, which depends on the Decisional Diffie-Hellman assumption.

Trace soundness: The proofs and signatures of knowledge ensure that the identity of the signer ek is actually $S_1 \cdot S_2$ (from σ_M), each c_i encrypts the same S_2 (from π_i'), the reporter returns S_2 (from π_{Rep}), and the tracer returns S_1 (from π_{ρ_t}). If an adversary is able to report the same signature for two different identities, then it forges a proof on a false statement that cannot be correctly extracted, which contradicts the extractability.

Non-frameability: As it is shown for the trace soundness, the proofs ensure that the report and trace mechanism are sound. Thus, to attack non-frameability the adversary must produce a fresh valid and traceable signature for an honest user. As for unforgeability, such an adversary can be used to extract the discrete logarithm of the public encryption key of an honest user, which is hard under the Decisional Diffie-Hellman assumption.

Reporter anonymity: Each reporter returns the same S_2 (according to the proofs of knowledge that we use in the protocol), and a zero-knowledge proof that gives no information about their identity. Therefore, an adversary cannot deduce the identity of the reporter.

The Role of the Zero-Knowledge Proofs on the Public Keys. We recall that each public key is associated with a proof of correctness, and that these proofs are verified before each signature. In what follows, we will show that this mechanism avoids a subtle attack on anonymity. Assume that the users do not prove the knowledge of their secret keys (*i.e.* $\mathsf{pk} = \mathsf{ek}$). In this case, an attacker $\mathcal{A}$ can break the anonymity of our construction using the following attack. $\mathcal{A}$ chooses the public keys $(\mathsf{pk}_0, \mathsf{pk}_1)$ of two honest users, picks $\mathsf{sk}_2 \xleftarrow{\$} \mathbb{Z}_p^*$, sets $\mathsf{ek}_2 \leftarrow g^{\mathsf{sk}_2}$, and sets $\mathsf{pk}_2 \leftarrow \mathsf{ek}_2$. $\mathcal{A}$ then picks $\gamma \xleftarrow{\$} \mathbb{Z}_p^*$, sets $\mathsf{ek}_3 \leftarrow \mathsf{ek}_\mathsf{T}^\gamma$, and sets $\mathsf{pk}_3 \leftarrow \mathsf{ek}_3$. $\mathcal{A}$ chooses a message m, sets $R \leftarrow \{\mathsf{pk}_0, \mathsf{pk}_1, \mathsf{pk}_2, \mathsf{pk}_3\}$ sends $(m, R, \mathsf{pk}_0, \mathsf{pk}_1, st)$ to the challenger, and receives a signature $\sigma = (h, c, (c_i, \pi_i')_{i=1}^n, \sigma_M)$. Since σ has been generated correctly, we have that $c = \mathsf{ek}_\mathsf{T}^\alpha \cdot S_1$ and $\forall\, i, c_i = \mathsf{ek}_i^\alpha \cdot S_2$ (where α denotes the discrete logarithm of h). $\mathcal{A}$ computes $S_2 \leftarrow c_2/h^{\mathsf{sk}_2}$ and $S_1' \leftarrow c/\left(\frac{c_3}{S_2}\right)^{\frac{1}{\gamma}}$. If $S_1' \cdot S_2 = \mathsf{ek}_0$, then $\mathcal{A}$ returns 0, else if $S_1' \cdot S_2 = \mathsf{ek}_1$, then $\mathcal{A}$ returns 1. We observe that:

$$S_1' = \frac{c}{\left(\frac{c_3}{S_2}\right)^{\frac{1}{\gamma}}} = \frac{\mathsf{ek}_\mathsf{T}^\alpha \cdot S_1}{\left(\frac{\mathsf{ek}_3^\alpha \cdot S_2}{S_2}\right)^{\frac{1}{\gamma}}} = \frac{\mathsf{ek}_\mathsf{T}^\alpha \cdot S_1}{(\mathsf{ek}_3^\alpha)^{\frac{1}{\gamma}}} = \frac{\mathsf{ek}_\mathsf{T}^\alpha \cdot S_1}{((\mathsf{ek}_\mathsf{T}^\gamma)^\alpha)^{\frac{1}{\gamma}}} = \frac{\mathsf{ek}_\mathsf{T}^\alpha \cdot S_1}{\mathsf{ek}_\mathsf{T}^{\alpha \cdot \frac{\gamma}{\gamma}}} = \frac{\mathsf{ek}_\mathsf{T}^\alpha \cdot S_1}{\mathsf{ek}_\mathsf{T}^\alpha} = S_1.$$

Thus, $S_1' \cdot S_2$ gives the identity of the signer with probability 1.

Efficiency of Our Protocol and Comparison. Similarly to our instantiation in Sect. 4, the protocol presented and instantiated in Sect. 5.1 has space and time complexity that is linear in the size of the ring. More explicitly, a signature can be computed with $11|R| - 3$ group exponentiations and verified with $10|R| - 4$ group exponentiations. A signature consists of $6|R|$ group elements and $4|R| - 2$ field elements. On the other hand, in our instantiation in Sect. 4, a signature can be computed with $5|R| + 21$ group exponentiations and 4 pairings, and verified with $3|R| + 23$ group exponentiations and 3 pairings. A signature consists of $2|R| + 20$ group elements and $|R| + 7$ field elements. Thus, our instantiation from Sect. 4 requires less group exponentiations, moreover, it generates reporter tokens of constant size, while the size of the tokens grows linearly with the number of users in the new construction. In return, our new construction can be instantiated with any prime order group, including pairing-free groups based on elliptic curves, which are known to optimize the size of the group elements and the computation cost of the operations for an equivalent level of security.

6 Concluding Remarks

We introduced a new instantiation of an RTR signature scheme that follows the generic construction in [14]. Our instantiation has space and time complexity linear in the size of the ring. Consequently, our instantiation significantly increases the efficiency of the construction in [14], but requires pairings. We also introduce a new RTR signature construction with similar complexity that does not require pairings and can be instantiated with any prime order group. In return, our construction requires more group exponentiations than our instantiation of [14]. An interesting open question is whether it is possible to design an RTR signature that simultaneously reaps the benefits of our instantiation and new construction. That is, we ask, is it possible to design an RTR signature that is (at least) as efficient as our instantiation of the construction from [14] *and* can be instantiated with any group?

References

1. Arun, V., Kate, A., Garg, D., Druschel, P., Bhattacharjee, B.: Finding safety in numbers with secure allegation escrows. In: The Network and Distributed System Security Symposium. Internet Society (2020)
2. Bender, A., Katz, J., Morselli, R.: Ring signatures: stronger definitions, and constructions without random oracles. In: Halevi, S., Rabin, T. (eds.) TCC 2006. LNCS, vol. 3876, pp. 60–79. Springer, Heidelberg (2006). https://doi.org/10.1007/11681878_4
3. Bonneau, J., Narayanan, A., Miller, A., Clark, J., Kroll, J.A., Felten, E.W.: Mixcoin: anonymity for bitcoin with accountable mixes. In: Christin, N., Safavi-Naini, R. (eds.) FC 2014. LNCS, vol. 8437, pp. 486–504. Springer, Heidelberg (2014). https://doi.org/10.1007/978-3-662-45472-5_31
4. Bootle, J., Cerulli, A., Chaidos, P., Ghadafi, E., Groth, J., Petit, C.: Short accountable ring signatures based on DDH. In: Pernul, G., Ryan, P.Y.A., Weippl, E. (eds.) ESORICS 2015. LNCS, vol. 9326, pp. 243–265. Springer, Cham (2015). https://doi.org/10.1007/978-3-319-24174-6_13
5. Bultel, X., Fraser, A., Quaglia, E.A.: Improving the efficiency of report and trace ring signatures. Cryptology ePrint Archive, Paper 2022/1293 (2022). https://eprint.iacr.org/2022/1293
6. Camenisch, J., Stadler, M.: Proof systems for general statements about discrete logarithms. In: Technical Report No. 260. Department of Computer Science, ETH Zurich (1997)
7. Chase, M., Lysyanskaya, A.: On signatures of knowledge. In: Dwork, C. (ed.) CRYPTO 2006. LNCS, vol. 4117, pp. 78–96. Springer, Heidelberg (2006). https://doi.org/10.1007/11818175_5

8. Chatterjee, S., Menezes, A., Rodrıguez-Henrıquez, F.: On instantiating pairing-based protocols with elliptic curves of embedding degree one. IEEE Trans. Comput. **66**(6), 1061–1070 (2017)

9. Chaum, D., van Heyst, E.: Group signatures. In: Davies, D.W. (ed.) EUROCRYPT 1991. LNCS, vol. 547, pp. 257–265. Springer, Heidelberg (1991). https://doi.org/10.1007/3-540-46416-6_22

10. Chaum, D., Pedersen, T.P.: Wallet databases with observers. In: Brickell, E.F. (ed.) CRYPTO 1992. LNCS, vol. 740, pp. 89–105. Springer, Heidelberg (1993). https://doi.org/10.1007/3-540-48071-4_7

11. Cramer, R., Damgård, I., Schoenmakers, B.: Proofs of partial knowledge and simplified design of witness hiding protocols. In: Desmedt, Y.G. (ed.) CRYPTO 1994. LNCS, vol. 839, pp. 174–187. Springer, Heidelberg (1994). https://doi.org/10.1007/3-540-48658-5_19

12. Fauzi, P., Meiklejohn, S., Mercer, R., Orlandi, C.: Quisquis: a new design for anonymous cryptocurrencies. In: Galbraith, S.D., Moriai, S. (eds.) ASIACRYPT 2019. LNCS, vol. 11921, pp. 649–678. Springer, Cham (2019). https://doi.org/10.1007/978-3-030-34578-5_23

13. Fiat, A., Shamir, A.: How to prove yourself: practical solutions to identification and signature problems. In: Odlyzko, A.M. (ed.) CRYPTO 1986. LNCS, vol. 263, pp. 186–194. Springer, Heidelberg (1987). https://doi.org/10.1007/3-540-47721-7_12

14. Fraser, A., Quaglia, E.A.: Report and trace ring signatures. In: Conti, M., Stevens, M., Krenn, S. (eds.) CANS 2021. LNCS, vol. 13099, pp. 179–199. Springer, Cham (2021). https://doi.org/10.1007/978-3-030-92548-2_10

15. Fujisaki, E., Suzuki, K.: Traceable ring signature. In: Okamoto, T., Wang, X. (eds.) PKC 2007. LNCS, vol. 4450, pp. 181–200. Springer, Heidelberg (2007). https://doi.org/10.1007/978-3-540-71677-8_13

16. Goldwasser, S., Micali, S.: Probabilistic encryption & how to play mental poker keeping secret all partial information. In: Proceedings of the Fourteenth Annual ACM Symposium on Theory of Computing, STOC. ACM (1982)

17. Groth, J., Ostrovsky, R., Sahai, A.: Perfect non-interactive zero knowledge for NP. In: Vaudenay, S. (ed.) EUROCRYPT 2006. LNCS, vol. 4004, pp. 339–358. Springer, Heidelberg (2006). https://doi.org/10.1007/11761679_21

18. Hevia, A., Mergudich-Thal, I.: Implementing secure reporting of sexual misconduct - revisiting WhoToo. In: Longa, P., Ràfols, C. (eds.) LATINCRYPT 2021. LNCS, vol. 12912, pp. 341–362. Springer, Cham (2021). https://doi.org/10.1007/978-3-030-88238-9_17

19. Kiayias, A., Tsiounis, Y., Yung, M.: Traceable signatures. In: Cachin, C., Camenisch, J.L. (eds.) EUROCRYPT 2004. LNCS, vol. 3027, pp. 571–589. Springer, Heidelberg (2004). https://doi.org/10.1007/978-3-540-24676-3_34

20. Kohlweiss, M., Miers, I.: Accountable metadata-hiding escrow: a group signature case study. Proc. Priv. Enhancing Technol. **2015**(2), 206–221 (2015)

21. Kuykendall, B., Krawczyk, H., Rabin, T.: Cryptography for# MeToo. Proc. Priv. Enhancing Technol. **2019**(3), 409–429 (2019)

22. Liu, J.K., Wei, V.K., Wong, D.S.: Linkable spontaneous anonymous group signature for ad hoc groups. In: Wang, H., Pieprzyk, J., Varadharajan, V. (eds.) ACISP 2004. LNCS, vol. 3108, pp. 325–335. Springer, Heidelberg (2004). https://doi.org/10.1007/978-3-540-27800-9_28

23. Maxwell, G.: CoinJoin: bitcoin privacy for the real world. In: Post on Bitcoin forum, vol. 3, p. 110 (2013)

24. Noether, S., Mackenzie, A., et al.: Ring confidential transactions. Ledger **1**, 1–18 (2016)

25. Rajan, A., Qin, L., Archer, D.W., Boneh, D., Lepoint, T., Varia, M.: Callisto: a cryptographic approach to detecting serial perpetrators of sexual misconduct. In: Proceedings of the 1st ACM SIGCAS Conference on Computing and Sustainable Societies, pp. 1–4 (2018)
26. Rivest, R.L., Shamir, A., Tauman, Y.: How to leak a secret. In: Boyd, C. (ed.) ASIACRYPT 2001. LNCS, vol. 2248, pp. 552–565. Springer, Heidelberg (2001). https://doi.org/10.1007/3-540-45682-1_32
27. Sakai, Y., Emura, K., Hanaoka, G., Kawai, Y., Matsuda, T., Omote, K.: Group signatures with message-dependent opening. In: Abdalla, M., Lange, T. (eds.) Pairing 2012. LNCS, vol. 7708, pp. 270–294. Springer, Heidelberg (2013). https://doi.org/10.1007/978-3-642-36334-4_18
28. Sasson, E.B., et al.: Zerocash: decentralized anonymous payments from bitcoin. In 2014 IEEE Symposium on Security and Privacy, pp. 459–474. IEEE (2014)
29. Schnorr, C.-P.: Efficient signature generation by smart cards. J. Cryptol. **4**, 161–174 (1991)
30. Stadler, M.: Publicly verifiable secret sharing. In: Maurer, U. (ed.) EUROCRYPT 1996. LNCS, vol. 1070, pp. 190–199. Springer, Heidelberg (1996). https://doi.org/10.1007/3-540-68339-9_17
31. Tyagi, N., Miers, I., Ristenpart, T.: Traceback for end-to-end encrypted messaging. In: Proceedings of the 2019 ACM SIGSAC Conference on Computer and Communications Security, pp. 413–430 (2019)
32. Xu, S., Yung, M.: Accountable ring signatures: a smart card approach. In: Quisquater, J.-J., Paradinas, P., Deswarte, Y., El Kalam, A.A. (eds.) CARDIS 2004. IIFIP, vol. 153, pp. 271–286. Springer, Boston, MA (2004). https://doi.org/10.1007/1-4020-8147-2_18

Flexible Scheduling of Transactional Memory on Trees

Costas Busch[1], Bogdan S. Chlebus[1], Maurice Herlihy[2], Miroslav Popovic[3], Pavan Poudel[1], and Gokarna Sharma[4(✉)] 🆔

[1] Augusta University, Augusta, GA, USA
{kbusch,bchlebus,ppoudel}@augusta.edu
[2] Brown University, Providence, RI, USA
herlihy@cs.brown.edu
[3] University of Novi Sad, Novi Sad, Serbia
miroslav.popovic@rt-rk.uns.ac.rs
[4] Kent State University, Kent, OH, USA
gsharma2@kent.edu

Abstract. We study the efficiency of executing transactions in a distributed transactional memory system. The system is modeled as a wired network with the topology of a tree. Contrary to previous approaches, we allow the flexibility for both transactions and their requested objects to move simultaneously among the nodes in the tree. Given a batch of transactions and objects, the goal is to produce a schedule of executing the transactions that minimizes the cost of moving the transactions and the objects in the tree. We consider both techniques for accessing a remote object with respect to a transaction movement. In the first technique, instead of moving, transactions send control messages to remote nodes where the requested objects are gathered. In the second technique, the transactions migrate to the remote nodes where they execute. When all the transactions use a single object, we give an offline algorithm that produces optimal schedules for both techniques. For the general case of multiple objects per transaction, in the first technique, we obtain a schedule with a constant-factor approximation of optimal. In the second technique, with transactions migrating, we give a k factor approximation where k is the maximum number of objects per transaction.

Keywords: Distributed system · Transactional memory · Shared object · Network · Communication cost

1 Introduction

Threads executed concurrently require synchronization to prevent inconsistencies while accessing shared objects. Traditional low-level thread synchronization mechanisms such as locks and barriers are prone to deadlock and priority inversion, among multiple vulnerabilities. The concept of *transactional memory* has emerged as a high-level abstraction of the functionality of distributed systems;

© The Author(s), under exclusive license to Springer Nature Switzerland AG 2022
S. Devismes et al. (Eds.): SSS 2022, LNCS 13751, pp. 146–163, 2022.
https://doi.org/10.1007/978-3-031-21017-4_10

see Herlihy and Moss [10] and Shavit and Touitou [25]. The idea is to designate blocks of program code as *transactions* to be executed atomically. Transactions are executed speculatively, in the sense that if a transaction aborts due to synchronization conflicts or failures then the transaction's execution is rolled back to be restarted later. A transaction commits if there are no conflicts or failures, and its effects become visible to all processes. If multiple transactions concurrently attempt to access the same object, then this creates a conflict for access and could trigger aborting some of the involved transactions. Scheduling transactions to minimize conflicts for access to shared objects improves the system's performance.

The processing units of a distributed transactional memory system are the nodes of a communication network, which is an integral part of the system. A transaction executing at a node may want to access shared memory objects residing in other nodes. This could be implemented such that the transaction coordinates access to the needed shared objects with the nodes hosting the objects. Such systems were studied by Herlihy and Sun [11], Sharma and Busch [23], and Siek and Wojciechowski [26]. The efficiency of executing a specific transaction may reflect the topology of the communication network that is part of a distributed system. For example, the amount of communication needed to execute a transaction interacting with some objects could be proportional to the distances in the network between all the nodes hosting the transaction and the objects.

To improve efficiency of processing transactions on shared objects, we may preemptively move objects and transactions among the nodes to schedule their presence at specific nodes at specific times. Moving transactions or program code among network nodes is currently used in several real-world applications. For example, Erlang Open Telecom Platform aids dynamic code upgrade by supporting transactional servers with hot code swapping whose call-back modules may be changed on the fly [1]. A job management system for a computer cluster may migrate a job to a different node, if the target nodes load is below the migration threshold and the migration overhead is acceptable, in order to achieve better load balancing among the nodes, see Hwang et al. [13]. A related system that uses live virtual machine migration to support autonomic adaptation of virtual computation environments is described by Ruth et al. [20].

Coordinating accessing objects to execute transactions may involve relocation of objects or transactions. Efficiency of such coordination may depend on additional model's specification which determines the very feasibility of moving transactions and objects across the network. In the *data-flow* model, transactions are static and objects move from one node to another to reach the nodes hosting transactions that require interacting with them; see Tilevich and Smaragdakis [27] and Herlihy and Sun [11]. In that model, a transaction initially requests the objects it needs, and executes after assembling them. After a transaction commits, it releases its objects, possibly forwarding them to pending transactions. In the *control-flow* model, objects are static and transactions move from one node to another to access the objects. Control-flow allows transactions to send control requests, in a manner similar to remote procedure calls, to the nodes where the required objects are located; see Arnold et al. [2] and Saad and Ravindran [22].

Contributions. We consider a flexible scheduling approach that combines the benefits of the data-flow and control-flow models. We study the *dual-flow* model that allows for both transactions and objects to move among the nodes to synchronize transactions and objects. We consider distributed systems whose networks interpreted as graphs have tree topologies. This represents many real-world networks. For example, the internet cloud consists of the cloud network, representing a root, the fog network gateways and/or the edge network gateways, as internal nodes, and the IoT devices as leaves, see Comer [8].

We study the efficiency of executing transactions by a distributed system represented as a tree in the dual-flow model. The efficiency is measured by the cost of communication. Scheduling transactions is considered in a batch setting, in which all the transactions are given at the outset, subject to the constraint that each node is assigned at most one original transaction. The initial position of shared objects are distributed arbitrarily among the nodes. We consider scheduling transactions in the general case of arbitrarily many shared objects, and also in a special case of a single shared object that needs to be accessed by all the transactions. Given a batch of transactions and objects residing at nodes of the system, the goal is to produce a schedule of executing transactions that minimizes the cost of moving transactions and objects among the nodes and sending control messages to facilitate executing the transactions. Such a schedule is computed by a centralized offline algorithm to be executed by the distributed system. We develop a centralized algorithm finding an optimal schedule in the case when all the transactions use a single object. The general case of multiple objects is studied in two models that determine if executing a transaction may involve sending control messages. For multiple shared objects and with transactions sending control messages, we give a centralized algorithm that finds a schedule with a constant-factor approximation of communication cost with respect to an optimal schedule. For multiple shared objects and with transactions migrating and not using control messages, we give a centralized algorithm that finds a schedule approximating an optimal one by a factor k that equals the maximum number of shared objects requested by a transaction.

Related Work. Attiya et al. [3], Busch et al. [5–7], and Sharma and Busch [23,24] considered transaction scheduling with provable performance bounds in the data-flow model. Saad and Ravindran [22], Palmieri et al. [17], Siek and Wojciechowski [26] studied scheduling transactions in the control-flow model. Palmieri et al. [17] also gave a comparative study of data-flow versus control-flow models for distributed transactional memory. A prototype distributed transactional memory system described by Saad and Ravindran [21] supports experimentation for both data-flow and control-flow models. Bocchino et al. [4] considered the dual-flow model by allowing programmers to either bring the data to the code of computation (transaction) or send the code of computation to the data. Hendler et al. [9] studied a lease based dual-flow model which dynamically determines whether to migrate transactions to the nodes that own the leases or to demand the acquisition of these leases by the node that originated the transaction.

Transaction scheduling in a distributed system with the goal of minimizing execution time was first considered by Zhang et al. [28]. Busch et al. [5] considered minimizing both the execution time and communication cost simultaneously. They showed that it is impossible to simultaneously minimize execution time and communication cost for all the scheduling problem instances in arbitrary graphs even in the offline setting. Specifically, Busch et al. [5] demonstrated a tradeoff between minimizing execution time and communication cost and provided offline algorithms optimizing execution time and communication cost separately. Busch et al. [7] considered transaction scheduling tailored to specific popular topologies and provided offline algorithms that minimize simultaneously execution time and communication cost. In a follow-up work, Poudel and Sharma [19] provided an evaluation framework for processing transactions in distributed systems. Busch et al. [6] studied online algorithms to schedule transactions arriving continuously. Distributed directory protocols have been designed by Herlihy and Sun [11], Sharma and Busch [23], and Zhang et al. [28], with the goal to optimize communication cost in scheduling transactions.

Alternative approaches to distributed transactional memory systems have been proposed in the literature by way of replicating transactional memory on multiple nodes and providing means to guarantee consistency of replicas. This includes work by Hirve et al. [12], Kim and Ravindran [14], Kobus et al. [15], Manassiev et al. [16], and Peluso et al. [18]. In this work, we use a single copy of each object. Replicas of objects help to improve reliability of the systems rather than decrease the communication overhead.

2 Technical Preliminaries

A distributed system can be modeled as weighted graph $G = (V, E, \mathrm{w})$ which in our case is a tree. There are n vertices in the set V, each representing a processing node. Edges in the set $E \subseteq V \times V$ represent communication links between nodes. The function $\mathrm{w} : E \to \mathbb{Z}^+$ assigns a weight to each edge representing a communication delay. We let $\mathrm{dist}(u, v)$ denote the shortest path distance between two vertices u and v.

The initial configuration of the distributed system consists of a set of transactions and shared objects distributed among the nodes. Each node hosts at most one transaction. During executing transactions, both shared objects and transactions can move among the nodes of a network, which we call the *dual-flow* model. If a transaction requests access to an object, that object may move to a different node, possibly closer to the requesting transaction. At the same time, the transaction can also migrate to the object's new location, or send a control message to that new location to access the object. The combined cost of executing a transaction is measured with relation to the distances traversed by shared objects, transaction code and control messages.

We consider the following two specializations of the dual-flow model for remote object access: (i) *Control-message* technique, where a transaction sends a control message to access the remote object. The control-message technique is motivated by a scenario in which each transaction performs a number of updates to an object bounded by a constant, with each update requiring a control message, for a total of a constant number of such messages. (ii) *Transaction-migration* technique, in which a transaction moves to the node where objects are located and no control messages are sent. This technique is motivated by the scenarios in which a transaction may issue a variable number of requests to an object, in which case it is advantageous to migrate the transaction to the object location to avoid potentially unbounded communication overhead.

We parameterize the costs of transmitting messages that carry transactions, objects, or control instructions. The cost of moving an object of size α over a unit weight edge is denoted by α. We denote the cost of sending a control message over a unit weight edge by β. The cost of moving a transaction over a unit weight edge is denoted by γ.

A scheduling algorithm determines a schedule to execute transactions, including movements of objects and transactions. A centralized algorithm takes as input a configuration of transactions and objects in the system as arranged at the outset. We assume that each node has this input available so that it can execute it locally. Formally, a *schedule* of executing transactions is a sequence of actions $s_1, s_2, \ldots$ to be performed by the nodes. An *action* s_i is a set of instructions to be performed by a node to facilitate processing transaction T_i. The *communication cost* of executing such a schedule is the sum of distances traversed by the shared objects, control messages, and transactions according to the schedule, weighted by the corresponding parameters α, β, and γ.

3   A Single Object

We assume a single shared object o of size $\alpha > 1$ positioned at the root node of a tree G. We develop an optimal scheduling algorithm denoted as SINGLE-OBJECT in the dual-flow model considering both techniques for accessing a remote object: control-message and transaction-migration.

A general idea of the algorithm in the control-message technique is as follows. First we find a set of intermediate nodes in G to move the object o to. These nodes are referred to as *supernodes*. An intermediate node v becomes a supernode if the cost of moving o from v to one of its children is greater than the cost of sending control messages from the transactions contained by the sub-tree of that child to v. Each supernode contains a set of transactions in its sub-tree which send control messages to that supernode to access object o. These transactions are added to the local execution schedule of the supernode following an iterative pre-order tree traversal in the sub-tree. We determine a subtree P containing paths in G that reach the supernodes from the root of G. Starting from the root, object o travels all the supernodes following the iterative pre-order tree traversal of P. Any transaction that lies along the path is added to the execution schedule $\mathcal{E}$ as soon as o reaches the respective node. When o reaches some supernode, the transactions from its local execution schedule get added to $\mathcal{E}$ in the respective order. The execution ends when all the transactions have been added to $\mathcal{E}$. The algorithm can be modified as follows if performed in the transaction-migration technique. Determine supernodes with respect to transaction migration cost rather than control messages cost. Migrate transactions to the corresponding supernodes instead of sending control messages to access the object. These modifications result in creating an algorithm of a comparable communication performance.

We elaborate on the details of the algorithm next. The cost of moving o over an edge of unit length is α. Let β represents the control message cost for a transaction to access object o at one unit away and $\alpha > \beta$. Let $\mathcal{T} = \{T_1, T_2, \ldots T_n\}$ be the set of n transactions issued to the nodes of G, one at each node. The first objectives are to determine the walk the object traverses and to find transaction execution schedule. Intuitively, since it costs more to move the object across a link than to send a control message through the link, we strive to move the object minimally, only when when this pays, and this approach is captured by the concept of supernodes. The object o first travels from the root up to a supernode. Transactions that lie along the path the object traverses execute as soon as the object reaches the respective nodes. The remaining transactions beyond that supernode and towards the leaves send control messages to the supernode to access the object. Then the object moves to the next supernode and transactions get executed following a similar approach.

The communication cost of an execution of the algorithm is determined by the location of supernodes. The set of supernodes is selected by referring to transaction loads and transaction counts at all nodes, which are defined as follows. A *transaction load* of a node v, denoted txload(v), is the sum of distances from v to the positions of transactions contained in the sub-tree of v, including v. The transaction load of v represents the cost of sending control messages due to the transactions contained in its sub-tree, assuming o is moved to v. A *transaction count* at node v, denoted txnum(v), is the total number of transactions contained in the sub-tree of node v, including v.

To identify supernodes, we start from the leaves of G and work through the ancestors towards the root. Let v_{cur} be a leaf node and v_{next} be the parent of v_{cur}. During the computation of supernodes, we can assume that the object is at the parent node v_{next} and check if it pays to move the object down to v_{cur}, since object moves away from the root. Let txload(v_{cur}) denote the control message cost incurred by the txnum(v_{cur}) number of transactions contained in the sub-tree of v_{cur}, including v_{cur}. If the object o moves to v_{cur}, the transactions contained in the sub-tree of v_{cur} can access o at v_{cur} and the cost becomes txload(v_{cur}) $+ \alpha \cdot$ dist(v_{cur}, v_{next}). Here, $\alpha \cdot$ dist(v_{cur}, v_{next}) is the cost incurred by the movement of object o from v_{next} to v_{cur}. Otherwise, these transactions send control messages to v_{next} to access o and the cost becomes txload(v_{cur}) $+$ txnum(v_{cur}) $\cdot \beta \cdot$ dist(v_{cur}, v_{next}). Object o will move to v_{cur} from v_{next} only if the control message cost from v_{cur} to v_{next}, due to the transactions contained

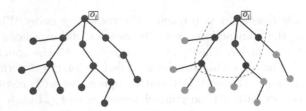

Fig. 1. Identification of supernodes by algorithm SINGLE-OBJECT. The tree on the left is G. The tree on the right is the same G after determining the status of nodes. Supernodes are colored blue. Nodes on the path from the root to a blue node are colored black. The dashed line delineates P obtained from G by pruning G of vertices beyond the supernodes, which are colored orange. (Color figure online)

in the sub-tree of v_{cur}, is more than or equal to the object movement cost from v_{next} to v_{cur}. After reaching a supernode, object o may need to move back to the root or intermediate nodes to visit other supernodes. To account for this and simplify the argument, we assume that the object moves over each edge twice, but this assumption will be revisited when we optimize the algorithm. If the following inequality holds

$$\text{txload}(v_{cur}) + 2\,\alpha \cdot \text{dist}(v_{cur}, v_{next}) \leq \text{txload}(v_{cur}) + \text{txnum}(v_{cur}) \cdot \beta \cdot \text{dist}(v_{cur}, v_{next}),$$

then we choose v_{cur} as a supernode. Otherwise, if v_{cur} is not the root, a new pair of v_{cur} and v_{next} is checked such that current v_{next} becomes new v_{cur} and the parent of current v_{next} becomes a new node v_{next}. If v_{cur} is the root, then it becomes a supernode.

Let P denote the *pruned tree*, which contains only the supernodes and nodes that need to be traversed on the way from the root to a supernode. Tree P is rooted the root of G. Figure 1 illustrates such a tree P. The object o is originally located at the root, from which it moves to the supernodes in a pre-order traversal manner. The transactions are executed along the way of the object's movement. Transactions at the nodes beyond the pruned tree P, marked by color orange in Fig. 1, either send control messages or move to access o to their closest supernodes. When object o reaches the respective supernode, these transactions are executed in order.

After computing the set of supernodes, the object performs a pre-order tree traversal starting from the root to visit all the supernodes. The transaction execution schedule $\mathcal{E}$ is computed as follows. First add transaction at the root to $\mathcal{E}$. During the pre-order tree traversal to visit the supernodes, if $\mathcal{E}$ does not contain the transaction at a visited node v, then add it to $\mathcal{E}$. If the visited node v is a supernode, add to $\mathcal{E}$ the transactions that sent control messages to v from the subtree rooted at v.

Next we show how to refine this approach, which is based on the assumption that during the computation of supernodes if the object moves from some parent node to the child node then it will ultimately move back from that child node to the parent. When the object reaches the last supernode, it does not move back because there is no any other supernode remained to visit. We define a *one-way path* to be such a path from v_{root} to the last supernode v_{last}, all the edges of which the object traverses only once. This v_{last} must be chosen in such a way that the total communication cost is minimized. A condition for computing a supernode is

$$2\alpha \cdot \text{dist}(v_{cur}, v_{next}) > \text{txnum}(v_{cur}) \cdot \beta \cdot \text{dist}(v_{cur}, v_{next}) \tag{1}$$

so it accounts for the object traversing each edge twice, which is not required for v_{last}. The object can move further down until the following holds

$$\alpha \cdot \text{dist}(v_{cur}, v_{next}) > \text{txnum}(v_{cur}) \cdot \beta \cdot \text{dist}(v_{cur}, v_{next}) \tag{2}$$

We find the last supernode v_{last} and the one-way path as follows. Let S be the initial set of supernodes computed considering that the object moves twice on each edge up to the supernode. In a one-way path, the object may move further down towards the leaf node satisfying the condition in Inequality (2). For each node $v \in S$, if the sub-tree of v contains multiple branches, there could be a number of possible paths for the object to move. There will always be a unique one-way path that minimizes the total cost. In each sub-tree of $v \in S$, we find the set of nodes $D(v)$ that are candidates for v_{last} using the condition in Inequality (2). Then the difference between the cost of selecting v as a supernode and $v_j \in D(v)$ as a supernode is computed. Among these differences for every $v \in S$, the one with the highest difference is chosen as the last supernode. Let $v_{ref} \in S$ and $v_k \in D(v_{ref})$ be the set of two nodes that provided the highest difference. Then v_k becomes v_{last} and is added to S. The path from v_{root} to v_{last} becomes the one-way-path and is visited at last following the pre-order tree traversal. Moreover, if a node between v_{ref} and v_{last} (including v_{ref}) in the one-way-path contains transactions in its sub-tree other than the one-way-path branch, it becomes a supernode to serve control requests to the transactions in those branches and is added to S.

We state following three lemmas whose proofs are immediate from the discussion:

Lemma 1. *If a node v does not belong to the pruned tree P, then the total number of transactions contained in the sub-tree of v is less than 2α.*

Lemma 2. *If v is a descendant of v_{last}, then the total number of transactions contained in the sub-tree of v is always less than α.*

Lemma 3. *For any transaction, the corresponding supernode for accessing the object always lies at or above its position along the path towards the root of G.*

Theorem 1. *Algorithm* SINGLE-OBJECT *schedules transactions with the optimal communication cost.*

Proof. Let S be the set of supernodes found for a tree G with respect to object o. We will show that any other selection of supernodes gives strictly higher communication cost and hence, S provides optimal communication cost.

To simplify the problem, without loss of generality, we assume that each edge of G has weight 1, $\beta = 1$ and $\alpha > \beta$. Let P be the pruned tree containing nodes only up to the supernodes starting from the root of G. Let $v_{last} \in S$ be the last supernode for object o to visit. Let C be the total communication cost of Algorithm SINGLE-OBJECT. Let $v \in S$ be a supernode in G, v_p be an ancestor of v with distance $dist(v_p, v) \geq 1$, and v_q be a descendant of v with $dist(v, v_q) \geq 1$. Based on the positions of v and v_q, it can have one of the following three cases:

Case (a): $v = v_{last}$. Then, by Lemma 2, we have that

$$txnum(v_p) \geq txnum(v) \geq \alpha > txnum(v_q) \tag{3}$$

Case (b): $v \neq v_{last}$, $v_q \notin P$, and the path from v to v_q contains no other supernode, in that v is the bottommost supernode in the current branch. Then, by Lemma 1, we have

$$txnum(v_p) \geq txnum(v) \geq 2\alpha > txnum(v_q) \tag{4}$$

Case (c): Either $v_q \in P$ or $v_q \notin P$ and the path from v to v_q contains at least one other supernode. Let $z \geq 1$ be the transactions that send control messages to v to access o.

We have following four subcases with respect to each supernode $v \in S$:

(i) *Choosing an ancestor of v as a supernode instead of v increases communication:*
   Let S_p be the set of nodes contained between v and v_p (excluding both). Suppose v_p be selected as a supernode instead of v. Then in Case (a) and Case (b), o moves only up to v_p, and in addition to the transactions issued to the sub-tree of v, all the transactions between v and v_p send control messages to v_p. But, in Case (c), since the sub-tree of v (excluding v) still contains another supernode $v_k \in S$, o still moves to v_k passing through v. When v was the supernode, $z \geq 1$ transactions could access o at v. Now, since v_p is selected as the supernode instead of v, all those z transactions send control messages to v_p to access o. So, the total communication cost C_{v_p} of selecting v_p as a supernode compared to that of selecting v in each case becomes:

$$C_{v_p} = \begin{cases} C - \alpha \cdot dist(v_p, p) + txnum(v) \cdot dist(v_p, v) \\ \quad + \sum_{v_k \in S_p} (txnum(v_k) - txnum(v)), & \text{Case (a)} \\ C - 2\alpha \cdot dist(v_p, p) + txnum(v) \cdot dist(v_p, v) \\ \quad + \sum_{v_k \in S_p} (txnum(v_k) - txnum(v)), & \text{Case (b)} \\ C + z \cdot dist(v_p, v), & \text{Case (c)} \end{cases}$$

In Case (a), from Inequality (3), since $txnum(v) \geq \alpha$, $C_{v_p} > C$. In Case (b), from Inequality (4), since $txnum(v) \geq 2\alpha$, $C_{v_p} > C$. Also, in case (c), $C_{v_p} > C$.

(ii) *Choosing a descendant of v as a supernode instead of v increases communication:*

Now, we analyze the communication cost of selecting a descendant node v_q as a supernode instead of $v \in S$. Let S_q be the set of nodes contained between v and v_q (excluding both). As v_q is a new supernode, object moves up to it. So, in Case (a) and Case (b), to get the change in total communication cost compared to C, we have to add object movement cost of o from v to v_q and subtract the control message cost for the transactions between v and v_q. Moreover, the transactions in the sub-tree of v_q will also send control messages only up to v_q. Thus, the total communication cost C_{v_q} of selecting node v_q as a supernode compared to C in Case (a) and Case (b) becomes:

$$
C_{v_q} = \begin{cases} C + \alpha \cdot \text{dist}(v, v_q) - \text{txnum}(v_q) \cdot \text{dist}(v, v_q) \\ \quad - \sum_{v_k \in S_q}(\text{txnum}(v_k) - \text{txnum}(v_q)), & \text{Case (a)} \\ C + 2\alpha \cdot \text{dist}(v, v_q) - \text{txnum}(v_q) \cdot \text{dist}(v, v_q) \\ \quad - \sum_{v_k \in S_q}(\text{txnum}(v_k) - \text{txnum}(v_q)), & \text{Case (b)} \end{cases}
$$

Let $\text{dist}(v, v_q) = k$ where $k \geq 1$. In Case (a), from Inequality (3), $\text{txnum}(v_q) < \alpha$. Let $\text{txnum}(v_q) = \alpha - j$, $1 \leq j < \alpha$. Following Lemma 2, the nodes between v and v_q (i.e., S_q) contain at most j number of transactions. The control message cost sent to v due to these transactions is: $\sum_{v_k \in S_q}(\text{txnum}(v_k) - \text{txnum}(v_q)) < j \cdot k$. Thus,

$$
C_{v_q} > C + \alpha \cdot k - (\alpha - j) \cdot k - j \cdot k > C.
$$

In Case (b), $\text{txnum}(v_q) < 2\alpha$ by the Inequality (4). Let $\text{txnum}(v_q) = 2\alpha - l$, for $1 \leq l < 2\alpha$. By Lemma 1, there are at most l transactions between v and v_q, and control message cost sent to v due to them is: $\sum_{v_k \in S_q}(\text{txnum}(v_k) - \text{txnum}(v_q)) < l \cdot k$. Thus

$$
C_{v_q} > C + 2\alpha \cdot k - (2\alpha - l) \cdot k - l \cdot k > C.
$$

Now, we analyze Case (c). Based on the position of v_q, it can have two sub-cases:

Case (c.1): $v_q \in P$. There is no extra movement of o and the $z \geq 1$ number of transactions that previously depend on v now send control messages to v_q to access o. So, the total communication cost C_{v_q} compared to C becomes: $C_{v_q} = C + z \cdot \text{dist}(v, v_q) > C$.

Case (c.2): $v_q \notin P$ but the path from v to v_q contains at least one other supernode in S. The node v_q lies below the bottommost supernode of current branch. Let $v_{bot} \in S$ be the bottommost supernode in the path between v and v_q. When v_q is selected as a supernode, there will be extra movement of object o from v_{bot} up to v_q. If $v_{bot} = v_{last}$, and o moves up to v_q. Otherwise, object o also needs to return back at v_{bot}. Let M represents the cost due to the movement of object o between v_{bot} and v_q, then,

$M > \alpha \cdot \text{dist}(v_{bot}, v_q)$. Thus, the total communication cost C_{v_q} compared to C in this case becomes: $C_{v_q} = C + z \cdot \text{dist}(v, v_q) + M > C$.

(iii) *Merging multiple supernodes at some ancestor node increases communication cost:*

Consider two supernodes $v_r, v_s \in S$ have a common ancestor v_y. Instead of v_r and v_s, let v_y be chosen as a supernode. Since v_y is ancestor of both v_r and v_s, following argument (i), total communication cost C_{v_y} of selecting v_y as a supernode instead of v_r and v_s is more compared to C.

(iv) *Splitting any supernode into multiple supernodes increases communication cost:*

Consider a supernode $v_j \in S$. Let v_x, v_z be two descendant nodes of v_j at two different sub-branches. Let v_x and v_z are chosen as two different supernodes instead of v_j. Since both v_x and v_z are descendants of v_j, following argument (ii), total cost $C_{v_{xz}}$ of selecting v_x, v_z as supernodes instead of v_j is more compared to C.

The set of supernodes S computed in algorithm SINGLE-OBJECT is unique. If any new node is added to S or any node in S is removed or replaced by another node, the total communication cost increases. This means that scheduling by algorithm SINGLE-OBJECT minimizes the communication cost. □

Next we consider the transaction-migration technique. Let γ be the cost of moving a transaction over a unit weight edge of G. Consider algorithm SINGLE-OBJECT modified such that transactions are moved to supernodes instead of sending control messages and the cost of moving transaction replaces the cost of sending control messages, in that we use the parameter γ instead of β. After these modification in algorithm SINGLE-OBJECT and its analysis, we obtain optimality similarly as stated in Theorem 1.

Theorem 2. *Algorithm* SINGLE-OBJECT *provides 2-approximation in communication cost without optimization.*

4   Multiple Objects

We provide two scheduling algorithms for multiple shared objects, which extend the single object algorithm above. For the *control message* technique, we present the algorithm denoted as MULTIPLEOBJECTS-CTRLMSG, which provides an $O(1)$-approximation. For the *transaction-migration* technique, our algorithm is denoted as MULTIPLEOBJECTS-TXMIGR, which provides $O(k)$-approximation, where k is the maximum number of shared objects accessed by a transaction.

We consider a set of shared objects $\mathcal{O} = \{o_1, o_2, \ldots, o_\delta\}$ initially positioned at arbitrary nodes of G. We assume that each object has size α. Each transaction in $\mathcal{T}$ accesses a subset of objects in $\mathcal{O}$. Let $\text{objs}(T_i) \subseteq \mathcal{O}$ be the set of objects accessed by transaction T_i. We assume that each object has a single copy and $home(o_i) \in V$ represents the home node at which object o_i is originally positioned. The ownership of an object is also transferred with the movement of that object. Similarly, $home(T_i) \in V$ represents the node at which transaction T_i is positioned.

The idea in the algorithms is to provide synchronized accesses to the objects with minimum cost while executing the transactions in order. We achieve this extending the techniques used in algorithm SINGLE-OBJECT. In particular, we compute supernodes w.r.t. each object and the transactions requiring those objects. We then perform iterative pre-order tree traversal to move each object to the respective supernodes and execute transactions in order.

For brevity, let T_i be a transaction that requires objects in objs$(T_i) = \{o_x, \ldots, o_z\}$. Let $sv_i(o_x), \ldots, sv_i(o_z)$ be the respective supernodes (computed using algorithm SINGLE-OBJECT w.r.t. each object) at which T_i can access $o_x, \ldots, o_z$, respectively. Then, one way of providing synchronised access to the required objects by T_i is to bring each object in objs(T_i) at the respective supernode (i.e., $sv_i(o_x), \ldots, sv_i(o_z)$) at the same time so that T_i can access them by sending control messages. This approach is used in the control-message technique. The other way is to gather all the objects in objs(T_i) at a single node $sv(T_i)$ (i.e., common supernode for T_i) and access them at that node by migrating T_i. This approach is used in the transaction-migration technique.

We now describe how transactions are executed in order and the objects are moved from one supernode to the next minimizing the communication cost. As in algorithm SINGLE-OBJECT, this can be achieved using iterative pre-order tree traversal algorithm in G, provided that there is a single reference point, i.e., root node. We find a *virtual root* (v'_{root}) of tree G as a single reference point.

In the control-message technique, any node of G can be selected as the virtual root (v'_{root}). In the transaction-migration technique, if all the objects are initially positioned at the same node, that node is selected as the virtual root of G. If objects are positioned at different nodes initially, we compute the virtual root with respect to the initial positions (home nodes) of transactions and the objects they access. The virtual root of tree G is the node in G from which the sum of distances to home nodes of all the transactions and the objects they access is the minimum, that is,

$$v'_{root} = v_i : W(v_i) = \min_{v \in V} W(v), \tag{5}$$

where

$$W(v) = \sum_{j=1}^{n} \left(\text{dist}(v, \text{home}(T_j)) + \sum_{o \in \text{objs}(T_j)} \text{dist}(v, \text{home}(o)) \right).$$

Multiple Objects with Control Messages. The algorithm for the control-message technique is named MULTIPLEOBJECTS-CTRLMSG. The algorithm runs in two phases.

Phase 1: We compute sets of supernodes $S(o_i)$ w.r.t. each object $o_i \in \mathcal{O}$ individually following algorithm SINGLE-OBJECT without optimization. For each

o_i, home(o_i) is assumed as the root of G during the computation of respective supernodes $S(o_i)$. If a transaction T_i requires an object o_j, T_i accesses o_j at supernode $sv(T_i(o_j)) \in S(o_j)$.

Phase 2: We find transaction execution schedule $\mathcal{E}$ and paths of movement for each object $o_i \in \mathcal{O}$ along their respective supernodes. For this, let a random node in G be selected as the virtual root v'_{root} of G. We perform an iterative pre-order tree traversal in G starting from v'_{root}. During the traversal, if there is a transaction T_j at current node v_{cur}, T_j is added to the schedule $\mathcal{E}$ and each object o_k required by T_j. In notation, $o_k \in \text{objs}(T_j)$) is scheduled to move to the respective supernode $sv_j(o_k)$. When the traversal of G completes, all the transactions get scheduled and the execution ends.

Lemma 4. *An object o may traverse an edge along the path from* home(o_i) *to* v'_{root} *at most three times.*

Theorem 3. *Algorithm* MULTIPLEOBJECTS-CTRLMSG *provides a 3-approximation of communication cost.*

Proof. Let $S(o_i)$ be the set of supernodes computed with respect to object $o_i \in \mathcal{O}$ following algorithm SINGLE-OBJECT without optimization. Let P_i be the pruned tree containing nodes only up to the supernodes $S(o_i)$ starting from home(o_i) in G. Let C_{obj} denotes the cost of moving object o_i at each edge inside P_i only once and C_{ctrl} denotes the communication cost incurred due to the control messages sent from transactions beyond P_i in G. By the analysis of algorithm SINGLE-OBJECT, o_i visits each edge of P_i at most twice during the execution. Theorem 1 shows that the set of supernodes computed in algorithm SINGLE-OBJECT provides the minimum communication cost and Theorem 2 shows that algorithm SINGLE-OBJECT without optimization provides 2-approximation. Thus, if $C_{OPT}(o_i)$ be the optimal communication cost for accessing o_i by a set of transactions T, then,

$$C_{obj} + C_{ctrl} \leq C_{OPT}(o_i) \leq 2(C_{obj} + C_{ctrl}) \tag{6}$$

and $C_{OPT} = \sum_{o_i \in \mathcal{O}} C_{OPT}(o_i)$.

The algorithm in MULTIPLEOBJECTS-CTRLMSG uses the same set of supernodes $S(o_i)$ computed in algorithm SINGLE-OBJECT without optimization and object o_i does not move beyond the pruned tree P_i. So, C_{ctrl} for MULTIPLEOBJECTS-CTRLMSG remains the same. From Lemma 4, object o_i may traverse an edge inside P_i at most 3 times. Thus, if $C_{ALG}(o_i)$ represents the total communication cost for accessing o_i by a set of transactions T, then,

$$C_{ALG}(o_i) \leq 3C_{obj} + C_{ctrl} \tag{7}$$

Equations (6) and (7) imply

$$C_{ALG}(o_i) \leq 3 \cdot C_{OPT}(o_i) \tag{8}$$

This gives the estimate

$$C_{ALG} = \sum_{o_i \subset \mathcal{O}} C_{ALG}(o_i) \le \sum_{o_i \in \mathcal{O}} (3 \cdot C_{OPT}(o_i)) \le 3 \cdot C_{OPT},$$

where C_{ALG} represents the total communication cost in MULTIPLEOBJECTS-CTRLMSG for executing all the transactions accessing multiple objects and C_{OPT} represents that of any optimal algorithm. □

Multiple Objects with Migration of Transactions. The algorithm for multiple objects implemented in the transaction-migration technique is named MULTIPLEOBJECTS-TXMIGR. First, we discuss the algorithm assuming all the objects are initially positioned at the same node, the virtual root v'_{root}, of G. Later, we relax the algorithm where objects can be positioned initially at arbitrary nodes in G.

The algorithm works in four phases. In Phase 1, we compute sets of supernodes with respect to individual object $o_i \in \mathcal{O}$. In Phase 2, we find a common supernode for each transaction $T \in \mathcal{T}$ where all the required objects for T can be gathered together. In Phase 3, we finalize the set of common supernodes. Finally, in Phase 4, we perform iterative pre-order tree traversal on G to create transaction execution schedule and object movement paths along the common supernodes. We describe each phase below.

Phase 1: In this phase, we compute supernodes with respect to each object $o_i \in \mathcal{O}$ using algorithm SINGLE-OBJECT without optimization where control message cost β over an edge is replaced with the transaction migration cost γ. Let $S(o_i)$ be the set of supernodes with respect to object $o_i \in \mathcal{O}$ and $sv(T(o_i)) \in S(o_i)$ represents the supernode for transaction T at which T accesses o_i. After this, each transaction $T_j \in \mathcal{T}$ has a set of respective supernodes $sv(T_j(o_i))$ to access each required object $o_i \in \text{objs}(T_j)$. Since all the objects in $\text{objs}(T_j)$ need to gather at a single node, a common supernode $sv(T_j)$ for transaction T_j is selected out of all $sv(T_j(o_i))$ in the next phase.

Phase 2: In this phase, we find a common supernode of objects $sv(T)$ for each transaction $T \in \mathcal{T}$. The objective of selecting a common supernode for a transaction is to allow all the required objects for that transaction to gather together at the common supernode. After that, the transaction is also migrated at the common supernode and all the required objects are accessed locally. For a transaction T, if all the supernodes $sv(T(o_i))$, $o_i \in \text{objs}(T)$, computed in Phase 1 are the same, it automatically becomes the common supernode for T. If they are different, then we select the one among $sv(T(o_i))$, $o_i \in \text{objs}(T)$, which is the closest from v'_{root}.

Phase 3: In this phase, we compute the final set of supernodes FinalSV in G where respective transactions and the required objects are gathered together.

From Phase 2, we have a set of common supernodes $sv(T)$ for each transaction $T \in \mathcal{T}$. For each common supernode $v \in sv(*)$, following information is maintained separately:

– numtxs(v): total number of transactions that selected v as a common supernode.
– objs(v): set of objects with respect to which the node v is a supernode.
– txs($v(o_i)$), $o_i \in$ objs(v): set of transactions requiring object o_i that have selected v as the common supernode.

Let P be the pruned tree containing the nodes of G only up to the common supernodes moving down from v'_{root}. Starting from every leaf node of P towards v'_{root}, we check at each node how many transactions have selected it as a common supernode. Particularly, if $v \in P$ is a leaf node in P and is selected as a common supernode with respect to the set of objects objs(v), then, we check if numtxs(v) $\cdot \gamma \geq 2\alpha \cdot$ |objs(v)|. If the condition is satisfied, v belongs to FinalSV with respect to all objects in objs(v). Otherwise, for each object $o_i \in$ objs(v), we check how many transactions requiring the object o_i have selected v as the common supernode in Phase 2. Let txs($v(o_i)$) be the set of transactions requiring object o_i that have selected v as a common supernode. If |txs($v(o_i)$)| $\cdot \gamma \geq 2\alpha$, v belongs to FinalSV. But if |txs($v(o_i)$)| $\cdot \gamma < 2\alpha$, we visit its parent node $parent(v)$, find the set of transactions txs($parent(v)(o_i)$) requiring object o_i that have selected $parent(v)$ as the common supernode. At the parent node $parent(v)$, we again check if (|txs($v(o_i)$)| + |txs($parent(v)(o_i)$)|) $\cdot \gamma \geq 2\alpha$. If the condition is met, $parent(v)$ belongs to FinalSV and all the transactions in txs($v(o_i)$) that previously selected node v as the common supernode now select $parent(v)$ as the common supernode. Otherwise, if the condition is not met, we repeat the same procedure by selecting the parent of $parent(v)$ and so on until the inequality

$$(|\text{txs}(v(o_i))| + |\text{txs}(parent(v)(o_i))| + \ldots) \cdot \gamma \geq 2\alpha$$

is satisfied or reach at v'_{root}. We apply this approach recursively until at each leaf node $v \in P$, numtxs(v)$\cdot \gamma \geq 2\alpha$ where P is the pruned tree containing nodes only up to final set of common supernodes FinalSV starting from v'_{root}.

Phase 4: In this phase, we find the transaction execution schedule $\mathcal{E}$ and the paths of movement for each object $o_i \in \mathcal{O}$ along their respective supernodes. We find the pruned tree P containing the nodes up to the common supernodes in FinalSV starting from v'_{root}. Then we perform iterative pre-order traversal on P starting from v'_{root}. At each current visited node v, if $v \in$ FinalSV, then all the transactions which have selected v as their common supernode (i.e., $sv(T_*) = v$) are added to the execution schedule $\mathcal{E}$. Additionally, the objects in $\mathcal{O}$ for which v is a common supernode (i.e., objs(v)) are scheduled to move at v. An object $o_k \in$ objs(v) remains at v until all the transactions that require o_k finish their executions. After all the transactions that require object $o_k \in$ objs(v) finish their executions, o_k can move to the next common supernode in the order where other transactions are waiting for it. When the traversal of P completes, all the transactions get scheduled and the algorithm ends.

Theorem 4. *Algorithm* MULTIPLEOBJECTS-TXMIGR *provides* k-*approximation in communication cost, where k is the maximum number of objects a transaction accesses.*

Proof. After computing the final set of common supernodes FinalSV, at the bottommost common super $v \in$ FinalSV in each branch of G, the number of transactions that require object o are at least 2α. These 2α number of transactions in the sub-tree of v may require $k \leq \delta$ number of objects in $\mathcal{O}$. Thus node v can be a common supernode for all those 2α transactions with respect to $k \leq \delta$ objects. During the execution, these k objects are moved from v'_{root} to v and the cost is $k \cdot 2\alpha \cdot \mathrm{dist}(v'_{root}, v)$. Instead, if we move those 2α transactions up towards some closest common supernode v_j that contains at least $k \cdot 2\alpha$ number of transactions, then the cost due to transaction migration increases by $2\alpha \cdot \mathrm{dist}(v_j, v)$ reducing the object movement cost by $k \cdot 2\alpha \cdot \mathrm{dist}(v_j, v)$. That means the total cost may increase by at most a k factor from optimal. $\qquad\square$

Arbitrary Initial Positions of Objects. We discuss algorithm MULTIPLEOBJECTS-TXMIGR with the relaxed setting where objects are located at arbitrary nodes of G initially. In this case, before Phase 1, we compute the virtual root v'_{root} of G using Eq. 5. All the objects in $\mathcal{O}$ are then moved to v'_{root}. After this, algorithm continues with Phase 1 to Phase 4 as it is. There is an extra cost incurred before Phase 1 due to the movements of objects from their home nodes to the virtual root. Let C_{extra} represents this cost due to the movements of objects from their home nodes to v_{root} which is:

$$C_{extra} = \sum_{o_i \in \mathcal{O}} \alpha \cdot \mathrm{dist}(\mathrm{home}(o_i), v'_{root}) \qquad (9)$$

Let FinalSV be the finalized set of common supernodes computed in Phase 3 of algorithm MULTIPLEOBJECTS-TXMIGR after moving all objects in $\mathcal{O}$ to v'_{root}. Let C_{mov} be the total cost due to the movements of objects from v'_{root} to their respective common supernodes in FinalSV following the iterative pre-order tree traversal. Now, let $S(o_i)$ be the sets of supernodes computed with respect to each object $o_i \in \mathcal{O}$ positioned at the respective home node and using algorithm SINGLE-OBJECT without optimization. Let $C_{opt-mov}$ denotes the total cost due to the movements of objects in their respective supernodes in $S(o_*)$ following iterative pre-order tree traversal. By Theorem 2, we have that $C_{opt-mov}$ is asymptotically optimal with respect to the objects movement cost.

If $C_{extra} + C_{mov} \leq k \cdot C_{opt-mov}$, then algorithm MULTIPLEOBJECTS-TXMIGR has performance as in Theorem 4 in the relaxed setting as well. Otherwise, by Eq. 5, it provides $O(\alpha \cdot k \cdot D)$-approximation in the relaxed setting because of the bound $\mathrm{dist}(\mathrm{home}(o), v'_{root}) \leq D$, where D is the diameter of tree G.

Acknowledgements. G. Sharma was supported by National Science Foundation under Grant No. CAREER CNS-2045597.

References

1. Armstrong, J.: Programming Erlang: Software for a Concurrent World. Pragmatic Bookshelf (2007)
2. Arnold, K., Scheifler, R., Waldo, J., O'Sullivan, B., Wollrath, A.: Jini Specification. Addison-Wesley Longman Publishing (1999)
3. Attiya, H., Gramoli, V., Milani, A.: Directory protocols for distributed transactional memory. In: Guerraoui, R., Romano, P. (eds.) Transactional Memory. Foundations, Algorithms, Tools, and Applications. LNCS, vol. 8913, pp. 367–391. Springer, Cham (2015). https://doi.org/10.1007/978-3-319-14720-8_17
4. Bocchino Jr., R.L., Adve, V.S., Chamberlain, B.L.: Software transactional memory for large scale clusters. In: PPOPP, pp. 247–258. ACM (2008)
5. Busch, C., Herlihy, M., Popovic, M., Sharma, G.: Time-communication impossibility results for distributed transactional memory. Distrib. Comput. 31(6), 471–487 (2018)
6. Busch, C., Herlihy, M., Popovic, M., Sharma, G.: Dynamic scheduling in distributed transactional memory. In: IPDPS, pp. 874–883. IEEE (2020)
7. Busch, C., Herlihy, M., Popovic, M., Sharma, G.: Fast scheduling in distributed transactional memory. Theory Comput. Syst. 65(2), 296–322 (2021)
8. Comer, D.E.: The Cloud Computing Book: The Future of Computing Explained. Chapman and Hall/CRC (2021)
9. Hendler, D., Naiman, A., Peluso, S., Quaglia, F., Romano, P., Suissa, A.: Exploiting locality in lease-based replicated transactional memory via task migration. In: Afek, Y. (ed.) DISC 2013. LNCS, vol. 8205, pp. 121–133. Springer, Heidelberg (2013). https://doi.org/10.1007/978-3-642-41527-2_9
10. Herlihy, M., Moss, J.E.B.: Transactional memory: architectural support for lock-free data structures. In: ISCA, pp. 289–300. ACM (1993)
11. Herlihy, M., Sun, Y.: Distributed transactional memory for metric-space networks. Distrib. Comput. 20(3), 195–208 (2007)
12. Hirve, S., Palmieri, R., Ravindran, B.: HiperTM: high performance, fault-tolerant transactional memory. Theoret. Comput. Sci. 688, 86–102 (2017)
13. Hwang, K., Dongarra, J., Fox, G.C.: Distributed and Cloud Computing: From Parallel Processing to the Internet of Things. Morgan Kaufmann Publishers, Burlington (2011)
14. Kim, J., Ravindran, B.: Scheduling transactions in replicated distributed software transactional memory. In: CCGrid, pp. 227–234. IEEE Computer Society (2013)
15. Kobus, T., Kokocinski, M., Wojciechowski, P.T.: Hybrid replication: state-machine-based and deferred-update replication schemes combined. In: ICDCS, pp. 286–296. IEEE Computer Society (2013)
16. Manassiev, K., Mihailescu, M., Amza, C.: Exploiting distributed version concurrency in a transactional memory cluster. In: PPOPP, pp. 198–208. ACM (2006)
17. Palmieri, R., Peluso, S., Ravindran, B.: Transaction execution models in partially replicated transactional memory: the case for data-flow and control-flow. In: Guerraoui, R., Romano, P. (eds.) Transactional Memory. Foundations, Algorithms, Tools, and Applications. LNCS, vol. 8913, pp. 341–366. Springer, Cham (2015). https://doi.org/10.1007/978-3-319-14720-8_16
18. Peluso, S., Ruivo, P., Romano, P., Quaglia, F., Rodrigues, L.E.T.: When scalability meets consistency: genuine multiversion update-serializable partial data replication. In: ICDCS, pp. 455–465. IEEE Computer Society (2012)

19. Poudel, P., Sharma, G.: GraphTM: an efficient framework for supporting trans-actional memory in a distributed environment. In: ICDCN, pp. 11:1–11:10. ACM (2020)
20. Ruth, P., Rhee, J., Xu, D., Kennell, R., Goasguen, S.: Autonomic live adaptation of virtual computational environments in a multi-domain infrastructure. In: ICAC, pp. 5–14. IEEE Computer Society (2006)
21. Saad, M.M., Ravindran, B.: HyFlow: a high performance distributed software transactional memory framework. In: HPDC, pp. 265–266. ACM (2011)
22. Saad, M.M., Ravindran, B.: Snake: control flow distributed software transactional memory. In: Défago, X., Petit, F., Villain, V. (eds.) SSS 2011. LNCS, vol. 6976, pp. 238–252. Springer, Heidelberg (2011). https://doi.org/10.1007/978-3-642-24550-3_19
23. Sharma, G., Busch, C.: Distributed transactional memory for general networks. Distrib. Comput. **27**(5), 329–362 (2014). https://doi.org/10.1007/s00446-014-0214-7
24. Sharma, G., Busch, C.: A load balanced directory for distributed shared memory objects. J. Parallel Distrib. Comput. **78**, 6–24 (2015)
25. Shavit, N., Touitou, D.: Software transactional memory. Distrib. Comput. **10**(2), 99–116 (1997)
26. Siek, K., Wojciechowski, P.T.: Atomic RMI: a distributed transactional memory framework. Int. J. Parallel Prog. **44**(3), 598–619 (2016)
27. Tilevich, E., Smaragdakis, Y.: J-Orchestra: automatic java application partition-ing. In: Magnusson, B. (ed.) ECOOP 2002. LNCS, vol. 2374, pp. 178–204. Springer, Heidelberg (2002). https://doi.org/10.1007/3-540-47993-7_8
28. Zhang, B., Ravindran, B., Palmieri, R.: Distributed transactional contention man-agement as the traveling salesman problem. In: Halldórsson, M.M. (ed.) SIROCCO 2014. LNCS, vol. 8576, pp. 54–67. Springer, Cham (2014). https://doi.org/10.1007/978-3-319-09620-9_6

Perpetual Torus Exploration by Myopic Luminous Robots

Omar Darwich[1], Ahmet-Sefa Ulucan[2], Quentin Bramas[1], Anissa Lamani[1(✉)], Anaïs Durand[3], and Pascal Lafourcade[3]

[1] University of Strasbourg, CNRS UMR 7357, ICUBE, Strasbourg, France
alamani@unistra.fr
[2] University of Strasbourg, Strasbourg, France
[3] University Clermont Auvergne, CNRS UMR 6158, LIMOS, Clermont-Ferrand, France

Abstract. We study perpetual torus exploration for swarm of autonomous, anonymous, uniform, luminous robots with a common chirality. We consider robots with only few capabilities. They have a finite limited vision (myopic), they can only see robots at distance one or two. We show that the problem is impossible with only two luminous robots and also with three oblivious robots (without light). We design an optimal algorithm for three luminous robots using two colors and with visibility one. We also propose an optimal algorithm with visibility two with four oblivious robots.

Keywords: Perpetual exploration · Luminous robots · Torus-shaped network

1 Introduction

Swarm robotics has drawn a lot of attention the past decade. Inspired by natural systems, a lot of investigations focused on how to reproduce autonomous behaviors observed in nature within artificial systems. Given a collection of autonomous mobile entities called robots, the main focus is to determine the minimum hypothesis in order for the robots to solve a given task. Robots can evolve either on a continuous 2D plane on which they can freely move or on a discrete universe, generally represented by a graph, where nodes indicate possible locations of the robots and the edges the possibility for the robots to move from one node to another.

In this paper, we assume that the mobile robots are autonomous (*i.e.* there is no central authority to coordinate their move), anonymous (*i.e.* they have no identity), uniform (*i.e.* they all execute the same algorithm) and luminous (*i.e.* they are endowed with lights of different colors). Moreover, they cannot communicate directly but are endowed by visibility sensors allowing them to sense their environment within a certain distance called visibility range. We assume myopic robots that can only sense at small distances. Robots operate in the well-known LCM model. That is, they operate in cycles which comprise three phases: Look, Compute, and Move. During the first phase (Look), robots take a snapshot of their environment using their visibility sensors. In the second phase (Compute), based on the taken snapshot, they first decide whether to move or remain idle and then whether they change their color. If they decide to move, they compute a

S. Devismes et al. (Eds.): SSS 2022, LNCS 13751, pp. 164–177, 2022.
https://doi.org/10.1007/978-3-031-21017-4_11

neighboring destination. Similarly, they compute a new color if they decide to change it. Finally, in the last phase (Move), they move to the computed destination (if any) and they change their color (if they decided to). We consider the fully synchronous model (FSYNC) in which all robots execute the LCM cycle synchronously and atomically.

In the following, we investigate the case in which the robots have to solve the perpetual exploration problem. In this problem, robots evolve in a discrete universe and have to ensure that each location (node) is visited by at least one robot infinitely often. We are interested in torus shaped networks and focus on optimal exclusive solutions with respect to both the visibility range and the number of robots. Exclusiveness add an additional constraint on robots behavior as they can neither occupy the same node simultaneously or traverse the same edge at the same time.

2   Related Work

The exploration problem is considered as one of the benchmarking tasks when it comes to robots evolving on graphs. Various topologies have been considered: lines [14], rings [1,9,12,15,16], tori [11], grids [2,4,5,10], cuboids [3], and trees [13]. Two variants of the problem has been investigated: (i) the perpetual exploration problem [1–3,17], considered in this paper, which requires the robots to visit each node of the graph infinitely often and (ii) the terminating exploration problem [9–15] which requires the robots to visit each node of the graph at least once and then stop moving.

Most of the investigations consider robots with unlimited visibility range allowing them to observe every node of the system [1,2,10–15]. Robots are in this case oblivious (*i.e.* they cannot remember past actions) and have to solve the terminating exploration problem. Myopic robots have also been considered in both variants of the problem [4,6,8,9,16]. When it comes to the perpetual exploration problem, an additional assumption has an impact on the feasibility of the task and the optimality of the proposed solutions. This assumption endow the robots with a common chirality. In fact, chirality is usually assumed when robots evolve in the continuous 2D Euclidean plan but some investigations have also considered it recently in the discrete universe. On finite grids, it has been shown that two (resp. three) synchronous robots with three colors (resp. one color) are sufficient to solve the problem when robots have visibility one and share a common chirality [6]. The case in which robots have no common chirality was investigated in [17]. It was proven that the problem is not solvable with only two robots having any finite number of colors and a finite visibility range. An optimal solution is also presented using only three robots having visibility range one, using only three colors. The case in which robots are oblivious and visibility range 2 was solved using five robots. In the case of infinite grids, assuming robots with visibility range one and few colors (O(1)), five (resp. six) synchronous robots are necessary and sufficient to solve the problem with (resp. without) the common chirality assumption [4,5]. Finally, in the case of cuboids, it has been shown in [3] that three synchronous robots with a common chirality endowed with five colors are necessary and sufficient to solve the perpetual exploration problem.

Contribution: We first present two impossibility results: we start by showing that the perpetual torus exploration problem is not solvable with only two robots if the number of colors is finite and their visibility range is limited. We then show that three oblivious robots are not sufficient to solve the PTE problem. Next, we propose two optimal solutions $\mathcal{A}_3^2$ and $\mathcal{A}_4^1$ with respect to both the number of robots and the number of colors for the case of visibility one and two respectively. Table 1 summarizes our contribution:

Table 1. Summary of our results.

Visibility	# Robots	# Colors	Algorithm
Finite	2	Finite	Impossible (Theorem 1)
Finite	3	1	Impossible (Theorem 2)
1	3	2	$\mathcal{A}_3^2$
2	4	1	$\mathcal{A}_4^1$

3   Model

We consider a set $\mathcal{R}$ of $n > 0$ robots located on a *torus*. A graph $G = (V, E)$ is a (l, L)-torus (or torus for short) if $|V| = l \times L$ and for any $v_{(i,j)} \in V$; $i \in [0, l-1]$, $j \in [0, L-1]$:

- $\{v_{(i,j)}, v_{((i+1) \bmod l, j)}\} \in E$, and
- $\{v_{(i,j)}, v_{(i,(j+1) \bmod L)}\} \in E$.

The order on the nodes of G forms a coordinate system. For example node $v_{(i,j)}$ is at coordinate (i, j), or, the node is at column i and row j. For simplicity we note node (i, j) instead of $v_{(i,j)}$. This order/coordinate is used for the analysis only, *i.e.*, robots cannot access it.

At each time instant called a *round*, the robots synchronously perform a *Look-Compute-Move* cycle. In the *Look* phase, a robot gets a snapshot of the subgraph induced by the nodes within distance $\Phi \in \mathbb{N}^*$ from its position. Φ is called the *visibility range* of the robots. The snapshot is not oriented in any way as the robots do not agree on a common North. However, it is implicitly ego-centered since the robot that performs a Look phase is located at the center of the subgraph in the obtained snapshot. Robots agree on a common chirality. Then, each robot *computes* a destination (either Up, Left, Down, Right or Idle) based only on the snapshot it received. Finally, it *moves* towards its computed destination. We also assume that robots are *opaque*, *i.e.*, they obstruct the visibility in such way that if three robots are aligned, the two extremities cannot see each other. We forbid any two robots to occupy the same node simultaneously. A node is *occupied* when a robot is located at this node, otherwise it is *empty*.

Robots may have *lights* with different colors that can be seen by robots within distance Φ from them. We denote by Cl the set of all possible colors. For simplicity, we assume that all tore has dimensions $l \times L$ where $l, L \geq n\Phi + 1$.

The *state* of a node is either the color of the light of the robot located at this node, if it is occupied, or $\perp$ otherwise. In the Look phase, the snapshot includes the state of the nodes (within distance Φ, including its current node). During the compute phase, a robot may decide to change the color of its light.

In all our algorithms, we also prevent any two robots from traversing the same edge simultaneously. Since we already forbid them to occupy the same position simultaneously, this means that we additionally prevent robots from swapping their position. Algorithms verifying this property are said to be *exclusive*. However, to be as general as possible, we do not make this additional assumption in our impossibility results.

In the following, we borrow some of the definitions already presented in [17].

Configurations. A *configuration* C in a torus $G(V, E)$ is a set of pairs (p, c), where $p \in V$ is an occupied node and $c \in Cl$ is the color of the robot located at p. A node p is empty if and only if $\forall c, (p, c) \notin C$. We sometimes just write the set of occupied nodes when the colors are clear from the context.

Views. We denote by G_r the *globally oriented view* centered at the robot r, *i.e.*, the subset of the configuration containing the states of the nodes at distance at most Φ from r, translated so that the coordinates of r is $(0, 0)$. We use this globally oriented view in our analysis to describe the movements of the robots: when we say "the robot moves Up", it is according to the globally oriented view. However, since robots do not agree on a common North, they have no access to the globally oriented view. When a robot looks at its surroundings, it instead obtains a snapshot. To model this, we assume that the *local view* acquired by a robot r in the Look phase is the result of an arbitrary *indistinguishable transformation* on G_r. The set $\mathcal{IT}$ of indistinguishable transformations contains the rotations of angle 0 (to have the identity), $\pi/2$, π and $3\pi/2$, centered at r. Moreover, since robots may obstruct visibility, the function that removes the state of a node u if there is another robot between u and r is *systematically* applied to obtain the local view. Finally, we assume that robots are *self-inconsistent*, meaning that different transformations may be applied at different rounds.

It is important to note that when a robot r computes a destination d, it is relative to its local view $f(G_r)$, which is the globally oriented view transformed by some $f \in \mathcal{IT}$. So, the actual movement of the robot in the *globally oriented view* is $f^{-1}(d)$. For example, if $d = Up$ but the robot sees the torus upside-down (f is the π-rotation), then the robot moves $Down = f^{-1}(Up)$. In a configuration C, $V_C(i, j)$ denotes the globally oriented view of a robot located at (i, j).

Algorithm. An algorithm $\mathcal{A}$ is a tuple $(Cl, Init, T)$ where Cl is the set of possible colors, $Init$ is a mapping from any considered torus to a non-empty set of initial configurations in that torus, and T is the transition function $Views \rightarrow \{Idle, Up, Left, Down, Right\} \times Cl$, where $Views$ is the set of local views. When the robots are in Configuration C, a configuration C' obtained after one round satisfies: for all $((i, j), c) \in C'$, there exists a robot in C with color $c' \in Cl$ and a transformation $f \in \mathcal{IT}$ such that one of the following conditions holds:

- $((i, j), c') \in C$ and $f^{-1}(T(f(V_C(i, j)))) = (Idle, c)$,
- $(((i - 1) \bmod l, j), c') \in C$ and $f^{-1}(T(f(V_C((i - 1) \bmod l, j)))) = (Right, c)$,

- $(((i+1) \bmod l, j), c') \in C$ and $f^{-1}(T(f(V_C((i+1) \bmod l, j)))) = (Left, c)$,
- $((i, (j-1) \bmod L), c') \in C$ and $f^{-1}(T(f(V_C(i, (j-1) \bmod L)))) = (Up, c)$, or
- $((i, (j+1) \bmod L), c') \in C$ and $f^{-1}(T(f(V_C(i, (j+1) \bmod L)))) = (Down, c)$.

We denote by $C \mapsto C'$ the fact that C' can be reached in one round from C ($n.b.$, $\mapsto$ is then a binary relation over configurations). An execution of Algorithm $\mathcal{A}$ in a torus G is then a sequence $(C_i)_{i \in \mathbb{N}}$ of configurations such that $C_0 \in Init(G)$ and $\forall i \geq 0$, $C_i \mapsto C_{i+1}$.

Definition 1 (Perpetual Torus Exploration). *An algorithm $\mathcal{A}$ solves the* Perpetual Torus Exploration *(PTE) problem if in any execution $(C_i)_{i \in \mathbb{N}}$ of $\mathcal{A}$ and for any node $(i, j) \in V$ of the torus and any time t, there exists $t' > t$ such that (i, j) is occupied in $C_{t'}$.*

Notations. $\vec{t}_{(i,j)}(C)$ denotes the translation of the configuration C of vector (i, j).

4   Impossibility Results

Lemma 1. *Let $\mathcal{A}$ be an algorithm using a set $\mathcal{R}$ of $n > 0$ robots. If $\mathcal{A}$ solves the exploration problem for any torus then, there exists a tori such that for any execution $(C_i)_{i \in \mathbb{N}}$ of $\mathcal{A}$ on this torus, there is a configuration C_i such that the distance between the two farthest robots is at least $2\Phi + 3$.*

Proof. We proceed by contradiction. Assume, there is an algorithm $\mathcal{A}$ that solves the PTE problem and let $0 < B$ be the farthest any of the robots will be from each other, in any torus. Let $(C_i)_{i \in \mathbb{N}}$ be the execution of $\mathcal{A}$ on a very large torus $l, L \gg B$. When all robots are at distance at most B, then the occupied positions are included in a square sub-grid of size $B \times B$. Since the number of possible configurations included in a sub-grid of size $B \times B$ is finite, there must be two indices t_1 and t_2, when the positions and colors of the robots in the corresponding sub-grids are the same, formally, such that $C_{t_2} = \vec{t}_{(i,j)}(C_{t_1})$ and $t_1 < t_2$ for a given translation $\vec{t}_{(i,j)}$. By making the adversary choose the same rotation, the movements done by the robots in configurations C_{t_1} and C_{t_2} are the same as each robot has the same globally oriented view in both configurations, only their positions on the torus change. Thus $C_{t_2+1} = \vec{t}_{(i,j)}(C_{t_1+1})$ and so on so forth, so that $\forall x$, $C_{t_2+x} = \vec{t}_{(i,j)}(C_{t_1+x})$. We obtain that the configurations are periodic with period $p = t_2 - t_1$, up to translation.

Suppose, that the torus being explored is of dimensions $l \times L$ with $l = 3np^3 \max(|i|, 1)$ and $L = 3np^3 \max(|j|, 1)$. The dimensions of the torus are proportional to the non-null scalar components of translation $\vec{t}_{(i,j)}$ i.e., $i3np^3 \equiv 0 \bmod l$ and $j3np^3 \equiv 0 \bmod L$. This means that,

$$(\vec{t}_{(i,j)})^{3np^3}(C_{t_1}) = \vec{t}_{(i3np^3, j3np^3)}(C_{t_1}) = \vec{t}_{(0,0)}(C_{t_1}) = C_{t_1}.$$

Since translation $\vec{t}_{(i,j)}$ is performed in p rounds, after $p \times 3np^3 = 3np^4$ rounds, all robots will retake their initial positions, so the whole configuration is periodic with period $3np^4$. In this setting, a node is visited infinitely often if and only if it is visited between round t_1 and $t_1 + 3np^4$. Now we have to prove that some nodes are left unvisited between round t_1 and $t_1 + 3np^4$.

Between time t_1 and $t_1 + 3np^4$, each robot visits at most $3np^4$ nodes, hence all the robots visit at most $n \times 3np^4$ nodes after t_1. However, there are at least $9n^2p^6 \leq l \times L$ nodes in the torus. Hence, there exist some nodes which are not visited infinitely often, which is a contradiction.

Note that we only proved there are some nodes that are not perpetually visited. Nevertheless, observe that at most nt_1 nodes are visited before t_1 and we can increase arbitrarily the chosen period p by a factor $f \in \mathbb{N}^*$ without changing the result (in particular t_1 does not depend on f). By taking $f \geq 1$ such that $9n^2(fp)^6 - 3n^2(fp)^4 > nt_1$, we have that the number of visited nodes (before or after t_1) is $nt_1 + 3n^2(fp)^4$ and is smaller than the number of nodes in the torus $(9n^2(fp)^6)$, hence there is at least one node that is never visited. This implies that the impossibility also holds for non-perpetual algorithms as well (where each node must be visited at most once).   □

We restate the following lemma proven in [5].

Lemma 2. *A robot with self-inconsistent compass and that sees no other robot, either stays idle or the adversary can make it alternatively move between two chosen adjacent nodes.*

Theorem 1. *It is impossible to solve the exploration problem with two myopic robots equipped with self-inconsistent compasses that agree on a common chirality.*

Proof. By Lemma 1, there is a torus and a configuration where the two robots are at distance $2\Phi + 3$ from each other. In this case the two robots are isolated. By Lemma 2, the two robots will remain idle or the adversary can make them alternatively move between two nodes, never being in vision from each other and never visiting another node.   □

Theorem 2. *It is impossible to solve the exploration problem with three anonymous, oblivious and myopic robots equipped with self-inconsistent compasses that agree on a common chirality.*

Proof. By Lemma 1, there is a torus and a configuration where the distance between the two farthest robots is $2\Phi + 3$ from each other. We have one of the two following possibilities, (i) there are three isolated robots, or (ii) there is an isolated robot and two robots in vision from each other.

In the first case, it is easy to see that the three isolated robots cannot explore the torus because, by Lemma 2, they have to stay idle or the adversary can make them alternatively move between two nodes, never being in vision from each other and never visiting another node.

In the second case, the two robots that see each other cannot travel together in a direction (because they have the same view). All they can do is get either closer to each other or further from each other. Formally, there is a point P at the middle of the two robots and, if they stay in vision, they will always be at the same distance from that point. The two robots can explore a subgrid $\Phi \times \Phi$ centered at a given middle point. This point is at distance at least $\frac{3\Phi}{2} + 2$ from the isolated robots.

If the two robots in vision gets isolated from one another, they will be at distance $\frac{\Phi}{2} + 1$ from the middle point. In this case, the closest robot to the originally isolated

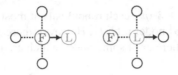

Fig. 1. Rules for moving straight.

robot will be at distance $\Phi + 1$. Now the three robots are isolated, and, as in the first case, they cannot explore the torus.   □

5   Visibility Range One: $\mathcal{A}_3^2$

We present an algorithm, denoted by $\mathcal{A}_3^2$, which assumes a visibility range one and uses three robots and two colors. By Theorem 1, $\mathcal{A}_3^2$ is optimal w.r.t. the number of robots, and by Theorem 2, $\mathcal{A}_3^2$ is also optimal w.r.t. the number of colors. Animations are made available online [7] to help the reader visualize the algorithm.

The idea of the algorithm is to make the robots alternate between exploring a row and exploring a column. To explore the whole torus, robots move so that all the nodes of the torus are explored eventually often. More precisely, after exploring row r_i and column c_j, the robots will proceed at exploring row $r_{i-1 \bmod L}$ and then column $c_{j-1 \bmod l}$ and so on.

Initially the robots are co-linear with respectively color L, F, F^1. The line of the torus on which they are located is considered as a row. The robot with color F which does not sense the robot of color L moves up changing its color to L while the two other robots move along their current row in the following manner: the robot initially with color L moves away from the one with color F and the remaining robot just follows it.

To explore a row (resp. column), one robot stays idle while the two others travel in a straight line along the nodes of the row (resp. column) being explored until they reach the idle robot. The idle robot is located on an neighboring row (resp. column). The idle robot has color L and is called the *landmark*. The two robots traveling together on a straight line have different colors. One robot, called the *follower*, has color F and the other robot, called the *leader*, has color L. To explore a row (resp. column), the two robots have to be next to each other on that row (resp. column). The follower always follows the leader and leader always moves away from the follower. This is done by executing the rules presented in Fig. 1.[2]

The tricky part of this algorithm is how robots switch from exploring a column to exploring a row and *vice versa*. When exploring a column, the robot left behind (aka the landmark) is on the right side of the traveling group. When the leader of the traveling group reaches the landmark, it moves away from the landmark on its current row and

---

[1] Note that any reachable configuration can be an initial configuration.

[2] In all figures, colored letters inside nodes indicate the color of the robots occupying the nodes. Moreover when a colored letter is given next to a node, it indicates which color the robot will take in the next round.

updates its color to F. Meanwhile, the follower continues to follow the leader. In the next round, the three robots are aligned on the same row. The landmark then moves away from the follower and remains on its row followed by the follower. These two robots become the new traveling group. Whereas the leader, moves to the next row so that it becomes on the left side of the traveling group. That is, the landmark and the leader switch their roles and the new traveling group proceed at the exploration of the row on which there are located. The rules relative to this operation are presented in Fig. 2. The corresponding sequence of configurations is illustrated in Fig. 3.

Fig. 2. Rules for switching from moving upward to sideward.

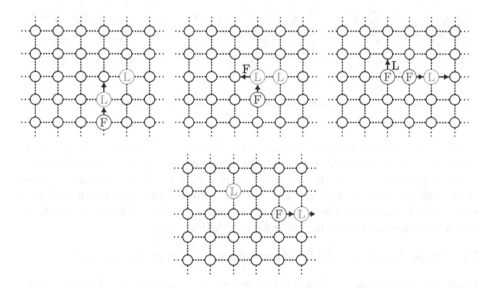

Fig. 3. Sequence of configurations when robots move from exploring a column to exploring a row.

The traveling group are now exploring a row, when they reach the landmark again, the landmark is this time, on the right side. The robots proceed to move to the next column to be explored. More precisely, when the leader reaches the landmark, it continues forward on its current row and changes its color to F. The follower also continues to move towards the leader. After one round, the robots will be in a L-shaped form with two robots colored F and one robot colored L. In the next round, the two robots on the left form the new traveling group and they both move to explore the new column. The robot on the right, moves down and changes its color to L, it becomes the new landmark. The set of rules relevant to this sequence is in Fig. 4 and the corresponding sequence of configurations are presented in Fig. 5.

Fig. 4. Rules for switching from moving upward to sideward.

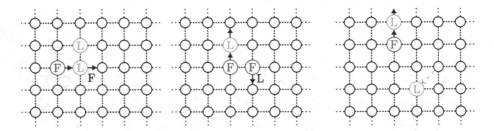

Fig. 5. Sequence of configurations when moving from exploring a row to exploring a column.

It is important to note that every node on a column/row is visited during the exploration of that column/row. Also, the landmark moves two nodes to the left and one node up when going from exploring a column to exploring a row. And, it moves one node to the right and two nodes downward when going from exploring a row to exploring a column. This means that between two consecutive columns (rows) exploration, the landmark moves one node to the left and one node downward.

Theorem 3. A_2^3 solves the PTE problem with three robots and two colors.

Proof. By induction on $l \times L$, where l is the number of columns and L is the number of rows of the torus.

We have validated the base case, for tori of size 4×4, using our simulation tool. Such a checking is easy since, from a given initial configuration, there is only one possible execution (the algorithm is well-defined and the execution is synchronous). So, we just have to execute the algorithm until reaching an already encountered configuration from which all the nodes have been visited.

We assume now that $\mathcal{A}_2^3$ solves the PTE problem in all tori $x \times y$ with $4 \le x \le l$ and $4 \le y \le L$ for some values $l, L \ge 4$ and show that $\mathcal{A}_2^3$ solves also the PTE problem in a torus of size $l \times (L + 1)$ and $(l + 1) \times L$.

Consider first the torus of size $l \times (L + 1)$. Then, it is easy to see that after adding one row, our algorithm still solves the PTE problem. Indeed, when robots are traveling upward (*i.e.* they are exploring a row), they move in a straight line periodically until they reach the landmark, so adding one row just increases by one the number of times they perform their periodic movement. And, when robots are traveling sideward (*i.e.* they are exploring a column), they visit all the nodes of the corresponding column.

Now, for the torus of size $(l + 1) \times L$. The same argument from the torus of size $l \times (L + 1)$ could be used. When robots are traveling sideward, they will perform an extra step for the added column. And, when they travel upward, they will revisit the same nodes visited during the exploration of rows.   □

6   Visibility Range Two: $\mathcal{A}_4^1$

We present an algorithm, denoted by $\mathcal{A}_4^1$, which assumes a visibility range two and uses four oblivious robots. $\mathcal{A}_4^1$ is optimal w.r.t. the number of colors. By Theorem 2, $\mathcal{A}_4^1$ is optimal w.r.t. the number of robots, for oblivious robots. Animations are made available online [7] to help the reader visualize the algorithm.

The idea of the algorithm is to make the robots explore the torus rows by rows in a given direction. This is achieved as follows: Three robots, referred to as the traveling group, move to explore three adjacent rows at the same time, and one robot is left behind to be used as their landmark. When the traveling group reaches the landmark, all four robots perform a three rounds sequence to move to the next rows to be explored.

When exploring the rows, the traveling group form a $>$ shape. That is, two robots are located on the same column separated by one empty node, denoted u. And, on the right of u, the third robot is placed. The three robots move to the right until they sense the landmark. Note that the direction is pointed by the third mentioned robot. Figure 6 presents the rules executed by the robots part of the traveling group.

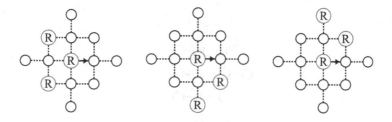

Fig. 6. Rules for three robots moving straight.

The landmark is left behind so that the traveling group knows when they are done exploring the current rows and have to move to the next ones. Note that the landmark is on the same row as the top most robot. When that robot is one node away from the landmark it goes down, same for the landmark since they have the same view. The bottom robot keeps going right because it does not see the landmark. And, the center robot stays idle. After one round, the robots form a T-shape. The rules executed by the robots are presented in Fig. 7.

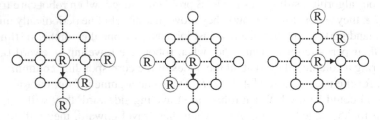

Fig. 7. Rules executed when robots initiate rows change.

From the T-shape, the robot move to create a reverse L shape *i.e.* the two robots in the center of the T-shape move down while the robot on the right goes left. Figure 8 presents the rules executed during this process.

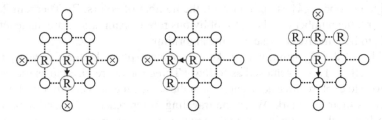

Fig. 8. Rules for the creation of the reverse L shape.

Within the reverse L shape, three robots are co-linear (the ones located on the long side). Among these robots, the one in the middle moves to the right to recreate the > shape while all the other robots remain idle. Refer to the rule presented Fig. 9. That is, after three rounds the robots changes rows and the > shape is built again.

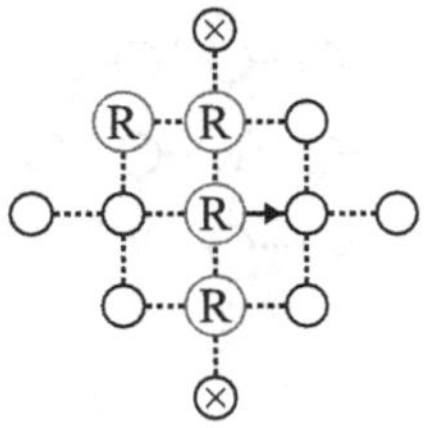

Fig. 9. Rule for restoring the > shape.

Now the three robots on the right form the new traveling group. The robots repeat the same behavior and hence start moving right until they reach the landmark once

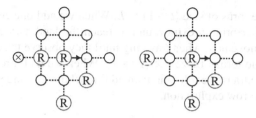

Fig. 10. Rules for the top most robot to keep traveling with the group.

more. There are two more rules to tell the top most robot in the traveling group to keep following the group even if it sees the landmark at the back. These rules are presented in Fig. 10.

It is important to note that the landmark changes its position two nodes to the right and one node down. The fact that it moves down makes the robots always explore a new row. Figure 11 presents the sequence of configuration during this process.

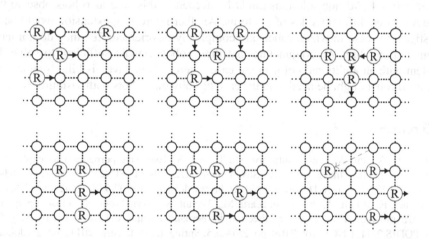

Fig. 11. Sequence for changing rows. The red dashed arrow highlights the movement of the landmark. (Color figure online)

Robots form initially the reverse L shape.

Theorem 4. $\mathcal{A}_1^4$ *solves the PTE problem with four oblivious robots.*

Proof. By induction on $l \times L$, where l is the number of columns and L is the number of rows of the torus.

Similar to the proof of Theorem 3, we have validated one base case for $l, L = 9$, using our simulation tool.

We assume now that $\mathcal{A}_1^4$ solves the PTE problem in all tori $x \times y$ with $9 \leq x \leq l$ and $9 \leq y \leq L$ for some values $l, L \geq 9$. We should show that $\mathcal{A}_1^4$ solves the PTE problem in the tore of size $l \times (L + 1)$ and $(l + 1) \times L$.

Consider first the torus of size $(l + 1) \times L$. When we add one column the traveling group will have to perform an extra round to reach the landmark again as the robots perform a periodic movement when traveling until they observe the landmark.

Now, consider the torus of size $l \times (L + 1)$. When we add a row. The robots will have to perform an extra row exploration: an additional three round sequence to change rows followed by the row exploration.   □

7 Conclusion

We presented two optimal solutions for the PTE problem with respect to both the number of robots and the number of colors when robots share a common chirality and have visibility one and two respectively. Indeed, we have shown that three robots endowed with two colors are necessary and sufficient to solve the problem when robots have visibility one and four oblivious robots are necessary and sufficient to solve the problem when robots have visibility two.

One direct open question is to extend the study to consider (L, l)-tori such that $l, L < n\varPhi + 1$. Ad-hoc solutions might be needed in this case as robots observe the same robots on different sides of the torus. Another interesting extension would be to investigate the case in which robots are completely disoriented, *i.e.*, they do not have a common chirality. We conjuncture that three robots remain sufficient to solve the problem with an additional color in the case where robots have visibility one and an additional robot might be needed in the case of oblivious robots with visibility two.

References

1. Blin, L., Milani, A., Potop-Butucaru, M., Tixeuil, S.: Exclusive perpetual ring exploration without chirality. In: Lynch, N.A., Shvartsman, A.A. (eds.) DISC 2010. LNCS, vol. 6343, pp. 312–327. Springer, Heidelberg (2010). https://doi.org/10.1007/978-3-642-15763-9_29
2. Bonnet, F., Milani, A., Potop-Butucaru, M., Tixeuil, S.: Asynchronous exclusive perpetual grid exploration without sense of direction. In: Fernàndez Anta, A., Lipari, G., Roy, M. (eds.) OPODIS 2011. LNCS, vol. 7109, pp. 251–265. Springer, Heidelberg (2011). https://doi.org/10.1007/978-3-642-25873-2_18
3. Bramas, Q., Devismes, S., Lafourcade, A.D.P., Lamani, A.: Beedroids: how luminous autonomous swam of UAVs can save the world? In: 11th International Conference on Fun with Algorithms (FUN 2022), LIPIcs (2022, to appear)
4. Bramas, Q., Devismes, S., Lafourcade, P.: Finding water on poleless using melomaniac myopic chameleon robots. In: FUN 2020, 10th International Conference on Fun with Algorithms, Favignana, Sicily, Italy, 28–30 September 2020. LiPICs (2020, to appear)
5. Bramas, Q., Devismes, S., Lafourcade, P.: Infinite grid exploration by disoriented robots. In: Georgiou, C., Majumdar, R. (eds.) NETYS 2020. LNCS, vol. 12129, pp. 129–145. Springer, Cham (2021). https://doi.org/10.1007/978-3-030-67087-0_9
6. Bramas, Q., Devismes, S., Lafourcade, P.: Optimal exclusive perpetual grid exploration by luminous myopic opaque robots with common chirality, pp. 76–85, 5–8 January 2021
7. Darwich, O., Ulucan, A.-S., Bramas, Q., Lamani, A., Durand, A., Lafourcade, P.: Perpetual Torus exploration by myopic luminous robots: the animations, April 2022. https://doi.org/10.5281/zenodo.6482690

8. Datta, A.K., Lamani, A., Larmore, L.L., Petit, F.: Ring exploration by oblivious agents with local vision. In: IEEE 33rd International Conference on Distributed Computing Systems, ICDCS 2013, 8–11 July 2013, Philadelphia, Pennsylvania, USA, pp. 347–356. IEEE Computer Society (2013)
9. Datta, A.K., Lamani, A., Larmore, L.L., Petit, F.: Enabling ring exploration with myopic oblivious robots. In: 2015 IEEE International Parallel and Distributed Processing Symposium Workshop, IPDPS 2015, Hyderabad, India, 25–29 May 2015, pp. 490–499. IEEE Computer Society (2015)
10. Devismes, S., Lamani, A., Petit, F., Raymond, P., Tixeuil, S.: Terminating exploration of A grid by an optimal number of asynchronous oblivious robots. Comput. J. **64**(1), 132–154 (2021)
11. Devismes, S., Lamani, A., Petit, F., Tixeuil, S.: Optimal torus exploration by oblivious robots. Computing **101**(9), 1241–1264 (2019)
12. Devismes, S., Petit, F., Tixeuil, S.: Optimal probabilistic ring exploration by semi-synchronous oblivious robots. Theor. Comput. Sci. (TCS) **498**, 10–27 (2013)
13. Flocchini, P., Ilcinkas, D., Pelc, A., Santoro, N.: Remembering without memory: tree exploration by asynchronous oblivious robots. Theor. Comput. Sci. **411**(14–15), 1583–1598 (2010)
14. Flocchini, P., Ilcinkas, D., Pelc, A., Santoro, N.: How many oblivious robots can explore a line. Inf. Process. Lett. **111**(20), 1027–1031 (2011)
15. Flocchini, P., Ilcinkas, D., Pelc, A., Santoro, N.: Computing without communicating: ring exploration by asynchronous oblivious robots. Algorithmica **65**(3), 562–583 (2013)
16. Ooshita, F., Tixeuil, S.: Ring exploration with myopic luminous robots. In: Izumi, T., Kuznetsov, P. (eds.) SSS 2018. LNCS, vol. 11201, pp. 301–316. Springer, Cham (2018). https://doi.org/10.1007/978-3-030-03232-6_20
17. Rauch, A., Bramas, Q., Devismes, S., Lafourcade, P., Lamani, A.: Optimal exclusive perpetual grid exploration by luminous myopic robots without common chirality. In: Echihabi, K., Meyer, R. (eds.) NETYS 2021. LNCS, vol. 12754, pp. 95–110. Springer, Cham (2021). https://doi.org/10.1007/978-3-030-91014-3_7

Optimal Algorithms for Synchronous Byzantine k-Set Agreement

Carole Delporte-Gallet[1] , Hugues Fauconnier[1] , Michel Raynal[2] ,
and Mouna Safir[1,3]($\boxtimes$)

[1] IRIF, Université Paris Cité, Paris, France
{cd,hf,safir}@irif.fr
[2] Univ Rennes IRISA, CNRS, INRIA, Rennes, France
raynal@irisa.fr
[3] School of Computer Sciences, Mohammed VI Polytechnic University, Ben Guerir, Morocco
mouna.safir@um6p.ma

Abstract. Considering a system made up of n processes prone to Byzantine failures, k-set agreement allows each process to propose a value and decide a value such that at most k different values are decided by the correct (i.e., non-Byzantine) processes, in such a way that, if all the correct processes propose the same value v, they will decide v (when $k = 1$, k-set agreement boils down to consensus). This paper presents a two-round algorithm that solves Byzantine k-set agreement on top of a synchronous message-passing system. This algorithm is based on two new notions denoted by Square and Regions which allow processes to locally build a global knowledge on which processes proposed some values. Two instances of the algorithm are presented. Assuming $n = 3t$, where t is the maximum number of Byzantine, the first instance solves 2-set agreement. The second one solves the more general case $2t < n \leq 3t$, where $k = \frac{n-t}{n-2t}$ is an integer. These two algorithm instances are optimal with respect to the number of rounds executed by the processes (namely two rounds). Combined with previous results, this article "nearly closes" the solvability of Byzantine k-set agreement in synchronous message-passing systems (more precisely, the only remaining case for which it is not known whether k-set agreement can or cannot be solved is when $k = \frac{n-t}{n-2t}$ is not an integer).

Keywords: Agreement problem · Byzantine process · Knowledge · k-set agreement · Message-passing · Synchronous system

1 Introduction

Coordination Problems. Coordination problems are central in the design of distributed systems where a set of n processes have to exchange information and synchronize in order to agree in one way or another (otherwise, they would behave as independent Turing machines, and the system would no longer be a distributed system). In such a context, this paper is about the process coordination captured by *k-set agreement* (initially introduced in the context of asynchrony and process crash failures [4]). Notice that

S. Devismes et al. (Eds.): SSS 2022, LNCS 13751, pp. 178–192, 2022.
https://doi.org/10.1007/978-3-031-21017-4_12

the value k can be seen as the degree of coordination associated with the corresponding instance of the k-set agreement problem. The smaller k, the more coordination among the processes: $k = 1$ means the strongest possible coordination (namely consensus).

Computing Model. The present paper considers a very adversarial context where, within the set of n processes, up to $t < n$ processes can commit Byzantine failures [8]. The processes are denoted $p_1, ..., p_n$ and $\Pi = \{p_1, ..., p_n\}$.

Let us remind that a Byzantine process is a process whose behavior is not the one defined by the code it should execute (i.e., it executes an arbitrary code, unknown by the non-Byzantine processes). The processes that are not Byzantine are said to be *correct*. Let us remind that, in the traditional Byzantine failure model adopted here, a process crash (unanticipated halt) is considered as a Byzantine failure.

In the context of the asynchronous computing model with process crashes, it has been shown in [6] that consensus cannot be solved even if a single process may crash, and in [2, 7, 11] that k-set agreement cannot be solved if k or more processes may crash. These computability bounds remain trivially true in the asynchronous Byzantine process failure model. So, the present article considers the classical fully connected synchronous message-passing computing model with reliable link [1, 10]. In this model the progress of the processes is governed by a sequence of rounds they execute. Each round is composed of three consecutive steps, such that

- during the first step, each (correct) process sends a message to all the processes,
- during the second step, each (correct) process receives the messages sent to it during the current round (let us notice that a Byzantine process can send different messages–or no message at all– to different correct processes),
- during the third step, each (correct) process executes the same local computation (involving the set of messages it received).

The fundamental property of the synchronous model lies in the fact that a message sent by a correct process to a correct process during a round is received and processed by its receiver during the very same round (this property provides the seed exploited by the correct processes in order to ensure termination).

k-Set Agreement in Synchronous Byzantine Systems. k-set agreement can be seen as a concurrent object that provides the processes with a single operation denoted propose(). This operation takes the value proposed by the invoking process as input parameter and returns the value it decides. The behavior of k-set agreement is defined by the following properties.

- Validity. If all the correct processes propose the same value v, no correct process decides a value different from v.
- Agreement. At most k different values are decided by the correct processes.
- Termination. The invocation of propose() by a correct process terminates.

Previous Works and Content of the Article. It is shown in [3, 5] that, in the synchronous Byzantine failure model, there is no algorithm solving k-set agreement when

$$\left[(n - t \geq k + 1) \wedge (n \leq 2t + \frac{t}{k}) \right] \bigvee \left[(n - t < k + 1) \wedge (k \leq t) \right].$$

Moreover, on the positive side, a one-round synchronous algorithm is presented in [5] which solves k-set agreement in the presence of up to t Byzantine processes when

$$\left[(n \geq 2t+1) \wedge \lfloor \tfrac{n-t}{n-2t} \rfloor + 1 \leq k)\right] \bigvee \left[(n \leq 2t) \wedge (t < k)\right].$$

It follows that, from a t-resilience point of view, the previous conditions cover all the possible/impossible cases except the case $2t < n \leq 3t$. More precisely, it is shown in [5] that, when $2t < n \leq 3t$, on one side there exists an algorithm that solves $\left(\lfloor \tfrac{n-t}{n-2t} \rfloor + 1\right)$-set agreement in one round, and on the other side it is impossible to solve $\left(\lfloor \tfrac{t}{n-2t} \rfloor\right)$-set agreement. Unfortunately, these possibility/impossibility results and the fact that $\lfloor \tfrac{n-t}{n-2t} \rfloor + 1 - \lfloor \tfrac{t}{n-2t} \rfloor = 2$, do not allow us to conclude whether or not it is possible to solve $\lfloor \tfrac{n-t}{n-2t} \rfloor$-set agreement in two rounds. This case (namely, $k = \lfloor \tfrac{n-t}{n-2t} \rfloor$) is the target of this article, that presents a generic two-round optimal k-set algorithm in two different instances:

- one that, assuming $n = 3t$ and $t > 1$, solves 2-set agreement,
- one that, assuming $2t < n \leq 3t$ and that $\lfloor \tfrac{n-t}{n-2t} \rfloor$ is an integer, solves k-set agreement for $k = \lfloor \tfrac{n-t}{n-2t} \rfloor$.

This algorithm relies on new notions denoted by Square and Regions, which allows a correct process to locally build a global knowledge (obtained in two rounds) on which each process propose a value. While the algorithm is simple, the proofs of its two instances are not.

Roadmap. The article is organised as follows. In Sect. 2 we present the basic k-set algorithm and proves it for $n = 3t$, $k = 2$, and $t > 1$. In Sect. 2.5 we consider the algorithm in a more general setting, namely $2t < n \leq 3t$ and $k = \tfrac{n-t}{n-2t}$ is an integer. In Sect. 3 we show that the two instances of the proposed algorithm are also optimal with respect to the number of rounds. Finally, in Sect. 4 we provide the conclusions. As we will see, this article introduces new notions (Square and Regions on matrices of values) and some parts of the proofs are pretty technical.

2 k-Set Agreement for $n = 3t$, $k = 2$ and $t > 1$

2.1 Algorithm: Local Data Structures

Each process p_i manages a local matrix $M_i[1..n][1..n]$ such that $M_i[i][i]$ is initialized with v_i, the value it proposes and each other $M_i[j][k]$, where $j, k \neq i$, is initialised to a default value denoted $\bot$. $M_i[j][k]$ contains p_i's knowledge on the value known by p_j as the value proposed by p_k [9,12].

2.2 Algorithm: Code of p_i

A process p_i first builds its local matrix (in two synchronous rounds) and then exploits its content to decide a value. The code executed by p_i is described in Algorithm 1. It is self-explanatory as far as the rounds are concerned. The statement at the end of the second round (based on Squares and Regions) is developed in Sect. 2.4.

```
operation propose(v_i) is
(1)   M_i[i][i] ← v_i;
──────────────── round 1 ────────────────
(2)   send the value M_i[i][i] to all the processes;
(3)   when p_i receives value v from p_j do M_i[i][j] ← v;
──────────────── round 2 ────────────────
(4)   send the vector V_i = M_i[i][*] to all the processes;
(5)   when p_i receives a vector V from p_j do M_i[j] ← V;
──────────────── at the end of round 2 ────────────────
(6)   if p_i finds a Square or Regions in M_i
(7)       then return(v_i)
(8)       else return(⊥)
(9)   end if.
```

Algorithm 1: Algorithm executed by p_i (two synchronous rounds)

2.3 Properties of a Matrix M_i

Claim. If p_i and p_j are two correct processes then, the row corresponding to process p_j in M_i and the one corresponding to p_j in M_j are equal: $M_i[j][*] = M_j[j][*]$.

Proof. Since p_j is a correct process, it sends $M_j[j][*]$ to p_i in the second round, and as p_i is also a correct process, then it receives this vector and writes it in $M_i[j][*]$. Then: $M_i[j][*] = M_j[j][*]$. □

Claim. Let p_i, p_j and p_k be three correct processes. We have $M_i[k][*] = M_j[k][*]$.

Proof. Let p_i, p_j and p_k be three correct processes, then from the previous Claim we have: $M_i[k][*] = M_k[k][*]$ and $M_j[k][*] = M_k[k][*]$. This implies that $M_i[k][*] = M_j[k][*]$. Which means that p_j and p_i have the same vision on p_k. □

$$M_3 = \begin{pmatrix} v_3 & v_3 & v_3 & * & * & v_3 \\ v_3 & v_3 & v_3 & * & * & v_3 \\ v_3 & v_3 & v_3 & * & * & v_3 \\ * & * & * & * & * & * \\ * & * & * & * & * & * \\ v_3 & v_3 & v_3 & * & * & v_3 \end{pmatrix}$$

Fig. 1. Matrix M_3 (Square example)

$$\begin{matrix} & & R_1 & \bar{R} & R_2 \\ & & \downarrow & \downarrow & \downarrow \end{matrix}$$
$$M_2 = \begin{pmatrix} v & v & v & v & w & w \\ v & v & v & v & w & w \\ * & * & * & * & * & * \\ * & * & * & * & * & * \\ v & v & w & w & w & w \\ v & v & w & w & w & w \end{pmatrix}$$

Fig. 2. Matrix M_2 (Regions example)

2.4 Basic Patterns: Squares and Regions

During the second round each process p_i will analyze its matrix M_i in order to decide. This analysis is based on patterns appearing in M_i, that we name *Square* and *Regions*. When a process finds one of the patterns, it will decide its own proposed value, otherwise it will decide the default value ⊥.

Finding Square S. We say that p_i finds a Square S, when (1) there exists a subset S of processes of size $n - t$ containing p_i, such that (2) for every two processes p_j and p_k of S, the value of $M_i[j][k]$ is equal to $M_i[i][i]$, i.e.,

1. $|S| = n - t$ and $p_i \in S$,
2. $\forall p_j, p_k \in S, \ M_i[j][k] = M_i[i][i]$.

Example: Let us take $n = 6, t = 2$ and $k = 3$. p_3 is a correct process with proposed value v_3 and M_3 is its corresponding matrix as presented in Fig. 1. In this example p_3 finds the Square $S = \{p_1, p_2, p_3, p_6\}$.

Finding Regions (R_1, R_2). We say that p_i finds Regions (R_1, R_2), if it has not found a Square and there exist two subsets of Π, R_1 and R_2 such that:

1. $p_i \subset R_1$,
2. $|R_1| = |R_2| = t$,
3. $R_1 \cap R_2 = \emptyset$,
4. $\forall \, k \in R_1, \forall \, \ell \in \Pi - R_2 : M_i[k][\ell] = v$,

Since p_i does not find a Square, one of the $M_i[k][\ell]$ values for $k \in R_1$ and $\ell \in R_2$ is different from v, let w be that value.

5. $\forall \, k \in R_1, \ell \in R_2 : M_i[k][\ell] = w$,
6. $\forall \, k \in R_2, \ell \in \Pi - R_1 : M_i[k][\ell] = w$,
7. $\forall \, k \in R_2, \ell \in R_1 : M_i[k][\ell] = v$.

If for every k and l, $M_i[k][l]$ is equal to v, then p_i finds a Square as it is not the case by hypothesis, there exists another value. Property (5) says that this value is unique. Properties (4) and (5) mean that all the lines corresponding to R_1 are equals between them. Properties (6) and (7) mean the same thing for R_2. From the properties (4) to (7), as soon as the lines corresponding to R_1 and R_2 are concerned, a column contains the same value but there is a disagreement for the column corresponding to $\Pi - R_2 - R_1$. These properties do not impose any conditions on the lines corresponding to $\Pi - R_2 - R_1$.

Example: Let us take $n = 6, t = 2$ and $k = 3$, suppose that p_2 is a correct process with initial value v and that M_2 is its corresponding matrix, with the values represented in Fig. 2. In this example p_2 finds Regions (R_1, R_2), with $R_1 = \{p_1, p_2\}$, and $R_2 = \{p_5, p_6\}$.

2.5 Proof of Correctness of Algorithm 1

After the construction of its matrix, a process p_i checks if its matrix contains a Square S. If it is the case, p_i might be in an execution of the algorithm where all the processes of S, including itself, are correct and have the same initial value. As the size of S is $n - t$, the t remaining may be Byzantine. By validity it has to decide its initial value. Consequently if a process finds a Square it has to decide its initial value.

It may happen that in fact, we can have an execution, where some processes of S are byzantine and send a different vector at round two to another correct process p_j. In this case, even if p_j has the same initial values as p_i, it does not find a Square. Since this execution is no longer compatible with an execution where all correct processes have the same initial value, the validity does not imply that it has to decide a particular value.

Let us now present an example of execution in the case where there are three sets of processes $A1$, $A2$ and Byz of size t (see the examples in Fig. 3, 4 and 5). The processes of $A1$ (processes p_1 and p_2) are correct and have a_1 as initial value. The processes of $A2$ (processes p_3 and p_4) are correct and have a_2 as initial value. The processes of Byz (processes p_5 and p_6) are Byzantine, they send $a1$ to processes of $A1$ pretending to have $a1$ as initial value and send $a2$ to processes of $A2$ pretending to have a_2 as initial value. The processes of Byz sends to a process of $A1$, say p_1, that they received $a1$ from processes in $A1$ and Byz, and to a process of $A2$, say p_2, that they received a_2 from processes in $A2$ and Byz. One process of Byz sends to another process of $A1$ (this is possible as $t > 1$), say p_j, that it has received from at least one process in $A1$ and Byz a value different from a_1. Process p_1 finds a Square and decide a_1 (Fig. 3), p_2 finds a Square and decide a_2 (Fig. 4), while p_j does not find a Square. To achieve 2-set agreement it has to decide either a_1 or a_2. At this point the notion of Region is helpful. Process p_j does not find a Square but it finds Regions (A_1, A_2) (Fig. 5). This pattern proves that the processes of Byz are byzantine, and have lied to produce a Square somewhere else and it decides a_1.

$$
M_1
\begin{pmatrix}
a_1 & a_1 & a_2 & a_2 & a_1 & a_1 \\
a_1 & a_1 & a_2 & a_2 & a_1 & a_1 \\
a_1 & a_1 & a_2 & a_2 & a_2 & a_2 \\
a_1 & a_1 & a_2 & a_2 & a_2 & a_2 \\
a_1 & a_1 & * & * & a_1 & a_1 \\
a_1 & a_1 & * & * & a_1 & a_1
\end{pmatrix}
\quad
M_2
\begin{pmatrix}
a_1 & a_1 & a_2 & a_2 & a_1 & a_1 \\
a_1 & a_1 & a_2 & a_2 & a_1 & a_1 \\
a_1 & a_1 & a_2 & a_2 & a_2 & a_2 \\
a_1 & a_1 & a_2 & a_2 & a_2 & a_2 \\
* & * & a_2 & a_2 & a_2 & a_2 \\
* & * & a_2 & a_2 & a_2 & a_2
\end{pmatrix}
\quad
M_j
\begin{pmatrix}
a_1 & a_1 & a_2 & a_2 & a_1 & a_1 \\
a_1 & a_1 & a_2 & a_2 & a_1 & a_1 \\
a_1 & a_1 & a_2 & a_2 & a_2 & a_2 \\
a_1 & a_1 & a_2 & a_2 & a_2 & a_2 \\
* & * & * & * & * & * \\
* & * & * & * & * & *
\end{pmatrix}
$$

$A_1 \quad A_2 \quad Byz$

Fig. 3. p_1's matrix: square   **Fig. 4.** p_2' matrix: square   **Fig. 5.** p_j'matrix: regions

If a process does not find a Square or Regions it decides $\bot$.

We show in the next lemmas that if two correct processes decide two different values different from $\bot$ by finding a Square or Regions then all the other processes will decide by Square or Regions one of these values. This achieves the agreement property of the 2-set agreement.

Lemma 1. *If a correct process p_i decides a value different from $\bot$, then it has found a Square or Regions, and it decides its initial value.*

Proof. Let p_i be a correct process, in the second round, p_i analyses its corresponding matrix M_i. If it finds a Square or Regions it decides its initial value, otherwise $\bot$. These instructions correspond to Lines 6, 7 and 8 of Algorithm 1 □

Lemma 2. *If a correct process p_i finds a Square S_i, there is at least one subset of S_i of size t including only correct processes.*

Proof. Let p_i find a Square S_i such that $|S_i| = n - t$. As there are at most t Byzantine processes and $n = 3t$, it follows that at least $n - 2t = t$ processes in S_i are correct. □

Let R_3 be $\Pi - R_2 - R_1$.

Lemma 3. *If a correct process p_i finds Regions (R_1, R_2), then all the processes of R_1 are correct and (1) either all the processes of R_3 are Byzantine and all the processes of R_2 are correct, (2) or all the processes of R_3 are correct and all the processes of R_2 are Byzantine.*

Proof. We have $n = 3t$, let p_i be a correct process in R_1 that finds Regions (R_1, R_2). By the definition of Regions (items 2 and 3), R_1, R_2 and R_3 contain t processes and are disjoint.

If all the processes of R_2 are Byzantine, since there are at most t Byzantine processes and $|R_2| = t$, then processes of $R_1 \cup R_3$ are correct.

If a process of R_2 is correct, let p_k be this process and let p_ℓ be a process of R_3. By item 4, p_i receives v from p_ℓ at the first round. By item 6, p_k sends to p_i at the second round M_k with $M_k[\ell] = w$, which is the value that p_k pretends to have received from p_ℓ at the first round. If both the processes are correct then $w = v$, but by the definition of Regions, we have $v \neq w$, since p_k is correct then p_ℓ is Byzantine. Then all processes in R_3 are Byzantine, because we have at most t Byzantine and $|R_3| = t$, thus the processes of $R_1 \cup R_2$ are correct.

In general, either processes in R_2 are Byzantine and the processes of $R_1 \cup R_3$ are correct, or R_3 are Byzantine and the processes of $R_1 \cup R_2$ are correct. □

Lemma 4. *If a correct process p_i decides v by Regions (R_1, R_2), then all the processes of $R_1 \cup R_2$ are correct and the other processes are Byzantine.*

Proof. If p_i decides by Regions(R_1, R_2), it means that it did not find a Square. By Lemma 3, processes of R_1 are correct and either processes of R_2 are Byzantine or processes of R_3 are byzantine.

Since p_i did not find a Square, a $M[k][\ell]$ value for some $p_k \in R_3$ and p_ℓ in $R_1 \cup R_3$ is different from v. Let z be that value.

If p_ℓ belongs to $R_1 \backslash \{p_i\}$: by Lemma 3, p_ℓ is correct then it sends the same value v to p_i and p_k at the first round, while p_k sends z to p_i at the second round, as a received value from p_ℓ. Therefore p_k is Byzantine. Thus processes of R_3 are Byzantine and $R_1 \cup R_2$ are correct.

If p_ℓ is in R_3: p_i received v from p_ℓ at the first round, and z from p_k as a received value from p_ℓ at the second round. Thus at least one of the two processes p_k and p_ℓ is Byzantine, since they both belong to R_3 from Lemma 3, processes of R_3 are Byzantine and those of $R_1 \cup R_2$ are correct. □

Lemma 5. *If a correct process p_i decides v by a Square S_i, and another correct process p_j decides v' by a Square S_j, with $v \neq v'$, then all the correct processes decide either v or v'.*

Proof. Let p_i (respectively p_j) be a correct process that finds a Square S_i (resp. S_j) and let v (resp. v') be its initial value with $v \neq v'$. Let us show that every correct process decides either v or v'.

By Lemma 2, there is a subset SS_i of size t of correct processes in S_i and there is a subset SS_j of size t of correct processes in S_j. By item (2) of the definition of Square, all the processes in SS_i have v as initial value and all the processes in SS_j have v'. Such that $v \neq v'$, SS_i and SS_j arc disjoint and $|S_i \cap S_j| = t$

A process in $S_i \cap S_j$ sent v to the processes of SS_i, and v' to those in SS_j, so this process is Byzantine. Consequently correct processes are exactly $SS_i \cup SS_j$.

Let p_k be a correct process, without loss of generality, assume that p_k is in SS_i. As processes of SS_i and SS_j are correct, they send the same vector to p_k, p_i and p_j in the second round, which means that:

1. a correct process may, following its initial value, find the Square S_i or the Square S_j,
2. if a correct process does not find a Square, it finds, following its initial value, at least Regions (SS_i, SS_j) or Regions (SS_j, SS_i) and decides its initial value.

So either a process decides by the Square or by Regions, in both case it decides its initial value v or v'.   □

We are now ready to prove that for $n = 3t$ and $t > 1$, Algorithm 1 is a t-resilient algorithm that solves 2-set agreement, in two rounds.

In the following, we prove separately the three properties, namely Validity, and Agreement, and Termination.

Lemma 6 [Validity]. *If all the correct processes propose the same value, they decide this value.*

Proof. Let C be the set of correct processes that propose v. Since we have at most t Byzantine, then $|C| \geq 2t$. Let p_i be a correct process, S a subset of C of size $2t$, $p_i \in S$. Then all the processes in S have as initial value v and send v to all the processes at the first round. For every process p_s in S we have $M_s[s][s'] = v$ for all s' in S and that value will be send to p_i at the second round, then p_i will find at least the Square S, and whatever the Square it finds, it decides v, and all the processes in C will decide v.   □

Lemma 7 [Termination]. *All the correct processes decide.*

Proof. All the correct processes will execute the two synchronous rounds and will decide at the end of the second round.   □

Lemma 8 [Agreement]. *At most two values are decided by correct processes.*

Proof. Let's suppose we have three decided values, then at least two of them are different from $\perp$. To show the agreement, we need to prove that if two values v and v' different from $\perp$ are decided, then all the correct processes decide v or v'.

Let p_i and p_j be two correct processes that decide v or v' different from $\perp$ ($v \neq v'$), by Lemma 1, the decided values are their initial value.

– If p_i and p_j decide by a Square, then from Lemma 5, all the correct processes decide v or v'.

– Else without loss of generality assume that p_i decides v by Regions (R_1, R_2), $|R_1| = |R_2| = t$, $R_1 \cap R_2 = \emptyset$. Furthermore by Lemma 4, processes of $R_1 \cup R_2$ are correct and other processes are Byzantine.

By definition of Regions, a process in R_1 has v as initial value. As p_j decides v' its initial value is v'. As it is correct and not in R_1, it is in R_2. By the definition of Regions, all the processes of R_2 have v' as initial value.

Let p_k be a correct process, then it is in R_1 or in R_2 and its initial value is v or v'. Either it finds a Square, and decides its initial value v, or p_k does not find a Square S, in this case p_k finds Regions (R_1, R_2) or (R_2, R_1), because the correct processes of $R_1 \cup R_2$ send the same value to p_i and to p_k. So p_k decides its initial value v or v'.   □

Finally, from Lemmas 6, 7 and 8, we have:

Theorem 1. *For $n = 3t$ and $t > 1$, Algorithm 1 is a t-resilient algorithm that solves 2-set agreement in two rounds.*

k-set Agreement for for $2t < n \leq 3t$ and $k = \frac{n-t}{n-2t}$ is Integer

This section shows that Algorithm 1 works for $2t < n \leq 3t$ when $\frac{n-t}{n-2t}$ is an integer. Its adaptation to this new setting requires some modifications in the way Regions are found.

2.6 Finding Regions $\{R_\ell : \ell = 1, ..., k\}$

We say that p_i finds Regions $\{R_\ell : \ell = 1, \ldots, k\}$, if it has not found a Square and there exist k subsets of Π, $R_1, \ldots, R_k$ such as:

1. $p_i \in R_1$,
2. $\forall \alpha \in \{1, \ldots, k\}, |R_\alpha| = n - 2t$,
3. $\forall \alpha, \beta \in \{1, \ldots, k\}$ and $\alpha \neq \beta, R_\alpha \cap R_\beta = \emptyset$, the Regions are disjoint,
4. $\forall \alpha \in \{1, \ldots, k\}, \forall x, y \in R_\alpha, M_i[x][*] = M_i[y][*]$, the lines in each Region are equal,
5. $\forall \alpha \in \{1, \ldots, k\}, \forall x, y, x', y' \in R_\alpha, M_i[x][y] = M_i[x'][y']$, all the values of a certain Region are equal,
   Let $val.R_\alpha$ be the value of $M_i[x][y]$ for any $x, y \in R_\alpha$
6. $\forall \alpha, \beta \in \{1, \ldots, k\}$ and $\alpha \neq \beta, val.R_\alpha \neq val.R_\beta$, the values of two Regions are different,
7. $\forall \alpha \in \{1, \ldots, k\}, \forall y \in R_\alpha, \forall x \in \bigcup_{r=1}^{k} R_r, M_i[x][y] = val.R_\alpha$,
   Let $\bar{R} = \Pi - \bigcup_{r=1}^{k} R_r$.
8. $\forall \alpha \in \{1, \ldots, k\}, \forall x \in R_\alpha, \forall y \in \bar{R}, M_i[x][y] = val.R_\alpha$.

The idea behind "finding a Square" is the same that in the previous section. The Regions are defined in such a way that if k correct processes decide k different values by Square, then any other processes find Regions.

Lemma 9. *If a correct process p_i decides a value different from $\perp$, then it either finds a Square S or Regions $\{R_\ell : \ell = 1, \ldots, k\}$, and it decides its initial value.*   □

Proof. Let p_i be a correct process, in the second round, p_i has its own matrix M_i, and decides $\perp$ at line 8 if it did not find a Square or Regions at line 6. If it decides at line 7, it decides its own value.   □

Lemma 10. *If a correct process p_i finds Regions $\{R_\ell : \ell = 1, \ldots, k\}$, the size of the subsets $\bar{R} = \Pi - \bigcup_{\ell=1}^{k} R_\ell$ and $\bigcup_{\ell \neq 1}^{k} R_\ell$ is t.*

Proof. From condition 2 of the definition of Regions $|R_1| = n - 2t$. By hypothesis of the studied case, we have $k = \frac{n-t}{n-2t}$ since the size of the Regions are equal (condition 2) and we have k distinct Regions (condition 3) then: $|\bigcup_{\ell \neq 1}^{k} R_\ell| = (k-1)(n-2t) = t$ and $|\bar{R}| = n - k(n-2t) = t$.   □

Lemma 11. *If a correct process p_i decides by Regions $\{R_\ell : \ell = 1, \ldots, k\}$, then all processes of R_1 are correct, and (1) either processes of $\bar{R} = \Pi - \bigcup_{\ell=1}^{k} R_\ell$ are Byzantine and processes of $\bigcup_{l \neq 1} R_\ell$ are correct, or (2) processes of $\bar{R}$ are correct and processes of $\bigcup_{l \neq 1} R_\ell$ are Byzantine.*   □

Proof. Let p_i be a correct process that decides v_i by Regions $\{R_\ell : \ell = 1, \ldots, k\}$, let T_1 be the subset $\bigcup_{r \neq 1} R_\ell$. By definition of Regions $\{R_\ell : \ell = 1, \ldots, k\}$, if p_j is a correct process and v_j is it's initial value, from condition 6 we have:

1. $\forall p_j \in T_1, v_j \neq v_i$
   From the fact that p_j sends its initial value to p_i and p_i puts it in $M_i[i][j]$ and the condition 8, we have:
2. $\forall p_j \in \bar{R}, v_j = v_i$.

If all processes of T_1 are Byzantine, since there is at most t Byzantine processes and by Lemma 10, $|T_1| = t$, then processes of $\bar{R}$ and R_1 are correct.

Otherwise there is a correct process in T_1. Let p_r be a correct process of T_1 and p_m be a process of $\bar{R}$, p_i receives v_i from p_m at the first round, and v from p_r at the second round that it puts in $M_i[r][*]$. As p_r is correct, $M_i[r][m]$ is the value that p_m sent to p_r at the first round as it's initial value, if p_m is a correct process then $v' = v$ but by definition of Regions $v \neq v'$. Then all processes in $\bar{R}$ arc Byzantine, since we have at most t Byzantine and by Lemma 10, $|\bar{R}| = t$, then processes of T_1 and R_1 are correct.

So either processes in T_1 are Byzantine and processes of $\bar{R}$ and R_1 are correct, or processes of $\bar{R}$ are Byzantine and processes of T_1 and R_1 are correct.   □

Lemma 12. *If a correct process p_i decides by Regions R_ℓ (line 6), then all the processes of $\bigcup_{\ell=1}^{k} R_\ell$ are correct and the other are Byzantine.*

Proof. Let p_i be a correct process that decides v by Regions R_ℓ. Let S_1 be the subset $\bigcup_{l \neq 1} R_\ell$.

By Lemma 11, processes of R_1 are correct and either processes of S_1 or $\bar{R}$ are Byzantine. By condition 6 and 8, if p_i decides by a Square S, then $S = \bar{R} \cup R_1$. In this case for p_k and p_j in $R_1 \cup \bar{R}$, $M[k][j]$ is equal to v.

Since p_i didn't found a Square, the conditions 4 and 5 imply that some $M[k][j]$ values for $p_k \in \bar{R}$ and p_j in $R_1 \cup \bar{R}$ is different from v. Let w be that value.

If $p_j \in R_1$ with $p_j \neq p_i$, since p_j is correct, it sends the same value to p_i and p_k at the first round. p_k sent w instead of v to p_i at the second round, as the received value from p_j, then p_k is Byzantine. Thus processes of $\bar{R}$ are Byzantine and $R_1 \cup S_1$ are correct.

If $p_j \in \bar{R}$, then by condition 7, p_i received $val.R_1$ from p_j at the first round, and $w \neq val.R_1$ from p_k as a received value from p_j at the second round. Thus at least one of the two processes p_k and p_j is Byzantine, since they belong to $\bar{R}$ from Lemma 11, processes of $\bar{R}$ are Byzantine and those of $R_1 \cup S_1$ are correct.   □

Lemma 13. *If k correct processes decide distinct $\{v_\ell : \ell = 1, ..., k\}$ by Squares S_ℓ, then all the correct processes will eventually decide one of the v_ℓ distinct values.*

Proof. Let $\{p_i, i = 1, ..., k\}$ be k different correct processes with their k corresponding distinct initial values $\{v_i, i = 1, ..., k\}$ that decide there own value by finding a Square $\{S_i, i = 1, ..., k\}$ of size $n - t$. Then all these sets are disjoint.

As each set S_i is of size $n - t$, there exists there are k subsets $\{T_i, i = 1, ..., k\}$ of size $n - 2t$ of correct processes. As a process of T_i and a process of T_j have different initial value then: $\forall i, j; i \neq j \implies T_i \cap T_j = \emptyset$.

The size of $\cup_{g=1}^{g=k} T_g$ is $k(n - 2t)$, then $K = \Pi - \cup_{g=1}^{g=k} T_g$ is of size t. So for each i from 1 to k, $S_i = T_i \cup K$.

A process of K sends v_1 to p_1 in T_1 and v_2 to p_2 in T_2 ($k \geq 2$), so it is a Byzantine process.

Let us show that any correct process decides one of the v_i values. By the claims of Sect. 2.3 (Identical lines), any two correct processes have the same rows for processes in $\cup_{g=1}^{g=k} T_g$.

By the Byzantine behaviour of K, a correct process p_i in T_i:

1. May find a Square $T_i \cup K$ and decides v_i,
2. If it does not find a Square, it finds the Regions thanks to the sets $\{T_i, i = 1, ..., k\}$.

Example: Let us take $n = 10, k = 3$ and $t = 4$. Let us consider three correct processes p_1, p_2 and p_3 with their respective distinct initial values v_1, v_2 and v_3, that decide by Squares S_1, S_2 and S_3 their initial values. Looking at the matrix of Fig. 6, if $v_\alpha = v_1$ (resp v_2, v_3) then this is process p_1's matrix (resp p_2, p_3).

Let p_ℓ be a correct process, and let us suppose that $p_\ell \in S_1$ then it has as an initial value v_1. From the matrix we can tell that each correct process will eventually find the Regions R_ℓ thanks to claims of Sect. 2.3 and decides its initial value. And by the Byzantine behaviour of the faulty processes if $v_\alpha = v_1$ then p_ℓ will find a Square S_1 and decides v_1.   □

2.7   Proof of Correctness of the Algorithm

We are now ready to prove that when $2t < n \leq 3t$ and $\frac{n-t}{n-2t}$ is an integer, General Algorithm is a t-resilient algorithm for solving $\frac{n-t}{n-2t}$-set agreement. In the following we separately prove each the three properties defining k-set agreement in the presence of Byzantine failures, (Validity, Termination, and Agreement).

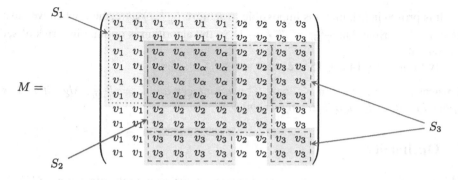

Fig. 6. View of correct processes

Lemma 14 [Validity]. *If all the correct processes propose the same value, they decide that value.*

Proof. Let C be the set of correct processes that propose v. Since we have at most t Byzantine, then $|C| \geq n-t$. Let S a subset of size $n-t$ of C. Let p_i be a correct process. Let S a subset of size $n - t$ of C that contains p_i. Then all the processes in S have as initial value v and sends v to all the processes at the first round. All the processes p_c in S have $M_c[c][c'] = v$ for all c' in S and that value will be send to p_i at the second round, then $M_i[c][c'] = v$ for all c, c' in S (including p_i). So we have:

(1) $S = n - t$ and $p_i \in S$, and
(2) $\forall c, c' \in S \ M_i[c][c'] = M_i[c][c']$.

Then p_i finds at least the Square S and whatever the Square it finds, it decides v. □

Lemma 15 [Termination]. *All the correct processes will eventually decide.*

Proof. All the correct processes will execute the two synchronous rounds and will decide at the end of the second round. □

Lemma 16 [Agreement]. *At most k values are decided by correct processes.*

Proof. We prove this result by contradiction. Assume we have at least $k + 1$ decided values. Therefore k of them are different from $\perp$. We will show that all correct processes decide one of these k values. By Lemma 9, if a correct process decides some value different from $\perp$, it is its initial value. So we have k processes, each process decides its initial value, and all these values are different:

- If these k processes decide different values by a Square, then from Lemma 13, all the correct processes decide one of the k values.
- Else, if a correct process p_i decides by Regions R_ℓ, then by Lemma 12, processes of $\bigcup_{\ell=1}^{k} R_\ell$ are correct and the other processes are Byzantine.
  Let p_j be a correct process of $\bigcup_{\ell=1}^{k} R_\ell$ from Lemma 3, all the lines concerning processes in $\{R_\ell\}$ of M_i are equal to the lines concerning processes in $\{R_\ell\}$ of M_j. If p_j does not find a Square, it finds at least Regions R_ℓ. In all the case it decides its initial value that is one of the k values. □

It is proved in [5], that it is impossible to achieve $\left(\frac{t}{n-2t}\right)$-agreement when we have $2t < n \leq 3t$. Note that $\frac{t}{n-2t} = \frac{n-t}{n-2t} - 1$. So the algorithm is optimal in terms of set agreement.

By Lemma 16, 14 and 15, we get

Theorem 2. *When $2t < n \leq 3t$, $\frac{n-t}{n-2t}$ is an integer, and $k = \frac{n-t}{n-2t}$, Algorithm 1 is optimal on the value k of k-set agreement.*

3   Optimality

This section proves that the proposed algorithm (together with the algorithm of [5]) is optimal in term of number of rounds. To this end we first prove the following lemma.

Lemma 17. *If a process has v as initial value and receives v from $n - l$ processes (including itself) then if it decides after one round, it decides v.*

Proof. Let p be a process, and v be its initial value. p has to decide in one round, if it receives v from $n - t$ processes, it may be in an execution where these $n - t$ processes are correct, so by validity of the k-set agreement, it has to decide v.   □

Let us first consider the case $t = 1$.

Theorem 3. *For $n \geq 3$, $t = 1$, there is no algorithm for 2-set agreement in 0 round.*

Proof. By contradiction, let $\mathcal{A}$ be an algorithm that works in 0 round. A process p_i decides based on its initial value, since it can be in an execution where processes have the same initial value, to ensure validity, it must decide its own value.

In an execution where 3 processes are correct, each decides its own value. If the values are different then there are 3 different decided values, thus this algorithm doesn't achieve 2-set agreement.   □

Theorem 4. *For $n = 3$, $t = 1$, there is a one-round algorithm $\mathcal{A}$ for 2-set agreement.*

Proof. Each process sends its own value, if a process receives 2 identical values to its own, it decides its own value else it decides $\perp$.

[Validity] If all the correct processes have the same value, since there is at most one Byzantine process, each correct process receives at least 2 identical values and by Lemma 17 decides it.

[Agreement] If the 3 processes are correct, they receive the same values. Let v_i be p_i's initial value. If all the values are different, the processes decide $\perp$. If at least 2 values are identical, for example $v_1 = v_2$, then, p_1 and p_2 decide v_1, there will be at most 2 decided values. Finally, if there are exactly 2 correct processes, we will have at most 2 decided values.

[Termination] All the correct processes execute a single round and decide.   □

By Theorem 3 and 4, $\mathcal{A}$ is optimal in term of the number of rounds. As it is impossible to achieve consensus for $n = 3$ and $t = 1$ [8], we get the following result.

Theorem 5. *For $n = 3$, $t = 1$, $\mathcal{A}$ is optimal, both in term of set agreement and number of rounds.*

Let us now consider the case $t > 1$.

Theorem 6. *For $n = 3t$ and $t > 1$, there is no one-round 2-set agreement algorithm.*

Proof. We suppose that we have an algorithm that allows to have 2-set agreement in one round.

We decompose Π in 3 sets of size t: S_0, S_1 and S_2. Let v_0, v_1 and v_2 be three different initial values. Since t is greater than 2, there are at least two processes in each set. Let p_i and q_i be two processes of S_i. p_i and q_i have v_i as initial value.

We consider now an execution e where all the processes are correct.

The execution e is indistinguishable for q_i from an execution where processes of $S_{(i+1) \bmod 3}$ are byzantine and send v_i to p_i and $v_{(i+2) \bmod 3}$ to $p_{(i+2) \bmod 3}$. That execution, is indistinguishable for p_i from an execution, where processes of S_i and $S_{(i+1) \bmod 3}$ are correct and processes of $S_{(i+1) \bmod 3}$ have v_i as initial value. By Lemma 17, p_i decides v_i in e. In the same way $p_{(i+2) \bmod 3}$ decides $v_{(i+2) \bmod 3}$. Thus by the agreement property of 2-set agreement q_i has to decide v_i or $v_{(i+2) \bmod 3}$.

In the same way, q_i has to decide v_i or $v_{(i+1) \bmod 3}$.

To satisfy both, q_i has to decides v_i in the execution e.

In execution e, all the processes are correct, for each $i = 0, 1, 2$, process q_i decides v_i. Then there are at least 3 different decisions contradicting the agreement property of 2-set agreement. $\square$

The following theorem can be proved in the same way.

Theorem 7. *For $2t < n \leq 3t$ and $t > 1$, there is no one-round algorithm for k-set agreement, where, $\frac{n-t}{n-2t}$ is an integer and $k = \frac{n-t}{n-2t}$.*

4 Conclusion

We have presented a simple two-round algorithm for synchronous 2-set agreement in a system of $n = 3t$ processes in which up to $t > 1$ processes may be Byzantine. This algorithm is based on new notions (denoted Square and Regions) which allow each process p_i to capture the global knowledge of which every proposed value is known by each other process (such that "p_i knows that p_j knows the value proposed by p_k"). Extending the notion of Regions, we have shown that the same two-round algorithm solves Byzantine k-set agreement for the case where $k = \frac{n-t}{n-2t}$ is a positive integer, in a system such that $2t < n \leq 3t$. While the statement of the algorithm is simple, its proofs (based on the notion of Square and Regions) are not.

Combining the results of this article with the results presented in [3,5][1], "nearly closes" the solvability (possibility and impossibility) of Byzantine k-set agreement in synchronous message-passing systems. More precisely, the only remaining case is when $k = \frac{n-t}{n-2t}$ is not an integer for which we do not know whether $\lfloor \frac{n-t}{n-2t} \rfloor$-set agreement is solvable (but we know that we can solve $(\lfloor \frac{n-t}{n-2t} \rfloor + 1)$-set agreement in two rounds, and that it is impossible to solve $(\lfloor \frac{n-t}{n-2t} \rfloor - 1)$-set agreement).

---

[1] For $k > 1$, all these algorithms use at most 2 rounds.

Acknowledgments. C. Delporte-Gallet, H. Fauconnier and M. Safir have been partially supported by the French projects: DUCAT (ANR-20-CE48-0006), Distributed Network Computing through the Lens of Combinatorial Topology, and FREDDA (ANR-17-CE40-0013) devoted to the development of formal methods in order to improve and ease the design of distributed algorithms.

M. Raynal has been partially supported by the French project ByBloS (ANR-20-CE25-0002-01) devoted to the design of modular building blocks for distributed applications.

References

1. Attiya, H., Welch, J.: Distributed Computing, Fundamentals, Simulation and Advanced Topics. Wiley Series on Parallel and Distributed Computing, 2nd edn., p. 414. New Jersey (2004)
2. Borowsky, E., Gafni, E.: Generalized FLP impossibility results for t-resilient asynchronous computations. In: Proceedings of the 25th ACM Symposium on Theory of Computing (STOC'93), pp. 91–100. ACM Press (1993)
3. Bouzid, Z., Imbs, D., Raynal, M.: A necessary condition for Byzantine k-set agreement. Inf. Process. Lett. **116**(12), 757–759 (2016)
4. Chaudhuri, S.: More choices allow more faults: set consensus problems in totally asynchronous systems. Inf. Comput. **105**(1), 132–158 (1993)
5. Delporte-Gallet, C., Fauconnier, H., Safir, M.: Byzantine k-set agreement. In: Georgiou, C., Majumdar, R. (eds.) NETYS 2020. LNCS, vol. 12129, pp. 183–191. Springer, Cham (2021). https://doi.org/10.1007/978-3-030-67087-0_12
6. Fischer, M.J., Lynch, N.A., Paterson, M.S.: Impossibility of distributed consensus with one faulty process. J. ACM **32**(2), 374–382 (1985)
7. Herlihy, M.P., Shavit, N.: The topological structure of asynchronous computability. J. ACM **46**(6), 858–923 (1999)
8. Lamport, L., Shostack, R., Pease, M.: The Byzantine generals problem. ACM Trans. Program. Lang. Syst. **4**(3), 382–401 (1982)
9. Raynal, M.: Distributed Algorithms For Message-passing Systems, p. 510. Springer, Heidelberg (2013). https://doi.org/10.1007/978-3-642-38123-2. ISBN 978-3-642-38122-5
10. Raynal, M.: Fault-tolerant Message-passing Distributed Systems: An Algorithmic Approach, p. 480. Springer, Heidelberg (2018). https://doi.org/10.1007/978-3-319-94141-7.pdfISBN 978-3-319-94140-0
11. Saks, M., Zaharoglou, F.: Wait-free k-set agreement is impossible: the topology of public knowledge. SIAM J. Comput. **29**(5), 1449–1483 (2000)
12. Wuu, G.T.J., Bernstein, A.J.: Efficient solutions to the replicated log and dictionary problems. In: Proceeding of the 3rd Annual ACM Symposium on Principles of Distributed Computing (PODC 1984), pp. 233–242. ACM Press (1984)

Reaching Consensus in the Presence of Contention-Related Crash Failures

Anaïs Durand[1], Michel Raynal[2(✉)], and Gadi Taubenfeld[3]

[1] LIMOS, Université Clermont Auvergne CNRS UMR 6158, Aubière, France
[2] IRISA, CNRS, Inria, Univ Rennes, 35042 Rennes, France
raynal@irisa.fr
[3] Reichman University, 4610101 Herzliya, Israel

Abstract. While consensus is at the heart of many coordination problems in asynchronous distributed systems prone to process crashes, it has been shown to be impossible to solve in such systems where processes communicate by message-passing or by reading and writing a shared memory. Hence, these systems must be enriched with additional computational power for consensus to be solved on top of them. This article presents a new restriction of the classical basic computational model that combines process participation and a constraint on failure occurrences that can happen only while a predefined contention threshold has not yet been bypassed. This type of failure is called λ-*constrained crashes*, where λ defines the considered contention threshold. It appears that when assuming such contention-related crash failures and enriching the system with objects whose consensus number is $k \geq 1$, consensus for n processes can be solved for any $n \geq k$ assuming up to k failures. The article proceeds incrementally. It first presents an algorithm that solves consensus on top of read/write registers if at most one crash occurs before the contention threshold $\lambda = n - 1$ has been bypassed. Then, it shows that if the system is enriched with objects whose consensus number is $k \geq 1$, then
- when $\lambda = n - k$, consensus can be solved despite up to k λ-constrained crashes, for any $n \geq k$, and
- when $\lambda = n - 2k + 1$, consensus can be solved despite up to $2k - 1$ λ-constrained crashes, assuming k divides n.

Finally, impossibility results are presented for the number of λ-constrained failures that can be tolerated.

Keywords: Consensus algorithm · Asynchronous system · Atomic register · Concurrency · Consensus number · Contention · λ-constrained failure · Participating process · Process crash failure · Read/write register

1 Introduction

Consensus and Contention-Related Crash Failures. Consensus is one of the most important problems encountered in crash-prone asynchronous distributed systems. Its statement is pretty simple. Let us consider a system of n asynchronous sequential processes denoted $p_1, ..., p_n$. Each process p_i is assumed to propose a value and, if it does

© The Author(s), under exclusive license to Springer Nature Switzerland AG 2022
S. Devismes et al. (Eds.): SSS 2022, LNCS 13751, pp. 193–205, 2022.
https://doi.org/10.1007/978-3-031-21017-4_13

not crash, must decide a value (Termination property) such that no two processes decide different values (Agreement property) and the decided value is a proposed value (Validity property). Despite its very simple statement, consensus is impossible to solve in the presence of asynchrony and process crashes, even if a single process may crash, be the communication medium message-passing [6], or atomic read/write registers [10].

In a very interesting way, Fischer, Lynch, and Paterson presented in Sect. 4 of [6] an algorithm for asynchronous message-passing systems that solves consensus if a majority of processes do not crash and the processes that crash do it initially (the number of crashes being unknown to the other processes [19]). This poses the following question: Can some a priori knowledge on the timing of failures impact the possibility/impossibility of consensus in the presence of process crash failures? As the notion of "timing" is irrelevant in an asynchronous system, Taubenfeld replaced the notion of time with the notion of contention degree and, to answer the previous question, he introduced in [18] the explicit notion of *weak failures*, then renamed *contention-related crash failures* in [5].

More precisely, given a predefined contention threshold λ, a λ-constrained crash failure is a crash that occurs while process contention is smaller or equal to λ. Considering read/write shared memory systems and $\lambda = n - 1$, a consensus algorithm is presented in [5, 18] that tolerates one λ-constrained crash (*i.e.*, at most one process may crash, which may occur only when the contention degree is $\leq (n - 1)$), and it is shown that this bound (on the number of failures) is tight. [1] In addition, upper and lower bounds for solving the k-set agreement problem [2] in the presence of multiple contention-related crash failures for $k \geq 2$ are presented in [5, 18].

Motivation: Why λ-Constrained Failures? The first and foremost motivation for this study is related to the basics of computing, namely, increasing our knowledge of what can (or cannot) be done in the context of asynchronous failure-prone distributed systems. Providing necessary and sufficient conditions helps us determine and identify under which type of process failures the fundamental consensus problem is solvable.

As discussed and demonstrated in [5], the new type of λ-constrained failures enables the design of algorithms that can tolerate several traditional "any-time" failures plus several additional λ-constrained failures. More precisely, assume that a problem can be solved in the presence of t traditional failures but cannot be solved in the presence of $t + 1$ such failures. Yet, the problem might be solvable in the presence of $t_1 \leq t$ "any-time" failures plus t_2 λ-constrained failures, where $t_1 + t_2 > t$.

Adding the ability to tolerate λ-constrained failures to algorithms that are already designed to circumvent various impossibility results, such as the Paxos algorithm [12] and indulgent algorithms in general [7, 8], would make such algorithms even more robust against possible failures. An indulgent algorithm never violates its safety property and eventually satisfies its liveness property when the synchrony assumptions it relies on are satisfied. An indulgent algorithm which in addition (to being indulgent) tolerates λ-constrained failures may, in many cases, satisfy its liveness property even before the synchrony assumptions it relies on are satisfied.

---

[1] The consensus algorithm described in [5, 18] does not use adopt/commit objects as done in the present article. As we will see, this object is crucial for the present paper.

When facing a failure-related impossibility result, such as the impossibility of consensus in the presence of a single faulty process, discussed earlier [6], one is often tempted to use a solution that guarantees no resiliency at all. We point out that there is a middle ground: tolerating λ constrained failures enables to tolerate failures some of the time. Notice that traditional t-resilient algorithms also tolerate failures only some of the time (i.e., as long as the number of failures is at most t). After all, *something is better than nothing*. As a simple example, an algorithm is described in [6], which solves consensus despite asynchrony and up to $t < n/2$ processes crashes if these crashes occur initially (hence no participating process crashes).

Content of the Article. This article investigates the interplay between asynchrony, process crashes, contention threshold, and the computability power of base objects as measured by their consensus number [9]. Let us recall that the consensus number of an object O (denote $CN(O)$) is the maximal number of processes for which consensus can be solved despite any number of process crashes (occurring at any time) with any number of objects O and read/write registers. If there is no such integer, $CN(O) = +\infty$. An object the consensus number of which is k is called kCONS object. After a presentation of the computing model, the article is made up of three main sections.

- Section 3 presents a consensus algorithm built on top of read/write registers (RW), which tolerates one process crash occurring before the contention degree bypasses $(n - 1)$.
- Section 4 generalizes the previous algorithm by presenting two (reduction) algorithms that solve consensus on top of objects whose consensus number is $k \geq 1$.
    - The first algorithm tolerates up to k process crashes that may occur before the contention degree bypasses $n - k$.
    - The second algorithm, assumes k divides n, and tolerates up to $2k - 1$ process crashes that may occur before the contention degree bypasses $n - 2k + 1$.
- Finally, Sect. 5 presents impossibility results that address the limits of the proposed approach.

A Short Look at Consensus Solvability. The article [19] was one of the very first articles (if not the first one) that considered the case of initial failures for distributed tasks solvability. The reader will find in [4, 13] an approach to task solvability based on the theory of knowledge. When considering the close case of synchronous network-based systems the reader will find in [20] an overview of results for the case of consensus algorithms where links can appear and disappear at every communication step.

The usual notion of fault tolerance states that algorithm is crash-resilient if, in the presence of crash faults, all the non-faulty processes complete their operations and terminate. The article [17] considers a weaker liveness property namely a limited number of participating correct processes are allowed not to terminate in the presence of faults. As stated in [17] "sacrificing liveness for few of the processes allows us to increase the resiliency of the whole system".

2   Computing Model

Process and Communication Model. The system is composed of n asynchronous sequential processes denoted $p_1, ..., p_n$. The index of p_i is the integer i. Asynchronous means that each process proceeds at its own speed, which can vary with time and remains unknown to the other processes [14, 16].

A process can crash (a crash is an unexpected premature halt). Given an execution, a process that crashes is said to be *faulty* in that execution, otherwise, it is *correct*. Let us call *contention* the current number of processes that started executing. A λ-constrained crash is a crash that occurs before the contention degree bypasses λ.

The processes communicate through a shared memory made of the following base objects:

- Read/write atomic registers (RW).
- Atomic objects with consensus number $k \geq 1$ (these objects, denoted kCONS, will be used in Sect. 4).
- Adopt/commit objects (see below).

The Adopt-Commit Object. This object can be built in asynchronous read/write systems prone to any number of process crashes. Hence, its consensus number is 1. It was introduced by Gafni in [11]. It provides the processes with a single operation (that a process can invoke only once) denoted ac_propose(). This operation takes a value as input parameter and returns a pair $\langle tag, v \rangle$, where $tag \in \{\texttt{commit}, \texttt{adopt}\}$ and v is a proposed value (we say that the process decides a pair). The following properties define the object.

- *Termination.* A correct process that invokes ac_propose() returns from its invocation.
- *Validity.* If a process returns the pair $\langle -, v \rangle$, then v was proposed by a process.
- *Obligation.* If the processes that invoke ac_propose() propose the same input value v, only the pair $\langle \texttt{commit}, v \rangle$ can be returned.
- *Weak agreement.* If a process decides $\langle \texttt{commit}, v \rangle$ then any process that decides returns the pair $\langle \texttt{commit}, v \rangle$ or $\langle \texttt{adopt}, v \rangle$.

Process Participation. As in message-passing systems(see e.g., [1,3,15]), it is assumed that all the processes participate in the algorithm. (Equivalently, a process that does not participate is considered as having crashed initially). A process participates in the algorithm as soon as it has written in the shared memory.

Proposed Values. Without loss of generality, it is assumed that the values proposed in a consensus instance are non-negative integers, and $\perp$ is greater than any proposed value.

3   Base Algorithm ($k = 1$): Consensus from Read/Write Registers

This section presents an algorithm that solves consensus on top of RW registers[2] while tolerating one crash that occurs before the contention degree bypasses $\lambda = n - 1$.

---

[2] As their consensus number is 1, RW registers are 1CONS objects.

3.1 Presentation of the Algorithm

Shared Base Objects. The processes cooperate through the following shared objects.

- $INPUT[1..n]$ is an array of atomic single-writer multi-reader registers. Each of its entries is initialized to $\bot$, a value that cannot be proposed by the processes and is greater than any of these values. $INPUT[i]$ will contain the value proposed by p_i.
- DEC is a multi-writer multi-reader atomic register, the aim of which is to contain the decided value. It is initialized to $\bot$.
- $LAST$ will contain the index of a process.
- AC is an adopt/commit object.

Local Objects. Each process p_i manages:

- three local variables denoted val_i, res_i and tag_i, and
- two arrays denoted $input1[1..n]$ and $input2[1..n]$.

The initial values of the previous local variables are irrelevant. The value proposed by p_i is denoted in_i.

---

operation propose(in_i) **is**   code for p_i
(1) $INPUT[i] \leftarrow in_i$;
(2)   **repeat** $input1_i \leftarrow$ asynchronous non-atomic reading of $INPUT[1..n]$;
             $input2_i \leftarrow$ asynchronous non-atomic reading of $INPUT[1..n]$
       until $\big(input1_i = input2_i \wedge input1_i$ contains at most one $\bot\,\big)$ **end repeat**;
(3) $val_i \leftarrow \min\big($values deposited in $input1_i[1..n]\big)$;
(4)   **if** $(\exists\, j$ such that $input1_i[j] = \bot)$ **then** $LAST \leftarrow j$ **end if**;
(5) $\langle tag_i, res_i \rangle \leftarrow AC$.ac_propose($val_i$);
(6)   **if** $(tag_i = \mathtt{commit} \vee LAST = i)$ **then** $DEC \leftarrow res_i$ **else** wait$(DEC \neq \bot)$ **end if**;
(7)   return(DEC).

Algorithm 1: Consensus tolerating one $(n-1)$-constrained failure (on top of atomic RW registers)

Behavior of a Process p_i. (Algorithm 1) When a process p_i invokes propose(in_i), it first deposits the value in_i in $INPUT[i]$ (Line 1) and waits until the array $INPUT[1..n]$ contains at least $(n-1)$ entries different from their initial value $\bot$ (Line 2). Because at most one process may crash, and the process participation assumption, the wait statement eventually terminates.

After this occurs, p_i computes the smallest value deposited in the array $INPUT[1..n]$ (Line 3, remind that $\bot$ is greater than any proposed value). If $INPUT[1..n]$ contains an entry equal to $\bot$, say $INPUT[j]$, p_i observes that p_j is a belated process (or p_j the only process that may crash and it crashed before depositing its value in $INPUT[j]$) and posts this information in the shared register $LAST$ (Line 4).

Then, p_i champions its value val_i for it to be decided. To this end, it uses the underlying adopt/commit object, namely, it invokes AC.ac_propose(val_i) from which it obtains a pair $\langle tag_i, res_i \rangle$ (Line 5). There are three possible cases for a process p_i; at the end of which it decides at Line 7.

- If $tag_i = $ adopt, due to the Weak Agreement property of the object AC, no value different from res_i can be decided. Consequently, p_i writes res_i in the shared register DEC (Line 6) and returns it as the consensus value (Line 7).
- The same occurs if, while $tag_i = $ adopt, p_i is such that $LAST = i$. In this case, p_i has seen all the entries of the array $INPUT[1..n]$ filled with non-$\bot$ values and imposes res_i as the consensus value.
- If p_i is such that $tag_i = $ adopt $\wedge\ LAST \neq i$, it waits until it sees $DEC \neq \bot$, and decides.

3.2   Proof of Algorithm 1

Lemma 1. *Algorithm 1 satisfies the* Validity *property of consensus.*

Proof. It is easy to see that a value written in DEC is obtained from the adopt/commit object at Line 5. Moreover, due to Line 1 and Line 3 (where $\bot$ is greater than any proposed value), only values proposed to consensus can be proposed to the adopt/commit object. $\Box_{Lemma\ 1}$

Lemma 2. *Let us consider an execution in which no process crashes. Algorithm 1 satisfies the* Agreement *property of consensus.*

Proof. Let p_ℓ be the last process that writes the value it proposes in $INPUT[1..n]$. It follows from Line 3 that p_ℓ computes the smallest value in the array, and from Line 2 and Line 4 that, no index different from ℓ can be assigned to $LAST$. There are then two cases according to the value of the pair $\langle tag, res \rangle$ returned at Line 5.

- If a process p_k obtains $\langle \text{commit}, res \rangle$, it follows from the Weak Agreement property of the adopt/commit object that any other process can obtain $\langle \text{commit}, res \rangle$ or $\langle \text{adopt}, res \rangle$ only. We then have $DEC = res$ after the execution of Line 6. This is because the assignment at Line 6 can be executed only by a process that obtained $\langle \text{commit}, res \rangle$ or by p_ℓ (which is p_{LAST}) which obtained $\langle \text{commit}, res \rangle$ or $\langle \text{adopt}, res \rangle$ from its invocation of the AC object.
- If at Line 5 no process obtains $\langle \text{commit}, - \rangle$, it follows from Line 6 that only p_ℓ assigns a value to DEC, and consequently, no other value can be decided.

$\Box_{Lemma\ 2}$

Lemma 3. *Let us consider executions in which one process crashes. Algorithm 1 satisfies the* Agreement *property of consensus.*

Proof. Let us recall that by assumption (namely, contention related crash failures) if a process p_k crashes, it can do it only when the contention is lower or equal to $(n-1)$. We consider two cases.

- If p_k crashes initially (i.e., before writing the value it proposes in $INPUT[k]$, this array will eventually contain $(n-1)$ non-$\perp$ entries, and all the correct processes will consequently compute the same minimal value val that they will propose to the underlying adopt/commit object (Line 5). It then follows from the Obligation property of this object that all the correct processes will obtain the same pair $\langle \text{commit}, res \rangle$, from which we conclude that a single value can be decided.
- The process p_k crashes after it writes the value it proposes in $INPUT[k]$. There are two cases.
  - When exiting the repeat loop (Line 2), the local array $input1_i$ of all processes does not contain $\perp$. In this case, we are as in the previous item (replacing $INPUT[1..n]$ with one $\perp$ value by $INPUT[1..n]$ with no $\perp$ value).
  - There is an entry x such that, when exiting Line 2, there is some process p_i where $input1_i[x] = \perp$ and all other entries are different than $\perp$ (let call A this set of processes), while other process p_j is such that all entries of $input1_j$ are different than $\perp$ (set B). p_x is the last process to write into $INPUT$ and belongs to B.

    Notice that p_k is not the last process to write into $INPUT$ since it crashes when the contention threshold is lower or equal to $(n-1)$. Thus $x \neq k$ and p_x is correct.

    Processes of set A write x in $LAST$ at Line 4. Thus $LAST$ contains the identity of a correct process. The rest of the proof is the same as the proof of Lemma 2. $\square_{Lemma\ 3}$

Lemma 4. *Algorithm 1 satisfies the* Termination *property of consensus.*

Proof. Due to the assumption that all the processes participate and at most one process can crash, no process can block forever at Line 2.

Hence, all the correct processes invoke $AC.\text{ac\_propose}(val_i)$ and, due the Termination of the adopt/commit object, return from their invocation. If the tag commit is returned at some correct process p_k, this process assigns a value to DEC. If the tag is adopt, we claim that the process p_k such that $k = LAST$ is a correct process. Hence, it then assigns a non-$\perp$ value to DEC. So, in all cases, we have eventually $DEC \neq \perp$, which concludes the proof.

Proof of the claim. If $LAST = k$ at Line 6, there is a process p_i that wrote k in $LAST$ at Line 4. This means that p_i found $input1_i[k] = \perp$ at Line 4 and every other entry of $input1_i$ was different than $\perp$. Thus, we conclude that the contention threshold $\lambda = n - 1$ was attained when p_i wrote k in $LAST$. But, by assumption, no process crashes after the contention threshold $\lambda = n - 1$ has been attained. So, p_k is a correct process. $\square_{Lemma\ 4}$

Theorem 1. *Let* $\lambda = n - 1$. *Considering an asynchronous RW system, Algorithm 1 solves consensus in the presence of at most one λ-constrained failure.*

Proof. The proof follows from the previous lemmas. $\square_{Theorem\ 1}$

We notice that this bound is tight. When using only atomic registers, there is no consensus algorithm for n processes that can tolerate two $(n-1)$-constrained crash failures (Corollary 1, [5, 18]).

4   General Algorithms ($k \geq 1$): Consensus from Objects whose Consensus Number is k

The algorithms described in this section are built of top of RW registers and kCONS objects. As we are about to see, they are reductions to Algorithm 1. At Line 5, They exploit the additional power provided by objects whose consensus number is k. We present below two consensus algorithms:

- Algorithm 2, which tolerates up to k $(n - k)$-constrained failures, and
- Algorithm 3, which tolerates up to $2k-1$ $(n-2k+1)$-constrained failures, assuming k divides n.

4.1   Presentation of Algorithm 2

Shared Objects. Algorithm 2 uses the same shared registers DEC, $LAST$, and AC as Algorithm 1. It also uses:

- An array $INPUT[1..\lceil n/k \rceil]$ where each entry $INPUT[x]$ (instead of being a simple read/write register) is a kCONS object, and
- A Boolean array denoted $PARTICIPANT[1..n]$, initialized to [false, ..., false].

Behavior of a Process p_i. Algorithm 2 is very close to Algorithm 1.

- The lines N1 and N2 are new. They aim to ensure that no process will block forever despite up to k crashes.
- The lines with the same number have the same meaning in both algorithms.
- Each set of at most k processes p_i, p_j, etc. such that $\lceil i/k \rceil = \lceil j/k \rceil$, defines a cluster of processes that share the same kCONS object. Consequently, all the processes of a cluster act as if they were a single process, namely, no two different values can be written in $INPUT[\lceil i/k \rceil]$ by processes belonging to the same cluster.

4.2   Further Explanations

Before proving Algorithm 2, let us analyze it with two questions/answers.

Question 1. Can Algorithm 2 where $k \geq 1$, tolerates $(k+1)$ $(n-(k+1))$-constrained process crashes?

The answer is "no." This is because if $(k+1)$ processes crash, for example, initially (as allowed by the $(n-(k+1))$-constrained assumption), the other processes will remain blocked forever in the loop of Line N2. This entails the second question.

```
operation propose(in_i) is                                        code for p_i
(N1)    PARTICIPANT[i] ← true;
(N2)    repeat participant_i ← asynchronous reading of PARTICIPANT[1..n]
        until participant_i[1..n] contains at most k entries with false end repeat;
(1-M)   INPUT[⌈i/k⌉] ← kCONS[⌈i/k⌉].propose(in_i);
(2-M)   repeat input1_i ← asynchronous non-atomic reading of INPUT[1..⌈n/k⌉];
               input2_i ← asynchronous non-atomic reading of INPUT[1..⌈n/k⌉]
        until input1_i = input2_i ∧ input1_i contains at most one ⊥ end repeat;
(3)     val_i ← min(values deposited in input1_i);
(4)     if (∃ j such that input1_i[j] = ⊥) then LAST ← j end if;
(5)     ⟨tag_i, res_i⟩ ← AC.ac_propose(val_i);
(6)     if (tag_i = commit ∨ LAST = ⌈i/k⌉)
                    then DEC ← res_i else wait(DEC ≠ ⊥) end if ;
(7)     return(DEC);
```

Algorithm 2: Consensus tolerating up to k $(n - k)$-constrained failures (on top of kCONS objects)

Question 2. Are the lines N1-N2 needed?

Let us consider Algorithm 2 without the lines N1-N2 and with $k = 2$, and let us examine the following possible scenario which involves five processes $p_1, ..., p_5$. So, p_1 and p_2 belong the cluster 1, p_3 and p_4 belong the cluster 2, and p_5 belongs to cluster 3. Let us assume that the value in_5 proposed by p_5 is smaller than the other proposed values.

- Process p_1 executes Line 1-M and writes in $INPUT[1]$.
- Process p_3 executes Line 1-M and writes in $INPUT[2]$.
- Both processes p_1 and p_3 execute Line 4 and write the cluster number 3 in $LAST$.
- Then, process p_5 executes from Line 1-M until Line 4.
- Then, the processes p_1, p_3, and p_5 execute Line 5, and obtain the tag adopt.
- Then p_5 crashes. It follows that p_5 will never write in DEC which forever remains equal to ⊥.
- Then p_2 and p_4 execute Line 1-M to Line 4, and obtain adopt from the adopt/commit object.
- It follows that, when the processes p_1, p_2, p_3, and p_4 execute Line 6 they remain forever blocked in the wait statement.

Hence, Lines N1 and N2 cannot be suppressed from Algorithm 2.

4.3 Proof of Algorithm 2

Theorem 2. *Let $n \geq k$ and $\lambda = n - k$. Considering an asynchronous RW system enriched with k-CONS objects, Algorithm 2 solves consensus in the presence of at most k λ-constrained crash failures.*

Proof. Let us first observe that, as at most k processes may crash, no process can block forever at Line N2.

Now, let us show that the lines N1-N2 cannot entail a process to block forever at any line from 1-M to 7. To this end, let us consider the n processes are partitioned in clusters of at most k processes so that p_i belongs to the cluster identified $\lceil i/k \rceil$. A cluster crashes if all its processes crash. A cluster is alive if at least one of its processes does not crash. There are two cases.

- Each cluster contains at least one process that does not crash, so all the clusters are alive. It follows that, when a process executes Line 4 and assigns a cluster identity to $LAST$, it is the identity of an alive cluster, from which follows that (if needed due to the predicate of Line 4) a correct process will be able to write a value in DEC, thereby preventing processes from being blocking forever in the wait statement at Line 6.
- All the processes in a cluster crash. Let us notice that at most one cluster can crash.[3] In this case, considering the clusters (instead of the processes) and replacing n by $\lceil n/k \rceil$, we are in the same case as in the proof of Lemma 3.

$\square_{Theorem\,2}$

4.4   When k Divides n: Tolerating $k - 1$ Classical Any-Time Failures

Let us consider the case where crash failures are not constrained. Those are the classical crashes that can occur at any time (they are called *any-time* failures in [5]). It is known that there is no consensus algorithm for $n \geq k+1$ processes that can tolerate k any-time failures, using registers and wait-free consensus objects for k processes [9]. In such a model, Algorithm 2 has the property captured by the following theorem.

Theorem 3. *If k divides n, Algorithm 2 tolerates $k - 1$ any-time failures.*

Proof. Using the cluster terminology defined in the previous proof, k divides n, each cluster contains k processes exactly. As at most $(k - 1)$ processes may crash, it follows that all the clusters must be alive. The rest of the proof is the same as the proof of Theorem 2.

$\square_{Theorem\,3}$

4.5   When k Divides n: Tolerating $2k - 1$ Contention-Related Crash Failures

Algorithm 3. Let Algorithm 3 be the same as Algorithm 2, except that line 3,
"**until** $participant_i[1..n]$ contains at most k entries with `false` **end repeat**;"
is replaced with,
"**until** $participant_i[1..n]$ contains at most $2k - 1$ entries with `false` **end repeat**;"
Then, the following theorem holds.

Theorem 4. *Assume that k divides n, $n \geq 2k - 1$, and $\lambda = n - 2k + 1$. Considering an asynchronous RW system enriched with k-CONS objects, Algorithm 3 solves consensus in the presence of up to $(2k - 1)$ λ-constrained crash failures.*

Proof. Using the cluster terminology defined in the proof of Algorithm 2, k divides n, implies that each cluster contains k processes exactly. As at most $2k - 1$ processes may crash, it follows that all the clusters, except maybe one, must be alive. The rest of the proof is similar to the proof of Theorem 2.

$\square_{Theorem\,4}$

---

[3] If k does not divides n, and the cluster that crashes contains less than k processes, no other cluster can crash.

5   Impossibility Results

This section presents impossibility results for an asynchronous model which supports atomic read/write registers and kCONS objects, in which λ-constrained and any-time crash failures are possible. Let an *initial* crash failure be the crash of a process that occurs before it executes its first access to an atomic read/write register.

Hence, there are three types of crash failures: initial, λ-constrained, and any-time. Let us say that a failure type T1 is *more severe* than a failure type T2 (denoted T1 > T2) if any crash failure of type T2 is also a crash failure of type T1 but not vice-versa. Considering an n-process system, the following severity hierarchy follows from the definition of the failure types: any-time > $(n-1)$-constrained > $(n-2)$-constrained $\cdots$ > 1-constrained > initial (let us observe that any-time is the same as n-constrained and initial is the same as 0-constrained).

Consensus with λ-constrained failures.

Theorem 5. *For every $\ell \geq 0$, $k \geq 1$, $n > \ell + k$, and $\lambda = n - \ell$, there is no consensus algorithm for n processes, using atomic RW registers and kCONS objects, that tolerates $(\ell + k)$ λ-constrained crash failures (even when assuming that there are no any-time crash failures).*

Proof. Assume to the contrary that for some $\ell \geq 0$, $k \geq 1$, $n > \ell + k$, and $\lambda = n - \ell$, there is a consensus algorithm, say A, that (1) uses atomic registers and kCONS objects, and (2) tolerates $\ell + k$ λ-constrained crash failures.

Given any execution of A, let us remove any set of ℓ processes by assuming they fail initially (this is possible because $(n - \ell)$-constrained > initial). It then follows (from the contradiction assumption) that the assumed algorithm A solves consensus in a system of $n' = n - \ell$ processes, where $n' > k$, using atomic registers and k-cons objects.

However, in a system of $n' = n - \ell$ processes, process contention is always lower or equal to n', from which follows that, in such an execution, n'-constrained crash failures are the same as any-time failures. Thus, algorithm A can be used to generate a consensus algorithm A' for $n' = n - \ell$ processes, where $n' > k$, that (1) uses only atomic registers and k-cons objects, and (2) tolerates k any-time crash failures. But, this is known to be impossible as shown in [9]. A contradiction. $\square_{Theorem\ 5}$

Consensus Using Atomic Registers Only. For the special case of consensus using atomic registers only, the equation $n > \ell + k$ becomes $n > \ell + 1$. The following corollary is then an immediate consequence of Theorem 5.

Corollary 1. *For every $0 \leq \ell < n - 1$ and $\lambda = n - \ell$, there is no consensus algorithm for n processes, using atomic RW registers, that can tolerate $(\ell+1)$ λ-constrained crash failures (even when assuming that there are no any-time crash failures). In particular, when $\ell = 1$, there is no consensus algorithm for n processes that can tolerate two $(n-1)$-constrained crash failures.*

Consensus with λ-constrained and any-time failures.

Theorem 6. *For every $\ell \geq 0$, $k \geq 1$, $n > \ell + k$, $g \geq 0$, and $\lambda = n - \ell$, there is no consensus algorithm for n processes, using atomic RW registers and kCONS objects, that, tolerates $(\ell + k - g)$ λ-constrained crash failures and g any-time crash failures.*

Proof. Follows immediately from Theorem 5 by observing that any-time crash failures belong to a more severe type of a failure than λ-constrained crash failures when $\lambda < n$, and is the same as a λ-constrained crash failure when $\lambda = n$. $\square_{Theorem\,6}$

6 Conclusion

This article has investigated the computability power of the pair made up of process participation plus contention-related crashes, when one has to solve consensus in an n-process asynchronous shared memory system enriched with objects the consensus number of which is equal to k. It has been shown that for $n \geq k$, consensus can be solved in such a context in the presence of up to k process crashes if these crashes occur before process contention has attained the value $\lambda = n - k$. Furthermore, for the case where k divides n, it has been shown that consensus can be solved in such a context in the presence of up to $2k - 1$ process crashes if these crashes occur before process contention bypasses the threshold $\lambda = 2n - k + 1$.

The corresponding consensus algorithms have been built in an incremental way. Namely, a read/write algorithm based on adopt/commit object has first been given, and then generalized by replacing atomic read/write registers by objects whose consensus number is k. Developments of the power/limit of this approach have also been presented, increasing our knowledge on an important topic of fault-tolerant process synchronization in asynchronous distributed systems.

Acknowledgments. M. Raynal has been partially supported by the French projects ByBloS (ANR-20-CE25-0002-01) and PriCLeSS (ANR-10-LABX-07-81) devoted to the design of modular building blocks for distributed applications.

References

1. Attiya, H., Welch, J.L.: Distributed Computing: Fundamentals, Simulations And Advanced Topics, 2nd edn., p. 414. Wiley-Interscience, New Jersey (2004). ISBN 0-471-45324-2
2. Chaudhuri, S.: More choices allow more faults: set consensus problems in totally asynchronous systems. Inf. Comput. **105**(1), 132–158 (1993)
3. Cachin, Ch., Guerraoui, R., Rodrigues, L.: Reliable And Secure Distributed Programming, p. 367. Springer, Heidelberg (2011). https://doi.org/10.1007/978-3-642-15260-3
4. Castañeda, A., Gonczarowski, Y.A., Moses, Y.: Unbeatable consensus. Distrib. Comput. **35**(2), 123–143 (2022). https://doi.org/10.1007/s00446-021-00417-3
5. Durand, A., Raynal, M., Taubenfeld, G.: Contention-related crash-failures: definitions, agreement algorithms and impossibility results. Theoret. Comput. Sci. **909**, 76–86 (2022)
6. Fischer, M.J., Lynch, N.A., Paterson, M.S.: Impossibility of distributed consensus with one faulty process. J. ACM **32**(2), 374–382 (1985)
7. Guerraoui R.: Indulgent algorithms. In: Proceedings of the 19th Annual ACM Symposium on Principles of Distributed Computing (PODC 2000), pp. 289–297. ACM Press (2000)

8. Guerraoui, R., Raynal, M.: The information structure of indulgent consensus. IEEE Trans. Comput. **53**(4), 453–466 (2004)
9. Herlihy, M.P.: Wait-free synchronization. ACM Trans. Program. Lang. Syst. **13**(1), 124–149 (1991)
10. Loui, M., Abu-Amara, H.: Memory requirements for agreement among unreliable asynchronous processes. Adv. Comput. Res. **4**(163–183), 3–5 (1987)
11. Gafni E.: Round-by-round fault detectors: unifying synchrony and asynchrony. In: Proceedings of the 17th ACM Symposium on Principles of Distributed Computing (PODC), pp. 143–152. ACM Press (1998)
12. Lamport, L.: The part-time parliament. ACM Trans. Comput. Syst. **16**(2), 133–169 (1998)
13. Moses, Y., Rajsbaum, S.: A layered analysis of consensus. SIAM J. Comput. **31**(4), 989–1021 (2002)
14. Raynal, M.: Concurrent Programming: Algorithms Principles And Foundations, p. 515. Springer, Heidelberg (2013). https://doi.org/10.1007/978-3-642-32027-9. ISBN 978-3-642-32026-2
15. Raynal, M.: Fault-tolerant Message-passing Distributed Systems: An Algorithmic Approach, p. 492. Springer, Heidelberg (2018). https://doi.org/10.1007/978-3-319-94141-7. ISBN 978-3-319-94140-0
16. Taubenfeld, G.: Synchronization Algorithms And Concurrent Programming, p. 423. Pearson Education/Prentice Hall, Hoboken (2006)
17. Taubenfeld G.: A closer look at fault tolerance. Theor. Comput. Syst. **62**(5) :1085–1108 (2018). (First version in Proceedings of PODC 2012, 261–270)
18. Taubenfeld, G.: Weak failures: definitions, algorithms and impossibility results. In: Podelski, A., Taïani, F. (eds.) NETYS 2018. LNCS, vol. 11028, pp. 51–66. Springer, Cham (2019). https://doi.org/10.1007/978-3-030-05529-5_4
19. Taubenfeld, G., Katz, S., Moran, S.: Initial failures in distributed computations. Int. J. Parallel Prog. **18**(4), 255–276 (1989). https://doi.org/10.1007/BF01407859
20. Winkler, K., Schmid, S.: An Overview of recent results for consensus in directed dynamic networks. Bull. Eur. Assoc. Theor. Comput. Sci. **2**(128), 30 (2019)

Self-stabilizing Byzantine Fault-Tolerant Repeated Reliable Broadcast

Romaric Duvignau[1], Michel Raynal[2], and Elad M. Schiller[1(✉)]

[1] Chalmers University of Technology, Gothenburg, Sweden
{duvignau,elad}@chalmers.se
[2] IRISA, CNRS, Inria, Univ Rennes, 35042 Rennes, France
michel.raynal@irisa.fr

Abstract. We study a well-known communication abstraction called Byzantine Reliable Broadcast (BRB). This abstraction is central in the design and implementation of fault-tolerant distributed systems, as many fault-tolerant distributed applications require communication with provable guarantees on message deliveries. Our study focuses on fault-tolerant implementations for message-passing systems that are prone to process-failures, such as crashes and malicious behaviors.

At PODC 1983, Bracha and Toueg, in short, BT, solved the BRB problem. BT has optimal resilience since it can deal with up to $t < n/3$ Byzantine processes, where n is the number of processes. The present work aims at the design of an even more robust solution than BT by expanding its fault-model with self-stabilization, a vigorous notion of fault-tolerance. In addition to tolerating Byzantine and communication failures, self-stabilizing systems can recover after the occurrence of *arbitrary transient-faults*. These faults represent any violation of the assumptions according to which the system was designed to operate (as long as the algorithm code remains intact).

We propose, to the best of our knowledge, the first self-stabilizing Byzantine fault-tolerant (SSBFT) solution for repeated BRB (that follows BT's specifications) in signature-free message-passing systems. Our contribution includes a self-stabilizing variation on a BT that solves asynchronous single-instance BRB. We also consider the problem of recycling instances of single-instance BRB. Our SSBFT recycling for time-free systems facilitates the concurrent handling of a predefined number of BRB invocations and, by this way, can serve as the basis for SSBFT consensus.

1 Introduction

Fault-tolerant distributed systems are known to be hard to design and verify. High-level communication primitives can facilitate such complex challenges. These primitives can be based on low-level ones, *e.g.,* the one that allows processes to send a message to only one other process at a time. Hence, when an algorithm wishes to broadcast message m to all processes, it can send m individually to every other process. But, if the sender fails during this broadcast, perhaps only some of the processes have received m. Even in the presence of network-level support for broadcasting or multicasting, failures can cause similar inconsistencies. To simplify the design of fault-tolerant distributed algorithms, such inconsistencies need to be avoided. Fault-tolerant broadcasts can simplify the development of fault-tolerant distributed systems, *e.g.*, State Machine Replication [1] and Set-Constrained Delivery Broadcast [2]. The weakest variant, named *Reliable Broadcast*, lets all non-failing processes agree on the set of delivered messages , including all messages they have broadcast. We aim to design a reliable broadcast that is more fault-tolerant than the state of the art.

The Problem. A process commits a Byzantine failure if it deviates from the algorithm instructions, say, by deferring (or omitting) messages that were sent by the algorithm or sending fake messages. Bracha and Toueg [3], BT from now on, proposed the communication abstraction of Byzantine Reliable Broadcast (BRB), which allows every process to invoke the brbBroadcast(v) operation and raise the brbDeliver() event upon message arrival. Following Raynal [1, Ch. 4], we consider the single-instance BRB problem (Definition 1), whose solution facilitates Byzantine Fault-Tolerant (BFT) binary and multivalued consensus [1].

Single-Instance BRB. We require the above operations to satisfy Definition 1.

Definition 1. *The operations* brbBroadcast(v) *and* brbDeliver() *satisfy:*

- **BRB-validity.** *Suppose a correct process BRB-delivers message m from a correct process p_i. Then, p_i had BRB-broadcast m.*
- **BRB-integrity.** *No correct process BRB-delivers more than once.*
- **BRB-no-duplicity.** *No two correct processes BRB-deliver different messages from p_i (who might be faulty).*
- **BRB-Completion-1.** *Suppose p_i is a correct sender. All correct processes BRB-deliver from p_i eventually.*
- **BRB-Completion-2.** *If a correct process BRB-delivers a message from p_i (who might be faulty), all correct processes BRB-deliver p_i's message eventually.*

Repeated BRB. Distributed systems may use, over time, an unbounded number of BRB instances. However, we require our solution to use, at any time, a bounded amount of memory. Thus, we also consider the recycling BRB invocations using bounded memory. We require the single-instance BRB object, O, to have an operation, called recycle(), that allows the recycling mechanism to locally reset O after all non-faulty processes had completed the delivery of O's message. Also, we require the mechanism to inform (the possibly recycled) O regarding its availability to take new missions. Specifically, the txAvailable() operation returns True when the sender can use O for broadcasting, and rxAvailable() returns True when O's new transmission has arrived at the receiver.

One may observe that the problem statement does not depend on the fault model or the design criteria. However, the proposed solution depends on all three. To clarify, we solve the single instance BRB using the requirements presented by Raynal [1, Ch. 4]. Then, we solve an extended version of the problem in which each BRB instance needs to be recycled so that an unbounded number of BRB instances can appear.

Fault Models. Recall that our BRB solution may be a component in a system that solves consensus. Thus, we safeguard against Byzantine failures by following the same assumptions that are often used when solving consensus. Specifically, for the sake of deterministic and signature-free solvability [4], we assume there are at most $t < n/3$ crashed or Byzantine processes, where n is the total number of processes. The proposed solutions are for message-passing systems that have no guarantees on the communication delay and without explicit access to the clock. These systems are also prone to communication failures, *e.g.*, packet omission, duplication, and reordering, as long as Fair Communication (FC) holds, *i.e.*, if p_i sends a message infinitely often to p_j, then p_j receives that message infinitely often. We use three different fault models with notations following Raynal [1]:

- $BAMP_{n,t}[FC, t < n/3]$. This is a Byzantine Asynchronous Message-Passing model with at most t (out of n) faulty nodes. The array $[FC, t < n/3]$ denotes the assumption list, *i.e.*, FC and $t < n/3$. We use this model for studying the problem of single-instance BRB since it has no synchrony assumptions.
- $BAMP_{n,t}[FC, t < n/3, BML, \Diamond P_{mute}]$. By Doudou *et al.* [5], processes commit muteness failures when they stop sending specific messages, but they may continue to send "I-am-alive" messages. For studying the repeated BRB problem, we enrich $BAMP_{n,t}[FC, t < n/3]$ with a muteness detector of class $\Diamond P_{mute}$ and assume Bounded Message Lifetime (BML). That is, in any unbounded sequence of BRB invocations, at the time that immediately follows the x-th invocation, the messages associated with the $(x-\lambda)$-th invocation (or earlier) are either delivered or lost, where λ is a known upper-bound.
- $AMP_n[FC, BML]$. Our repeated BRB solution for $BAMP_{n,t}[FC, t < n/3, BML, \Diamond P_{mute}]$ is based on this model, which does not consider any node failures.

Raynal [1] refers to an asynchronous system as *time-free* when it includes synchrony assumptions, *e.g.*, BML. Note that BML does not imply bounded communication delay since an unbounded number of messages can be lost between any two successful transmissions. At last, our muteness detector implementation follows an assumption about the number, Θ, of messages that some non-faulty processes can exchange without hearing from all non-faulty processes.

Self-stabilization. In addition to the failures above, we aim to recover after the occurrence of the last *transient-fault* [6,7]. These faults model any temporary violation of assumptions according to which the system was designed to operate. This includes the corruption of control variables, *e.g.*, the program counter and packet payloads, as well as operational assumptions, *e.g.*, at most $t < n/3$ processes are faulty. When modeling the system, we assume these violations can bring the system to an arbitrary state from which a *self-stabilizing system* should recover. Such a system must satisfy the task requirements only after the system has finished recovering from the occurrence of the last transient fault, cf [6,7].

Related Work. In the context of reliable broadcast, there are non-self-stabilizing BFT [1,10–12] and self-stabilizing crash-tolerant solutions [13] (even for total order broadcast [13, 23–25]). We focus on BT [3] to which we propose a self-stabilizing variation. BT is the basis for advanced BFT algorithms for solving consensus [14] and is based on Toueg's simpler abstraction called no-duplicity broadcast [15] (ND-broadcast). It includes all of Definition 1's requirements except for BRB-Completion-2. Maurer and Tixeuil [16] consider an abstraction that is somewhat simpler than ND-broadcast since they only consider BRB-no-duplicity (and none of the other requirements of Definition 1). They provide a single-instance synchronous SSBFT broadcast, whereas we consider an asynchronous repeated BRB that follows Definition 1, which is taken from Raynal [1]. Raynal studies the exact power of all the essential communication abstractions in the area of fault-tolerant message-passing systems. We use the more useful definition provided by Raynal since we wish to connect our solution to all relevant protocols in the area, such as multivalued consensus.

We also consider a self-stabilizing BFT (SSBFT) mechanism for recycling BRB instances. This mechanism uses a muteness detector inspired by Doudou *et al.* [5]. Even though Doudou *et al.* consider the consensus problem while we consider here repeated BRB, both works share the same motivation, *i.e.*, circumventing known impossibilities, *e.g.*, the one by Fischer, Lynch, and Paterson [17].

Our Contribution. We present SSBFT BRB—a fundamental module for dependable distributed systems, which is obtained via a transformation of the non-self-stabilizing BT algorithm while preserving BT's resilience optimality. In the absence of transient-faults, our asynchronous solution for single-instance BRB achieves operation completion within a constant number of asynchronous communication rounds. After the occurrence of the last transient-fault, the system recovers eventually (while assuming execution fairness among the non-faulty processes). The amount of memory used by the proposed algorithm is bounded. The communication costs of the studied and proposed BRB algorithms are similar, *i.e.*, $\mathcal{O}(n^2)$ messages per BRB instance. Our contribution also includes an SSBFT recycling mechanism for $\mathsf{BAMP}_{n,t}[\mathsf{FC}, \Diamond\mathsf{P}_{\mathsf{mute}}, \mathsf{BML}]$ named the *independent round counter* (IRC) algorithm. Implementing an SSBFT IRC is a non-trivial challenge since this counter should facilitate an unbounded number of increments, yet it has to use only a constant amount of memory. Using novel techniques for dealing with integer overflow events, the proposed solution recovers from transient faults eventually and has communication cost of $\mathcal{O}(n)$ messages per BRB instance.

To the best of our knowledge, we propose the first self-stabilizing BFT solutions for the problems of IRC and repeated BRB (that follows BT's problem specifications [1, Ch. 4]). As said, BRB and IRC consider different fault models. Section 2 defines $\mathsf{BAMP}_{n,t}[\mathsf{FC}, t < n/3]$ and self-stabilization. The non-self-stabilizing BT algorithm for $\mathsf{BAMP}_{n,t}[\mathsf{FC}, t < n/3]$ is studied in Sect. 3. Our SSBFT variation on BT for $\mathsf{BAMP}_{n,t}[\mathsf{FC}, t < n/3]$ is proposed in Sect. 4. Our IRC solution is presented in two steps. A self-stabilizing IRC for time-free node-failure-free systems appears in Sect. 5. We revise these settings into $\mathsf{BAMP}_{n,t}[\mathsf{FC}, \Diamond\mathsf{P}_{\mathsf{mute}}, \mathsf{BML}]$ (Sect. 6) and propose our novel SSBFT IRC solution. Section 7 compares the overhead of the studied and proposed solutions when executing δ BRB instances concurrently. This straightforward extension is imperative for practical deployments and usage in implementations of solutions to harder problems, e.g. multivalued consensus [1].

Due to the page limit, a detailed version of this work (which includes the complete proofs) appears in the complementary technical report [9].

2   System Settings for $\mathsf{BAMP}_{n,t}[\mathsf{FC}, t < n/3]$

The fault model considered in this section is for asynchronous message-passing systems that have no guarantees on the communication delay. Also, the algorithm cannot explicitly access the clock (or timeouts). The system consists of a set, $\mathcal{P}$, of n fail-prone nodes (or processes) with unique identifiers. Any pair of nodes $p_i, p_j \in \mathcal{P}$ has access to a bidirectional communication channel, $\mathsf{channel}_{j,i}$, that, at any time, has at most $\mathsf{channelCapacity}$ messages on transit from p_j to p_i (this assumption is due to an impossibility [7, Chapter 3.2]).

In the *interleaving model* [7], the node's program is a sequence of *(atomic) steps*. Each step starts with an internal computation and finishes with a single communication operation, *i.e.*, a message *send* or *receive*. The *state*, s_i, of node $p_i \in \mathcal{P}$ includes all of p_i's variables and incoming channels. The term *system state* (or configuration) refers to the tuple $c = (s_1, s_2, \cdots, s_n)$. We define an *execution (or run)* $R = c[0], a[0], c[1], a[1], \ldots$ as an alternating sequence of system states $c[x]$ and steps $a[x]$, such that each $c[x + 1]$, except for the starting one, $c[0]$, is obtained from $c[x]$ by $a[x]$'s execution. The *legal executions* (LE) set refers to all the executions in which the task requirements (Sect. 1) hold.

Arbitrary Node Failures. Byzantine faults model any fault in a node including crashes, and arbitrary malicious behaviors. Here the adversary lets each node receive the arriving messages and calculate their state according to the algorithm. However, once a node (that is captured by the adversary) sends a message, the adversary can modify the message in any way, arbitrarily delay it or omit it. The adversary can also send fake messages, *i.e.*, not according to the algorithm. For the sake of solvability [4], the number, t, of Byzantine failures needs to be less than one-third of the number, n, of nodes. The set of non-faulty indexes is denoted by *Correct*, so that $i \in Correct$ when p_i is a correct node.

Transient-Faults. We consider any temporary violation of the assumptions according to which the system was designed to operate. We refer to these violations as *transient-faults* and assume that they can corrupt the system state arbitrarily (while keeping the program code intact). The occurrence of a transient fault is rare. Thus, we assume the last transient fault occurs before the system execution starts [7]. Also, it leaves the system to start in an arbitrary state.

Dijkstra's Self-stabilization. An algorithm is *self-stabilizing* w.r.t. LE, when every execution R of the algorithm reaches within a finite period a suffix $R_{legal} \in LE$ that is legal. Namely, Dijkstra [8] requires $\forall R : \exists R' : R = R' \circ R_{legal} \wedge R_{legal} \in LE \wedge |R'| \in Z^+$, where the operator $\circ$ denotes that

$R = R' \circ R''$ is the concatenation of R' with R''. This work assumes execution fairness during the period in which the system recovers from the occurrence of the last arbitrary transient fault. We say that an execution is *fair* when every step of a correct node that is applicable infinitely often is executed infinitely often and fair communication is kept. Since transient faults are rare, this fairness assumption is seldom needed and even then, it is only needed for the period of recovery.

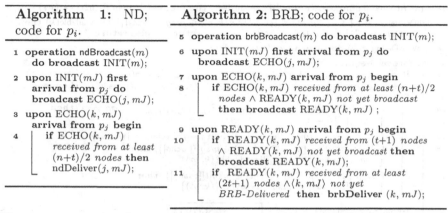

(When a message arrives from p_j to the receiver, we add the suffix J to the field name.)

3   The Non-Self-Stabilizing BT Algorithm

BT [3] is a BRB solution for $\mathsf{BAMP}_{n,t}[\mathsf{FC}, t < n/3]$, which is based on ND-broadcast [15]. It includes all of the BRB requirements except BRB-Completion-2. We review ND-broadcast before BT.

ND-Broadcast. Algorithm 1 presents ND-broadcast, and assumes that every correct node invokes ND-broadcast at most once. Node p_i initiates the ND-broadcast of m_i by sending INIT(m_i) to all nodes (line 1). Upon this message's first arrival to p_j, it disseminates the fact that p_i has initiated m's ND-broadcast by sending ECHO(i, m) to all nodes (line 2). Upon this message arrival to p_k from more than $(n+t)/2$ different nodes, p_k is ready to ND-deliver $\langle i, m_i \rangle$ (line 4).

BRB-Broadcast. Algorithm 2 satisfies the BRB requirements. The first difference between the ND-broadcast and BRB algorithms is when ND-delivery of $\langle j, m \rangle$ is replaced with the broadcast of READY(j, m). This broadcast indicates that p_i is ready to BRB-deliver $\langle j, m \rangle$ as soon as it receives sufficient support, *i.e.*, the arrival of READY(j, m), which tells that $\langle j, m \rangle$ can be BRB-delivered. Note that BRB-no-duplicity protects from the case in which p_i broadcasts READY(j, m) while p_j broadcasts READY(j, m'), such that $m \neq m'$.

The new part of the BRB algorithm (lines 9 to 11) includes two if-statements. The first one (line 10) makes sure that every correct node receives READY(j, m) from at least one correct node before BRB-delivering $\langle j, m \rangle$. This is done via

---

Algorithm 3: SSBFT BRB with instance recycling interface; p_i's code

---

12 **types:** brbMSG := {init, echo, ready};

13 **variables:** $msg[\mathcal{P}][\text{brbMSG}] := [[\emptyset, \ldots, \emptyset]]$ /* most recently sent/received message */

14 $wasDelivered[\mathcal{P}] := [\text{False}, \ldots, \text{False}]$ /* indicates whether the message was delivered */

15 **required interfaces:** txAvailable() and rxAvailable(k)

16 **provided interfaces:** recycle(k) **do** $\{(msg[k], wasDelivered[k]) \leftarrow ([\emptyset, \emptyset, \emptyset], \text{False})\};$

17 mrg(mJ, j) **do** {**foreach** $s \in$ brbMSG, $p_k \in \mathcal{P}$ **do if** $s \neq init \vee \not\exists s = init, (k, m), (k, m') \in$
    $(msg[j][s] \cup mJ[s]) : m \neq m'$ **then** $msg[j][s] \leftarrow msg[j][s] \cup mJ[s]\};$

18 **operations:** brbBroadcast(v) **do** {**if** txAvailable() **then** recycle(i); $msg[i][\text{init}] \leftarrow \{v\}$}

19 brbDeliver(k) **do** {**if** $\exists_m (2t+1) \leq |\{p_\ell \in \mathcal{P} : (k, m) \in msg[\ell][\text{ready}]\}| \wedge$rxAvailable($k$) **then**
    $wasDelivered[k] \leftarrow wasDelivered[k] \wedge m \neq \bot$; **return** m **else return** $\bot\};$

20 brbWasDelivered(k) **do return** $wasDelivered[k];$

21 **do-forever begin**

22 | **if** $\exists_{(j,m)\in msg[i][\text{echo}]} m \notin msg[j][\text{init}] \vee \exists_{(j,m)\in msg[i][\text{ready}]} \neg((n+t)/2 < |\{p_\ell \in \mathcal{P} :$
    $(j, m) \in msg[\ell][\text{echo}]\}| \vee (t+1) \leq |\{p_\ell \in \mathcal{P} : (j, m) \in msg[\ell][\text{ready}]\}|)$ **then** recycle(i);

23 | **foreach** $p_k \in \mathcal{P}$ **do**

24 | | **if** $|msg[k][\text{init}]| > 1 \vee \exists_{s \neq init} \exists_{p_j \in \mathcal{P}} \exists_{(j,m),(j,m') \in msg[k][s]} m \neq m'$ **then**

25 | | | $msg[k][s] \leftarrow \emptyset$

26 | | **if** $\exists_{m \in msg[k][\text{init}]} msg[i][\text{echo}] = \emptyset$ **then** $msg[i][\text{echo}] \leftarrow \{(k, m)\};$

27 | | **if** $\exists_m (n+t)/2 < |\{p_\ell \in \mathcal{P} : (k, m) \in msg[\ell][\text{echo}]\}|$ **then**

28 | | | $msg[i][\text{ready}] \leftarrow msg[i][\text{ready}] \cup \{(k, m)\}$

29 | | **if** $\exists_m (t+1) \leq |\{p_\ell \in \mathcal{P} : (k, m) \in msg[\ell][\text{ready}]\}|$ **then**

30 | | | $msg[i][\text{ready}] \leftarrow msg[i][\text{ready}] \cup \{(k, m)\}$

31 | **broadcast** MSG($brb = msg[i]$, $\boxed{irc = \text{txMSG}()}$);

32 **upon** MSG($brbJ$, $\boxed{ircJ}$) **arrival from** p_j **do** {mrg($brbJ, j$); $\boxed{\text{rxMSG}(brbJ, ircJ, j)}$}

---

the broadcasting of READY(j, m) as soon as p_i received it from at least $(t+1)$ different nodes (since t of them can be Byzantine).

The second if-statement (line 11) makes sure that no two correct nodes BRB-deliver different pairs (in the presence of plausibly fake READY$(j, \text{-})$ messages sent by Byzantine nodes, where the symbol '-' stands for any legal value). That is, the delivery of a BRB-broadcast is done only after the first reception of the pair $\langle j, m \rangle$ from at least $(2t+1)$ (out of which at most t are Byzantine). The receiver then knows that there are at least $t+1$ correct nodes that can make sure that the condition in line 10 holds eventually for all correct nodes.

4 Self-stabilizing Byzantine-Tolerant Single-Instance BRB

Algorithm 3 proposes our SSBFT BRB solution for BAMP$_{n,t}$[FC, $t < n/3$]. The key idea is to offer (i) a variation of Algorithm 2 so that its operations always complete even when starting from an incorrect state, (ii) interfaces for accessing the current status and value of the broadcast, as well as (iii) interfaces for coordinating the recycling of a given BRB object. This way, the recycling coordination mechanism (Sect. 5 and Sect. 6) can make sure that no BRB object is recycled before all correct nodes deliver its result. Also, once all correct nodes have delivered a message, the BRB object can be recycled eventually. The line numbers of Algorithm 3 continue the ones of the previous algorithms, and the boxed code fragments in lines 31 to 32 are irrelevant to our single-instance BRB.

Variables and Message Structure. The message MSG() unifies the different messages of Algorithm 2. The array $msg[][]$ stores both the information that is sent and received by these messages. Specifically, $msg_i[i][]$ stores the information that p_i broadcasts (line 31) and for any $j \neq i$ the entry $msg_i[j][]$ stores the information coming from p_j (line 17). Also, we define the type brbMSG (line 12) for storing information related to BRB-broadcast messages, *e.g.*, $msg_i[i][\text{init}]$ stores the information that BRB-broadcast disseminates of INIT() messages and the aggregated content of READY() messages appear in $msg_i[i][\text{ready}]$.

Algorithm Details. The brbBroadcast(v) operation (line 18) invokes BRB-broadcast instances with v. The invocation causes Algorithm 3 to follow Algorithm 2's logic (lines 19 and 26 to 30). It also includes consistency tests (line 22).

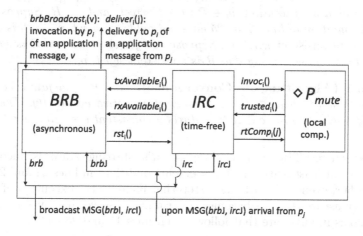

Fig. 1. Integrating the BRB (Sect. 4), IRC (Sect. 5), and $\Diamond P_{mute}$ (Sect. 6) protocols.

Interfaces for Coordinating the Recycling of a Given BRB Object. Recall that Algorithm 3 has an interface to a recycling mechanism of BRB instances (Sect. 5). The interface between the proposed BRB and recycling mechanism includes the recycle(), txAvailable(), and rxAvailable() operations, see Fig. 1 (the interface between IRC and $\Diamond P_{mute}$ is irrelevant to Algorithm 3). The function recycle$_i$(k) lets the recycling mechanism locally reset $msg_i[k][]$ with the notation $f_i()$ denoting that p_i executes the function f. For the single-instance BRB (without recycling), define txAvailable() and rxAvailable(k) to return True.

Interfaces for Accessing the Delivered Value and Current Status. Algorithm 2 informs the application about message arrival by raising brbDeliver() (line 11).

Our SSBFT BRB solution takes another approach in which the application is pulling information from Algorithm 3 by invoking the brbDeliver() operation (line 19), which returns $\perp$ (line 19) when no message is ready to be delivered. Otherwise, the arriving message is returned. Note that once brbDeliver$_i(k)$: $i, k \in Correct$ returns a non-$\perp$ value, brbDeliver$_i(k)$ returns a non-$\perp$ value in all subsequent invocations. For the sake of satisfying BRB-integrity in a self-stabilizing manner, line 19 records the fact that the non-$\perp$ message was delivered at least once by storing True in $wasDelivered_i[k]$. The application can access the value stored in $wasDelivered_i[k]$ by invoking brbWasDelivered$_i(k)$ (line 20).

Algorithm 3's Correctness. Theorem 1 shows that consistency (Definition 2) is regained eventually while Theorem 2 proves BRB-completion. Our proposal satisfies BRB's requirements since any completed BRB instance is eventually recycled (cf. Sect. 1). Showing that a recycled SSBFT BRB object satisfies BRB's requirements is obtained by arguments similar to the ones of the non-self-stabilizing BT algorithm, and the complete proof appears in [9].

Definition 2 (Consistent executions of Algorithm 3). *We use the term* active *for node* $p_i \in \mathcal{P}$ *when referring to the case of* $msg_i[i][\text{init}] \neq \emptyset$. *Let* R *be an Algorithm 3's execution,* $p_i \in \mathcal{P} : i \in Correct$, *and* $c \in R$. *Suppose the if-statement condition of line 22 or 25 does not hold in* c *w.r.t.* p_i. *In this case, we say that* c *is* inconsistent *w.r.t.* p_i. *Suppose every system state in* R *is consistent w.r.t.* p_i. *In this case, we say that* R *is* consistent *w.r.t.* p_i.

Theorem 1 (Algorithm 3's Convergence). *Let* R *be a fair execution of Algorithm 3 in which* $p_i \in \mathcal{P} : i \in Correct$ *is active eventually. The system eventually reaches a state* $c \in R$ *that starts a consistent execution w.r.t.* p_i.

Proof Sketch for Theorem 1. Suppose R's starting state is inconsistent w.r.t. p_i. I.e., at least one of the if-statement conditions in lines 22 and 25 holds. Since R is fair, eventually p_i takes a step that includes the execution of lines 22 to 25, which assures that p_i becomes consistent. Observe that once consistency holds, it holds in any state that follows c, cf. lines 17 and 26 to 32.

$$\square_{Theorem}\ 1$$

Theorem 2 (BRB-Completion-1). *Let* R *be a consistent Algorithm 3's execution in which* $p_i \in \mathcal{P}$ *is active. Eventually,* $\forall i, j \in Correct :$ brbDeliver$_j(i) \neq \perp$.

Proof of Theorem 2. Since p_i is correct, it broadcasts MSG($brbJ = msg_i[i]$,-) infinitely often. By fair communication, every correct $p_j \in \mathcal{P}$ receives MSG($brbJ$) $= (m,$-$)$ eventually. Thus, $\forall j \in Correct : msg_j[i][\text{init}] = \{m\}$ due to line 17. Also, $\forall j \in Correct : msg_j[j][\text{echo}] \supseteq \{(i, m)\}$ since node p_j obverses that the if-statement condition in line 26 holds (for the case of $k_j = i$). Thus, p_j broadcasts MSG($brbJ = msg_j[j]$,-) infinitely often. By fair communication, every correct node $p_\ell \in \mathcal{P}$ receives MSG($brbJ$,-) eventually. Thus, $\forall j, \ell \in Correct : msg_\ell[j][\text{echo}] \supseteq \{(i, m)\}$ (line 17). Since $n - t > (n+t)/2$, node p_ℓ observes that $(n+t)/2 < |\{p_x \in \mathcal{P} : (i, m) \in msg_\ell[x][\text{echo}]\}|$ holds, i.e., the if-statement condition in line 27 holds, and thus, $msg_\ell[\ell][\text{ready}] \supseteq \{(i, m)\}$ holds.

Note that, since $t < (n+t)/2$, faulty nodes cannot prevent a correct node from broadcasting $\text{MSG}(brbJ = mJ, \text{-}) : mJ[\text{ready}] \supseteq \{(i, m)\}$ infinitely often, say, by colluding and sending $\text{MSG}(brbJ = mJ, \text{-}) : mJ[\text{ready}] \supseteq \{(i, m')\} \wedge m' \neq m$. By fair communication, every correct $p_y \in \mathcal{P}$ receives $\text{MSG}(brbJ = mJ, \text{-})$ eventually. Thus, $\forall j, y \in Correct : msg_y[j][\text{ready}] \supseteq \{(i, m)\}$ holds (line 17). Therefore, whenever p_y invokes $\text{brbDeliver}_y(i)$ (line 19), the condition $\exists_m (2t+1) \leq |\{p_\ell \in \mathcal{P} : (k_y = i, m) \in msg_y[\ell][\text{ready}]\}|$ holds, and thus, m is returned.

$\square_{Theorem}$ 2

5   Self-stabilizing Recycling in Node-Failure-Free Systems

Before proposing our SSBFT algorithm for BRB instance recycling (Sect. 6), we study a non-crash-tolerant yet self-stabilizing recycling algorithm. *I.e.,* towards a solution for $\text{BAMP}_{n,t}[\text{FC}, \Diamond\text{P}_{\text{mute}}, \text{BML}]$, the *independent round counter* (IRC) task is presented. And, we implement $\text{txAvailable}()$ and $\text{rxAvailable}(k)$ (Fig. 1).

When non-self-stabilizing node-failure-free systems are considered, the operations $\text{txAvailable}()$ and $\text{rxAvailable}(k)$ can be implemented using prevailing mechanisms for automatic repeat request (ARQ), which uses unbounded counters. These mechanisms are often used for guaranteeing reliable communications by letting the sender collect acknowledgments from all receivers. Each message is associated with a unique message number, which the sender obtains by adding one to the previous message number after all acknowledgments arrived. From that point in time, the previous message number is obsolete and can be recycled. For the case of self-stabilizing node-failure-free systems, the challenge is to deal with integer overflow events. Specifically, when an algorithm considers the counters to be unbounded but the studied system has bounded memory, transient faults can trigger integer overflow events. The solution presented here shows how to overcome this challenge via our recycling technique and a mild synchrony assumption.

Independent Round Counters (IRCs). We consider n independent counters, such that each counter, cnt_i, can be incremented by a unique node, p_i, via the invocation of $\text{increment}_i()$, which returns the new round number or $\perp$ when the invocation is (temporarily) disabled. Suppose $p_i, p_j \in \mathcal{P}$ are correct. Node p_j can fetch cnt_i's value via the invocation of $\text{fetch}_j(i)$, which returns the most recent and non-fetched cnt_i's value or $\perp$ when such value is unavailable. We define the IRC task using the following requirements.

- **IRC-integrity-1.** Let $S_{i,j} = (s_0, \ldots, s_x) : x < B$ be a sequence of p_i's round numbers that p_j fetched—we are only interested in B most recent ones, where B is a predefined constant. It holds that $\forall s_y \in S_{i,j} : y < B - 1 \implies s_y + 1 \bmod B = s_{y+1}$. *I.e.,* no correct node IRC-fetches a value more than once from the counter of any other correct node (considering the B most recent IRC-fetches).
- **IRC-integrity-2.** Correct nodes that IRC-fetch from cnt_i do so in the order in which cnt_i was incremented (considering the B most recent IRC-fetches).
- **IRC-preemption.** Suppose p_i IRC-increments cnt_i to s. IRC-increment is (temporarily) disabled until all correct nodes have fetched s from p_i's counter.

Algorithm 4: time-free IRC; code for p_i

---

33 **constants:** B: a bound on the integer size, *e.g.*, $2^{64}-1$.

34 **variables:** $cur[\mathcal{P}], nxt[\mathcal{P}] = [[-1,-1], \ldots, [-1,-1]]$: a pair of round numbers—one pair per node, where $cur[i]$ is p_i's current round number and $nxt[i]$ is the next one. Also, $cur[j]$ and $nxt[j]$ are the most recently received, and resp., delivered round num. from p_j;

35 $lbl[\mathcal{P}] = [0, \ldots, 0]$: labels corresponding to $cur[i]$, where $lbl[j]$ stores the most recently received label from p_j.

36 **required interfaces:** recycle(k), trusted(), $\boxed{\text{invoc(), rtComp}(j);}$

37 **provided interface:** txAvailable() **do** {**return** increment() $\neq \perp$}

38 rxAvailable(k) **do** {**return** fetch(k) $\neq \perp$}

39 **macro:** behind(d, s, c) **do** {**return** $s \in \{x \bmod B : x \in \{c - d\lambda, \ldots, c\}\}$}

40 **operation** increment() /* trusted() $= \mathcal{P}$ for the crash-free version */ **begin**

41 | **if** $cur[i] = -1 \vee \exists j \in$ trusted() : $lbl[j] \leq 2(\text{channelCapacity} + 1)$ **then return** $\perp$;

42 | **else** $\boxed{\text{invoc();}}$ $cur[i] \leftarrow cur[i] + 1 \bmod B$; recycle($j$); **return** $cur[i]$;

43 **operation** fetch(k) **do** {**if** behind($1, cur[k], nxt[k]$) **then return** $\perp$ **else** {$nxt[k] \leftarrow cur[k]$; **return** $nxt[k]$}};

44 **operation** txMSG(j) {**return** (True, $cur[i], lbl[j]$))}

45 **operation** rxMSG($brbJ, ircJ = (aJ, sJ, \ell J), j$) **begin**

46 | **if** $\neg aJ \wedge$ behind($2, cur[i], sJ$) $\wedge lbl[j] = \ell J$ **then**

47 | | {$\boxed{\text{rtComp}(j);}$ $lbl[j] \leftarrow \min\{B, \ell J + 1\}$; **return** }

48 | **if** $\neg$behind($1, sJ, cur[i]$) **then** {$cur[j] \leftarrow sJ$; recycle(j)};

49 | **send** MSG(False, $nxt[j], \ell J$) **to** p_j;

50 **do forever broadcast** MSG($brb = msg[i]$, $irc = $ txMSG());

51 **upon** MSG($brbJ, ircJ$) arrival from p_j **do** {$mrg(brbJ, j)$; rxMSG($brbJ, ircJ, j$)}

We also require IRC to be completed eventually (IRC-completion) and to only allow the fetching of authentic values (IRC-validity), cf. [9] for details. Note that an IRC algorithm can implement the interface functions txAvailable() and rxAvailable(k) by returning increment() $\neq \perp$ and fetch(k) $\neq \perp$, resp.

Time-Free System Settings for $\mathsf{AMP_n[FC, BML]}$. The IRC solution proposed in this section requires time-free system settings, which we define by revising $\mathsf{BAMP_{n,t}[FC, t < n/3]}$ into $\mathsf{AMP_n[FC, BML]}$. The latter model does not consider node failures but includes Assumption 3, as we explain further.

Suppose, due to a transient fault, cnt_i is smaller than p_j's copy of cnt_i by $x \in \mathbb{Z}^+$, thus node p_i will have to complete x rounds before p_j could IRC-fetch a non-$\perp$ value. We overcome this by following Assumption 3.

Assumption 3 (Bounded Message Lifetime, BML). *Suppose a correct $p_i \in \mathcal{P}$ repeatedly completes an unbounded number of round-trips with every correct $p_j \in \mathcal{P}$. Suppose p_j receives message $m(s)$ from p_i immediately before $c \in R$, where s is the round number. Assume B is a bound for integers and $cur_i[i] - s \leq \lambda$ holds in c, where $\lambda \in \mathbb{Z}^+$: channelCapacity $< \lambda < B/6$ is a known upper-bound.*

Self-stabilizing IRC for $\mathsf{AMP_n[FC, BML]}$. Algorithm 4 presents a self-stabilizing solution for crash-free systems. The idea is to make sure that any node that had IRC-incremented its round counter defers any further IRC-increments until all nodes have acknowledged the latest IRC-increment. To that end, acknowledgments are used. Note that the line numbers of Algorithm 4 continue the ones of Algorithm 3. Also, the $\boxed{\text{boxed}}$ code in lines 42 and 47 are irrelevant to the IRC solution studied in this section. We remind that the implementation of recycle() (line 36) is provided by Algorithm 3, line 16. Also, for this section only, let us assume that $trusted_i() = \mathcal{P}$.

Constants and Variables. All integers used by Algorithm 4 have a maximum value, which we denote by B (line 33) and require to be large, say, $2^{64} - 1$. The arrays $cur[]$ and $nxt[]$ (line 34) store a pair of round numbers. The entry $cur[i]$ is p_i's current round number and $nxt[i]$ is the next one. Also, $cur[j]$ and $nxt[j]$ store the most recently received, and resp., delivered round numbers from p_j. The array $lbl[]$ holds labels that correspond to the number in $cur[i]$, where $lbl[j]$ is the most recently received label from p_j (line 34).

The increment() *Operation.* This operation allows the caller to IRC-increment the value of its round number modulo B. It also returns the new round number. However, if the previous invocation has not finished, the operation is disabled and the $\perp$ value is returned. Line 41 tests whether the round number is ready to be incremented. In detail, recall that in this section, we assume $trusted_i() = \mathcal{P}$. Now line 41 checks whether this is the first round, *i.e.*, a round number of -1, or the previous round has finished, *i.e.*, the labels indicate that every node has completed at least $2(\text{channelCapacity} + 1)$ round-trips. By that, the proposed solution overcomes packet loss and duplication over non-FIFO channels, see [20].

The fetch(k) *Operation.* It returns, exactly once, the most recently received round number. Line 43 tests whether a new round number has arrived. If not, $\perp$ is returned. Otherwise, the new round number is returned (line 43). In detail, due to Assumption 3, immediately after the arrival of $m(s)$ to p_j from p_i, $s \notin \{x \bmod B : x \in \{c - \lambda, \ldots, c\}\}$ implies that s is newer than $cur_j[i]$. Thus, p_i can use $behind_i(1, cur_i[k], nxt_i[k])$ (line 43) for testing the freshness of $cur_i[k]$ w.r.t. $nxt_i[k]$. If it is fresh, $fetch_i()$ updates $nxt_i[k]$ with the returned number.

The txMSG() *and* rxMSG() *Operations.* These operations let the sender, and resp. receiver, process messages. Algorithm 4's $MSG()$ message has two fields: brb and irc, where brb is related to Algorithm 3. Recall that when a message arrives from p_j, the receiving-side appends J to the field name, *i.e.*, $brbJ$ and $ircJ$. The field irc is composed of ack, which indicates a required acknowledge, seq, which is the sender's round, and lbl, which is the corresponding label to seq that the sender uses for the receiver. The operation txMSG() is used when the sender transmits (line 44). It specifies that acknowledgment is required, *i.e.*, $ack = \text{True}$ as well as includes the sender's current round, *i.e.*, $cur[i]$, and the corresponding label that the sender uses for the receiver $p_j \in \mathcal{P}$, *i.e.*, $lbl[j]$.

The operation rxMSG() processes messages arriving either to the sender or receiver. On the sender-side, when an acknowledgment arrives from the receiver, p_j, the sender checks whether the message has fresh round and label (line 46). In this case, the label is incremented to indicate round-trip completion. In detail, p_i uses $behind_i(2, cur_i[j], sJ)$ for testing if the arriving round, sJ, is fresh by asking whether sJ is not a member of $\{cur_j[i] - 2\lambda, \ldots, cur_j[i]\}$, see Assumption 3. As we see next, we need to consider the receiver's test (line 48), which can cause a non-fresh value to be a member of $\{x \bmod B : x \in \{c - 2\lambda, \ldots, c\}\}$, but not $\{x \bmod B : x \in \{c-\lambda, \ldots, c\}\}$. On the receiver-side, p_i uses $\mathsf{behind}_i(1, sJ, cur_i[j])$ to test whether a new round arrived, *i.e.*, whether sJ is a member of $\{cur_j[i] - 2\lambda, \ldots, cur_j[i]\}$. In this case, the local round number is updated (line 48) and the interface function $\mathsf{recycle}_i(j)$ is called (line 16). Note that whenever the receiver gets a message, it replies (line 49). That acknowledgment specifies that no further replies are required, *i.e.*, $ack = \mathsf{False}$, as well as the most recently delivered round number, *i.e.*, $nxt[i]$, and label, ℓJ.

The Do-Forever Loop and Message Arrival. The processing of messages (for sending and receiving) is along the lines of Algorithm 3, and thus, can be piggybacked. The do-forever loop broadcasts MSG() to every node (line 50). The operation txMSG() is used for setting the $ircJ$ field. Upon message arrival, the receiver passes the arriving values to rxMSG() for processing (line 51).

6   SSBFT BRB Recycling via Muteness Detection

Algorithm 4 presents our self-stabilizing BFT recycling mechanism for the time-free model of $\mathsf{BAMP}_{n,t}[\mathsf{FC}, t < n/3, \mathsf{BML}, \Diamond\mathsf{P}_{\mathsf{mute}}]$, which we obtain by enriching $\mathsf{BAMP}_{n,t}[\mathsf{FC}, t < n/3, \mathsf{BML}]$ with $\Diamond P_{mute}$, a detector for muteness failures that we define in this section. Our SSBFT recycling mechanism appears in Algorithm 4, including the $\boxed{\text{boxed}}$ code lines. It is for $\mathsf{BAMP}_{n,t}[\mathsf{FC}, \Diamond\mathsf{P}_{\mathsf{mute}}, \mathsf{BML}]$ and uses a muteness detector, which this section presents. Algorithm 4 lets p_i restart its local detector via a call to $\mathsf{invoc}_i()$ (line 42) and uses $\mathsf{rtComp}_i(j)$ (line 47) for reporting the completion of a round-trip between p_i and p_j. Our proof, which appear in [9] due to the page limit, shows that the algorithm can consider $\mathsf{trusted}_i() \subseteq \mathcal{P}$ due to $\Diamond P_{mute}$'s properties.

Muteness Failures. Let Alg be an algorithm that attaches a round number, $seq \in \mathbb{Z}^+$, to its messages, $m(seq)$. Suppose $\exists c_\tau \in R$ after which p_j stops forever replying to p_i's $m(seq)$. In this case, we say that p_j is *mute* to p_i w.r.t. $m(seq)$.

Specifications of $\Diamond P_{mute}$. We specify this class of muteness detectors.
Muteness Strong Completeness: Eventually, every mute node is forever suspected w.r.t. round s by every correct node (or the round number changes).
Eventual Strong Accuracy: Eventually $\exists c_\tau \in R$: no correct node is suspected.

Our Solution in a Nutshell. Existing non-BFT implementations of perfect failure detectors [21,22] might let p_i suspect any $p_j \in \mathcal{P}$ whenever p_i was able to complete Θ round-trips with other nodes but not with p_j, where Θ is a predefined constant. But, a Byzantine node might anticipate the sender's messages and reply before the arrival of prospective messages. Using this attack, the adversary may accelerate the (fake) completion round-trips and let the detector suspect non-faulty nodes. We propose to use Assumption 4 for defending against the above attacks that use speculative acknowledgments. Specifically, when testing if the Θ threshold has been exceeded, p_i ignores the round-trips that were completed

---

Algorithm 5: class $\Diamond P_{mute}$ detector; code for p_i

---

52 **constants:** B: a predefined bound on the integer size, say, $2^{64} - 1$.

53 **variables:** $rt[\mathcal{P} \setminus \{p_i\}][\mathcal{P} \setminus \{p_i\}]$: round trip counters, initially all entries are set to zero;

54 **interface functions:**

55 invoc() **do** $\{rt \leftarrow [[0,\ldots,0],\ldots,[0,\ldots,0]]\}$;

56 rtComp(j) **do** $\{\{\textbf{foreach } p_k \in \mathcal{P} \setminus \{p_i, p_j\} \textbf{ do } rt[k][j] \leftarrow \min\{B, rt[k][j] + 1\}\}$
    $rt[j] \leftarrow [0,\ldots,0];\}$

57 trusted() **do return** $\{p_j \in \mathcal{P} : (\sum_{x \in withoutTopItems(t,j)} x) < \Theta\}$ **where** $\{rt[j][\ell]\}_{p_\ell \in \mathcal{P}}$ is a
    multi-set with all the values in $rt[j][]$ and $withoutTopItems(t,j)$ is the same multi-set after
    the removal of the top t values;

---

with the top t nodes, say, $p_1, \ldots, p_t$, that had the highest number of round-trips
with p_i. W.l.g. suppose the adversary captured nodes $P_{byz} = p_{n-t}^{byz}, \ldots, p_{n-1}^{byz}$. On
the one hand, the adversary aims at letting the P_{byz} nodes to rapidly complete
round trips with p_i. While on the other hand, p_i ignores (when testing whether
the Θ threshold has been exceeded) any of the P_{byz} nodes that completes round
trips faster than any of the nodes $p_1, \ldots, p_t$. In other words, any adversarial
strategy that lets any of the P_{byz} nodes to complete more round trips with p_i
than the nodes $p_1, \ldots, p_t$ cannot cause a "haste" muteness detection of a correct
node. Algorithm 5 implements our solution, see [9] for details.

Assumption 4. *Let $\sum_{x \in withoutTopItems_{i,c}(t,j)} x$ be the total number of round
trips that p_i has completed until c when excluding the values from the top t
nodes. We assume that if $\Theta \leq \sum_{x \in withoutTopItems_{i,c}(t,j)} x$, p_j is mute to p_i w.r.t.
$m(s)$.*

7 Discussion

To the best of our knowledge, this paper presents the first SSBFT algorithms for
IRC and repeated BRB (that follows Definition 1) for hybrid asynchronous/time-
free systems. As in BT, the SSBFT BRB algorithm takes several asynchronous
communication rounds of $\mathcal{O}(n^2)$ messages per instance whereas the IRC algorithm takes $\mathcal{O}(n)$ messages but requires synchrony assumptions.

The two SSBFT algorithms are integrated via specified interfaces and message piggybacking (Fig. 1). Thus, our SSBFT repeated BRB solution increases
BT's message size only by a constant per BRB, but the number of messages per
instance stays similar. The integrated solution can run an unbounded number of
(concurrent and independent) BRB instances. The advantage is that the more
communication-intensive component, *i.e.*, SSBFT BRB, is not associated with
any synchrony assumption. Specifically, one can run δ concurrent BRB instances,
where δ is a parameter for balancing the trade-off between fault recovery time
and the number of BRB instances that can be used (before the next δ concurrent instances can start). The above extension mitigates the effect of the fact
that, for the repeated BRB problem, muteness detectors are used and mild synchrony assumptions are made in order to circumvent well-known impossibilities,

e.g., [17]. Those additional assumptions are required for the entire integrated solution to work. To the best of our knowledge, there is no proposal for a weaker set of assumptions for solving the studied problem in a self-stabilizing manner.

We note that the above extension facilitates the implementation of FIFO-ordered delivery SSBFT repeated BRB. Here, each of the δ instances is associated with a unqiue label $\ell \in \{0, \dots, \delta - 1\}$. The implementation makes sure that no node p_i delivers a BRB message with label $\ell > 0$ before all the BRB messages with labels in $\{0, \dots, \ell - 1\}$. (For the case of $\ell = 0$, the delivery is unconditional.)

We hope that the proposed solutions, *e.g.*, the proposed recycling mechanism and the hybrid composition of time-free/asynchronous system settings, will facilitate new SSBFT building blocks.

Acknowledgments. The work of E. M. Schiller was partly supported by the CyReV project (2019-03071) funded by VINNOVA, the Swedish Governmental Agency for Innovation Systems.

References

1. Raynal, M.: Fault-tolerant message-passing distributed systems - an algorithmic approach. Springer, Cham (2018). https://doi.org/10.1007/978-3-319-94141-7
2. Auvolat, A., Raynal, M., Taïani, F.: Byzantine-tolerant set-constrained delivery broadcast. In: OPODIS 2019-International Conference on Principles of Distributed Systems, pp. 1–23. ACM (2019)
3. Bracha, G., Toueg, S.: Asynchronous consensus and broadcast protocols. J. ACM **32**(4), 824–840 (1985). Also appeared at ACM PODC. **1983**, 12–26 (1985)
4. Pease, M.C., Shostak, R.E., Lamport, L.: Reaching agreement in the presence of faults. J. ACM **27**, 228–234 (1980)
5. Doudou, A., Garbinato, B., Guerraoui, R., Schiper, A.: Muteness failure detectors: specification and implementation. In: Hlavička, J., Maehle, E., Pataricza, A. (eds.) EDCC 1999. LNCS, vol. 1667, pp. 71–87. Springer, Heidelberg (1999). https://doi.org/10.1007/3-540-48254-7_7
6. Altisen, K., Devismes, S., Dubois, S., Petit, F.: Introduction to distributed self-stabilizing algorithms. Synth. Lect. Distrib. Comput. Theory **8**(1), 1–165 (2019)
7. Dolev, S.: Self-Stabilization. MIT Press, Cambridge (2000)
8. Dijkstra, E.W.: Self-stabilizing systems in spite of distributed control. Commun. ACM **17**, 643–644 (1974)
9. Duvignau, R., Raynal, M., Schiller, E.M.: Self-stabilizing Byzantine-tolerant broadcast. arXiv preprint arXiv:2201.12880 (2022)
10. Bonomi, S., Decouchant, J., Farina, G., Rahli, V., Tixeuil, S.: Practical Byzantine reliable broadcast on partially connected networks. In: 2021 IEEE 41st International Conference on Distributed Computing Systems (ICDCS), pp. 506–516. IEEE (2021)
11. Guerraoui, R., Komatovic, J., Kuznetsov, P., Pignolet, Y., Seredinschi, D., Tonkikh, A.: Dynamic Byzantine reliable broadcast. In: OPODIS, vol. 184, pp. 23:1–23:18. LIPIcs, Schloss Dagstuhl (2020)
12. Albouy, T., Frey, D., Raynal, M., Taïani, F.: Byzantine-tolerant reliable broadcast in the presence of silent churn. In: Johnen, C., Schiller, E.M., Schmid, S. (eds.) SSS 2021. LNCS, vol. 13046, pp. 21–33. Springer, Cham (2021). https://doi.org/10.1007/978-3-030-91081-5_2

13. Lundström, O., Raynal, M., M. Schiller, E.: Self-stabilizing uniform reliable broadcast. In: Georgiou, C., Majumdar, R. (eds.) NETYS 2020. LNCS, vol. 12129, pp. 296–313. Springer, Cham (2021). https://doi.org/10.1007/978-3-030-67087-0_19

14. Mostéfaoui, A., Raynal, M.: Intrusion-tolerant broadcast and agreement abstractions in the presence of Byzantine processes. IEEE Trans. Parall. Distrib. Syst. **27**, 1085–1098 (2016)

15. Toueg, S.: Randomized Byzantine agreements. In: Proceedings of the Third Annual ACM Symposium on Principles of Distributed Computing, pp. 163–178 (1984)

16. Maurer, A., Tixeuil, S.: Self-stabilizing Byzantine broadcast. In: 2014 IEEE 33rd International Symposium on Reliable Distributed Systems, pp. 152–160. IEEE (2014)

17. Fischer, M.J., Lynch, N.A., Paterson, M.: Impossibility of distributed consensus with one faulty process. J. ACM **32**, 374–382 (1985)

18. Duvignau, R., Raynal, M., Schiller, E.M.: Self-stabilizing Byzantine- and intrusion-tolerant consensus. arXiv preprint arXiv:2110.08592 (2021)

19. Georgiou, C., Marcoullis, I., Raynal, M., Schiller, E.M.: Loosely-self-stabilizing Byzantine-tolerant binary consensus for signature-free message-passing systems. In: Echihabi, K., Meyer, R. (eds.) NETYS 2021. LNCS, vol. 12754, pp. 36–53. Springer, Cham (2021). https://doi.org/10.1007/978-3-030-91014-3_3

20. Dolev, S., Hanemann, A., Schiller, E.M., Sharma, S.: Self-stabilizing end-to-end communication in (bounded capacity, omitting, duplicating and non-FIFO) dynamic networks. In: Richa, A.W., Scheideler, C. (eds.) SSS 2012. LNCS, vol. 7596, pp. 133–147. Springer, Heidelberg (2012). https://doi.org/10.1007/978-3-642-33536-5_14

21. Beauquier, J., Kekkonen-Moneta, S.: Fault-tolerance and self-stabilization: impossibility results and solutions using self-stabilizing failure detectors. Int. J. Syst. Sci. **28**, 1177–1187 (1997)

22. Blanchard, P., Dolev, S., Beauquier, J., Delaët, S.: Practically self-stabilizing Paxos replicated state-machine. In: Noubir, G., Raynal, M. (eds.) NETYS 2014. LNCS, vol. 8593, pp. 99–121. Springer, Cham (2014). https://doi.org/10.1007/978-3-319-09581-3_8

23. Lundström, O., Raynal, M., Schiller, E.M.: Self-stabilizing indulgent zero-degrading binary consensus. In: International Conference on Distributed Computing and Networking 2021, pp. 106–115 (2021)

24. Lundström, O., Raynal, M., Schiller, E.M.: Self-stabilizing multivalued consensus in asynchronous crash-prone systems. In: 2021 17th European Dependable Computing Conference (EDCC), pp. 111–118. IEEE (2021)

25. Lundström, O., Raynal, M., Schiller, E.M.: Self-stabilizing total-order broadcast. arXiv preprint arXiv:2209.14685 (2022)

Capacity Planning for Dependable Services

Rasha Faqeh[1]([✉]), André Martin[1][ID], Valerio Schiavoni[2][ID], Pramod Bhatotia[3],
Pascal Felber[2]([✉])[ID], and Christof Fetzer[1][ID]

[1] TU Dresden, Dresden, Germany
{rasha.faqeh,andre.martin,christof.fetzer}@tu-dresden.de
[2] University of Neuchâtel, Neuchâtel, Switzerland
{valerio.schiavoni,pascal.felber}@unine.ch
[3] TU Munich, Munich, Germany
pramod.bhatotia@cit.tum.de

Abstract. Fault-tolerance techniques depend on replication to enhance availability, albeit at the cost of increased infrastructure costs. This results in a fundamental trade-off: Fault-tolerant services must satisfy given availability and performance constraints while minimising the number of replicated resources. These constraints pose *capacity planning* challenges for the service operators to *minimise replication costs without negatively impacting availability*.

To this end, we present PCRAFT, a practical system to enable capacity planning of dependable services. PCRAFT's capacity planning is based on a hybrid approach that combines empirical performance measurements with probabilistic modelling of availability based on fault injection. In particular, we integrate traditional service-level availability mechanisms (active route anywhere and passive failover) and deployment schemes (cloud and on-premises) to quantify the number of nodes needed to satisfy the given availability and performance constraints. Our evaluation based on real-world applications shows that cloud deployment requires fewer nodes than on-premises deployments. Additionally, when considering on-premises deployments, we show how passive failover requires fewer nodes than active route anywhere. Furthermore, our evaluation quantifies the quality enhancement given by additional integrity mechanisms and how this affects the number of nodes needed.

1 Introduction

Dependability is a must-have requirement for modern Internet-based services. These services must be *highly available, integrity protected, secure* and offer high assurance of *performance* to users, in terms of response time and throughput. Service providers can use replication to achieve high availability and more reliable services, and deploy them either using an on-premises cluster or on a public cloud. However, such techniques regardless of the chosen deployment *(i)* increase the complexity and the costs of the supporting infrastructure, and *(ii)*

S. Devismes et al. (Eds.): SSS 2022, LNCS 13751, pp. 222–238, 2022.
https://doi.org/10.1007/978-3-031-21017-4_15

degrade the observed performance of the applications. To address the problem of performance assurance, the service providers provision extra physical resources. However, over-provisioning increases the operational costs without improving availability. This represents an important problem: *how to achieve the required level of availability and performance while maintain affordable costs?* We tackle this problem directly by providing a capacity planning process.

We consider a scenario of a service that uses a cluster of server nodes that run stateless [23] or soft-state [3] applications. The service has a target through-put and availability requirements. To fulfil these requirements, applications are replicated on different nodes. However, nodes crash and are replaced with new ones, mainly to enhance or guarantee availability of the services. This can be implemented using simple replication techniques such as *active route anywhere* (ARA) or *passive failover* (PF). *Active route anywhere* provisions more nodes to process users requests than required to meet the target performance. The extra nodes fulfil this objective as long as sufficiently many stay available. *Passive failover* also requires extra nodes to be provisioned but they are passively wait-ing in a standby pool: when an active node fails, it is replaced by one from the pool. After repairing the node, it is returned to the pool to handle new failures.

We consider two physical deployment schemes: *on-premises cluster* and *public cloud.* The scheme has direct consequences on the fault-tolerance properties as well as the associated costs. Cloud providers largely rely on the passive failover approach, restarting virtual machines (or lately containers) of a failed node on a functional one. Doing so, they can meet service level agreements (SLAs) under several classes of *nines* [8]. Note that the service provider only has to pay for the nodes actively participating in the cluster without the need to pay for the nodes that passively exist in the pool. Conversely, when compared to an on-premises deployment, resource sharing in the cloud (*e.g.,* co-located virtual machines) impacts the observed performance, leading to a degraded response time and unexpected variations [25]. This degradation is perceived by clients as service unavailability if it exceeds a certain (negative) threshold. On the other hand, on-premises solutions must provide and pay for both the active nodes in the cluster and the passive nodes in the pool.

Even when the service is available and serves requests, because of transient hardware faults these requests may be incorrectly processed and produce incor-rect results. Therefore, mechanisms such as instruction level redundancy [22] are often used to protect the integrity of the execution by detecting which execu-tions are incorrectly processed, yet at the price of decreased performance and corresponding capacity.

Our system, PCRAFT,[1] proposes a capacity planning process that is based on a combination of empirical performance measurements with availability and integrity probabilistic modelling. We consider the costs of deploying dependable applications in terms of both the number of nodes used and the integrity of the service provided. This simpler cost model allows us to easily reason about the

---

[1] **P**erformant, **C**heap, **R**eliable and **A**vailable **F**ault **T**olerance.

total cost of ownership of a cluster and to consider the number of nodes as a building block for more complex schemes.

PCRAFT integrates two availability techniques in its process: *passive failover* and *active route anywhere*. PF consists of loosely coupled and independent servers with failover capabilities. To tolerate f failures, at least f extra nodes should be available in a standby pool. By default, these nodes are in *cold* mode, *i.e.*, they are only started when needed. ARA uses active replication to deploy f additional, fully functional nodes behind a load-balancer that dispatches requests to all of them. The service performance is ensured only if at most f nodes crash. In addition, PCRAFT uses *instruction level redundancy* (ILR) [22] to protect node integrity from transient faults. ILR replicates data flow instructions and executes two instruction streams in parallel, leveraging the instruction-level parallelism of modern CPUs. To do so, PCRAFT relies on the HAFT [13] framework, which additionally exploits hardware transactional memory (HTM) [30] to recover from faults.

Previous studies on capacity planning mainly modelled the system performance with varying workloads and resource conditions [16,17,24,26] assuming an always available reliable infrastructure. Studies that quantify the availability in the event of different types of failures ignored the effect of failures on the performance [12,27]. Similarly, the combined effect of faults on availability and performance [7,18–20] did not quantify the number of nodes needed to ensure both the performance and availability levels. Further details on availability techniques and related work on dependability studies are found in the extended technical report [5].

In this paper, we propose the following contributions. *(i)* We introduce PCRAFT, a capacity planning process that is based on a combination of empirical experimentation and modelling to quantify the number of nodes needed to assure availability and performance levels. *(ii)* We develop a collection of probabilistic models to measure the availability of services when incorporated with various failures and recovery behaviour via different fault-tolerance approaches and physical deployment schemes. *(iii)* We measure the integrity of the service by combining integrity models with fault-injection.

2   System Design

Fault Model. We assume a dependable service built using a cluster of server nodes with three sources of failures: (1) Availability failures at the node level regardless of the cause. We assume fail-stop failures that either crash nodes or make them non-responsive, *e.g.*, failing hardware, software, disks, memory. We also assume that server nodes fail independently but do not exclude that many nodes can fail simultaneously. We exclude failure types that cause multiple nodes to fail due to a single failure, *e.g.*, network failures or software bugs that deterministically crashes applications. (2) Performance failures: requests cannot be served due to limited capacity, *i.e.*, the number of available nodes is too low. (3) Integrity failures: nodes are available but requests are served incorrectly without any error notification, in particular silent data corruption (SDC) [22] which leads to non-malicious Byzantine behaviour. SDCs are transient hardware faults caused by single event upsets, *e.g.,* one bit-flip in a CPU register or miscomputation in a CPU execution unit. Note that memory and caches are protected against bit-flips due to the use of ECC which is assumed to exist in all modern servers.

In this paper, we consider a service as *dependable*[2] if *(i)* the availability is above a predetermined threshold, *(ii)* whenever the service is available, there is sufficient capacity to ensure performance, and *(iii)* the service data integrity is protected.

Architecture. We consider a distributed n-tier service, with a front-end load balancer, a middle-tier cluster of server nodes and a connected back-end persistent storage. We focus on the middle-tier (*i.e.,* web, application, caching servers) to be available and well-performing. We assume the load balancer to be always available (*e.g.,* using replication [10]) and the back-end resources to be able to scale accordingly.

The load balancer intercepts the client requests and distributes them to the homogeneous cluster of servers nodes. A node becomes saturated when serving the maximum throughput (requests per unit time) with an acceptable latency (application-dependent response time threshold). Adding more requests to the node after saturation will cause the latency perceived by users to be monotonically increasing as more requests are added to the node's local queue (sharing model [20]). Alternatively, the server prematurely rejects the requests if the server is saturated—assuming no queues (constant bit rate model [20])—with users subsequently re-sending the rejected requests. In PCRAFT, we adapt the constant bit rate model for server nodes to control the upper bound of the latency perceived by users.

Dependable Services. The service consists of a cluster of nodes. Its throughput is the sum of the throughput of each node, while the latency is the average latency of all nodes that constitute the cluster. The service is available if at least a single node in the cluster is available, but with a degraded performance. To consider the service dependable, it must fulfils both the availability constraints (*e.g.,* three 9's) and the performance constraints (*e.g.,* target throughput and response time threshold). Additionally, the integrity mechanisms must be implemented at the node level to enhance the integrity of the served requests.

To meet our performance requirements, we can predict—based on single node performance—the number of nodes needed. Typically, we first assume that all nodes are always available. Since nodes can actually fail, in a second step we increase the availability by over-provisioning the number of nodes in the cluster. Over-provisioning might take the form of ARA in which fully functional extra nodes are added to the service cluster, or simply by replacing a failed node from a standby pool of nodes with PF. The number of nodes needed for the over-provisioning varies based on the type of deployment—on-premises or in the cloud. This is due to the availability mechanisms which are implemented in the cloud to assure the availability level for a single node that must meet the SLA.

---

[2] It is possible to extend the dependability definition to include other attributes *e.g.,* security, privacy, etc.

However, single node provisioning is typically insufficient to meet the availability constraints of a dependable service. Finding the adequate number of nodes in each case requires solving the capacity planning problem for this service.

Note, we extrapolate the behaviour of a cluster using a single node performance, however, in reality, sharing resources in a cluster might degrade the performance of a single node. The degradation in the node performance when deployed within a cluster can be captured by (1) considering various performance degradation percentages of the standalone node performance e.g., 10%, 20% etc., then, (2) we calculate the required number of nodes based on the degraded node performance. The exact performance degradation percentage can be verified at runtime.

Capacity Planning Process. The process consists of two-phases. First, we empirically benchmark the performance of a single server node. Second, we model the availability behaviour and parameterise the models using the values from the first phase to identify how many server nodes we need to ensure the dependability requirements.

Experimentation phase — Assuming an always available node, we profile the service that consists of a single node along two dimensions: performance and integrity. First, we benchmark the performance of both the native application (*native*) and the integrity protected version of the application (*ft*). We refer to the throughput of the single node in both cases as $NodT_{native}$ and $NodT_{ft}$, respectively. Note that usually $NodT_{ft} < NodT_{native}$. The service target throughput $SerT$ is defined by the service provider as $(Num_{native} \times NodT_{native})$ or $(Num_{ft} \times NodT_{ft})$. For different node types (*native* and *ft*), we can calculate Num_{native} and Num_{ft} as an estimation for the number of nodes needed in the cluster to fulfil the service target performance assuming nodes do not fail and without any over-provisioning of nodes. Note that usually $Num_{ft} > Num_{native}$ to fulfil the same $SerT$. Second, we inject integrity faults with a service that uses *native* and *ft* nodes to benchmark the integrity behaviour in each case. The results of the fault injection is subsequently used to estimate the integrity behaviour of applications in the presence of integrity faults.

Modelling phase — We build availability models for a cluster of nodes that implements over-provisioning using ARA or PF mechanisms with a cloud or on-premises deployment. The model can be used to first estimate the availability level achieved by the basic number of nodes Num calculated in the previous phase. Then, by comparing the availability achieved to the target availability defined by the service provider, we over-provision iteratively the number of nodes in the cluster until the availability constraint is met. In addition to availability models, we build integrity models for *native* and *ft* to estimate the integrity behaviour of nodes in the cluster when deployed in the cloud.

3   Implementation

In the second phase of the process, we build continuous-time Markov chain (CTMC) models a probabilistic model checker tool called PRISM [14]. The models, which capture the availability and the integrity behaviour, consist of possible

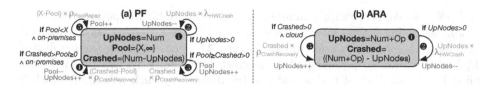

Fig. 1. State machine for a cluster of nodes using passive failover (left) or active route anywhere (right) as over-provisioning in the availability models for the cloud and on-premises deployments. Rectangles represent the states while arrows are transitions with associated rates. The system fails at rates of λ's and recovers at rates of ρ's.

states and possible transitions between them with their respective rates (failure and repair rates). We assume all rates have inter-event times that are exponentially distributed [29]. CTMC suffers from well-known state space explosion problems. To reduce the generated number of states, we follow two approaches. First, we attempt to aggregate states together. Specifically, we use homogeneous nodes in the cluster and so they exhibit similar failure and repair behaviour. It is thus not necessary to distinguish between which node in the cluster failed. Rather, we can simply keep track of up nodes (*UpNodes*). Second, performability analysis generally uses a hierarchy of models instead of monolithic ones in order to combine both availability and performance and hence reduce the number of generated states. In this paper, instead of solving performance models, we use the empirical measurements to feed the availability models, which further reduces the number of states needed.

For our models, we explore the following server node types: *(i) native* nodes without any special software/hardware hardening mechanisms implemented at the node level (standard nodes), and *(ii) ft* nodes which are integrity protected using the HAFT [13] approach. Additionally, we consider two deployments, in the *cloud* and *on-premise*, as well as two over-provisioning techniques, *active route anywhere* and *passive failover*.

Availability Models. In the availability models (Fig. 1), we inject hardware crash faults at different rates and consider the different over-provisioning techniques and deployments schemes. The two node types do not differ in their availability models at the node level because they use the same hardware. However, the performance achieved by each type is different and we need to use a higher number of *ft* nodes compared to *native* nodes to fulfil the same performance constraints. This results in different availability levels achieved in a cluster by each type of node (see later in Fig. 6).

Passive failover — Figure 1(a) presents the state machine diagram for the availability models of PF deployed in the cloud or on-premises. The PF technique assumes the existence of a pool that has a number of *cold nodes* that are turned off and hence do not fail. With a cloud deployment, the number of nodes passively waiting in the pool is unlimited (*Pool* = ∞) compared with concrete value (*Pool* $\geq$ 0) for the on-premises case. The cluster initially consists of *UpNodes*. We start with a number of nodes that fulfil the performance constraint assuming always available nodes, *i.e.*, $UpNodes = Num$ (❶). A fault at rate $\lambda_{HWCrash}$ crashes a node in the cluster (❷), hence reducing the number of *UpNodes*. Because *UpNodes* nodes can crash independently, this rate is multiplied by the number of nodes that can be affected by such a fault. A crashed node can be recovered by replacing it with a node from the pool with a rate of $\rho_{CrashRecovery}$ (❸). This rate is affected by the number of available nodes in the pool (❸ and ❹). This would increase the *UpNodes* while, additionally, decreasing the *Pool* size in an on-premises deployment. The crashed nodes from the pool may be repaired (❺) and returned back to the pool to use if needed at rate of $\rho_{PoolRepair}$, which would increase the number of available nodes inside the pool. Note that ❹ and ❺ are special cases for the on-premises deployment.

To calculate the availability achieved by such a model, we use "rewards" in the PRISM tool to represent the time spent in each state in a one year time period. The cluster traverses different states according to the failures and recovery rates, and the time spent in a state where $UpNodes = Num$ represents the cluster availability. If the time spent outside this state does not exceed the downtime specified by the availability constraints (*e.g.*, three 9's availability = 8.77 h downtime per year), the cluster is considered available and well-performing.

Active route anywhere — Figure 1(b) presents the state machine diagram for the availability models of ARA deployed in the cloud or on-premises. In ARA, in addition to the initial number of nodes needed to fulfil performance constraints (Num), we additionally use over-provisioned nodes (OP) which are actively participating in the cluster. Therefore, the number of active nodes in the cluster is $UpNodes = Num + OP$ (❶). A fault $\lambda_{HWCrash}$ crashes a node in the cluster (❷), hence reducing the number of *UpNodes*. Unlike PF, this rate is multiplied by all active nodes including the over-provisioned nodes ($UpNodes$). In a cloud deployment (❸), the failed node is replaced automatically by another node at rate of $\rho_{CrashRecovery}$, which increments *UpNodes*.

We calculate the cluster availability by considering the time spent in a state where $UpNodes \geq Num$. Consequently, at most OP nodes can fail simultaneously without violating the availability and performance constraints. Note that the cluster can have $UpNodes < Num$ at any time, but it is considered available and well-performing as long as it does not violate the availability constraint.

Integrity Models. In the integrity models, we inject integrity faults considering the different node types and deployments schemes. *ft* nodes implementing the HAFT approach have two modes of execution. HAFT implements instruction level redundancy to detect any violation to computation integrity. The first mode implements a fail-stop model, specifically, once a violation is detected, computation is stopped (ft_{ilr}). The second mode targets the availability, specifically, after an integrity failure is detected, instead of aborting, the execution is retried using transactions (ft_{tx}). Figure 2 presents the state machine diagram for integrity models of a node deployed in the cloud or on-premises. The node starts with *Correct* state. A transient fault can result in corruption of the state (SDC), crash of the application or masking of the fault. If not masked, a transient fault transfers the node in a *Corrupt* state at rate of λ_{SDC} (❶) or in a *Crash* state at rate of $\lambda_{HWcrash}$ (❷). Note that using ft_{ilr} nodes, this rate also includes the crashes resulting from aborting the application after detecting a transient fault. A ft_{tx} node detects transient faults at rate of $\lambda_{Detected}$ and transfers the node into *Retry* state (❸). A node in a *Retry* state is able to either recover the state at rate of $\rho_{RetryTx}$ and revert the node back into *Correct* state (❹), or if retry is not successful, abort execution and transfer the node into *Crash* state at rate of $\rho_{CrashTx}$ (❺). Both types of nodes do not have any mechanism to recover from crashed states. However, if deployed in the cloud, a node with *Crash* state is automatically replaced by another node to match the SLA agreement at a rate of $\rho_{CrashRecovery}$ (❻). When deployed on-premises, assuming enough resources in the pool, the node transfers back to *Correct* state. Additionally, the corruption of a node may be manually detected at a rate of $\rho_{SDCRecovery}$, which reverts the node back into *Correct* state (❼).

The integrity level achieved is captured by measuring the normalised time spent by the node in each state: *Correct* as correct time, *Corrupt* as corrupted time, *Crash* combined with *Retry* as downtime. Note that over-provisioning of nodes does not help to reduce the time in *Corrupt* state, since it produces multiple nodes with similar integrity behaviour. Alternatively, a different integrity protection technique should be implemented at the node level.

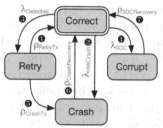

Fig. 2. State machine for integrity models of the different nodes.

4   Evaluation

In this section we illustrate how PCRAFT's two phase methodology can be used. In a first step we benchmark a single server node deployed with *native*, ft_{ilr} and ft_{tx} nodes using a stateless web server application and two soft-state applications. Then, we parameterise the models built in PCRAFT to calculate the availability and the integrity behaviour at the cluster level and decide the required capacity.

Our evaluation answers the following questions: (1) How much performance, *i.e.*, throughput and latency, can be achieved by a single node of types *native*, ft_{ilr} and ft_{tx}? (2) What is the effect of the deployment scheme (cloud vs. on-premises) on the availability level achieved by a single node, without over-provisioning? (3) What is the effect of using a cluster of nodes on the availability achieved, without over-provisioning? (4) How many extra nodes are needed to ensure a given availability and performance constraints when using ARA and PF with different deployment schemes? (5) How a single node of types *native*, ft_{ilr} and ft_{tx} deployed in the cloud would behave when transient faults exist?

Experimental Settings. All experiments use a dedicated on-premises deployment. The experimental part attempts to identify the performance of a single node $NodT$, which can then be used to identify the number of nodes (Num) required to achieve the cluster target performance $(SerT)$ assuming always the available nodes. Sharing resources in the cloud, might result in a lower single node performance $NodT$, however, using SLA, at higher costs, we can request stronger machines that have minimal performance comparable to the performance of the on-promises machines, otherwise, we can use similar experimental path as presented here to obtain the required Num in the cloud deployment. In this paper, we want to study the pure effect of over-provisioning and node types on the availability of the cluster. We therefore assume $NodT$ to be the same for nodes deployed in the cloud or on-premises, and we use the same number of nodes (Num) in each deployment to achieve $SerT$.

Each server node has an Intel Xeon E3-1270 v5 CPU clocked at 3.6 GHz. The CPU has 4 cores with 8 hyper-threads (2 per core) and 8 MB of L3-cache. The server has 64 GB memory running Ubuntu 14.04.5 LTS with Linux 4.4. The workload generators run on a server with two 14-core Intel Xeon E5-2683 v3 CPUs at 2 GHz with 112 GB of RAM and Ubuntu 15.10. All machines have a 10 Gb/s Ethernet NIC connected to a dedicated network switch.

We use the following three real-world applications: Apache web server (v2.2.11) [11], memcached (v1.4.21) [6] and Redis (v2.8.7) [21]. Furthermore, we deploy the applications in three variants: *native* unmodified application, ft_{ilr} built using the HAFT LLVM tool chain [13] with ILR, and ft_{tx} which additionally execute the application inside transactions.

4.1   Experimental Measurements

Apache Web Server. Our first set of experiments study the Apache `httpd` web server (Fig. 3). We evaluate the throughput vs. latency ratio and the overall CPU usage. We first measure the achievable throughput and latency of the three node variants under test, and the CPU utilisation during the execution of the benchmarks. We use the *wrk2* workload generator [28] to measure the throughput and latency based on fixed request rates issued to the master server. The following three workloads are used. *(i) static content:* the web server fetches static content (such as images or CSS files); *(ii) dynamic content:* the web server fetches dynamic content generated by PHP scripts (v5.4.0); and *(iii) real workload:* the web server operates under real-world conditions by retrieving a WordPress blog page with a MySQL server database at the back-end. We gradually increase the submission rate of HTTP requests until the response times hit unacceptable levels (*e.g.,* > 1 second).

Figure 3a shows the results for static content. The x-axis shows the measured response rate of the submitted requests while the y-axis shows the corresponding latency. The measured response rate is often lower than the introduced request rate when the system is saturated, giving the impression of the line going backwards suddenly since the data points are sorted by the introduced request rate which is constantly increasing, as seen in top graphs of Fig. 3. For dynamic content, Fig. 3b depicts the results to fetch a PHP script that solely employs

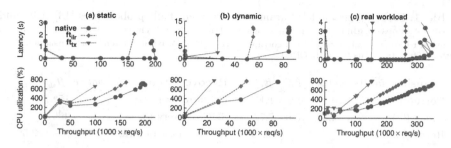

Fig. 3. Apache throughput vs. latency (top) and CPU utilisation (bottom) with 3 different workloads: static (a), dynamic (b) and real-world (c).

an empty for-loop iterating 10^3 times to basically simulate some CPU-intensive workload. Lastly, Fig. 3c presents the results under real workload for blog-like web pages. As expected, the *native* execution outperforms the other variants, with 200 thousand requests per seconds (kreq/s) to fetch static content. With ft_{tx} we reach only half the throughput, *i.e.*, 100 kreq/s, whereas ft_{ilr} improves the performance (up to 155 kreq/s for static content) but without the ability to properly handle detected errors. For dynamic content, we observe similar trends. The *native* mode excels with a peak of roughly 86 kreq/s, followed by ft_{ilr} and ft_{tx}, respectively at 52 and 23 kreq/s. Surprisingly, for blog-like web pages, the peak performance for both *native* and *ft* is much higher than when solely retrieving static content or a plain PHP page without any database interaction. We observe a peak performance of 321 kreq/s for *native*, and respectively 260 and 160 kreq/s for the two *ft* variants. This effect can be explained by lower thread contention upon database lookups happening for each request.

In terms of CPU utilisation, as expected we observe an increase as more requests are being issued. In general, all the variants are strictly CPU-bound (the limiting factor is our hardware) and the injected workloads manage to fully saturate all CPU cores. However, the *ft* variants saturate the CPU much more quickly than the *native* execution. For example, with static content we reach roughly the 800% CPU limit with a throughput of around 200 kreq/s. This is confirmed by a corresponding increase in response latency. This behaviour is expected since *ft* requires more CPU cycles (for the instrumented instructions) and thus saturates the CPU more quickly. Similarly, CPU consumption also increases for the benchmarks that retrieve dynamic content, either with and without database interaction.

Key-Value Stores: Memcached and Redis. Next, we evaluate two widely-used key-value stores: memcached and Redis. To measure throughput vs. latency with memcached, we rely on Twitter's *mcperf* [15] tool. For Redis, we use YCSB [4] with workload A, which comprises 50% read and 50% update operations. Figure 4 shows the results for both systems.

Table 1. Probabilistic models parameters: transient fault probabilities [13] (left) and recovery times (right). [a]Common values for failover in HA cluster is 1–30 s [9]. [b]Amazon reported 6 h to manually recover from corrupted state [1]. [c]Maximum latency of transaction retry with 5,000 instructions (2.0 GHz CPU).

Transient faults	native	ft_{ilr}	ft_{tx}	Recovery time	native	ft_{ilr}	ft_{tx}
Corrupt (%)	26.19	0.8	1.17	Crash recovery (s)	15[a]		
Crash (%)	12.49	75.0	7.72	SDC recovery (h)	6[b]		
Retry (%)	–	–	66.99	Retry transaction (μs)	–	–	2.5[c]

Memcached reaches a peak throughput at 886 kreq/s for *native* and 600 kreq/s for ft_{tx}. The ft_{ilr} variant is close to *native*, with only a 12% difference overall. Since memcached is limited by the memory bandwidth (8 GB/s on our hardware), there is only a small increase in CPU utilisation once the system is saturated.

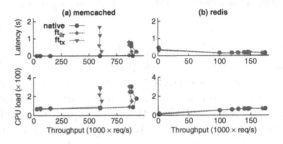

Fig. 4. Memcached (a) and Redis (b): throughput vs. latency (top) and CPU load (bottom).

With Redis, we observe a peak at around 120 kreq/s before the latency starts climbing. Interestingly, there is almost no visible overhead for the *ft* variants in comparison to *native*. This is because Redis is single-threaded while *ft* harnesses multi-core technology for ILR, as confirmed by the fact that CPU usage slightly increases as more requests are being processed, yet never exceeds 100% (*i.e.*, 1 core).

In summary, we observe across all applications an average throughput (*NodT*) of about 71% for ft_{tx} in comparison to *native* execution. If we use ft_{ilr}, the throughput climbs up to 92% of *native* performance.

4.2　Dependability Evaluation

We next use the models described in Sect. 3 to evaluate the availability and integrity under faults for single nodes and a cluster of nodes, to calculate the required capacity.

Models Settings. Table 1 presents the main parameters used in the models. The table consists of two parts. The first part presents the probabilities of state transitions in the integrity models from *Correct* state to any of the other states (*Corrrupt, Crash, Retry*) when transient faults are injected in a node of a given type (*native*, ft_{ilr} and ft_{tx}). These values are produced using fault injection experiments on a wide range of applications in the HAFT paper [13] (Table 4). The second part presents the time needed to recover the different failed states back to *Correct* state. The techniques include replacing a crashed node by either failover to a new node (*CrashRecovery*), the manual repair of a

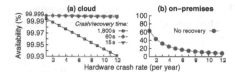
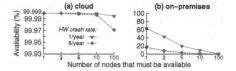

Fig. 5. Availability of a single-node for one year when deployed in the cloud (a) and on-premises (b), without over-provisioning.

Fig. 6. Availability of a service under a given crash fault rates and without over-provisioning.

node with SDC state (*SDCRecovery*) and the recovery of a node with a detected transient fault by retrying a transaction (*RetryTx*). Note that recovery times can be converted into rates assuming the second (s) as the basic time unit, using $RecoveryRate = 1/RecoveryTime$. In the rest of this section we use the values presented in the table unless otherwise specified.

Availability of Single Node Deployment. We want to study the availability achieved by deploying a single node without any over-provisioning techniques (*i.e.*, PF or ARA) in the cloud compared to on-premises. The cloud differs from on-premises deployment in its ability to automatically fail over by replacing a failed node with another one from a hypothetically unlimited pool, so as to satisfy the SLA agreement. The cloud automatic failover is modelled with $Pool = \infty$ and three values for $CrashRecovery = \{15\,s, 60\,s, 1800\,s\}$, while on-premises uses $Pool = 0$. Both deployments use $Num = 1$ to model a single node in the cluster. Figure 5 shows the results of injecting hardware crash faults with rates from once to 12 per year (x-axis) and the availability achieved in one year (y-axis) for a node deployed in cloud (a) and on-premises (b). The availability calculated represents the operational availability $upTime/totalTime$, where *up* time assumes that Num nodes are operational and *total* time is one year.

Figure 5 (a) shows that the cloud deployment can achieve at least five 9's for a single node in terms of yearly availability. With slower recovery time (1800 s), the achieved availability of at least three 9's is consistent with what most current cloud providers would provide for a single node [2]. Figure 5 (b) shows that on-premises cannot achieve the required availability levels even with very low fault rate, and availability quickly degrades with higher fault rates. The more sever degradation in the availability is due to missing repairs in the on-premises deployment, which indicates the need for the over-provisioning techniques to ensure the required availability.

Service Target Throughput with Failure Free Nodes. In the experimental phase, we measured throughput of a single node (*NodT*) for the different node types and calculated the average throughput degradation for ft_{ilr} and ft_{tx} with respect to a *native* node. By defining the *SerT* as multiples of $NodT_{native}$, we can calculate the number of nodes Num needed to achieve a service target throughput for all node types using $SerT/NodT$. For example, for $SerT = 1$, we need either one *native* node or two nodes of either ft_{ilr} or ft_{tx} type. Similarly,

Table 2. Number of active nodes needed (base + extra) for *cloud* and *on-premises* deployments with ARA to achieve $10\times$ native throughput ($SerT$) and three 9's availability level (HCR = $\lambda_{HWcrash}$, CR = $\rho_{CrashRecovery}$).

Node	Base	HCR:	1/year			6/year		
		CR: 15 s	1 min	30 min	15 s	1 min	30 min
native	10	0	0	0	0	0	1
ft_{ilr}	11	0	0	0	0	0	1
ft_{tx}	15	0	0	0	0	0	1

(a) cloud

Node	Base	HCR: 1/year	6/year
native	10	35	113
ft_{ilr}	11	37	121
ft_{tx}	15	46	152

(b) on-premises

we need either 10 *native*, 11 ft_{ilr} or 15 ft_{tx} nodes to handle $SerT = 10$. The given nodes are considered sufficient to fulfil the performance constraints of the service under the assumptions that *(i)* nodes do not fail and *(ii)* the backend infrastructure scales with the number of nodes in the cluster. If the backend infrastructure does not scale with the number of nodes, contention will increase on the backend resources, hence reducing $NodT$ and increasing the response time. In this case, more nodes are required to achieve the same $SerT$, which should then be determined experimentally.

Availability of Multiple Node Deployments. The service requires Num of nodes to achieve the performance constraints assuming always available nodes. Nodes do, however, crash in practice, which leads to degraded service performance. We want to study the effect of nodes crashing on the overall service availability using different deployments schemes when no over-provisioning techniques are used. In Fig. 6, we vary the number of nodes in the cluster (x-axis) when deployed in the cloud (a) and on-premises (b), and calculate the availability achieved at the cluster level (y-axis) when hardware crash faults are injected with two rates (1 and 6 per year). We measure the availability of cluster with $UpNodes = Num$ during one year, *i.e.*, the yearly percentage of time that the service is able to fulfill its performance requirement. We observe that, as we increase the number of nodes expected to be operational, the availability of the service deployed in the cloud remains high, while it degrades fast on-premises even with low fault rate. Therefore, deploying a service on-premises requires over-provisioning to ensure that performance requirements are met.

Capacity for Dependable Service. A dependable service that relies on a cluster of nodes to achieve a target QoS requires the cluster to satisfy availability constraints, in addition to protecting the integrity of the service. To that end, we can use over-provisioning (*e.g.*, PF or ARA) to meet the availability objectives as well as integrity protection techniques to enhance the integrity of the service (*e.g.*, HAFT). We use the capacity planning process in two ways: *i)* to define the number of nodes needed for a dependable service built using different node types, deployment schemes and over-provisioning techniques, and *ii)* to quantify the integrity of the service.

(1) Number of Nodes Needed. For *cloud deployments*, Table 2 (a) shows the number of nodes needed for a dependable service that has a performance constraint $SerT = 10 \times NodT_{native}$ and service availability of at least three 9's. We consider *CrashRecovery* times for the automatic failover as 15 s, 1 min and 30 min, and hardware crash rates of 1 and 6 per year per node. If the availability achieved does not satisfy the required level, extra nodes are provisioned as ARA nodes. The deployment types differ in their "base" number of nodes, yet they all achieve high availability levels of at least three 9's except with high crash rate and slow failover time (HCR = 6/year and CR = 30 min). In this case, it is enough to have a single extra ARA node over-provisioned in the cloud to meet the required availability level.

For *on-premises deploy-*
ment, we consider both
ARA in Table 2 (b) and
PF in Table 3 as over-
provisioning techniques.
The tables consider a service required throughout
$SerT = 10 \times NodT_{native}$
and a service availabil-
ity of at least three 9's.
Table 2 (b) shows that the

Table 3. Number of nodes needed (base + pool) for *on-premises* deployment with PF to achieve 10× native throughput $(SerT)$ and three 9's availability (HCR=$\lambda_{HWcrash}$, CR=$\rho_{CrashRecovery}$, PR=$\rho_{PoolRepair}$).

Node	Base	HCR: CR: PR:						Extra pool nodes					
			1/year						6/year				
		15 s		1 min		30 min		15 s		1 min		30 min	
		−	1 h	−	1 h	−	1 h	−	1 h	−	1 h	−	1 h
native	10	18	1	18	1	19	1	30	1	30	1	50	5
ft_{ilr}	11	19	1	19	1	20	1	33	1	33	1	57	5
ft_{tx}	15	24	1	24	1	27	1	42	1	42	1	63	5

dependable service requires a number of active nodes *UpNodes* equal to the sum of the "base" nodes needed for performance and the over-provisioned ARA nodes. For example, a service that requires 10 *native* nodes also needs, assuming a crash rate of 1 per year, 35 additional active nodes to ensure three 9's availability. To understand this high number of over-provisioned nodes, consider that an on-premises deployment can achieve only 10% availability with a cluster of 10 nodes (Fig. 6), which is very low compared to the required level of 99.9%. Additionally, ARA nodes are active nodes and can fail due to crash failures. Therefore, we need to over-provision many nodes to ensure that at least 10 are available at any time, except for the allowed downtime (8.77 h per year for three 9's). Note that the number of base nodes for each type is different, which also affects the number of additional ARA nodes.

Table 3 shows that a dependable service requires a number of nodes equal to the sum of "base" active node needed for performance and the over-provisioned nodes as PF. The table considers *CrashRecovery* times for the failover from the pool as 15 s, 1 min and 30 min and hardware crash rates of 1 and 6 per year per node. Additionally, we consider two cases for handling crashed nodes upon failed-over to a node from the pool: "no repair" (denoted by −) and "1 h repair". If repaired, a crashed node can return to the pool and be used for further failover upon need. The table indicates that the number of nodes required to fulfil the availability constraints is dramatically reduced when repairing crashed nodes, as compared to the "no repair" case. For example, for a crash rate of 1 per year and 15 s failover time, a service would require, in order to achieve three 9's availability using 10 *native* active nodes, 18 additional passive nodes in the pool if there are no repair vs. one if the pool is repaired at a rate of one per hour.

Comparing Table 2 (b) and Table 3, one can see that PF requires fewer nodes than ARA. Indeed, passive nodes in the pool work in cold mode (turned off) and not exposed to crashes.

(2) Integrity of the Service. To study how different nodes behave when transient faults are injected, we use the integrity models presented in Fig. 2. If not masked, a transient fault can crash the node or corrupt its internal state with probabilities that vary between different node types due to their ability to tolerate transient faults, as seen in Table 1. Note that *native* nodes do not implement any integrity protection mechanism, while *ft* nodes are hardened against data corruption. Transition rates between *Correct* state and other states (*Corrupt*, *Crash*, *Retry*) are defined by the injected transient faults rate multiplied by the corresponding probability.

Figure 7 presents the normalised time that each node type spends in *Correct* (available), *Corrupt* (available but integrity is not preserved) and *Down* (unavailable, crashed or under repair) states in one month in the cloud. The figure shows that with low transient fault rates, all nodes spend most of their time in *Correct* state. By increasing fault rates, nodes spends more time in *Corrupt* or *Crash* states. Specifically, *native* nodes spend 0.2–5.5%

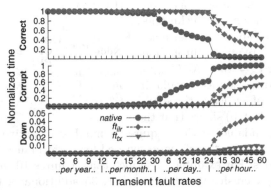

Fig. 7. Normalised time spent by the different node types in correct, corrupted and down states after injecting transient faults.

of time in *Corrupt* state with faults in the month range and 6–58% with faults in the day range, whereas these percentages decrease to 0.007–0.18% and 0.2–4.3% with ft_{ilr} and 0.0026–0.07% and 0.07–1.67% with ft_{tx} for the same ranges, respectively. With high fault rates, ft_{tx} spends more time than ft_{ilr} in *Correct* state and less in *Corrupt* or *Down* states. This is due to the use of transactions to recover from a detected fault in ft_{tx}, as compared to the slower failover recovery in ft_{ilr}. Therefore, ft_{tx} is not only more reliable, but also more available than the other node types. Service dependability should not only consider the availability of the nodes in the cluster, but also the integrity of the available nodes, since they may spend a considerable amount of time in *Corrupt* state if integrity mechanisms are not implemented.

5 Conclusion

We have developed a capacity planning process (PCRAFT) to quantify the number of nodes needed to ensure the dependability of stateless services. We consider availability, integrity and performance failures for cloud-based and on-premises deployments. PCRAFT combines a two-phase process—empirical and modelling-based. In the *empirical phase*, we characterise the performance and integrity of the service at the node level to parameterise the *modelling phase*, in which we implement probabilistic models to estimate the availability and integrity of service. Our evaluation of PCRAFT using Apache, memcached and Redis shows that both availability and performance are important to leverage the benefits of dependability mechanisms.

References

1. Amazon S3 availability event (2008). https://status.aws.amazon.com/s3-20080720.html
2. Amazon S3 service level agreement (2019). https://aws.amazon.com/s3/sla/
3. Birman, K., Freedman, D.A., Huang, Q., Dowell, P.: Overcoming CAP with consistent soft-state replication. Computer **45**(02), 50–58 (2012)
4. Cooper, B.F., Silberstein, A., Tam, E., Ramakrishnan, R., Sears, R.: Benchmarking cloud serving systems with YCSB. In: Proceedings of the 1st ACM Symposium on Cloud Computing, pp. 143–154 (2010)
5. Faqeh, R., Martin, A., Schiavoni, V., Bhatotia, P., Felber, P., Fetzer, C.: PCRAFT: capacity planning for dependable stateless services. arXiv preprint arXiv:2206.07368 (2022)
6. Fitzpatrick, B.: Distributed caching with Memcached. Linux J. **2004**(124), 5 (2004)
7. Ghosh, R., Trivedi, K.S., Naik, V.K., Kim, D.S.: End-to-end performability analysis for infrastructure-as-a-service cloud: an interacting stochastic models approach. In: 2010 IEEE 16th Pacific Rim International Symposium on Dependable Computing, pp. 125–132. IEEE (2010)
8. Greene, W., Lancaster, B.: Carrier-grade: five nines, the myth and the reality. Pipeline Mag. **3**(11), 1–12 (2007)
9. High availability failover optimization, tuning HA timers, PAN-OS 6.0.0 (2013). https://knowledgebase.paloaltonetworks.com/KCSArticleDetail?id=kA10g000000ClOSCA0
10. HAProxy: www.haproxy.org
11. Apache HTTPD: https://httpd.apache.org/
12. Kim, D.S., Machida, F., Trivedi, K.S.: Availability modeling and analysis of a virtualized system. In: 2009 15th IEEE Pacific Rim International Symposium on Dependable Computing, pp. 365–371. IEEE (2009)
13. Kuvaiskii, D., Faqeh, R., Bhatotia, P., Felber, P., Fetzer, C.: HAFT: hardware-assisted fault tolerance. In: Proceedings of the Eleventh European Conference on Computer Systems, pp. 1–17 (2016)
14. Kwiatkowska, M., Norman, G., Parker, D.: PRISM: probabilistic model checking for performance and reliability analysis. ACM SIGMETRICS Perform. Eval. Rev. **36**(4), 40–45 (2009)
15. mcperf: https://github.com/twitter-archive/twemperf

16. Mohamad, R.P., Kolovos, D.S., Paige, R.F.: Resource requirement analysis for web applications running in a virtualised environment. In: 2014 IEEE 6th International Conference on Cloud Computing Technology and Science, pp. 632–637. IEEE (2014)

17. Mohan, S., Alam, F.M., Fowler, J.W., Gopalakrishnan, M., Printezis, A.: Capacity planning and allocation for web-based applications. Decis. Sci. **45**(3), 535–567 (2014)

18. Nagaraja, K., Gama, G., Bianchini, R., Martin, R.P., Meira, W., Nguyen, T.D.: Quantifying the performability of cluster-based services. IEEE Trans. Parallel Distrib. Syst. **16**(5), 456–467 (2005)

19. Nagaraja, K., Li, X., Bianchini, R., Martin, R.P., Nguyen, T.D.: Using fault injection and modeling to evaluate the performability of cluster-based services. In: 4th USENIX Symposium on Internet Technologies and Systems (2003)

20. Qian, H., Medhi, D., Trivedi, K.: A hierarchical model to evaluate quality of experience of online services hosted by cloud computing. In: 12th IFIP/IEEE International Symposium on Integrated Network Management (IM 2011) and Workshops, pp. 105–112. IEEE (2011)

21. Redis: https://redis.io

22. Reis, G.A., Chang, J., Vachharajani, N., Rangan, R., August, D.I.: SWIFT: software implemented fault tolerance. In: International Symposium on Code Generation and Optimization, pp. 243–254. IEEE (2005)

23. Rodriguez, A.: Restful web services: the basics. IBM Developer Works **33**, 18 (2008)

24. Roy, N., Dubey, A., Gokhale, A., Dowdy, L.: A capacity planning process for performance assurance of component-based distributed systems. In: Proceedings of the 2nd ACM/SPEC International Conference on Performance engineering, pp. 259–270 (2011)

25. Schad, J., Dittrich, J., Quiané-Ruiz, J.: Runtime measurements in the cloud: observing, analyzing, and reducing variance. Proc. VLDB Endow. **3**(1–2), 460–471 (2010)

26. Tootaghaj, D.Z., et al.: Evaluating the combined impact of node architecture and cloud workload: characteristics on network traffic and performance cost. In: 2015 IEEE International Symposium on Workload Characterization, pp. 203–212. IEEE (2015)

27. Undheim, A., Chilwan, A., Heegaard, P.: Differentiated availability in cloud computing SLAs. In: 2011 IEEE/ACM 12th International Conference on Grid Computing, pp. 129–136. IEEE (2011)

28. wrk2 (2015). https://github.com/giltene/wrk2

29. Xue, Z., Dong, X., Ma, S., Dong, W.: A survey on failure prediction of large-scale server clusters. In: Eighth ACIS International Conference on Software Engineering, Artificial Intelligence, Networking, and Parallel/Distributed Computing (SNPD 2007), vol. 2, pp. 733–738. IEEE (2007)

30. Yoo, R.M., Hughes, C.J., Lai, K., Rajwar, R.: Performance evaluation of Intel transactional synchronization extensions for high-performance computing. In: Proceedings of the International Conference on High Performance Computing, Networking, Storage and Analysis, pp. 1–11 (2013)

Lower Bound for Constant-Size Local Certification

Virgina Ardévol Martínez[1], Marco Caoduro[2], Laurent Feuilloley[3(✉)]⬤,
Jonathan Narboni[4]⬤, Pegah Pournajafi[5], and Jean-Florent Raymond[6]⬤

[1] LAMSADE, Université Paris Dauphine, Paris, France
[2] Laboratoire G-SCOP, Univ. Grenoble Alpes, Grenoble, France
[3] Univ Lyon, CNRS, INSA Lyon, UCBL, LIRIS, UMR5205, Villeurbanne, France
`laurent.feuilloley@univ-lyon1.fr`
[4] LaBRI, Université de Bordeaux, CNRS, Bordeaux, France
[5] ENS Lyon, LIP, Univ. Lyon, UCBL, CNRS Lyon, Lyon, France
[6] CNRS, LIMOS, Université Clermont Auvergne, Clermont-Ferrand, France

Abstract. Given a network property or a data structure, a local certification is a labeling that allows to efficiently check that the property is satisfied, or that the structure is correct. The quality of a certification is measured by the size of its labels: the smaller, the better. This notion plays a central role in self-stabilization, because the size of the certification is a lower bound (and often an upper bound) on the memory needed for silent self-stabilizing construction of distributed data structures.

When it comes to the size of the certification labels, one can identify three important regimes: the properties for which the optimal size is polynomial in the number of vertices of the graph, the ones that require only polylogarithmic size, and the ones that can be certified with a constant number of bits. The first two regimes are well studied, with several upper and lower bounds, specific techniques, and active research questions. On the other hand, the constant regime has never been really explored.

The main contribution of this paper is the first non-trivial lower bound for this low regime. More precisely, we show that by using certification on just one bit (a binary certification), one cannot certify k-colorability for $k \geq 3$. To do so, we develop a new technique, based on the notion of score, and both local symmetry arguments and a global parity argument. We hope that this technique will be useful for establishing stronger results.

We complement this result with an upper bound for a related problem, illustrating that in some cases one can do better than the natural upper bound.

1 Introduction

Local certification consists in assigning labels to the vertices of a network, to allow them to check locally that some property holds [9]. Historically, the concept appeared implicitly in the study of self-stabilization, where in addition to computing the solution of the problem, the vertices would compute some additional

S. Devismes et al. (Eds.): SSS 2022, LNCS 13751, pp. 239–253, 2022.
https://doi.org/10.1007/978-3-031-21017-4_16

information that would allow fast checking of the solution (i.e. a certification of the solution). The most classic example is maybe the problem of computing a spanning tree, where in addition to computing the pointer to its parents, every vertex stores its distance to the root [2]. Such additional information is an overhead in the memory used, hence, it is a natural goal to minimize its size. In [4], Blin, Fraigniaud, and Patt-Shamir proved that for a standard notion of self-stabilization called *silent stabilization* and up to some hypothesis, the space needed for certification is the same as the space needed for self-stabilization

More recently, the question of the certification of properties of the network itself, and not the correctness of a data structure built on top of it, has attracted a lot of attention. This paper follows this direction, and we will only consider certification of graph properties.

Let us now give a more precise intuition of what a local certification is (proper definitions will be given in Sect. 2). We denote the number of vertices of a graph by n. For a graph property P, we will say that it has a local certification of size s if:

- for any graph G such that P holds, there exists an assignment of labels of size $s(n)$ per vertex that can "convince" all the vertices that P is satisfied,
- for any graph G such that P *does not hold*, for any assignment of labels of size $s(n)$ per vertex, there is at least one vertex that detects that the property is not satisfied.

At the level of the vertices, the behavior is the following; every vertex runs the same local decision algorithm that takes as input all the information available in a neighborhood (i.e. a local view), and outputs a decision: *accept* or *reject*. For positive instances, all the vertices are convinced, that is, they all accept. For negative instances, at least one vertex rejects.

There are actually many possible models, depending on the notion of neighborhood considered, the presence of identifiers and how vertices can use them, etc. Two classic models are proof-labeling schemes [19] and locally checkable proofs [17]. The precise model is not essential for the discussion that follows, hence we delay their definitions to the model section.

1.1   Three Typical Regimes for the Certificate Sizes

As said earlier, a natural goal in the study of local certification is to minimize the size of the certificates. It is well-known that the optimal size is always in $O(n^2)$, since one can always use the adjacency matrix as a certificate and make the vertex check the consistency of this matrix with their neighborhoods, as well as check that the property holds in the graph described by the matrix [19, Theorem 3.2].

Also, for any subquadratic function f, it is possible to engineer a property for which the optimal size is $f(n)$ [19, Corollary 2.4]. In other words, if we consider the certificate size as the complexity of a property, there is no gap in the complexity of certification. Nevertheless, for all the natural properties that have been studied, the optimal certificate size only belongs to one of the following three regimes (already identified in [17]): polynomial, (poly)logarithmic, and constant size. For example, there is no known natural properties with certificate size $\Theta(\log \log n)$, or $\Theta(\log^* n)$, or $\Theta(2^{\sqrt{\log n}})$.

In this paper, we are interested in lower bounds for the constant size regime. But let us provide a quick overview of the three regimes, in order to give the full picture and later discuss the novelty of our techniques.

Polynomial Regime. It is known that the $\Theta(n^2)$ size is needed for some specific properties, such as having a non-trivial automorphism [17, Theorem 6.1] or having chromatic number at least 4 (up to polylog factors) [17, Theorem 6.4]. Even innocent-looking properties such as having diameter 3 or being triangle-free require certificates of size $\Omega(n)$ [6, Theorem 1] and $n/e^{O(\sqrt{n})}$ [7, Proposition 5], respectively.

Polylogarithmic Regime. The regime of (poly)logarithmic certificate size has attracted a lot of attention recently, and is often referred to as *compact certification* (or LogLCP in [17]). The best-known local certification is the certification of acyclicity (that is, the verification of the class of trees) for which the optimal size is $\Theta(\log n)$ (by a straightforward adaptation of [19, Lemma 2.2]). It has been proved recently that planarity and bounded-genus [8,12,13] have logarithmic certification, and that MSO properties on graphs of bounded treedepth [10] and bounded treewidth [16] have respectively $\Theta(\log n)$ and $O(\log^2 n)$ local certifications. An important open question in the area is to establish whether any graph class defined by a set of forbidden minors has a compact certification. Partial results are known for small minors [5] or minors with specific shapes (namely paths [10, Corollary 2.7] and planar graphs [16, Corollary 3]). Finally, let us mention one key result of the area, even if it is concerned with a data structure instead of a graph property: the optimal certificate size for a minimum spanning tree is $\Theta(\log n \log W)$, where W is the maximum weight [18].

Constant Size Regime. First, let us note that for some properties, no certificate is needed. For example, checking that the graph is a cycle can be done by simply having every vertex check that it has exactly two neighbors (we will always assume that the graph is connected, thus there must be only one cycle).

Now, let us make a connection with a class of *construction problems*. A key class of problems in distributed computing is the construction of locally checkable labelings [21], or LCLs for short. These are problems that have constant-size output per node and whose correctness can be checked by inspecting a local neighborhood. Examples of LCLs are maximal independent sets, maximal matchings, and minimal dominating sets at some distance d. There is now a very large literature on computing such labelings. The problem that has attracted the most interest is the one of vertex coloring: given an integer k, how fast can we compute an assignment of colors to the vertices, such that for every edge the endpoints have different colors. We refer to the monograph [3] for distributed graph coloring.

For any LCL, we can design a certification question:

Question 1. How many bits are needed to certify that the graph has a solution?

Most classic LCL problems are designed so that any graph has a solution; for example, any graph has a maximal matching. But it is not true for any LCL; for example, given a positive integer $k \in \mathbb{N}$, not all graphs are k-colorable.

When a solution exists, and can be checked by inspecting each vertex and its direct neighbors, it is trivial to design a certification for the question above: get a solution, give every vertex its output in this solution as a certificate, and for the verification, let the vertices run the local checking. Specifically, to certify that a graph is k-colorable, one can find a proper k-coloring, and then give to every vertex its color as a certificate. It is then easy for the vertices to check this certification: every vertex checks that no neighbor has been given the same color as itself. This certification uses certificates of $\lceil \log k \rceil$ bits, and the key question that we would like to answer is:

Question 2. Can we do better than $\lceil \log k \rceil$ bits to certify that a graph is k-colorable?

This question was already listed in [9] as one of the key open questions in the field, and in the following section, we will review a few reasons why it is a question worth studying.

1.2 Motivation for Studying the Constant-Size Regime

In local certification, and more generally in theoretical computer science, the focus is usually not on the precise constants in the complexities, thus one might consider the questions above to be non-essential. Let us list a few reasons why Questions 1 and 2 are actually important.

An arena for New Lower Bound Techniques. The lower bound techniques that we have for local certification are mainly of two types (see the survey [9] for precise citations and more detailed sketches).

First, there are the techniques based on counting arguments, also called cut-and-plug techniques, that can be rather sophisticated but boils down to the following fact: if we use $o(\log n)$-bit labels in *yes*-instances (that is, correct instances) then some (set of) labels will appear in different places of an instance (or in different instances), because there are n vertices and $o(n)$ different labels. Using this, one can build a *no*-instance and derive a contradiction. This is the technique used to show almost all lower bounds in the logarithmic regime.

The second classic technique is a reduction from communication complexity, which we will not sketch here, but simply mention that it works better for the polynomial regime.

At this point, two things are clear: (1) we have only two main techniques, and they are now very well understood, and (2) they do not solve all our problems. In particular, they do not seem to apply to the $o(\log n)$ regime. One can hope that by trying to give a negative answer to Question 2, we will create new techniques, and that these techniques could be useful to establish new lower bounds.

A Point of View on the Encoding of LCLs. As mentioned earlier, the study of LCLs now plays a key role in our understanding of locality in distributed computing. By asking Question 1, we are basically asking about how we express such problems. Beyond the size of the encoding, a key question is what are the different encodings for an LCL? Are there some that are more useful or more compact? Such consideration could have an impact on techniques that heavily rely on precise encodings, such as round elimination [23] and local conflict colorings [15, 20].

Beyond the Constant Regime. Up to now, we have considered the question of k-coloring with constant k, thus Question 2 was about the constant regime *per se*. But actually, one could let k depend on n, and the question is meaningful for labels of size up to $\Theta(\log n)$ (which corresponds to coloring with $\Theta(n)$ colors). Hence, we are not only playing with constants when studying Question 2 in the general case. Note that if we could show that k-coloring requires labels of size $\Theta(\log k)$ for all the range of k, then we would also have fairly natural problems strictly between constant and logarithmic, which would be new and interesting in itself.

A Candidate for Disproving the Trade-off Conjecture. One of the remaining important open questions in local certification is the following, which we will call the *trade-off conjecture*.

Question 3. Suppose that there exists a local certification with labels of size $f(n)$ for some property, where every vertex would check its radius at distance 1. Is it true that there always exists a certification with labels of size $O(f(n)/t)$ if we allow the vertices to see at distance t in the graph?

This question and variants of it were raised in [11,14,22]. In these papers, the authors basically prove (among other results) that the answer is positive if the certification uses only spanning trees and a uniform certification (giving the same information to every vertex). Since these are the main tools used for certification in the logarithmic and polynomial regimes, the constant regime (and its extension beyond constant, discussed above) seems to be the place to find potential counterexamples. Note that for the constant regime, one could try to disprove the conjecture with $\alpha f(n)/t$, for some given constant α. And it seems like a reasonable approach, since it is difficult to imagine how the trade-off conjecture could be true for coloring-like problems: even if the vertices can see further, how can we save bits to certify colorability? In order to prove such a counterexample, we first need to have proper lower bounds for distance 1, that is, to answer Question 2.

1.3   Our Results and Techniques

In this paper, we give the first non-trivial lower bound for the certification of k-colorability. This is the first step of a research direction that we hope to be successful, and in terms of result it is a small step, in the sense that our answer to Question 2 is restricted in several ways. The first restriction we make is that instead of proving a $\log k$ lower bound, we prove that it is not possible to certify k-colorability for any $k \geq 3$, if we use *exactly one bit* (that is, only two different labels). We will call this a *binary certification*. The second restriction is that we take a model that is not the most powerful one. In our result, a vertex has access to the following information: its identifier, its label, and the multiset of labels of its neighbors. That is, a vertex cannot see further than its direct neighbors and cannot access the identifiers of its neighbors (which corresponds to the original proof-labeling scheme model [19], but not to the generalizations, such as locally checkable proofs [17]), and there is no port number.

To prove this result, we introduce a new technique. Similarly to the cut-and-plug technique mentioned earlier, we reason about one or several *yes*-instances and prove that we can craft a *no*-instance where the vertices would accept. But the reasoning is different, since counting arguments based on the pigeon-hole principle applied to the certificates can only lead to $\Omega(\log n)$ lower bounds. First, we define the notion of *score* for a neighborhood and prove that if two vertices have been given different labels but have the same score, then we can build a *no*-instance that is accepted. Then we prove that this necessarily happens in some well-chosen graphs, thanks to a series of local symmetry arguments, and a global parity argument. This technique has a similar flavor as the fooling views technique used for triangle detection in he CONGEST model [1].

We complement this main result by proving that in some cases (namely distance-2 3-colorability) one can actually go below the size of the natural encoding. As we will see, this happens because graphs that are distance-2 3-colorable have a very specific shape. This illustrates why establishing lower bounds for such problems is not so easy: the fact that the graph can (or cannot) be colored with a given number of colors implies that it has a given structure, and this structure could in theory be used in the certification to compress the natural $\log k$-bit encoding.

2 Models and Definitions

We denote by $\mathbb{N}$ the set of non-negative integers, and by $|A|$ the cardinality of a set A. All graphs in this paper are simple and connected. The vertex-set and the edge-set of a graph G are denoted by $V(G)$ and $E(G)$, respectively. The *closed neighborhood* of a vertex $v \in V(G)$, denoted by $N[v]$, is defined by $N[v] = N(v) \cup \{v\}$ where $N(v) = \{u \in V(G) : uv \in E(G)\}$ is the neighborhood of v. We denote the complete graph on n vertices by K_n. A *proper k-coloring* of the vertex-set of a graph G is a function $\phi : V(G) \rightarrow \{1, 2, \ldots, k\}$ such that if $xy \in E(G)$, then $\phi(x) \neq \phi(y)$. In other words, it is an assignment of colors to the vertices of G using at most k colors, such that the endpoint of every edge receive different colors. We say that G is *k-colorable* if it admits a proper k-coloring.

Let $f : \mathbb{N} \rightarrow \mathbb{N}$ be a function. We say that a graph G on n vertices is equipped with an *identifier assignment* of range $f(n)$ if every vertex is given an integer in

$[1, f(n)]$ (its *identifier*, or *ID* for short) such that no two vertices of the graph are given the same number. Typically, $f(n)$ is some polynomial of n, and in this paper it has to be at least n^3 (but we did not try to optimize this parameter).

A *certificate assignment* of size s of a graph G is a labeling of the vertices of G with strings of length s, that is, a function $\ell \colon V(G) \to \{0,1\}^s$. A *binary certificate assignment* is a certificate assignment with $s = 1$.

As hinted earlier, there are many variants for the definition of local certification. An important aspect is the type of algorithm that the vertices run. This is a local algorithm, in the sense that the vertices can see only a neighborhood in the graph, but this neighborhood can be at distance 1, constant, non-constant etc. Another important aspect is the symmetry-breaking hypothesis: whether there are identifiers, whether the vertices can see the identifiers of their neighbors, whether they can distinguish these neighbors, etc. In this paper, we use the following notion.

Definition 1. *A* local decision algorithm *is an algorithm that runs on every vertex of a graph. It takes as input the identifier of the vertex, the certificate of the vertex, and the multiset of certificates of its neighbors, and outputs a decision,* accept *or* reject.

Definition 2. *Fix a function $f : \mathbb{N} \to \mathbb{N}$. A proof-labeling scheme of size s for a property P is a local decision algorithm A such that the following holds: for every graph G and every identifier assignment of range $f(|V(G)|)$ of G there exists a certificate assignment of size s of G such that A accepts on every vertex in $V(G)$, if and only if, the graph G has property P.*

Notice that the proof-labeling scheme depends on the chosen function f.

In the proofs, as a first step, we will prove the result in a weaker anonymous model.

Definition 3. *An* anonymous proof-labeling scheme *is the same as a proof-labeling scheme, but the graphs are not equipped with identifiers (or equivalently, the outcome of the local decision algorithm is invariant by a change of the identifiers).*

For a graph G with identifier id and labeling ℓ, the *view* of a vertex v in (G, id, ℓ) in the proof-labeling scheme is a tuple $(M_v, \mathrm{id}(v))$ where M_v is the multiset

$$\{(\ell(u), \mathrm{id}(u)) : u \in N[v]\}.$$

In the anonymous case, the *view* of a vertex v is only the multiset defined above.

3 k-colorability Does Not Have a Binary Certification

This section contains our main contribution. We prove that k-colorability does not have a binary certification when $k \geq 3$. Recall that for $k = 2$, k-colorabily indeed has a binary certification (take the colors as certificates).

3.1 Indistinguishability Setting

Let us first clarify the proof strategy with Lemma 1. It is a classic strategy, that we detail for completeness.

Lemma 1. *Let s be a positive integer, $f : \mathbb{N} \to \mathbb{N}$ be a function, and $\Lambda \subseteq \mathbb{N}$ be a set of indices. If for every $i \in \Lambda$ there exist a connected graph G_i with identifier $\mathrm{id}_i : V(G_i) \to [1, f(|V(G_i)|)]$, and there exists a connected graph H such that*

1. *G_i is k-colorable for every $i \in \Lambda$,*
2. *H is not k-colorable,*
3. *for every set of labelings $\{\ell_i\}_{i \in \Lambda}$, where $\ell_i : V(G_i) \to \{0,1\}^s$ is a labeling of size s of G_i, there exists a labeling $\ell : V(H) \to \{0,1\}^s$ of size s of H and an identifier $\mathrm{id} : V(H) \to [1, f(|V(H)|)]$ such that for every view in (H, id, ℓ) there exists $i \in \Lambda$ such that the view is the same as some view in $(G_i, \mathrm{id}_i, \ell_i)$,*

then k-colorability cannot be certified by certificates of size s.

In case G and H do not have identifiers, the same holds with removing the identifier functions and f from the statement of the Lemma.

Proof. Suppose there exists a local certification of size s for k-colorability. Then, in particular, for every $i \in \Lambda$, there exists a labeling ℓ_i for the graph G_i such that the verifier algorithm accepts on every vertex. For this set of labelings $\{\ell_i\}_{i \in \Lambda}$, consider the labeling ℓ and the identifier assignment id of H described in item (3) of the Lemma. The verifier algorithm accepts on every vertex of (H, id, ℓ) because its view is the same as a view in $(G_i, \mathrm{id}_i, \ell_i)$ for some $i \in \Lambda$. This contradicts the fact that H is not k-colorable. $\square$

3.2 Notion of Score

Let ℓ be a binary labeling of a graph G, and let $v \in V(G)$. The *score* of v in ℓ, denoted by $\mathrm{score}_\ell(v)$ or $\mathrm{score}(v)$ if there is no confusion, is defined as follows:

$$\mathrm{score}_\ell(v) = |\{u \in N[v] : \ell(u) = 1\}|.$$

Given a k-regular graph G and a binary labeling ℓ of G, the *score matrix* of (G, ℓ) is a $2 \times (k+2)$ matrix S with rows labeled with 0 and 1 and columns labeled from 0 to $k+1$. Let $S_{i,j}$ denote the (i,j) element of S. We set

$$S_{1,0} = S_{0,k+1} = 1,$$

and for $i = 0, 1$, $j = 0, 1, \ldots, k+1$, and $(i,j) \neq (1,0), (0, k+1)$ we set

$$S_{i,j} = |\{v \in V(G) : \ell(v) = i, \mathrm{score}(v) = j\}|.$$

3.3 Our Graph Construction and Its Properties

Fix an integer $k \geq 3$. We build a graph as follows: take the disjoint union of three copies of K_{k+1}. For $i = 1, 2, 3$, let a_i and b_i be two distinct vertices in the i-th copy. Then, remove the edges a_1b_1, a_2b_2, and a_3b_3 from the graph, and add the edges b_1a_2, b_2a_3, and b_3a_1 to it. We denote the resulting graph by N_k. See Fig. 1. In the figure, each set C_t, $t \in \{1, 2, 3\}$ induces a K_{k-1} in the graph and a_t and b_t are complete to C_t, i.e. every vertex of C_t is connected by an edge to a_t and to b_t.

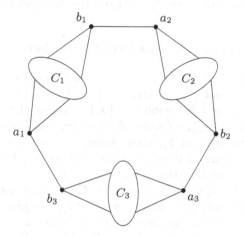

Fig. 1. The graph N_k.

Lemma 2. *For every $k \geq 3$, the graph N_k is k-colorable.*

Proof. For every $t \in \{1, 2, 3\}$, color a_t and b_t with color t and color the $k - 1$ vertices in C_t with the $k - 1$ colors $\{1, 2, \ldots, k\} \setminus \{t\}$. It is easy to check that this is a proper coloring of the vertex-set of N_k and as $k \geq 3 = t$, we have used exactly the k colors $\{1, 2, \ldots, k\}$.   □

Lemma 3. *Assume $k \geq 3$ is an integer and set $G = N_k$. If $\ell : V(G) \to \{0, 1\}$ is a binary labeling of G, and S is the score matrix of (G, ℓ), then there exists an integer $j \in \{0, 1, \ldots, k + 1\}$ such that $S_{0,j}S_{1,j} \neq 0$.*

Proof. If there exists a vertex with label 0 whose neighbors all have label 0 as well, then $S_{0,0} = 1$, and since by definition, $S_{1,0} = 1$, choosing $j = 0$ gives us the required result. Similarly, if there exists a vertex with label 1 whose neighbors all have label 1 as well, then $S_{1,k+1} = 1$, and as $S_{1,k+1} = 1$, choosing $j = k + 1$ gives us the required result. Hence, from now on, we may assume that

there exists no vertex in G that has the same label as all its neighbors.   (1)

Notice that for all $t \in \{1,2,3\}$, for all $u, v \in C_t$, we have $N[u] = N[v]$, thus score$(u) =$ score(v). If two distinct vertices u and v of C_t have different labels, then by choosing $j =$ score(v), we have $S_{0,j} S_{1,j} \neq 0$. So, we may assume that for every $t \in \{1,2,3\}$,

$$\text{all the vertices of } C_t \text{ have the same label.} \qquad (2)$$

Thanks to (2), for the rest of this proof and by abuse of notion, we use the term *the label of C_t* for referring to the common label of the vertices of C_t, and we denote it by $\ell(C_t)$. Also, notice that by (1), if $\ell(C_t) = i$, where $i \in \{0,1\}$, then at least one of the vertices a_t and b_t must receive the label $1 - i$. Thus, for every $t \in \{1,2,3\}$,

$$\text{at least one of } a_t \text{ and } b_t \text{ has a label different from the one of } C_t. \qquad (3)$$

Since there are three indices $\{1,2,3\}$, but only two labels $\{0,1\}$, there exist $t, t' \in \{1,2,3\}$ such that $t \neq t'$ and $\ell(a_t) = \ell(a_{t'})$. By symmetry, we may assume $\ell(a_1) = \ell(a_2) = \hat{i}$ for some $\hat{i} \in \{0,1\}$. Notice that for every $u \in C_1$, $N[u] \setminus \{a_1\} = N[b_1] \setminus \{a_2\}$, so score$(u) =$ score(b_1). Thus if the label of C_1 is different from the label of b_1, then choosing $j =$ score(b_1) completes the proof. So, we may assume that $\ell(C_1) = \ell(b_1)$. Therefore, by (3), we must have $\ell(C_1) \neq \ell(a_1)$. Consequently, $\ell(b_1) = \ell(C_1) = 1 - \hat{i}$.

Now, if $\ell(b_3) = 1 - \hat{i}$, then for every $u \in C_1$ we have score$(a_1) =$ score(u). And because $\ell(C_1) \neq \ell(a_1)$, choosing $j =$ score(a_1) completes the proof. Hence we assume $\ell(b_3) = \hat{i}$. Now, because of (1), there must be a vertex u in the neighborhood of b_3 with label $1 - \hat{i}$. As we already have $\ell(a_3) = \hat{i}$, we must have $u \in C_3$, and therefore by (2), $\ell(C_3) = 1 - \hat{i}$.

Moreover, if $\ell(C_2) = 1 - \hat{i}$, then we have score$(a_2) =$ score(b_1), and as a_2 and b_1 have different labels, choosing $j =$ score(a_2) completes the proof. So, we also assume that $\ell(C_2) = \hat{i}$. Thus $\ell(C_2) = \ell(a_2) = \hat{i}$. Therefore, by (3), we must have $\ell(b_2) = 1 - \hat{i}$. Now, notice that the neighbors of a_3 all have label $1 - \hat{i}$, thus by (1), we must have $\ell(a_3) = \hat{i}$.

The labels of vertices of G, with all the assumptions so far, are as shown in Fig. 2.

To conclude, consider a_1 and a vertex $u \in C_3$. In their closed neighborhoods, they both have twice the label $\hat{i}$ and $k - 1$ times the label $1 - \hat{i}$, so score$(a_3) =$ score(u). Moreover, they have different labels. So, by choosing $j =$ score(a_3) we have the required result. $\qquad \square$

3.4 Anonymous Case

Theorem 1. *For every $k \geq 3$, k-colorability is not certifiable by binary certificates in the anonymous model.*

Proof. Let G be the graph N_k and H be a complete graph on $k + 1$ vertices. Let ℓ be a binary labeling of G, and let S be the score matrix of (G, ℓ). Since G is k-colorable and H is not, by Lemma 1, to prove the theorem, it is enough to

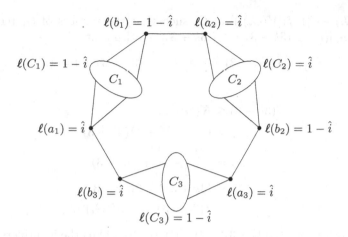

$\ell(b_1) = 1 - \hat{i}$ $\ell(a_2) = \hat{i}$

$\ell(C_1) = 1 - \hat{i}$

$\ell(C_2) = \hat{i}$

C_1

C_2

$\ell(a_1) = \hat{i}$

$\ell(b_2) = 1 - \hat{i}$

$\ell(b_3) = \hat{i}$

C_3

$\ell(a_3) = \hat{i}$

$\ell(C_3) = 1 - \hat{i}$

Fig. 2. The labels at the end of the proof of Lemma 3.

find a binary labeling $\ell' : V(H) \rightarrow \{0, 1\}$ of H such that every view in (H, ℓ') is a view in (G, ℓ).

By Lemma 3, there exists $j \in \{0, 1, \ldots, k + 1\}$ such that $S_{0,j}$ and $S_{1,j}$ are non-zero. So, if $j = 0$ (resp. $j = k + 1$), then there exists a vertex $v \in V(G)$ such that $\ell(v) = 0$ (resp. $\ell(v) = 1$) and all its neighbors have label 0 (resp. 1). If $0 < j < k + 1$, then there exist two distinct vertices $u, v \in V(G)$ such that $\ell(u) = 0$, $\ell(v) = 1$, and there are j vertices of label 1 in $N(u)$, and $j - 1$ vertices of label 1 in $N(v)$.

Let $V(H) = U \cup V$ such that $|U| = k + 1 - j$ and $|V| = j$. If $j \in \{0, k + 1\}$, then U or V is an empty set. Notice that the condition on the cardinalities of U and V implies that $U \cap V = \varnothing$. Define:

$$\ell'(w) = \begin{cases} 0 & w \in U \\ 1 & w \in V \end{cases}$$

Notice that if $j = 0$ or $j = k + 1$, then $\ell'(\cdot) = 0$ or $\ell'(\cdot) = 1$ respectively.

The view of each vertex of U in H is the same as the view of u in G and the view of each vertex of V in H is the same as the view of v in G. So, every view in H is the same as some view in G. □

3.5 Extension to Identifiers

Theorem 2. *For every $k \geq 3$, k-colorability is not certifiable by binary certificates in the proof-labeling scheme model when the range of the identifiers for a graph on n vertices is $f(n) = n^3 + 3n$.*

Proof. Set $K = (k + 1)^2 + 1$ and $\Lambda = \{1, 2, \ldots, K\}$.

Let $G_1, G_2, \ldots, G_K$ be K connected graphs each isomorphic to N_k. Notice that $|V(G_i)| = 3k + 3$. For $i \in \Lambda$, consider an identifier

$\mathrm{id}_i : V(G_i) \rightarrow [1, f(|V(G_i)|)]$ of G_i such that the vertices of G_i receive ID's in the range $[(i-1)(3k+3)+1, i(3k+3)]$. Notice that

$$(i-1)(3k+3)+1 \geq (1-1)(3k+3)+1 = 1,$$

and

$$
\begin{aligned}
i(3k+3) &\leq K(3k+3) \\
&= ((k+1)^2+1)(3k+3) \\
&= \frac{(3k+3)^3}{27} + (3k+3) \\
&\leq (3k+3)^3 + 3(3k+3) \\
&= f(3k+3) = f(|V(G_i)|).
\end{aligned}
$$

So, $[(i-1)(3k+3)+1, i(3k+3)] \subseteq [1, f(|V(G_i)|)]$. Thus the identifiers id_i exist.

Let H be a complete graph on $k+1$ vertices. Notice that each G_i is k-colorable and H is not. Hence, by Lemma 1, to prove the theorem, it is enough to define an identifier $\mathrm{id} : V(H) \rightarrow [1, f(|V(H)|)]$ and a binary labeling assignment $\ell : V(H) \rightarrow \{0,1\}$ of H such that every view in (H, id, ℓ) is the same as a view in $(G_i, \mathrm{id}_i, \ell_i)$ for some $i \in \Lambda$.

Let $S^{(i)}$ be the score matrix of (G_i, ℓ_i). By Lemma 3, for every $i \in \Lambda$, there exists $j \in \{0, 1, \ldots, k+1\}$ such that $S_{0,j}^{(i)} S_{1,j}^{(i)} \neq 0$. Therefore, by the pigeonhole principle, there exists an integer $j \in \{0, 1, \ldots, k+1\}$ and a subset Λ_0 of Λ such that $|\Lambda_0| \geq k+1$ and for all $i \in \Lambda_0$, we have $S_{0,j}^{(i)} S_{1,j}^{(i)} \neq 0$. Notice that $j \in \{0, 1, \ldots, k+1\}$, hence $|\Lambda_0| \geq k+1 \geq k+1-j$ and $|\Lambda_0| \geq k+1 \geq j$. Thus, we can find j distinct vertices $v_1, v_2, \ldots, v_j \in \bigcup_{i \in \Lambda_0} V(G_i)$ with label 1 and score j, and $k+1-j$ distinct vertices $v_{j+1}, v_{j+2}, \ldots, v_{k+1} \in \bigcup_{i \in \Lambda_0} V(G_i)$ with label 0 and score j. Notice that in case that $j = 0$ (resp. $j = k+1$), then the first (resp. the second) set of vertices in empty.

Now, assume $V(H) = \{u_1, u_2, \ldots, u_{k+1}\}$.

First, define an identifier $\mathrm{id} : V(H) \rightarrow [1, f(|V(H)|)]$ as follows:

$$\mathrm{id}(u_t) = \mathrm{id}(v_t) \text{ for every } t \in \{1, 2, \ldots, k+1\}.$$

Notice that by this definition, for all t, we have:

$$\mathrm{id}(u_t) \in \bigcup_{i \in \Lambda} [(i-1)(3k+3)+1, i(3k+3)] = [1, K(3k+3)].$$

On the other hand:

$$K(3k+3) = \frac{(3k+3)^3}{27} + (3k+3) = (k+1)^3 + 3(k+1) = f(|V(H)|),$$

and therefore the image of id is a subset of $[1, f(|V(H)|)]$.

Second, define a binary labeling $\ell : V(H) \rightarrow \{0, 1\}$ as follows:

$$\ell(u_t) = \begin{cases} 1 & t \leq j \\ 0 & j+1 \leq t \end{cases}.$$

Notice that if $j = 0$ or $j = k + 1$, then $\ell'(\cdot) = 0$ or $\ell'(\cdot) = 1$ respectively.

Thus, for every t, $1 \le t \le k + 1$, the view of vertex u_t in (H, id, ℓ) is exactly the view of vertex v_t in some of the G_i's, $i \in \Lambda_0$. □

4 Going Below $\lceil \log k \rceil$

In this section, we illustrate that in some cases one can go below the natural upper bound. More precisely, we exhibit an LCL whose natural encoding uses k different labels, and for which one can find a certification that a solution exists with strictly less than k labels. The problem we use is *distance-2 3-coloring*, which is the same as 3-coloring except that even having two vertices at distance 2 colored the same is forbidden. The natural encoding consists in giving the colors (that are between 1 and 3) to the vertices, but we show that one can actually certify distance-2 3-colorability with just two different certificates.

Lemma 4. *A connected graph G is distance-2 3-colorable if and only if it is a cycle of length $0 \bmod 3$ or a path.*

Proof. First, let G be a connected distance-2 3-colorable graph. Each vertex and its neighbors form a set of vertices that are pairwise at distance at most 2, so they should all have different colors. Since there are only three available colors, G has maximum degree at most 2. Thus, G is a path or a cycle.

If G is a path, then we are done, so assume G is a cycle. Assume that the cycle is $v_1, v_2, \ldots, v_k, v_1$. Consider a proper distance-2 3-coloring of G with colors $\{0, 1, 2\}$. Notice that if a vertex v of G has color $i \bmod 3$, then necessarily, its two neighbors have colors $(i - 1) \bmod 3$ and $(i + 1) \bmod 3$. Without loss of generality, assume that the color of v_1 is 1 and the color of v_2 is 2. Let $[t]$ denote the remainder of t divided by 3. So, $[t] \in \{0, 1, 2\}$. We prove by induction on t that v_t has color $[t]$ for every $t \in \{1, 2, \ldots, k\}$. This holds by assumption for $t = 1, 2$. Now let $t \ge 3$ and assume that $v_{t'}$ has color $[t']$ for every $t' < t$. By the induction hypothesis, the color of v_{t-1} is $[t - 1]$, hence the colors of its two neighbors, namely v_{t-2} and v_t, are $[t]$ and $[t+1]$. Again, by induction hypothesis, the color of v_{t-2} is $[t - 2] = [t + 1]$. Thus the color of v_t must be $[t]$, proving the statement. Therefore, the color of v_k is $[k]$. Finally, notice that because v_1 has color 1, and v_2 has color 2, the color of v_k must be 0. Therefore $[k] = 0$, meaning that the length of the cycle, k is equal to $0 \bmod 3$.

Second, in both cycles of length $0 \bmod 3$ and in paths, it is possible to find a proper distance-2 3-coloring, by simply choosing the color of one vertex and propagating the constraints. □

Theorem 3. *One can certify distance-2 3-colorable graphs with a binary certification.*

Proof. By Lemma 4, it is enough to prove that paths and cycles of length 0 mod 3 can be recognized with a binary certification. The idea of the certification is to give certificates of the form: $\ldots, 1, 0, 0, 1, 0, 0, 1, 0, 0, \ldots$.

Let us describe first the verifier algorithm of a vertex v:

1. If the degree is strictly more than 2, reject,
2. If the degree is 2, accept if and only if, $\text{score}(v) = 1$, that is, among v and its neighbors, exactly one has a 1 as certificate.
3. If the degree is 1, accept.

Because of Item 1, only paths and cycles can be accepted. For paths, the following labeling makes every vertex accept: choose one endpoint u, and give label 1 to a vertex v, if and only if, the distance from u to v is $0 \mod 3$. For cycles of length 0 mod 3, the following labeling makes every vertex accept: choose an orientation and an arbitrary vertex u, and again give label 1 if and only the distance from u to v in the sense of the orientation is $0 \mod 3$. It is easy to see that in cycles of length different from $0 \mod 3$, at least one vertex will reject with Item 2.

Hence, we have a proper certification that a graph is a path or a cycle of length $0 \mod 3$, with only two different labels (that is, just one bit). □

5 Challenges and Open Questions

We have proved the one bit is not enough for certifying k-colorability for $k \geq 3$. We conjecture that the answer to Question 2 is negative, that is, that $\lceil \log k \rceil$ is the optimal certification size for k-colorability.

There are several challenges to overcome before one can hope to prove the conjecture. First, it would be nice to have a more general model, where the vertices can see their neighbors' identifiers, or at least distinguish them, and even better, where the vertices can see at a larger distance. At least the first step in this direction might work by using some Ramsey argument, but then losing the upper bound on the identifier range. Second, it might be necessary to use graphs of large chromatic number that do not have large cliques as subgraph, and these have complicated structures.

A different direction is to understand other LCLs, and to try to see which ones have a certification that is more efficient than the natural encoding (such as distance-2 3-coloring) and which do not. Maybe in this direction, one could characterize exactly which properties can be certified with one bit.

Acknowledgements. This work originates from the 2021 "Journées Graphes et Algorithmes" (JGA) workshop. We thank the organizers for this opportunity. We also thank the reviewers for useful suggestions.

References

1. Abboud, A., Censor-Hillel, K., Khoury, S., Lenzen, C.: Fooling views: a new lower bound technique for distributed computations under congestion. Distrib. Comput. **33**(6), 545–559 (2020). https://doi.org/10.1007/s00446-020-00373-4
2. Afek, Y., Kutten, S., Yung, M.: Memory-efficient self stabilizing protocols for general networks. In: van Leeuwen, J., Santoro, N. (eds.) WDAG 1990. LNCS, vol. 486, pp. 15–28. Springer, Heidelberg (1991). https://doi.org/10.1007/3-540-54099-7_2

3. Barenboim, L., Elkin, M.: Distributed graph coloring: fundamentals and recent developments. Synth. Lect. Distrib. Comput. Theory **4**(1), 1–171 (2013)
4. Blin, L., Fraigniaud, P., Patt-Shamir, B.: On proof-labeling schemes versus silent self-stabilizing algorithms. In: Felber, P., Garg, V. (eds.) SSS 2014. LNCS, vol. 8756, pp. 18–32. Springer, Cham (2014). https://doi.org/10.1007/978-3-319-11764-5_2
5. Bousquet, N., Feuilloley, L., Pierron, T.: Local certification of graph decompositions and applications to minor-free classes. In: OPODIS 2021, vol. 217, pp. 22:1–22:17 (2021)
6. Censor-Hillel, K., Paz, A., Perry, M.: Approximate proof-labeling schemes. Theor. Comput. Sci. **811**, 112–124 (2020)
7. Crescenzi, P., Fraigniaud, P., Paz, A.: Trade-offs in distributed interactive proofs. In DISC 2019, vol. 146, pp. 13:1–13:17 (2019)
8. Esperet, L., Lévêque, B.: Local certification of graphs on surfaces. Theor. Comput. Sci. **909**, 68–75 (2022)
9. Feuilloley, L.: Introduction to local certification. Discret. Math. Theor. Comput. Sci. **23**(3) (2021)
10. Feuilloley, L., Bousquet, N., Pierron, T.: What can be certified compactly? compact local certification of MSO properties in tree-like graphs. In: PODC'22, pp. 131–140. ACM (2022)
11. Feuilloley, L., Fraigniaud, P., Hirvonen, J., Paz, A., Perry, M.: Redundancy in distributed proofs. Distrib. Comput. **34**(2), 113–132 (2020). https://doi.org/10.1007/s00446-020-00386-z
12. Feuilloley, L., Fraigniaud, P., Montealegre, P., Rapaport, I., Rémila, E., Todinca, I.: Local certification of graphs with bounded genus. CoRR, abs/2007.08084 (2020)
13. Feuilloley, L., Fraigniaud, P., Montealegre, P., Rapaport, I., Rémila, É., Todinca, I.: Compact distributed certification of planar graphs. Algorithmica **83**(7), 2215–2244 (2021)
14. Fischer, O., Oshman, R., Shamir, D.: Explicit space-time tradeoffs for proof labeling schemes in graphs with small separators. In: OPODIS 2021, vol. 217, pp. 21:1–21:22 (2021)
15. Fraigniaud, P., Heinrich, M., Kosowski, A.: Local conflict coloring. In: Dinur, I., (ed.) FOCS 2016, pp. 625–634 (2016)
16. Fraigniaud, P., Montealegre, P., Rapaport, I., Todinca, I.: A meta-theorem for distributed certification. In: Parter, M. (ed.) SIROCCO 2022. LNCS, vol. 13298. Springer, Cham (2022). https://doi.org/10.1007/978-3-031-09993-9_7
17. Göös, M., Suomela, J.: Locally checkable proofs in distributed computing. Theory Comput. **12**(1), 1–33 (2016)
18. Korman, A., Kutten, S.: Distributed verification of minimum spanning trees. Distrib. Comput. **20**(4), 253–266 (2007)
19. Korman, A., Kutten, S., Peleg, D.: Proof labeling schemes. Distrib. Comput. **22**(4), 215–233 (2010)
20. Maus, Y., Tonoyan, T.: Local conflict coloring revisited: linial for lists. In: Attiya, H. (ed.) DISC 2020, vol. 179, pp. 16:1–16:18 (2020)
21. Naor, M., Stockmeyer, L.J.: What can be computed locally? SIAM J. Comput. **24**(6), 1259–1277 (1995)
22. Ostrovsky, R., Perry, M., Rosenbaum, W.: Space-time tradeoffs for distributed verification. In: Das, S., Tixeuil, S. (eds.) SIROCCO 2017. LNCS, vol. 10641, pp. 53–70. Springer, Cham (2017). https://doi.org/10.1007/978-3-319-72050-0_4
23. Suomela, J.: Using round elimination to understand locality. SIGACT News **51**(3), 63–81 (2020)

Collaborative Dispersion by Silent Robots

Barun Gorain[1], Partha Sarathi Mandal[2], Kaushik Mondal[3],
and Supantha Pandit[4(✉)]

[1] Indian Institute of Technology Bhilai, Sejbahar, India
barun@iitbhilai.ac.in
[2] Indian Institute of Technology Guwahati, Guwahati, India
psm@iitg.ac.in
[3] Indian Institute of Technology Ropar, Punjab, India
kaushik.mondal@iitrpr.ac.in
[4] Dhirubhai Ambani Institute of Information and Communication Technology,
Gandhinagar, Gujarat, India
pantha.pandit@gmail.com

Abstract. In the dispersion problem, a set of k co-located mobile robots must relocate themselves in distinct nodes of an unknown network. The network is modeled as an anonymous graph $G = (V, E)$, where the graph's nodes are not labeled. The edges incident to a node v with degree d are labeled with port numbers in the range $\{0, 1, \ldots, d-1\}$ at v. The robots have unique IDs in the range $[0, L]$, where $L \geq k$, and are initially placed at a source node s. Each robot knows only its ID, however, it does not know the IDs of the other robots or the values of L or k. The task of the dispersion was traditionally achieved based on the assumption of two types of communication abilities: (a) when some robots are at the same node, they can communicate by exchanging messages between them, and (b) any two robots in the network can exchange messages between them.

This paper investigates whether this communication ability among co-located robots is absolutely necessary to achieve the dispersion. We established that even in the absence of the ability of communication, the task of the dispersion by a set of mobile robots can be achieved in a much weaker model, where a robot at a node v has the access of following very restricted information at the beginning of any round: (1) am I alone at v? (2) did the number of robots at v increase or decrease compared to the previous round?

We propose a deterministic distributed algorithm that achieves the dispersion on any given graph $G = (V, E)$ in time $O\left(k \log L + k^2 \log \Delta\right)$, where Δ is the maximum degree of a node in G. Further, each robot uses $O(\log L + \log \Delta)$ additional memory. We also prove that the task of the dispersion cannot be achieved by a set of mobile robots with $o(\log L + \log \Delta)$ additional memory.

B. Gorain, K. Mondal, and S. Pandit—Acknowledge the support of the Science and Engineering Research Board (SERB), Department of Science and Technology, Govt. of India (Grant Number: CRG/2020/005964). B. Gorain also acknowledges the support of SERB (Grant Number: MTR/2021/000118), and the Research Initiation Grant supported by IIT Bhilai, India. P. S. Mandal acknowledges a partial support of SERB (Grant Number: MTR/2019/001528).

Keywords: Autonomous mobile robots · Anonymous graphs ·
Dispersion · Deterministic algorithm · Time and memory complexity

1 Introduction

1.1 Background

The dispersion problem in a graph using mobile robots became popular in recent times. In this problem, a set of k mobile robots, starting from one or multiple source nodes of a graph, must relocate themselves in the nodes of the graph so that no two robots are located on a single node. This problem was first introduced by Augustine and Moses Jr. [3]. In the last few years, this problem got attention from various researchers and has been studied over various models. This problem has several practical applications. The most prominent application is the charging of self-driving electric cars in charging stations [3]. It is assumed that charging a car is a more time-consuming and costly task than relocating the car to a nearby free charging station. So it is better to spread the cars such that each charging station gets one at any time instead of a long queue in a single station. The dispersion problem is closely related to several problems on a graph network such as exploration [6,7,10], scattering [4,11,24], load balancing [12], token distribution [8,13,14], and many more. In the previous studies of dispersion, it is assumed that, if two robots are co-located at the same node, they can communicate and exchange any amount of information. It enables the robots to learn the number of co-located robots in the node, their IDs, the previous histories, etc.

1.2 Motivation and Problem Definition

Our work is motivated by the recent work on gathering by Bouchard et al. [5]. In the problem of gathering [2,23], a set of mobile robots, starting from different nodes of an unknown graph, must meet at a node and declare that they all met. In all the prior works related to gathering, the mobile robots are assumed to have the capability of communication: any two robots can communicate if they are co-located at a node. Bouchard et al. [5] asked the following fundamental question: whether the capability of communication between co-located robots is necessary for gathering? They showed that gathering can be achieved without communication by a set of co-located mobile robots. Here, it is assumed that a robot at any node can see how many robots are co-located with it in any round.

The task in the dispersion is the opposite of gathering. Here, a set of co-located mobile robots must be relocated to different nodes of the graph. Similar to the problem of gathering, in all the prior works in the dispersion, the capability of communication between co-located robots is assumed. Therefore, it is natural to ask whether this communication capability is absolute necessary to achieve the dispersion.

1.3 The Model

Let $G = (V, E)$ be a connected graph with n nodes. The nodes of the graph are anonymous but the edges incident to a node v of degree d are labeled arbitrarily by unique port numbers $0, 1, \ldots, d-1$. Thus, every edge in E is associated with two independent port numbers, one corresponding to each of its end nodes. Let s be a specified source node in V and initially $k \le n$ mobile robots are placed at s. Each mobile robot has a unique integer ID represented as a binary string in the range $[0, L]$, $k - 1 \le L$.

A mobile robot knows its own ID, but does not know the IDs of the other robots or the values of L and k. The robots move in synchronous rounds, and at most one edge can be traversed by a robot in every round. Each round is divided into two different stages. In the first stage, each robot at a node v does any amount of local computations. In the second stage, a robot moves along one of the edges incident to v or stays at v.

The robots are silent: there is no means of communication between any two robots in the graph. A robot M at a node v has access to the following two local information at the beginning of a round: (1) am I alone at v? (2) did the number of robots at v increase or decrease compared to the previous round?

The robots use three binary variables named *alone*, *increase* and *decrease* in order to store the above mentioned local information. In any round t, if there is only one robot at v, then *alone* = *true*, else *alone* = *false*. If a robot M decides to stay at a node v in the t-th round, and if the number of robots that left v in the t-th round is more than the number of robots that entered v, then *decrease* = *true* for M at the beginning of the $(t+1)$-th round. If a robot M decides to stay at a node v in the t-th round, and if the number of robots that left v in the t-th round is less than the number of robots that entered v, then *increase* = *true* for M at the beginning of the $(t+1)$-th round. Otherwise, both *increase* and *decrease* are *false* at the beginning of the $(t + 1)$-th round.

Whenever a robot M entered a node v in some round t using a port from another node, it learns the incoming port through which it reaches v and the degree of v. If two robots decide to move along the same edge from the same or different end nodes in the same round, none of them can detect other's movement.

1.4 Our Contribution

So far, all the works on dispersion problem require two types of communication abilities between the robots: (1) when some robots are at the same node, they can communicate by exchanging messages between them (2) any two robots in the network can exchange messages between them. This paper shows that neither of the above communication abilities is required to achieve dispersion. We propose a deterministic algorithm in our described model, that runs in time $O(k \log L + k^2 \log \Delta)$, where k and Δ are the number of robots and the maximum degree of the underlying graph, respectively. The additional memory used by the robots is $O(\log L + \log \Delta)$. We further prove that $\Omega(\log L + \log \Delta)$ additional memory is necessary to achieve dispersion in our model.

It can be noted here that with the sufficient amount of memory available to each robot, dispersion can be achieved by the following trivial algorithm: the robot with ID i starts moving according to depth-first search in round i where the edges are visited in the increasing order of their port numbers. The robot settles down at the first node that some other robot has not previously occupied.

Hence, our main contribution in this paper is to design an efficient dispersion algorithm by a set of silent robots with asymptotically optimal memory.

Due to restriction in page limit, the proofs of the lemmas and theorems, the figures, and the pseudocodes are deferred to the full version of the paper.

1.5 Related Works

The dispersion problem was first introduced by Augustine and Moses Jr. [3]. In this paper, the authors considered this problem when the number of robots (i.e., k) equals the number of vertices (i.e., n) and all the robots are initially co-located. Along with arbitrary graphs, they also study various special classes of graphs such as paths, rings, and trees. They proved that, for any graph G of diameter D, any deterministic algorithm must take $\Omega(\log n)$ bits of memory by each robot and $\Omega(D)$ rounds. For arbitrary graphs with m edges, they provided an algorithm that requires $O(m)$ rounds where each robot requires $O(n \log n)$ bits of memory. For paths, rings, and trees, they provided algorithms such that each robot requires $O(\log n)$ bits of memory and takes $O(n)$ rounds. Further, their algorithm takes $O(D^2)$ rounds for rooted trees, and each robot requires $O(\Delta + \log n)$ bits of memory. All their algorithms work under the local communication model, i.e., co-located robots can communicate among themselves. Kshemkalyani and Ali [15] proposed five different dispersion algorithms for general graphs starting from arbitrary initial configurations. Their first three algorithms require $O(m)$ time and each robot requires $O(k \log \Delta)$ bits of memory, where m is the number of edges and Δ is the degree of the graph. These three algorithms differ on the system model and what, where, and how the used data structures are maintained. Their fourth and fifth algorithms work in the asynchronous model. Their fourth algorithm uses $O(D \log \Delta)$ bits of memory at each robot and runs in $O(\Delta^D)$ rounds, where D is the graph diameter. Their fifth algorithm uses $O(\max(\log k, \log \Delta))$ bits memory at each robot and uses $O((m-n)k)$ rounds. All their algorithms work use local communication model. In [16], Kshemkalyani et al. provided a novel deterministic algorithm in arbitrary graphs in a synchronous model that requires $O(\min(m, k\Delta) \log k)$ rounds and $O(\log n)$ bits of memory by each robot. However, they assumed that the robots know the maximum degree and number of edges. Shintaku et al. [25] studied the dispersion problem of [16] without the knowledge of maximum degree and number of edges and provided an algorithm that uses the same number of rounds and $\log(\Delta + k)$ bits of memory per robot which improves upon the memory requirement of [16]. Recently Kshemkalyani et al. [19] came up with an improved algorithm where it requires $O(\min(m, k\Delta))$ rounds, however, the memory requirement remains the same as in [25]. All the algorithms in [16,25] works under the local communication model. The dispersion problem was studied on dynamic rings by Agarwalla et al. [1]. In [21], Molla et al. introduced fault-tolerant in dispersion problem in a ring in the presence of the Byzantine robots. The results are further extended by the authors in [22] where dispersion on general graphs in presence of Byzantine robots are considered. In all these algorithms, local communication model is considered. Molla et al. [20] used randomness in dispersion problem. They gave an algorithm where each robot uses $O(\log \Delta)$ bits of memory. They also provided a matching lower bound of $\Omega(\log \Delta)$ bits for any randomized algorithm to solve the dispersion problem. They extended the problem to a general k-dispersion problem where $k > n$ robots need to disperse over n nodes such that at most $\frac{k}{n}$ robots are at each node in the final configuration. Recently, Das et al. [9] studied dispersion on anonymous robots and provided a randomized dispersion algorithm where each robot uses $O(\log \Delta)$ bits of memory. In both the works, local communication model is considered. There are works [17,18] in the global communication model as well where robots can communicate even if they are located in different nodes. Results in these papers include dispersion on grids as well as general graphs. In all the results mentioned above, robots communicate either locally or globally.

2   Dispersion on Graphs

In this section, we propose an algorithm that achieves dispersion in any anonymous graph in time $O(k \log L + k^2 \log \Delta)$ and with $O(\log L + \log \Delta)$ additional memory. Before we describe our algorithm, we overview how previous results on dispersion work where co-located robots with limited memory can exchange arbitrary amounts of messages between them. The proposed algorithms in the previous works on dispersion rely on exploring nodes of the graph using depth-first search (DFS). At the beginning, all the robots are at a node s and the smallest ID robot settles at s and the other robots move to an adjacent node according to DFS. The robots learn about the smallest ID by exchanging their IDs among co-located robots. In any round, the robot with the smallest ID among the co-located robots settles at the current node and other robots move to an adjacent empty neighbor. Here, the self-placement of a robot at an 'empty' node represents 'coloring' of already visited nodes in DFS traversal. Therefore, even if the graph is anonymous, DFS traversal can still be executed by the mobile robots. The difficulty arises due to limited memory, the robots may not store the entire path it follows while traversing nodes before it settles down at an empty node. Specifically, suppose that all the unsettled robots reach a node v (which is already occupied by some other robot) during DFS. If the robots observe that each of the neighbor of v is already visited (the robot can learn this by visiting the neighbors of v and observing that some other mobile robots already occupy these neighbors), then as per DFS, all the unsettled robots must backtrack to the node u from which it visited v and then search for another empty neighbor of u. If there is no empty neighbor of u, backtrack again and continue until an empty node is found. Without sufficient memory, the robots cannot do this backtracking process by themselves. Here, the capability of communications between co-located robots again comes for rescue. Each robot stores the incoming port through which it enters the empty node where it settled down. The information of this port serves as the pointer to backtrack from a particular node. When the set of unsettled robots unable to find any empty neighbor of a node v, they have to backtrack. The robot which settled at v provides the port information for backtracking to these unsettled robots. Therefore, the above DFS like dispersion strategy can be executed with $O(\log \Delta)$ memory at each robot, where Δ is the maximum degree of a node in the graph.

The difficulty arises when the co-located robots do not have the capability of communication. Specifically, the following major issues may arise in the absence of communication.

- Each mobile robot only knows its own label but is unable to know other robots' labels without direct communication. Therefore, a strategy like a robot with the 'minimum' or 'maximum' label settled down will not work.
- With limited memory and lack of communication, a robot may not learn sufficiently long path information that is needed for backtracking.

Our algorithm runs in several iterations. We call a node v *full* in an iteration j, if v is occupied by a robot at the end of the iteration j. Otherwise, it is called *empty*. Also, for any node v, the node adjacent to v and connected through the port i from v is denoted by $v(i)$.

In each iteration of our algorithm, except the last iteration, an empty node becomes full and no full node becomes empty. Therefore, if k robots are initially present at the start node, the task of dispersion is completed within $k - 1$ iterations. An additional iteration is required to identify that the dispersion is completed.

Each iteration of the algorithm has two phases. In Phase 1, a leader election algorithm is executed and a robot M is elected as the leader from a set of robots R. In Phase 2, an empty node is occupied by a mobile robot that is either the robot elected recently or a robot elected previously.

A detailed description of the algorithm with the high-level idea is described below. During the description of each major step of the algorithm, we explicitly mention the purpose of the respective steps, the difficulty of implementing the steps with existing techniques, and how to overcome such difficulties.

2.1 The Algorithm

High Level Idea and Preliminaries: The proposed algorithm executes in several iterations. Each iteration of the algorithm consists of Phase 1 and Phase 2. In Phase 1, a leader among the robots situated at s is elected. In Phase 2, one empty node is occupied by a robot. Phase 2 requires several communications between robots. Since there is no means of direct communication, we adopt the idea proposed in [5] which enables the robots to communicate between them by utilizing the robot's movement as the tool of communication. We describe later how this communication process is executed while describing Phase 2 of our algorithm.

The robots collectively execute the following tasks in each iteration.

- Execution of Phase 1.
- Execution of Phase 2. This phase includes five major steps. (1) Informing all robots (those who will participate in Phase 2 that Phase 1 ended. (2) Finding an empty node. (3) Propagate information whether an empty node was found or not to the robots 'participating' in Phase 2. (4) Movement of the robots for occupying the empty node. (5) Termination detection.

Each of the above tasks involves the movement of the robots. A robot may decide to move in a particular round to achieve one of the following goals.

- To elect the leader.
- To transmit some information.
- To search or occupy an empty node.

The movement of a robot for a specific purpose may create confusion for other robots, who are affected by this movement. This is because a robot may decide to move to find an empty node, but some other robots may learn this movement to initiate some message transmission. Therefore special care must be taken to avoid such ambiguity. Our algorithm overcomes such ambiguity by allotting a unique 'slot' to each of the five above mentioned steps for Phase 2 and one slot for Phase 1. Specifically, each round in a consecutive block of six rounds is dedicated to exactly one of the above six steps required to execute Phase 1 and Phase 2. That is, a robot moving in round $6i + j$ means different to the algorithm than a robot moving in round $6i + j'$ for $j \neq j'$ and $0 \leq j, j' \leq 5$. For $0 \leq j \leq 5$, we call a round j-dedicated, if the round number is of the form $6m + j$ for some positive integer m.

During the algorithm's execution, each robot maintains a variable $status$. At any point of time the $status$ of a robot can be one of following.

- $active$: These robots participates in Phase 1 and one of the $active$ robots is elected as 'leader' in Phase 1 of any iteration.
- $master$ and $follower$: The robot, elected as the leader in Phase 1 of an iteration, changes its $status$ to $master$ in the very first iteration of the algorithm. In the subsequent iterations, the leader changes its $status$ to $follower$.
- $idle$: A robot with this $status$ does not take part in the algorithm anymore. During our algorithm's execution, each robot eventually becomes $idle$.

Initially, all robots are $active$. The algorithm terminates when $status$ of each robot becomes $idle$.

With the above details, we are ready to describe the details of the dispersion algorithm. We start by describing Phase 1 of the algorithm.

Phase 1 (Electing Leader). Only the $active$ robots start executing this phase. The robots execute the steps of this phase only in 1-dedicated rounds. The $active$ robots at s start this phase in round 1 if this is the first iteration of the algorithm. Otherwise, if $decrease = true$ in some 5-dedicated round at s (this event signifies that the activities in the last iteration are ended), then all the *active* nodes start executing Phase 1 in the next 1-dedicated round.

Without the ability of communication by message passing, the labels of the robots are used to elect a leader among co-located robots at s. On a high level, a robot 'leave' s if a bit of its label is 1, else stay. Since the labels of two robots are different, there must be at least a position in their labels where the bits are different. Therefore, if, a robot moves when a bit of its label is 1 and does not move if the bit is 0 or all the bits of its labels are already processed, then the two robots must occupy different nodes within z rounds where z is the length of the label of the node with maximum ID. Careful implementation of this process ensures that after z rounds, exactly one robot stays at s and elects itself as the leader. However, this raises a difficulty. The difficulty is that the labels of the robots are not necessarily of the same length. For example, suppose that the label of one robot is '10' and the other is '100'. If the robots process the bits of their label from left to right, then in this case, there is no way one can identify the position of the labels where the bits differ. This difficulty can be overcome by processing the bits from right to left instead of left to right as no label can end with a zero if read from right to left.

Let $l(M)$ be the reverse binary string corresponding to the label of the robot M. Also, let δ be the degree of s. Without loss of generality, we assume that the degree of s is at least 2. Otherwise, each robot moves to the adjacent node of s and starts the algorithm from the node.

Each robot M executes a subroutine called PROCESSBIT(M, j) for the j-th bit of its reverse label $l(M)$, for all $j = 1, 2, 3, \ldots$ until the leader is elected. If $|l(M)| < j$ for a robot M, then the j-th bit is treated as zero while executing PROCESSBIT(M, j).

Each call of subroutine PROCESSBIT is executed for six consecutive 1-dedicated rounds. On a high level, after executing subroutine PROCESSBIT(M, j), two robots whose j-th bits are not the same, gets separated. After executing subroutine PROCESSBIT(M, j), one of the following events happens.

- If all robots at s have the same j-th bit, then after executing subroutine PROCESSBIT(M, j) all of them stay at s and participate in the next call of the subroutine for the $(j + 1)$-th bit.
- Otherwise, the robots whose j-th bit are 1 move to $s(\delta - 1)$ and remain there until a robot is elected as the leader. Other robots with j-th bit 0, stay at s and participate in the next call of this subroutine for the $(j + 1)$-th bit.

Executing the above steps for $j = 1, 2, \ldots$, eventually, exactly one robot remains at s. This robot changes its *status* to *master* in the first iteration and *follower* in subsequent iterations. After learning that the leader is elected, the other robots return to s, and Phase 1 of the current iteration ends with this. The details of the subroutine PROCESSBIT are described below.

Description of the Subroutine PROCESSBIT: The robots at s use the set of variables *engage*, *move*, *candidate*, and *election*. At the beginning of Phase 1 of any iteration, for all the robots at s, *engage* $= true$, *move* $= 0$, *candidate* $=$

false and *election* = *false*. At the beginning of each call of the subroutine PROCESSBIT, all the robots at s have *engage* = *true* and these robots only participate in the first four 1-dedicated rounds. In the first 1-dedicated round, if the number of robots at s is more than one, then the robots with the j-th bit of its reverse label 1 move through port 0 by setting the variable *move* = 1. This activity in round 1 resulted in a possible 'split' in the set of robots at s. The robots with j-th bit 0 stayed at s and the other robots move to $s(0)$. Hence, the robots who stayed at s observe *decrease* = *true* in the next round learns about this split. However, the robots that moved to $s(0)$ do not have any idea about this split as it may happen that all the robots moved to $s(0)$.

If some of the robots at s have j-th bit 0 and others have j-th bit 1, a split happens in the 1st 1-dedicated round. The 2nd 1-dedicated round is for the robots at $s(0)$ to learn about this split. For this purpose, the robots at s, move to $s(0)$ in the 2nd 1-dedicated round after setting *move* − 2. The robots at $s(0)$ (came to $s(0)$ in the first 1-dedicated round) observe *increase* = *true* and hence learn the fact that some robots from s visited $s(0)$ and therefore a split happened in the 1st 1-dedicated round. The 3rd 1-dedicated round is for all the robots currently at $s(0)$ to come back to s. In the 4th 1-dedicated round, the robots whose j-th bit are 1, move to $s(\delta - 1)$ and set *engage* = *false*.

If all robots at s have the j-th bit 0, then in the 1st 1-dedicated round no robots move from s and each of them has *move* = 0. Since these robots observe *decrease* = *false*, they learned that no split happened and did not move in the 2nd 1-dedicated round, and hence no robot participates in the 3rd or 4th 1-dedicated round. Hence at the end of the 4th 1 dedicated round, all the robots at s have *move* = 0, *engage* = *true*.

If all the robots at s have the j-th bit 1, then in the 1st 1-dedicated round all robots move from s to $s(0)$ and each has *move* = 1. In the 2nd 1-dedicated round, no robots visit $s(0)$ (as there is no robot has left s). Hence the robots at $s(0)$ see *increase* = *false* after the 2nd 1-dedicated round and learn that no split happened at s. In the 3rd 1-dedicated round these robots move back to s and set *move* = 0. Hence no robot participates in the 4th 1-dedicated round.

The 5th and 6th 1-dedicated rounds are participated by the robots only if there was only one robot at s in the 1st 1-dedicated round. In this case, this robot had set *candidate* = *true*, and the subroutine identifies this robot as the leader. At this point, all the other robots must have set *engage* = *false* and are in $s(\delta - 1)$. To 'inform' the robots at $s(\delta - 1)$ that the leader is elected, the robot at s (with *candidate* = *true*) moves to $s(\delta - 1)$. Hence, in the 6th 1-dedicated round, robots at $s(\delta - 1)$, after observing *increase* = *true* in the 5th 1-dedicated round, learn that the leader is elected, and move back to s after setting *election* = *true*, *engage* = *true* and *move* = 0. The robot with *candidate* = *true* also returns to s in the 6th 1-dedicated round and changes its *status* to *master* if the current iteration is the first iteration of the algorithm, else changes its *status* to *follower*.

Phase 2 (Occupying an Empty Node). All the robots except those who became *idle* participate in this phase. In this phase, one empty node is occupied by a robot. On a high level, let $v_1, v_2, \ldots, v_{p-1}$ be the nodes that became full in consecutive iterations and v_1 is a neighbor of s. Let $r_1, r_2, \ldots, r_{p-1}$ be the robots that are in $v_1, v_2, \ldots, v_{p-1}$, respectively, before Phase 2 of the current iteration starts. Then the leader elected in Phase 1 of the current iteration moves to v_1, r_1 moves to v_2, r_2 moves to v_3 and so on and, finally r_{p-1} moves to an empty neighbor of v_{p-1}.

During the execution of our algorithm, there is a unique *master* robot, and the other robots are either *follower*, or *active*, or *idle*.

We define *parent* and *child* of the robots with *status master* and *follower* in an iteration. Let *master* (resp. *follower*) be at node v at the start of Phase 2 of some iteration. The parent of a *master* robot r (resp. *follower* robot) is the node u from where the *master* (resp. *follower*) is entered at v for the first time. If the *master* (resp. *follower*) is at s, then its parent is defined as null. Similarly, the *child* of a *master* or *follower* robot is the node to which the robot will move at the end of the current iteration.

Since the graph is anonymous, the *parent* and *child* of a robot are identified by the port numbers through which its parent and child can be reached from the robot's current position, respectively. Initially at s, all the robots have *parent* = $NULL$ and *child* = 0.

We first describe the high level description of the task the robots collectively execute in Phase 2. Let M_p be the unique *master* robot at v_p. Let $M_{p-1}, M_{p-2}, \ldots, M_1$ be the *follower* robots at the nodes $v_{p-1}, v_{p-2}, \ldots, v_1$, respectively, such that v_j is the parent of the robot M_{j+1}, $v_1 = s$ and M_1 is the leader that is elected in Phase 1 of current iteration. In this phase, the *master* robot M_p searches for an empty neighbor of its current node v_p. While searching, the *master* robot visits the neighbors of v_p using the edges incident to v_p in the increasing order of their port numbers, starting from 0 until it finds an empty node. Intuitively, if *master* finds an empty node, it goes to v_{p-1} and 'informs' M_{p-1} to move to v_p and then M_p moves to that empty node. The robot M_{p-1}, after learning the information that M_p is going to leave v_p, 'informs' M_{p-2} to occupy v_{p-1} and then move to v_p. This procedure of information exchange and moving forward goes on until M_1 moves to v_2 and with this, Phase 2 ends.

If the *master* robot does not find any empty neighbor, it informs the same to the robot r_{p-1} and then changes its *status* to *idle*. The robot r_{p-1}, upon learning that the *master* is *idle*, changes its *status* to *master* and initiates searching for an empty neighbor. This process continues until an empty node is found and then occupied by the *master* robot. phase ends when r_1 leaves s and occupies a previously occupied node by a *follower* robot or empty.

There are certain difficulties in implementing the above explained procedures.

1. How can the robot learn through which port from the current node it can reach its parent?
2. How to propagate 'information' to the robot residing at the parent node?
3. How to learn through which port v_p is reachable from v_{p-1}?

The learning of the port that leads to the parent by a robot is gained in the previous iteration itself. To elaborate this, first consider the very first iteration of our algorithm. In Phase 1 of the first iteration, a robot is elected as leader and the *status* of this robot is *master*. In Phase 2, this *master* finds $s(0)$ empty and hence moves to $s(0)$. While moving to $s(0)$, this *master* robot learned the incoming port q of the edge from s to $s(0)$ and set *parent* $= q$. Suppose that the *master* and every *follower* robot knows their parent port till iteration t. Then consider the execution of $t + 1$-th iteration. In Phase 1 of this iteration, a robot r is elected as leader and sets its *status* as *follower*. In Phase 2, the *master* robot, after finding an empty neighbor, assigns its parent port to the port number through which it entered to its empty neighbor. The *follower* robots at the time of occupying the new node updates its parent port through which it entered its new position.

The second and third difficulties can be resolved together as follows. First, we explain below how a robot r can exchange a binary string α with a robot r' reachable through the port number p from its current node.

Message Transmission Using the Movement of Mobile Robots: Let a robot r decided to transmit the string α to a robot r' reachable from the current node of r through port p.

First, r waits for the first available 4-dedicated round. Call this round as the 1st 4-dedicated round. Then for each $i \geq 1$, the robot moves through port p in the i-th 4-dedicated round if the i-th bit of α is 1 and comes back to v in the next round. On the receiving end of this communication, the robot r' decodes α by identifying the event *increase* = *true* in every 4-dedicated round at its current node as a 1 and identifying an event *increase* = *false* in every 4-dedicated round as 0. The difficulty here is how the receiving robot knows when this communication process ends. To overcome this, we use the idea of *transformed binary encoding*. For any binary string α, replace every '1' by '11' and '0' by '10'. Note that the transformed binary encoding of any binary string can not contain the sub string '00'. Hence, the robot recognizes the observation of two consecutive zeros as the end of transmission.

Using this technique, the *master* robot transmits one of the following information to its parent in Phase 2.

1. "I am a *master* robot, I found an empty neighbor though port p". This message is encoded as $1011 \cdot B_p$, where the transformed binary encoding of the integer p is denoted by B_p.
2. "I am a *master* robot, I did not find any empty neighbor". This message is encoded as 1111.

Upon receiving the message (1), the *follower* robot decodes the integer p transmits the following message to the robot connected through its parent port:
3. "I am a *follower* robot, I am going to move forward through port *child*. This message can be encoded as $1011 \cdot B_{child}$.

The *follower* then moves through the port p, updates *parent* as the incoming port at the destination node and *child* $= p$. If a *follower* robot receives the message (2), it changes its *status* to *master* and start vising each of its neighbors in the increasing order of the port number starting from port $child + 1$. When the *follower* robot at s receives the message (1) or (3), it moves through port *child* and with this Phase 2 and hence the current iteration ends. If the *follower* robot at s receives the message (2), then it changes its *status* to *master*, and start searching for an empty neighbor starting from port $child + 1$. The iteration ends once the robot leaves s.

We now give the detailed descriptions of the algorithms of the robots with different *status* in Phase 2.

Description of Subroutine FOLLOWER (M): A robot M with *status* *follower* executes the subroutine FOLLOWER(M). The robot uses a binary variable *forward*. If the robot is at s, i.e., this robot is elected as leader in Phase 1 of the current iteration, then *forward* = 0. For the other *follower* robots, which are not in s, have *forward* = 1. If the robot at s is not the only robot at s, i.e., *alone* = *false*, then this robot moves through its *child* port in the next available 2-dedicated round and comes back to s in the next round (steps 5–8). The *follower* robots which are not is s, waits until *increase* = *true* in a 0-dedicated round or in a 2-dedicated round. Suppose the robot finds *increase* = *true* in a 2-dedicated round. In this case, it learns that the current iteration is not the last and send the same information to the robot present in the adjacent node by moving through its *child* port in the next 2-dedicated round and comes back to its position in the next round. Once this step is executed, the robot calls subroutine LEARN_SIGNAL, where it waits until *increase* = *true* in a 4-dedicated round. After that, it learns the message from the robot connected through its child port by identifying *increase* = *true* as a 1 in a 4-dedicated round and *increase* = *false* as a 0 in the same round until two consecutive 4-dedicated rounds have *increase* = *false*. It then decodes the integer p and the three bit string γ. If $\gamma = 1111$, the robot learns that the robot connected through its child port is a *master* robot and it is now *idle*. After learning this information, the *follower* robot changes its *status* to *master* and set *recent* = *true*. After that, it starts executing the subroutine MASTER(M). If γ is either 1011 or 1110, then the robot calls subroutine SEND_SIGNAL(α, *parent*), where $\alpha = 1110 \cdot B_{child}$. After this transmission is complete, the robot moves through port p in the next 5-dedicated round and updates *parent* as the incoming port through which it entered the empty node, and *child* = p. In step 4, if the robot observes *increase* = *true* in a 0-dedicated round, it learns that the current iteration is the last iteration and the *follower* robot connected through its parent port is now *idle*. It moves through port *child* in the next available 0-dedicated round and changes its *status* to *idle*.

Description of the Subroutine MASTER (M): A robot with *status* *master* executes the subroutine MASTER(M). If *recent* = *true*, then the robot was a *follower* robot at the beginning of the current iteration and changed its *status* to *master* because the previous *master* robot did not find any empty neighbor in the current iteration and is now *idle*. In this case, the robot executes from step 9 of the algorithm, according to which, it starts searching for an empty neighbor in its neighborhood (steps 9–15). If *recent* = *false*, then the robot waits until *increase = true* in a 0-dedicated round or in a 2-dedicated round. If it observes *increase = true* in a 2-dedicated round, then it learns that the current iteration is not the last iteration of the algorithm. It then searches for an empty neighbor in its neighborhood (steps 9–15). If an empty neighbor is found through port p', the robot executes the subroutine SEND_SIGNAL with $\alpha = 101 \cdot B_{p'}$ through the port *parent*. It then moves to its empty neighbor in the next 5-dedicated round through the port p', updates *child = 0*, *parent* as the port through which it entered this empty node, and sets *recent = false*.

Description of Subroutine Active (M): The *active* robots at s execute the subroutine ACTIVE(M) in Phase 2. The robots will execute the subroutine LEARN_SIGNAL to learn the port p and γ which was transmitted by the robot connected through its child port by executing the subroutine SEND_SIGNAL. If $\gamma = 1111$, then the robots at s learn that the robot connected through its child port was a *master* robot, and it does not find any empty neighbor. Therefore, the *follower* robot at s is going to become *master* and will start searching for an empty neighbor starting from port *child*. Since 3-dedicated rounds are used in search of an empty neighbor by a *master* robot, the *active* robots observe how many times the event *decrease = true* in a 3-dedicated round occurs at s. If there are total j times *decrease = true* occurs then that signifies $s(child + 1), s(child+2), \ldots, s(child+j)$ are full. Accordingly, the robots at s update their $child = child + j + 1$.

2.2   Correctness and Analysis

The following lemma will be useful to show that a unique leader is elected in Phase 1 of any iteration.

Lemma 1. *In Phase 1 of any iteration of our algorithm, for $j \geq 1$, let U_j be the set of robots at s and U'_j be the set of robots at $s(\delta - 1)$ before the call of the subroutine PROCESSBIT(M, j) by every robot in $U_j \cup U'_j$. If $|U_j| > 1$ then, the following statements are true.*

1. *All the robots in U_j have engage = true, candidate = false, move = 0, election = false.*
2. *All the robots in U'_j have engage = false, candidate = false, move = 1, election = false.*
3. *Let $U_j(1)$ be the robots in U_j with $j + 1$-th bit at its reverse label 1 and $U_j(0) = U_j \setminus U_j(1)$. If $U_j(1) = U_j$ or $U_j(0) = U_j$, then, $U_{j+1} = U_j$ and $U'_{j+1} = U'_j$; otherwise, $U_{j+1} = U_j(0)$, $U'_{j+1} = U'_j \cup U_j(1)$.*

The lemma below proves that one robot is always elected as a leader in Phase 1.

Lemma 2. *If $m > 1$ robots are at s in the beginning of some iteration, then at the end of Phase 1 of that iteration, exactly one robot changes its status to either master or follower.*

The following two lemmas (Lemma 3 and Lemma 4) help us to show that some robots always find an empty neighbor for movement in Phase 2.

Lemma 3. *Before any iteration of the algorithm, if the number of robots at s is at least 2, then one of the following statements is true.*

1. *The master robot has an empty neighbor*
2. *one of the follower robot has an empty neighbor.*
3. *s has an empty neighbor.*

Lemma 4. *In any iteration of the algorithm, following statements are true.*

1. *At the beginning of the iteration, there is a simple path P from s to the node where the master node is present and the internal nodes of this path contains follower robots. Also, for any node w in this path, the next node w' is connected to w through port child of the robot present at w.*
2. *All the robots which are not in any node in P are idle.*
3. *If the number of robots at s is at least 2, then exactly one empty node becomes full and no full nodes become empty after the iteration.*

The following theorems ensure the termination of the algorithm after the k-th iteration.

Theorem 1. *Each robot becomes idle by the k-th iteration.*

Following lemmas and theorems give the time and memory complexity of the proposed algorithm.

Lemma 5. *The algorithm executes at most $k \log L$ 1-dedicated rounds.*

Lemma 6. *The total number of 2-dedicated round used is $O(k^2)$.*

Lemma 7. *The total number of 4-dedicated round is $O(k^2 \log \Delta)$.*

Lemma 8. *The total number of 5-dedicated round is $O(k^2)$.*

Lemma 9. *The total number of 3-dedicated round used across all the iterations is $O(\min\{k\Delta, k^2\})$.*

Lemma 10. *The total number of 0-dedicated round is at most k.*

Theorem 2. *The algorithm terminates in time $O(k \log L + k^2 \log \Delta)$ and each robot uses $O(\log L + \log \Delta)$ additional memory.*

We show that every robot's amount of additional memory in the algorithm is indeed asymptotically optimal. In [20], the authors proved $\Omega(\log \Delta)$ lower bound of memory requirement by any randomized algorithm for each robot for dispersion. The same proof gives $\Omega(\log \Delta)$ lower bound of memory for any deterministic algorithm. Hence it is enough to prove the lower bound $\Omega(\log L)$ which we do in the following theorem.

Theorem 3. *In the proposed communication model, dispersion can not be achieved by a set of mobile robots if the memory available to the robots is $o(\log L)$.*

3 Conclusion

This paper introduces an algorithm that achieved dispersion without communication between the robots using asymptotically optimal additional memory. Here, the task of dispersion is achieved under the assumption that the robots have access to two local information at any node: (1) whether the robot is alone at the node (2) whether the number of robots changes at the node compared to the previous round. A natural question arises: whether dispersion can be achieved with lesser local information. To be specific, it will be quite interesting to study whether the information of a robot is alone or not at a node is sufficient to achieve dispersion. Also, improving the time complexity of our algorithm in the proposed model or proving a lower bound of the same can be explored in the future. Another natural question is how to achieve dispersion when the robots starts from multiple source nodes in the graph.

References

1. Agarwalla, A., Augustine, J., Moses Jr, W.K., Madhav, S.K., Sridhar, A.K.: Deterministic dispersion of mobile robots in dynamic rings. In: ICDCN, pp. 19:1–19:4 (2018)
2. Alpern, S., Gal, S.: The Theory of Search Games and Rendezvous. International Series in Operations Research and Management Science, vol. 55. Kluwer, Netherlands (2003)
3. Augustine, J., Moses Jr, W. K.: Dispersion of mobile robots: a study of memory-time trade-offs. In: ICDCN, pp. 1:1–1:10 (2018)
4. Barrière, L., Flocchini, P., Barrameda, E.M., Santoro, N.: Uniform scattering of autonomous mobile robots in a grid. Int. J. Found. Comput. Sci. **22**(3), 679–697 (2011)
5. Bouchard, S., Dieudonné, Y., Pelc, A.: Want to gather? no need to chatter! In: PODC, pp. 253–262 (2020)
6. Brass, P., Cabrera-Mora, F., Gasparri, A., Xiao, J.: Multirobot tree and graph exploration. IEEE Trans. Robot. **27**(4), 707–717 (2011)
7. Brass, P., Vigan, I., Xu, N.: Improved analysis of a multirobot graph exploration strategy. In: ICARCV, pp. 1906–1910 (2014)
8. Broder, A.Z., Frieze, A.M., Shamir, E., Upfal, E.: Near-perfect token distribution. In: Kuich, W. (ed.) ICALP 1992. LNCS, vol. 623, pp. 308–317. Springer, Heidelberg (1992). https://doi.org/10.1007/3-540-55719-9_83
9. Das, A., Bose, K., Sau, B.: Memory optimal dispersion by anonymous mobile robots. In: Mudgal, A., Subramanian, C.R. (eds.) CALDAM 2021. LNCS, vol. 12601, pp. 426–439. Springer, Cham (2021). https://doi.org/10.1007/978-3-030-67899-9_34
10. Dereniowski, D., Disser, Y., Kosowski, A., Pajak, D., Uznanski, P.: Fast collaborative graph exploration. Inf. Comput. **243**, 37–49 (2015)
11. Elor, Y., Bruckstein, A.M.: Uniform multi-agent deployment on a ring. Theor. Comput. Sci. **412**(8–10), 783–795 (2011)
12. Ghosh, B., et al.: Tight analyses of two local load balancing algorithms. In: STOC, pp. 548–558 (1995)

13. auf der Heide, F.M., Oesterdiekhoff, B., Wanka, R., et al.: Strongly adaptive token distribution. Algorithmica **15**(5), 413–427 (1996)
14. Herley, K.T.: A note on the token distribution problem. Inf. Process. Lett. **38**(6), 329–334 (1991)
15. Kshemkalyani, A.D., Ali, F.: Efficient dispersion of mobile robots on graphs. In: ICDCN, pp. 218–227 (2019)
16. Kshemkalyani, A.D., Molla, A.R., Sharma, G.: Fast dispersion of mobile robots on arbitrary graphs. In: Dressler, F., Scheideler, C. (eds.) ALGOSENSORS 2019. LNCS, vol. 11931, pp. 23–40. Springer, Cham (2019). https://doi.org/10.1007/978-3-030-34405-4_2
17. Kshemkalyani, A.D., Molla, A.R., Sharma, G.: Dispersion of mobile robots on grids. In: Rahman, M.S., Sadakane, K., Sung, W.-K. (eds.) WALCOM 2020. LNCS, vol. 12049, pp. 183–197. Springer, Cham (2020). https://doi.org/10.1007/978-3-030-39881-1_16
18. Kshemkalyani, A.D., Molla, A.R., Sharma, G., Dispersion of mobile robots using global communication: Dispersion of mobile robots using global communication. J. Parallel Distrib. Comput. **161**, 100–117 (2022)
19. Kshemkalyani, A.D., Sharma, G.: Near-optimal dispersion on arbitrary anonymous graphs. CoRR abs/2106.03943 (2021)
20. Molla, A.R., Moses, W.K.: Dispersion of mobile robots: the power of randomness. In: Gopal, T.V., Watada, J. (eds.) TAMC 2019. LNCS, vol. 11436, pp. 481–500. Springer, Cham (2019). https://doi.org/10.1007/978-3-030-14812-6_30
21. Molla, A.R., Mondal, K., Moses, W.K.: Efficient dispersion on an anonymous ring in the presence of weak byzantine robots. In: Pinotti, C.M., Navarra, A., Bagchi, A. (eds.) ALGOSENSORS 2020. LNCS, vol. 12503, pp. 154–169. Springer, Cham (2020). https://doi.org/10.1007/978-3-030-62401-9_11
22. Molla, A.R., Mondal, K., Moses Jr. W.K.: Byzantine dispersion on graphs. In: IPDPS, pp. 942–951 (2021)
23. Pelc, A.: Deterministic rendezvous in networks: A comprehensive survey. Networks **59**(3), 331–347 (2012)
24. Shibata, M., Mega, T., Ooshita, F., Kakugawa, H., Masuzawa, T.: Uniform deployment of mobile agents in asynchronous rings. In: PODC, pp. 415–424 (2016)
25. Shintaku, T., Sudo, Y., Kakugawa, H., Masuzawa, T.: Efficient dispersion of mobile agents without global knowledge. In: Devismes, S., Mittal, N. (eds.) SSS 2020. LNCS, vol. 12514, pp. 280–294. Springer, Cham (2020). https://doi.org/10.1007/978-3-030-64348-5_22

Time Optimal Gathering of Myopic Robots on an Infinite Triangular Grid

Pritam Goswami$^{(\boxtimes)}$ (iD), Avisek Sharma (iD), Satakshi Ghosh (iD), and Buddhadeb Sau (iD)

Jadavpur University, 188, Raja S.C. Mallick Road, Kolkata 700032, India
{pritamgoswami.math.rs,aviseks.math.rs,
satakshighosh.math.rs,buddhadeb.sau}@jadavpuruniversity.in

Abstract. This work deals with the problem of gathering n oblivious mobile entities, called robots, at a point (not known beforehand) placed on an infinite triangular grid. The robots are considered to be myopic, i.e., robots have limited visibility. Earlier works of gathering mostly considered the robots either on a plane or on a circle or on a rectangular grid under both full and limited visibility. In the triangular grid, there are two works to the best of our knowledge. The first one is by Cicerone et al. [ICDCN'2021] on arbitrary pattern formation where full visibility is considered. The other one by Shibata et al. [IPDPS(W)'2021] which considers seven robots with 2-hop visibility that form a hexagon with one robot in the center of the hexagon in a collision-less environment under a fully synchronous scheduler.

In this work, we first show that gathering on a triangular grid with 1-hop vision of robots is not possible even under a fully synchronous scheduler if the robots do not agree on any axis. So one axis agreement has been considered in this work (i.e., the robots agree on a direction and its orientation). We have also shown that the lower bound for time is $\Omega(n)$ epochs when n number of robots are gathering on an infinite triangular grid. An algorithm is then presented where a swarm of n number of robots with 1-hop visibility can gather within $O(n)$ epochs under a semi-synchronous scheduler. So the algorithm presented here is time optimal.

Keywords: Gathering · Triangular grid · Swarm robot · Limited visibility

1 Introduction

1.1 Background and Motivation

A swarm of robots is a collection of a large number of robots with minimal capabilities. In the present research scenario on robotics, researchers are interested

P. Goswami, A. Sharma and S. Ghosh—Full time research scholars in Jadavpur University.

in these swarms of robots as these inexpensive robots can collectively do many tasks which earlier were done by single highly expensive robots with many capabilities. The wide application of these swarm of robots in different fields (e.g., search and rescue operations, military operations, cleaning of large surfaces, disaster management, etc.) grabbed the interest of researchers in the field of swarm robotics.

The goal of the researches in this field is to find out the minimum capabilities the robots need to have to do some specific tasks like *gathering* [10,12], *dispersion* [3], *arbitrary pattern formation* [5] etc. These capabilities are considered when modeling a robot for some specific task. Some of the well known robot models are $\mathcal{OBLOT}$, $\mathcal{FSTA}$, $\mathcal{FCOM}$ and $\mathcal{LUMI}$. In each of these models, the robots are *autonomous* (i.e. there is no central control for the robots), *anonymous* (i.e. the robots do not have any unique identifier), *homogeneous* (i.e. all the robots upon activation execute the same deterministic algorithm), *identical* (i.e. robots are physically identical). In the $\mathcal{OBLOT}$ model the robots are considered to be *silent*(i.e. robots do not have any direct means of communication) and oblivious (i.e. the robots do not have any persistent memory so that they can remember their earlier state). In $\mathcal{FSTA}$ model, the robots are *silent* but not *oblivious*. In $\mathcal{FCOM}$, the robots are not *silent* but are *oblivious*. And in $\mathcal{LUMI}$ model, the robots are neither *silent* nor *oblivious*. Their are many works that have been done considering these four robot models [4–6,11,12,16]. In this paper, we have considered the weakest $\mathcal{OBLOT}$ model, among these four models.

The activation time of the robots is a huge factor when it comes to the robots doing some tasks. A scheduler is said to be controlling the activation of robots. Mainly there are three types of schedulers that have been used vastly in literature. *Fully synchronous* (FSYNC) scheduler where the time is divided into global rounds of the same length and each robot is activated at the beginning of each round, *semi-synchronous* (SSYNC) scheduler where time is divided into equal-length rounds but all robots may not be activated at the beginning of each round and *asynchronous* (ASYNC) scheduler where any robot can get activated any time as there is no sense of global rounds. Among these, FSYNC and SSYNC schedulers are considered to be less practical than ASYNC scheduler. Still, it has been used in many works [16] as providing algorithms for a more general and more realistic ASYNC scheduler is not always easy. In this paper, we have considered the SSYNC scheduler.

Vision is another important capability that robots have. The vision of a robot acquires information about the positions of other robots in the environment. A robot can have either full or restricted visibility. In [4,8,10,11,15] authors have modeled the robots to have infinite or full vision. The biggest drawback of full vision is that it is not possible in practical applications due to hardware limitations. So in [2,12,18], authors considered *limited visibility*. A robot with limited visibility is called a myopic robot. A myopic robot on the plane is assumed to see only up to a certain distance called *visibility range*. In graphs though, the vision of a robot is assumed to be all the vertices within a certain hop from the vertex on which the robot is located. Other than *limited vision*, robots can have *obstructed vision* where even if the vision of a robot is infinite it might get obstructed by other robots in front of it. This model is also more practical than using point robots that can see through other robots. So in [6], obstructed vision model has been considered.

In this paper, we are interested in the problem of *gathering*. The *gathering problem* requires a swarm of robots that are placed either on a plane or on a graph, to move to a single point that is not known to the robots a priori (Ideal Gathering Configuration). In this work, we have considered the robots on an infinite triangular grid having the least possible vision of 1-hop under the SSYNC scheduler. Our solution also works under obstructed vision model as a robot needs no information about other robots who are not directly adjacent to it.

Earlier Gathering problem has been considered under limited vision on the plane [12], but movements of robots are not restricted in the plane as there are infinitely many paths between any two points on a plane. So it would have been interesting to consider this problem on discrete terrain where the movement of a robot is restricted. And since grid network has wide application in various fields it was natural to study this problem under different kinds of grids. Now an infinite regular tessellation grid is one of the 3 types of infinite regular grids namely, infinite square grid, infinite triangular grid, and infinite hexagonal grid [13]. Our goal is to solve this problem for any infinite regular tessellation grid with the least possible vision for a robot. In [18] a solution has already been provided by the authors where the terrain is an infinite square grid embedded on a plane and the robots can either move diagonally from one grid point to another or moves along the edges of the grid. But in their work, the robots can see up to a distance of 2 units (each edge length of the grid is considered to be one unit). So in this paper, by providing a solution for the infinite triangular grid, where a robot can see only up to a unit of distance, we reached a little closer to our goal of providing a solution for this problem for any infinite regular tessellation grid. Furthermore, we also drew motivation for framing this problem for an infinite triangular grid from the application perspective of it. In [19], authors have shown that for some robots with sensors the coverage will be maximum if the robots are forming a triangular grid and the length of each edge is $\sqrt{3}s$ where s is the sensing radius for the sensors on the robots. So coverage wise triangular grid is better than any other regular tessellation grid. For these specific reasons, we have considered this problem on this specific terrain.

The literature on this problem is very rich. In the following subsection, we have provided a glimpse of the rich literature that lead us to write this paper.

1.2   Earlier Works

In this paper, we are specifically focused on the problem of *gathering*. Earlier the problem was mainly studied considering the robots on a plane [1,4]. But currently, many researchers have been interested in gathering on the discrete environment as well, [10,11,14,15] as movements in graphs become more restricted which is practical in real-life scenarios. In [15], Klasing et al. studied the gathering problem on a ring and proved that it is impossible to gather on a ring without multiplicity detection. In [10], D'Angelo et al. first characterized the problem of gathering on a tree and finite grid. He has proved that gathering even with global-strong multiplicity detection is impossible if the configuration is periodic or, symmetric with the line of symmetry passing through the edges of the grid.

Another capability of these robots is their vision. After activation, a robot takes a snapshot of its surroundings to collect information about the positions of the other robots. Gathering has been studied extensively where robots are assumed to have full or infinite visibility [1, 4, 8–11, 14, 15]. But in the application, it is impossible due to hardware limitations. So, in [2] Ando et al. provided an algorithm where indistinguishable robots with a limited vision on a plane without any common coordinate system converge to a point under a semi-synchronous scheduler. In [12] Flocchini et al. have produced a procedure that guides robots with a limited vision on a plane to gather at a single point in finite time. In their work, they have assumed the robots have agreement on the direction and orientation of the axes under an asynchronous scheduler. In [17], the authors have shown that gathering is possible by robots on a circle with agreement on the clockwise direction even if a robot can not see the location at an angle π from it, under a semi-synchronous scheduler. Gathering under limited visibility where the robots are placed in a discrete environment has been recently studied by the authors in [18] where algorithms have been provided with both one and two-axis agreement under viewing range 2 and 3 simultaneously and square connectivity range $\sqrt{2}$ under asynchronous scheduler.

1.3 Our Contribution

Recently, in [7], the authors have provided an algorithm for robots on a triangular grid to form any arbitrary pattern from any asymmetric initial configuration. In their work, they have assumed that the target configuration can have multiplicities also. So the algorithm provided in [7] can be used for gathering where the target configuration contains only one location for each robot. But in their work, they assumed the robots have full visibility which is impractical as in application robots can't have an infinite vision. Also, their algorithm works only when the initial configuration is asymmetric.

Considering limited vision this problem has earlier been done in the euclidean plane in [12]. But in the plane, the movement of a robot is not at all restricted as there are infinitely many paths between any two points on the plane. Also, the authors have considered two axis agreement which makes the robot more powerful which is against the motivation of research on swarm robot algorithms where we need to find the minimum capabilities for the robots to do a specific task.

In [18], the authors have presented a technique for gathering under limited visibility under an infinite rectangular grid. In their work, they have presented two algorithms. In the first algorithm, they have considered two axis agreement and a vision of 2× edge length of the grid. And in the second algorithm considering one axis agreement and vision of 3× edge length of the grid for any robot they have provided an algorithm where the robots may not gather but will surely be on a horizontal segment of unit length (Relaxed Gathering Configuration). Both of these algorithms are not collision-free. Also, observe that none of their algorithms are able to gather if the visibility for each robot is 1× edge length of the grid.

In our work, we have given a characterization of the gathering problem of myopic robots with 1-hop vision on a triangular grid with any connected initial configuration. We have shown that myopic robots with 1-hop visibility on an infinite triangular grid which agree on the direction of both axis can not gather even under a fully synchronous scheduler if they do not agree on the orientation of any axis. So assuming that myopic robots on an infinite triangular grid have 1-hop (i.e. 1× length of an edge of the triangular grid) visibility and they agree on the direction and orientation of any one of the three lines that generate the infinite triangular grid, we have provided an algorithm 1-HOP 1-AXIS GATHER (Algorithm 1) which gathers these robots on a single grid point within $O(n)$ epochs under semi-synchronous scheduler where n is the number of myopic robots on the grid. Where one epoch is a time interval such that within which each robot has been activated at least once. We have also shown that any gathering algorithm on a triangular grid must take $\Omega(n)$ epochs where n is the number of robots placed on the infinite triangular grid. Therefore the algorithm we presented in this paper is asymptotically time optimal.

In the following Table 1 we have compared our work with the works in [7, 12, 18].

Table 1. Comparison table

SL. No.	Algorithm	Axis agreement	Visibility	Ideal/Relaxed gathering
1	Algorithm in [7]	No axis agreement	Full visibility	Ideal
2	Algorithm in [12]	Two axis	$V \in \mathbb{R}(> 0)$	Ideal
3	1st Algorithm in [18]	Two axis	2× edge length	Ideal
4	2nd Algorithm in [18]	One axis	3× edge length	Relaxed
5	1-HOP 1-AXIS GATHER(**This paper**)	One axis	1× edge length	Ideal

2 Models and Definitions

2.1 Model

An infinite triangular grid $\mathcal{G}$ is a geometric graph where each vertex v is placed on a plane and has exactly six adjacent vertices and any induced sub-graph K_3

forms an equilateral triangle. Let $R = \{r_1, r_2, r_3, \ldots r_n\}$ be n robots placed on the vertices of an infinite triangular grid $\mathcal{G}$.

Robot Model: The robots are considered to be-
   autonomous: there is no centralized control.
   anonymous: robots do not have any unique identifier (ID).
   homogeneous: robots execute same deterministic algorithm.
   identical: robots are identical by their physical appearance.

The robots are placed on the vertices of an infinite triangular grid $\mathcal{G}$ as a point. The robots do not have any multiplicity detection ability i.e., a robot can not decide if a vertex contains more than one robot or not. The robots do not agree on some global coordinate system, but each robot has its own local coordinate system with itself at the origin and handedness. However, the robots may agree on the direction and orientation of the axes. Based on that we consider the following model.

One Axis Agreement Model: In the one axis agreement model all robots agree on the direction and orientation of any specific axis. Note that any vertex v of the infinite triangular grid $\mathcal{G}$ is at the intersection of three types of lines. In this work, the robots will agree on the orientation and direction of any one of these three types of lines and consider it as its y-axis. Note that in this model the robots have a common notion of up and down but not about left or right.

As an input, a robot takes a snapshot after waking. This snapshot contains the position of other robots on $\mathcal{G}$ according to the local coordinates of the robot. In a realistic setting due to limitations of hardware, a robot might not see all of the grid points in a snapshot. So to limit the visibility of the robots we have considered the following visibility model.

Visibility: In k-hop visibility model, each robot r can see all the grid points which are at most at a k-hop distance from r. In this paper, the robots are considered to have 1-hop visibility (i.e. $k = 1$). Note that when $k = 1$, a robot placed on a vertex v of the infinite triangular grid $\mathcal{G}$ can only see the adjacent six vertices of v.

The robots operate in *LOOK-COMPUTE-MOVE (LCM)* cycle. In each cycle a previously inactive or idle robot wakes up and does the following steps:

LOOK: In this step after waking a robot placed on $u \in V$ takes a snapshot of the current configuration visible to it as an input. In this step, a robot gets the positions of other robots expressed under its local coordinate system.

COMPUTE: In this step a robot computes a destination point x adjacent to its current position, where $x \in V$ according to some deterministic algorithm with the previously obtained snapshot as input.

MOVE: After determining a destination point $x \in V$ in the previous step the robot now moves to x through the edge $ux \in E$. Note that if $x = u$ then the robot does not move.

After completing one *LCM* cycle a robot becomes inactive and again wakes up after a finite but unpredictable number of rounds and executes the *LCM* cycle again.

Scheduler Model: Based on the activation and timing of the robots there are mainly three types of schedulers in the literature,

Fully Synchronous: In the case of a fully synchronous (FSYNC) scheduler time can be divided logically into global rounds where the duration of each round and each step of each round is the same. Also, each robot becomes active at the start of each round (i.e. the set of the active robot at the beginning of each round is the whole of R).

Semi-synchronous: A semi-synchronous (SSYNC) scheduler is a more general version of a fully synchronous scheduler. In the case of a semi-synchronous scheduler, the set of active robots at the beginning of a round can be a proper subset of R. i.e. all the robots might not get activated at the beginning of a round. However, every robot is activated infinitely often.

Asynchronous: An Asynchronous (ASYNC) scheduler is the most general model. Here a robot gets activated independently and also executes the *LCM* cycles independently. The amount of time spent in each cycle and the inactive phase may be different for each robot and also for the same robot in two different cycles. This amount of time is finite but unbounded and also unpredictable. Hence there is no common notion of time. Moreover, a robot with delayed computation may compute at a time when other robots have already moved and changed the configuration. Thus the robot with delayed computation now computes with an obsolete configuration as input.

In this paper, we have considered the scheduler to be semi-synchronous. The scheduler that controls the time and activation of the robots can be thought of as an adversary. Observe that the semi-synchronous scheduler can be controlled as a fully synchronous scheduler as SSYNC is more general than FSYNC but not vice-versa. Also, an adversary can decide the local coordinate system of a robot (obeying the agreement rules of axes and orientation). However, after deciding on the coordinate system of a robot it can not be changed further.

2.2 Notations and Definitions

Definition 1 (Infinite Triangular Grid). *An infinite triangular grid $\mathcal{G}$ is an infinite geometric graph $G = (V, E)$, where the vertices are placed on $\mathbb{R}^2$ having coordinates $\{(k, \frac{\sqrt{3}}{2}i) : k \in \mathbb{Z}, i \in 2\mathbb{Z}\} \cup \{(k + \frac{1}{2}, \frac{\sqrt{3}}{2}i) : k \in \mathbb{Z}, i \in 2\mathbb{Z} + 1\}$ and two vertices are adjacent if the euclidean distance between them is 1 unit.*

It is to be noted that robots do not have access to this coordinates. This coordinates are used simply for describing the infinite triangular grid $\mathcal{G}$.

Definition 2 (Configuration). *A configuration formed by a set of robots R, denoted as $\mathcal{C}_R$ (or, simply $\mathcal{C}$) is the pair $(\mathcal{G}, f)$ where, f is a map from V to $\{0, 1\}$. For $v \in V$, $f(v) = 1$ if and only if there is at least one robot on the vertex v.*

Definition 3 (Visibility Graph). *A visibility graph $G_{\mathcal{C}}$ for a configuration $\mathcal{C} = (\mathcal{G}, f)$ is the sub graph of $\mathcal{G}$ induced by set of vertices $\{v \in V : f(v) = 1\}$.*

It is not hard to produce a configuration $\mathcal{C}$ with disconnected $G_{\mathcal{C}}$, such that there exists no deterministic algorithm which can gather a set of robots starting from $\mathcal{C}$. So in this work, it is assumed that initially the visibility graph is connected and any algorithm that solves the gathering problem should maintain this connectivity during its complete execution.

Definition 4 (Extreme). *A robot r is said to be an **extreme** robot if the following conditions hold in its visibility:*

1. *There is no other robot on the positive y-axis of r.*
2. *Either left or right open half of r is empty.*

2.3 Problem Definition

Suppose, a swarm of n robots is placed on the grid points of an infinite triangular grid $\mathcal{G}$. The gathering problem requires devising an algorithm such that after some finite time all robots assemble at exactly one grid point and stay forever gathered at that grid point.

3 Impossibility Result

The proof of the impossibility result stated in Theorem 1 is omitted here due to page constraint. In Fig. 1 the reasoning is discussed in brief. Check the full version of the paper for the detailed discussion.

Theorem 1. *Gathering in a triangular grid is impossible without agreement on the orientation of any axis even when agreement on direction is present and under a fully synchronous scheduler and 1-hop visibility.*

Due to Theorem 1 we have considered one axis agreement model and devised an algorithm considering 1-hop vision under semi-synchronous scheduler.

4 Gathering Algorithm

In this section, an algorithm 1-HOP 1-AXIS GATHER (Algorithm 1) is provided that will work for a swarm of n myopic robots with one axis agreement and 1-hop visibility under a semi-synchronous scheduler. Note that under one axis agreement a robot can divide the grids into two halves based on the agreed line as the y-axis. An **extreme** robot r will always have either left or right open half

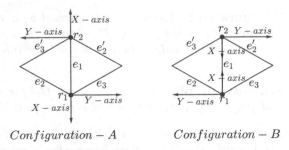

$Configuration - A$ $Configuration - B$

Fig. 1. In the diagram the robots agree on direction of both the axes but do not agree on the orientation of the axes. Now, the initial Configuration-A transforms into Configuration-B after a round and similarly Configuration-B transforms into Configuration-A after a round creating a deadlock situation.

empty. Thus it is easy to see that when any one of the open halves is non-empty and r is on a grid point v, two adjacent grid points of v on the empty open half and another adjacent grid point of v on y-axis and above r will always be empty. In this situation, r can uniquely identify the remaining three adjacent grid points of v (one on the y-axis and below r and the remaining two are on the non-empty half) based on the different values of their $y - coordinates$. So an **extreme** robot can uniquely name them as v_1, v_2 and v_3 such that $y - coordinate$ of v_i is less than $y - coordinate$ of v_{i+1} and $i \in \{1, 2\}$ (Fig. 2). We denote position v_j of an **extreme** robot r as $v_j(r)$ where $j \in \{1, 2, 3\}$. Note that for a non-**extreme** robot r, there are two $v_2(r)$ and two $v_3(r)$ positions as r have either both open halves empty or both open halves non empty. In the algorithm 1-HOP 1-AXIS GATHER (1), an **extreme** robot r moves to $v_1(r)$ if there is a robot on $v_1(r)$ and there is no robot on $v_3(r)$. r does not move when there is only a robot on $v_3(r)$ or there are robots only on $v_3(r)$ and $v_1(r)$. In the other remaining cases, if r sees at least one robot on the adjacent vertices it moves to $v_2(r)$. An **extreme** robot terminates when it does not see any other robot on the adjacent vertices.

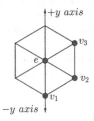

Fig. 2. e is an **extreme** robot it can uniquely identify the positions of v_1, v_2 and v_3 if it sees right or left open half non empty.

If r is not an **extreme** robot, then it only moves if there is no robot with $y - coordinate$ greater than zero within its vision and there are two robots on both of its $v_2(r)$ positions. In this scenario the robot r moves to $v_1(r)$.

In Fig. 3 we have shown all possible views when a robot r moves and in which direction it moves. In Fig. 3 suppose a robot r is placed on the node denoted by a black solid circle. The grid points that are encircled are occupied by other robots. For all the views of r in $View - I$, r moves to $v_1(r)$ and for all the views of r in $View - II$, r moves to $v_2(r)$.

Algorithm 1: 1-HOP 1-AXIS GATHER (for a robot r)

Data: Position of the robots on the adjacent grid points of r on triangular grid
  $\mathcal{G}$.
Result: A vertex on $\mathcal{G}$ adjacent to r, as destination point of r.
if *r is extreme* **then**
> **if** *There is no robot on the adjacent grid points* **then**
>> terminate;
>
> **else if** *There is a robot only on $v_3(r)$ or there are robots only on both $v_1(r)$*
>   *and $v_3(r)$* **then**
>> do not move;
>
> **else if** *There is a robot on $v_1(r)$ and no robot on $v_3(r)$* **then**
>> move to $v_1(r)$;
>
> **else**
>> move to $v_2(r)$;

else
> **if** *There is a robot on both $v_2(r)$ and no robot on the vertices with*
>   *$y - coordinate > 0$* **then**
>> move to $v_1(r)$;
>
> **else**
>> do not move;

4.1 Correctness Results:

The intuition of the Algorithm 1 is that the width of the configuration decreases while the visibility graph stays connected by the movement of the robots. The following results will make this intuition more concrete. Before that let us have some definitions which will be needed in the proof of the results.

Definition 5 (Layer). *Let H be a straight line perpendicular to the agreed direction of $y-axis$ such that there is at least one robot on some grid points on H, then H is called a layer.*

Definition 6 (Top most layer, H_t). *H_t or top most layer of a configuration $\mathcal{C}$ is a layer such that there is no layer above it.*

Definition 7 (Vertical line, L_v). *Let L_v be a line that is parallel to the agreed direction of the y-axis such that there is at least one robot on some grid point on L_v, then L_v is called a vertical line.*

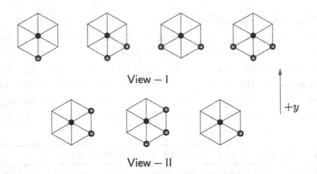

Fig. 3. All possible views of a robot r placed on a node indicated by a black solid circle when r decides to move. Encircled point represents a robot occupied node For all views in $View - I$, r moves to $v_1(r)$ position and for all views in $View - II$, r moves to $v_2(r)$ position.

Definition 8 (Left edge, e_l). *Left edge of a configuration C or, e_l is the vertical line such that there is no other vertical line on the left of e_l.*

Definition 9 (Right edge, e_r). *Right edge of a configuration C or, e_r is the vertical line such that there is no other vertical line on the right of e_r.*

Definition 10 (Width of a configuration C). *Width of a configuration $w(C)$ is defined as the distance between e_l and e_r.*

Definition 11 (Depth of a vertical line L_v). *Depth of a vertical line L_v is defined as the distance between the layers H_t and the layer on which the lowest robot on L_v is located. We denote the depth of line L_v as $d(L_v)$.*

Figure 4 shows all the entities of the above definitions. A brief overview of the correctness proof is given below along with the statements of the results. Detailed proofs of all the following results are in the full version of the paper due to page constraints.

Overview of the Correctness Proof: In Lemma 1, we have proved that the visibility graph will remain connected throughout the execution of the algorithm. It is necessary to prove this as otherwise, the robots may gather in several clusters on the infinite triangular grid. Then we have shown that in Lemma 6 the width of the configuration will decrease in finite time. Now when the width of the configuration becomes one then there are only two vertical lines that contain robots. These lines are left edge e_l and right edge e_r. Now in this scenario from Lemma 2 the robots on the topmost layer will always move below and the depth of both e_l and e_r never increases (by Lemma 5). So the depth of both the right and left edge now decreases in each epoch. Hence within finite time, the depth will also become one for either e_l or e_r. And in this scenario when the topmost layer shifts down again, all the robots gather at one grid vertex (Theorem 2).

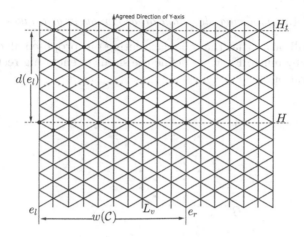

Fig. 4. diagram of a configuration C mentioning layer (H), top most layer (H_t), vertical line (L_v), left edge (e_l), right edge (e_r), width of the C $(w(C))$ and depth of the vertical line e_l $(d(e_l))$.

Lemma 1. *If at the start of some round the configuration formed by the robots has connected visibility graph then after execution of Algorithm 1 at the end of that round the visibility graph of the configuration remains connected.*

Lemma 2. H_t *of the configuration C, always shift down in one epoch until the gathering is complete.*

Lemma 3. *Robots on e_l or e_r which are not **extreme** do not move.*

Lemma 4. *A robot r which is lowest on e_l or e_r never moves down to $v_1(r)$.*

Lemma 5. *Neither $d(e_l)$ nor $d(e_r)$ ever increase as long as the position of the corresponding vertical line is same.*

Lemma 6. *If $w(C) > 0$ at a round t_0 then there exists a round $t > t_0$ such that $w(C)$ decreases.*

Theorem 2. *Algorithm 1-hop 1-axis Gather guarantees that there exists a round $t > 0$ such that a swarm of n myopic robots on an infinite triangular grid G with 1-hop visibility and one axis agreement will always gather after completion of round t under semi-synchronous scheduler starting from any initial configuration C for which visibility graph G_C is connected.*

4.2 Complexity Analysis

First we observe that it will take at least $\Omega(n)$ epochs to gather n number of robots. One can check that it is the case when all robots are on a single vertical line. We state this in the following Theorem 3. For the detailed calculations see the full version of the paper.

Theorem 3. *Any gathering algorithm on a triangular grid takes $\Omega(n)$ epoch.*

Now we shall prove that the robots executing our proposed algorithm do not go downwards by much. First, we define the smallest enclosing rectangle for the initial configuration.

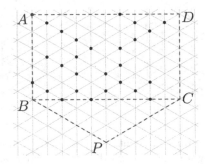

Fig. 5. $ABCD$, smallest enclosing rectangle

Definition 12 ($\mathcal{SER}$). *A rectangle $\mathcal{R} = ABCD$ is said to be the smallest enclosing rectangle ($\mathcal{SER}$) (Fig. 5) of the initial configuration if it is the smallest in dimension satisfying the following:*

1. *All robots in the initial configuration are inside $\mathcal{R}$*
2. *All vertices of $ABCD$ are on some grid points*
3. *AB and CD side is parallel to the axis agreed by all the robots*
4. *BC is the lower side of the rectangle.*

Next, we define a polygon that shall contain all the robots throughout the algorithm.

Definition 13 (Bounding Polygon). *Let $\mathcal{R} = ABCD$ be the $\mathcal{SER}$ of the initial configuration. Let P the point below BC line such that $\angle CBP = \angle BCP = \pi/6$. Then the polygon $\mathcal{P} = ABPCDA$ is said to be the Bounding Polygon.*

We show that no robot executing Algorithm 1 ever steps out of the bounding polygon (Lemma 7). Using Lemma 7, Theorem 4 proves that Algorithm 1 terminates within $O(n)$ epochs. The proofs are in the appendix due to page limitations.

Lemma 7. *No robot executing the Algorithm 1 ever steps out of the bounding polygon.*

Theorem 4. *The algorithm 1-hop 1-axis Gather takes at most $O(n)$ epochs to gather all the robots.*

5   Conclusion

Gathering is a classical problem in the field of swarm robotics. The literature on the gathering problem is vast as it can be considered under many different robot models, scheduler models, and environments. Limited vision is very practical when it comes to robot models. To practically implement any algorithm considering a robot swarm having full visibility is impossible. So, we have to transfer the research interest towards providing algorithms that work under limited visibility also. This paper is one achievement towards that goal.

In this paper, we have done a characterization of gathering on an infinite triangular grid by showing that it would not be possible to gather from any initial configuration to a point on the grid if the myopic robots having a vision of 1-hop do not have any axis agreement even under the FSYNC scheduler. Thus, considering one axis agreement we have provided an algorithm that gathers n myopic robots with a vision of 1-hop under the SSYNC scheduler within $O(n)$ epochs. We have also shown that the lower bound of time for gathering n robots on an infinite triangular grid is $\Omega(n)$. So our algorithm is time optimal.

For an immediate course of future research, one can think of solving the gathering problem by considering myopic robots on an infinite triangular grid making the algorithm collision-free (where no collision occurs except at the vertex of gathering) and under an asynchronous scheduler. Another interesting work would be to find out if there is any class of configurations for which gathering on a triangular grid will be solvable even without one axis agreement.

Acknowledgement. First and second Authors are supported by UGC, the Government of India. The third author is supported by the West Bengal State government Fellowship Scheme.

References

1. Agmon, N., Peleg, D.: Fault-tolerant gathering algorithms for autonomous mobile robots. SIAM J. Comput. **36**(1), 56–82 (2006). https://doi.org/10.1137/050645221
2. Ando, H., Oasa, Y., Suzuki, I., Yamashita, M.: Distributed memoryless point convergence algorithm for mobile robots with limited visibility. IEEE Trans. Rob. Autom. **15**(5), 818–828 (1999). https://doi.org/10.1109/70.795787
3. Augustine, J., Jr., W.K.M.: Dispersion of mobile robots: a study of memory-time trade-offs. In: Bellavista, P., Garg, V.K. (eds.) Proceedings of the 19th International Conference on Distributed Computing and Networking, ICDCN 2018, Varanasi, India, 4–7 January 2018, pp. 1:1–1:10. ACM (2018). https://doi.org/10.1145/3154273.3154293
4. Bhagat, S., Gan Chaudhuri, S., Mukhopadhyaya, K.: Fault-tolerant gathering of asynchronous oblivious mobile robots under one-axis agreement. In: Rahman, M.S., Tomita, E. (eds.) WALCOM 2015. LNCS, vol. 8973, pp. 149–160. Springer, Cham (2015). https://doi.org/10.1007/978-3-319-15612-5_14
5. Bose, K., Adhikary, R., Kundu, M.K., Sau, B.: Arbitrary pattern formation on infinite grid by asynchronous oblivious robots. Theor. Comput. Sci. **815**, 213–227 (2020). https://doi.org/10.1016/j.tcs.2020.02.016

6. Bose, K., Kundu, M.K., Adhikary, R., Sau, B.: Arbitrary pattern formation by asynchronous opaque robots with lights. Theor. Comput. Sci. **849**, 138–158 (2021). https://doi.org/10.1016/j.tcs.2020.10.015

7. Cicerone, S., Fonso, A.D., Stefano, G.D., Navarra, A.: Arbitrary pattern formation on infinite regular tessellation graphs. In: ICDCN'21: International Conference on Distributed Computing and Networking, Virtual Event, Nara, Japan, 5–8 January 2021, pp. 56–65. ACM (2021). https://doi.org/10.1145/3427796.3427833

8. Cicerone, S., Di Stefano, G., Navarra, A.: Gathering of robots on meeting-points: feasibility and optimal resolution algorithms. Distrib. Comput. **31**(1), 1–50 (2017). https://doi.org/10.1007/s00446-017-0293-3

9. Cicerone, S., Di Stefano, G., Navarra, A.: Gathering synchronous robots in graphs: from general properties to dense and symmetric topologies. In: Censor-Hillel, K., Flammini, M. (eds.) SIROCCO 2019. LNCS, vol. 11639, pp. 170–184. Springer, Cham (2019). https://doi.org/10.1007/978-3-030-24922-9_12

10. D'Angelo, G., Stefano, G.D., Klasing, R., Navarra, A.: Gathering of robots on anonymous grids and trees without multiplicity detection. Theor. Comput. Sci. **610**, 158–168 (2016). https://doi.org/10.1016/j.tcs.2014.06.045

11. D'Angelo, G., Stefano, G.D., Navarra, A.: Gathering six oblivious robots on anonymous symmetric rings. J. Discrete Algorithms **26**, 16–27 (2014). https://doi.org/10.1016/j.jda.2013.09.006

12. Flocchini, P., Prencipe, G., Santoro, N., Widmayer, P.: Gathering of asynchronous robots with limited visibility. Theoret. Comput. Sci. **337**(1), 147–168 (2005). https://doi.org/10.1016/j.tcs.2005.01.001

13. Grunbaum, B., Shephard, G.C.: Tilings and Patterns, New York (1987)

14. Klasing, R., Kosowski, A., Navarra, A.: Taking advantage of symmetries: gathering of many asynchronous oblivious robots on a ring. Theor. Comput. Sci. **411**(34–36), 3235–3246 (2010). https://doi.org/10.1016/j.tcs.2010.05.020

15. Klasing, R., Markou, E., Pelc, A.: Gathering asynchronous oblivious mobile robots in a ring. Theor. Comput. Sci. **390**(1), 27–39 (2008). https://doi.org/10.1016/j.tcs.2007.09.032

16. Luna, G.A.D., Flocchini, P., Prencipe, G., Santoro, N.: Black hole search in dynamic rings. In: 41st IEEE International Conference on Distributed Computing Systems, ICDCS 2021, Washington DC, USA, 7–10 July 2021, pp. 987–997. IEEE (2021). https://doi.org/10.1109/ICDCS51616.2021.00098

17. Luna, G.A.D., Uehara, R., Viglietta, G., Yamauchi, Y.: Gathering on a circle with limited visibility by anonymous oblivious robots. In: Attiya, H. (ed.) 34th International Symposium on Distributed Computing, DISC 2020, 12–16 October 2020, Virtual Conference. LIPIcs, vol. 179, pp. 12:1–12:17. Schloss Dagstuhl - Leibniz-Zentrum für Informatik (2020). https://doi.org/10.4230/LIPIcs.DISC.2020.12

18. Poudel, P., Sharma, G.: Time-optimal gathering under limited visibility with one-axis agreement. Information **12**(11), 448 (2021). https://doi.org/10.3390/info12110448

19. Zhang, H., Hou, J.C.: Maintaining sensing coverage and connectivity in large sensor networks. Ad Hoc Sens. Wirel. Networks **1**(1–2), 89–124 (2005). http://www.oldcitypublishing.com/journals/ahswn-home/ahswn-issue-contents/ahswn-volume-1-number-1-2-2005/ahswn-1-1-2-p-89-124/

Card-Based ZKP Protocol for Nurimisaki

Léo Robert[1,2](✉) ⓘ, Daiki Miyahara[3,4] ⓘ, Pascal Lafourcade[1,2] ⓘ,
and Takaaki Mizuki[4,5] ⓘ

[1] Université Clermont-Auvergne, CNRS, Mines de Saint-Étienne,
Saint-Étienne, France
{leo.robert,pascal.lafourcade}@uca.fr
[2] LIMOS, 63000 Clermont-Ferrand, France
[3] The University of Electro-Communications, Tokyo, Japan
[4] National Institute of Advanced Industrial Science and Technology, Tokyo, Japan
[5] Cyberscience Center, Tohoku University, Sendai, Japan

Abstract. Proving to someone else the knowledge of a secret without
revealing any of its information is an interesting feature in cryptography.
The best solution to solve this problem is a *Zero-Knowledge Proof* (ZKP)
protocol.

Nurimisaki is a Nikoli puzzle. The goal of this game is to draw a kind
of abstract painting ("Nuri") that represents the sea with some capes
("Misaki") of an island (represented by white cells). For this, the player
has to fulfill cells of a grid in black (representing the sea) in order to draw
some capes while respecting some simple rules. One of the specificity of
the rules of this game is that the cells called "Misaki" can only have one
white neighbour and all white cells need to be connected. In 2020, this
puzzle has been proven to be NP-complete.

Using a deck of cards, we propose a physical ZKP protocol to prove
that a player knows a solution of a Nurimisaki grid without revealing
any information about the solution.

Keywords: Zero-knowledge proof · Pencil Puzzle · Card-based
cryptography · Nurimisaki

1 Introduction

The democratization of computers and network systems has fuelled the virtu-
alization of interactions and processes such as communication, payments, and
elections. Proving the knowledge of some secret without revealing any bit of
information from that secret is crucial in our today's society. This issue can be
applied to numerous contexts.

We thank the anonymous referees, whose comments have helped us to improve the
presentation of the paper. This work was supported in part by JSPS KAKENHI Grant
Numbers JP18H05289 and JP21K11881. This study was partially supported by the
French ANR project ANR-18-CE39-0019 (MobiS5).

For instance, a client would like to connect to a server via a password without revealing the password. Another example is database management, where an entity could ask if a piece of information is in a database without asking for factual data. A third example can be given in the electronic voting system where the voters want to be sure that the ballots are correctly mixed (without revealing how the mix was done).

A cryptographic tool exists for all the previous examples, called a *Zero-Knowledge Proof* (ZKP) protocol. It enables a prover P to convince a verifier V that P knows a secret s without revealing anything other than it. A ZKP protocol must verify the following three properties:

- **Completeness:** If P knows s then the protocol ends without aborting (meaning that V is convinced that P has s);
- **Soundness:** If P does not have s then V will detect it;
- **Zero-Knowledge:** V learns nothing about s.

In practice, ZKP protocols are typically executed by computers. However, their understanding is difficult for the uninitiated. We take a more direct approach to the notion of ZKP and construct a protocol using physical objects like playing cards and envelopes. It allows us to present the notion of ZKP protocols without deep mathematical backgrounds and also to extend the existing literature.

The first physical ZKP protocol [7] for a Sudoku grid was constructed using a deck of cards. Since this novel protocol was devised, several teams in the world have proposed physical ZKP protocols using a deck of cards for pencil puzzles, such as Sudoku [19,25], Akari [1], Takuzu [1], Kakuro [1,13], KenKen [1], Makaro [2], Norinori [5], Slitherlink [11], Suguru [16], Nurikabe [17], Ripple Effect [22], Numberlink [20], Bridges [21], Cryptarithmetic [8], Shikaku [23], and Nonogram [3,18].

Why shall we propose a new card-based ZKP protocol for another Nikoli puzzle? For us, it is similar to the question: Why shall we prove that a puzzle is NP-complete? People want to know if a puzzle is NP-complete in order to know if the puzzle is difficult or not for a computer to solve it. Card-based ZKP protocols are quite similar; once a puzzle is shown to be NP-complete, a natural question is: Can we design a physical ZKP protocol? This is an intellectual challenge on the puzzle. Moreover, each puzzle has different rules and specificity, which force us to imagine new physical ZKP techniques. For instance, consider a Nikoli puzzle, Nurimisaki, which we will deal with in this paper; then, its rules combine for the first time some connectivity, neighbourhood restriction, and straight line with counting, as seen later. A previous work [24] (in Japanese, unpublished) proposed a card-based ZKP protocol for Nurimisaki. Yet, the protocol is not optimal since it prepares another grid to verify the rules (so the number of cards is large). Moreover, elaborate but complex techniques are used (*e.g.*, using another grid to represent the in-spanning-tree of P's solution). In contrast, our protocol has a more direct approach with closer interaction to the real game. Before giving our contributions, let us define the rules of the Nurimisaki puzzle.

Fig. 1. Nurimisaki example (left) with its solution (right).

Nurimisaki Rules. Figure 1 shows a puzzle instance of Nurimisaki. The goal for Nurimisaki puzzle is to color in black some cells on the grid, under the following rules:

1. A cell with a circle is called a "Misaki". A Misaki has only one cell of its neighbours (vertically or horizontally) remaining white and the rest black.
2. The number written in a Misaki cell indicates the number of white cells in straight line from the Misaki. If there is no number, any number of white cells is allowed.
3. White cells without a circle cannot be a Misaki.
4. A 2 × 2 square cannot be composed of only black or white cells.
5. White cells are connected.

Nurimisaki puzzle was recently proven NP-complete in [9]; hence, it is a natural question to construct a physical ZKP protocol for this fun puzzle. Although Goldwasser *et al.* [6] proved that any NP-complete problem has its corresponding interactive ZKP protocol, simple physical ZKP protocols are always sollicited as mentioned above.

Contributions. We propose a physical ZKP protocol that only uses cards and envelopes. We rely on some classical existing card-based sub-protocols in order to be able to construct our ZKP protocol. The main difficulty in this Nurimisaki game that seems to be simple, is that existing techniques proposed in the literature since few years cannot be applied directly. The main trick is to find an encoding that allows us to apply several sub-protocols in the right order to obtain a secure ZKP protocol. For this, we propose an original way to combine several techniques to design our ZKP protocol with a reasonable amount of cards and manipulations.

Outline. In Sect. 2, we introduce our encoding scheme using cards in order to represent a gird of the game and a solution. We also give some sub-protocols that are used in our construction. In Sect. 3, we give our ZKP protocol for Nurimisaki. Before concluding in the last section, we give the security proof of our ZKP protocol in Sect. 4.

2   Preliminaries

We explain the notations and sub-protocols used in our constructions.

Cards and Encoding. The cards we use in our protocols consist of clubs ♣♣ $\cdots$, hearts ♡♡ $\cdots$, and numbered cards 1 2 $\cdots$, whose backs are identical ?. We encode three colors {black, white, red} with the order of two cards as follows:

$$♣♡ \to \text{black}, \quad ♡♣ \to \text{white}, \quad ♡♡ \to \text{red}. \tag{1}$$

We call a pair of face-down cards ? ? corresponding to a color according to the above encoding rule a *commitment* to the respective color. We also use the terms, a *black commitment*, a *white commitment*, and a *red commitment*. We sometimes regard black and white commitments as bit values, based on the following encoding scheme:

$$♣♡ \to 0, \quad ♡♣ \to 1. \tag{2}$$

For a bit $x \in \{0, 1\}$, if a pair of face-down cards satisfies the encoding (2), we say that it is a commitment to x, denoted by $\underbrace{?\ ?}_{x}$.

We also define two other encoding [22, 26]:

- ♣-scheme: for $x \in \mathbb{Z}/p\mathbb{Z}$, there are p cards composed of $p-1$ ♡s and one ♣, where the ♣ is located at position $(x+1)$ from the left. For example, 2 in $\mathbb{Z}/4\mathbb{Z}$ is represented as ♡♡♣♡.
- ♡-scheme: it is the same encoding as above but the ♡ and ♣ are reversed. For instance, 2 in $\mathbb{Z}/4\mathbb{Z}$ is represented as ♣♣♡♣.

2.1   Pile-Shifting Shuffle [15, 26]

This shuffling action means to *cyclically* shuffle piles of cards. More formally, given m piles, each of which consists of the same number of face-down cards, denoted by $(\mathbf{p}_1, \mathbf{p}_2, \ldots, \mathbf{p}_m)$, applying a *pile-shifting shuffle* (denoted by $\langle \cdot \| \cdots \| \cdot \rangle$) results in $(\mathbf{p}_{s+1}, \mathbf{p}_{s+2}, \ldots, \mathbf{p}_{s+m})$:

$$\left\langle \underbrace{\boxed{?}}_{\mathbf{p}_1} \middle\| \underbrace{\boxed{?}}_{\mathbf{p}_2} \middle\| \cdots \middle\| \underbrace{\boxed{?}}_{\mathbf{p}_m} \right\rangle \to \underbrace{\boxed{?}}_{\mathbf{p}_{s+1}} \underbrace{\boxed{?}}_{\mathbf{p}_{s+2}} \cdots \underbrace{\boxed{?}}_{\mathbf{p}_{s+m}},$$

where s is uniformly and randomly chosen from $\mathbb{Z}/m\mathbb{Z}$. Implementing a pile-shifting shuffle is simple: we use physical cases that can store a pile of cards, such as boxes and envelopes; a player (or players) cyclically shuffles them manually until everyone (*i.e.*, the prover P and the verifier V) loses track of the offset.

2.2 Input-Preserving Five-Card Trick [12]

Given two commitments to $a, b \in \{0, 1\}$ based on the encoding rule (2), this sub-protocol [4,12] reveals only the value of $a \vee b$ as well as restores commitments to a and b: $\underbrace{\boxed{?}\ \boxed{?}}_{a}\ \underbrace{\boxed{?}\ \boxed{?}}_{b} \rightarrow a \vee b\ \&\ \underbrace{\boxed{?}\ \boxed{?}}\ \underbrace{\boxed{?}\ \boxed{?}}$.

The original sub-protocol [4,12] was designed for computing AND $(a \wedge b)$, but we adjust it to compute OR $(a \vee b)$:

1. Add helping cards and swap the two cards of the commitment to b so that we have the negation $\bar{b}$, as follows:

$$\underbrace{\boxed{?}\ \boxed{?}}_{a}\ \underbrace{\boxed{?}\ \boxed{?}}_{b} \rightarrow \underbrace{\boxed{?}\ \boxed{?}}_{a}\ \boxed{\heartsuit}\ \underbrace{\boxed{?}\ \boxed{?}}_{\bar{b}}\ \boxed{\heartsuit}\ \boxed{\clubsuit}\ \boxed{\clubsuit}\ \boxed{\clubsuit}.$$

2. Rearrange the sequence of cards and turn over the face-up cards as:

$$\boxed{?}\ \boxed{?}\ \boxed{\heartsuit}\ \boxed{?}\ \boxed{?}\ \boxed{\heartsuit}\ \boxed{\clubsuit}\ \boxed{\clubsuit}\ \boxed{\clubsuit}\ \boxed{\clubsuit} \rightarrow \begin{matrix} \boxed{?}\ \boxed{?}\ \boxed{\heartsuit}\ \boxed{?}\ \boxed{?} \\ \boxed{\heartsuit}\ \boxed{\clubsuit}\ \boxed{\clubsuit}\ \boxed{\clubsuit}\ \boxed{\clubsuit} \end{matrix} \rightarrow \begin{matrix} \boxed{?}\ \boxed{?}\ \boxed{?}\ \boxed{?}\ \boxed{?} \\ \boxed{?}\ \boxed{?}\ \boxed{?}\ \boxed{?}\ \boxed{?} \end{matrix}.$$

3. Regarding cards in the same column as a pile, apply a pile-shifting shuffle to the sequence:

$$\left\langle \begin{matrix}\boxed{?}\\\boxed{?}\end{matrix} \middle\| \begin{matrix}\boxed{?}\\\boxed{?}\end{matrix} \middle\| \begin{matrix}\boxed{?}\\\boxed{?}\end{matrix} \middle\| \begin{matrix}\boxed{?}\\\boxed{?}\end{matrix} \middle\| \begin{matrix}\boxed{?}\\\boxed{?}\end{matrix} \right\rangle \rightarrow \begin{matrix} \boxed{?}\ \boxed{?}\ \boxed{?}\ \boxed{?}\ \boxed{?} \\ \boxed{?}\ \boxed{?}\ \boxed{?}\ \boxed{?}\ \boxed{?} \end{matrix}.$$

4. Reveal all the cards in the first row.
   (a) If it is $\boxed{\clubsuit}\ \boxed{\clubsuit}\ \boxed{\heartsuit}\ \boxed{\heartsuit}\ \boxed{\heartsuit}$ (up to cyclic shifts), then $a \vee b = 0$.
   (b) If it is $\boxed{\heartsuit}\ \boxed{\clubsuit}\ \boxed{\heartsuit}\ \boxed{\clubsuit}\ \boxed{\heartsuit}$ (up to cyclic shifts), then $a \vee b = 1$.
5. After turning over all the face-up cards, apply a pile-shifting shuffle.
6. Reveal all the cards in the second row; then, the revealed cards should include exactly one $\boxed{\heartsuit}$.
7. Shift the sequence of piles so that the revealed $\boxed{\heartsuit}$ is the leftmost card and swap the two cards of the commitment to $\bar{b}$ to restore commitments to a and b.

2.3 Mizuki–Sone Copy Protocol [14]

Given a commitment to $a \in \{0,1\}$ along with four cards ♣♡♣♡, the Mizuki–Sone copy protocol [14] outputs two commitments to a:

$$\boxed{?}\boxed{?}\,\boxed{♣}\boxed{♡}\boxed{♣}\boxed{♡} \;\rightarrow\; \boxed{?}\boxed{?}\;\boxed{?}\boxed{?}.$$
$$\underbrace{}_{a} \qquad\qquad \underbrace{}_{a}\;\underbrace{}_{a}$$

1. Turn all cards face-down and set the commitments as follows:

2. Apply a pile-shifting shuffle as follows:

3. Reveal the two above cards to obtain either a or $\bar{a}$ as follows:

2.4 How to Form a White Polyomino [17]

We introduce the generic method of [17] to address the connectivity constraint (rule 5). Given a grid where all cells are black, it enables P to make white connected cells, *i.e.*, *white-polyomino*, without revealing anything to V. We first describe two crucial sub-protocols: the chosen pile protocol and the 4-neighbor protocol.

Chosen Pile Protocol [5]. The chosen pile protocol allows P to choose a pile of cards without V knowing which one. This pile can be manipulated and all the commitments are replaced to their initial order afterward.

This protocol is an extended version of the "chosen pile cut" proposed in [10]. Given m piles $(\mathbf{p}_1, \mathbf{p}_2, \ldots, \mathbf{p}_m)$ with $2m$ additional cards, the *chosen pile protocol* enables a prover P to choose the i-th pile $\mathbf{p}_i$ (without revealing the index i) and revert the sequence of m piles to their original order after applying other operations to p_i.

1. Using $m-1$ ♣s and one ♡, P places m face-down cards encoding $i-1$ in the ♡-scheme (denoted by *row 2*) below the given piles, *i.e.*, only the i-th card is ♡. We further put m cards encoding 0 in the ♡-scheme (denoted by *row 3*):

2. Considering the cards in the same column as a pile, apply a pile-shifting shuffle to the sequence of piles.
3. Reveal all the cards in *row 2*. Then, exactly one ♡ appears, and the pile above the revealed ♡ is the i-th pile (and hence, P can obtain $\mathbf{p}_i$). After this step is invoked, other operations are applied to the chosen pile. Then, the chosen pile is placed back to the i-th position in the sequence.
4. Remove the revealed cards, *i.e.*, the cards in *row 2*. (Note, therefore, that we do not use the card ♡ revealed in Step 3.) Then, apply a pile-shifting shuffle.
5. Reveal all the cards in *row 3*. Then, one ♡ appears, and the pile above the revealed ♡ is $\mathbf{p}_1$. Therefore, by shifting the sequence of piles (such that $\mathbf{p}_1$ becomes the leftmost pile in the sequence), we can obtain a sequence of piles whose order is the same as the original one without revealing any information about the order of the input sequence.

Sub-protocol: 4-Neighbor Protocol [17]. Given pq commitments placed on a $p \times q$ grid, a prover P has a commitment in mind, which we call a *target* commitment. The prover P wants to reveal the target commitment and another one that lies next to the target commitment (without revealing their exact positions). Here, a verifier V should be convinced that the second commitment is a neighbor of the first one (without knowing which one) as well as V should be able to confirm the colors of both the commitments. To handle the case where the target commitment is at the edge of the grid, we place commitments to red (as "dummy" commitments) in the left of the first column and below the last row to prevent P from choosing a commitment that is not a neighbor. Thus, the size of the expanded grid is $(p + 1) \times (q + 1)$. This sub-protocol proceeds as follows.

1. P and V pick the $(p + 1)(q + 1)$ commitments on the grid from left-to-right and top-to-bottom to make a sequence of commitments: ?? ?? ?? ?? ⋯ ?? .
2. P uses the chosen pile protocol to reveal the target commitment.
3. P and V pick all the four neighbors of the target commitment. Since a pile-shifting shuffle is a cyclic reordering, the distance between commitments are kept (up to a given modulo). That is, for a target commitment (not at any the edge), the possible four neighbors are at distance one for the left or right one, and $p + 1$ for the bottom or top one so that P and V can determine the positions of all the four neighbors.
4. Among these four neighbors, P chooses one commitment using the chosen pile protocol and reveals it.
5. P and V end the second and first chosen pile protocols.

Forming White-Polyomino. Assume that there is a grid having $p \times q$ cells. P wants to arrange white commitments on the grid such that they form a white-polyomino while V is convinced that the placement of commitments is surely a white-polyomino. The sub-protocol proceeds as follows.

1. P and V place a commitment to black (*i.e.*, ♣♡) on every cell and commitments to red as mentioned above so that they have $(p+1)(q+1)$ commitments on the board.

2. P uses the chosen pile protocol to choose one black commitment that P wants to change.

   (a) V swaps the two cards constituting the chosen commitment so that it becomes a white commitment (recall the encoding (1)).

   (b) P and V end the chosen pile protocol to return the commitments to their original positions.

3. P and V repeat the following steps exactly $pq - 1$ times.

   (a) P chooses one white commitment as a target and one black commitment among its neighbors using the 4-neighbor protocol; the neighbor is chosen such that P wants to make it white.

   (b) V reveals the target commitment. If it corresponds to white, then V continues; otherwise V aborts.

   (c) V reveals the neighbor commitment (chosen by P). If it corresponds to black, then P makes the neighbor white or keep it black (depending on P's choice) by executing the following steps; otherwise V aborts.

      i. If P wants to change the commitment, P places face-down club-to-heart pair below it; otherwise, P places a heart-to-club pair: $\boxed{?}\,\boxed{?} \rightarrow$
   $$\begin{array}{cc} \boxed{?}\,\boxed{?} & \text{or} \quad \boxed{?}\,\boxed{?} \\ \boxed{?}\,\boxed{?} & \boxed{?}\,\boxed{?} \\ \clubsuit \ \heartsuit & \heartsuit \ \clubsuit \end{array}.$$

      ii. Regarding cards in the same column as a pile, V applies a pile-shifting shuffle to the sequence of piles: $\left\langle \begin{smallmatrix} \boxed{?} \\ \boxed{?} \end{smallmatrix} \,\middle\|\, \begin{smallmatrix} \boxed{?} \\ \boxed{?} \end{smallmatrix} \right\rangle \rightarrow \begin{smallmatrix} \boxed{?}\,\boxed{?} \\ \boxed{?}\,\boxed{?} \end{smallmatrix}.$

      iii. V reveals the two cards in the second row. If the revealed right card is $\boxed{\heartsuit}$, then V swaps the two cards in the first row; otherwise V does nothing.

   (d) P and V end the 4-neighbor protocol.

V is now convinced that all the white commitments represent a white-polyomino. Therefore, this method allows a prover P to make a solution that only P has in mind, guaranteed to satisfy the connectivity constraint.

2.5   Sum in $\mathbb{Z}$ [22]

We give a brief overview of the protocol described in [22] for the addition of elements in $\mathbb{Z}/2\mathbb{Z}$ with a result in $\mathbb{Z}$. This allows to compute $S = \sum_{i=1}^{n} x_i$ with $S \in \mathbb{Z}$ and $x_i \in \mathbb{Z}/2\mathbb{Z}$ for $i \in \{1, \ldots, n\}$. The idea is to compute the sum inductively; when starting by the two first elements x_1 and x_2, they are transformed into $x_1 - r$ and $x_2 + r$ for uniformly random $r \in \mathbb{Z}/2\mathbb{Z}$. Then $x_2 + r$ is revealed (no information about x_2 leaks since r is random), and the cards of $x_1 - r$ is shifted by $x_2 + r$ positions to encode value $(x_1 - r) + (x_2 + r) = x_1 + x_2$. Note that this result is in $\mathbb{Z}/(p+1)\mathbb{Z}$ (or simply $\mathbb{Z}$ since the result is less than p) for elements x_1, x_2 in $\mathbb{Z}/p\mathbb{Z}$.

3   ZKP Protocol for Nurimisaki

We present our ZKP protocol for Nurimisaki. Hereinafter, we consider an instance of Nurimisaki as a rectangular grid of size $p \times q$.

3.1   Setup Phase

The verifier V and the prover P place black commitments on all the cell of the $p \times q$ grid and place red commitments ("dummy" commitments) around the grid so that we have $(p+1)(q+1)$ commitments.

3.2   Connectivity Phase

P and V apply the protocol given in Sect. 2.4: a white-polyomino is formed according to P's solution. Now, V reveals all the commitments corresponding to Misaki to check that they are indeed white. After this phase, V is convinced that white commitments are connected (rule 5).

3.3   Verification Phase

The verifier V is now checking that the other rules are satisfied.

No 2×2 square (rule 4). We use an adapted verification phase of the one in [17] for checking that 2×2 square are not composed of only white (black) commitments. Note that for an initial grid $p \times q$, there are $(p-1)(q-1)$ possible squares of size 2×2. Thus P and V consider each of those squares (in any order) and apply the following:

1. P chooses a white commitment and a black one among the four commitments via the chosen-pile protocol (Sect. 2.4).
2. V reveals both commitments marked by P in the previous step. If there are exactly a white commitment and a black one, V continues; otherwise, abort.

Misaki (rule 1 and 2). V wants to check that each Misaki cell (cell with a circle) has only one of its neighbours white and others black. Moreover, when a Misaki has a number in it, V wants to check that the straight line formed by white cells starting from the Misaki cell has the corresponding number of white cells.

  P and V first consider Misaki cells with a number. For each Misaki cell (not at a border) with a number i in it, apply the following:

1. P and V add black commitments (*i.e.*, "dummy" commitments) at the border of the grid. This ensures that we delimit correctly the number of white commitments in a straight line.
2. For each of the four neighbours, P and V form a pile composed of $i+1$ commitments for each direction (top, bottom, left, right).

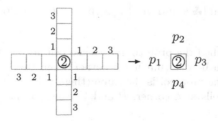

3. P and V puts numbered cards under each pile as follows:
$$\begin{array}{|c|c|c|c|} \hline p_1 & p_2 & p_3 & p_4 \\ \hline 1 & 2 & 3 & 4 \\ \hline \end{array}.$$

4. P and V shuffle the piles and reveal the first commitment of each pile. If there is exactly one commitment corresponding to white then V continues. Otherwise, V aborts.

5. V reveals the next i commitments of the pile with the first white commitment. If there are only white commitments for the first $i - 1$ commitments and a black commitment for the last one, then V continues; otherwise, aborts.

After this step, V is convinced that Misaki cells with a number are well-formed. In the case where there is no number, the first step consists of forming a pile with only one commitment. Hence, V is convinced that Misaki cells without a number satisfy only rule 1 but not rule 2 since any number of white cells could form the straight line[1].

No circle, no Misaki (rule 3). V needs to check that white cells without a circle are not Misaki, meaning that any white cell of the grid has at least two of its neighbours white. This rule is somewhat challenging to verify without leaking information on the solution because the number and location of white cells are part of the solution (and must not be publicly revealed).

If the targeted cell is black then there is nothing to verify since any configurations could occur. Yet, if the targeted cell is white then there are at least (but it could be more) two neighbours that are white. The idea is to set the value of targeted cell being 5 if it is white and 0 if it is black. Then we add the neighbours to it (white is 0, and black is 1). If the cell is black then the sum is always less than or equal to 4 (which is permitted by the rules to have all black). But if the cell is white then the permitted value for the sum is less than or equal to 7 (a Misaki is equal to 8) for a targeted cell that is not at a border.

For a given cell, called targeted cell c_t, we look at its neighbors (up to 4). The idea of verifying that a white cell is not a Misaki is to first sum the four neighbors (where a white cell is equal to 0 and a black cell is equal to 1). Then by choosing another encoding, the targeted cell can be equal to 5 for white and 0 for black. Finally, adding the sum of the neighbors with c_t gives at most 4 for black c_t (which is permitted by the rules) and at most 7 for white c_t in a valid configuration and 8 or 9 for invalid configuration.

1. Copy all the commitments using the copy protocol (Sect. 2.3). The number of copies for a $p \times q$ grid is $2(2pq - p - q)$;
2. Sum the four neighbours by considering that a white commitment is equal to 0 and a black commitment is equal to 1. The result is given in the $\heartsuit$-scheme (*i.e.*, there are four ♣s and one ♡ at position corresponding to the result of the sum).

---

[1] Note that we described the protocol for Misaki cell not at the border of the grid. If a Misaki cell is at a border (but not a corner) then the 4-neighbours becomes the 3-neighbours and the protocol is the same (there will be only three piles instead of four). For Misaki cells at a corner, P and V consider the 2-neighbours (thus only two piles).

3. For the targeted cell, add 3 $\heartsuit$ s in the middle of the commitment as:

$$\text{white: } \boxed{\heartsuit}\,\boxed{\clubsuit} \rightarrow \boxed{\heartsuit}\,\boxed{\heartsuit}\,\boxed{\heartsuit}\,\boxed{\heartsuit}\,\boxed{\clubsuit} = 5,$$
$$\text{black: } \boxed{\clubsuit}\,\boxed{\heartsuit} \rightarrow \boxed{\clubsuit}\,\boxed{\heartsuit}\,\boxed{\heartsuit}\,\boxed{\heartsuit}\,\boxed{\heartsuit} = 0.$$

White is now 5 and black is 0 in the $\clubsuit$-scheme.

4. Sum the result of the two previous steps (the sum of the four neighbours and the inner cell). The result is encoded in the $\heartsuit$-scheme.
5. Reveal the last and penultimate cards. If a $\boxed{\heartsuit}$ appears then abort; otherwise, continue.

4   Security Proofs

Our protocol needs to verify three security properties given as theorems.

Theorem 1 (Completeness). *If P knows the solution of a Nurimisaki grid, then P can convince V.*

Proof. First, notice that P convinces V in the sense that the protocol does not abort which mean that all the rules are satisfied. The protocol can be split in two: (1) the connectivity and (2) the verification phases.

(1) Since P knows the solution, the white cells are connected and hence can always choose a black commitment at step 2 to swap it to white. Notice that there exists a proof for the connectivity in [17].
(2) The verification of 2×2 square will not abort since if P has the solution then for any given 2×2 square there always exist a white commitment and a black commitment. For the Misaki rules, each Misaki cell has three of its neighbors black and one white; thus, the first commitment of piles p_1, p_2, p_3, p_4 will reveal exactly three black and one white commitments. Then, when looking at pile p_i of the first commitment corresponding to white, the number of white commitments corresponds to the number in the inner cell. Thus the protocol will continue. Finally, the non-Misaki rule is verified. Since P has the solution, any white cell (with no circle in it) has at least two white neighbors. Thus if the inner cell is white then the sum will start to 5 and the maximal value is 7 because a solution has at least two whites so at most two black commitments (of value 1 in this step). So the protocol will continue and hence V will be convinced that P has the solution.   □

Theorem 2 (Soundness). *If P does not provide a solution of the $p \times q$ Nurimisaki grid, P is not able to convince V.*

Proof. Suppose that P does not know the solution, hence at least one of the rules is not verified. If the white cells are not connected then P cannot choose a black commitment at step 2 hence V will detect it. Notice that there is also the proof of this phase in [17].

If P does not have the solution, then one of the verification phase will fail. We apply a case distinction for those verifications. Assume first that there is a block of 2×2 square composed of only white (black) commitments, then P cannot choose, during the chosen-pile protocol, two distinct commitments (*i.e.*, a black and a white) thus the revealed commitments will attest to V that P does not have the solution. Second, assume that a Misaki cell is not well-formed in the sense that either (1) the number of white neighbour is not equal to 1 or that (2) the number of white cells in straight line does not correspond to the number of the Misaki cell. For (1) the neighbours are revealed (after a shuffle) so V will notice the number of white commitments; for (2) all the commitments next to the white neighbour are revealed thus V will also notice if there is a flaw. The last verification is for white cells which are not Misaki. It is equivalent of saying that any white cell (without a circle in it) has at least two white neighbours. If a white cell has only one white neighbour then during the sum process, then $c_t = 5$ (because the central cell is white) and the total for its neighbours is 3 (because there are 3 black commitments and 1 white). The final sum is then equal to 8, since V will look at the last and penultimate card of the sum (corresponding to a sum equal to 9 and 8) then V will detect that a white card is a Misaki. Notice that a sum equals to 9 means the white cell is surrounded by 4 black cells. It is not possible since white cells are connected.   □

Theorem 3 (Zero-knowledge). *V learns nothing about P's solution of the given grid G.*

Proof. We use the same proof technique as in [7], namely the description of an efficient *simulator* which simulates the interaction between an honest prover and a cheating verifier. The goal is to produce an indistinguishable interaction from the verifier's view (with the prover). Notice that the simulator does not have the solution but it can swap cards during shuffles. Informally, the verifier cannot distinguish between two protocols, one that is run with the actual solution and one with random commitments. The simulator acts as follows: The simulator constructs a random connected white polyomino. During the 2×2 square verification, the simulator will swap cards to choose white and black commitments. For the Misaki verification, the simulator swaps three commitments to black for three piles and one to white for the last pile. The latter will also be modified by the simulator to contain the correct numbers of white commitments (and the last commitment to black). During the non-Misaki verification, when the sum is computed, the simulator swaps the cards to always put ♣ cards in position 8 and 9 (for the cell not at the edge, but the latter is done the same way).

The simulated and real proofs are indistinguishable hence V learns nothing from the connectivity and verification phases. Finally, we conclude that the protocol is zero-knowledge.   □

5   Conclusion

We proposed a physical ZKP protocol for Nurimisaki that uses only cards and envelopes. The most difficult part was to prove that cells are not Misaki without leaking their color. Of course, we combined this part with the rest of the verifications that are stated by other rules. This new approach clearly demonstrates that showing that some cells do not have some properties is often more difficult than proving an explicit property without leaking any information.

References

1. Bultel, X., Dreier, J., Dumas, J.G., Lafourcade, P.: Physical zero-knowledge proofs for Akari, Takuzu, Kakuro and KenKen. In Demaine, E.D., Grandoni, F. (eds.) Fun with Algorithms, volume 49 of LIPIcs, pp. 8:1–8:20 (2016)
2. Bultel, X., et al.: Physical zero-knowledge proof for Makaro. In: Izumi, T., Kuznetsov, P. (eds.) SSS 2018. LNCS, vol. 11201, pp. 111–125. Springer, Cham (2018). https://doi.org/10.1007/978-3-030-03232-6_8
3. Chien, Y.-F., Hon, W.-K.: Cryptographic and physical zero-knowledge proof: from Sudoku to Nonogram. In: Boldi, P., Gargano, L. (eds.) FUN 2010. LNCS, vol. 6099, pp. 102–112. Springer, Heidelberg (2010). https://doi.org/10.1007/978-3-642-13122-6_12
4. den Boer, B.: More efficient match-making and satisfiability: The five card trick. In: Quisquater, J., Vandewalle, J. (eds.) EUROCRYPT 1989. LNCS, vol. 434, pp. 208–217. Springer, Berlin, Heidelberg (1989). https://doi.org/10.1007/3-540-46885-4_23
5. Dumas, J.-G., Lafourcade, P., Miyahara, D., Mizuki, T., Sasaki, T., Sone, H.: Interactive physical zero-knowledge proof for Norinori. In: Du, D.-Z., Duan, Z., Tian, C. (eds.) COCOON 2019. LNCS, vol. 11653, pp. 166–177. Springer, Cham (2019). https://doi.org/10.1007/978-3-030-26176-4_14
6. Goldwasser, S., Micali, S., Rackoff, C.: The knowledge complexity of interactive proof-systems. In: STOC 1985, pp. 291–304, New York. ACM (1985)
7. Gradwohl, R., Naor, M., Pinkas, B., Rothblum, G.N.: Cryptographic and physical zero-knowledge proof systems for solutions of Sudoku puzzles. Theory Comput. Syst. **44**(2), 245–268 (2009)
8. Isuzugawa, R., Miyahara, D., Mizuki, T.: Zero-knowledge proof protocol for cryptarithmetic using dihedral cards. In: Kostitsyna, I., Orponen, P. (eds.) UCNC 2021. LNCS, vol. 12984, pp. 51–67. Springer, Cham (2021). https://doi.org/10.1007/978-3-030-87993-8_4
9. Iwamoto, C., Ide, T.: Computational complexity of Nurimisaki and Sashigane. IEICE Trans. Fundam. **103**(10), 1183–1192 (2020)
10. Koch, A., Walzer, S.: Foundations for actively secure card-based cryptography. In M. Farach-Colton, M., Prencipe, G., Uehara, R. (eds.) Fun with Algorithms, volume 157 of LIPIcs, pp. 17:1–17:23, Dagstuhl. Schloss Dagstuhl (2021)
11. Lafourcade, P., Miyahara, D., Mizuki, T., Robert, L., Sasaki, T., Sone, H.: How to construct physical zero-knowledge proofs for puzzles with a "single loop" condition. Theor. Comput. Sci. **888**, 41–55 (2021)
12. D. Miyahara, et al.: Card-based ZKP protocols for Takuzu and Juosan. In Farach-Colton, M., Prencipe, G., Uehara, R. (eds.) Fun with Algorithms, volume 157 of LIPIcs, pp. 20:1–20:21, Dagstuhl. Schloss Dagstuhl (2021)
13. Miyahara, D., Sasaki, T., Mizuki, T., Sone, H.: Card-based physical zero-knowledge proof for Kakuro. IEICE Trans. Fundam. **102-A**(9), 1072–1078 (2019)
14. Mizuki, T., Sone, H.: Six-card secure AND and four-card secure XOR. In: Deng, X., Hopcroft, J.E., Xue, J. (eds.) FAW 2009. LNCS, vol. 5598, pp. 358–369. Springer, Heidelberg (2009). https://doi.org/10.1007/978-3-642-02270-8_36

15. Nishimura, A., Hayashi, Y.I., Mizuki, T., Sone, H.: Pile-shifting scramble for card-based protocols. IEICE Trans. Fundam. **101-A**(9), 1494–1502 (2018)
16. Robert, L., Miyahara, D., Lafourcade, P., Libralesso, L., Mizuki, T.: Physical zero-knowledge proof and np-completeness proof of suguru puzzle. Inf. Comput. **285**(Part), 104858 (2022)
17. Robert, L., Miyahara, D., Lafourcade, P., Mizuki, T.: Card-based ZKP for connectivity: applications to Nurikabe, Hitori, and Heyawake. New Gener. Comput. **40**, 149–171 (2022)
18. Ruangwises, S.: An improved physical ZKP for Nonogram. In: Du, D.-Z., Du, D., Wu, C., Xu, D. (eds.) COCOA 2021. LNCS, vol. 13135, pp. 262–272. Springer, Cham (2021). https://doi.org/10.1007/978-3-030-92681-6_22
19. Ruangwises, S.: Two standard decks of playing cards are sufficient for a ZKP for Sudoku. New Gener. Comput. **40**, 49–65 (2022)
20. Ruangwises, S., Itoh, T.: Physical zero-knowledge proof for Numberlink puzzle and k vertex-disjoint paths problem. New Gener. Comput. **39**(1), 3–17 (2021)
21. Ruangwises, S., Itoh, T.: Physical ZKP for connected spanning subgraph: applications to bridges puzzle and other problems. In: Kostitsyna, I., Orponen, P. (eds.) UCNC 2021. LNCS, vol. 12984, pp. 149–163. Springer, Cham (2021). https://doi.org/10.1007/978-3-030-87993-8_10
22. Ruangwises, S., Itoh, T.: Securely computing the N-variable equality function with 2N cards. Theor. Comput. Sci. **887**, 99–110 (2021)
23. Ruangwises, S., Itoh, T.: How to physically verify a rectangle in a grid: a physical ZKP for Shikaku. In Fraigniaud, P., Uno, Y. (eds.), Fun with Algorithms, volume 226 of LIPIcs, pp. 24:1–24:12. Schloss Dagstuhl (2022)
24. Saito, K.: Physical zero-knowledge proof for the pencil puzzle Nurimisaki. Graduation Thesis, The University of Electro-Communications, Tokyo (2020)
25. Sasaki, T., Miyahara, D., Mizuki, T., Sone, H.: Efficient card-based zero-knowledge proof for Sudoku. Theor. Comput. Sci. **839**, 135–142 (2020)
26. Shinagawa, K.: Card-based protocols using regular polygon cards. IEICE Trans. Fundam. **100-A**(9), 1900–1909 (2017)

Consensus on Demand

Jakub Sliwinski, Yann Vonlanthen$^{(\boxtimes)}$, and Roger Wattenhofer

ETH Zürich, Zürich, Switzerland
yvonlanthen@ethz.ch

Abstract. Digital money can be implemented efficiently by avoiding consensus. However, no-consensus designs are fundamentally limited, as they cannot support general smart contracts, and similarly they cannot deal with conflicting transactions.

We present a novel protocol that combines the benefits of an asynchronous, broadcast-based digital currency, with the capacity to perform consensus. This is achieved by selectively performing consensus a posteriori, i.e., only when absolutely necessary. Our on-demand consensus comes at the price of restricting the Byzantine participants to be less than a one-fifth minority in the system, which is the optimal threshold.

We formally prove the correctness of our system and present an open-source implementation, which inherits many features from the Ethereum ecosystem.

Keywords: Consensus · Reliable broadcast · Blockchain · Fault tolerance · Cryptocurrency

1   Introduction

Following the famed white paper of Satoshi Nakamoto [30], a plethora of digital payment systems (cryptocurrencies) emerged. The basic functionality of such payment systems are money transfer transactions. These transactions are stored in a distributed ledger, a fault-tolerant and cryptographically secured append-only database. Most cryptocurrencies have a ledger where transactions are *totally ordered*, effectively forcing all participants of the system to perform the state transitions sequentially. This sequential verification of all transactions is considered the main bottleneck of distributed ledger solutions [12].

However, in reality, most transactions have no dependencies between each other. For example, a transaction from Alice to Bob and a transaction from Charlie to Dani can be performed in any order. Verifying such independent transactions in parallel offers a vast efficiency improvement. Indeed, recent research proposes *"no-consensus"* payment systems that do not order independent transactions [12,29]. Such systems can achieve unbounded transaction throughput, as all transactions can be verified in any order, in parallel.

However, no-consensus payment systems suffer from fundamental limitations, as they lack the means to deal with conflicting inputs: If Charlie sets up two transactions, one for Alice, one for Bob, but Charlie does not have enough funds

© The Author(s), under exclusive license to Springer Nature Switzerland AG 2022
S. Devismes et al. (Eds.): SSS 2022, LNCS 13751, pp. 299–313, 2022.
https://doi.org/10.1007/978-3-031-21017-4_20

for both transactions, no-consensus payment system might end up in a deadlock, with Charlie ultimately losing access to her account, and neither Alice nor Bob getting paid. The same problem fundamentally prevents no-consensus systems from supporting general smart contracts, where many uncoordinated parties might issue conflicting inputs to the same smart contract at the same time (Fig. 1).

We are faced with a choice: either we use a total ordering currency which cannot scale to a high transaction throughput, or we use a parallel no-consensus verification system that is functionally restricted, and cannot resolve conflicting transactions.

In this work we propose a system which combines the advantages of both approaches. Our system offers all of the benefits of no-consensus systems, such as in principle unbounded throughput and powerful resiliency to network attacks. Our design first tries to verify every transaction without performing consensus. Only if a transaction cannot be verified on this "fast path", we invoke a consensus routine to resolve potential conflicts.

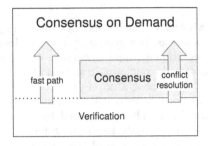

Fig. 1. A high level overview of our protocol.

Our contributions are as follows:

1. We present a protocol we call ConsensusOnDemand. Assuming access to an existing consensus protocol, ConsensusOnDemand is a wrapper algorithm where the first phase offers the benefits of no-consensus systems. In situations where conflicting inputs cannot be processed by pure no-consensus systems (and only those situations), ConsensusOnDemand invokes the consensus instance to resolve the deadlock. The wrapper protocol is resilient to completely asynchronous network conditions as long as $n > 5f$, where n is the total number of participants and f is the number of Byzantine participants. The common case (no consensus) is optimal with regard to latency and does not rely on complex broadcast primitives.

   Thus, we combine the power of processing unrelated inputs in parallel with the ability to resolve conflicting inputs when needed and pave the way for implementations of systems with unbounded throughput and full smart contract functionality.
2. We exhibit our idea in the context of online payments. We describe our protocol, including the pseudocode, and prove the algorithm's correctness.
3. We implement our design as a digital currency following a no-consensus approach enhanced with consensus on demand. A smart contract is used as the example consensus instance. Our implementation is built on top of the Ethereum client *go-ethereum*, and thus features a network discovery protocol and advanced wallets, while being compatible with the Ethereum ecosystem.

2 Model

We distinguish between clients and servers. Clients are free to enter and leave the system as they please. Servers are in charge of securing the system. We assume that the set of servers Π is fixed and known to all servers.

Clients and servers that follow the protocol are said to be honest. Byzantine clients or servers are subject to arbitrary behavior and might collude when attempting to compromise the system's security. We assume there are no more than f Byzantine servers and that the set of Byzantine servers is static. Further, let $n = |\Pi|$. We assume that $n > 5f$, in other words, less than one-fifth of servers are Byzantine.

Servers are connected all-to-all with authenticated links. Communication is **asynchronous** i.e. messages are delivered with arbitrary delays. We assume standard cryptographic primitives to hold, more specifically, MACs and signatures cannot be forged.

Finally, the model might have to be restricted further in order to reflect the assumptions needed for the choice of the underlying consensus instance. For the consensus algorithm chosen for our implementation (see Sect. 8) we indeed assume synchronous communication.

3 Problem Statement

We formulate the problem in the context of a cryptocurrency. Initially, the state of the system consists of a known assignment of currency amounts to clients. The system's purpose is to accept transactions, where a transaction $t = (sender, sn, recipient, amount)$ moves an *amount* of currency from a *sender* to a *recipient*. Each client can issue transactions as the sender, where the sequence number sn starts from 0 and increases by 1 for each transaction.

Definition 1. *Two transactions t and t' are said to conflict, if they have the same sender and sequence number but $t \neq t'$, i.e., the recipient or the amount differ.*

Existing broadcast-based payment systems [3,12] provide the guarantees of a Byzantine reliable broadcast for every transaction:

Definition 2. *Each honest server observes transactions from a set of conflicting transactions $\{t_0, t_1, ...\}$. Byzantine reliable broadcast satisfies the following properties:*

1. **Totality:** *If some honest server accepts a transaction, every honest server will eventually accept the same transaction.*
2. **Agreement:** *No two honest servers accept conflicting transactions.*
3. **Validity:** *If every honest server observes the same transaction (there are no conflicting transactions), this transaction will be accepted by all honest servers.*

The totality and agreement properties guarantee consistent state of the system and that at most one transaction per unique $(sender, sn)$ pair can be accepted, thus preventing double-spends.

Validity ensures that if the client issued only one transaction for a given sequence number, the transaction will indeed be accepted. However, otherwise the definition does not guarantee termination. In other words, if the client issues conflicting transactions, the system might deadlock and never decide on accepting any of them.

Through the use of this weak abstraction, broadcast-based payment systems combine many benefits, such as resilience to complete asynchrony and fast acceptance. The standout advantage is perhaps the inherent ability to parallelize the processing of independent transactions, resulting in unbounded throughput through horizontal scaling [5,29].

The crucial assumption that well-behaved clients will not issue conflicting transactions is warranted for a rudimentary payment system. However, it inherently precludes more advanced applications where conflicting inputs naturally occur, such as uncoordinated parties issuing conflicting inputs to a smart contract. To support the full range of blockchain applications, a stronger guarantee needs to hold:

Definition 3. *Each honest server observes transactions from a set of conflicting transactions $\{t_0, t_1, ...\}$.* ***Consensus*** *satisfies the following properties:*

1. *All properties of Byzantine reliable broadcast, and*
2. **Termination:** *Every honest server eventually accepts one of the observed transactions.*

The objective of this work is to combine the benefits of broadcast-based designs with the power of consensus: a) non-conflicting transactions are to be processed in a broadcast-based fashion: each honest server broadcasting one acknowledgement for a transaction is enough to accept it; and b) consensus is supported to resolve conflicts (Table 1).

4   Related Work

Broadcast-based Protocols. In 2016 Gupta [20] points out that a payment system does not require consensus. Later, Guerraoui et al. [19] prove that the consensus number of a cryptocurrency is indeed 1 in Herlihy's hierarchy [21].

Both Guerraoui et al. [12] and Baudet et al. [5] propose a payment scheme where the ordering of transactions is purely determined by the transaction issuer.

Table 1. A comparison of existing solutions and ConsensusOnDemand (CoD). The CoD wrapping of a consensus is asynchronous and leaderless, and thus any potentially stronger assumptions are inherited from the consensus instance being used.

	Bitcoin and Ethereum [30]	Ouroboros [22]	Algorand [17]	PBFT [10]	Red Belly [13]	BEAT [15]	Broadcast-based [12]	CoD + PBFT	CoD + BEAT
Energy-efficient		✓	✓	✓	✓	✓	✓	✓	✓
Deterministic finality		✓	✓	✓	✓	✓	✓	✓	✓
Permissionless	✓	✓	✓						
Leaderless					✓	✓	✓		✓
Asynchronous						✓	✓		✓
Parallelizable							✓	✓	✓
Consensus	✓	✓	✓	✓	✓	✓		✓	✓

In their simplest form those currencies rely on Byzantine reliable broadcast, as originally defined by Bracha and Toueg [8]. Srikanth and Toueg [39] as well as Bracha [7] propose well-known Byzantine reliable broadcast algorithms with $\mathcal{O}(n^2)$ message complexity per instance. We use Bracha's Double-Echo algorithm [7] as a fundamental building block and comparison to our approach.

The Cascade protocol [37] promises similar benefits, while being permission-less, i.e., participants are free to enter and leave the system as they please.

Other approaches have proposed a probabilistic Byzantine reliable broadcast [18]. By dropping determinism, efficiency is gained, more specifically $\mathcal{O}(n \log(n))$ messages are shown to be sufficient for each transaction. Our implementation relies on a practical and widely adopted probabilistic broadcast protocol.

Instead, it is possible to drop the *totality* property of Byzantine reliable broadcast and build a payment system where servers distribute themselves proof (a list of signatures) that they are indeed in the possession of the claimed funds. This was also proposed by Guerraoui et al. [12], based on a digital signature approach inspired by Malkhi and Reiter [27]. The message complexity is hereby improved to $\mathcal{O}(n)$.

Remedying the Consensus Bottleneck. Early work by Pedone et al. [32] and Lamport [25] recognizes that *commuting* transactions do not need to be ordered in the traditional state machine replication (SMR) problem with crash failures. Follow-up protocols also deal with Byzantine faults and show fundamental lower-bounds [26,33,35].

Removing global coordination in favor of weaker consistency properties also receives a lot of attention outside the area of state machine replication. Conflict-free Replicated Data Types (CRDT) [9,34] provide a principled approach to performing concurrent operations optimistically, and have recently also been applied to permissioned blockchains [31].

It is often tricky to compare protocols, as they can differentiate themselves in one of the many dimensions, such as synchrony, fault-tolerance and fast path latency [6]. A recent protocol called Byblos [6] achieves 5-step latency in a partially synchronous network when $n > 4f$. Suri-Payer et al. [40] improve the fast path latency to 2 communication steps, in the absence of Byzantine behavior.

Kursawe's optimistic Byzantine agreement protocol [23] features a fast path paired with a consensus protocol in the slow path, with each component being modular. While Kursawe's proposed fast path requires synchronous rounds and no Byzantine failures to happen, our protocol features the same optimal fast path of a single round-trip, while not relying on synchrony and tolerating f Byzantine servers. This comes at the cost of requiring $n \geq 5f + 1$ servers. This bound has been shown to be optimal by Martin et al. [28]. Kuznetsov et al. [24] have recently shown the lower bound to be $n \geq 5f - 1$ in the special case where the set of *proposers* (clients) is a subset of *acceptors* (servers). Their insight is to disregard the acknowledgement of a provably misbehaving server. Although we do not assume the required special case, as in our model the set of clients is external to servers and changing freely, the assumption might well be warranted in other contexts, wherein their approach is applicable to our work.

Our protocol improves upon the solutions of Kursawe and Kuznetsov et al. by being leaderless and asynchronous even in the slow path. This is crucial as leader-based protocols have been shown to be susceptible to throughput degradation in the case of even one slow replica [1,2,11,15,43]. Song et al. [38] solution is probably most similar to ours, as their Bosco algorithm provides the same decision latency as ours. However, their solution does not focus on reducing the number of invocations of the underlying consensus, meaning that consensus is still performed for every decision.

Sharding is the process of splitting a blockchain architecture into multiple chains, allowing parallelization as each chain solves the state replication task separately. The improvement brought forward in this area [4] is orthogonal to the one we address in this work. Indeed, while having multiple shards allows systems to parallelize operations overall, inside each shard transactions still need to be processed sequentially.

Implementations. Recent systems that remove or reduce the need for consensus have shown great promise in terms of practical scalability. More specifically, Astro [12] is able to perform 20,000 transactions per second, in a network of 200 nodes, with transactions having a latency of less than a second. A similar system by Spiegelman et al. [14] that uses consensus without creating overhead achieves 160,000 tx/s with about 3 s latency in a WAN. The Accept system [29] scales linearly, and has been shown to achieve 1.5 Million tx/s.

5   A Simple Payment System

We describe a digital currency called BroadcastCoin that serves as a foundation. The protocol disseminates transactions through separate instances of Byzantine reliable broadcast. Crucially, the protocol does not rely on transactions being executed sequentially.

As explained in Sect. 3, clients start with a given account balance. Clients can access a server to submit transactions $t = (sender, sn, recipient, amount)$. We assume that all transactions are signed using public-key cryptography and that servers only handle transactions with valid signatures. Clients can go offline whenever they please, but are required to keep track of the number of transactions they have performed so far, in order to choose correct, i.e. increasing, sequence numbers.

The BroadcastCoin algorithm determines the agreed order of transactions of a given client to be executed. A transaction accepted by the underlying Byzantine reliable broadcast instance is executed (i.e., the funds are moved) as soon as all previous transactions belonging to the corresponding sender are executed, and enough funds are available in the sender's balance.

The **BroadcastCoin** interface of a server (bc) exports the following events:

- **Request**: $\langle bc.\text{Transfer} \mid s, sn, r, a \rangle$: Allows a client s to submit a transaction with sequence number sn sending a units of cryptocurrency to a recipient client r.
- **Request**: $\langle bc.\text{RequestBalance} \mid c \rangle$: Retrieves the amount of cryptocurrency client c currently owns.
- **Indication**: $\langle bc.\text{Balance} \mid c, a \rangle$: Amount a of cryptocurrency currently owned by client c.

In Byzantine reliable broadcast algorithms, a transaction t typically undergoes the following steps before being accepted:

1. *Dissemination*: A server broadcasts t received by a client by sending it to all servers.
2. *Verification*: Servers acknowledge t if they have never acknowledged a conflicting transaction t'.
3. *Approval*: Servers that receive more than $\frac{n+f}{2}$ acknowledgements for a transaction, broadcast an APPROVE message. Servers also broadcast an APPROVE message, if they see more than $f + 1$ approvals. A server that receives more than $2f + 1$ approvals, accepts the transaction.

Algorithm 1. BroadcastCoin

1: **Uses:**
2:     Authenticated Perfect Point-to-Point Links, **instance** al
3:     Byzantine Reliable Broadcast, **instance** rb
4:
5: **upon event** ⟨bc.Init | *initialDistribution*⟩ **do**
6:     $currentSN := [](-1);$ ▷ dictionary initialized with -1
7:     $pending := \{\};$ ▷ empty set
8:     $balance := initialDistribution;$ ▷ dictionary
9:
10: **upon event** ⟨bc.RequestBalance | *client*⟩ **do**
11:     **trigger** ⟨bc.Balance | *client, balance[client]*⟩;
12:
13: **upon event** ⟨bc.Transfer | [*sender, sn, recipient, amount*]⟩ **do**
14:     $t := [sender, sn, recipient, amount];$
15:     **trigger** ⟨rb.Broadcast | [*sender, sn*], t⟩;   ▷ will be changed in Section 6
16:
17: **upon event** ⟨rb.Deliver | [*sender, sn*], t⟩ **do**
18:     $pending[t.sender] = pending[t.sender] \cup t;$
19:
20: **upon** $\exists t \in pending$ **such that** $isValidToExecute(t)$ **do**
21:     $balance[t.sender] = balance[t.sender] - t.amount;$
22:     $balance[t.recipient] = balance[t.recipient] + t.amount;$
23:     $currentSN[t.sender] = currentSN[t.sender] + 1;$
24:     $pending[t.sender] = pending[t.sender] \setminus t;$
25:
26: **procedure** $isValidToExecute(t)$ **is**
27:     **return** $currentSN[t.sender] = t.sn - 1 \wedge balance[t.sender] \geq t.amount;$
28:

---

6   Consensus on Demand

This section presents the core of our contribution that improves upon Broadcast-Coin by providing higher functionality as well as lower latency in the fast path. The Byzantine reliable broadcast instance *rb* is substituted by two steps. A best-effort broadcast primitive is used to disseminate transactions efficiently. Then the first transaction *t* for a given (*sender, sn*) received by a server is the input value proposed in the corresponding ConsensusOnDemand instance. ConsensusOnDemand uses an underlying consensus instance to provide conflict resolution when necessary. We stress that the combination of the broadcast and consensus steps can be implemented in a variety of ways. The version we present in the following consists of best-effort broadcast paired with consensus as defined in Definition 3, while in Sect. 7 we mention a different combination. As before, a transaction traverses three stages:

1. *Dissemination:* The transaction is broadcast to all servers.
2. *Verification:* Servers issue an acknowledgement for the first valid transaction they observe for a given (*sender, sn*) pair. If at any point, a server observes a

quorum of more than $\frac{n+3f}{2}$ acknowledgements for a transaction t, the server accepts t.

3. *Consensus (opt.):* If after receiving $n - f$ acknowledgements servers observe conflicting acknowledgments, they propose the transaction for which they have observed the most acknowledgements up to this point to the consensus instance identified by the $(sender, sn)$ pair. The transaction decided by the consensus routine is then accepted immediately, if the transaction hasn't already been accepted by the fast path.

Note that the first stage is identical to the first stage in the Byzantine reliable broadcast considered in Sect. 5. Although the acceptance condition is also similar, it is performed without the additional broadcast round of APPROVE messages. This means that in the common case, transactions are accepted with less delay. The final stage consists of performing consensus if necessary.

The crux of this construction is that a transaction accepted by the fast path should never conflict with a transaction accepted in the slow path. This holds true, since if a transaction t can be accepted by an honest server in the fast path, even though conflicting transactions exists, then every other honest server is guaranteed to observe a majority of acknowledgements for t in a quorum of size $n - f$. Thus, all honest servers will propose t to the underlying consensus instance, and by its validity property, every server will eventually also accept t.

Figure 2 illustrates this argument in the case where $n = 5f + 1$. There are $3f + 1$ honest servers that acknowledge t and f honest servers that acknowledge t'. By issuing acknowledgements for t, the adversary could bring some servers to accept the transaction t in the fast path. Hence, ConsensusOnDemand should never accept t'. This can be guaranteed, as every quorum containing more than $n - f$ servers (such as Q_1) has a majority of servers acknowledging t. Thus, every server will propose t to the consensus instance, which will accept t due to its validity property. Theorem 3 proves this intuition.

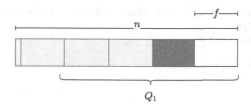

Fig. 2. The two shades of gray represent the share of honest servers acknowledging t (light gray) and t' (dark gray). The adversary is depicted in white, and can acknowledge either transaction. While a server might see more than $4f$ acknowledgments for t, no server sees a majority of acknowledgements for t' in a quorum of $n - f$ servers.

Algorithm 2. ConsensusOnDemand

1: **Implements:**
2:     Consensus, **instance** fc for the (sender, sn) tuple
3:
4: **Uses:**
5:     Consensus, **instance** con
6:     Authenticated Perfect Point-to-Point Links, **instance** al
7:
8: **upon event** $\langle fc.\text{Init} \rangle$ **do**
9:     $accepted, con\_proposed :=$ False;
10:    $acks := [n](\perp);$ ▷ array of size n initialized with $\perp$
11:
12: **upon event** $\langle fc.\text{Propose} \mid t \rangle$ **do**
13:    **for all** q **in** Π **do**
14:        **trigger** $\langle al.\text{Send} \mid q, [\text{ACK}, t] \rangle$
15:    **end for**
16:
17: **upon event** $\langle al.\text{Deliver} \mid p, [\text{ACK}, t] \rangle$ **do**
18:    **if** $acks[p] = \perp$ **then**
19:        $acks[p] := t;$
20:    **end if**
21:
22: **upon exists** $t \neq \perp$ **such that** $\#(\{p \in \Pi \mid acks[p] = t\}) \geq \frac{n+3f}{2}$ **and** $accepted =$
      False **do**
23:    $accepted :=$ True;
24:    **trigger** $\langle fc.\text{Accept} \mid t \rangle;$
25:
26: **upon exists** $p, q \in \Pi$ **such that** $acks[p] \neq acks[q]$ **and** $\#(\{p \in \Pi \mid acks[p] \neq$
      $\perp\}) \geq n - f$ **and** $con\_proposed =$ False **do**
27:    $majority := argmax_{t \in T}(\#(\{p \in \Pi \mid acks[p] = t\})$
28:    $con\_proposed :=$ True;
29:    **trigger** $\langle con.\text{Propose} \mid majority \rangle$
30:
31: **upon event** $\langle con.\text{Accept} \mid t \rangle$ **such that** $accepted =$ False **do**
32:    $accepted :=$ True;
33:    **trigger** $\langle fc.\text{Accept} \mid t \rangle;$
34:

Theorem 1. *ConsensusOnDemand satisfies Validity.*

Proof. If every honest server observes the same transaction t, then every honest server broadcasts an acknowledgment for t. Thus every server is guaranteed to eventually observe at least $n - f$ acknowledgements for t. Since $f < \frac{n}{5}$, it follows that $\frac{n+3f}{2} < n - f$, thus every server eventually accepts t.

Theorem 2. *ConsensusOnDemand satisfies Termination.*

Proof. If every honest server observes the same transaction t, by the same argument as in Theorem 1, every server accepts t in a single message round-trip. If an honest server observes too many conflicting acknowledgments to accept a transaction on the fast path, then at least two honest servers have issued conflicting transactions. Hence, eventually, every correct server will propose a transaction to the consensus instance *con*. By *termination* of consensus, *con* will eventually accept a transaction, and thus every honest server will eventually accept a transaction.

Theorem 3. *ConsensusOnDemand satisfies Agreement.*

Proof. First, let us assume that a server accepts a transaction t without using the consensus instance. This means that the server has seen more than $\frac{n+3f}{2}$ acknowledgments for t. This implies that more than $\frac{n+3f}{2} - f = \frac{n+f}{2}$ honest servers have acknowledged t.

Before proposing, every server waits for the arrival of $n-f$ acknowledgements, out of which at least $n-2f$ come from honest servers. Together, both sets contain more than $\frac{n+f}{2} + n - 2f = \frac{3(n-f)}{2}$ acknowledgements coming from honest servers. However, there are no more than $n - f$ honest servers, meaning that both sets have more than $\frac{3(n-f)}{2} - (n - f) = \frac{n-f}{2}$ acknowledgements in common. This implies that acknowledgements for t will be the most received acknowledgement at every honest server.

Therefore, every honest server will either accept t though its fast path or, if there is a conflicting transaction, propose t to the consensus instance. Due to its validity property, no honest server will accept a value different from t, thus satisfying agreement.

If no server observes more than $\frac{n+3f}{2}$ acknowledgments for a single transaction, then all honest servers will fall back to the consensus instance, and due to its agreement property, the agreement of ConsensusOnDemand is also satisfied.

7   Discussion

Throughput. No-consensus payment systems have been shown to scale linearly with more computing resources [5,12]. In particular the simple design of Mathys et al. [29] can be directly applied as the implementation of the fast path of our design, and their result supports our claim that the fast path of our protocol has in principle unbounded throughput.

Slow Path Abuse. In ConsensusOnDemand, malicious clients can increase the likelihood that consensus needs to be performed by submitting conflicting transactions intentionally.

Due to the completely asynchronous communication model, in our protocol servers keep listening for potentially conflicting acknowledgements of past transactions that might trigger a consensus invocation. This requirement can be avoided by replacing best-effort broadcast in the fast path with (probabilistic) reliable broadcast. In this configuration, servers for which the fast path succeeds do not have to participate in the slow path at all, as thanks to reliable broadcast's totality property, every honest server is guaranteed to eventually be able to complete the fast path. This modification would make it harder for malicious clients to intentionally invoke consensus, but on the other hand a more complicated broadcast primitive would be used (two echo rounds instead of one).

Intentional abuse of the slow path can also be addressed through game-theoretic means. Economic incentives, such as fees, can be set up so that intentional consensus invocation is adequately costly for a malicious client. The subject of incentive schemes in blockchain systems is broad, as different aspects of the system's functionality need to be considered depending on the application. It is thus left outside the scope of this paper.

Fast Path-Only Synchronization. We presented ConsensusOnDemand in the form where the consensus outcome is accepted by the servers without further steps. Consider the following addition to our protocol. Suppose a server s has not acknowledged a transaction t in the fast path, and later t is the result of consensus. Even though s might have acknowledged a conflicting transaction t' in the fast path, let now s broadcast a fast path acknowledgement for t. By introducing this rule, we ensure that all honest servers that observe the consensus outcome additionally issue a fast path acknowledgement. Afterwards, all accepted transactions can be determined only following the fast path condition.

In this setup, any records of consensus performed by the system can be forgotten, as any agent synchronizing with the state of the system conveniently only needs to be supplied with the fast path acknowledgements.

8   Implementation

We implement the BroadcastCoin protocol described in Algorithm 1 by utilizing the core of the *go-ethereum* client for Ethereum. The main modules that are of relevance are briefly described below.

Transactions: There are two types of transactions in Ethereum. We only support transactions that lead to message calls, and do not support transactions that lead to contract creation. Transactions are broadcast using the Ethereum Wire Protocol [16] that probabilistically disseminates blocks through gossip with a sample size of $\sqrt{n}$.

Blocks: The fundamental building blocks of Ethereum also lay at the core of our protocol. However, instead of using a single chain of blocks to totally order transactions, blocks are used to broadcast batches of acknowledgments. This is done by including all transactions that should be signed in a block created by the server. The block signature proves the authenticity of all acknowledgments. The *parentHash* field of a block is also kept, in order to refer to the previous block, which allows for easier *synchronization* between servers.

Blockchain: As every server issues its own chain of blocks, we re-purpose the blockchain abstraction to keep track of all chains in a DAG and allow for synchronization with new clients in future extensions.

Mining: We replace the proof-of-work engine with our own logic that determines which transactions from the transaction pool are safe to be acknowledged. Acknowledgements are batched in blocks, signed and broadcast every 5 s.

Transaction Pool: The transaction pool module is managing new transactions in Ethereum. Most functions and data structures shown in the pseudocode of Algorithm 1 are closely matching the implementation of this module.

We complete the implementation of our protocol by enhancing the no-consensus payment system with the ConsensusOnDemand algorithm. We do so by plugging in a simple consensus algorithm built on the Ethereum Rinkeby testnet. More specifically, we provide a smart contract that is able to perform consensus for any $(sender, sn)$ instance. The contract terminates either when $f + 1$ equal proposals for t are collected, in which case it immediately accepts t. Alternatively, once $2f + 1$ proposals are collected, the contract accepts the most frequent input. The smart contract is called *Multishot* and its implementation can be found in [42], while the appendix of the arXiv version [36] shows the pseudocode and the correctness proof of this algorithm.

While our algorithm is agnostic to the underlying consensus algorithm used, this simple smart contract allows us to demonstrate the effectiveness of ConsensusOnDemand, while keeping our implementation in the Ethereum ecosystem.

These few modules make up most of the changes that were required for us to leverage a large part of the existing *go-ethereum* infrastructure. This allows us to take advantage of the network discovery protocol [16] and the support for hardware wallets. Moreover, our server can simultaneously function as a client, which can be controlled through a variety of interfaces. While the regular JavaScript console can be used, the client can also be addressed via a standard web3 JSON-RPC API accessible through HTTP, WebSockets and Unix Domain Sockets. The complete infrastructure is open source [41].

References

1. Amir, Y., Coan, B., Kirsch, J., Lane, J.: Prime: byzantine replication under attack. IEEE Trans. Dependable Secure Comput. **8**, 564–577 (2011)
2. Antoniadis, K., Desjardins, A., Gramoli, V., Guerraoui, R., Zablotchi, I.: Leaderless consensus. In: 2021 IEEE 41st International Conference on Distributed Computing Systems (ICDCS), pp. 392–402 (2021)
3. Auvolat, A., Frey, D., Raynal, M., Taïani, F.: Money transfer made simple: a specification, a generic algorithm, and its proof. arXiv preprint arXiv:2006.12276 (2020)
4. Avarikioti, G., Kokoris-Kogias, E., Wattenhofer, R.: Divide and scale: formalization of distributed ledger sharding protocols. arXiv preprint arXiv:1910.10434 (2019)
5. Baudet, M., Danezis, G., Sonnino, A.: Fastpay: high-performance byzantine fault tolerant settlement. In: Proceedings of the 2nd ACM Conference on Advances in Financial Technologies, pp. 163–177 (2020)

6. Bazzi, R., Herlihy, M.: Clairvoyant state machine replication. Inf. Comput. **285**, 104701 (2021)
7. Bracha, G.: Asynchronous byzantine agreement protocols. Inf. Comput. **75**(2), 130–143 (1987)
8. Bracha, G., Toueg, S.: Asynchronous consensus and broadcast protocols. JACM **32**(4), 824–840 (1985)
9. Burckhardt, S., Gotsman, A., Yang, H., Zawirski, M.: Replicated data types: specification, verification, optimality. In: Proceedings of the 41st ACM SIGPLAN-SIGACT Symposium on Principles of Programming Languages, pp. 271–284. POPL 2014, Association for Computing Machinery, New York, NY, USA (2014)
10. Castro, M., Liskov, B.: Practical byzantine fault tolerance and proactive recovery. ACM Trans. Comput. Syst. (TOCS) **20**(4), 398–461 (2002)
11. Clement, A., Wong, E., Alvisi, L., Dahlin, M., Marchetti, M.: Making byzantine fault tolerant systems tolerate byzantine faults. In: Proceedings of the 6th USENIX Symposium on Networked Systems Design and Implementation, pp. 153–168. NSDI 2009, USENIX Association, USA (2009)
12. Collins, D., et al.: Online payments by merely broadcasting messages. In: 2020 50th Annual IEEE/IFIP International Conference on Dependable Systems and Networks (DSN), pp. 26–38. IEEE (2020)
13. Crain, T., Natoli, C., Gramoli, V.: Red belly: a secure, fair and scalable open blockchain. In: 2021 IEEE Symposium on Security and Privacy (SP), pp. 466–483. IEEE (2021)
14. Danezis, G., Kokoris-Kogias, L., Sonnino, A., Spiegelman, A.: Narwhal and tusk: a DAG-based mempool and efficient BFT consensus. In: Proceedings of the 17th European Conference on Computer Systems, pp. 34–50 (2022)
15. Duan, S., Reiter, M.K., Zhang, H.: Beat: asynchronous BFT made practical. In: Proceedings of the 2018 ACM SIGSAC Conference on Computer and Communications Security, pp. 2028–2041. CCS 2018 (2018)
16. Foundation, E.: Ethereum wire protocol (eth) (2021). https://github.com/ethereum/devp2p/blob/master/caps/eth.md
17. Gilad, Y., Hemo, R., Micali, S., Vlachos, G., Zeldovich, N.: Algorand: scaling byzantine agreements for cryptocurrencies. In: Proceedings of the 26th symposium on operating systems principles, pp. 51–68 (2017)
18. Guerraoui, R., Kuznetsov, P., Monti, M., Pavlovic, M., Seredinschi, D.A., Vonlanthen, Y.: Scalable byzantine reliable broadcast (extended version). arXiv preprint arXiv:1908.01738 (2019)
19. Guerraoui, R., Kuznetsov, P., Monti, M., Pavlovič, M., Seredinschi, D.A.: The consensus number of a cryptocurrency. In: Proceedings of the 2019 ACM Symposium on Principles of Distributed Computing - PODC 2019 (2019)
20. Gupta, S.: A non-consensus based decentralized financial transaction processing model with support for efficient auditing. Arizona State University (2016)
21. Herlihy, M.: Wait-free synchronization. ACM Trans. Program. Lang. Syst. (TOPLAS) **13**(1), 124–149 (1991)
22. Kiayias, A., Russell, A., David, B., Oliynykov, R.: Ouroboros: a provably secure proof-of-stake blockchain protocol. In: Katz, J., Shacham, H. (eds.) CRYPTO 2017. LNCS, vol. 10401, pp. 357–388. Springer, Cham (2017). https://doi.org/10.1007/978-3-319-63688-7_12
23. Kursawe, K.: Optimistic byzantine agreement. In: 21st IEEE Symposium on Reliable Distributed Systems, 2002. Proceedings, pp. 262–267. IEEE (2002)

24. Kuznetsov, P., Tonkikh, A., Zhang, Y.X.: Revisiting optimal resilience of fast byzantine consensus. In: Proceedings of the 2021 ACM Symposium on Principles of Distributed Computing, pp. 343–353 (2021)
25. Lamport, L.: Generalized consensus and paxos (2005)
26. Lamport, L.: Lower bounds for asynchronous consensus. Distrib. Comput. **19**(2), 104–125 (2006)
27. Malkhi, D., Reiter, M.: A high-throughput secure reliable multicast protocol. J. Comput. Secur. **5**(2), 113–127 (1997)
28. Martin, J.P., Alvisi, L.: Fast byzantine consensus. IEEE Trans. Dependable Secure Comput. **3**(3), 202–215 (2006)
29. Mathys, M., Schmid, R., Sliwinski, J., Wattenhofer, R.: A limitlessly scalable transaction system. In: 6th International Workshop on Cryptocurrencies and Blockchain Technology (CBT), Copenhagen, Denmark (2022)
30. Nakamoto, S.: Bitcoin: a peer-to-peer electronic cash system (2009). http://www.bitcoin.org/bitcoin.pdf
31. Nasirifard, P., Mayer, R., Jacobsen, H.A.: Fabriccrdt: a conflict-free replicated datatypes approach to permissioned blockchains. In: Proceedings of the 20th International Middleware Conference, pp. 110–122. Middleware 2019 (2019)
32. Pedone, F., Schiper, A.: Generic broadcast. In: Jayanti, P. (ed.) DISC 1999. LNCS, vol. 1693, pp. 94–106. Springer, Heidelberg (1999). https://doi.org/10.1007/3-540-48169-9_7
33. Pires, M., Ravi, S., Rodrigues, R.: Generalized paxos made byzantine (and less complex). Algorithms **11**(9), 141 (2018)
34. Preguiça, N.: Conflict-free replicated data types: an overview. arXiv preprint arXiv:1806.10254 (2018)
35. Raykov, P., Schiper, N., Pedone, F.: Byzantine fault-tolerance with commutative commands. In: Fernàndez Anta, A., Lipari, G., Roy, M. (eds.) OPODIS 2011. LNCS, vol. 7109, pp. 329–342. Springer, Heidelberg (2011). https://doi.org/10.1007/978-3-642-25873-2_23
36. Sliwinski, J., Vonlanthen, Y., Wattenhofer, R.: Consensus on demand. arXiv preprint arXiv:2202.03756 (2022)
37. Sliwinski, J., Wattenhofer, R.: Asynchronous proof-of-stake. In: 23rd International Symposium on Stabilization, Safety, and Security of Distributed Systems (SSS) (2021)
38. Song, Y.J., van Renesse, R.: Bosco: one-step byzantine asynchronous consensus. In: Taubenfeld, G. (ed.) DISC 2008. LNCS, vol. 5218, pp. 438–450. Springer, Heidelberg (2008). https://doi.org/10.1007/978-3-540-87779-0_30
39. Srikanth, T.K., Toueg, S.: Simulating authenticated broadcasts to derive simple fault-tolerant algorithms. Distrib. Comput. **2**(2), 80–94 (1987)
40. Suri-Payer, F., Burke, M., Wang, Z., Zhang, Y., Alvisi, L., Crooks, N.: Basil: breaking up BFT with acid (transactions). In: Proceedings of the ACM SIGOPS 28th Symposium on Operating Systems Principles, pp. 1–17 (2021)
41. Vonlanthen, Y.: Cascadeth (2021). https://github.com/yannvon/cascadeth
42. Vonlanthen, Y.: Multishot (2021). https://github.com/yannvon/aposteriori
43. Yin, M., Malkhi, D., Reiter, M.K., Gueta, G.G., Abraham, I.: Hotstuff: BFT consensus with linearity and responsiveness. In: Proceedings of the 2019 ACM Symposium on Principles of Distributed Computing, pp. 347–356 (2019)

Better Incentives for Proof-of-Work

Jakub Sliwinski$^{(\boxtimes)}$ and Roger Wattenhofer

ETH Zurich, Zürich, Switzerland
{jsliwinski,wattenhofer}@ethz.ch

Abstract. This work proposes a novel proof-of-work blockchain incentive scheme such that, barring exogenous motivations, following the protocol is guaranteed to be the optimal strategy for miners. Our blockchain takes the form of a directed acyclic graph, resulting in improvements with respect to throughput and speed.

More importantly, for our blockchain to function, it is not expected that the miners conform to some presupposed protocol in the interest of the system's operability. Instead, our system works if miners act selfishly, trying to get the maximum possible rewards, with no consideration for the overall health of the blockchain.

1 Introduction

A decade ago, Satoshi Nakamoto presented his now famous Bitcoin protocol [11]. Nakamoto assembled some stimulating techniques in an attractive package, such that the result was more than just the sum of its parts.

The Bitcoin blockchain promises to order and store transactions meticulously, despite being anarchistic, without a trusted party. Literally anybody can participate, as long as "honest nodes collectively control more CPU power than any cooperating group of attacker nodes." [11]

In Sect. 6 of his seminal paper, Nakamoto argues that it is rational to be honest thanks to block rewards and fees. However, it turns out that Nakamoto was wrong, and rational does not imply honest. If a miner has a fast network *and/or* a significant fraction of the hashing power, the miner may be better off by not being honest, holding blocks back instead of immediately broadcasting them to the network [2].

If the material costs and payoffs of mining are low, one can argue that the majority of miners will want to remain honest. After all, if too many miners stop conforming to the protocol, the system will break down. However, the costs and payoffs of participation vary over time, and a majority of miners remaining altruistic is never guaranteed. Strategies outperforming the protocol may or may not be discovered for different blockchain incentive designs. However, as long as it is not proven that no such sophisticated strategy exists, the system remains in jeopardy.

S. Devismes et al. (Eds.): SSS 2022, LNCS 13751, pp. 314–328, 2022.
https://doi.org/10.1007/978-3-031-21017-4_21

1.1 Blockchain Game

Typical blockchains, such as Bitcoin's, take the form of a rooted tree of blocks. During the execution of the protocol, players continually create new blocks that are appended to the tree as new leaves. Creating blocks is computationally intensive, so that the network creates a specific number of blocks in a given time period, such as one block every ten minutes on average in Bitcoin. One path of blocks, such as the longest path, is distinguished as the main chain and keeps being extended by addition of new leaves. The network's participants want to create blocks that remain incorporated into the main chain, as these blocks are rewarded. Ideally, the leaves would be added in sequence, each leaf appended to the previous leaf. However, by chance or malice, it is inevitable that some leaves are appended to the same block and create a "fork". Then, it is uncertain which one will end up extending the main chain. According to typical solutions, one of the competing leaves is eventually chosen as being in the main chain, and the creator of the other leaf misses out on block rewards. This approach introduces some unwanted incentives and a potential to punish other players. Even worse, some factors such as network connectivity start to play a role and might influence the behaviour of players.

1.2 Our Contribution

We propose a blockchain design with an incentive scheme guaranteeing that deviating from the protocol strictly reduces the overall share and amount of rewards. All players following the protocol constitute a strict, strong Nash equilibrium. Our approach is to ensure that creating a fork will always be detrimental to all parties involved. Our design allows blocks to reference more than one previous block; in other words, the blocks form a directed acyclic graph (DAG). We prove that miners creating a new block have an incentive to always reference all previously unreferenced blocks. Hence, all blocks are recorded in the blockchain and no blocks are discarded.

1.3 Intuitive Overview

In Sect. 2 we describe the terms to define our protocol.

In Sect. 3 we explain the protocol and how to interpret the created DAG. In terms of security, our design is identical to known proof-of-work blockchains, as similarly to other protocols, we identify the main chain to achieve consensus. Intuitively, each new block should reference all previous terminal blocks known to the miner and automatically extend the main chain. In Subsect. 3.1, we explain how to use the main chain to process and totally order all blocks [7].

In Sect. 4 we construct and discuss our reward scheme.

In Subsect. 4.1 we explain how to label some blocks as stale, such that blocks mined by honest miners are not labeled as stale, but blocks withheld for a long time are labeled as stale. Stale blocks do not receive any rewards.

The core idea of the incentive scheme is to penalize every block by a small amount for every block that it "competes" with.

In Sect. 5 we discuss related work.

2   Model and Preliminaries

2.1   Rounds

We assume a network with a message diffusion mechanism that delivers messages to all connected parties (similarly to Bitcoin's network).

Similarly to foundational works in the area [3] we express the network delay in terms of rounds. Communication is divided into rounds, such that when a player broadcasts a message, it will be delivered to all parties in the network in the next round. Thus each round can be viewed as: 1) receiving messages sent in the previous round, 2) computing (mining) new blocks, 3) broadcasting newly found blocks to all other players.

Rounds model the network delay for the purpose of analysis. However, the protocol itself is not concerned with the division of time into rounds in any way, and only relies on the network delay being correspondingly bounded.

2.2   Players

To avoid confusion in how we build on previous work, we stick to the usual terminology of *honest* players and an *adversary*. The players that conform to the protocol are called honest. A coalition of all parties that considers deviating from the protocol is controlled by an adversary. We gradually introduce new elements, and eventually show that by deviating from the protocol, the adversary reduces its share and amount of rewards. Hence, rational becomes synonymous with honest.

The adversary constitutes a minority as described in Sect. 2.5, otherwise the adversary can take over the blockchain by simply ignoring all actions by honest players.

The adversary is also more powerful than honest players. First of all, we consider the adversary as a single entity. The adversary does not have to send messages to itself, so the mine/send/receive order within a round does not apply to the adversary. Moreover, the adversary gets to see all messages sent by honest players in round r before deciding its strategy of round r. After seeing the honest messages, the adversary is not allowed to create new blocks again in this round. Moreover, the adversary controls the order that messages arrive to each player.

2.3   Blocks

Blocks are the messages that the players exchange, and a basic unit of the blockchain. Formally, a block B is a tuple $B = \langle \mathcal{T}_B, \mathcal{R}_B, c, \eta \rangle$, where:

- $\mathcal{T}_B$ is the content of the block

- $\mathcal{R}_B$ is a set of references (hashes) to previously existing blocks, i.e. $\mathcal{R}_B = \{h(B_1), \ldots, h(B_m)\}$
- c is a public key of the player that created the block
- η is the proof-of-work nonce, i.e., a number such that for a hash function h and difficulty parameter D, $h(B) < D$ holds.

The content of the block $\mathcal{T}_B$ depends on the application. In general, $\mathcal{T}_B$ contains some information that the block creator wishes to record in the blockchain for all participants to see. We consider blockchain properties independently of the content $\mathcal{T}_B$. The content $\mathcal{T}_B$ is discussed in the arXiv version [16].

The creator of B holds the private key corresponding to c. The creator can later use the key to withdraw the reward for creating B. The amount of reward is automatically determined by the protocol, and at the core of our contribution in Sect. 4.

2.4 DAG

$\mathcal{R}_B$ includes at least one hash of a previous block, which might be the hash of a special *genesis* block $\langle \emptyset, \emptyset, \perp, 0 \rangle$. The hash function is pre-image resistant, i.e. it is infeasible to find a message given its hash. If a block B' includes a reference to another block B, B' must include $h(B)$, and hence has to be created after B.

A directed cycle of blocks is impossible, as the block which was created earliest in such a cycle cannot include a hash to the other blocks that were created later. Consequently, the blocks always form a directed acyclic graph (*DAG*) with the genesis block as the only root (block without any parent) of this DAG.

2.5 Mining

Creating a new block is achieved by varying η to find a hash value that is smaller than the difficulty parameter $\mathcal{D}$, i.e., $h(\langle \mathcal{T}_B, \mathcal{R}_B, c, \eta \rangle) < \mathcal{D}$. Creating blocks in this way is called *mining*. Blocks are called honest if mined by an honest player, or adversarial if mined by the adversary.

By varying $\mathcal{D}$, the protocol designer can set the probability of mining a block with a single hashing query arbitrarily. The difficulty $\mathcal{D}$ could also change during the execution of the protocol to adjust the rate at which blocks are created. We leave the details of changing $\mathcal{D}$ to future work, and assume $\mathcal{D}$ to be constant.

The honest players control the computational power to mine α blocks in expectation in one round. The computational power of the adversary is such that the expected number of blocks the adversary can mine in one round is equal to β. The adversary does not experience a delay in communication with itself, so the adversary might mine multiple blocks forming a chain in one round.

Assumptions. The following assumptions are made in order to satisfy the prerequisites of Lemma 2, which was proven in [6]. Lemma 2 links our work to traditional blockchains. Intuitively, the lemma states that a traditional blockchain works with respect to the most basic requirement. If one believes a blockchain to function in this basic way under some other assumptions, those assumptions can be used instead, and our results would apply in the same way.

Because of the delay in communication, the effective computational power of the honest players corresponds to the probability $\alpha' \approx \alpha e^{-\alpha}$ [6] that in a given round exactly one honest player mines a block.

1. The honest players have more mining power: $\alpha' \geq \beta(1 + \epsilon)$ for a constant $\epsilon > 0$.
2. The difficulty D is set such that the expected number of blocks mined within one round is less than one: $\alpha + \beta < 1$.

2.6 Action Space

The state of the blockchain is only updated through discovery and broadcasting of new blocks, hence the adversary can only vary its behaviour with respect to the following factors:

- the blocks being mined i.e. the contents, the included references etc.
- when to announce any of the mined blocks
- the set of agents to whom to send a given block[1].

3   The Block DAG

The protocol by which the honest players construct the block DAG is simple:

- Attempt to mine new blocks.
- Reference in $\mathcal{R}_B$ all unreferenced blocks observed.
- Broadcast newly mined blocks immediately.

Each player stores the DAG formed by all blocks known to the player. For each block B, one of the referenced blocks B_i is the parent $B_i = P(B)$, and B is the child of $P(B)$. The parent is automatically determined based on the DAG structure. The parent-child edges induce the *parent tree* from the DAG.

The players use Algorithm 1 by [17] to select a chain of blocks going from the genesis block to a leaf in the parent tree. The selected chain represents the current state of the blockchain; it is called the *main* chain. The main chain of a player changes from round to round. Players adopt main chains that may be different from each other, depending on the blocks observed.

Let $past(B)$ denote the set of blocks reachable by references from B and the DAG formed by those blocks. The protocol dictates referencing all blocks that otherwise would not be included in $past(B)$. Then, by creating a new block B, the creator communicates only being aware of blocks in $past(B)$. Based on $past(B)$, we determine $P(B)$ as the end of the main chain (Algorithm 1) of the DAG of the player when creating a new block B [7].

---

[1] Honest agents disseminate all received blocks, so by sending a block to a subset of agents, the adversary can delay other agents from seeing a block for only one round.

Algorithm 1: Main chain selection algorithm.

Input: a block tree T
Output: block B - the end of the selected chain
1 $B \leftarrow genesis$ `// start at the genesis block.`
2 **while** B *has a child in* T **do**
3 | $B \leftarrow$ *heaviest child of* B `// continue with the child of B`
                                                    `// with most nodes in its subtree.`
4 **return** B

Definition 1 (Determining Parent). *For a given block B, the block returned by Algorithm 1 in the parent tree of $past(B) \setminus \{B\}$ is the parent of B.*

Lemma 2 by [6], encapsulates the notion that a blockchain (represented by the parent tree in our description) functions properly with respect to a basic requirement. Intuitively, it states that from any point in time, the longer one waits, the more probable it becomes that some honest block mined after that point in time is contained in a main chain of each honest player. The probability of the contrary decreases exponentially with time.

Lemma 2 (Fresh Block Lemma). *For all $r, \Delta \in \mathbb{N}$, with probability $1 - e^{-\Omega(\Delta)}$, there exists a block mined by an honest player on or after round r that is contained in the main chain of each honest player on and after round $r + \Delta$.*

Lemma 2 can be proved with respect to other chain selection rules, for instance picking the child with the longest chain instead of the heaviest child as in Algorithm 1. Our work can be applied equally well using such chain selection rules.

If the protocol designer has control over some factor x, probability of the form $e^{-\Omega(x)}$ can be set arbitrarily low with relatively small variation of x. Probability of the form $e^{-\Omega(x)}$ is called negligible[2].

3.1   Block Order

We will now explain, how all blocks reachable by references will be ordered, following the algorithm of [7]. According to the resulting order, the contents of blocks that fall outside of the main chain can be processed, as if all blocks formed one chain.

Definition 3. *Each player processes blocks in the order $Order(B)$, where B is the last block of the main chain.*

Note the order of executing the FOR loop in line 6 of the Algorithm 2 has to be the same for each player for them to receive consistent orders of blocks. Algorithm 2 processes B_i's in the order of inclusion in $\mathcal{R}_B$, but the order could be alphabetical or induced by the chain selection rule.

Based on lines numbered 5–8 we can state Corollary 4.

---

[2] Probabilities of this form are often disregarded completely in proofs [14].

Algorithm 2: $Order(B)$: a total order of blocks in $past(B)$.

Input: a block B
Output: a total order of all blocks in $past(B)$
1 On the first invocation, $visited(\cdot)$ is initialized to *false* for each block.
2 **if** $visited(B)$ **then return** $\emptyset$
3 $visited(B) \leftarrow true$ // Blocks are visited depth-first.
4 **if** $B = genesis$ **then return** (B)
5 $O \leftarrow Order(P(B))$ // Get the order of $P(B)$ recursively.
6 **for** $i = 1, \ldots, m$ **do**
7 $\quad | \quad O \leftarrow O.append(Order(B_i))$ // Append newly included blocks.
8 $O \leftarrow O.append(B)$ // Append B at the end.
9 **return** O

Corollary 4. *$Order(B)$ extends $Order(P(B))$ by appending all newly reachable blocks not included yet in $Order(P(B))$.*

Lemma 5. *Any announced block becomes referenced by a block contained in the main chain of any honest player after Δ rounds with probability $1 - e^{-\Omega(\Delta)}$.*

Proof. Suppose a block B is announced at round r. By Lemma 2, some honest block A mined in the following Δ rounds is contained in the main chains adopted by honest players after round $r + \Delta$. Since A is honest, $B \in past(A)$.   □

By Lemma 5 all announced blocks are eventually referenced in the main chains of honest players. Since for the purpose of achieving consensus we rely on the results of [6] and [7], we state Corollary 6.

Corollary 6. *The protocol achieves consensus properties corresponding to [6] and [7].*

4   Reward Schemes

4.1   Stale Blocks

We now introduce a mechanism to distinguish blocks that were announced within a reasonable number of rounds from blocks that were withheld by the miner for an extended period of time. Such withheld blocks are called *stale*. Honest miners broadcast their blocks immediately, so stale blocks can be attributed to the adversary. In our incentive scheme, stale blocks will not receive any rewards and will also be ignored for the purpose of determining other block rewards. Thus we ensure that it is pointless for the adversary to wait too long before broadcasting its blocks.

The basic definition of whether a block A is stale is termed with respect to some other block B. We are only interested in blocks B that form the main chain. When the main chain is extended, the sets of stale and non-stale blocks are preserved (and extended). Hence, stale-ness is determined by the eventual main chain.

Definition 7. *Given a block B, the set of stale blocks S_B is computed by Algorithm 3. Then, $\bar{S}_B = past(B) \setminus S_B$. If $A \in S_B$ we call A stale.*

The constant p of Algorithm 3 is chosen by the protocol designer. Intuitively, given a main chain ending with block B that references another block A, we judge A by the distance one needs to backtrack along the main chain to find an ancestor of A. If the distance exceeds p, A is stale.

We call $P^i(B)$ the ith *ancestor of* B and B is a *descendant* of $P^i(B)$[3]. By $LCA(B_1, B_2)$ (lowest common ancestor) we denote the block that is an ancestor of B_1 and an ancestor of B_2, such that none of its children are simultaneously an ancestor of B_1 and an ancestor of B_2.

For blocks A and B, $D(A, B)$ is the distance between A and B in the parent tree, i.e. $D(A, P(A)) = 1$, $D(A, P(P(A))) = 2$, etc.

Algorithm 3: Compute S_B.

Input: a block B
Output: a set S_B
1 **if** $B = genesis$ **then return** $\emptyset$
2 $S \leftarrow S_{P(B)}$ // Copy $S_{P(B)}$ for blocks in $past(P(B))$.
3 **for** $A \in past(B) \setminus past(P(B))$ **do**
4     $X = LCA(A, B)$
5     $Age = D(X, B)$ // age = distance from B to LCA.
6   **if** $Age > p$ **then**
7         $S = S \cup \{A\}$ // A is stale iff age is bigger than p
8 **return** S

Corollary 8 shows that when the main chain is extended, the stale-ness of previously seen blocks is preserved.

Corollary 8. *If $A \in past(P(B))$ then $A \in S_B \iff A \in S_{P(B)}$.*

Proof. Line 2 in Algorithm 3 sets S_B as the same as $S_{P(B)}$, while the following FOR loop adds only blocks $A \notin past(P(B))$. □

Theorem 9 establishes the most important property of stale-ness. The probability that the adversary can successfully make an honest block stale decreases exponentially with p, and is negligible.

Theorem 9 (Honest Blocks are Not Stale). *Let B be an honest block mined on round r. With probability $1 - e^{-\Omega(p)}$, after round $r + O(p)$ each honest player H adopts a main chain ending with a block B_H such that $B \in \bar{S}_{B_H}$.*

The proof appears in the arXiv version of the paper [16].

---

[3] Note that ancestors and descendants are defined based on the parent tree and not based on other non-parent references building up the DAG.

4.2   Discussion of Flat Rewards

Consider coupling the presented protocol with a reward mechanism $\mathcal{R}^0$ that, intuitively speaking, grants some flat amount b of reward to all non-stale blocks, and 0 reward to stale blocks. $\mathcal{R}^0$ is a special case of the reward scheme properly defined in Definition 12.

Corollary 10. *Under the reward scheme $\mathcal{R}^0$, honest players are rewarded proportionally to the number of blocks they mine, except with negligible probability.*

Proof. By Theorem 9 honest blocks are not stale, so honest miners receive rewards linear in the number of blocks they mined. The adversary might only decrease its rewards by producing stale blocks, otherwise the adversary is rewarded in the same way.   □

Note that $\mathcal{R}^0$ achieves the same fairness guarantee as the Fruitchains protocol to be discussed in Sect. 5.3—honest blocks are incorporated into the blockchain as non-stale, while withholding a block for too long makes it lose its reward potential. Both protocols rely on the honest majority of participants to guarantee this fairness.

The Fruitchains protocol relies critically on merged-mining [12] (also called 2-for-1 POW [3]) fruits and blocks. While fruits are mined for the rewards, blocks are supposed to be mined entirely voluntarily with negligible extra cost. The reward scheme $\mathcal{R}^0$ avoids this complication.

Granting flat amount of reward for each non-stale block leaves a lot of room for deviation that goes unpunished. In the case of the Fruitchains protocol, mining blocks does not contribute rewards in any way. Hence, any deviation with respect to mining blocks (which decide the order of contents) is free of any cost for the adversary. In the context of cryptocurrency transactions, a rational adversary should always attempt to double-spend.

In the case of $\mathcal{R}^0$, the adversary can refrain from referencing some recent blocks, and suffer no penalty. However, attempting to manipulate the order of older blocks would render the adversary's new block stale, and hence penalize. Thus, we view even the base case $\mathcal{R}^0$ of the presented reward scheme as a strict improvement over the Fruitchains protocol.

4.3   Penalizing Deviations

Central to our design is the approach to treating forks i.e. blocks that "compete" by referencing the same parent block and not each other. Typically, blockchain schemes specify that one of the blocks eventually "loses" and the creator misses out on some rewards, essentially discouraging competition. However, there are ways of manipulating this process to one's advantage, and the uncertainty of which block will win the competition introduces unneeded incentives. We penalize all parties involved in creating a fork.

The *conflict set* introduced in Definition 11 contains the blocks that "compete" with a given block. Stale blocks are excluded, as we ignore them for the purpose of computing rewards. Like stale-ness, the conflict set is defined with respect to some other block A. Again, we are only interested in blocks A that form the main chain, and the conflict set indicated by the eventual main chain.

The conflict set of a non-stale block B contains all non-stale blocks X that are not reachable by references from B, and B is not reachable by references from X (Fig. 1).

Definition 11 (Conflict Set). *For blocks A and B where $B \in \bar{S}_A$,*

$$X_A(B) = \{X : X \in \bar{S}_A \wedge X \notin past(B) \wedge B \notin past(X)\}.$$

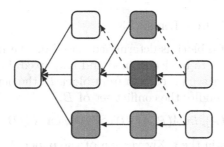

Fig. 1. An example of a conflict set. The gray blocks constitute the conflict set of the blue block. The dashed arrows are references and the solid arrows are parent references. (Color figure online)

Intuitively, the scheme we propose awards every block some amount of reward b decreased by a penalty c multiplied by the size of the conflict set. The ultimate purpose of the properties we establish is to make sure that rational miners want to minimize the conflict set of the blocks they create, following the protocol as a consequence.

Definition 12 (Rewards). *A reward scheme $\mathcal{R}^{c,b}$ is such that given the main chain ending with a block A, each block $B \in past(A)$ is granted $\mathcal{R}_A^{c,b}(B)$ amount of reward:*

$$\mathcal{R}_A^{c,b}(B) = \begin{cases} 0, & \text{if } B \in S_A \text{ or } D(A, LCA(A,B)) \leq 2p. \\ b - c|X_A(B)|, & \text{otherwise.} \end{cases}$$

We write $\mathcal{R}^c$ for $\mathcal{R}^{c,b}$ if b is clear from context, or just $\mathcal{R}$ if c is clear from context.

In our reward scheme, the reward associated with a given block are decreased linearly with the size of the block's conflict set. We need to ensure that no block reward is negative, otherwise the reward scheme would break down. Lemma 13 shows that it is only possible for the conflict set to reach certain size; the probability that the conflict set of a block is bigger than linear in p is negligible.

Intuitively, it is because stale blocks cannot be part of a conflict set, and after enough time has passed from broadcasting some block B, new blocks either reference B or are stale.

As a consequence, we establish in Corollary 14 that the rewards are non-negative.

Lemma 13. *Let $x \geq p$ and B be a block. The probability that any honest player adopts a main chain ending with a block A such that $|X_A(B)| > xp$ is $e^{-\Omega(x)}$.*

The proof appears in the arXiv version of the paper [16].

Corollary 14 (Rewards Are Non-Negative). *Let B be a block. The probability that any honest player adopts a main chain ending with a block A such that $\mathcal{R}_A^{c,b}(B) < 0$ is $e^{-\Omega(\frac{b}{cp})}$.*

Proof. Follows directly from Lemma 13.   □

The conflict set of a block is determined based on the main chain. At some point, the reward needs to be determined and stay fixed. Lemma 15 shows that if the main chain has grown far enough from block B, the new block A appended to the chain will not modify the conflict set of B.

Lemma 15. *If $D(P(A), LCA(P(A), B)) > 2p$ then $X_A(B) = X_{P(A)}(B)$*

The proof appears in the arXiv version of the paper [16].

The rewards in Definition 12 are only assigned as non-zero to blocks B such that $D(A, LCA(A, B)) > 2p$, where A is the block at the end of the main chain. By Corollary 16, these non-zero rewards are not modified by the blocks extending the main chain and remain fixed.

Corollary 16 (Rewards Are Final).

$$\forall B \in past(A) : \mathcal{R}_{P(A)}(B) \neq 0 \implies \mathcal{R}_A(B) = \mathcal{R}_{P(A)}(B).$$

Proof. $\mathcal{R}_A^{c,b}(B)$ is non-zero only if $D(A, LCA(A, B)) > 2p$. The corollary follows from Lemmas 8 and 15 and induction.   □

The properties we have established so far culminate in Theorem 17.

Theorem 17. *Deviating from the protocol reduces the adversary's rewards and its proportion of rewards $\mathcal{R}^{c,b}$, except with negligible probability.*

The proof appears in the arXiv version of the paper [16].

4.4   Nash Equilibria

Theorem 17 follows from Lemma 2 and hence holds for the same action space as considered in [6], i.e. attempting to mine any chosen blocks and withholding or releasing blocks at will. Hence, for this action space, minimizing the conflict set of mined blocks is in the interest of the miner. The adversary is considered as a coordinated minority coalition of players, hence the constants p, c, b can be set such that all players following the protocol constitute a strict, strong Nash equilibrium. In other words, all agents and all minority coalitions of agents strictly prefer to follow the protocol to any alternative strategy.

Corollary 18. *All players following the protocol constitute a strict, strong Nash equilibrium.*

However, there exist other Nash equilibria, such as the example given in the arXiv version of the paper [16]. The presented equilibrium is based on a player threatening to induce penalties for other players by suffering penalties herself. Intuitively speaking, we suggest all Nash equilibria where some player does not follow the protocol are of this nature, but we do not formalize this concept. However, if the adversary wishes to spend resources solely to influence the behaviour of rational miners, there are always ways to achieve this outside the scope of any reward scheme, such as bribery (see Sect. 5.4).

4.5 Hurting Other Players

When designing a reward scheme, it might be seen as fair if each honest player is rewarded irrespectively of the strategies of other players. Such fairness principle is enjoyed by the Fruitchains protocol and our reward scheme $\mathcal{R}^0$. However, those schemes inevitably trivialize some aspect of the game and leave potential for deviation that goes unpunished. A relaxation of this principle is stated in Corollary 19 based on Theorem 17 and its proof.

Corollary 19. *Under the reward scheme $\mathcal{R}^{c,b}$, by deviating from the protocol the adversary can only reduce the rewards of other players by forfeiting at least the same amount.*

We observe that the property stated in Corollary 19 prevents the existence of selfish mining strategies such as those concerning Bitcoin and other traditional blockchains (see Sect. 5.1). Such strategies pose a threat since they enable forfeiting some rewards to penalize other players to an even bigger extent.

5   Related Work

The model of round-based communication in the setting of blockchain was introduced in [3]. This paper formalizes and studies the security of Bitcoin.

5.1   Selfish Mining

Selfish mining is a branch of research studying a type of strategies increasing the proportion of rewards obtained by players in a Bitcoin-like system. Selfish mining exemplifies concerns stemming from the lack of proven incentive compatibility. Selfish mining was first described formally in [2], although the idea had been discussed earlier [10]. Selfish mining strategies have been improved [15] and generalized [13]. Selfish mining is not applicable to our incentive scheme.

5.2 DAG

The way we order all blocks for the purpose of processing them was introduced in [7]. The authors consider an incentive scheme to accompany this modification. Their design relies on altruism, as referring extra blocks has no benefit, other than to creators of referred blocks. Hence, rational miners would never refer them, possibly degenerating the DAG to a blockchain similar to Bitcoin's. Some other shortcomings are discussed by the authors.

The authors of [8] contribute an experimental implementation of the directed acyclic graph structure and ordering of [7], in particular its advantages with respect to the throughput.

5.3 Fruitchains

Fruitchains [14] is the work probably the closest related to ours. Fruitchains is a protocol that gives a guarantee that miners are rewarded somewhat proportionally to their mining power. The objective might seem similar to ours, but there are fundamental differences. To achieve fairness, similarly to existing solutions, the Fruitchains protocol requires the majority of miners to cooperate without an incentive. In other words, in order to contribute to the common good of the system, players must put in altruistic work. In contrast, we strive for a protocol such that any miner simply trying to maximize their share or amount of rewards will inadvertently conform to the protocol.

The Fruitchains protocol rewards mining of "fruits", which are a kind of blocks that do not contribute to the security of the system. The Fruitchains protocol relies on merged-mining[4] also called 2-for-1 PoW in [3]. In addition to fruits, the miners can mine "normal" blocks (containing the fruits) with minimal extra effort and for no reward. The functioning and security of the system depends only on mining normal blocks according to the protocol.

Miners are asked to reference the fruits of other miners, benefiting others but not themselves, similarly to [7]. The probability of not doing so having any effect is negligible, since majority of the miners are still assumed to reference said fruits.

The resulting system-wide cooperation guarantees fairness, inevitably removing many game-theoretic aspects from the resulting game. In particular, misbehaviour does not result in any punishment. It is common to analyze blockchain designs with respect to the expected cost of a double-spend attempt. In the case of Fruitchains, while the probability of double-spends being successful is similar to previous designs, the *cost* of attempting to double-spend is nullified. As a result, any miner might attempt to double-spend constantly at no cost, which we view as a serious jeopardy to the system.

In the absence of punishments, we also argue that not conforming to the protocol is often simpler. Since transaction fees are shared between miners, including transactions might be seen as pointless altogether. Mining only fruits with

---

[4] One of the first mentions of merged-mining as used today is [12], although the general idea was mentioned as early as [4].

dummy, zero-fee transactions, while not including the fruits of others (or not mining for blocks altogether), would relieve the miner of a vast majority of the network communication.

Another game-theoretic issue of the Fruitchains protocol is that while it prescribes sharing of the transaction fees, miners might ask transaction issuers to disguise the fee as an additional transaction output, locking it to a specific miner, potentially benefiting both parties and disrupting the protocol.

As argued in Sect. 4, the reward scheme $\mathcal{R}^0$ is an improvement over Fruitchains in the same vein, achieving the same result while avoiding some of the complications.

In contrast to Fruitchains protocol, the approach of reward schemes $\mathcal{R}^{c,b}$ is to employ purely economic forces, clearly incentivizing desired behaviour while making sure that deviations are punished.

5.4 Bribery

Recently, there have been works highlighting the problems of bribery, e.g. [1,5,9]. A bribing attacker might temporarily convince some otherwise honest players (either using threats or incentives) to join the adversary. Consequently, the adversary might gain more than half of the computational power, taking over the system temporarily.

Such bribery might be completely external to the reward scheme itself, for example the adversary might program a smart contract (perhaps in another blockchain) that provably offers rewards to miners that show they deviate from the protocol [5]. Hence, no permissionless blockchain can be safe against this type of attack.

6   Conclusions

Mining is a risky business, as block rewards must pay for hardware investments, energy and other operation costs. At the time of this writing, the Bitcoin mining turnover alone is worth over \$10 billion per year, which is without a doubt a serious market. Miners in this market are professionals, who will make sure that their investments pay off. Yet, many believe that a majority of miners will follow the protocol altruistically, in the best interests of everybody, the "greater good".

We argue that assuming altruistic miners is not strong enough to be a foundation for a reliable protocol. In this work, we introduced a blockchain incentive scheme such that following the protocol is guaranteed to be the optimal strategy.

We showed that our design is tolerant to miners acting rationally, trying to get the maximum possible rewards, with no consideration for the overall health of the blockchain.

To the best of our knowledge, our design is the first to provably allow for rational mining. Nakamoto [11] needed "honest nodes collectively control more CPU power than any cooperating group of attacker nodes". With our design it is possible to turn the word honest into the word rational.

References

1. Bonneau, J.: Why buy when you can rent? - bribery attacks on bitcoin-style consensus. In: Financial Cryptography and Data Security - FC 2016 International Workshops, BITCOIN, VOTING, and WAHC, Christ Church, Barbados, 26 February 2016, Revised Selected Papers, pp. 19–26 (2016)
2. Eyal, I., Sirer, E.G.: Majority is not enough: bitcoin mining is vulnerable. In: 18th International Conference on Financial Cryptography and Data Security, pp. 436–454 (2014)
3. Garay, J., Kiayias, A., Leonardos, N.: The bitcoin backbone protocol: analysis and applications. In: 34th Annual International Conference on the Theory and Applications of Cryptographic Techniques, pp. 281–310 (2015)
4. Jakobsson, M., Juels, A.: Proofs of work and bread pudding protocols. In: Secure Information Networks, pp. 258–272 (1999)
5. Judmayer, A., et al.: Pay-to-win: incentive attacks on proof-of-work cryptocurrencies. Technical report, Cryptology ePrint Archive, Report 2019/775 (2019)
6. Kiayias, A., Panagiotakos, G.: On trees, chains and fast transactions in the blockchain. In: 5th International Conference on Cryptology and Information Security in Latin America (2017)
7. Lewenberg, Y., Sompolinsky, Y., Zohar, A.: Inclusive block chain protocols. In: 19th International Conference on Financial Cryptography and Data Security, pp. 528–547 (2015)
8. Li, C., Li, P., Xu, W., Long, F., Yao, A.C.: Scaling nakamoto consensus to thousands of transactions per second. arXiv preprint arXiv:1805.03870 (2018)
9. McCorry, P., Hicks, A., Meiklejohn, S.: Smart contracts for bribing miners. In: Financial Cryptography and Data Security - FC 2018 International Workshops, BITCOIN, VOTING, and WTSC, Nieuwpoort, Curaçao, 2 March 2018, Revised Selected Papers, pp. 3–18 (2018)
10. mtgox (2010). https://bitcointalk.org/index.php?topic=2227.msg29606#msg29606
11. Nakamoto, S.: Bitcoin: a peer-to-peer electronic cash system (2008)
12. Nakamoto, S.: https://bitcointalk.org/index.php?topic=1790.msg28696#msg28696 (2010)
13. Nayak, K., Kumar, S., Miller, A., Shi, E.: Stubborn mining: generalizing selfish mining and combining with an eclipse attack. In: 1st IEEE European Symposium on Security and Privacy (2016)
14. Pass, R., Shi, E.: Fruitchains: a fair blockchain. In: Symposium on Principles of Distributed Computing, pp. 315–324 (2017)
15. Sapirshtein, A., Sompolinsky, Y., Zohar, A.: Optimal selfish mining strategies in bitcoin. In: 20th International Conference on Financial Cryptography and Data Security, pp. 515–532 (2016)
16. Sliwinski, J., Wattenhofer, R.: Better incentives for proof-of-work. arXiv preprint arXiv:2206.10050 (2022)
17. Sompolinsky, Y., Zohar, A.: Secure high-rate transaction processing in bitcoin. In: 19th International Conference on Financial Cryptography and Data Security, pp. 507–527 (2015)

Brief Announcements

Brief Announcement: Self Masking for Hardening Inversions

Paweł Cyprys[1], Shlomi Dolev[1(✉)], and Shlomo Moran[2]

[1] Ben-Gurion University of the Negev, Beersheba, Israel
dolev@cs.bgu.ac.il
[2] Technion Israel Institute of Technology, Haifa, Israel

Abstract. The question whether one way functions (i.e., functions that are easy to compute but hard to invert) exist is arguably one of the central problems in complexity theory, both from theoretical and practical aspects. While proving that such functions exist could be hard, there were quite a few attempts to provide functions which are one way "in practice", namely, they are easy to compute, but there are no known polynomial time algorithms that compute their (generalized) inverse (or that computing their inverse is as hard as notoriously difficult tasks, like factoring very large integers).

In this paper we study a different approach. We introduce a simple heuristic, called self masking, which converts a given polynomial time computable function f into a self masked version $[f]$, which satisfies the following: for a random input x, $[f]^{-1}([f](x)) = f^{-1}(f(x))$ w.h.p., but a part of $f(x)$, which is essential for computing $f^{-1}(f(x))$ is *masked* in $[f](x)$. Intuitively, this masking makes it hard to convert an efficient algorithm which computes f^{-1} to an efficient algorithm which computes $[f]^{-1}$, since the masked parts are available in $f(x)$ but not in $[f](x)$.

We apply this technique on variants of the subset sum problem which were studied in the context of one way functions, and obtain functions which, to the best of our knowledge, cannot be inverted in polynomial time by published techniques.

1 Introduction

The question whether one way functions (i.e., functions that are easy to compute but hard to invert) exist is arguably one of the central problems in complexity theory, both from theoretical and practical aspects.

e.g., it is known that the existence of one way functions implies, and is implied by, the existence of pseudo random number generators (see e.g. [5] for a constructive proof of this equivalence).

While proving that one way functions exist could be hard (since it would settle affirmatively the conjecture that $P \neq NP$), there were quite a few attempts to provide functions which are one way "in practice" – namely, they are easy to compute, but there are no known polynomial time algorithms which compute their (generalized) inverses.

S. Devismes et al. (Eds.): SSS 2022, LNCS 13751, pp. 331–334, 2022.
https://doi.org/10.1007/978-3-031-21017-4_22

In this paper we suggest a heuristic, called *self masking*, to cope with published attacks on previous attempts to construct one way functions. Specifically, the self masking versions of polynomial time computable functions "hide" in the outputs of these functions parts which are essential for computing their inverse. This brief announcement contains the necessary definitions, related previous results and a short survey of the main results of the paper. For a more detailed exposition the reader is referred to [4].

1.1   Preliminaries

To make the presentation self contained and as short as possible, we present only definitions which are explicitly used in our analysis. For a more comprehensive background on one way functions and related applications see, e.g., [5,6].

The notation $x \in_{\mathcal{U}} D$ indicates that x is a member of the (finite) set D, and that for probabilistic analysis we assume a uniform distribution on D.

Following [5], we define one way functions using the notion of *polynomial time function ensembles*.

Definition 1. *A polynomial time function ensemble* $f = (f_k)_{k=1}^{\infty}$ *is a polynomial time computable function that, for a strictly increasing sequence* $(n_k)_{k=1}^{\infty}$ *and a sequence* $(m_k)_{k=1}^{\infty}$, f_k *maps* $\{0,1\}^{n_k}$ *to* $\{0,1\}^{m_k}$. *Both* n_k *and* m_k *are bounded by a polynomial in* k *and are computable in time polynomial in* k. *The domain of* f_k *is denoted by* $D_k = \{0,1\}^{n_k}$.[1]

Definition 2. *Let* $f = (f_k)_{k=1}^{\infty}$ *be a polynomial time function ensemble. Then* f *is one way function if for any polynomial time algorithm AL, and for all but finitely many* k's, *the probability that* $AL(f_k(x)) \in f_k^{-1}(f_k(x))$ *for* $x \in_{\mathcal{U}} D_k$ *is negligible (i.e., asymptotically smaller than* $|x|^{-c}$ *for any* $c > 0$) .

1.2   Previous Work

Quite a few attempts to construct one way functions - typically in the context of public key cryptosystems - are based on the hardness of variants of the subset sum problem. However, algorithmic attacks which compute the inverses of the suggested functions in expected polynomial time were later found for all these attempts.

The public key cryptosystem of Merkle and Hellman [9] uses an easy to solve variant of the subset sum problem, in which the input sequence is super increasing, which is transformed to a sequence in which the super increasing structure is concealed. This cryptosystem was first broken by Shamir in [11], and subsequently more sophisticated variants of it were broken too [2].

Super increasing sequences are a special case of *low density* instances of the subset sum problem. These low density instances were also solved efficiently [1, 3,7]. A comprehensive survey of these methods and of the corresponding attacks can be found in [10].

---

[1] For definiteness, inputs whose length ℓ is different from m_k for all k are mapped to 1^{ℓ}.

1.3 Contribution

The basic variant of the self masking technique replaces a (polynomial time computable) function f by a self masking version, denoted $[f]$, as follows: Let $y = f(x)$ for arbitrary x in the domain of f, and let $|x|$ denote the length of x. Then a self masked version $[y] = [f](x)$ is obtained by replacing two "critical" substrings, z_1 and z_2, of y, of length $|x|^{\Omega(1)}$, by $z_1 \oplus z_2$[2]. Intuitively, z_1 and z_2 are critical in the sense that they are essential for computing $f^{-1}(y)$.

An immediate concern raised by this method is that it might significantly increase the number of preimages associated with the masked output value $[f](x)$, e.g. that $[f]^{-1}([f](x))$ may contain exponentially many preimages of $[f](x)$ even if $f^{-1}(f(x))$ contains only few elements. We cope with this difficulty by showing that, by carefully selecting the parameters of the transformation, this is not the case, and in fact that we can guarantee that, w.h.p., $[f]^{-1}([f](x)) = \{x\}$, i.e. $[f]$ is univalent.

We demonstrate this technique on functions associated with variants of the subset sum problem, which were widely used in the context of one way functions (see e.g. [6–9]).

In the detailed presentation of our results, given in [4], we first introduce the self masked subset sum problem, and prove that this problem is NP hard. Then we define function ensembles associated with the self masked subset sum problem, and present conditions under which the resulted functions are univalent w.h.p.. Then we demonstrate that applying the self masking technique on *super increasing* instances of the subset sum problem produces function which cannot be inverted by the known attacks on cryptosystems based on super increasing sequences. We extend this result further by showing that applying the self masking technique on *low density* instances of the subset sum problem provides functions which cannot be inverted by the known attacks on low density instances of the (unmasked) subset sum problem, given, e.g., in [1,7,10]. We conclude by discussing applications of the self masking technique on *high density* instances of the subset sum problem.

References

1. Brickell, E.F.: Solving low density knapsacks. In: Chaum, D. (ed) Advances in cryptology, pp. 25–37. Springer (1984).https://doi.org/10.1007/978-1-4684-4730-9_2
2. Brickell, E.F.: Breaking iterated knapsacks. In: Blakley, G.R., Chaum, D. (eds.) CRYPTO 1984. LNCS, vol. 196, pp. 342–358. Springer, Heidelberg (1985). https://doi.org/10.1007/3-540-39568-7_27
3. Coster, M.J., Joux, A., LaMacchia, B.A., Odlyzko, A.M., Schnorr, C.P., Stern, J.: Improved low-density subset sum algorithms. Comput. Complex. **2**(2), 111–128 (1992)

---

[2] $z_1 \oplus z_2$ denotes bitwise XOR of the binary representations of z_1 and z_2; leading zeros are assumed when these representations are of different lengths.

4. Cyprys, P., Dolev, S., Moran, S.: Self masking for hardering inversions - preliminary version. Cryptology ePrint Archive, Paper 2022/1274 (2022). https://eprint.iacr.org/2022/1274

5. Håstad, J., Impagliazzo, R., Levin, L.A., Luby, M.: A pseudorandom generator from any one-way function. SIAM J. Comput. **28**, 12–24 (1999)

6. Impagliazzo, R., Naor, M.: Efficient cryptographic schemes provably as secure as subset sum. J. Cryptol. **9**(4), 199–216 (1996)

7. Lagarias, J.C., Odlyzko, A.M.: Solving low-density subset sum problems. J. ACM (JACM) **32**(1), 229–246 (1985)

8. Lyubashevsky, V., Palacio, A., Segev, G.: Public-key cryptographic primitives provably as secure as subset sum. In: Micciancio, D. (ed.) TCC 2010. LNCS, vol. 5978, pp. 382–400. Springer, Heidelberg (2010). https://doi.org/10.1007/978-3-642-11799-2_23

9. Merkle, R., Hellman, M.: Hiding information and signatures in trapdoor knapsacks. IEEE Trans. Inf. Theory **24**(5), 525–530 (1978)

10. Odlyzko, A.M.: The rise and fall of knapsack cryptosystems. In: In Cryptology and Computational Number Theory, pp. 75–88. A.M.S (1990)

11. Shamir, A.: A polynomial-time algorithm for breaking the basic Merkle - Hellman cryptosystem. IEEE Trans. Inf. Theory **30**(5), 699–704 (1984). https://doi.org/10.1109/TIT.1984.1056964

Brief Announcement: Dynamic Graph Models for the Bitcoin P2P Network: Simulation Analysis for Expansion and Flooding Time

Antonio Cruciani[1(✉)] and Francesco Pasquale[2]

[1] Gran Sasso Science Institute, L'Aquila, Italy
antonio.cruciani@gssi.it
[2] Università di Roma "Tor Vergata", Roma, Italy
francesco.pasquale@uniroma2.it

Abstract. The network formation process in the Bitcoin protocol is designed to hide the global network structure: while most of the nodes of the network can be easily discovered, the existence or not of an edge between two nodes is only known by the two endpoints.

In [Becchetti et al., SODA2020] the authors propose a random graph generative model resembling the network formation process in the Bitcoin protocol and they prove that it generates an expander graph, with high probability. In this paper we extend that model to obtain two dynamic random graph models that continue to evolve forever. We run extensive simulations to measure "expansion" of the snapshots of the dynamic graphs (i.e., how "well-connected" they are) and "flooding time" (i.e., how long it takes a message starting at some node to reach all, or almost all, the nodes).

Keywords: Dynamic graphs · Markov chains · P2P networks

1 Introduction

Bitcoin is a cryptocurrency proposed in 2008 by an unknown person or group of people under the pseudonym of Satoshi Nakamoto [8]. Nodes in the Bitcoin system are connected toward an unstructured peer-to-peer network [2] running on top of the Internet. The first version of the Bitcoin software was released by Satoshi Nakamoto in January 2009. The most widely used implementation coming from that initial release, named Bitcoin-core [9], is currently under active development. In this paper we are concerned with dynamic graph models inspired by the network formation process of the Bitcoin P2P network. After an initial bootstrap in which they rely on DNS seeds for node discovery, nodes running the Bitcoin-core implementation turn to a fully-decentralized policy to regenerate their neighbors when their degree drops below the configured threshold [5]. Each node has a "target out-degree value" and a "maximum in-degree value" (respectively 8 and 125, in the default configuration) and it locally stores a large list of (ip addresses of) "active" nodes. Every time the number of current

© The Author(s), under exclusive license to Springer Nature Switzerland AG 2022
S. Devismes et al. (Eds.): SSS 2022, LNCS 13751, pp. 335–340, 2022.
https://doi.org/10.1007/978-3-031-21017-4_23

neighbors of a node is below the configured target value it tries to create new connections with nodes sampled from its list. The list stored by a node is initially started with nodes received in response to queries to DNS seeds, then it is periodically advertised to its neighbors and updated with the lists advertised by the neighbors. While most of the nodes of the network can be easily discovered [11], the existence or not of an edge between two nodes is only known by the two endpoints. Indeed, discovering the network structure has been recently an active research topic [6].

Our Contribution. RAES *(Request a link, then Accept if Enough Space)* [3] is a directed random graph model defined by three parameters $n \in \mathbb{N}, d \in \{1, \ldots, n - 1\}, c > 1$, in which each one of n nodes has out-degree exactly d and in-degree at most cd. The random graph is generated according to the following discrete random process: Starting from the empty graph, at every round each node u with out-degree $d_u^{out} < d$ picks $d - d_u^{out}$ nodes *uniformly at random (u.a.r.)* (with repetitions) and, for each such node v, u "requests" a directed link (u, v); If a node v receives a number of link-requests that would make its in-degree larger than cd, then v rejects all requests received in the current round, otherwise v accepts all requests of the round. The process terminates when all nodes have out-degree d (and in-degree at most cd). In this paper we consider an undirected version of RAES and we extend the random graph model in two ways generating *dynamic* random graphs that perpetually evolve. We run extensive simulations of both models to grasp the "stationary" structural properties of the dynamic random graphs and we measure the *flooding time*, i.e., how long it takes a message starting at a random node to reach all (or almost all) the nodes of the graph. For the E-RAES model, the simulations show that the flooding time is short (i.e., compatible with a logarithmic growth, as a function of the number of nodes), for every value of the edge-disappearance rate p. For the V-RAES model, the simulations show that, as long as the fraction of nodes that leave the network at any round is not too large, e.g., if it stays below 70%, a message starting at a random node typically quickly reaches nearly all of the nodes.

Related Work. The topology of the Bitcoin network is hidden by the network formation protocol. However several approaches in the last decade proved effective in revealing some portion of the network [6,7]. A random network model for unstructured P2P networks has been introduced and analyzed by Pandurangan et al. [10]. Their model was inspired by the Gnutella P2P network and is based on the existence of a *host server* that maintains a *cache* of constant size with addresses of nodes accepting connections that can be reached at any time by other nodes. Bagchi et al. [1] studied the number of adversarial and random faults that an expander graph can tolerate while preserving approximately the same expansion factor. Becchetti et al. [3] introduced and analyzed the *RAES* network formation model, in which after a logarithmic number of rounds the network evolution terminates in a state in which every node has a specified out-degree and in-degree upper bounded by a constant. More recently [4] they also introduced and studied a similar model in which nodes can also join and leave the network, but the in-degree of the nodes is not upper bounded by a constant.

2   Edge-Dynamic RAES (E-RAES)

The E-RAES model is defined by four parameters, n, d, c, and p, where $n \in \mathbb{N}$ is the number of nodes, $d \in \mathbb{N}$ is the *minimum target degree*, $c \cdot d$ with $c \geqslant 1$ is the *maximum acceptable degree*, and $p \in [0, 1]$ is the *edge-failure probability*. Starting from an arbitrary initial graph $G_0 = (V, E_0)$, the set of n nodes remains fixed while the set of edges evolves, at each round, in three steps.

- **Step 1:** For each node $u \in V$, let N_u^1 be the set of neighbors of u at the beginning of Step 1. If $|N_u^1| < d$ then u samples $d - |N_u^1|$ nodes from the set $V \setminus N_u^1$, independently and u.a.r. with replacement, and connects to them.

- **Step 2:** For each node $u \in V$, let N_u^2 be the set of neighbors of u at the beginning of Step 2. If $|N_u^2| > c \cdot d$ then u samples $|N_u^2| - (c \cdot d)$ neighbors from the set N_u^2, independently and u.a.r. with replacement, and disconnects from them.

- **Step 3:** Each edge $\{u, v\}$ currently in the graph disappears with probability p, independently of the other edges.

The E-RAES model defines a Markov chain with the set of all graphs with n nodes as state space. We want to study how fast the information spreads from a node to all the other nodes when the network evolution is *stationary*. In principle, it would be possible to give theoretical bounds on the number of rounds needed to reach stationarity; however, the analysis of such a Markov chain appears far from easy. For the purpose of this paper, we use an heuristic criterion based on the stabilization of the *spectral gap* of the snapshots of the dynamic graph. In Fig. 1a there is a representative sample of the evolution of the spectral gap during the first rounds of the E-RAES model. It shows that the spectral gap stabilizes after a few rounds. At that point we start the simulation of the flooding process and we measure the number of rounds until the flooding is complete. Figure 1b shows some of the results of the simulations. Each point in the plot is the average flooding time over 100 runs. The picture quite clearly highlights that the flooding time, as a function of the number of nodes, is compatible with a logarithmic growth, for every value of the edge-failure probability p. The value of p seems to determine the multiplicative constant of the logarithm. Notice that in the

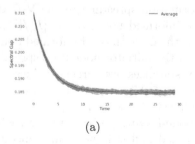

(a)

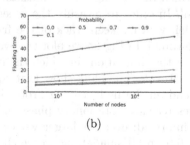

(b)

Fig. 1. (a) Evolution of the spectral gap for an ERAES with 2^{15} nodes, d = 4, and c = 1.5 starting from the empty graph. (b) Semi-log-plot of the average flooding time over an E-RAES with d = 4, c = 1.5, $2^9 \leqslant n \leqslant 2^{15}$, and p = 0, 0.1, 0.5, 0.7, 0.9.

simulations the message-passing step of the flooding process is scheduled *after* the edge-failure step of the E-RAES model, i.e., when for values of p larger than 0.1 the snapshot of the graph is typically disconnected. Thus, the results show that the time required to get all nodes informed is quite short even when every snapshot of the dynamic graph is completely sparse and disconnected.

3   Vertex-Dynamic RAES (V-RAES)

The V-RAES model is defined by four parameters, λ, d, c, and q, where $\lambda > 0$ is the *arrival rate* of new nodes, d and $c \cdot d$ are the *minimum target degree* and the *maximum acceptable degree* as in the E-RAES model, and $q \in [0,1]$ is the *node-leaving probability*. Starting from an arbitrary initial graph $G_0 = (V_0, E_0)$, at each round t the graph evolves in four steps.

- **Step 0:** $N_\lambda(t)$ new nodes join the graph, where $N_\lambda(t)$ is a Poisson random variable with rate λ.
- **Step 1:** For each node u, let N_u^1 be the set of neighbors of u at the beginning of Step 1. If $|N_u^1| < d$ then u samples $d - |N_u^1|$ nodes from the set $(V_t \setminus N_\lambda(t)) \setminus N_u^1$, independently and u.a.r. with replacement, and connects to them.
- **Step 2:** For each node u, let N_u^2 be the set of neighbors of u at the beginning of Step 2. If $|N_u^2| > c \cdot d$ then u samples $|N_u^2| - (c \cdot d)$ neighbors from the set N_u^2, independently and u.a.r. with replacement, and disconnects from them.
- **Step 3:** Each node u disappears with probability q, independently of the other nodes, together with its incident edges.

The size of the vertex set V_t in the V-RAES model converges to λ/q. For the purpose of our simulations we thus consider the network evolution for the V-RAES model to have reached a stationary regime when the number of nodes in the network is close to λ/q. Since nodes join and leave the network at any round, a message sent from an initiator node might not reach neither all the nodes in the graph nor a large fraction of them. It turns out that, when about 90% of the nodes disappear at every round, in about 60% of the simulations all the informed nodes left at the second round of the flooding process. On the other hand, when no more than half of the nodes disappear at every round, the fraction of times in which the message of the initiator node fails to spread in the network is very small. In order to measure the speed of information spreading in the V-RAES model, we thus keep track of the fraction of informed nodes $\alpha_t := |I_t|/|V_t|$ at each round. In Fig. 2a we plot the evolution of the fraction α_t of informed nodes, for all the simulations in which the message of the initiator node does spread in the network. The plots show that α_t quickly stabilizes over precise values that depend on the node-leaving probability q: for $q \leqslant 0.7$ the number of informed nodes reaches a stationary phase in which almost all the nodes in the network are informed; even for larger values of the node-leaving probability, e.g., when $q = 0.9$, in all simulations in which the informed nodes do not simultaneously disappear within the first few rounds, the fraction of informed nodes at any round stabilizes around 80%. As a measure of *flooding time* in the V-RAES model, we thus can consider the number of rounds required to reach the stable

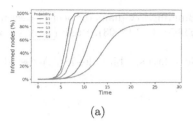
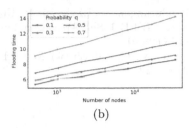

(a)

(b)

Fig. 2. (a) Evolution of the fraction of informed nodes α_t for a V-RAES with $d = 4, c = 1.5$, $\lambda/q = 2^{15}$, and $q = 0.1, 0.3, 0.5, 0.7, 0.9$. (b) Semi-log-plot of the average flooding time for a V-RAES with $d = 4, c = 1.5$, $2^9 \leqslant \lambda/q \leqslant 2^{15}$, and $q = 0.1, 0.3, 0.5, 0.7$.

value α_t, as it is determined by the node-leaving probability q. For example, in Fig. 2b we plot the number of rounds required by the flooding process to reach a fraction α_t of informed nodes of at least 90%, for all the values of the node-failure probability q such that the fraction of informed nodes stabilizes above 90%. The picture clearly highlights that such number of rounds is compatible with a logarithmic growth, as a function of λ/q.

References

1. Bagchi, A., Bhargava, A., Chaudhary, A., Eppstein, D., Scheideler, C.: The effect of faults on network expansion. Theory Comput. Syst. **39**(6), 903–928 (2006). Preliminary version in SPAA'04
2. Barkai, D.: Peer-to-peer computing: technologies for sharing and collaborating on the net. Intel Press (2001)
3. Becchetti, L., Clementi, A., Natale, E., Pasquale, F., Trevisan, L.: Finding a bounded-degree expander inside a dense one. In: Proceedings of the Fourteenth Annual ACM-SIAM Symposium on Discrete Algorithms, pp. 1320–1336. SIAM (2020)
4. Becchetti, L., Clementi, A., Pasquale, F., Trevisan, L., Ziccardi, I.: Expansion and flooding in dynamic random networks with node churn. In: 2021 IEEE 41st International Conference on Distributed Computing Systems (ICDCS), pp. 976–986. IEEE (2021)
5. Core, B.: Bitcoin Core 0.11 (ch 4): P2P Network. https://en.bitcoin.it/wiki/Bitcoin_Core_0.11_(ch_4):_P2P_Network. Accessed 21 Apr 2022
6. Delgado-Segura, S., et al.: TxProbe: discovering bitcoin's network topology using orphan transactions. In: Goldberg, I., Moore, T. (eds.) FC 2019. LNCS, vol. 11598, pp. 550–566. Springer, Cham (2019). https://doi.org/10.1007/978-3-030-32101-7_32
7. Miller, A., et al.: Discovering bitcoin's public topology and influential nodes. et al. (2015)
8. Nakamoto, S.: Bitcoin: A peer-to-peer electronic cash system. https://bitcoin.org/bitcoin.pdf (2008)
9. Nakamoto, S., et al.: Bitcoin core. https://github.com/bitcoin/bitcoin. Accessed 21 Apr 2022

10. Pandurangan, G., Raghavan, P., Upfal, E.: Building low-diameter peer-to-peer networks. IEEE J. Sel. Areas Commun. **21**(6), 995–1002 (2003). Preliminary version in FOCS'01
11. Yeow, A.: Global Bitcoin Nodes Distribution. https://bitnodes.io/. Accessed 21 Apr 2022

Brief Announcement: Fully Lattice Linear Algorithms

Arya Tanmay Gupta[✉] and Sandeep S. Kulkarni

Computer Science and Engineering, Michigan State University, East Lansing, USA
{atgupta,sandeep}@msu.edu

Abstract. This paper focuses on analyzing and differentiating between lattice linear problems and lattice linear algorithms. It introduces a new class of algorithms called *(fully) lattice linear algorithms*, that induce a partial order among all states and form *multiple lattices*. An initial state locks the system into one of these lattices. We present a lattice linear self-stabilizing algorithm for minimal dominating set.

Keywords: Self-stabilization · Lattice linear problems · Lattice linear algorithms · Minimal dominating set · Convergence time

1 Introduction

A multiprocessing system involves several processes running concurrently. These systems can provide a substantially larger computing power over a single processor. However, increased parallelism requires increased coordination, thereby increasing the execution time.

The notion of detecting predicates to represent problems which induce partial order among the global states (lattice linear problems) was introduced in [2]. If the states form a partial order, then the nodes can be allowed to read old data and execute asynchronously. In [4], we introduced *eventually lattice linear algorithms*, for problems where states do not naturally form a partial order (non-lattice linear problems), which induce a partial order among the feasible states. In this paper, we differentiate between the partial orders in lattice linear problems and those induced by lattice linear algorithms in non-lattice linear problems.

The paper is organized as follows. In Sect. 2, we elaborate the preliminaries and some background on lattice linearity. In Sect. 3, we present a fully lattice linear algorithm for minimal dominating set. In Sect. 4, we study the convergence time of algorithms traversing a lattice of states. We discuss related work in Sect. 5 and conclude in Sect. 6.

2 Preliminaries and Background

In this paper, we are mainly interested in graph algorithms where the input is a graph G, $V(G)$ is the set of its nodes and $E(G)$ is the set of its edges. For a

S. Devismes et al. (Eds.): SSS 2022, LNCS 13751, pp. 341–345, 2022.
https://doi.org/10.1007/978-3-031-21017-4_24

node $i \in V(G)$, Adj_i is the set of nodes connected to i by an edge, and Adj_i^x are the set of nodes within x hops from i, excluding i.

Each node in $V(G)$ stores a set of variables, which represent its *local state*. A *global state* is obtained by assigning each variable of each node a value from its respective domain. We use S to denote the set of all possible global states. A global state $s \in S$ is represented as a vector, where $s[i]$ itself is a vector of the variables of node i.

Each node in $V(G)$ is associated with actions. Each action at node i checks the values of nodes in $Adj_i^x \cup \{i\}$ (where the value of x is problem dependent) and updates its own variables. A *move* is an event in which some node i updates its variables based on the variables of nodes in $Adj_i^x \cup \{i\}$.

S is a *lattice linear state space* if its states form a lattice. The nature of the partial order, present among the states in S which makes it *lattice linear*, is elaborated as follows. Local states are totally ordered and global states are partially ordered. We use '$<$' to represent both these orders. For a pair of global states s and s', $s < s'$ iff $(\forall i : (s[i] < s'[i] \lor s[i] = s'[i])) \land (\exists i : (s[i] < s'[i]))$. We use the symbol '$>$' which is the opposite of '$<$', i.e. $s > s'$ iff $s' < s$. In the lattice linear problems in [2], s transitions to s' where $s < s'$.

Certain problems can be represented by a predicate $\mathcal{P}$ such that for any node i, if i is violating $\mathcal{P}$, then it must change its state, or else the system will not satisfy $\mathcal{P}$. If i is violating $\mathcal{P}$ in some state s, then it is forbidden in s. Formally,

Definition 1. *[2]* FORBIDDEN$(i, s, \mathcal{P}) \equiv \neg\mathcal{P}(s) \land (\forall s' > s : s'[i] = s[i] \implies \neg\mathcal{P}(s'))$.

The predicate $\mathcal{P}$ is *lattice linear* with respect to the lattice induced in S iff s not being optimal implies that there is some forbidden node in s. Formally,

Definition 2 *[2]* **Lattice Linear Predicate $\mathcal{P}$.** $\forall s \in S$: FORBIDDEN$(s, \mathcal{P})$ $\implies \exists i$: FORBIDDEN$(i, s, \mathcal{P})$.

A problem P is a *lattice linear problem* iff it can be represented by a lattice linear predicate. Otherwise, P is a *non-lattice linear problem*.

Many lattice linear problems studied in [2], such as stable marriage problem, single source shortest path problem, are lattice linear problems. These problems have only one optimal state. In lattice linear problems [2], the global states form a lattice. The system must initialize in the infimum of the lattice. If $\mathcal{P}(s)$ is false in a state s, then there exists at least one node i that is forbidden in s (Definition 2). If a forbidden i does not change its state, then $\mathcal{P}(s)$ remains false (Definition 1). A move causes the system to traverse up in the lattice. The goal is to reach the lowest state in the lattice where $\mathcal{P}(s)$ is true, which is optimal.

3   Lattice Linear *Algorithms*: Minimal Dominating Set

In non-lattice linear problems such as minimal dominating set (MDS), the states do not form a partial order naturally, as for a given non-optimal state, it cannot be determined that which nodes are forbidden.

We introduce the class of fully lattice linear algorithms, which partition the state space into subsets $S_1, S_2, \cdots, S_w (w \geq 1)$, where each subset forms a lattice. The initial state locks the system into one of these lattices and algorithm executes until an optimal state is reached. The optimal state is always the supremum of that lattice. In this section, we describe a fully lattice linear algorithm for MDS.

Definition 3 *Minimal dominating set. In the MDS problem, the task is to choose a minimal set of nodes $\mathcal{D}$ in a given graph G such that for every node in $V(G)$, either it is present in $\mathcal{D}$, or at least one of its neighbours is in $\mathcal{D}$. Each node i stores a variable $st.i$ with domain $\{IN, OUT\}$; $i \in \mathcal{D}$ iff $st.i = IN$.*

We describe the algorithm as Algorithm 1.

Algorithm 1 *Algorithm for MDS.*

REMOVABLE-DS(i) $\equiv st.i = IN \wedge (\forall j \in Adj_i \cup \{i\} : ((j \neq i \wedge st.j = IN) \vee$
$\qquad (\exists k \in Adj_j, k \neq i : st.k = IN)))$.
ADDABLE-DS(i) $\equiv st.i = OUT \wedge (\forall j \in Adj_i, st.j = OUT)$.
UNSATISFIED-DS(i) $\equiv$ REMOVABLE-DS(i)$\vee$ ADDABLE-DS(i).
FORBIDDEN-DS(i) $\equiv$ UNSATISFIED-DS(i) $\wedge (\forall j \in Adj_i^2 :$
$\qquad \neg$UNSATISFIED-DS(j) $\vee id.i > id.j)$.
Rules for node i:
FORBIDDEN-DS(i) $\longrightarrow st.i = \neg st.i$.

To demonstrate that Algorithm 1 is lattice linear, we define state value and rank, assumed as imaginary variables associated with the nodes, as follows:

$$\text{STATE-VALUE-DS}(i, s) = \begin{cases} 1 & \text{if UNSATISFIED-DS(i) in state s} \\ 0 & \text{otherwise} \end{cases}$$

$$\text{RANK-DS}(s) = \sum_{i \in V(G)} \text{STATE-VALUE-DS}(i, s).$$

The lattice is formed with respect to the state value. Specifically, the state value of a node can change from 1 to 0 but not vice versa. Therefore RANK-DS always decreases until it becomes zero at the supremum.

Lemma 1. *Any node in an input graph does not revisit its older state while executing under Algorithm 1.*

Proof. In Algorithm 1, if a node i is forbidden, then no node in Adj_i^2 moves.

If i is forbidden and addable at time t, then any other node in Adj_i is out of the DS. When i moves in, then any other node in Adj_i is no longer addable, so they do not move in after t. As a result i does not have to move out after moving in. Similarly, a forbidden and removable i does not move in after moving out.

Let that i is dominated and out, and $j \in Adj_i$ is removable forbidden. j will move out only if i is being covered by another node. Also, while j turns out of the DS, no other node in Adj_j^2, and consequently in Adj_i, changes its state. As a result i does not have to turn itself in because of the action of j.

From the above cases, we have that i does not change its state to $st.i$ after changing its state from $st.i$ to $st'.i$ throughout the execution of Algorithm 1. $\square$

Theorem 1. *Algorithm 1 is self-stabilizing and (fully) lattice linear.*

Proof. From Lemma 1, if G is in state s and RANK-DS(s) is non-zero, then at least one node is forbidden in s, so RANK-DS decreases monotonously until it becomes zero. For any node i, we have that its state value decreases whenever i is forbidden and never increases. Thus Algorithm 1 is self-stabilizing.

We have a partial order among the states, where if the rank of a state s is nonzero, then it transitions to a state s' such that $s < s'$ where for some i forbidden in s, $s[i] < s'[i]$. Here, $s < s'$ iff RANK-DS(s) > RANK-DS(i). This shows that Algorithm 1 is lattice linear. □

Example 1. Let G_4 be a graph where $V(G_4) = \{v_1, v_2, v_3, v_4\}$ and $E(G_4) = \{\{v_1, v_2\}, \{v_3, v_4\}\}$. For G_4 the lattices induced under Algorithm 1 are shown in Fig. 1; each vector represents a global state $(st.v_1, st.v_2, st.v_3, st.v_4)$. □

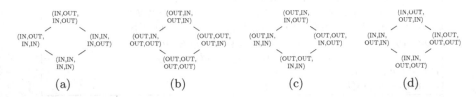

Fig. 1. The lattices induced by Algorithm 1 on the graph G_4 described in Example 1.

Remark: The lattices in Fig. 1 present the skeleton of the partial order among the states. Here, in a non-optimal state, if only one forbidden node moves, then the resulting state s' is a parent of s. If more than one nodes move, then the resulting state s' is not a parent of s, but is reachable from s through the lattice.

4   Convergence Time in Traversing a Lattice of States

Theorem 2. *Given an LLTS on n processes, with the domain of size not more than m for each process, the acting algorithm will converge in $n \times (m-1)$ moves.*

Proof. Assume for contradiction that the underlying algorithm converges in $x \geq n \times (m-1) + 1$ moves. This implies, by pigeonhole principle, that at least one of the nodes i is revising their states $st.i$ after changing to $st'.i$. If $st.i$ to $st'.i$ is a step ahead transition for i, then $st'.i$ to $st.i$ is a step back transition for i and vice versa. For a system containing a lattice linear state space, we obtain a contradiction since step back actions are absent in such systems. □

Corollary 1. *Consider the case where the nodes have multiple variables. Furthermore, in each node, atmost r of these variables, $var_1.i, ..., var_r.i$ (with domain sizes $m'_1, ... m'_r$ respectively) contribute independently to the construction of the lattice. Then the LLTS will converge in $n \times \left(\sum_{j=1}^{r} (m'_j - 1) \right)$ moves.* □

Corollary 2. *(From Theorem 2 and Theorem 1) Algorithm 1 converges in n moves.*

5   Related Work

Lattice Theory: Lattice linear problems are studied in [2]. In [4], we have extended the theory presented in [2] to develop eventually lattice linear self-stabilizing algorithms for some non-lattice linear problems. Such algorithms impose a lattice among the feasible states of the state space.

In this paper, we present a (fully) lattice linear algorithm for maximal dominating set, which imposes a partial order among all states and converges faster.

Dominating Set: Self-stabilizing algorithms for the minimal dominating set problem are proposed in [1,3,6]. The best convergence time among these works is $4n$ moves. The algorithm presented in [4], takes $2n$ moves to converge.

In this paper, the fully lattice linear algorithm that we present converges in n moves and is fully tolerant to consistency violations. This is an improvement as compared to the results presented in the literature.

6   Conclusion

In this paper, we study the differences between the structure of partial order induced in lattice linear problems and non-lattice linear problems. We present a fully lattice linear self-stabilizing algorithm for the minimal dominating set. This is the first lattice linear algorithm for a non-lattice linear problem. This algorithm converges in n moves. We provide upper bounds to the convergence time for an algorithm traversing an arbitrary lattice linear state space. A technical report for this paper, containing its extended version, is available at [5].

It is still an open question whether fully lattice linear algorithms for minimal vertex cover and maximal independent set problems can be developed.

References

1. Chiu, W.Y., Chen, C., Tsai, S.-Y.: A 4n-move self-stabilizing algorithm for the minimal dominating set problem using an unfair distributed daemon. Inf. Process. Lett. **114**(10), 515–518 (2014)
2. Garg, V.K.: Predicate Detection to Solve Combinatorial Optimization Problems. In: Association for Computing Machinery, pp. 235–245. New York (2020)
3. Goddard, W., Hedetniemi, S.T., Jacobs, D.P., Srimani, P.K., Zhenyu, X.: Self-stabilizing graph protocols. Parallel Process. Lett. **18**(01), 189–199 (2008)
4. Gupta, A.T., Kulkarni, S.S.: Extending lattice linearity for self-stabilizing algorithms. In: Johnen, C., Schiller, E.M., Schmid, S. (eds.) SSS 2021. LNCS, vol. 13046, pp. 365–379. Springer, Cham (2021). https://doi.org/10.1007/978-3-030-91081-5_24
5. Gupta, A.T., Kulkarni, S.S.: Lattice linear algorithms. CoRR abs/2209.14703, 2022
6. Xu, Z., Hedetniemi, S.T., Goddard, W., Srimani, P.K.: A synchronous self-stabilizing minimal domination protocol in an arbitrary network graph. In: Das, S.R., Das, S.K. (eds.) IWDC 2003. LNCS, vol. 2918, pp. 26–32. Springer, Heidelberg (2003). https://doi.org/10.1007/978-3-540-24604-6_3

Brief Announcement: Distributed Reconfiguration of Spanning Trees

Siddharth Gupta[1], Manish Kumar[2(✉)], and Shreyas Pai[3]

[1] University of Warwick, Coventry, UK
`siddharth.gupta.1@warwick.ac.uk`
[2] Ben-Gurion University of the Negev, Be'er Sheva, Israel
`manishk@post.bgu.ac.il`
[3] Aalto University, Espoo, Finland
`shreyas.pai@aalto.fi`

Abstract. In a reconfiguration problem, given a problem and two feasible solutions of the problem, the task is to find a sequence of transformations to reach from one solution to the another such that every intermediate state is also a feasible solution to the problem. In this paper, we study the distributed spanning tree reconfiguration problem and we define a new reconfiguration step, called *k-simultaneous add and delete*, in which every node is allowed to add at most k edges and delete at most k edges such that multiple nodes do not add or delete the same edge.

We first show that, if the two input spanning trees are rooted then we can transform one into another in one round using a single 1-simultaneous add and delete step in the CONGEST model. Therefore, we focus our attention towards unrooted spanning trees and show that transforming an unrooted spanning tree into another using a single 1-simultaneous add and delete step requires $\Omega(n)$ rounds in the LOCAL model. We additionally show that transforming an unrooted spanning tree into another using a single 2-simultaneous add and delete step can be done in $O(\log n)$ rounds in the CONGEST model.

Keywords: Spanning trees · Reconfiguration · Distributed algorithms

1 Introduction

A *reconfiguration problem* asks the following computational question: Given two different configurations of a system, is it possible to transform one to the other in a step-by-step fashion such that the intermediate solutions are also feasible? Spanning trees are important in classic distributed models such as LOCAL and

S. Gupta—Supported by Engineering and Physical Sciences Research Council (EPSRC) grant no: EP/V007793/1.
M. Kumar—Supported by the Rita Altura trust chair in computer science, and by the Lynne and William Frankel Center for Computer Science, BGU, Israel.
S. Pai—Supported in part by the Academy of Finland, Grant 334238.

S. Devismes et al. (Eds.): SSS 2022, LNCS 13751, pp. 346–351, 2022.
https://doi.org/10.1007/978-3-031-21017-4_25

CONGEST[1] as they can be used for efficient routing and aggregation. It is desirable to change the current spanning tree to a better spanning tree depending on the routing demands. Each node can just delete the old incident edges and add the new edges, but this is resource intensive as some nodes may have to simultaneously change a lot of incident edges. Efficiently computing a reconfiguration schedule for spanning trees in a distributed manner allows the system to change from one spanning tree to another in a way that each node is responsible for initiating only a limited amount of changes in one step. And since each intermediate structure is a spanning tree, these intermediate structures can be used to perform the required operations till the next steps are performed.

In the distributed spanning tree reconfiguration problem, we have two spanning trees T_1, T_2 of a graph G such that each node $v \in V$ knows its incident edges in T_1 and T_2. The nodes need to efficiently compute a reconfiguration schedule that converts T_1 to T_2 using k-*simultaneous add and delete steps*, where in each step, each node is allowed to add at most k incident edges to the spanning tree and delete at most k incident edges from the spanning tree. In any given step, multiple nodes cannot add or delete the same edge. A valid reconfiguration schedule is a sequence of steps where we start from T_1 and reach T_2 such that the intermediate structure obtained after each step is a spanning tree.

If T_1 and T_2 are rooted spanning trees, where each node knows its parent pointer, then each node v can tell its neighbours that it wants to add its parent in T_2 and delete its parent in T_1. If v sees that its parent wants to do the opposite operation on the same edge, it does nothing. Hence each edge is added or deleted by at most one node. Therefore, in this setting, the nodes can compute in 1-round, a reconfiguration schedule using a single 1-simultaneous add and delete step. But in the case of unrooted trees, this strategy fails as it crucially relies on the parent pointer information to coordinate between the nodes. Therefore, the natural question arises: what can we do in the case of unrooted spanning trees? In this work, we present two results that answer this question:

1. A lower bound that shows computing a single step 1-simultaneous add and delete reconfiguration schedule requires $\Omega(n)$ rounds in the LOCAL model.
2. An algorithm that computes a single step 2-simultaneous add and delete reconfiguration schedule in $O(\log n)$ rounds in the CONGEST model.

1.1 Related Work

The problem of spanning tree reconfiguration is very well studied in the centralized setting. A transformation step in the centralized setting is defined as follows: two spanning trees T and T' of a graph G are reachable in one step iff there exists two edges $e \in T$ and $e' \in T'$ such that $T' = (T \setminus e) \cup e'$. In the

---

[1] In the LOCAL model [9], a communication network is abstracted as an n-node graph. In synchronous *rounds* each node can send an arbitrary size message to each of its neighbors. The CONGEST model [11] is similar to the LOCAL model with the additional constraint that each message has size $O(\log n)$ bits.

centralized setting, any spanning tree can be reconfigured into any other spanning tree in polynomial time [7] and finding a *shortest reconfiguration sequence* between two directed spanning trees is polynomial-time solvable [8]. Therefore, more constrained versions of the problem have been studied. For instance, the reconfiguration problem is PSPACE-complete when each spanning tree in the sequence has *at most (and at least) k leaves* (for $k \geq 3$) [3]. On the other hand, reconfiguration is polynomial-time solvable if the intermediate spanning trees are constrained to have large maximum degree and small diameter while it is PSPACE-complete if we have small maximum degree constraints and NP-hard with large diameter constraints [4]. The only previous work on distributed spanning tree reconfiguration that we are aware of is [12]. The authors of [12] show how to solve reconfiguration of rooted spanning tree in an asynchronous message passing system using local exchange operation between pairs of incident edges, in $O(n)$ rounds and requires $O(\log n)$ bits memory at each process. Distributed reconfiguration has been studied for Coloring [1,2], Vertex Cover [5], and MIS [6].

2   Distributed Spanning Tree Reconfiguration

2.1   1-Simultaneous Add and Delete Requires $\Omega(n)$ Rounds

We begin by stating a folk result which will be the basis for the proof of the main lower bound in the subsequent theorem. We state our lower bounds in the LOCAL model, but since any CONGEST algorithm is also a LOCAL algorithm, the lower bound also holds in the CONGEST model.

Lemma 1. *Rooting a tree T at an arbitrary node is a global problem, i.e. it requires $\Omega(n)$ rounds in the LOCAL model.*

Theorem 1. *Solving the distributed spanning tree reconfiguration problem in one step of 1-simultaneous add and delete requires $\Omega(n)$ rounds in the LOCAL model.*

Proof. For sake of contradiction let $\mathcal{A}$ be a LOCAL algorithm that computes a one step reconfiguration schedule in $o(n)$ rounds. We will show that $\mathcal{A}$ can be used to root an unrooted tree in $o(n)$ rounds in the LOCAL model. Let $T = (V, E)$ be the tree that we wish to root. For each node $v \in V$ create a copy v' which will be simulated by v, and add edges $\{v, v'\}$ as well as $\{u', v'\}$ for all neighbours u of v. Let V' be the set of all the nodes v', E' be the set of edges of the form $\{u', v'\}$, and $M = \{\{v, v'\} \mid v \in V\}$. Now we want to run algorithm $\mathcal{A}$ where the source spanning tree is $T_1 = (V \cup V', E \cup M)$, the destination spanning tree is $T_2 = (V \cup V', E' \cup M)$, and the communication network is $T_1 \cup T_2$.

Any R-round LOCAL algorithm on $T_1 \cup T_2$ can be simulated on network T in R rounds by having v simulate the behaviour of v'. Since $\mathcal{A}$ produces a reconfiguration schedule that uses one step of 1-simultaneous add and delete, each node will delete at most one edge and add at most one edge in order to go from T_1 to T_2. Node v will output as its parent the edge in E that is to be deleted by v, if such an edge exists.

These parent pointers correspond to a valid rooting because nodes in V must delete $n-1$ edges of T_1 in one step for the reconfiguration schedule of $\mathcal{A}$ to be correct. This is only possible if $n-1$ nodes of T delete exactly one incident edge of T and the remaining node r does not delete any incident edge. The neighbours of r in T must delete the incident edge that is pointing to r as nobody else can delete this edge. Then we can repeat this argument inductively on all nodes that are i-hops away from r and we show that the parent pointers form a valid rooting of T with root node r.

Thus, a rooting of T was output in the LOCAL model in $o(n)$ rounds, which is impossible by Lemma 1. Thus $\mathcal{A}$ cannot exist, which proves the theorem. □

2.2   2-Simultaneous Add and Delete in $O(\log N)$ Rounds

We first describe an edge orientation procedure that is essentially the rake and compress algorithm of [10]. The output of Algorithm 1 has the property that each node has at most two outgoing edges. It is well known that this orientation can be computed very efficiently as opposed to a rooting of the tree.

Algorithm 1: ORIENT(T)

1 $T' \leftarrow$ empty graph
2 **while** $T \neq \emptyset$ **do**
3      $H \leftarrow$ nodes in T with degree at most 2
4   Add to T' the nodes of H with their incident edges in T oriented outward, breaking ties arbitrarily
5   Remove H from T
6 **end**
7 **return** oriented tree T'

Lemma 2. *The while loop of Algorithm 1 runs for $O(\log n)$ iterations. Moreover each iteration can be implemented in $O(1)$ rounds in the CONGEST model.*

Proof. If α fraction of the nodes have degree at most 2 then we can write average degree as at least $3(1-\alpha)$ because $(1-\alpha)$ fraction of the nodes must have degree at least 3. Average degree of a tree (or a forest) is 2, which implies $2 \geq 3(1-\alpha)$. So an $\alpha \geq 1/3$ fraction of the nodes are removed in each iteration. Therefore the number of iterations is at most $O(\log n)$.

To execute an iteration in the CONGEST model, each node just needs to know its degree in the current tree T. So in the each iteration, nodes in H that remove themselves can send a message to their neighbours to decrease their degree. □

Now we show how this orientation can be used to compute a reconfiguration schedule. We run Algorithm 1 on the source spanning tree T_1 and the target spanning tree T_2 separately and obtain two orientations such that each node

Fig. 1. This figure shows how node v_1 computes reconfiguration schedule using the orientation procedure. The bold edges belong to T_1 and the dashed edges belong to T_2

in the graph has at most 2 outgoing edges in T_1 and at most 2 outgoing edges in T_2 (see Fig. 1). Now, each node v decides it will add its outgoing edges of T_2 and it will delete its outgoing edges of T_1. If v decides to add and delete the same incident edge e, it updates its decision to not change e. Then v sends the decisions along the outgoing edges. If for a single edge, one end point has decided to add and the other has decided to delete, then both nodes update their decision on this edge to do nothing. It is easy to see that these decisions form one step of 2-simultaneous add and delete where all edges of $T_1 \setminus T_2$ are deleted and all edges of $T_2 \setminus T_1$ are added. This proves the following theorem.

Theorem 2. *The distributed spanning tree reconfiguration problem can be solved in one step of 2-simultaneous add and delete. Computing this reconfiguration schedule takes $O(\log n)$ rounds in the CONGEST model.*

References

1. Bonamy, M., Ouvrard, P., Rabie, M., Suomela, J., Uitto, J.: Distributed recoloring. In: DISC 2018 (2018)
2. Bousquet, N., Feuilloley, L., Heinrich, M., Rabie, M.: Distributed recoloring of interval and chordal graphs. In: OPODIS 2021 (2021)
3. Bousquet, N., et al.: Reconfiguration of spanning trees with many or few leaves. In: ESA 2020 (2020)
4. Bousquet, N., et al.: Reconfiguration of spanning trees with degree constraint or diameter constraint. In: STACS 2022 (2022)
5. Censor-Hillel, K., Maus, Y., Peled, S.R., Tonoyan, T.: Distributed vertex cover reconfiguration. In: ITCS 2022 (2022)
6. Censor-Hillel, K., Rabie, M.: Distributed reconfiguration of maximal independent sets. J. Comput. Syst. Sci. **112**, 85–96 (2020)
7. Ito, T., et al.: On the complexity of reconfiguration problems. TCS **412**(12–14), 1054–1065 (2011)
8. Ito, T., Iwamasa, Y., Kobayashi, Y., Nakahata, Yu., Otachi, Y., Wasa, K.: Reconfiguring directed trees in a digraph. In: Chen, C.-Y., Hon, W.-K., Hung, L.-J., Lee, C.-W. (eds.) COCOON 2021. LNCS, vol. 13025, pp. 343–354. Springer, Cham (2021). https://doi.org/10.1007/978-3-030-89543-3_29
9. Linial, N.: Locality in distributed graph algorithms. SIAM J. Comput. **21**(1), 193–201 (1992)
10. Miller, G.L., Reif, J.H.: Parallel tree contraction part 1: fundamentals. Adv. Comput. Res. **5**, 47–72 (1989)

11. Peleg, D.: Distributed Computing: A Locality-Sensitive Approach. SIAM, Philadelphia (2000)
12. Yamauchi, Y., Kamiyama, N., Otachi, Y.: Distributed reconfiguration of spanning trees. In: Johnen, C., Schiller, E.M., Schmid, S. (eds.) SSS 2021. LNCS, vol. 13046, pp. 516–520. Springer, Cham (2021). https://doi.org/10.1007/978-3-030-91081-5_40

Brief Announcement: Mutually-Visible Uniform Circle Formation by Asynchronous Mobile Robots on Grid Plane

Yoshiaki Ito$^{(\boxtimes)}$, Yonghwan Kim$^{(\boxtimes)}$ ⓘ, and Yoshiaki Katayama$^{(\boxtimes)}$ ⓘ

Nagoya Institute of Technology, Aichi, Japan
`y.ito.987@stn.nitech.ac.jp`, `{kim,katayama}@nitech.ac.jp`

Abstract. In this paper, we consider the *Uniform Circle Formation* problem, which is a problem to locate all robots uniformly (*i.e.,* with equal central angle) on the circumference of a common circle on infinite grid plane. We first introduce an algorithm to achieve *Uniform Circle Formation* using 5 colors with diameter $\mathcal{O}(N)$, and present another algorithm to achieve *Uniform Circle Formation* satisfying *Complete Visibility* (*i.e.,* no three robots are collinear) using 4 colors with diameter $\mathcal{O}(N^2)$ (*optimal*) under assumptions such that robots agree on the only one axis, are opaque, operate asynchronously, and do not know the number of robots.

Keywords: Uniform circle formation · Complete visibility · Autonomous mobile robot · Luminous model

1 Introduction

Since basic computational theoretical models of autonomous mobile robot system consisting of multiple mobile computational entities (called *robots*) with low functionality was first introduced by Suzuki *et al.* [1], various models are considered based on the capabilities of the robots and the assumptions of the entire system. Many studies are investigated to clarify the relationship between the model and the solvability of the given problem.

The *circle formation* problem is one of pattern formation problems in which the robots form a circle in a certain region. The main difficulty of the problem is how to provide to all robots information for forming a common circle, *e.g.,* the position of the center and the radius of the circle. Therefore, to form a circle, some sophisticated manner is required to provide these necessary information to the robots. Many studies of the circle formation problem are investigated on the Euclidean plane [2], however, the problem on an infinite grid is first introduced by Adhikary *et al.* [3]. In the case of grid plane, each robot can be located only on the grid point and moves only along the line between two adjacent points. Therefore, the shape of a circle on the grid plane is not perfectly formed as that on the Euclidean plane. If a grid point does not exist on the circumference of the circle, a robot cannot be located on the circumference of the circle; hence, the robot is placed on the nearest grid point. In [3], the authors consider *Luminous Model* using 7 colors of a light equipped on the robot and assume that all robots agree on the direction and orientation of one axis. This algorithm guarantees a circle formation but not its uniformity. That is, the position of the robots forming the circle is allowed to be biased (*i.e., non-uniform* circle formation).

In this paper, we consider the *uniform* circle formation algorithm with fewer numbers of light. Moreover, we also consider the *Uniform Circle Formation* that satisfies *Complete Visibility* by opaque (*i.e.,* non-transparent) robots; no three robots are collinear. We assume that all robots agree on the direction and orientation of one axis (Y-axis), are opaque, do not know the number of robots, and operate asynchronously. Under these assumptions, we introduce an algorithm to achieve *Uniform Circle Formation* using only 5 colors with $\mathcal{O}(N)$ diameter, where N is the number of robots. To the best of our knowledge, this is the first algorithm for *Uniform Circle Formation* on grid plane. Furthermore, we present another algorithm, which is an extension of the first one, to achieve *Uniform Circle Formation* with *Complete Visibility*. The diameter $\mathcal{O}(N^2)$ is optimal to achieve *Complete Visibility*.

2   Model and Problem Definition

Let $R = \{r_1, r_2, ..., r_N\}$ be the set of N autonomous mobile robots. Robots are indistinguishable by their appearance, execute the same algorithm, and have no memory (*i.e.,* oblivious). Each robot can be located only at the point on the grid, and two or more robots cannot exist at the same point on the grid. All robots agree on the orientation and direction of Y-axis; however, they do not agree on the chirality. No robot knows the total number of robots N.

We consider *Luminous Model* [2]: Each robot maintains a constant-sized visible memory called *light* that can be observed by other robots. Each light can be set by one among the constant numbers of colors. Moreover, every robot has an unlimited visibility range; however, robots are opaque: a robot cannot observe some other robots if there is another robot between them.

Each robot performs one of the three operations: *Look, Compute,* and *Move*. In *Look* operation, a robot obtains the positions (based on its local coordinate system centered on itself) and the colors of all other (visible) robots' lights as well as the color of its own light. Note that some robots cannot be observed because of their opaqueness. In *Compute* operation, a robot computes its color of light and its destination according to the given algorithm with the other robot's positions and colors, as well as its own color obtained in *Look* operation. Furthermore, as a result of *Compute*, each robot immediately changes its color of light when *Compute* operation is terminated (if necessary). In *Move* operation, a robot moves to the destination computed in *Compute* operation. A robot can move to only one of the four points adjacent to the current point in one *Move* operation. The movement of each robot is *atomic* (*i.e.,* instant move); thus, each robot is

never observed by any other robots while it is moving. In this paper, we assume
an asynchronous (ASYNC) scheduler; There is no assumption on the timing of
each robot's operation. This means that all robots perform their operations in
an unpredictable time instant and duration.

Here we define the **Uniform Circle Formation Problem** as follows: Given
a set of robots that is initially located on distinct points on infinite grid. Algorithm $\mathcal{A}$ solves the uniform circle formation problem if $\mathcal{A}$ satisfies all the following conditions: (1) $\mathcal{A}$ eventually terminates; $\mathcal{A}$ eventually reaches a configuration
such that no robot can move, and (2) When $\mathcal{A}$ terminates, all robots are located
on the circumference of the same circle with equal center angle; if a point does
not exist on the circumference of the circle, a robot should be on the nearest
point on the grid plane. Furthermore, we say that an algorithm achieves *Complete Visibility*, if every (opaque) robot can observe all other robots when the
algorithm terminates.

3   Uniform Circle Formation

In this section, we propse an algorithm for solving the *Uniform Circle Formation* problem under ASYNC. The proposed algorithm consists of the following
three phases. Each robot is equipped with a light that emits one of five colors of
$\{A, B, \mathsf{EvenCorner}, \mathsf{OddCorner}, \mathsf{Done}\}$; colors $\mathsf{EvenCorner}$ and $\mathsf{OddCorner}$ are used
to share information (the center and diameter of the circle), color Done for ter-
mination detection, and colors A and B are required to change the robots' phase.
The light is initially set by A.

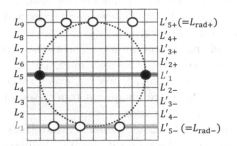

Fig. 1. Notations of horizontal lines

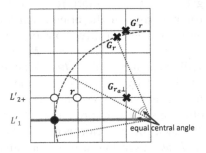

Fig. 2. Example of $G_r, G'_r, G'_{r_a\perp}$

Preliminaries: We introduce some notations as follows. Let L_1 be the line
parallel to X-axis (*i.e.*, horizontal line) containing the robot with the smallest
Y-coordinate (Fig. 1). We call the horizontal line above L_1 L_2, as the same
manner, we also call every horizontal line $L_3, L_4, \cdots$, respectively (Fig. 1). Let
L'_1 be the horizontal line where there are two robots whose lights are $\mathsf{EvenCorner}$,
$\mathsf{OddCorner}$, or Corner (in Fig. 1, two black robots presents the robots with such
color). We call each horizontal line above line L'_1 $L'_{2+}, L'_{3+}, L'_{4+}, \cdots$, respectively

in order from bottom. As the same manner, we call each horizontal line below line L'_1 L'_{2-}, L'_{3-}, L'_{4-}, $\cdots$, respectively. Moreover, we call two horizontal lines radius apart from L'_1 L_{rad+} and L_{rad-} respectively. Let G_r be the exact location of robot r to achieve *Uniform Circle Formation*, and we denote the nearest point on grid to G_r as G'_r (Fig. 2). When robot r is located on line L_i, we denote the foot of a perpendicular from G'_r to L_i as $G'_{r_a \perp}$ (in Fig. 2, i is 2).

Line Formation Phase: The first phase locates all robots on the same horizontal line. Since all robots agree on the direction and orientation of Y-axis, they can be lined up on L_1. All robots changes their light from A into B (Fig. 3(a)).

Diameter Determination Phase: In this phase, the two robots at both end of robots aligned on L_1 become the reference robots which provide the diameter and the center of a circle to inform them to all other robots. After the Line Formation Phase, the two reference robots move in the negative direction of the Y-axis to grasp the total number of robots N (Fig. 3(b)). If N is an even number, the light is changed to EvenCorner, otherwise, OddCorner. After that, they move back to where they were before changing their lights (Fig. 3(c)), and the other robots move up (L'_{2+}) or down (L'_{2-}) so that the number of robots in L'_{2+} and (L'_{2-}) are the same (as possible) (Fig. 3(d) and (e)). Note that the difference in the number of robots on L'_{2+} and on L'_{2-} is at most 2 (Fig. 3(f) and (h)).

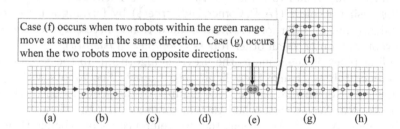

Fig. 3. Two examples of partitioning into two groups (depends on a scheduler)

Circle Formation Phase: In this phase each robot moves to the point that achieves *Uniform Circle Formation* based on the two reference robots. Now the robots at both ends on L'_{2+} (resp. L'_{2-}) move to L'_{rad+} (resp. L'_{rad-}) (Fig. 4(a)). After all robots other than the reference robots reach L'_{rad+} and L'_{rad-}, the robot at both ends of L'_{rad+} moves to G'_r (Fig. 4(b)). After all robots on L'_{rad+} have been moved, the robots on L'_{rad-} begin to move to G'_r by referring to the robots on the upper side of L'_1. Each robot changes its color into Done when it reaches G'_r. Finally, two reference robots move to G'_r (if necessary). Note that all robots need to know the exact number of robots N to move to G'_r, and this can be calculated by referring to the locations and lights of two reference robots (Fig. 4(c)).

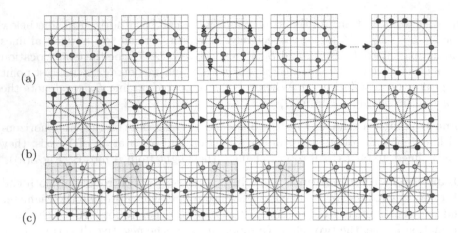

Fig. 4. Example of the movements of robots in the third phase

4 Uniform Circle Formation with Complete Visibility

Uniform Circle Formation achieved by the algorithm in Sect. 3 may include three collinear robots, which means that some robots cannot observe each other. Now we extend the algorithm to achieve *Uniform Circle Formation* with *Complete Visibility* using 4 colors ({A, B, Corner, 2ndCorner}) by forming a larger circle. In this algorithm, no color for termination detection is necessary because every robot eventually observes all other robots (*Complete Visibility*).

The first phase is the same as the previous algorithm. In the second phase, two reference robots change their lights into Corner. The robots with light B move upward or downward as the same manner of the previous one. When two reference robots observe each other, they move away until the distance between them becomes $(N - 2)^2$. After that, the two reference robots change their light into 2ndCorner. If each robot with light B at the end of L'_{2+} or L'_{2-} observes two reference robots with lights 2ndCorner, it moves to $G'_{r_a\perp}$ and changes its light to A when it reaches $G'_{r_a\perp}$. When each robot with light A on L'_{2+} (resp. L'_{2-}) observes that all robots on L'_{2-} (resp. L'_{2+}) have lights A, it moves to G'_r and changes its light into B again when it reaches G'_r. Finally, if two reference robots move to G'_r (if necessary). As a result, *Uniform Circle Formation* with *Complete Visibility* is achieved. This diameter $((N - 2)^2)$ is a necessary and sufficient condition to achieve *Complete Visibility*.

Acknowledgements. This work was supported in part by JSPS KAKENHI Grant Numbers 19K11823, 20KK0232, and Foundation of Public Interest of Tatematsu.

References

1. Suzuki, I., Yamashita, M.: Distributed anonymous mobile robots: formation of geometric patterns. SIAM J. Comput. **28**(4), 1347–1363 (1999)

2. Flocchini, P., Prencipe, G., Santoro, N. (eds.): Distributed Computing by Mobile Entities, Current Research in Moving and Computing. Lecture Notes in Computer Science, vol. 11340. Springer, Cham (2019)
3. R. Adhikary, M.K.Kundu, and B.Sau. Circle formation by asynchronous opaque robots on infinite grid. Comput. Sci. **22**(1) (2021)

Brief Announcement: Self-stabilizing Total-Order Broadcast

Oskar Lundström[1], Michel Raynal[2], and Elad M. Schiller[1(✉)]

[1] Chalmers University of Technology, Gothenburg, Sweden
osklunds@student.chalmers.se elad@chalmers.se
[2] Institut Universitaire de France IRISA, Rennes, France
michel.raynal@irisa.fr

1   Introduction

Our study aims at the design of an even more reliable solution. We do so through the lenses of *self-stabilization*—a very strong notion of fault-tolerance. In addition to node and communication failures, self-stabilizing algorithms can recover after the occurrence of *arbitrary transient faults*; these faults represent any violation of the assumptions according to which the system was designed to operate (as long as the algorithm code stays intact). This work proposes the first (to the best of our knowledge) self-stabilizing algorithm for total-order (uniform reliable) broadcast for asynchronous message-passing systems prone to process failures and transient faults. As we show, the proposed solution facilitates the elegant construction of self-stabilizing state-machine replication using bounded memory.

We study the TO-URB problem (Definition 1). It uses the operations TO-broadcast (for sending application messages) and TO-deliver (for receiving them).

Definition 1. *TO-URB requires the satisfaction of the following.*

- ***TO-validity.*** *Suppose a process TO-delivers m. Message m was previously TO-broadcast by its sender, which is denoted by $m.sender$.*

- ***TO-integrity.*** *A process TO-delivers m at most once.*

- ***TO-delivery.*** *Suppose a process TO-delivers m and later TO-delivers m'. No process TO-delivers m' before m.*

- ***TO-completion-1.*** *Suppose a non-faulty process TO-broadcasts m. All non-faulty processes TO-delivers m.*

- ***TO-completion-2.*** *Suppose a process TO-delivers m. All non-faulty processes TO-deliver m.*

S. Devismes et al. (Eds.): SSS 2022, LNCS 13751, pp. 358–363, 2022.
https://doi.org/10.1007/978-3-031-21017-4_27

It is known that TO-broadcast's implementation requires the computability power of consensus, but FIFO-URB does not. Thus, our reference architecture (Fig. 1) includes consensus and a failure detector for eventually identifying faulty nodes. It also uses the communication abstraction of FIFO-URB, which is simpler than TO-URB since it does not require the computability power of consensus. One can specify FIFO-URB by substituting the TO-delivery requirement of Definition 1 with the following FIFO-delivery requirement. Suppose a process FIFO-delivers m and later FIFO-delivers m', such that the sender is the same, i.e., $m.sender = m'.sender$. Then, no process FIFO-delivers m' before m.

Fault Model. We study an asynchronous message-passing system that has no guarantees on the communication delay and the algorithm cannot explicitly access the local clock. We assume that this asynchronous system is prone to (detectable) fail-stop failures after which the failed node stops taking steps forever. We also consider communication failures, e.g., packet loss, duplication, and reordering, as long as fair communication holds, i.e., a message that is sent infinitely often is received infinitely often. We say that the faults above are *foreseen* since they are

emulation of state-machine replication		
reliable broadcast with total-order delivery		
multivalued consensus	failure detector	reliable broadcast with FIFO delivery
message-passing system		

Fig. 1. The context of the studied problems (appear in bold font)

known at the design time. In addition, we consider *transient faults*, i.e., any temporary violation of assumptions according to which the system was designed to operate, e.g., state corruption due to soft errors. These transient faults arbitrarily change the system state in unpredictable manners (while keeping the program code intact). Thus, we assume that these violations bring the system to an arbitrary state from which a *self-stabilizing system* should recover. Once the system has recovered, it must never violate the task specifications.

Related Work. This work uses several external building blocks. I.e., FIFO-URB [2], binary [3] and multivalued consensus [4] solutions for self-stabilizing systems that their scheduler is seldom fair [1]. Specifically, after the occurrence of the last transient fault, fairness eventually holds, but only for the period that is sufficient for enabling recovery. Note that, in the absence of transient faults, correctness is demonstrated without any fairness assumptions. Since transient faults are rare, these fairness assumption is seldom needed.

Our Contribution. We present a fundamental module for dependable distributed systems: a self-stabilizing fault-tolerant TO-URB for asynchronous message passing systems. Our solution assumes the availability of self-stabilizing algorithms for FIFO-URB and multivalued consensus. In the absence of transient faults, our asynchronous solution for self-stabilizing TO-URB completes within a constant number of communication rounds. After the occurrence of the last transient fault, the system recovers eventually (while assuming execution fairness among the non-faulty processes). The amount of memory used by the proposed algorithm as well as its communication costs are bounded. To the best of our knowledge, we propose the first self-stabilizing TO-URB solution.

The detailed version of this work appears in a complementary technical report [5].

2 Self-stabilizing Bounded-Memory TO-URB

We present a self-stabilizing algorithm that uses bounded memory for implementing TO-URB. It uses FIFO-URB broadcasts for disseminating the messages that were sent via TO-broadcast. It defers the delivery of these FIFO broadcasts (in the buffers of FIFO-URBs) until sufficient information allows all nodes to decide on their total-order.

To that end, the URB objects report the message numbers, per sender, of messages that are ready-to-be-delivered. By collecting these reports from the nodes, the solution can decide, via a multivalued consensus, on the set of messages that all trusted nodes are ready to deliver. Specifically, it agrees on the vector of message numbers, one number per sender, that all nodes are ready to deliver their respective messages (and all earlier messages). Thus, the result of the agreement defines a common set of messages that all nodes are ready to deliver. Since the message numbers in the set are known to all nodes, one can use a straightforward deterministic total-order for delivering these buffered messages in the same order.

Overview of the Proposed Solution (Fig. 2). Before going through the overview, we highlight its key parts.

1. Upon the invocation of toBroadcast(m), disseminate the application message m by using FIFO-URB for broadcasting toURB(m), which is the name of the URB messages that need to be totally ordered before delivery.

2. Do forever
   (a) Query all trusted nodes about the system's consensus round numbers and the vector, $allReady_i$, of ready-to-be-delivered messages.
   (b) Recycle unused consensus objects; use round numbers info. from step (a).
   (c) If the set of consensus round numbers (collected in line 2a) include just one number, continue to the next consensus round by proposing $allReady_i$. Once the consensus has been completed, p_i delivers the buffered messages that their individual message numbers, per sender, are not greater than the respective entries in the agreed vector.

Going Through the Overview of Fig. 2. The array $CS[]$ stores three multivalued consensus objects, where the proposed values are $(seq, ready)$. The field seq is a round number of a multivalued consensus invocation that moderates

---

variables: $CS[0..2] = [\bot, \bot, \bot]$: consensus objects, where the proposed values are $(seq, ready)$, seq is a consensus round number, and $ready$ is a vector of URB message numbers (one number per node).

$obsS = 0$: a local copy of the highest, possibly obsolete, consensus round number.

macros: $needFlush()$: indicates the need for flushing the buffer, *i.e.*, all URBs have been completed, or the number of messages exceeds a predefined constant, δ.

1. **operation** toBroadcast(m) **do** FIFO-URB the message m along with the message name toURB.

2. **do forever**

   (a) <u>Collect info. about round numbers and buffered messages.</u> Query all trusted nodes, p_j, about $obsS_j$, $getSeq_j()$, which is the highest consensus round number known to p_j, and $maxReady_j()$, which is a vector of p_j's ready-to-be-delivered toURB() messages. Use the arriving values for calculating:

     i. $maxSeq_i$: the greatest collected consensus round number.

     ii. $allSeq_i$: the set of all collected consensus round numbers.

     iii. $allReady_i$: a vector of message numbers, per sender, of the ready-to-deliver broadcasts that all nodes can perform.

   (b) <u>Recycle unused consensus objects.</u> Nullify $CS[]$'s unused entries, *i.e.*, assign $\bot$ to any $CS[k]$, for which $k \in \{0, 1, 2\}$ is not one of the following:

     i. $obsS_i$ mod 3, but only when $obsS < getSeq_i()$, *i.e.*, $CS[]$'s highest consensus round number, $getSeq_i()$, is higher than the locally highest obsolete round number, $obsS_i$. The reason is that p_i still uses this entry.

     ii. $getSeq_i()$ mod 3 since there might be another node that is using it.

     iii. $maxSeq_i+1$ mod 3 but only when $|allSeq_i| = 1$, *i.e.*, there is a single consensus round number. This is because one should not nullify the next entry since another node might have already started to use it.

   (c) <u>Agree on the delivery order.</u> If one collected consensus round number exists and it is time to flush the toURB() buffer, *i.e.*, $needFlush() = $ True, call $CS_i[maxSeq_i + 1$ mod $3].propose(maxSeq_i+1, allReady_i)$. If other nodes have higher rounds than p_i or the current consensus object has completed, then:

     i. If the current object has been completed, deliver all messages that their individual consensus round numbers are not greater than the agreed ones.

     ii. Finish the current consensus round, *i.e.*, $obsS \leftarrow obsS + 1$.

Fig. 2. An overview of the proposed solution; code for $p_i \in \mathcal{P}$

the ordered delivery of URB messages. The field $ready$ is a vector of URB message numbers (one number per node)—each number, say $ready[j]$, moderates the URB messages sent by p_j. The integer $obsS$ holds the consensus round number that is locally considered to be the highest one, but possibly obsolete. Once p_i delivers the messages associated with $CS[obsS$ mod $3].result()$ (and the earlier ones), p_i considers $obsS_i$ as obsolete. Node p_i recycles $CS[obsS$ mod 3] once it knows that all other trusted nodes also consider $obsS$ as an obsolete round number. The proposed solution uses $CS[]$ cyclically by considering $obsS$'s value modulus three. As explained in [5], we use global reset for dealing with the event of *obsS*'s integer overflow.

Since the proposed solution defers message delivery, there is a need to guarantee that such delivery occurs eventually. To that end, the macro *needFlush*() identifies two cases in which the buffered messages should be flushed (*i.e.*, *needFlush*() returns True): (i) the number of deferred messages exceeds a predefined constant, and (ii) there are no active URBs.

As mentioned, the invocation of toBroadcast(m) (line 1) leads to FIFO-URB of toURB(m). The do forever loop (line 2) makes sure that these toURB() messages can be delivered according to an order that all nodes agree on. To that end, a query is sent (line 2a) to all nodes, p_j, about their current consensus round number, $obsS_j$, and the highest round numbers stored in $CS[]$, $getSeq_j()$, as well as the current status of their ready-to-deliver FIFO-URBs, *i.e.*, $maxReady_j()$. Node p_i uses the arriving and local information (line 2a) for calculating (i) the message numbers of all-nodes ready-to-deliver broadcasts, *i.e.*, $allReady_i$, (ii) the maximum consensus round number, $maxSeq_i$, and (iii) the set of all consensus round numbers that p_i is aware of, *i.e.*, $allSeq_i$.

This information allows p_i to recycle stale entries in $CS_i[]$. Specifically, line 2b nullifies entries that are not used (or about to be used). Also, if there is just one collected consensus round number, *i.e.*, $|allSeq_i| = 1$, and it is time to flush the buffer of the toURB() messages, as indicated by $needFlush_i()$, then p_i continues to the next agreement round by proposing the pair $(maxSeq_i + 1, allReady_i)$. As mentioned, such agreement on the value of the vector *allReady* allows all nodes to deliver, in the same order, all the messages that their message numbers, per sender p_k, is not greater than $allReady[k]$.

If p_i notices that other nodes use a higher consensus round number than its own (which implies that they have already continued to the next consensus round) or its current consensus object has been completed, p_i can deliver the buffered messages (line 2c). Specifically, it tests whether the current consensus object has been completed. If so, it then delivers all messages that their individual message numbers are not greater than the one agreed by the completed object (line 2(c)i). In any case, it finishes the current consensus round by incrementing the agreement round number, *obsS* (line 2(c)ii).

3 Discussion

We proposed, to the best of our knowledge, the first self-stabilizing algorithm for total-order uniform reliable broadcast. This is built atop self-stabilizing algorithms for FIFO-URB and multivalued consensus. Our complementary technical report [5] includes an application for the proposed solution, *i.e.*, a self-stabilizing state-machine replication. We encourage the use of our solution and techniques when designing distributed systems that must recover from transient faults.

Acknowledgments. The work of E. M. Schiller was partly supported by the CyReV project (2019-03071) funded by VINNOVA, the Swedish Governmental Agency for Innovation Systems.

References

1. Dolev, S., Petig, T., Schiller, E.M.: Self-stabilizing and private distributed shared atomic memory in seldomly fair message passing networks. Algorithmica. Also appears in CoRR abs/1806.03498 (2022)
2. Lundström, Oskar, Raynal, Michel, M. Schiller, Elad: Self-stabilizing uniform reliable broadcast. In: Georgiou, Chryssis, Majumdar, Rupak (eds.) NETYS 2020. LNCS, vol. 12129, pp. 296–313. Springer, Cham (2021). https://doi.org/10.1007/978-3-030-67087-0_19
3. Lundström, O., Raynal, M., Schiller, E.M.: Self-stabilizing indulgent zero-degrading binary consensus. In: 22nd Distributed Computing and Networking ICDCN, pp. 106–115 (2021)
4. Lundström, O., Raynal, M., Schiller, E.M.: Self-stabilizing multivalued consensus in asynchronous crash-prone systems. In: 17th European Dependable Computing Conference, EDCC, pp. 111–118. IEEE (2021)
5. Lundström, O., Raynal, M., Schiller, E.M.: Self-stabilizing total-order broadcast. CoRR abs/2209.14685 (2022)

Brief Announcement: Secure and Efficient Participant Authentication—Application to Mobile E-Voting

Kun Peng$^{(\boxtimes)}$

Shenzhen, China
Kun_Peng_CPU@hotmail.com

Abstract. With Popularity of smart phones, more and more users tend to use them in e-voting activities. However, mobile devices has weak computing power and sometimes cannot support costly cryptographic operations. Vote validity proof is usually an inefficient ZK proof for the prover and liable to have poor performance on mobile devices. To overcome the bottleneck for mobile voters, an efficient protocol is proposed in this paper.

1 Introduction

With the development of ubiquitous computing, more and more users are using mobile devices to enjoy network services like e-voting through dynamic omnipresent wireless networks. Suppose there are some voters in a network system. They move around and may log in the election system through a wireless connection in a dynamic location. There are many such systems in practical applications, and usually there is an authentication mechanism in any wireless network such that legal users can be authenticated and given access. An important security property of network application is user privacy. Namely, the voters do not want to be traced and hope to log into communication networks anonymously. When users' privacy is required, their authentication is a challenge. Especially, we should be aware that mobile users often use low-capability devices like mobile phone. So authentication of them must be efficient in computation. Moreover, to save power consumption of mobile devices in wireless networks, communicational efficiency must be high as well.

A straightforward solution to anonymous authentication is pseudonym. Every legal user registers at an authority, which issues a pseudonym to him. To prevent the authority from knowing the pseudonyms he issues, blind signature is usually employed to generate them such that every pseudonym is a digital signature signed by the authority using his private key without any knowledge of the signed message. Although the users can use their pseudonyms to show that they

K. Peng—Sponsored by Huawei Technology

are legal users certified by the authority, this straightforward authentication mechanism is vulnerable to replay attack. The pseudonyms may be intercepted (no matter in plaintext in a normal communication pattern or in ciphertext in an encrypted communication pattern) or revealed (by the network authentication agent who receives and verifies the pseudonyms) and then used by illegal users. Although interception-based replay attacks may be avoided by employing some special encryption functions of fresh nonces, attacks using revealed secret from conspiring verifiers are difficult to prevent.

A common method to realize anonymous authentication is to verify that a user is a member of a group of legal users without revealing his identity. Suppose there is a group of users S, which contains n users $A_1, A_2, \ldots, A_n$. When logging in, a user in the group only needs to prove that he is a member of the group and gives no more identity information. A simple solution to this mechanism is to give every member in the group the same password or secret key such that every member can authenticate himself in the same way. However, this simple solution has two drawbacks: complex maintenance and easy revealing. Firstly, it is complex to maintain the group. There must be a group manager to initiate and distribute the password or secret key and register new users. Moreover, when a member is deleted from the group, a new password or secret key must be generated and distributed to all the left members. In addition, when one member leaks his password or key, an update in the whole group is needed. Another problem in this solution is the attack using revealed secret just like in the pseudonym-based solution as the password or secret key may be intercepted in the air or revealed by the verifiers.

We want to design a dynamic and efficient anonymous authentication technology based on proof of membership in a user group. Firstly, it should be highly dynamic such that no initiation, registration or maintenance is needed for any group. So a temporary user can join a dynamic group in real time. Secondly, intensive employment of costly public key cryptographic operations should be avoided. With these two requirements, a user can still be authenticated without revealing his identity. Our idea of dynamic anonymous authentication is that every legal user publishes a public commitment to a secret only known by himself such that a user can dynamically choose a group of legal users in real time and prove that he knows the secret opening to one of the users' public commitments in the group. A straightforward method to implement this idea is the so-called zero knowledge proof of partial knowledge by Cramer *et al* in [1], which requires a user in S to give n parallel zero knowledge proofs, each corresponding to a user's secret. Of course, the user does not know other users' secrets, so the $n-1$ instances of proof of knowledge of their secrets are prepared off-line by the user without being challenged. The only on-line challenged proof is the proof of his knowledge of his own secret. As all the n instances of proof are indistinguishable, a verifier or observer cannot extract which secret the user knows. An OR logic between the n instances of proof guarantees that at least one of them is randomly challenged and thus implies knowledge of the corresponding secret. This method has an obvious drawback: low efficiency. It costs a prover $O(n)$ public key operations, each costing a few exponentiations. When mobile users employ low-capability devices to log in a wireless network, this authentication method is too costly.

In this paper, a new anonymous authentication scheme is proposed for mobile voters in wireless networks. A user can use it to prove that he is legal voter (a member of any dynamic user group) without revealing which member in the group he is. It achieves zero knowledge privacy and so reveals no information to verifiers and observers. Random and fresh challenges are employed in it to prevent the replay attack. No complex initiation, maintenance or updating operation is needed in the new anonymous authentication technique. The new anonymous authentication scheme mainly depends on hash functions and so is very efficient in both computation and communication. A voter only needs one public key operation (which costs one exponentiation) in his proof, while all his other operations are hash functions. As outputs of hash functions are usually much smaller than the integers used in public key cryptography, the new anonymous authentication scheme transfers very few large integers (e.g. those integers used in public key cryptographic operations, which are usually hundreds of bits long). It is especially suitable for wireless networks with mobile users using low-capability devices with limited power consumption, while an e-voting scheme is designed as an example of its application. It is more flexible than the traditional e-voting solutions [2–8] and does not compromised security or efficiency.

2   Efficient Anonymous Authentication for Legal Voters

Suppose a voter includes himself in a legally registered voter group $A_1, A_2, \ldots, A_n$, whose membership gives the network access he needs. Each A_i has a secret x_i in Z_q, which is the secret knowledge he uses for authentication. Each secret x_i has a public commitment $y_i = g^{x_i} \bmod p$. Public commitments of the voter in the group, denoted as S, form a commitment list $y_1, y_2, \ldots, y_n$. To prove he is a member of S, A_i can prove his knowledge of at least one of $\log_g y_1, \log_g y_2, \ldots, \log_g y_n$ without revealing i using the proof protocol in Fig 1 where $H()$ is a one-way and collision-resistent hash function from G to Z_{2^L}. As the bit length of the output of $H()$, L is usually much smaller than $\log_2 p$, the bit length of the integers used in the public key cryptographic operations in G.

The idea in the proof protocol is not complex. A verifier sets up n different Diffie-Hellman keys, each of whose discrete logarithm is the product of two key roots. The two key roots for the ith Diffie-Hellman key include a constant key root chosen by the verifier and $\log_g y_i$. The verifier then seals a random secret message m into n commitments, using $H()$ and the n Diffie-Hellman keys. The verifier publishes the n commitments and his Diffie-Hellman commitment of his key root and then asks the prover to extract m. Obviously, the prover can extract m if he knows one of the n Diffie-Hellman keys, while Diffie-Hellman assumption implies that he knows the ith Diffie-Hellman key if and only if he knows $\log_g y_i$. Therefore, passing the authentication protocol in Fig 1 implies that the prover knows one of $\log_g y_1, \log_g y_2, \ldots, \log_g y_n$ under Diffie-Hellman assumption.

This new authentication protocol is quite efficient in computation. Especially the prover only needs a low constant computational cost independent of n in the

Suppose A_t needs to authenticate to a verifier using his secret x_t where $1 \leq t \leq n$.

1. A verifier randomly chooses an integer r from Z_q and a random message m from Z_{2^L}. He calculates and conceals

$$z_i = y_i^r \bmod p \text{ for } i = 1, 2, \ldots, n.$$

The verifier calculates and publishes

$$c_i = H(z_i) \oplus m \text{ for } i = 1, 2, \ldots, n$$
$$z = g^r \bmod p.$$

2. A_t publishes

$$u = H(z_t) \oplus c_t$$

where $z_t = z^{x_t} \bmod p$.

3. The verifier verifies

$$u = m.$$

He accepts the authentication iff this equation holds.

Fig. 1. Efficient anonymous authentication

protocol. Moreover, as L is usually much smaller than $\log_2 p$, most integers transferred in the protocol are much smaller than the integers in G. So the protocol is much more efficient in communication than the solutions heavily depending on public key cryptographic operations like groups signature and ring signature. In addition, in the protocol, any voter can dynamically choose any user group and include himself in it immediately. So real time anonymous authentication service is provided and no initiation or maintenance work is needed. Therefore, the protocol is especially suitable for mobile users in wireless networks. Correctness of the protocol is straightforward and any interested reader can follow the proof protocol step by step to check it. Its soundness is proved in Theorem 1, while it is proved to be honest-verifier zero knowledge in Theorem 2.

Theorem 1. *Passing the protocol guarantees the user's knowledge of discrete logarithm of one of $y_1, y_2, \ldots, y_n$ under the Diffie-Hellman assumption.*

Proof: Passes the protocol implies

$$u = m$$

and thus the user knows m. As the only published information about m is

$$c_i = H(z_i) \oplus m \text{ for } i = 1, 2, \ldots, n,$$

the user must know a z_I where $1 \leq I \leq n$. So according to the Diffie-Hellman assumption, the user must know $x_I = \log_g y_I$ as

$$z_I = g^{x_I r} \bmod p$$

and r is kept secret from the prover.   □

Theorem 2. *The protocol achieves honest-verifier zero knowledge.*

Proof: The transcript of the protocol contains $c_1, c_2, ..., c_n, z, u$. A party without any knowledge of any secret can simulate the proof transcript as follows.

1. He randomly chooses an integer r from Z_q and a random message m from Z_{2^L}.
2. He calculates $z = g^r \bmod p$ and $z_i = y_i^r \bmod p$ for $i = 1, 2, ..., n$.
3. He calculates $c_i = H(z_i) \oplus m$ for $i = 1, 2, ..., n$
4. He sets $u = m$.

In both the real transcript of the protocol with an honest verifier and the simulated transcript,

- u is uniformly distributed in Z_{2^L}.
- z is uniformly distributed in G.
- $c_i = H(z_i) \oplus u$ for $i = 1, 2, ..., n$ where $z_i = y_i^{\log_g z} \bmod p$.

As the two transcripts have just the same distribution, the transcript of the protocol can be simulated without any difference by a party without any knowledge of any secret if the verifier is honest and does not deviate from the proof protocol. So the protocol achieves honest-verifier zero knowledge.   □

Note that proof of zero knowledge of the protocol in Theorem 2 assumes that the verifier is honest and does not deviate from the proof protocol. It is very common and actually necessary in many proof protocols.

References

1. Cramer, R., Damgård, I., Schoenmakers, B.: Proofs of partial knowledge and simplified design of witness hiding protocols. In: Desmedt, Y.G. (ed.) CRYPTO 1994. LNCS, vol. 839, pp. 174–187. Springer, Heidelberg (1994). https://doi.org/10.1007/3-540-48658-5_19
2. Peng, K., Bao, F.: Efficient proof of validity of votes in homomorphic e-voting. In: NSS 2010, pp. 17–23 (2010)
3. Peng, K.: Theory and practice of secure e-voting systems. In: Theory and Practice of Cryptography Solutions for Secure Information Systems, pp. 428–498 (2013)
4. Peng, K.: Efficient homomorphic e-voting based on batch proof techniques – an improvement to secure mpc application. In: PST 2022, pp. 1–8 (2022)

5. Peng, K., Bao, F.: A shuffling scheme with strict and strong security. In: SecureWare 2010, pp. 201–206 (2010)
6. Peng, K., Bao, F.: Efficient vote validity check in homomorphic electronic voting. In: Lee, P.J., Cheon, J.H. (eds.) ICISC 2008. LNCS, vol. 5461, pp. 202–217. Springer, Heidelberg (2009). https://doi.org/10.1007/978-3-642-00730-9_13
7. Peng, K., Bao, F.: Practicalization of a range test and its application to e-auction. In: Martinelli, F., Preneel, B. (eds.) EuroPKI 2009. LNCS, vol. 6391, pp. 179–194. Springer, Heidelberg (2010). https://doi.org/10.1007/978-3-642-16441-5_12
8. Peng, K., Aditya, R., Boyd, C., Dawson, E., Lee, B.: Multiplicative homomorphic e-voting. In: Canteaut, A., Viswanathan, K. (eds.) INDOCRYPT 2004. LNCS, vol. 3348, pp. 61–72. Springer, Heidelberg (2004). https://doi.org/10.1007/978-3-540-30556-9_6

Author Index

Printed in the United States
by Baker & Taylor Publisher Services

Printed in the United States
by Baker & Taylor Publisher Services